Begin **Databases**

21.81

Ow 4/07.

Beginning Visual Basic® 2005 Databases

Thearon Willis

WILEY

Wiley Publishing, Inc.

Beginning Visual Basic® 2005 Databases

Published by
Wiley Publishing, Inc.
10475 Crosspoint Boulevard
Indianapolis, IN 46256
www.wiley.com

Copyright © 2006 by Wiley Publishing, Inc., Indianapolis, Indiana

Published simultaneously in Canada

ISBN: 0-7645-8894-X

Manufactured in the United States of America

10 9 8 7 6 5 4 3 2 1

1B/QR/RR/QV/IN

Library of Congress Cataloging-in-Publication Data:

Willis, Thearon.
  Beginning Visual Basic 2005 databases / Thearon Willis.
    p. cm.
  Includes bibliographical references and index.
  ISBN-13: 978-0-7645-8894-5 (paper/website)
  ISBN-10: 0-7645-8894-X (paper/website)
  1. Web databases. 2. Client/server computing. 3. Microsoft Visual BASIC. I. Title.
  QA76.9.W43W42 2005
  005.2'768--dc22
                          2005013967

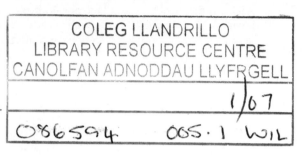

About the Author

Thearon Willis is a senior consultant with over 20 years of programming experience. He started writing applications using the Basic language in 1980 and later moved on to Visual Basic and finally to Visual Basic.Net. He began working with databases in 1987 and has been hooked on writing database applications ever since. He has experience with SQL Server, Oracle, and DB2 but works with SQL Server on a daily basis. Thearon has programmed in several other languages, some of which include C++, Assembler, Pascal, and COBOL. However, he enjoys Visual Basic.Net the best as it provides the features needed to quickly build Windows and Web applications as well as components and Web Services. He currently develops intranet applications, Web Services, and server-side and client-side utilities using Visual Basic.Net. Most of these applications and utilities are database-driven and make use of XML and XSL.

Thearon lives with his wife, Margie, and daughter, Stephanie, in the Raleigh, North Carolina area.

Credits

Acquisitions Editor
Katie Mohr

Development Editor
Sydney Jones

Technical Editor
Todd Meister

Production Editor
Pamela Hanley

Project Coordinator
Michael Kruzil

Copy Editor
Nancy Rapoport

Editorial Manager
Mary Beth Wakefield

Vice President & Executive Group Publisher
Richard Swadley

Vice President and Publisher
Joseph B. Wikert

Proofreading and Indexing
TECHBOOKS Production Services

For my dearest love

Contents

Contents

Contents

Contents

Contents

Acknowledgments

As always, I want to thank my wife, Margie, and my daughter, Stephanie, for the patience they have shown while I write another book. Without their love and support, none of this would be possible.

Introduction

This book teaches Visual Basic 2005 developers the concepts and skills necessary to write VB 2005 database applications that can be used throughout their enterprises. Although the book touches on database design concepts, its focus is on using ADO.NET to access and manipulate data in relational databases. This book covers all data providers in ADO.NET briefly, but focuses on using the OleDb Data Provider for accessing Access databases, the SQL Data Provider for accessing SQL Server databases, and the Oracle Data Provider for accessing Oracle databases. Most of the examples in this book involve writing database applications for SQL Server and Oracle.

You will learn how to use queries, views, and stored procedures to efficiently access and manipulate data from your applications. I provide examples and instruction on accessing data from Windows applications, ASP.NET applications, and Web Services. You'll also be exposed to more advanced concepts, such as writing business logic components and data access components, as well as how to read and write data from the Windows Registry. You will also learn how to encrypt and decrypt data using the .NET encryption classes and how to hash passwords to further secure your access to your data.

Who Is This Book For

This book was designed for the developer who wants to learn how to write database applications using Visual Basic 2005 and back-end databases such as Microsoft Access, Microsoft SQL Server, and Oracle.

There are two kinds of developers for whom this book is ideal:

❑   The *beginning VB 2005 developer* who already has some experience with Visual Basic 2005 developing Windows and ASP.NET applications. You've read *Beginning VB 2005* and are ready to learn database programming using VB 2005. Congratulations, you've made a great choice and will learn the skills and concepts necessary to write efficient database applications.

❑   The *experienced VB 2005 developer* who is new to database programming. You've also made a great choice, as you will hone your VB 2005 skills while you learn the skills and concepts necessary to write efficient database applications.

What This Book Covers

The ADO.NET classes offer a lot of features and functionality, much more than one book can cover in detail. This is especially true given all of the overloaded operators and methods available in these classes. However, the goal of this book is to teach you the concepts for efficiently accessing and manipulating data in enterprise applications. A brief review of database design concepts will help you understand relational database design.

ADO.NET is covered thoroughly so that you can get a firm grasp on this important data access technology in the .NET Framework. Hands-on examples and Try It Out exercises are provided to help you put into practice the topics that you read about.

This book is not intended to be used as a reference but as a teaching tool on building database applications using Visual Basic 2005. To that end, this book walks you through the process of building the various pieces of a single application chapter by chapter.

❑ Chapter 1 provides an overview of the components that make up Access, SQL Server, and Oracle databases as well as a refresher on relational database design and normalization.

❑ Chapters 2 and 3 provide an overview of ADO.NET and the data wizards available in Visual Studio 2005.

❑ Chapters 4 through 7 give you hands-on experience writing queries in Access and executing Access queries in your VB 2005 applications.

❑ Chapters 8 through 13 give you hands-on experience writing stored procedures and views in both SQL Server and Oracle, and executing those stored procedures and views from your VB 2005 application. You also build and enhance a business logic component and data access component starting in Chapter 10.

❑ Chapter 14 shows you how to use your business logic and data access components in an ASP.NET application to display and update data in your back-end databases.

❑ Chapter 15 shows you how to create a Web Service that also uses your business logic and data access components to produce report data.

❑ Finally, Chapter 16 shows you how to access your Web Service from both a Windows and Web application.

What You Need to Run the Examples

The following list describes the software components that you will need to complete the Try It Out exercises in each chapter.

❑ **All chapters:** Visual Studio 2005 Standard, Professional or Team System edition

❑ **Chapters 3 through 8:** Microsoft Office (2000, XP, or 2003 editions) or Microsoft Access (2000, XP, or 2003 editions)

❑ **Chapter 3 and Chapters 8 through 16:** You will need access to SQL Server 2005 or Oracle 10g installed locally on your machine or on your network.

Conventions

This book uses several different styles of text and layout to help differentiate between the different kinds of information. Here are examples of the styles used and an explanation of what they mean.

Try It Out   **How Do They Work?**

1. Each step has a number.

2. Follow the steps.

3. Then read the How It Works section that follows to find out what's going on.

   These notes hold important, not-to-be-forgotten, mission-critical details that are directly relevant to the surrounding text.

Bullets appear indented, with each new bullet marked as follows:

❑ *Important words* are in italics.

❑ Text you are required to type is in **bold**.

Code has several styles. If I am talking about a word in the text—for example, when discussing a `For...Next` loop—it's in `this font`. If it's a block of code that can be typed as a program and run, then it's also in a gray box:

```
Private Sub mnuHelpAbout_Click(ByVal sender As Object, _
    ByVal e As System.EventArgs) Handles mnuHelpAbout.Click

    Dim objAbout As New About
    objAbout.ShowDialog(Me)
    objAbout = Nothing

End Sub
```

Sometimes you'll see code in a mixture of styles, like this:

```
Private Sub mnuHelpAbout_Click(ByVal sender As Object, _
    ByVal e As System.EventArgs) Handles mnuHelpAbout.Click

    Dim objAbout As New About
    objAbout.ShowDialog(Me)
    objAbout.Dispose()
    objAbout = Nothing

End Sub
```

In cases like this, the code with a white background is code you are already familiar with; the line highlighted in gray is a new addition to the code since you last looked at it.

Customer Support

We always value hearing from our readers, and we want to know what you think about this book: what you liked, what you didn't like, and what you think we can do better next time. You can send us your comments either by returning the reply card in the back of the book or by e-mail to `feedback@wrox.com`. Please be sure to mention the book title in your message.

How to download the sample code for the book

When you visit the Wrox site (`wrox.com`) simply locate the title through our Search facility or by clicking the Download Code link at the top of the main page; then find the book in the title list. Click the HTTP or FTP link for the book to download the code.

The files that are available for download from our site have been archived using WinZip. When you have saved the attachments to a folder on your hard drive, you need to extract the files using a decompression program such as WinZip or PKUnzip. When you extract the files, the code is usually extracted into chapter folders. When you start the extraction process, ensure that your software (WinZip or PKUnzip) is set to use folder names.

Errata

We've made every effort to ensure that there are no errors in the text or in the code. However, no one is perfect and mistakes do occur. If you find an error in one of our books, such as a spelling mistake or a faulty piece of code, we would be very grateful for feedback. By sending in errata, you may save another reader hours of frustration, and, of course, you will be helping us provide even higher quality information. Simply e-mail the information to `support@wrox.com`; your information will be checked and, if correct, posted to the errata page for that title, or used in subsequent editions of the book.

To find errata on the Web site, go to `wrox.com` and simply locate the title through our Advanced Search or title list or by going to the Help Center using the link at the bottom of the main page. Click the View Errata link, which is to the right of the book's title.

E-mail support

If you wish to directly query a problem in the book with an expert who knows the book in detail, then e-mail `support@wrox.com` with the title of the book and the last four numbers of the ISBN in the subject field of the e-mail. A typical e-mail should include the following things:

❑   The title of the book, the last four digits of the ISBN (894X), and the page number of the problem in the Subject field

❑   Your name, contact information, and the problem in the body of the message

We won't send you junk mail. We need the details to save your time and ours. When you send an e-mail message, it will go through the following chain of support:

❑   **Customer support:** Your message is delivered to our customer support staff, who are the first people to read it. They have files on most frequently asked questions and will answer anything general about the book or the Web site immediately.

❑   **Editorial:** Deeper queries are forwarded to the technical editor responsible for that book. They have experience with the programming language or particular product, and are able to answer detailed technical questions on the subject.

❑   **The authors:** Finally, in the unlikely event that the editors cannot answer your problem, they will forward the request to the author. We do try to protect authors from any distractions to their writing; however, we are quite happy to forward specific requests to them. All Wrox authors help with the support on their books. They will e-mail the customer and the editor with their response, and again all readers should benefit.

The Wrox support process can offer support only for issues that are directly pertinent to the content of our published title. Support for questions that fall outside the normal scope of a book's support is provided via the community lists of our http://p2p.wrox.com/ forum.

p2p.wrox.com

For author and peer discussion, join the P2P forums. Our unique system provides programmer-to-programmer contact on mailing lists, forums, and newsgroups, all in addition to our one-to-one e-mail support system. If you post a query to P2P, you can be confident that it is being examined by the many Wrox authors and other industry experts who are present on our mailing lists. At p2p.wrox.com you will find a number of different lists that will help you, not only while you read this book, but also as you develop your own applications. Particularly appropriate to this book are the Visual Basic and VBA forums, the Database forums, and the DotNet forums.

To subscribe to a forum, just follow these steps:

1. Go to http://p2p.wrox.com/.
2. Register using the Register link from the left menu bar or log in if you are already a member.
3. Navigate to the appropriate forum.
4. Click the Subscribe to This Forum link for the forum you wish to join.

Why this system offers the best support

You can choose to join the mailing lists, or you can receive them as a weekly digest. If you don't have the time, or facility, to receive the mailing list, you can search our online archives. Junk and spam mail is deleted and your own e-mail address is protected by the unique Lyris system. Queries about joining or leaving lists, and any other general queries about lists, should be sent to listsupport@p2p.wrox.com.

Beginning Visual Basic® 2005 Databases

Databases

Most Visual Basic 2005 applications that you write use data in some form or fashion. Where you retrieve that data from depends on what your application is doing. One of the most common types of applications that you are likely to write is a database application, which retrieves and processes data from a database.

Although there are different kinds of databases and different manufacturers, the databases that you are most likely to encounter are Microsoft Access, Microsoft SQL Server, and Oracle. This chapter explores the components that make up each of these common databases at a high level to help you gain a better understanding of how they work.

To help you understand how databases are put together, you look also at relational database design. This topic describes the relationships between the different tables in your database and how they can be designed for optimal performance.

At the end of the chapter, you build the sample databases that are used throughout the rest of this book. You'll be using these databases to perform the *Try It Out* exercises in each of the chapters.

In this chapter, you:

- ❑ Learn which components make up a Microsoft Access database
- ❑ Learn which components make up a Microsoft SQL Server database
- ❑ Learn which components make up an Oracle database
- ❑ Learn about relational database design
- ❑ Build the sample databases used throughout the rest of this book

Access Databases

Access databases are common and can be found on most computers, especially if the sample databases were installed along with Microsoft Access as a standalone product or as part of Microsoft Office.

People use Access databases for a variety of reasons but mainly because they are *standalone databases*, meaning that you can create an Access database and then send that database to someone else who, if he or she has Microsoft Access installed, can open and use your database. These databases are easy to use, and Access provides many wizards to help you create a functional database in no time at all.

The database engine for Access is the Microsoft Access program MSACCESS.EXE. This database engine can create, open, and edit Access databases and manage the components that make up the database. The database engine is responsible for all the work that controls the database and the data contained in it.

You can run this program by clicking Start on the taskbar and then clicking Run. In the Run dialog box, enter **MSACCESS** and click OK. Microsoft Access starts, and depending on which version of Microsoft Access you have, you may be prompted with a dialog box to open or create a new database. The bottom line is that you can see the database engine at work and the user interface that it provides.

Although an Access database may look simple at first glance, it contains a lot of components, typically referred to as *objects*. All you see as a user is a database file that you can copy and distribute through a variety of channels. The brains behind the actual database itself is the database engine.

In this section, you explore some components that make up an Access database to gain a deeper understanding and appreciation for the complexities that make up an Access database.

Database file

An Access database consists of one complex file that stores the various objects that make up the database. You have probably seen the classic sample database Northwind.mdb. When you open this database, you can view the tables, queries, forms, and reports. These are some of the objects contained in this database file and are controlled by the database engine.

Access database files have an .mdb file extension and each database can contain tables, queries, forms, reports, pages, macros, and modules, which are referred to as *database objects*. That's a lot of information in one large file, but Microsoft Access manages this data quite nicely.

Forms, reports, pages, macros, and modules are generally used to enable users to work with and display data contained in the database. You will be writing Visual Basic 2005 applications to do this, so the only database objects you're really concerned about at the moment are tables and queries.

Tables

A *table* contains a collection of data, which is represented by one or more columns, and one or more rows of data. Columns are typically referred to as *fields* in Microsoft Access, and the rows are referred to as *records*. Each field in a table represents an attribute of the data stored in that table. For example, a field named First Name would represent the first name of an employee or customer. This field is an attribute of an employee or customer. Records in a table contain a collection of fields that form a complete record of information about the data stored in that table. For example, suppose a table contains two fields, First

Name and Last Name. These two fields in a single record describe the name of a single person, as illustrated in Figure 1-1.

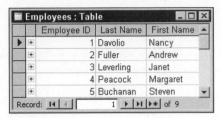

Figure 1-1

Queries

A *query* in a database is a group of Structured Query Language (SQL) statements that enable you to retrieve and update data in your tables. Queries can be used to select or update all the data in one or more tables or to select or update specific data in one or more tables.

SQL enables you to insert, update, and delete data in a database. Microsoft Access provides wizards and visual tools that enable beginning programmers to write queries without having to know SQL.

Using database query objects can make your Visual Basic 2005 code simpler because you have fewer SQL statements included in your code. Database query objects can also make your programs faster because database engines can compile queries when you create them, whereas the SQL statement in a Visual Basic 2005 program needs to be reinterpreted every time it's used. They also provide ease of maintenance because changing a query in your database affects only the database and not your compiled program, which may have been distributed to one or more users.

To understand the implications that queries can have on your programs, you need to learn some basic SQL, which you do in Chapter 4.

SQL Server Databases

A SQL Server database is more complex than an Access database and the actual database engine for SQL Server is made up of multiple components. Also, unlike in an Access database, you cannot simply copy a SQL Server database file and distribute it because SQL Server databases consist of multiple files. Procedures must be followed before you can copy and distribute the database files for a SQL Server database.

SQL Server comes in several editions, such as Microsoft SQL Server 2005 Express, Standard edition, and Enterprise edition. However, the components that make up the SQL Server database engine are virtually the same for all editions.

Many components, other than the database engine and database files, make up SQL Server. These include such components as Replication, Data Transformation Services (DTS), Analysis Services, Meta Data Services, and English Query. However, those components are beyond the scope of this book, as you will be focusing your attention on the actual objects that make up a SQL Server database.

SQL Server is a relational database consisting of many components, each of which contains multiple objects. In the following sections, you examine the main objects that make up a SQL Server database. While you will not examine each and every object of a database, rest assured that what you do learn here will serve you well, laying the foundation for what you will be doing throughout the rest of this book.

A SQL Server database consists of at least two files: a data file and a log file. The data file contains all the data that makes up a SQL Server database, such as tables, indexes, and stored procedures. You examine these objects shortly. The log file contains transaction logs, which are records of changes made to the database.

When you initially create a SQL Server database, the data file and log file are created by SQL Server; the data file has an .mdf extension and the log file has an .ldf extension. As your database grows and you run out of room on the hard drive, your database administrator may create a secondary data file on a separate hard drive. It will typically have an .ndf file extension. Creating a secondary data file for a database typically happens only with large enterprise databases, as most hard drives today can hold multiple database files on a single drive, given the drives extremely large capacity.

Data files

The data file contains multiple objects that make up a database. Table 1-1 lists the various objects that make up a database and are contained in the data file. While you will not be exploring each of these objects in detail, it is helpful to know that they exist and what they do.

Table 1-1: SQL Server Data File Objects

Object	Description
Tables	Contains the data in a database, organized in a row-column format.
Keys	Primary keys provide a unique value for each row of data in a table. Foreign keys provide a relationship between two tables using a column in one table and the primary key in another table.
Indexes	Provides pointers to rows in a table in a similar fashion that the index in this book provides pointers to specific topics.
Constraints	Provides a means by which you can enforce the integrity of a database, such as not allowing a column to contain a NULL value.
Stored Procedures	A single SQL statement or group of SQL statements compiled into a single execution plan.
Views	A SQL SELECT statement that returns a virtual table.
Triggers	A special class of stored procedures that are automatically executed when an Insert, Update, or Delete statement is executed against a table.
Defaults	A default value that is inserted into a column in a table when no value is supplied.

Object	Description
User-Defined Functions	A group of SQL statements that can be encapsulated into a subroutine that can be called by views and stored procedures.
User-Defined Data Types	User-defined data types are based on system data types and enable you to create a data type with attributes that can be applied to all your tables.
User	Identifies a user with a database.
Roles	A group containing certain permissions in the database to which you add users, effectively assigning the same permissions to each user.

Tables

Tables are core objects that exist in the data file and contain information about your business. For example, you could create an employee table like the one shown in Figure 1-1 that contains information about each employee in your organization.

Each table that you define is made up of columns and rows. Each column represents an attribute about the information stored in your table, such as an employee's first or last name. Collectively, the columns form a row in your table that represents a single occurrence of the information that the table represents. (Refer to the Employees table in Figure 1-1.)

Keys

Each table in your database usually, but not necessarily, has a column that uniquely identifies each row of data with a *primary key*. No two rows in a table can contain the same primary key, and SQL Server enforces this rule. Primary key columns are usually defined using a *globally unique identifier* (*Guid*), which is a unique value generated based on internal values in your computer. No two computers will ever generate the same unique identifier.

Primary keys may also contain other values such as an employee's employee number, which could consist of alpha and numeric characters. Also, primary key columns cannot contain NULL values. A NULL value is one missing: it does not exist.

When a primary key is created on a table, SQL Server automatically creates a unique index for the primary key on the table. Creating a unique index ensures that no two primary keys can contain the same value. Indexes are covered in detail in the next section. Using the index on the primary key column provides fast, efficient access to the data when using the primary key to access data in a table.

Foreign keys point to the primary key in another table. A foreign key in one row of a table points to an exact row of data in another table. A foreign key value cannot be inserted into a table if the row of data that it is pointing to in another table does not exist. This is just one of the constraints placed on foreign keys that help ensure referential integrity.

Referential integrity enforces the defined relationships between tables when records are inserted or deleted. You cannot insert a foreign key value for a row of data that does not exist in another table. Referential integrity also prevents you from deleting a row of data that is referenced by a foreign key. To do so, you must first delete the row of data containing the foreign key or update the column using a NULL value. Only then are you able to delete the row containing the primary key.

Referential integrity is based on the relationship between foreign and primary keys and ensures that key values are consistent across all tables. Referential integrity is automatically enforced by SQL Server and prevents a user from updating a primary or foreign key in a manner that would break the integrity of the data.

Indexes

An *index* is an object associated with tables and is built using one or more columns from a table. An index stores information from columns (usually primary and foreign key columns) and the exact location of that data within the table. Thus, using an index to access information in the table is very efficient, as SQL Server will use the information contained in the index to find the exact location of the row of data that you want retrieve or update.

SQL Server contains two main types of indexes: clustered and non-clustered.

Clustered indexes sort the data in the table rows by key, providing an efficient means of accessing data in the table. However, because a clustered index sorts the data in the table, a table can contain only one clustered index. You can think of a clustered index like a phone book. The columns that define the index (for example, the last name followed by an initial) are used to sort the table rows. A clustered index stores the data rows of the table in the bottom leaf of the index. This means that the index consists of the index entries pointing to each row of data, and the data rows are stored at the end of the index.

Non-clustered indexes store the keys of the table in the index and contain pointers to where the data actually resides in the table. The pointer in a non-clustered index is called a *row locator* because it actually locates the row of data in the table.

Indexes can be unique or not. Unique indexes unique do not allow duplicate keys (keys that contain the same data value), and indexes that are not defined as unique can contain duplicate keys. Index keys should not be confused with primary keys in a table. An index key can be generated for any column in a table that is used to access the data in the table.

The last index that I want to cover is the *full-text index*. This type of index is used on columns that contain the TEXT data type. This is a data type that can store large amounts of data, up to 2 gigabytes worth. This index enables you to search through the text in a column containing this data type for specific keywords.

Stored procedures

A *stored procedure* is a single SQL statement or group of SQL statements compiled into an execution plan and stored under a unique name in the database. It is executed as a unit. A stored procedure can have multiple SQL statements to perform such tasks as selecting data from one table and updating data in another table.

Stored procedures increase application performance in a couple of ways. First, they enable fewer SQL statements to be transmitted across the network, as you send only the name of the stored procedure and any parameters it may require.

Second, stored procedures are similar to procedures and functions in other programming languages, as they can contain input and output parameters and can return values. They use logic to control the flow of processing, and numerous functions and SQL statements can be used in stored procedures.

You can use stored procedures to execute routine functions, such as selecting, inserting, updating, and deleting data. A single stored procedure can be executed by multiple applications, thus providing code reuse. You learn more about stored procedures in Chapter 9.

Views

A view is like a virtual table containing data from one or more tables. A view is stored in the database as the actual SQL statements that are contained in the view, such as a stored procedure. When the view is referenced, the virtual table is created using the SQL statements that are contained in the view.

Views are generally used to enable users to see data from multiple tables in one view, thereby giving the illusion that the data exists as one table or group of data. This provides a couple of benefits. First, by providing the impression that all of the data is in one table, the complexities of the database are hidden from the user. Second, it provides a security mechanism in that you can grant a user access to the view but not to the actual tables from which the view is derived, and you can limit the data a user sees.

Because a view is like a virtual table, you can execute SQL SELECT statements against a view, thereby selecting only the data from the view that you need to see. You can also limit the results by using a SQL Where clause and order the results using a SQL Order By clause. You learn more about these basic SQL clauses starting in Chapter 4 and more about views in Chapter 9.

Log files

Each database that you create has its own transaction log. The transaction log contains transactions that have been applied against your database. A *transaction* is the execution of a group of SQL statements as one logical unit of work. SQL Server automatically manages transactions in the transaction log, generating a before-and-after picture of the data in a table that is changed. This means that you can execute an update query to update a row of data and SQL Server logs a record of the data before it was changed and after it was changed. This allows for backward and forward recovery of the data in your database.

SQL Server manages transaction logging automatically. You can, however, use transactions in your stored procedures to perform automatic recovery of the data that your stored procedures changed. You can also use transactions in the ADO.NET classes that provide data access to your database. Transactions are covered in more depth in Chapter 11.

Oracle Databases

Just as SQL Server databases are more complex than Access databases, Oracle databases are more complex than SQL Server databases. Because Oracle was designed to be platform independent, its architecture is more complex, and a single database in Oracle consists of more files than a SQL Server database.

Oracle comes in multiple editions: Enterprise, Standard, and Personal. However, the database engine components are virtually the same for all editions. Each edition supports features not found in the previous edition. For example, the Standard edition supports multiple processors, whereas the Personal edition does not. Likewise, the Enterprise edition supports transparent application failover support, but the Standard edition does not.

Oracle consists of many components in addition to the database engine, including components that perform data analysis, help you manage XML and image data, manage applications and clusters, and monitor and manage database performance. However, those components are beyond the scope of this book, which focuses on the components that make up an Oracle database.

Because Oracle is a relational database, it contains numerous components, and each component contains many objects. In this section, you look at the main objects that make up an Oracle database. While the topics presented here provide only a cursory overview, this information will help you throughout the rest of the book.

The following sections describe the five file types created when you create an Oracle database.

Data files

Data files are perhaps the most important files that make up your database and perhaps among the most complex. When an Oracle database is created, a single data file is created. However, you can create multiple data files, and most typical production databases contain at least two data files.

Data files are complex because they contain the various objects that make up your database. In Oracle terminology, these objects are known as *segments*. Because of the complexities of an Oracle data file, Table 1-2 contains only a partial list of the various objects, which you can compare to SQL Server data files.

Table 1-2: Oracle Data File Objects

Object	Description
Tables	Contains the data in a database, organized in a row-column format.
Keys	Primary keys provide a unique value for each row of data in a table. Foreign keys provide a relationship between two tables using a column in one table and the primary key in another table.
Indexes	Provides pointers to rows in a table similar to the fashion that the index in this book provides pointers to specific topics.
Constraints	Provides a means by which you can enforce the integrity of a database, such as not allowing a column to contain a NULL value.
Stored Procedures	A group of SQL statements compiled into a single execution plan.
Views	A SQL SELECT statement that returns a virtual table.
Triggers	A special class of stored procedures that are automatically executed when an Insert, Update, or Delete statement is executed against a table.
Functions	A group of SQL statements that can be encapsulated into a subroutine that can be called by views and stored procedures.
User	Identifies a user with a database.
Roles	A group containing certain permissions in the database to which you add users, effectively assigning the same permissions to each user.

Tables

Tables in Oracle perform the same function as they do in SQL Server — they contain information about your business.

Keys

Keys in Oracle perform the same function as they do in SQL Server — they uniquely identify each row of data in a table.

Indexes

Indexes in Oracle perform the same function as they do in SQL Server — they provide efficient access to the data in your tables. However, Oracle contains many different kinds of indexes, as outlined in this section.

B*Tree indexes contain four subtypes of indexes: The *Index Organized Table* index performs the same function as the *clustered index* in SQL Server, which is to sort and store the data in the table by the primary key.

The *B*Tree cluster index,* or *index clustered table,* stores blocks of data from multiple tables prejoined on the keys. This enables you to select data using a clustered key (a primary and foreign key, for example) and from the block that contains the rows related to that clustered key.

The *reverse key index* stores the keys in an index with the key value in reverse order, and is primarily used on keys that contain sequential numbers. For example, suppose your primary keys started with a sequential number of 1000. The next primary key would be 1001, and then 1002, and so on. The reverse key index stores the primary keys in the index as 0001, 1001, and 2001. This allows the index keys to be inserted into the index spread out over multiple blocks, thereby increasing the efficiency of your index.

The *descending index* enables you to store the primary key for a table in the index in descending order. This is particularly useful when most of the data selected from a table is selected in descending order.

Bitmap indexes use a single index entry to point to many data rows in a single table. This type of index is particularly useful when indexing columns that contain simple values. For example, if a column contains a value of 0 or 1 or a value of Y or N, this index can use a single index entry to point to all rows of data that contain the specified value in your query.

A *function-based index* stores the computed results of a function in the index. A *function* is a subroutine that can be used to encapsulate SQL statements that are repetitively executed and that return a result. For example, the MAX function returns the maximum value in a column. Using a function-based index on tables that rarely change can increase the performance of your queries.

The *domain index* is a user-defined index that you build yourself. You can then tell Oracle about the index and the query optimizer will decide whether to use the index in your queries. This type of index is for advanced users; in particular, database administrators.

The *interMedia Text index* enables the searching of keywords in large text fields. This type of index is useful for specialized applications such as search engines that need to search huge amounts of text for keywords entered by the user.

Stored procedures

A stored procedure in Oracle is functionally equivalent to a stored procedure in SQL Server and stores a single or group of SQL statements compiled into an execution plan.

Views

Views in Oracle perform the same function as they do in SQL Server and are like virtual tables containing data from one or more tables.

Redo log files

Oracle's redo log files are functionally equivalent to log files in SQL Server and enable you to recover transactions made against the tables in your database. However, Oracle databases contain at least two redo log files and can contain more. They are used in a round-robin fashion, whereby the first redo log file is used until it gets full and then the second redo log file is used. When the second one is filled up, the first redo log file is reused.

Control files

Oracle uses a single control file per database to tell the database engine where to find the other files, such as the data and redo log files, associated with a database. It also contains other important information about your database, such as the database name and the date and time the database was created. The control file may also contain other information, such as the location of your archived redo log files.

Temp files

Temp files are used to store the intermediate results of large sort operations and large results sets from a query. This provides efficient use of system resources, as smaller sort operations and results sets are stored in the computer's memory.

Password files

Information concerning password files is closely guarded at Oracle and rightly so given the security concerns of corporations everywhere and the fact that Oracle is a very secure database. Be aware that every database contains password files used to authenticate users performing administrative functions against the database.

Relational Database Design

A *relational database* contains tables, rows, and columns that are related to one another. A relational database that has been properly normalized will have more tables that contain fewer columns, rather than a few tables containing lots of columns. A normalized relational database actually improves storage efficiency and performance, even though it physically contains more tables than a non-normalized database does. You will be reading about the process of normalization in the next section.

Each table in your database represents an object about your business, and each column in a table represents an attribute of the object that the table represents. A row in the table represents a unique entry for the object that the table defines.

To design a relational database, you must first identify all of the objects that will make up your database. The term *object* is used to represent a set of information. You can also use the term *entity* in place of object. An entity is an object that refers to a person, place, or thing. If you know that you will be building an application that manages employees in your organization, you first identify which objects represent the information about an employee. For example, an employee is an object and the employee's manager is an object.

Next, you want to identify which attributes make up the employee and manager objects. Tables 1-3 and 1-4 illustrate the attributes that have been identified for these objects.

Table 1-3: Employee Attributes

Attribute	Description
Employee Name	The name of the employee
Phone Number	The phone number for the employee
Location	The location where the employee works (for example, city, building, or branch office)
Job Title	The job title of the employee

Table 1-4: Manager Attributes

Attribute	Description
Manager Name	The name of the manager
Phone Number	The phone number for the manager
Location	The location where the manager works (for example, city, building, or branch office)

Now that you have identified all the attributes for these objects, you must identify the tables to which these attributes should be assigned. You can begin by defining the tables that will go into your database, as shown in the Figure 1-2. Notice that the Employee Name and Manager Name have been separated into two fields. This enables you to select and order employees and managers by first or last name.

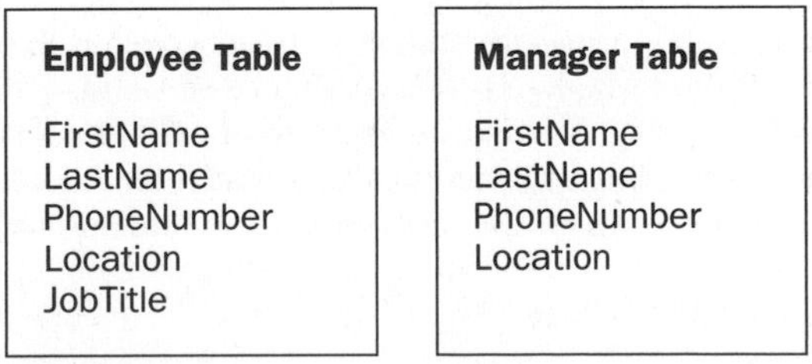

Employee Table

FirstName
LastName
PhoneNumber
Location
JobTitle

Manager Table

FirstName
LastName
PhoneNumber
Location

Figure 1-2

You'll also notice that the field names have been defined using *Pascal casing*. Pascal casing is where the first letter of each word is in uppercase, such as FirstName. You can choose to use a field name with spaces in it, such as First Name, or with an underscore in it, such as First_Name. Whichever method you choose to use is fine. However, keep in mind that using field names containing spaces forces you to use special coding conventions to encapsulate the field name so that the database recognizes it as a single name and not two separate names. Therefore, it's a good practice to not use spaces in field names.

Tables 1-3 and 1-4 illustrate the information that you need, but there is no relationship between the employee and manager. Therefore, you need to create another table that ties the information from these two tables together. Let's call this new table Manager Employees. This will enable you to assign employees to managers.

Figure 1-3 shows the new table, which will form the relationships between the Employee and Manager tables. Because a manager can be responsible for more than one employee, the Manager Employees table contains four employee fields.

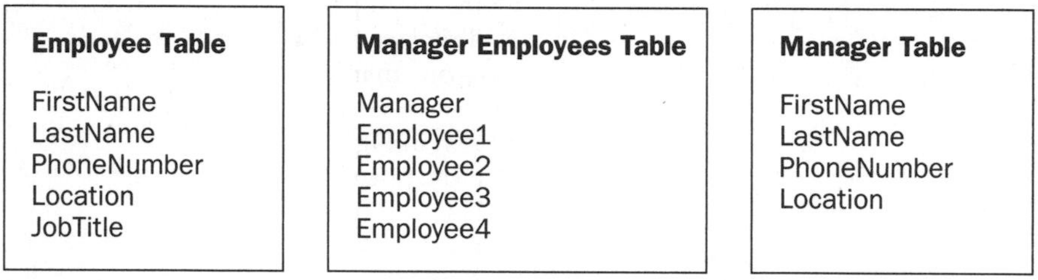

Employee Table	Manager Employees Table	Manager Table
FirstName LastName PhoneNumber Location JobTitle	Manager Employee1 Employee2 Employee3 Employee4	FirstName LastName PhoneNumber Location

Figure 1-3

This is the start of your relational database design. At this point, your database design is relational because the tables relate to one another; however, your design is not yet complete. To complete your database design, you must normalize it.

Normalization

Normalization is the process of using formal methods to eliminate duplicate data, and to separate data into multiple related tables. A normalized database offers improved database and application performance over a database that is not normalized, and over one that has been over-normalized. A normalized database also leads to more efficient data storage, as you eliminate repeating groups of data. Normalization also helps to make your tables easier to maintain.

As normalization increases, so do the number of joins required to access the data; however, relational database engines are optimized to handle normalized databases that require multiple joins. Joins are a logical relationship between two tables that enable you to access data in both tables in the same query. Joins are usually defined in the form of foreign key constraints. Joins are covered in more detail in Chapter 12.

Normalizing a logical database design involves using formal methods to separate the data into multiple, related tables. Each method is typically referred to as a *normal form*. There are three normal forms to a normalized database: *first normal form*, *second normal form*, and *third normal form*. An over normalized database is normalized to fourth and fifth normal forms (which are not covered here) and is rarely considered practical in relational database design. The normal forms listed here are discussed in the following sections:

- ❑ The first normal form eliminates repeating groups of data in a table. You create a separate table for each set of related data and identify each table with a primary key, which uniquely identifies each row of data.

- ❑ The second normal form creates separate tables for sets of values that apply to multiple records, and relates these tables with foreign keys.

- ❑ The third normal form eliminates columns that do not depend on the primary key.

First normal form

You want to apply the rules of normalization to your sample database design, shown previously. In the first normal form, you need to eliminate repeating groups of data, and create separate tables for each set of related data. You must also identify a primary key for each table.

The Manager Employees table contains repeating groups of data so this table is a prime candidate for the first normal form. This table already provides a relationship between a manager and employees, but you need to eliminate the repeating groups of data (for example Employee1, Employee2). You'll remove the four individual Employee fields in this table and replace them with a single Employee field. This table will then provide a one-to-many relationship — one manager to many employees.

All tables must have a primary key assigned, as shown in Figure 1-4. A primary key will uniquely identify each record contained in a table. Notice that the primary keys shown in Figure 1-4 contain a prefix of the table name and contain a suffix of ID. This naming convention will help identify all primary and foreign keys and which table they belong to. Of course, you can use any naming convention that you like, but find one that works well for you and use it consistently in your database design.

Notice that the Manager Employees table contains a primary key for itself, which will uniquely identify each record contained in this table. It also contains the primary keys from the Manager and Employee tables. These keys, as used in this table, are known as foreign keys, as a table may contain only one primary key.

Let's look at how you can identify the primary and foreign keys in a table using the naming convention that has been incorporated here. The Manager Employees table contains a field called ManagerEmployeeID. Because this key contains the name of the table and a suffix of ID, you know that this is the primary key for this table. Likewise, you see two other fields in this table containing a suffix of ID. By looking at the names of these fields you can surmise that the field ManagerID is a foreign key to the Manager table, and that the field EmployeeID is a foreign key to the Employee table.

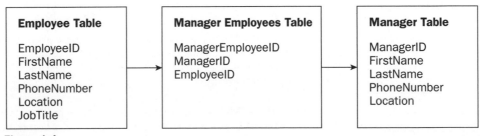

Employee Table

EmployeeID
FirstName
LastName
PhoneNumber
Location
JobTitle

Manager Employees Table

ManagerEmployeeID
ManagerID
EmployeeID

Manager Table

ManagerID
FirstName
LastName
PhoneNumber
Location

Figure 1-4

Second normal form

The rule for the second normal form dictates that you must create separate tables for sets of values that apply to multiple records and in multiple tables, and relate these tables with foreign keys.

Starting with the Employee table, you can see that multiple employees can work at the same location, as well as have the same job title. Therefore, following the rules of the second normal form, you need to create a separate table for Location and relate this new table to the Employee table with a foreign key. This provides a one-to-many relationship whereby you have one row in the Location table relating to multiple rows in the Employee table.

You also need to create a Job Title table and relate this table to the Employee table with a foreign key. This also provides a one-to-many relationship whereby you have one row in the Job Title table relating to multiple rows in the Employee table.

The next table that you want to examine for the rules of the second normal form is the Manager table. Again, you have a Location field, and multiple managers could work at the same location. Because you have already defined a Location table, you merely need to create a foreign key field in the Manager table pointing to the Location table.

With the addition of these new tables, your database design would now look like the one shown in Figure 1-5.

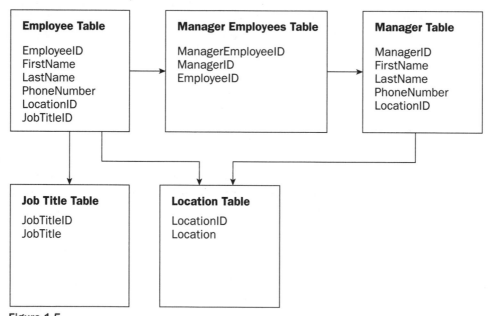

Figure 1-5

Third normal form

The rules of the third normal form dictate that you eliminate columns that do not depend on the primary key. Given the database design shown in Figure 1-5, you have no columns that match this description. All columns in all tables depend on the primary key to identify each row uniquely.

Building the Case Study Databases

In the rest of this book, you use some sample databases to work through the exercises in the chapters. These sample databases should be available to you either on your machine or another machine on your network and depend on whether you have SQL Server and/or Oracle installed.

Starting in Chapter 4, you use an Access database that you either create or download from the Wrox Web site for this book. In Chapter 9 you start using either a SQL Server or Oracle database to complete the rest of the exercises in this book. You can choose which database you want to use or you can use both and create two sets of applications, one for each database.

This section covers the schemas for these databases and provides instructions for creating the databases. In order to create these databases, you will need to download the database scripts for this book from the Wrox Web site or manually enter the scripts as shown in the *Try It Out* exercises.

The application that you build starting in Chapter 4 will be a Project Time Tracker application. This application enables employees to enter the amount of time that they spend on a variety of projects and enables managers to view various reports to track the amount of time employees enter. Additionally, this application provides administrative functions that enable you to manage the data for projects, groups, and users.

As you progress through the chapters in this book, you enhance the application by adding functionality and features. The application starts out using a Microsoft Access database so that you can learn how to access and manage data in this type of database and using one type of ADO.NET provider. An ADO.NET provider is a software component that exposes data and connection information from a database to ADO.NET.

In Chapter 9 you switch over to either a SQL Server or Oracle database, depending on what you choose. Examples from that point on are shown using both SQL Server and Oracle. This exposes you to another type of ADO.NET provider and shows you how to access and manage data in relational databases.

Access schema

The schema shown in Figure 1-6 lists the tables that need to be created in your Access database along with the column attributes and the primary and foreign key relationships. There are two main tables in this schema: Groups and Projects.

Ultimately, users will be assigned to groups; thus, a Groups table has been defined. This table contains group names, such as Finance and Human Resources. The Projects table will contain various projects defined to be worked on. These projects will be ultimately displayed in a user's timesheet so that they can enter the amount of time they spend on each project.

Some projects may be applicable to multiple groups; thus, a GroupProjects table has been defined with foreign keys pointing to the Groups and Projects tables. As you get further along in your development, you'll be retrieving a list of all projects assigned to a specific group from this table.

The primary keys in this schema as well as the schemas for SQL Server and Oracle will all use Guids. This will enable you to port the data from one database to another and ensure that the primary keys across all databases remain unique. A Guid contains a combination of 32 characters and numbers grouped together and separated by four dashes.

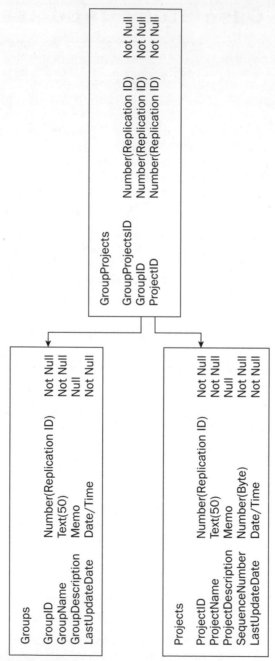

Figure 1-6

If you choose to create your own Access database instead of using the sample Access database available from the Wrox Web site, you can follow the instructions in the next *Try It Out* to create the database:

Try It Out   Creating the ProjectTimeTracker Access Database

1. Start Microsoft Access by clicking Start on the taskbar and then clicking Run.

2. In the Run dialog box, enter MSACCESS and then click OK.

3. Depending on which version of Microsoft Access you have, you may see the Microsoft Access dialog box prompting you to create a new database or open an existing database. Or you may see the New File window docked on the right-hand side of Microsoft Access. Either way, you want to create a new blank database, so choose the Blank Database option.

4. The File New Database dialog box will appear, prompting you to choose a location to create your database and to enter a database name. By default, a database name of db1.mdb has been entered. Choose the location in which to create this database and enter a filename of ProjectTimeTracker.mdb. Then click the Create button to have this database created.

5. The shortcut bar on the left side of the window contains two tabs: Objects and Groups. Under the Objects tab, the shortcut for Tables is selected by default. In the main window three options exist to create tables. You want to double-click the first option: Create table in Design view.

6. The table designer contains three columns: Field Name, Data Type, and Description. The General tab at the bottom of the designer contains the data type attributes after a data type has been chosen. Using Table 1-5, enter the field names, data types, and data type attributes to create the Groups table.

Table 1-5: Groups Table Fields

Field Name	Data Type	Data Type Attributes
GroupID	Number	Field Size = Replication ID; Required = Yes, Indexed = Yes (No Duplicates)
GroupName	Text	Field Length = 50, Required = Yes, Allow Zero Length = No
GroupDescription	Memo	Required = No, Allow Zero Length = Yes
LastUpdateDate	Date/Time	Required = Yes

7. After you enter all the field names and data types and set their attributes, click GroupID in the Field Name column, and then click the Edit menu and choose Primary Key or click the Primary Key icon on the toolbar to set this field as the primary key for the table.

8. To save your table, click the File menu and choose Save or click the Save icon on the toolbar. In the Save As dialog box, enter a name of Groups and then click OK.

9. Close the table designer by clicking on the X in the upper-right corner of the window.

10. The next table that you want to create is the Projects table. Double-click Create table in Design view to open the table designer. Enter the field names, data type, and data type attributes as shown in Table 1-6.

Table 1-6: Projects Table Fields

Field Name	Data Type	Data Type Attributes
ProjectID	Number	Field Size = Replication ID, Required = Yes, Indexed = Yes (No Duplicates)
ProjectName	Text	Field Length = 50, Required = Yes, Allow Zero Length = No
ProjectDescription	Memo	Required = No, Allow Zero Length = No
SequenceNumber	Number	Field Size = Byte, Required = Yes
LastUpdateDate	Date/Time	Required = Yes

11. Click ProjectID in the Field Name column and then click the Edit menu and choose the Primary Key menu item or click the Primary Key icon on the toolbar to set this field as the primary key for the table.

12. Click the File menu and choose Save or click the Save icon on the toolbar. In the Save As dialog box, enter a name of Projects and then click OK.

13. Close the table designer by clicking the X in the upper-right corner of the window.

14. The next table that you want to create is the GroupProjects table. Double-click Create table in Design view to open the table designer. Enter the field names, data type, and data type attributes as shown in Table 1-7.

Table 1-7: GroupProjects Table Fields

Field Name	Data Type	Data Type Attributes
GroupProjectID	Number	Field Size = Replication ID, Required = Yes, Indexed = Yes (No Duplicates)
GroupID	Number	Field Size = Replication ID, Required = Yes, Indexed = Yes (Duplicates OK)
ProjectID	Number	Field Size = Replication ID, Required = Yes, Indexed = Yes (Duplicates OK)

15. Click GroupProjectID in the Field Name column and then click the Edit menu and choose Primary Key or click the Primary Key icon on the toolbar to set this field as the primary key for the table.

16. Click the File menu and choose Save item or click Save. In the Save As dialog box, enter a name of GroupProjects and then click OK.

17. Close the table designer by clicking the X in the upper-right corner of the window.

18. You now need to create a relationship between the GroupProjects table and the Groups and Projects tables. Click the Tools menu and choose Relationships or click the Relationships icon.

19. In the Show Table dialog box, select all three tables and click the Add button. Then click the Close button to close the Show Table dialog box.

20. The Relationships designer now shows all three tables. Click the GroupID column in the GroupProjects table and drag it over to the Groups table and drop it on the GroupID column. This causes the Edit Relationships dialog box to be displayed, as shown in Figure 1-7.

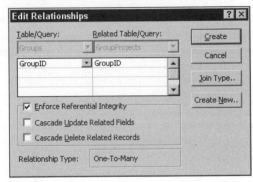

Figure 1-7

21. Click the Enforce Referential Integrity check box and click Create to create the relationship.

22. Click the ProjectID column in the GroupProjects table and drag it over to the Projects table and drop it on the ProjectID column. When the Edit Relationships dialog box is displayed, check the Enforce Referential Integrity check box and click Create to create the relationship.

23. Click the File menu and choose Save or click the Save icon to save your relationships.

24. Close the Relationships designer by clicking the X in the upper-right corner of the designer.

25. Close Access by clicking the File menu and choosing Exit or by clicking the X in the upper-right corner of the window.

How It Works

You start by creating your tables. As part of this process, you designate the first field name in each table as the primary key. This tells Access that this column is the primary key of the table and Access implements the rules to enforce this column as a primary key, including not allowing NULL values in this field and preventing you from entering duplicate values in this field. Access also creates an index on this column, providing efficient access to the data in these tables when accessed using the primary key.

After your tables are created, you define the relationships between your tables using the Relationships designer. By dragging the foreign key from the GroupProjects table to the primary key of the Groups table, you create a one-to-many relationship between the Groups and GroupProjects tables. This means that one row of data in the Groups table corresponds to many rows in the GroupProjects table. You do the same thing for the Projects table, creating a one-to-many relationship between the Projects and GroupProjects tables.

SQL Server schema

The Access schema was small compared to the SQL Server schema shown in Figure 1-8. You will be doing a limited amount of work on the Project Time Tracker application in Access. Most of your development of this application will be done in either SQL Server or Oracle. Therefore, the schema for SQL Server and Oracle will be larger and comprise all the tables that make up the ProjectTimeTracker database.

Because you've already seen the Groups, Projects, and GroupProjects tables, they won't be covered again. Instead, you'll focus on the other tables shown in the schema. Before you look at the other tables, however, take note of the data types used in the Groups, Projects, and GroupProjects tables. These data types have been converted from Access data types to SQL Server data types. A complete data type cross reference is available in Appendix A.

Of particular interest is the data type for the primary keys. SQL Server has a native data type, called a UniqueIdentifier, that supports Guids as seen in the schema. SQL Server also provides a built-in function that can generate Guids to be inserted into a column with this data type. However, you generate the Guids from your program using the built-in .NET Framework function called Guid.NewGuid().

Let's start by examining the Users table. This table contains all users with access to the application and the basic information about the users. You may have noticed that the Password column is five times the size of the LoginName column. This is because you will be hashing the user's password when inserting a new user in Chapter 11. A hashed password can be almost five times the size of the original password so this column has been designed to handle a hashed password based on a password that is a maximum length of 15 characters.

Also note that there is a foreign key relationship to the Groups table. Every user will be assigned to a group and this key provides the relationship between the Groups and Users tables.

Also notice that there is a foreign key relationship to the Roles table. Every user will be assigned to a role. The Roles table contains the various roles that may be assigned, such as Administrator, Manager, and User. The Roles table contains a column called Ranking. The roles will be defined by rank, so a role of Administrator has a higher ranking than Manager, and the Manager role has a higher ranking than User. You use this column later when selecting and displaying data from this table.

Finally, notice that there is a foreign key reference from the ManagerID column to the UserID column. A manager is a user like anyone else, only with a different role. This column allows a NULL value to be inserted because you may not want to assign a manager to a user when you enter a user. Once updated with a value, this column contains the UserID of the manager, enabling you to retrieve the user information for each user as well as information about his or her manager.

The last two tables in this schema are TimeSheets and TimeSheetItems. The TimeSheets table contains the basic information about a timesheet for any given week for a user. Notice that this table contains two foreign key references to the Users table. The first foreign key, UserID, is the foreign key that points to the user of this timesheet. The second foreign key, ManagerID, points to the manager who has approved the timesheet; this will be the manager of the user.

The last table in this schema is the TimeSheetItems table. This table contains a row of data for each project that is assigned to the user in the GroupProjects table. It also contains a row of data for each project for each day for which the user enters data (see Figure 1-8).

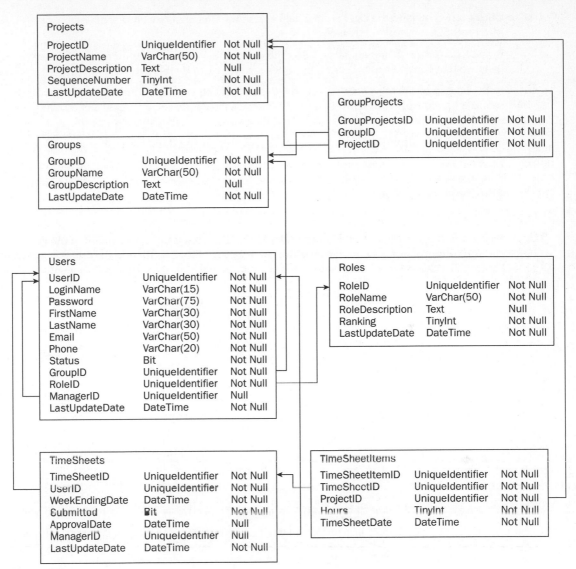

Figure 1-8

The steps in the following Try It Out assume that the physical database, ProjectTimeTracker, has been created by you or your DBA and that you have the appropriate permissions to create objects, such as tables and indexes, in that database.

Try It Out   **Creating the ProjectTimeTracker SQL Server Database**

1. Start Visual Studio 2005.

2. View the Server Explorer window and then click the Auto Hide icon on the title bar so that the Server Explorer window stays visible.

3. Right-click the Data Connections node and choose Add Connection from the context menu.

4. Click Change next to the Data Source field and in the Change Data Source dialog box, select Microsoft SQL Server and then click OK.

5. In the Add Connection dialog box, select the name of the computer running the SQL Server instance that contains your ProjectTimeTracker database in the Server name field.

6. In the Log on to the server section, choose the type of authentication that your account has been set up with (consult your DBA if you did not set up the database and create an account yourself). If you are using a specific User ID and Password, check the Save my password check box.

7. Select the ProjectTimeTracker database in the Select or enter a database name combo box.

8. Click the Test Connection button to verify your credentials. If the test did not succeed, verify your credentials and contact your DBA if necessary. When you are done, click OK to close the Add Connection dialog box.

9. Expand the Data Connection node that you just created.

10. Right-click the Tables node and choose Add New Table from the context menu. In the designer, add the columns and column attributes for the Projects table according to the schema shown in Figure 1-8. When you are done, your designer should look like the one shown in Figure 1-9.

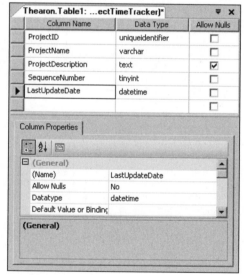

Figure 1-9

11. You now need to set the primary key for this table. Click the ProjectID column and click the Table Designer menu and select the Set Primary Key menu item or click the Set Primary Key icon on the toolbar. The Primary Key icon will be displayed in the row selector for the ProjectID column.

12. Save the table by clicking the File menu and selecting the Save Table1 menu item or by clicking the Save Table1 icon on the toolbar. In the Choose Name dialog box, enter a table name of Projects and then click OK. Finally, close the designer for the Projects table.

13. Repeat Steps 10 through 12 for the rest of the tables shown in the schema in Figure 1-8. The primary key for each table is the first column listed in each table. Don't worry about the foreign key relationships, as you add those in the next few steps.

14. At this point, all of your tables have been created and their primary keys have been set. You need to add the foreign key relationships between your tables. Double-click the GroupProjects table. When the Table Designer is displayed, click the Table Designer menu and choose Relationships or click the Relationships icon on the toolbar. The Foreign Key Relationships dialog box is displayed and this is where you define the primary and foreign relationships between your tables.

15. Click the Add button in the Foreign Key Relationships dialog box. In the Properties window, click the Tables and Columns Specification property as shown in Figure 1-10. Then click the elipse button for this property to display the Tables and Columns dialog box.

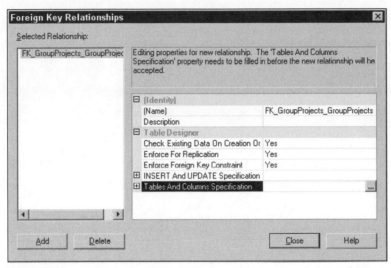

Figure 1-10

16. In the Tables and Columns dialog box, select the Groups table in the Primary key table combo box and then click in the empty row under this combo box and select GroupID in the combo box that is displayed. In the first row under the Foreign key table column, select GroupID in the combo box that is displayed there as shown in Figure 1-11. When you are done, click OK to return to the Foreign Key Relationships dialog box.

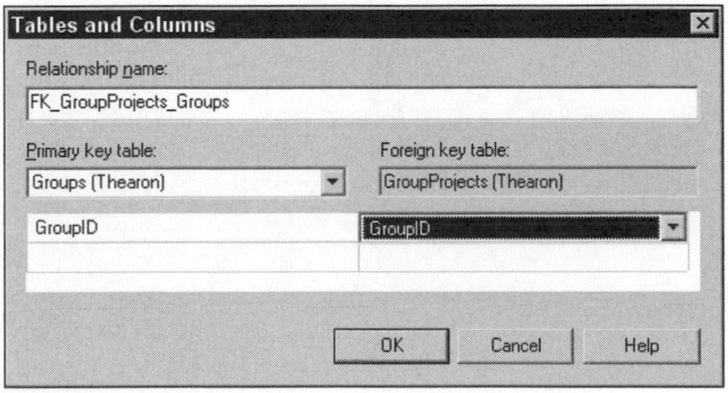

Figure 1-11

17. Click the Add button in the Foreign Key Relationships dialog box to add another relationship. In the Properties window, click the Tables and Columns Specification property and then click the elipse button for this property to display the Tables and Columns dialog box.

18. In the Tables and Columns dialog box, select the Projects table in the Primary key table combo box and then click in the empty row under this combo box and select ProjectID in the combo box that is displayed. In the first row under the Foreign key table column, select ProjectID in the combo box that is displayed there and then click OK to return to the Foreign Key Relationships dialog box.

19. Click Close to close the Foreign Key Relationships dialog box. Next, click the Save icon on the toolbar to save the GroupProjects table. You are prompted with the tables that will be saved in your database, which are the tables affected by this relationship. Click Yes to proceed.

20. Using Table 1-8, repeat Steps 14 through 19 to create the rest of the foreign key relationships in your database.

Table 1-8: Foreign Key Relationships

Foreign Key Table	Foreign Key	Primary Key Table	Primary Key
Users	ManagerID	Users	UserID
Users	GroupID	Groups	GroupID
Users	RoleID	Roles	RoleID
TimeSheets	UserID	Users	UserID
TimeSheets	ManagerID	Users	UserID
TimeSheetItems	TimeSheetID	TimeSheets	TimeSheetID
TimeSheetItems	ProjectID	Projects	ProjectID

How It Works

Using Visual Studio 2005, you connect to the SQL Server instance that contains your ProjectTimeTracker database in the Server Explorer window using a Data Connection. You are then able to use Visual Studio 2005 to create the tables within your database.

During the process of creating your tables, you set the primary key on each table, effectively creating a clustered index on the table based on the primary key. After all the tables are created, you create the foreign key relationships between the tables, joining the foreign key in one table to the primary key in another table. This causes a relationship to be formed between your tables and enforces the values that can be inserted into a table containing a foreign key. The table containing a foreign key will not allow you to insert a value in the foreign key column that does not exist in the primary key column of the primary table.

Oracle schema

The Oracle schema, shown in Figure 1-12, is similar to the SQL Server schema shown in Figure 1-8. The only differences between these schemas are the data types. Every database vendor has its own implementation for data types and the differences are usually subtle. Therefore, there's no need to cover the details of the schema again. Refer to Appendix A for a complete data type conversion between the different databases.

However, I do want to point out the data type used for primary keys in this schema. Oracle, like SQL Server, has a data type that supports Guids. Unfortunately, Oracle's implementation of this data type does not support the Guids you are used to seeing in Windows. The RAW(16) data type in Oracle supports Guids without the dashes, and Oracle even has a built-in function to generate Guids, Sys_Guid. This function also generates Guids without the dashes.

Because you will be generating the Guids from your program and will be porting the data from the Access database to either a SQL Server or Oracle database in Chapter 8, I chose to implement the primary key as a Char(36) data type in Oracle. This will enable you to port the data from Access to Oracle without any special considerations or the need to massage the data during the porting.

The steps in the following *Try It Out* assume that the physical database, ProjectTimeTracker, has been created by you or your DBA. Visual Studio 2005 does not support creating tables in an Oracle database in the designer as you did for SQL Server.

To that end, the process that you'll use for creating the tables, primary keys, and foreign key relationships will be performed through a SQL script. Therefore, you need to use your Oracle client tools — namely, iSQL Plus* or any other third-party tools that you normally use to run SQL scripts against Oracle.

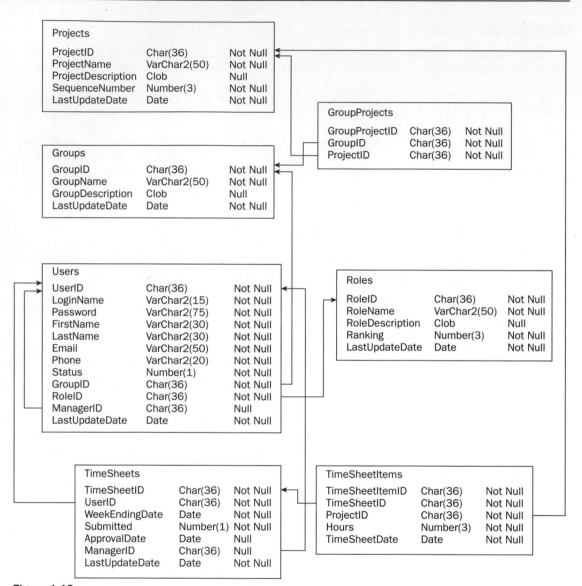

Figure 1-12

Try It Out   **Creating the ProjectTimeTracker Oracle Database**

1. Start SQL Plus or your favorite third-party tool for running SQL scripts against an Oracle database.

2. Enter and execute the following script to create your tables:

```
---------------------------------------------------------------------
-- Tables
---------------------------------------------------------------------
CREATE TABLE Projects
(
    ProjectID char(36) NOT NULL,
    ProjectName varchar2(50) NOT NULL,
    ProjectDescription clob NULL,
    SequenceNumber number(3) NOT NULL,
    LastUpdateDate date NOT NULL
);

CREATE TABLE Groups
(
    GroupID char(36) NOT NULL,
    GroupName varchar2(50) NOT NULL,
    GroupDescription clob NULL,
    LastUpdateDate date NOT NULL
);

CREATE TABLE GroupProjects
(
    GroupProjectID char(36) NOT NULL,
    GroupID char(36) NOT NULL,
    ProjectID char(36) NOT NULL
);

CREATE TABLE Users
(
    UserID char(36) NOT NULL,
    LoginName varchar2(15) NOT NULL,
    Password varchar2(75) NOT NULL,
    FirstName varchar2(30) NOT NULL,
    LastName varchar2(30) NOT NULL,
    Email varchar2(50) NOT NULL,
    Phone varchar2(20) NOT NULL,
    Status number(1) NOT NULL,
    GroupID char(36) NOT NULL,
    RoleID char(36) NOT NULL,
    ManagerID char(36) NULL,
    LastUpdateDate date NOT NULL
);

CREATE TABLE Roles
(
    RoleID char(36) NOT NULL,
    RoleName varchar2(50) NOT NULL,
    RoleDescription clob NULL,
```

```
    Ranking number(3) NOT NULL,
    LastUpdateDate date NOT NULL
);

CREATE TABLE TimeSheets
(
    TimeSheetID char(36) NOT NULL,
    UserID char(36) NOT NULL,
    WeekEndingDate date NOT NULL,
    Submitted number(1) NOT NULL,
    ApprovalDate date NULL,
    ManagerID char(36) NULL,
    LastUpdateDate date NOT NULL
);

CREATE TABLE TimeSheetItems
(
    TimeSheetItemID char(36) NOT NULL,
    TimeSheetID char(36) NOT NULL,
    ProjectID char(36) NOT NULL,
    Hours number(3) NOT NULL,
    TimeSheetDate date NOT NULL
);
```

3.   Enter and execute the following script to create the primary keys in the tables you just created:

```
----------------------------------------------------------------------
-- Primary Keys
----------------------------------------------------------------------
ALTER TABLE Projects ADD
(
    CONSTRAINT PK_Projects PRIMARY KEY (ProjectID)
);

ALTER TABLE Groups ADD
(
    CONSTRAINT PK_Groups PRIMARY KEY (GroupID)
);

ALTER TABLE GroupProjects ADD
(
    CONSTRAINT PK_GroupProjects PRIMARY KEY (GroupProjectID)
);

ALTER TABLE Users ADD
(
    CONSTRAINT PK_Users PRIMARY KEY (UserID)
);

ALTER TABLE Roles ADD
(
    CONSTRAINT PK_Roles PRIMARY KEY (RoleID)
);

ALTER TABLE TimeSheets ADD
```

```
(
    CONSTRAINT PK_TimeSheets PRIMARY KEY (TimeSheetID)
);

ALTER TABLE TimeSheetItems ADD
(
    CONSTRAINT PK_TimeSheetItems PRIMARY KEY (TimeSheetItemID)
);
```

4. Finally, you need to create the foreign key relationships between your tables, so enter and execute the following script:

```
---------------------------------------------------------------------
-- Foreign Key Relationships
---------------------------------------------------------------------
ALTER TABLE GroupProjects ADD
(
    FOREIGN KEY (GroupID) REFERENCES Groups (GroupID),
    FOREIGN KEY (ProjectID) REFERENCES Projects (ProjectID)
);

ALTER TABLE Users ADD
(
    FOREIGN KEY (ManagerID) REFERENCES Users (UserID),
    FOREIGN KEY (GroupID) REFERENCES Groups (GroupID),
    FOREIGN KEY (RoleID) REFERENCES Roles (RoleID)
);

ALTER TABLE TimeSheets ADD
(
    FOREIGN KEY (UserID) REFERENCES Users (UserID),
    FOREIGN KEY (ManagerID) REFERENCES Users (UserID)
);

ALTER TABLE TimeSheetItems ADD
(
    FOREIGN KEY (TimeSheetID) REFERENCES TimeSheets (TimeSheetID),
    FOREIGN KEY (ProjectID) REFERENCES Projects (ProjectID)
);
```

How It Works

The first script that you run creates all the tables in the Oracle schema shown in Figure 1-11. At this point, the primary keys are not defined so you run the second script to alter the tables to add the constraints that set the primary key in each table. Finally, you run the last script to create the foreign key relationships between the tables.

Summary

This chapter has been quite diverse, covering the major components that make up an Access, SQL Server, and Oracle database. If you weren't already familiar with them, you should now understand the components of each of these databases and how they tie together to comprise a single database. You should also have gained a deeper appreciation for each of these databases and know which database will meet your business requirements for future projects that you may work on.

You also took a look at relational database design and the process of normalization. Armed with this information, you should be able to set out and design a database for your own use. As you become more familiar with the process of normalization through practical implementation, your skills for designing and normalizing a database will grow and the process will become easier.

At the end of the chapter, I walked you through the process of creating the sample databases that are used throughout the rest of this book. You built your Access database directly in Access, creating the tables, primary keys, and foreign key relationships. Using Visual Studio 2005, you connected to a SQL Server instance and used the designer within the Integrated Development Environment (IDE) to create the tables, set the primary keys, and build the foreign key relationships. The tables created in your Oracle database were created using scripts. You also used scripts to create the primary and foreign key relationships in those Oracle tables.

To summarize, you should know:

- ❑ A Microsoft Access database consists of a single file that contains all of the objects (e.g., tables, indexes, queries) in the database.

- ❑ A Microsoft SQL Server database comprises at least two files, and the data file contains all of the objects (e.g., tables, indexes, stored procedures, views) that make up the database.

- ❑ An Oracle database comprises at least five files, and the data file contains all of the objects (e.g., tables, indexes, stored procedures, views) that make up the database.

- ❑ A relational database contains tables, rows, and columns that are related to one another.

- ❑ The process of normalization involves normalizing your data through formal methods to eliminate duplicate data, and to separate data into multiple related tables.

- ❑ The three forms of normalization are known as first normal form, second normal form, and third normal form.

Chapter 2 provides an introduction to ADO.NET. ADO.NET comprises the data access classes that you'll be using to access and manage the data in your various databases.

An Introduction to ADO.NET

ADO.NET components are at the core of developing database applications and provide the necessary classes that enable you to connect to a data store and to retrieve, manipulate, and update data. Many components are available in ADO.NET, which is implemented under the `System.Data` namespace. This chapter provides an introduction to ADO.NET and the major components that you use throughout the rest of this book.

As you progress through this chapter, you examine some of the base classes in ADO.NET that enable you to connect to a database, execute SQL statements, and retrieve and update data in your databases. This chapter is meant to be an introduction to ADO.NET; you get more detailed hands-on experience with these classes in the upcoming chapters, and by the end of the book you will be quite comfortable with ADO.NET.

In this chapter, you:

❑   Get an introduction to ADO.NET and its architecture

❑   Learn about the different ADO.NET providers

❑   Learn about the `Connection` and `Command` components

❑   Learn about the `DataAdapter` and `DataReader` components

❑   Learn about the `DataSet` and `DataTable` components

ADO.NET Overview

ADO is an acronym for ActiveX Data Objects, which prior to ADO.NET and the .NET Framework was Microsoft's premier data access technology. Windows developers everywhere embraced this easy-to-use technology for building database applications for Windows and the Web. This technology provided a user-friendly interface for accessing data in any type of database and was accessible to developers coding in most any type of language.

One of the initial design goals for ADO.NET was to keep the programming model as closely related to ADO as possible so developers could leverage their existing experience with ADO and ramp up quickly with ADO.NET. While this is great for experienced developers, it is also an enormous benefit for new developers. You get to learn a data access technology that is easy to use and very flexible.

ADO.NET has matured since its first offering in the .NET Framework version 1.0. It has been extended to make it even more developer friendly and more powerful than ever before. In this section, you get a general overview of the ADO.NET architecture as well as the components that make up ADO.NET.

ADO.NET architecture

The ADO.NET architecture can be broken into three major components: Data Provider, DataSet, and DataTable. Figure 2-1 shows these major components at a high level. Notice that the Data Provider component has several subcomponents listed: DbConnection, DbCommand, DbDataAdapter, and DbDataReader. These are the base classes that the specific data provider components are inherited from. You will be using these components to connect to your database, execute SQL commands, retrieve data, and read data. These subcomponents are covered in more detail later in this chapter.

The Data Provider component has been implemented in several versions and these different versions all inherit from the base version shown in Figure 2-1. There is a version for accessing Open DataBase Connectivity (ODBC)–compliant databases, a version for accessing Object Linking and Embedding DataBase (OLE DB)–compliant databases, a version for accessing SQL Server databases, and a version for accessing Oracle databases. You examine all of these versions in more detail in Chapter 3.

Another major component in this architecture is the DataSet component. The DataSet component can be populated with data retrieved from the database by the DataAdapter component and can also contain a collection of DataTable components. Notice in Figure 2-1 that the line between the DataProvider and the DataSet contains arrows pointing both ways because the DataAdapter component not only retrieves data from the database and populates the DataSet but is also used to read data from the DataSet component and update the database.

The DataTable component can either be used in the DataSet component or used as a standalone component. This component can also be filled with data using either the DataAdapter or DataReader components. The line pointing between the DataTable and the Data Provider in Figure 2-1 is also a bi-directional line as the DataTable can be used by the DataAdapter to update the database.

A few other aspects of the ADO.NET architecture are worth noting. The first is that the architecture provides a disconnected data access model. This means that you connect to your database, get the data that you need, and then disconnect from the database. You work with the data offline in the DataSet or DataTable components. This provides high scalability for your applications as it allows more clients to connect to the database and retrieve data. This is particularly important in Web applications, where you could potentially have thousands of clients requesting data simultaneously.

The other important aspect of the architecture is that the DataSet and DataTable components were designed hand in hand with the XML classes in the .NET Framework. The DataSet and DataTable components use XML behind the scenes to store and manipulate the data. This makes it an ideal method for transporting data between programs and computers.

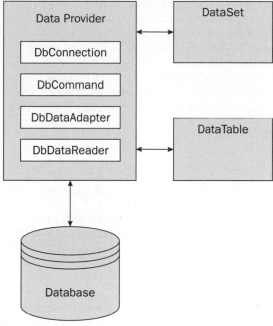

Figure 2-1

ADO.NET components

Now that you've had an overview of the ADO.NET architecture and are aware of the major components that make up ADO.NET, you can explore these major components in more detail. In this section you look at the Data Provider, DataSet and DataTable components.

As mentioned earlier, the Data Provider component comes in several versions. The following sections explore these versions in more depth so that you may gain a better understanding of them. This will enable you to make an informed decision about which version of the Data Provider to use when connecting to the various databases.

ODBC Data Provider

ODBC is a technology that predates OLE DB, and a few applications still use ODBC to connect to databases such as Access, SQL Server, and Oracle. Older databases support only ODBC as the data access technology. These could be older versions of SQL Server and Oracle or manufacturers of other databases such as Sybase.

This Data Provider uses the ODBC Driver Manager behind the scenes to communicate with databases that support the ODBC technology. Although this is not the most efficient Data Provider to use with the latest versions of SQL Server or Oracle, it is the most efficient Data Provider for databases that support only the ODBC technology.

Whenever you want to use a Data Provider in your VB 2005 programs, you must import the appropriate namespace. The ODBC Data Provider has been implemented in the System.Data.Odbc namespace, and all classes in this namespace are prefixed with Odbc. For example, the Connection component will be implemented in a class called OdbcConnection.

All the different versions of the Data Providers are implemented in their own namespaces and have their own classes. Although the different Data Providers are implemented in their own namespaces and have different class names, they provide a consistent interface. For example, the Connection component for the ODBC Data Provider is implemented in a class called OdbcConnection, while the Connection component for OLE DB is implemented in a class called OleDbConnection.

Both of these classes provide properties and methods that contain the same name, such as a ConnectionString property and an Open and Close method. The same holds true for the SQL Server and Oracle Data Providers. This makes it easy to switch between the different providers and work with an interface that you are already familiar with.

The Data Provider itself is broken into other components, as shown in Figure 2-1. You explore those components in more detail in sections that follow and throughout the rest of this book.

OLE DB Data Provider

This Data Provider is implemented in the System.Data.OleDb namespace and uses the OLE DB technology to provide data access to databases that implement the OLE DB technology. This includes all newer versions of databases such as Access, SQL Server, and Oracle.

If you need generic access to a variety of databases in your application you can use the OLE DB Data Provider. After you import the System.Data.OleDb namespace in your application, you will be able to make separate or simultaneous connections to Access, SQL Server, and Oracle databases and other databases that support OLE DB.

Using this Data Provider also enables you to create database-independent applications, meaning your code need not know which database it is connecting to. You need to take only one special consideration into account here and that is the connection string used by the OleDbConnection class to connect to the database. This connection string will be slightly different for Access, SQL Server, and Oracle. You could provide this connection string external to your program by means of the registry or a configuration file. That way, you can switch your compiled application from one database to another without changing any code or recompiling your application.

SQL Server Data Provider

This Data Provider is used exclusively with SQL Server and is implemented in the System.Data .SqlClient namespace. This Data Provider communicates with SQL Server directly through SQL Server's own protocol, providing optimized data access to SQL Server. This Data Provider can be used only with SQL Server version 7.0 and later. If you are accessing an earlier version of SQL Server, you need to use the OLE DB Data Provider.

If your application is being written exclusively to access a SQL Server database, use this Data Provider as it provides the best optimized performance.

Oracle Data Provider

The Oracle Data Provider is implemented in the `System.Data.OracleClient` namespace and as its name indicates, it provides access only to Oracle databases. Like its SQL Server counterpart, this Data Provider is used exclusively for Oracle and provides the most efficient access to Oracle databases. This Data Provider uses the Oracle client connectivity software to communicate with Oracle; thus, you need to install this software on the machine running your program from your Oracle CD before you can make use of this Data Provider.

Also note that this Data Provider supports only Oracle versions 8.1.7 and later. If your Oracle database is earlier than this version, you need to use the OLE DB Data Provider to access your Oracle database.

Again, like its SQL Server counterpart, this Data Provider provides the most efficient access to Oracle databases and should be used in applications that will access only Oracle databases.

Provider base

All of the different providers discussed so far inherit the various DB classes such as `DBConnection` and `DBCommand` from the provider base. Then each of the different providers adds functionality specific to the database provider that it is using to optimize its classes. For example, the Oracle Data Provider implements Oracle-specific functions to optimize that provider for accessing Oracle databases.

The classes in the provider base can be used to provide generic access to a variety of databases just as the OLE DB Data Provider can because that provider inherits from the provider base. You can specify the type of provider that the provider base should use at runtime, allowing you to dynamically configure the data provider to be used. You see an actual example of this in Chapter 8 when you migrate data from an Access database to either a SQL Server database or an Oracle database.

DataTable component

The `DataTable` component is one of the two main ADO.NET components used to store and manipulate data and is Data Provider independent. This component is implemented in the `System.Data` namespace and can be used by the various Data Providers you just explored. Each of those Data Providers can populate the `DataTable` component with data and use the `DataTable` component to update data in the database.

The `DataTable` component is an ideal component to use when working with data from a single table in your database. You can use this component to bind data to controls or work with the data in this component programmatically.

DataSet component

The `DataSet` component is another of the two main ADO.NET components used to store and manipulate data and is also Data Provider–independent. This component is implemented in the `System.Data` namespace and can be used by the various Data Providers you just explored. Each of those Data Providers can populate the `DataSet` component with data and use the `DataSet` component to update data in the database.

Because ADO.NET is designed to provide a disconnected model, the `DataSet` component needs to know a lot of information about the data, such as the structure of the data and the relationships of the data. To that end, the `DataSet` component consists of several collections, as shown in Figure 2-2.

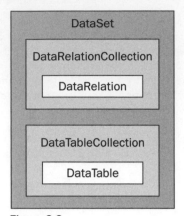

Figure 2-2

When you select data from your database and populate the DataSet component, the data and its related information is stored in the DataTable of the DataTableCollection, as shown in Figure 2-2. This not only includes the actual values of the columns in your SELECT statement, but also the column names and column attributes, such as whether the column is a VarChar or Integer data type. It also stores constraint information contained in the table from which the data was selected. For instance, if the column does not allow NULL values, the DataTable will also contain this information and not allow you to update the DataSet to set that column to null.

You can populate the DataSet component with multiple results sets. That is, you can perform multiple SELECT statements and add the results of each to the DataSet component as a DataTable. After you have multiple DataTables in the DataTableCollection, you can create a relationship between the tables using the DataRelation class.

A relationship between the DataTables is not automatically created; this is a process that you must perform as there may be no relationship between the tables at all. You create a DataRelation in the DataRelationCollection for each set of tables that has a relationship. For example, suppose you populated the DataSet component with the data from the Groups, Projects, and GroupProjects tables shown in your Access schema in Chapter 1.

In essence, you would have three DataTables in the DataTableCollection and would want to create a relationship between the Groups and GroupProjects table. You would then create a DataRelation in the DataRelationCollection for this relationship. Then you would create another DataRelation for the relationship between the Projects and GroupProjects tables.

A DataRelation is typically performed on the primary and foreign keys in your tables, in much the same manner as you create the primary and foreign key relationships in your database. A DataRelation performs the same function as the primary and foreign key relationships in your database. That is, it prevents you from breaking the relationship between the tables by updating data in the primary or foreign key columns that would break the relationship.

Starting in Chapter 3, you see how the DataSet component works; and in Chapter 4, you get first-hand experience with the DataSet component and start to explore it in more detail.

Connection Class

The Data Provider component shown in Figure 2-1 consists of many subcomponents or classes. One of those classes is the Connection class. Each version of the Data Provider component implements the same subcomponents. So for a Connection, classes exist for DB (Database), ODBC, OLE DB, SQL Server, and Oracle, and are named DBConnection, OdbcConnection, OleDbConnection, SqlConnection, and OracleConnection, respectively. These classes implement the same properties and methods.

In this section, you look at the OleDbConnection class in more detail. However, the properties and methods you examine here apply to the other Connection classes mentioned previously. Described here are the most common functions that you perform with the Connection class.

Common constructors

Almost every class in the .NET Framework has a constructor called New. Sometimes the constructor for a class does not accept any parameters, and sometimes the constructor is overloaded, meaning that multiple constructors accept different parameters.

The OleDbConnection class has two constructors: one that does not accept any parameters and one that accepts a connection string as input. This second constructor type is the most commonly used constructor for the OleDbConnection class.

The connection string used in the constructor provides the OleDbConnection class with all the information necessary to connect to a database. This typically includes the following common parameters:

- ❏ Provider
- ❏ Data Source
- ❏ Database
- ❏ User ID
- ❏ Password

This is not a complete list of parameters but the most commonly used parameters in a connection string. Let's take a look at each of these parameters in turn.

The Provider parameter specifies the driver that the OleDbConnection class uses to communicate with the database. The most common drivers are Microsoft.Jet.OLEDB.4.0 for Access, SQLOLEDB for SQL Server, and MSDAORA for Oracle. The actual drivers for the OdbcConnection class are different from the OLE DB drivers, and the MSDN Library that is installed with Visual Studio 2005 lists those drivers. Because the SqlConnection and OracleConnection classes have been designed specifically for SQL Server and Oracle, the Provider parameter is not needed for those classes.

The Data Source parameter is used to specify the server name of the computer on which the database is running. This parameter is used to make a network connection to that server to communicate with the database server. When connecting to an Access database, this specifies the path and database name.

The Database parameter is self-explanatory and specifies the database name where your data resides.

Finally, the User ID and Password parameters are used to specify your database login credentials — the User ID and Password defined in the database, not your Windows login credentials.

Now that you know what typical parameters are used for a connection string, take a look at some examples using these in a constructor for the OleDbConnection class. The connection string can be defined separately as a String variable and passed to the constructor as shown in the examples that follow or it can be passed to the constructor as a string constant.

The connection string shown in the following code snippet is connecting to an Access database. Notice that the Data Source parameter specifies the full path and database name of the database to which you want to connect. Because the Data Source contains all the information about the database and where it resides, the Database parameter has been omitted. Also note that the User ID and Password parameters have been omitted. This Access database does not implement a database password.

If the Access database has implemented a password, you would typically specify a User ID of Admin, which is the default user created when setting a password on an Access database. You would then specify the appropriate password in the Password parameter.

```
Dim strConnectionString As String = _
    "Provider=Microsoft.Jet.OLEDB.4.0;" & _
    "Data Source=C:\Program Files\Microsoft Office\Office11\Samples\Northwind.mdb;"
Dim objConnection As New OleDbConnection(strConnectionString)
```

A typical connection string to connect to a SQL Server database is shown in the next code fragment. The Data Source parameter specifies the server name of the computer running SQL Server. If SQL Server has been installed as a named instance, you specify the server name followed by a backslash followed by the instance name. SQL Server allows multiple instances to be installed on the same computer, and all instances other than the default instance (the first installation) must be uniquely identified by an instance name.

The Database parameter specifies the database in SQL Server to which you want to connect, and the User ID and Password parameters specify your database login credentials:

```
Dim strConnectionString As String = _
    "Provider=SQLOLEDB;Data Source=SCorporateDb;Database=pubs;" & _
    "User ID=sa;Password=foo"
Dim objConnection As New OleDbConnection(strConnectionString)
```

The Data Source parameter for an Oracle connection *does not* specify the server name on which your Oracle database is running. Instead it specifies the system identifier (SID) defined in your tnsnames.ora file, which was created when you installed and configured the Oracle client on your computer. The tnsnames.ora file contains the information necessary to connect to your Oracle database, such as the protocol to use, the server name, and the port number on which Oracle listens. It also specifies the database to use, which is why you do not specify the Database parameter, as shown in the following code snippet.

You do need to specify the User ID and Password parameters used to connect to your Oracle database.

```
Dim strConnectionString As String = _
    "Provider=MSDAORA;Data Source=OracleDB;" & _
    "User ID=system;Password=foo"
Dim objConnection As New OleDbConnection(strConnectionString)
```

Opening a connection

Opening the actual database connection is a straightforward process, as the Open method in the OleDbConnection class takes no parameters. However, because things could go wrong, it's important that you add error handling around the code that opens the database connection so you can catch the most typical errors.

In the following code snippet, a Try...Catch block has been implemented to handle any errors that occur during the opening of the database connection. In the Try block you specify the Open method to open your connection. If the Open method is successful, you write the connection state to the output window in the IDE. The State property of the OleDbConnection class returns the current state of the connection in a ConnectionState enumeration. Because the value returned is of little use to you, you specify the ToString method, which writes the member name in the enumeration.

The Try...Catch block has two Catch blocks to handle two types of errors. The first Catch block handles connection-level errors that occur while trying to open the database connection. The second Catch block handles the exception that is thrown when the database connection is already open. These Catch blocks write the error to the output window in the IDE.

```
Try
    objConnection.Open()
    Debug.WriteLine(objConnection.State.ToString)
Catch OleDbExceptionErr As OleDbException
    Debug.WriteLine(OleDbExceptionErr.Message)
Catch InvalidOperationExceptionErr As InvalidOperationException
    Debug.WriteLine(InvalidOperationExceptionErr.Message)
 End Try
```

Closing a connection

After you finish with your database connection, you close it to release the database resources held by the connection. Like the Open method, the Close method takes no parameters and is straightforward.

You can call the Close method on a connection that is not open because the Close method does not throw any exceptions when trying to close a connection that is already closed. Thus, the code to close the database connection is outside of the Try block shown in the previous snippet, as you always execute the code to close the connection. In the following code fragment, you are calling the Close method to close the database connection and then the Dispose method to release all resources held by the Connection object.

Calling the Dispose method provides a means to clean up the resources held by the connection object and keeps the memory usage of your program down by releasing unneeded resources. You could get away with not calling the Dispose method because at some point the Garbage Collector (GC) examines the Connection object, sees that it is no longer being used, and performs the cleanup. However, it is best coding practice to always call the Dispose method on objects that support it.

Finally, you release your reference to the Connection object by setting it to Nothing:

```
objConnection.Close()
objConnection.Dispose()
objConnection = Nothing
```

Command Class

The Command class is listed as one of the subcomponents of the Data Provider component shown in Figure 2-1. You know that a Command class exists for DB, ODBC, OLE DB, SQL Server, and Oracle, and that they are functionally equivalent. You also know that these different classes implement the same properties and methods.

Therefore, in this section you take a look at the OleDbCommand class in more detail. Keep in mind that the properties and methods that you examine here also apply to the other Command classes mentioned previously. The Command class provides a means for you to execute SQL statements, stored procedures, and views against your database. The SQL statements, stored procedures, and views that you execute can select, insert, update, and delete data in your database. You can also use the Parameters collection in the Command class to pass parameters to your SQL statements and stored procedures. You examine the Parameters collection in more depth starting in Chapter 4.

The OleDbCommand class provides several overloaded constructors. However, the one that you are most likely to use as you start coding database applications is the constructor shown in the next example. This constructor takes a String value that contains the SQL statements that you want executed and an OleDbConnection object representing the connection to your database. The database connection does not have to be open at this point; you just need a connection object that has been initialized through its constructor.

In the code that follows, a String variable defined as strSQL has been set to select the first and last names contained in the Employees table from an Oracle database. Notice that the table name has also been prefixed with the database owner, which in this case is HR.

You then declare a variable as an OleDbCommand class and initialize it through its constructor using the String variable defined in the first line of the code and a Connection object previously defined. At this point, you can use this Command object with a DataReader or DataAdapter to retrieve the data from your database.

```
Dim strSQL As String = _
    "SELECT FIRST_NAME, LAST_NAME FROM HR.EMPLOYEES"
Dim objCommand As New OleDbCommand(strSQL, objConnection)
```

Another constructor that you are likely to use is one in which you execute a stored procedure that accepts parameters. In a case like this, you can use the constructor shown in the previous code fragment or the constructor shown below. Irregardless, you have to set an additional property of the Command object: CommandType.

The CommandType property specifies how the CommandText property is to be interpreted. By default, the CommandType property is set to Text, which interprets the CommandText property as a SQL statement to be executed. Using the CommandType enumeration, you can select the appropriate value. In the following code fragment, this has been set to StoredProcedure, which indicates that you are executing a stored procedure.

Finally, you want to add a Parameter object to the Parameters collection of the Command object for each parameter that the stored procedure expects. In this case, the stored procedure expects only one parameter, which specifies the Employee ID of the employee.

The `Add` method of the `Parameters` collection is an overloaded method, meaning that you can choose from multiple `Add` methods. The one that you are most likely to use is shown in this code fragment. Here you specify the parameter name, the data type of the parameter, and the size of the parameter. In addition to adding the `Parameter` to the `Parameters` collection, you are also setting its value using the `Value` property.

After all the `Command` object's properties are set and the appropriate parameters are added to the `Parameters` collection, the `Command` object is ready to be used by the `DataAdapter` or `DataReader` objects.

```
Dim objCommand As New OleDbCommand
objCommand.Connection = objConnection
objCommand.CommandText = "SelectEmployee"
objCommand.CommandType = CommandType.StoredProcedure
objCommand.Parameters.Add("EmployeeID", OleDbType.Char, 9).Value = "PTC11962M"
```

DataAdapter Class

Figure 2-1 listed the `DataAdapter` as one of the subcomponents of the Data Provider. As with the `Connection` and `Command` classes, a `DataAdapter` class is provided for DB, ODBC, OLE DB, SQL Server, and Oracle. In this section, you examine the `DataAdapter` class for OLE DB. Keep in mind that the different versions are functionally equivalent.

The `DataAdapter` serves as a bridge between your database and your program. It is used to execute a `Command` object to retrieve data from the database and then fill a `DataSet` or `DataTable` object. It is also used to insert, update, or delete data in the database from a `DataSet` or `DataTable` object.

Because the `DataAdapter` is used to fill a `DataSet` and `DataTable` object, you start exploring the `DataTable` object in more detail in this section also. You get hands-on experience with both the `DataSet` and `DataTable` objects in subsequent chapters and learn a lot more about these classes and how they can be used.

Because the most common use of the `DataAdapter` is to retrieve data from your database and to populate a `DataTable` object with data, you look at the constructors used for this purpose.

In the previous section, the first constructor that you looked at for the `Command` class used a SQL string and the `Connection` object. The code fragment that follows uses the `Command` object that was shown in the previous example in the constructor for the `DataAdapter`.

The next line of code declares a new object representing a `DataTable` class. Notice that the `DataTable` is provider independent, in that it is not prefixed with DB, ODBC, OLE DB, SQL, or Oracle. The constructor for a `DataTable` does provide an overloaded list and is typically initialized with the table name parameter. Note that you do not have to use the table name specified in the FROM clause of your SQL statements; you can use any table name that you want.

Once the `DataAdapter` and `DataTable` objects have been initialized, you want to retrieve the data from the database and populate the `DataTable` object. This is done using the `Fill` method of the

DataAdapter. The Fill method also provides an overloaded list but the most common one is shown in the following code. Here you specify only the object representing the DataTable object.

After your DataTable object has been populated with data, the job of the DataAdapter is done and you should call the Dispose method to release the resources held by the DataAdapter and set it to Nothing The job of the Command object is also done at this point, so it would be a good idea to dispose of it and set it to Nothing to release resources and free up memory. Also, if you are not performing any more database operations, this would be a good point to close your database connection and call the Dispose method on it.

```
Dim objDataAdapter As New OleDbDataAdapter(objCommand)
Dim objDataTable As New Data.DataTable("Employees")
objDataAdapter.Fill(objDataTable)

objDataAdapter.Dispose()
objDataAdapter = Nothing
objCommand.Dispose()
objCommand = Nothing
```

Another common constructor used with the DataAdapter passes the SQL statements directly to the DataAdapter without using a Command object, as shown in the next code fragment. Here you pass the string variable for the SQL statement and the object representing the connection to your database. In the previous example you passed the Command object to the DataAdapter and the DataAdapter was able to extrapolate the connection information from it. In this constructor you use a string for the SQL statements, so the DataAdapter needs the Connection object so it knows how to communicate with the database to execute the SQL string.

```
Dim strSQL As String = _
    "SELECT FIRST_NAME, LAST_NAME FROM HR.EMPLOYEES"
Dim objDataAdapter As New OleDbDataAdapter(strSQL, objConnection)
Dim objDataTable As New Data.DataTable("Employees")
objDataAdapter.Fill(objDataTable)

objDataAdapter.Dispose()
objDataAdapter = Nothing
```

After you have a populated DataTable object, you can work with the data. The DataTable object contains a collection of rows, with each row containing a collection of items representing the columns in the row. This may all sound a little confusing but it is really quite simple, as illustrated in the next code fragment.

Here you declare an object for a DataRow, which will be used to access each row in the Rows collection of the DataTable object. Then you iterate through the rows of your table using a For Each loop.

Using the Item property of the DataRow object, you can access each column in the row as shown in the following code. This line of code prints the first and last names of each employee in the DataTable object to the output window in the IDE.

Finally, when you are done with the DataTable object, you call the Dispose method to release the resources held by the DataTable object and set it to Nothing to free the memory held by the object. This is extremely important because the DataTable object represents an in-memory data cache, meaning that all data contained in the DataTable object is loaded into memory; thus, you want to free up this memory as soon as possible.

```
Dim objDataRow As DataRow
For Each objDataRow In objDataTable.Rows
    Debug.WriteLine(objDataRow.Item("FIRST_NAME") & " " & _
        objDataRow.Item("LAST_NAME"))
Next
objDataTable.Dispose()
objDataTable = Nothing
```

You can use the Update method of the DataAdapter to update the database with the data in your DataTable object after modifications have been made to the data in the DataTable. When updating or inserting data into your relational database, you typically use a stored procedure to perform the insert or update and use the Command object to execute those stored procedures. Stored procedures enable you to execute one or more SQL statements and perform logic and validations in them. You see more of this starting in Chapter 4.

DataReader Class

The DataReader object is the final subcomponent of the Data Provider that you examine in this chapter. This object, like the other objects that you examined from Figure 2-1, has a class provided for DB, ODBC, OLE DB, SQL Server, and Oracle. Again, you examine the OLE DB version but the different versions are functionally equivalent.

The DataReader object provides a forward-only stream of data directly from your database. As its name implies, the DataReader object can only read data from your database. You should be aware that the DataReader, because it is reading data from the database, holds an open connection to the database. Thus, the Connection object that the DataReader object is using will be busy serving up the data to the DataReader and cannot be used for any other database operations.

This object provides the most efficient means of reading data from your database. The DataReader object is the object that you want to use to just read the data from your database from start to finish to populate a list on a form or to populate an array or collection. It can also be used to populate a DataSet or DataTable.

The DataReader class does not use a constructor to be initialized, rather, it is set using the ExecuteReader method of a Command object. The following code fragment assumes that you have already initialized a Command object with the SQL statements to be executed and that the database connection is open.

The first line of code declares an object for the DataReader and sets it using the ExecuteReader method of your Command object. After the DataReader is set, you are ready to start reading data using the Read method.

The next line of code sets up a While loop to read the records from the database. Each time the Read method of the DataReader is executed, another row of data is retrieved from the database. Using the Item property of the DataReader object, you can access the values of the columns that were specified in your SQL SELECT statement. The following code writes the first and last name of each employee selected from the Employees table to the output window in the IDE.

After all records have been read, it is important to close the `DataReader` using the `Close` method. This releases all resources held by the `DataReader` and allows the open database connection to be used for another operation or to be closed. You should set it to `Nothing` to free the memory being held by this object. You should also close your database connection if it is no longer needed.

```
Dim objReader As OleDbDataReader = objCommand.ExecuteReader()
While objReader.Read
    Debug.WriteLine(objReader.Item("FIRST_NAME") & " " & _
        objReader.Item("LAST_NAME"))
End While
objReader.Close()
objReader.Dispose()
objReader = Nothing
```

You explore many other properties for the `DataReader` in more detail in subsequent chapters. These include such properties as the `HasRows` property. This property will return a Boolean value indicating whether or not the `DataReader` contains any rows based on your SQL `SELECT` statement.

Summary

This chapter has provided you with a good foundation for understanding ADO.NET and its architecture. You have examined the major components that you use on a daily basis as you start to code database applications. As you work through the rest of the chapters in this book, you explore these components in more detail and see how they can help solve the various data access tasks that you'll face.

You should keep in mind that the ADO.NET Data Provider comes in multiple versions, each designed for a specific purpose. You should choose the appropriate version based on your application needs and the types of databases that your application will be accessing. Also keep in mind that no matter which version of the Data Provider you use, the properties and methods of the subcomponents are functionally equivalent.

To summarize, you should know:

- ❑ The various subcomponents of the Data Provider
- ❑ How to use the Connection object to connect to an Access, SQL Server, and Oracle database
- ❑ How to use the Command object to select data using a String variable containing SQL statements and how to select data using a stored procedure
- ❑ How to use the DataAdapter object to fill a DataTable object with data
- ❑ How to read data from the DataTable object
- ❑ How to read data using a DataReader

In Chapter 3, you get hands-on experience using all of the different versions of the Data Provider just covered and are exposed to the data wizards in Visual Studio 2005 and the components that it generates.

Exercises

Exercise 1

Create a Windows application that uses the OLE DB data provider to read data from the sample Northwind database that gets installed with Microsoft Office. The default location for this database is C:\Program Files\Microsoft Office\Office11\Samples and may vary depending on the version of Microsoft Office that you have and the path that was used during the installation.

Create a SELECT statement that selects the first and last names from the Employee table and use a DataAdapter object to populate a DataTable object with the data. Then read the data from the DataTable object and populate a list box control on your form.

You need to set a reference to the System.Data.dll namespace using the Add Reference dialog box and also import the System.Data and System.Data.OleDb namespaces in your form class.

The results from your application should look similar to the results shown in Figure 2-3.

Figure 2-3

Exercise 2

Create a Windows application that uses the OleDbDataReader to read data from the Employees table in the Northwind database. Display the results in a list box on a form and design your form so that it looks similar to the form in Exercise 1.

Use the same SQL SELECT statement that you used in the last exercise and follow the steps that you used to set a reference and import the System.Data and System.Data.OleDb namespaces.

Visual Studio 2005
Data Wizards

Visual Studio 2005 provides data wizards that assist you in creating connections to your database and retrieving and updating data. They do this by prompting you for the necessary information to connect to your database and to retrieve data. These wizards can be great time savers because they help new database developers get a simple database application up and running fast.

The Toolbox in Visual Studio 2005 contains data components that also assist you in quickly building simple database applications. These controls also interact with the data wizards in Visual Studio 2005, assist you in binding your data source to the controls on your form, and help you navigate through the data in your data source.

In this chapter, you:

❑   Learn how to automatically generate a DataSet object

❑   Learn how to bind a DataSet object to various controls

❑   Learn how to navigate through the data in a DataSet object

To complete the *Try It Out* exercises in this chapter, you need the sample Northwind.mdb database, which can be installed with Microsoft Office, access to SQL Server's Pubs database, or access to an Oracle database that has had the sample data installed.

Data Access Components

Every Windows application contains three components when building database applications using the data controls in the Toolbox: TableAdapter, DataSet, and BindingSource. The DataSet and BindingSource are located in the toolbox as shown in Figure 3-1. The TableAdapter is automatically generated as is the BindingSource and depends on the way you add data components to your application. Take a brief look at each of these data components in turn.

Figure 3-1

DataSet

The DataSet component is a cache of data stored in memory. It's a lot like a mini database engine, but its data exists in memory. The DataSet is very powerful. In addition to storing data in tables, it stores a rich amount of *metadata* — or data about the data. This includes things like table and column names, data types, and the information needed to manage and undo changes to the data. All of this data is represented in memory as XML. A DataSet can be saved to an XML file and then loaded back into memory very easily. It can also be passed in XML format over networks including the Internet.

Because the DataSet component stores all of the data in memory, you can scroll through the data both forward and backward, and can also make updates to the data in memory. The DataSet component is very powerful and you explore this component in more detail in Chapter 4. In this chapter, you simply use it to store data and bind it to a control on your form.

DataGridView

The DataGridView component is a container that allows you to bind data from your data source and have it displayed in a spreadsheet format (similar to Excel) that displays the columns of data horizontally and the rows of data vertically.

The DataGridView component also provides many properties that allow you to customize the appearance of the component itself as well as properties that allow you to customize the column headers and the display of data.

More important though are the quick links at the bottom of the Properties window for the DataGridView component, which allow you to customize the appearance of the DataGridView itself through several predefined format styles. You see this later in this chapter.

BindingSource

The `BindingSource` component acts like a bridge between your data source (`DataSet`) and your data bound controls (the controls that are bound to data components). Any interaction with the data from your controls goes through the `BindingSource` component, which in turn communicates with your data source.

For example, your `DataGridView` control is initially filled with data. When you request that a column be sorted, the `DataGridView` control communicates that intention to the `BindingSource`, which in turn communicates that intention to the data source.

The `BindingSource` component is the component that you bind to the `DataSource` property of your controls, as you see later in this chapter.

BindingNavigator

The `BindingNavigator` component provides a standard UI component that allows you to navigate through the records that are in your data source. It provides buttons that allow you to navigate to the first and previous records as well as to the next and last records. It also contains a display that shows you how many records there are in your database table as well as which record is currently displayed.

The `BindingNavigator` component is bound to your `BindingSource` component much like the `DataGridView` component is. When you click the Next button in the `BindingNavigator` component, it sends a request to the `BindingSource` component for the next record and the `BindingSource` component sends the request to the data source.

TableAdapter

There's one last component that I want to talk about — the `TableAdapter`. This component does not reside in the Toolbox but is automatically generated for you depending on how you add your data access components to your project.

The `TableAdapter` contains the query used to select data from your database and the connection information for connecting to your database. It also contains methods that fill the `DataSet` in your project with data from the database. You can also choose to have the `TableAdapter` generate insert, update, and delete statements based on the query that is used to select data.

Data Binding

Data binding means taking data referenced by your `BindingSource` and binding it to a control. In other words, the control receives its data from your `BindingSource`, which receives its data from your data source, and the data is automatically displayed in the control for the user to see and manipulate. In Visual Basic 2005, most controls support some level of data binding. Some are specifically designed for it, such as the `DataGridView`. In this first *Try It Out*, you bind data from a BindingSource component to a `DataGridView` control.

Try It Out   **Binding Data to a DataGridView Control**

To complete this exercise:

1.   Start Visual Studio 2005 and start a new project by clicking the Project link on the Recent
     Projects section of the Start page or by clicking the File menu and selecting New ⇨ Project.

2.   In the New Project dialog box, select a Windows Application template and enter a project name
     of DataGridView Binding. Click OK to create this project

3.   Click the Data tab in the Toolbox and then drag a DataGridView control from the Toolbox and
     drop it on your form. The DataGridView control displays a tasks list as shown in Figure 3-2.

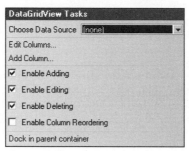

Figure 3-2

4.   Click the drop-down arrow in the Choose Data Source combo box and then click the Add
     Project Data Source link at the bottom of the list that is displayed. This causes the Data Source
     Configuration Wizard to be displayed.

5.   The Choose a Data Source Type screen allows you to choose the data source for your data. As you
     can see from this screen, shown in Figure 3-3, you have several options for a data source. You can
     click the Database icon for connecting to various databases such as Access, SQL Server and
     Oracle, the Web Service icon for connecting to a Web Service, and the Object icon for connecting
     to your business logic components. Click the Database icon and click the Next button.

086594

Visual Studio 2005 Data Wizards

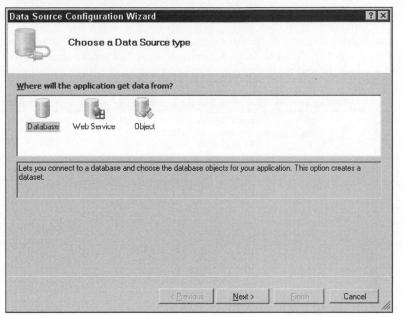

Figure 3-3

6. In the Choose Your Data Connection screen, click the New Connection button to invoke the Add Connection dialog box.

7. In the Add Connection dialog box, Microsoft SQL Server is the default data source. You want to change this to Access so click the Change button to invoke the Change Data Source dialog box.

8. In the Change Data Source dialog box, select Microsoft Access Database File and then click OK to be returned to the Add Connection dialog box.

9. In the Add Connection dialog box, click the Browse button and navigate to the samples folder for Microsoft office. By default, this is in the folder `C:\Program Files\Microsoft Office\Office11\Samples\` for a default installation of Microsoft Office 2003. Select the `Northwind.mdb` database and click the Open button to have the path and filename added to the Add Connection dialog box. Click OK in the Add Connection dialog box.

10. You are returned to the Choose Your Data Connection screen of the Data Source Configuration Wizard and you want to advance to the next step so click Next.

11. You are prompted with a message that says the connection you chose uses a local file that is not part of your project. Clicking Yes in this dialog box causes a copy of the database to be added to your project and the connection string to be modified to reference the local copy. Click Yes in this dialog box so that you work with a local copy that is part of your project.

12. The next step of the Data Source Configuration Wizard is the Save connection string to the application configuration file screen, which allows you to specify a name for the connection string. You can accept the default name and click the Next button.

13. The Choose Your Database Objects screen, shown in Figure 3-4, is the final screen of the Data Source Configuration Wizard. This screen allows you to select the objects that should be bound to your controls. Expand the Tables node and then expand the Customers node and select the fields shown in Figure 3-4. When you are done, click the Finish button to have your data source configured and bound to the DataGridView control.

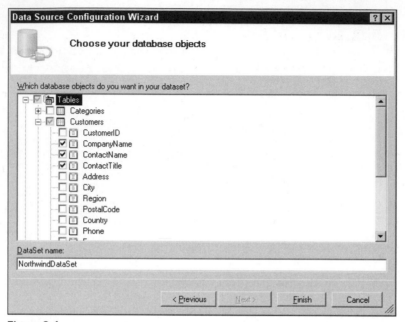

Figure 3-4

14. In the Properties window, click the Dock property for the DataGridView control and set it to Full.

15. At this point you can run your project to see the results. Click the Start button on the toolbar and your form is displayed with the DataGridView control populated with data.

You can click the column headers to have the data in the DataGridView sorted in ascending order. Clicking the same column header again sorts the data in descending order. Each sort order is indicated with an arrow pointing up for ascending and down for descending.

At this point, you have not written a single line of code to achieve these results, which just goes to prove how powerful the data wizards in Visual Basic 2005 are. When you are done viewing your data, close the form.

How It Works

The approach you take to creating a data-bound application in this *Try It Out* exercise is the most straightforward and the easiest. You start by adding a DataGridView control to your form, which causes you to be prompted with the DataGridView Tasks dialog box for the DataGridView as shown in Figure 3-2.

This dialog box allows you to create a new Data Source via the Data Source Configuration Wizard, which walks you through a series of steps. The first step is to identify the type of data source that you want to use. You are then allowed specify the type of database object that you want to use to retrieve your data and in this step you merely choose to use a specific table in your database and select specific columns from that table.

After you click the Finish button in the Data Source Configuration Wizard, several components are automatically generated and added to your project. These include the `NorthwindDataSet`, `CustomersBindingSource`, and `CustomersTableAdapter`, all of which can be viewed at the bottom of the IDE. The `CustomersBindingSource` was the actual component that was bound to the `DataSource` property of the `DataGridView` control.

Remember that the `BindingSource`'s job is to communicate the data needs of the control to the data source via the `TableAdapter`, which in this case is the `DataSet` containing all of the data. The `DataSet` is populated with data by the `TableAdapter` when your form is loaded.

The most important point of this exercise was the ease with which you were able to create a data bound application and the simple fact that you did not have to write a single line of code to achieve the end results.

In this next Try It Out exercise, you use several TextBox controls on your form and bind each text box to certain fields in your BindingSource. You then use a BindingNavigator control to navigate through the records in your DataSet.

Try It Out   Binding Data to TextBox Controls

To complete this exercise:

1.   In Visual Studio 2005, click the File menu and select New ➪ Project. In the New Project dialog box, select the Windows Application icon and enter a project name of TextBox Binding in the Name field and click OK.

2.   Add three Label controls and three TextBox controls to your form. Arrange the controls so that your form looks similar to Figure 3-5 and set the `Text` properties of the Label controls as shown in the figure.

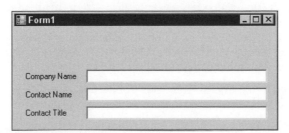

Figure 3-5

3. Click the first text box on your form and then expand the (DataBindings) property in the Properties window by clicking the plus sign next to it. Then click the Text property under the (DataBindings) property. Now click the drop-down arrow for the Text property.

    At this point, you see the Data Source window shown in Figure 3-6. Click the Add Project Data Source link to invoke the Data Source Configuration Wizard that you saw in the previous *Try It Out* exercise.

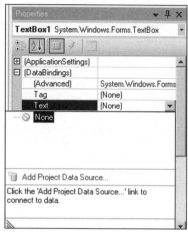

Figure 3-6

4. Select the Database icon in the Choose a Data Source Type screen and click the Next button.

5. In the Choose Your Data Connection screen, click the New Connection button to invoke the Add Connection dialog box.

6. In the Add Connection dialog box, Microsoft SQL Server is the default data source. You want to change this to Access so click the Change button to invoke the Change Data Source dialog box.

7. In the Change Data Source dialog box, select Microsoft Access Database File and then click OK to be returned to the Add Connection dialog box.

8. In the Add Connection dialog box, click the Browse button and navigate to the samples folder for Microsoft office. By default, this will be in the folder C:\Program Files\Microsoft Office\Office11\Samples\ for a default installation of Microsoft Office 2003. Select the Northwind.mdb database and click the Open button to have the path and filename added to the Add Connection dialog box. Click OK in the Add Connection dialog box.

9. You are returned to the Choose Your Data Connection screen of the Data Source Configuration Wizard and you want to advance to the next step so click Next.

10. You are prompted with a message that says the connection you chose uses a local file that is not part of your project. Click Yes in this dialog box so that you work with a local copy that is part of your project.

11. The next step of the Data Source Configuration Wizard is the Save connection string to the application configuration file screen which enables you to specify a name for the connection string. You can accept the default name and click the Next button.

12. The Choose Your Database Objects screen is the final screen of the Data Source Configuration Wizard. Expand the Tables node and then expand the Customers node and select the CompanyName, ContactName, and ContactTitle fields. Click the Finish button to have your data source configured.

13. Now click the drop-down arrow next to the Text property and then expand the Other Data Sources node, the Project Data Sources node, the NorthwindDataSet node, and finally the Customers node. Select the CompanyName field to have this text box bound to that field.

14. Click the second text box on your form and then click the Text property under the (DataBindings) property in the Properties window. Now click the drop-down arrow for the Text property and then expand the CustomersBindingSource node in the Data Source window and then click the ContactName field.

15. Click the third text box on your form and then click the Text property under the (DataBindings) property in the Properties window. Now click the drop-down arrow for the Text property, expand the CustomersBindingSource node in the Data Source window, and click the ContactTitle field.

16. Now go back to the Toolbox and drag a BindingNavigator control from the Data tab and drop it on your form. The BindingNavigator control is automatically docked to the top of the form.

17. In the Properties window, locate the BindingSource property and then click that field. Now click the drop-down arrow for the BindingSource property and choose CustomersBindingSource from the list.

18. Now click the Start button on the toolbar to run your project. Your form should look similar to the one shown in Figure 3-7. You can navigate through the records in your data source backward and forward, and you can go to the first and last record.

Figure 3-7

Clicking the Delete button deletes records from your DataSet but *does not* delete records from the database. Likewise, clicking the Add new button adds an empty record to your DataSet but not to the database. You would need to write some code to have the database updated with the changes from your DataSet.

The beauty of using the BindingNavigator control is that you've quickly built a form that navigates through the records of your database without writing a single line of code.

How It Works

You start this *Try It Out* exercise by adding three Label and TextBox controls to your form. You then set the `DataBindings` properties of the text boxes. When you choose to set the `Text DataBinding` property of the first text box, you are prompted to add a new data source, which again invokes the Data Source Configuration Wizard.

You use the Data Source Configuration Wizard in this exercise in the same manner as you did in the previous exercise. When you complete the Data Source Configuration Wizard, it automatically generates `DataSet`, `BindingSource`, and `TableAdapter` components. You can then choose which field in the `DataSet` to bind to the `DataBinding Text` property.

After you add the `BindingNavigator` control to your form, setting it up is a matter of simply choosing the `BindingSource` that was generated by the Data Source Configuration Wizard in the `BindingSource` property in the Properties window.

Again, this exercise has demonstrated the simplicity with which you can create data bound applications without writing any code.

Summary

This chapter has demonstrated the basics of binding data to controls on a form, specifically the `DataGridView` control and TextBox controls. You examined the necessary basic data access components required to retrieve data from an Access database and bind that data to your controls. You used the components provided in the Data tab of the Toolbox for your data access, and used the wizards to generate the necessary code to connect to the database and retrieve the data.

After working through this chapter, you should know:

❑ How to use the Data Source Configuration Wizard to create the data access components needed to perform data binding

❑ How to bind data to a `DataGridView` control

❑ How to bind data to TextBox controls and use the `BindingNavigator` control

In Chapter 4, you get an introduction to basic SQL statements and learn how to write SQL statements and create queries in Microsoft Access.

Exercises

Exercise 1

Create a Windows application containing a `DataGridView` control bound to the Northwind database. Follow the steps for creating a data source connection outlined in the "Binding Data to a DataGridView Control" *Try It Out* exercise in this chapter. When you get to the Choose Your Database Objects screen is the Data Source Configuration Wizard, expand the Products table and select the ProductName, UnitPrice, UnitsInStock, and UnitsOnOrder columns.

Exercise 2

Create a Windows application containing five Label and five TextBox controls and a `BindingNavigator`. Bind your data source to the Suppliers table in the Northwind database and select the Company Name, Address, City, Region, and Postal Code fields.

Basic SQL

Until now, you have been using the Data Source Configuration Wizard to select the columns from your tables that were shown from your data source. The Data Source Configuration Wizard provides a graphical user interface (GUI) that assists you by displaying all columns and all tables in your database.

Microsoft Access provides a Query Builder with a user interface (UI) not at all unlike the UI shown in the Data Source Configuration Wizard. In this chapter you build queries to select, insert, update, and delete data in Access. And while you are using the Query Builder in Access, you won't use the Design View (the UI) to create your queries. Instead, you enter your SQL statements in the SQL View of the Query Builder. This enables you to gain firsthand experience building queries using SQL statements.

The queries that you build in this chapter are used in the next several chapters as part of the Time Tracker application that you build throughout this book.

In this chapter, you:

- ❑ Learn about the SELECT SQL statement and build a query to select data
- ❑ Learn about the INSERT SQL statement and build a query to insert data
- ❑ Learn about the UPDATE SQL statement and build a query to update data
- ❑ Learn about the DELETE SQL statement and build a query to delete data

INSERT Statement

The logical starting point for discussing SQL statements is the INSERT statement, as your ProjectTimeTracker database currently has no data. The INSERT statement inserts rows of data in your tables. A single INSERT statement can be designed to insert multiple rows of data at one time or it can be designed to insert a single row of data. The latter is the more common use of the INSERT statement and this will be the syntax that you examine and use in this chapter.

The basic syntax for the INSERT statement is shown here:

```
INSERT INTO tablename
(column1, column2, ...)
VALUES (value1, value2, ...)
```

In the preceding syntax, the INSERT statement tells the database that you want to insert data into a table. The INTO keyword is optional in some databases and required in others. For example, Microsoft Access and Oracle require the INTO keyword whereas SQL Server does not. It's a good practice to always include the INTO keyword for clarity in your SQL statements.

The tablename parameter specifies the name of the table into which you want to insert data.

The second line of the syntax contains a list of column names into which the data should be inserted. This is a comma-separated list contained in parentheses and should contain every column name into which you are inserting data. If a column allows NULL values and you don't want to insert data into it, then you can omit that column from the list. Likewise, if a column has a default value inserted into it as part of the column definition, you can also omit that column from the list. You see more of this later when you build stored procedures in Chapter 9.

The last line of the syntax specifies the VALUES keyword followed by a list of data values contained in a comma-separated list that is also contained in parentheses. These values are typically parameters (placeholders) with the actual values supplied when the query is run. You can also specify literal string values, which are typically enclosed in single quotes, and numeric values, which are not. It should also be noted that built-in database functions, such as functions to retrieve the current date and time, can be used in this list. You see more on built-in functions later in this chapter.

In Chapter 1 I mentioned that you would be generating the Guids (globally unique identifiers) in VB 2005 that are inserted into your tables. To that end, you need to create a simple little program to generate the Guids that are used as input to your INSERT queries.

Try It Out   Building a Guid Generator

To create the Guid Generator:

1. Start Visual Studio 2005 and start a new project by clicking the New Project button on the Projects tab of the Start page or by clicking the File menu and selecting New ⇨ Project.

2. In the New Project dialog box, select a Windows Application template and enter a project name of Guid Generator. Click OK to create this project.

3. Set the following properties for Form1:
   - ❑ Set FormBorderStyle to FixedSingle.
   - ❑ Set MaximizeBox to False.
   - ❑ Set MinimizeBox to False.
   - ❑ Set Size to 430, 78.
   - ❑ Set StartPosition to Center Screen.
   - ❑ Set Text to Guid Generator.

4. Add a TextBox control and a Button control to the form and arrange them to look similar to the controls shown on the form in Figure 4-1.

5. Set the Name property of the TextBox to txtGuid.

6. On the Button control, set the Name property to btnGenerateGuid and the Text property to Generate Guid.

7. Double-click the Button control to add the btnGenerateGuid_Click procedure to your project and add the following code:

```
Private Sub btnGenerateGuid_Click(ByVal sender As System.Object, _
    ByVal e As System.EventArgs) Handles btnGenerateGuid.Click

    'Generate a new Guid
    txtGuid.Text = Guid.NewGuid.ToString.ToUpper()
End Sub
```

8. In the Class Name combo box at the top of the Code Editor, select txtGuid and in the Method Name combo box select the TextChanged event. Now add the following code to the txtGuid_TextChanged event handler procedure:

```
Private Sub txtGuid_TextChanged(ByVal sender As Object, _
    ByVal e As System.EventArgs) Handles txtGuid.TextChanged

    'Copy the Guid to the Clipboard
    Clipboard.SetText(txtGuid.Text)
End Sub
```

This is all the code you need to generate a Guid so start your project by clicking Start on the toolbar or by selecting the Debug menu and then selecting the Start menu item. When your form is displayed, the TextBox control is empty. Click the Generate Guid button to generate a Guid, as shown in Figure 4-1.

Figure 4-1

How It Works

You add one line of code in the btnGenerateGuid_Click procedure, which actually generates a new Guid. The Guid structure, implemented in the System namespace, represents a globally unique identifier. To generate a new Guid, you have to call the NewGuid method on the Guid structure. Because a Guid is a structure, you cannot simply load the value into the Text property of a TextBox control because the Text property accepts only a string value. Therefore, you have to convert the Guid generated to a string value using the ToString method:

```
'Generate a new Guid
txtGuid.Text = Guid.NewGuid.ToString.ToUpper()
```

By default, the alpha characters in a Guid are generated in lowercase. To convert the alpha characters to uppercase, you call the `ToUpper` method on the string. Converting the alpha characters to uppercase is a matter of personal preference and is not required.

You add one line of code to the `txtGuid_TextChanged` procedure. This procedure is invoked whenever the text in the text box changes. This procedure automatically copies the data in the TextBox control to the Windows Clipboard. The Clipboard class is implemented in the `System.Windows.Forms` name space and all you do is call the `SetText` method of the Clipboard class passing it the text in the `txtGuid` text box:

```
'Copy the Guid to the Clipboard
Clipboard.SetText(txtGuid.Text)
```

In essence, when you click the Generate Guid button, a new Guid is generated and placed in the TextBox control and the text in the TextBox is copied to the Windows Clipboard.

Every time you click the Generate Guid button, a new Guid is generated and the process described previously is repeated.

Now that you have a means of generating a Guid that can be used as input when inserting data into your tables, you want to create a query to insert a new project into the Projects table. This *Try It Out* uses the `ProjectTimeTracker` Access database that you created in Chapter 1.

Try It Out   Inserting a Project Query

To create an `INSERT` query:

1. Locate your `ProjectTimeTracker` Access database in Windows Explorer and double-click it, or start Microsoft Access and open your `ProjectTimeTracker` database.

2. In the navigation bar, click Queries; and in the list displayed, double-click Create query in Design view.

3. The Query Builder is shown in Design View by default and the Show Table dialog box is displayed. You do not want to add any tables, so click the Close button to close the Show Table dialog box.

4. You also do not want to use Design View to create this query, so on the toolbar click the View button or click the View menu and choose SQL View to switch the Query Builder to SQL view.

5. Enter the following query:

```
INSERT INTO Projects
    (ProjectID, ProjectName, ProjectDescription, SequenceNumber, LastUpdateDate)
VALUES (@ProjectID, @ProjectName, @ProjectDescription, @SequenceNumber,
    Date()+Time());
```

6. Now click the down arrow on the View button on the toolbar and select Design View or click the View menu and select the Design View. Notice that Design view of the Query Builder is populated with the data that you entered in your query, as shown in Figure 4-2.

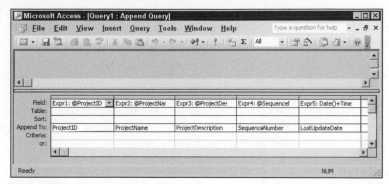

Figure 4-2

7. Switch back to SQL View and notice what Access has done to your query. It has replaced the the VALUES clause with a SELECT statement and added the AS keyword followed by Expr and a number after each parameter. This is the way that Access builds an INSERT SQL statement.

8. Click Save on the toolbar or click the File menu and choose Save. In the Save As dialog box, enter a query name of **usp_InsertProject**. After your query is saved, close the Query Builder window by clicking the X in its upper-right corner.

9. To test your new query, double-click the usp_InsertProject query shown in the list. You are prompted with a dialog box that informs you that you are about to run an append query that will modify data in your table. Click Yes to continue running the query.

10. You are prompted with a series of Enter Parameter Value dialog boxes and each dialog box lists the parameter name in the query, with the first being @ProjectID.

11. Start your Guid Generator program and generate a new Guid. Remember that when you click the Generate Guid button the new Guid that is generated is automatically copied to the Clipboard. Now switch back to Access and paste the new Guid into the Enter Parameter Value dialog box. Finally, click OK in the Enter Parameter Value dialog box to add this value to your query.

12. You are prompted for the @ProjectName parameter next. Enter a value of Vacation and click OK.

13. Next you are prompted for the @ProjectDescription parameter, so enter a value of Paid Vacation Day and click OK.

14. @SequenceNumber is the final parameter you are prompted for. Enter a value of 1 for this parameter, and click OK.

15. A dialog box informs you that you are about to append one row of data to your table. Click Yes to proceed.

16. Repeat Steps 9 through 15 and insert another row of data into the Projects table using the following information:

❑ @ProjectID : Generate a new Guid for this parameter

❑ @ProjectName: enter **Holiday**

❑ @ProjectDescription: enter **Paid Holiday**

❑ @SequenceNumber: enter **2**

17. To view the data that you just inserted, click the Tables icon in the navigation bar and then double-click the Projects table in the list. You will see two rows of data in this table, with the values that you entered.

How It Works

The first thing that you do in this exercise is enter the SQL statements for an INSERT query in the SQL View of the Query Builder. The first line of this query instructs Access that you want to insert data into the Projects table. The second line specifies the column names that you want to insert data into. The third line of this query specifies the parameters that will be used for the values that you want to insert. Here you use the column names prefixed with an at (@) sign. You could use any names you like, but I find that using the actual column names prefixed with an @ symbol makes the query easy to read and lets you know what data you are working with. It also makes this query easy to port to SQL Server, as it requires an @ symbol for its input parameters.

The last value in the list is not an input value that you will be supplying but consists of two built-in functions in Access. The Date function returns the current date and the Time function returns the current time. You concatenate the values returned by these two functions by using the plus (+) sign.

Every database has its own way of terminating SQL statements. In Microsoft Access and Oracle you terminate a SQL statement with a semicolon (;) which is what you do here. SQL Server does not need any terminators because it can determine where one SQL statement ends and where the next one begins.

```
INSERT INTO Projects
    (ProjectID, ProjectName, ProjectDescription, SequenceNumber, LastUpdateDate)
VALUES (@ProjectID, @ProjectName, @ProjectDescription, @SequenceNumber,
    Date()+Time());
```

When you switch to Design view in the Query Builder, Access converts your SQL statements and populates them in the designer. When you switch back to SQL view, you are able to see how Access converted your SQL statements into its own format.

What is particularly interesting is how Access replaces the VALUES clause that you entered. The complete converted query is shown next. Notice how Access changes the VALUES clause into a SELECT statement. Access uses expressions as input parameters to a query and encloses each value that you entered in square brackets followed by the AS clause and Expr followed by a number. These expressions are the input values that Access prompted you for when you ran the query.

```
INSERT INTO Projects ( ProjectID, ProjectName, ProjectDescription, SequenceNumber,
LastUpdateDate )
SELECT [@ProjectID] AS Expr1, [@ProjectName] AS Expr2, [@ProjectDescription] AS
Expr3, [@SequenceNumber] AS Expr4, Date()+Time() AS Expr5;
```

When you saved the query, you gave it a name of usp_InsertProject. You can name your queries anything that you like and the name can even contain spaces. However, queries that contain spaces in their names require special handling in your VB 2005 code because you need to enclose the query name in square brackets. Therefore, it is a best practice to avoid spaces in the names of your queries.

The prefix usp is typically used in enterprise relational databases such as SQL Server and Oracle. The prefix is an acronym for *user stored procedure* and helps distinguish stored procedures that a user writes from system stored procedures that are part of the database and that have a prefix of sp. Because action queries (Insert, Update, and Delete) in Access relate to stored procedures in other relational databases, I chose to have you use this prefix when naming the query.

The purpose for this is to save you time in converting the code in your project later. When you start Chapter 8, you switch over to SQL Server or Oracle and you use the same names for the stored procedures that you create in SQL Server or Oracle and for the queries that you create in the next few chapters. Once you make the switch, there will be very little VB 2005 code that you need to change.

The sequence numbers that you enter in your queries enable you to retrieve a list of projects sorted by the SequenceNumber column. You use a sequential number for standard project types such as Vacation, Holiday, Sick Day, and Personal Day and then a sequence number of 99 for all other projects. This enables you to display a list of projects with the standard project types just mentioned shown first; and then the actual programming projects shown last, as they all have a value of 99.

SELECT Statement

Now that you can insert data into your Access database, you'll want to explore the SELECT statement in detail to understand how you can select data from your Access database. In this section, you examine the basic syntax of the SELECT statement, which is shown here:

```
SELECT column1, column2, ...
    FROM tablename
    WHERE searchcondition
    ORDER BY orderexpression ASC|DESC
```

In the preceding syntax, the first line of the SELECT statement specifies the columns that you want included in the results of the SELECT statement, with each column name separated by a comma. You could optionally omit the column names and just include an asterisk (*), which would indicate that you want to select all the columns in the table.

The FROM clause specifies the table from which the SELECT statement retrieves its data, and the tablename parameter specifies the table name from which data should be selected.

The WHERE clause specifies an optional search condition used to restrict the amount of data returned by the SELECT statement. The searchcondition parameter specifies an expression that must be satisfied in order for a row of data to be included in the SELECT statement. This typically is something like columnname = value, where columnname specifies a specific column name in the table and value is some value that the column contains. You see more of this in the next several chapters.

The ORDER BY clause specifies an optional sort order of the results returned. The orderexpression parameter in the syntax specifies one or more column names that should be used in the sort expression. The optional ASC and DESC keywords specify the sort order, with ascending being the default.

As I mentioned earlier, this is just the basic syntax and you expand on this syntax as you work through the rest of the chapters. I explain the additional syntax as you incorporate it in your queries and stored procedures.

Now that you have some data in your `ProjectTimeTracker` Access database, it's time to create a query that selects all projects in the Projects table. The next *Try It Out* guides you through the steps of creating a `SELECT` query that selects this data and sorts the results returned based on a single column.

Try It Out   Creating a Select Project Query

To create a `SELECT` query:

1. Locate your `ProjectTimeTracker` database in Windows Explorer and double-click it or start Microsoft Access and open your `ProjectTimeTracker` database if it is not already open.

2. In the navigation bar to the left, click Queries and then in the list displayed, double-click Create query in Design view.

3. The Query Builder is shown in Design View and the Show Table dialog box is displayed. You do not want to add any tables so click the Close button to close the Show Table dialog box.

4. Nor do you want to use the Design View to create this query, as you'll code the SQL statements manually. Therefore, on the toolbar, click the View button or click the View menu and choose SQL View to switch the Query Builder to the SQL view.

5. Enter the following query:

```
SELECT ProjectID, ProjectName, ProjectDescription, SequenceNumber, LastUpdateDate
FROM Projects
ORDER BY SequenceNumber;
```

6. Click the Save button on the toolbar or click File and choose Save. In the Save As dialog box, enter a query name of `usp_SelectProjects`. After your query has been saved, close the Query Builder window by clicking the X in its upper-right corner.

7. To test your new query, double-click the `usp_ SelectProjects` query shown in the list. Your query is run and the results displayed are similar to those shown in Figure 4-3.

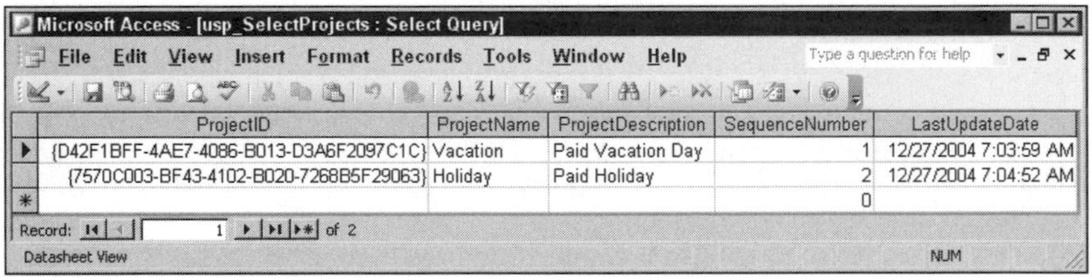

Figure 4-3

How It Works

The query that you build in this exercise is straightforward. You specify the column names that you want returned in the results on the first line of your `SELECT` query. The second line specifies the table name from which the `SELECT` statement should select data, and the third line specifies the sort order for the results.

You want the results sorted by sequence number so you specify the sequence number column in the `ORDER BY` clause. This causes the results to be sorted in ascending order.

```
SELECT ProjectID, ProjectName, ProjectDescription, SequenceNumber, LastUpdateDate
FROM Projects
ORDER BY SequenceNumber;
```

If you want the results sorted in descending order, you specify the DESC keyword after the column name as shown here.

```
ORDER BY SequenceNumber DESC;
```

You could have simply specified an asterisk in your SELECT statement instead of specifying each column. Using the asterisk returns all columns, but this is not a good practice to get into. You want to return only the columns in the table that you need.

If someone were to modify the table by adding more columns and you specify an asterisk in your SELECT statement, you would be retrieving more data than you actually need. This has a performance impact on your application if you have numerous extra columns and thousands of rows of data. A best practice is to retrieve only the data that your application needs to work with.

When you run your query, the results are displayed as shown in Figure 4-3. What's interesting to note is the data in the ProjectID column. When you supplied the Guid for the INSERT query you did not supply the brackets that are shown in Figure 4-3; Access adds those automatically and uses them internally to signify that this is a Guid and not just string data. You will not see those brackets in the data returned when you run this query from your VB 2005 program. This will become evident in Chapter 5 when you incorporate this query in your VB 2005 program.

UPDATE Statement

The UPDATE statement is also straightforward. You update specific columns in a table, setting a new value for each column. You need only specify the columns to be updated in the UPDATE statement and the remaining columns in the table remain unchanged.

To limit the rows of data that are updated, you specify a WHERE clause. This is not required; however, if it is not present in your UPDATE statement, all rows of data in the table are updated with the values specified in your UPDATE statement.

Take a look at the syntax for the UPDATE statement:

```
UPDATE tablename
SET column1 = value, column1 = value, ...
WHERE criteria
```

In the syntax, the tablename parameter represents that name of the table that you will be updating.

The SET keyword specifies a list of column = value pairs; each is separated with a comma. You specify a column name in your table and the value that it should be set to. The value can be a parameter, a literal value, or a computed value returned from built-in functions in the database.

The WHERE clause specifies the criteria, which limits the number of rows that are updated in the table. You typically update only a single row of data and specify the column that contains the primary key. You'll see this in action in the next exercise. If you want to update all the rows of data in the table, you omit the WHERE clause altogether.

In the following *Try It Out*, you create a query that updates a single row of data in the Projects table. To limit the update to a single row, you use the primary key column of ProjectID in the WHERE clause of your query. The primary key column must contain unique values, which ensures that only a single row of data is updated.

Try It Out   Updating a Project Query

To create an UPDATE query:

1. Locate your ProjectTimeTracker database in Windows Explorer and double-click it or start Microsoft Access and open your ProjectTimeTracker database if it is not already open.

2. In the navigation bar to the left, click Queries. Then, in the list displayed, double-click Create query in Design view.

3. The Query Builder is shown in Design View and the Show Table dialog box is displayed. Again, you do not want to add any tables so click the Close button to close the Show Table dialog box.

4. You also do not want to use Design View to create this query, so on the toolbar click the View button, or click View and choose SQL View to switch the Query Builder to the SQL view.

5. Enter the following query:

```
UPDATE Projects
SET ProjectName = @ProjectName,
    ProjectDescription = @ProjectDescription,
    SequenceNumber = @SequenceNumber,
    LastUpdateDate = Date()+Time()
WHERE ProjectID = @ProjectID;
```

6. Click the Save button on the toolbar or click File and choose Save. In the Save As dialog box, enter a query name of **usp_UpdateProject**. When your query has been saved, close the Query Builder window by clicking the X in its upper-right corner.

7. Before you can test your new query you need to get the Guid of an existing row of data in the Projects table. Run the usp_SelectProjects query and then copy the Guid of the row of data that you want to update. Copy the entire Guid, including the surrounding brackets.

8. To test your new query, double-click the usp_UpdateProject query shown in the list. You are prompted with a dialog box that informs you that you are about to run an UPDATE query that will modify data in your table. Click the Yes button to continue.

9. The Enter Parameter Value dialog box is displayed and prompts you for the first parameter, the @ProejctName parameter. Enter a value for the project name. If you do not want to change the current project name, enter the value that is currently in the row that you are updating. When you are done, click OK.

10. The next parameter that you are prompted for is @ProjectDescription. Enter a new or existing project description and then click OK.

11. The next parameter is the @SequenceNumber parameter. Again, enter a new value or the existing value. This field is set to handle a value from 0 to 255 so enter a valid value in that range. When you are done, click OK to proceed.

12. The last value that you are prompted for is the @ProjectID. This is the Guid value of the row of data that will be updated and that is used in the WHERE clause. Paste the Guid that you copied in this dialog box and then click OK.

13. You are now prompted with another dialog box informing you that you are about to update 1 row of data. Click Yes to proceed.

14. You can verify your update by running the usp_SelectProjects query.

How It Works

The UPDATE query that you build in this exercise updates a single row of data. You specify the UPDATE statement followed by the name of the table that you are updating data in. Then, using the SET keyword, you specify the column names followed by an equal sign and a parameter. Each column = value pair is separated by a comma. The LastUpdateDate column is not set to a value from a parameter but to a computed value using the built-in Date and Time functions.

Finally, you specify the WHERE clause and use the primary key column for the Projects table and specify a parameter for this. This limits the update to a single row. If the WHERE clause were omitted, all rows of data would have been updated to the same values that were specified in your parameters.

```
UPDATE Projects
SET ProjectName = @ProjectName,
    ProjectDescription = @ProjectDescription,
    SequenceNumber = @SequenceNumber,
    LastUpdateDate = Date()+Time()
WHERE ProjectID = @ProjectID;
```

When you run the usp_UpdateProject query, you have to specify the Guid, including the brackets, for the @ProjectID parameter. This is required only when running the query from Access. When you run the query from your VB 2005 program, you omit the brackets. The Data Provider that you use takes care of inserting the brackets for you.

Likewise, when you run the usp_SelectProjects query, the Data Provider that you use removes the brackets from the data that it returns. You see this in the next few chapters when you start building VB 2005 programs to execute these queries.

DELETE Statement

The DELETE SQL statement is by far the simplest SQL statement that you encounter. However, it is also a SQL statement that can cause you to lose a large amount of data if used improperly. The DELETE statement can delete all rows of data in a table, a single row, or a range of rows.

The syntax for the DELETE statement is very straightforward:

```
DELETE
FROM tablename
WHERE criteria
```

In the syntax, the `tablename` parameter represents the name of the table from which you will be deleting data.

The `WHERE` clause in the `DELETE` statement is like the `WHERE` clause in the `UPDATE` statement; it limits the amount of data that affected by the query. If the `WHERE` clause is omitted, all rows of data in the table are deleted. The `criteria` parameter specifies the criteria used to limit the delete operation to a range of rows or to a single row.

In the following *Try It Out*, you create a query that deletes a single project from the Projects table. The delete operation will be limited to deleting a single row by using the ProjectID column in the criteria of the `WHERE` clause.

Try It Out   Deleting a Project Query

To create a `DELETE` query:

1. Locate your `ProjectTimeTracker` database in Windows Explorer and double-click it or start Microsoft Access and open your `ProjectTimeTracker` database if it is not already open.

2. In the navigation bar to the left, click Queries. Then, in the list displayed, double-click Create query in Design view.

3. The Query Builder is shown in Design View and the Show Table dialog box is displayed. You do not want to add any tables so click the Close button to close the Show Table dialog box.

4. You also do not want to use Design view to create this query, so on the toolbar click the View button, or click View and choose SQL View to switch the Query Builder to the SQL view.

5. Enter the following query:

```
DELETE
FROM Projects
WHERE ProjectID = @ProjectID;
```

6. Click Save on the toolbar, or choose Save from the File menu. In the Save As dialog box, enter a query name of **usp_DeleteProject**. When your query has been saved, close the Query Builder window by clicking the X in its upper-right corner.

7. Before you can test this query, you need to get the Guid of an existing row of data from your Projects table. Run the `usp_SelectProjects` query and copy the Guid, including the brackets, from the row that you want to delete. When you are done, close the `usp_SelectProjects` query window.

8. Double-click the `usp_DeleteProject` query in the list. You are prompted with a dialog box informing you that you are about to run a `DELETE` query that will modify data in your table. Click Yes to proceed.

9. The Enter Parameter Value dialog box is displayed and prompts you for the `@ProjectID` parameter. Paste the Guid that you copied into this dialog box and then click OK to proceed.

10. The next dialog box that appears informs you that you are about to delete one row of data from your table. Click Yes to allow the query to run.

11. You can verify the success of the DELETE query by running the `usp_SelectProjects` query to confirm that the row you specified was deleted.

How It Works

The DELETE query that you build in this exercise deletes only a single row of data from the Projects table. You accomplish this by specifying the table name of Projects for the FROM keyword and specifying a criteria for the WHERE clause.

The ProjectID column is the primary key column in your table and contains unique values throughout the table. By supplying a Guid for the @ProjectID parameter, you are limiting the delete operation to a single row of data:

```
DELETE
FROM Projects
WHERE ProjectID = @ProjectID;
```

Before you move on to Chapter 5, you want to ensure that the Projects table contains the two rows of data shown in Figure 4-4. If these rows of data are not present, please insert them before continuing.

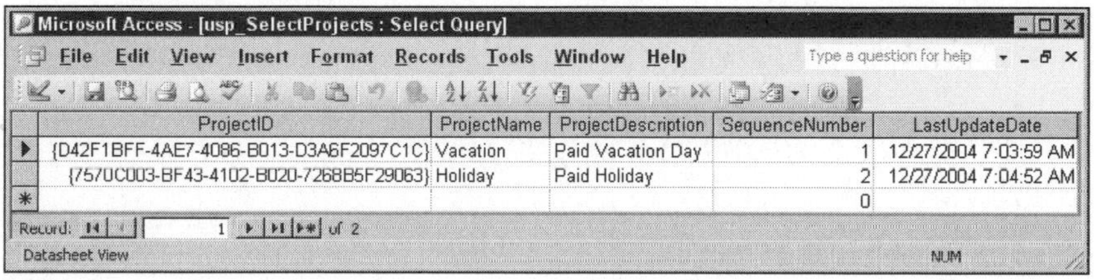

Figure 4-4

Summary

This chapter has been a primer for basic SQL statements. You expand your knowledge of SQL in the coming chapters. In this chapter, you took a look at the basic syntax for the SELECT, INSERT, UPDATE, and DELETE SQL statements.

After examining the syntax for each of these SQL statements, you built a query in Access using the SQL view of the Query Builder and not the Design view. This allowed you to gain firsthand experience at writing SQL statements that inserted, updated, deleted, and selected data.

You also had a chance to build a simple program that generated a Guid that could be used as input to your INSERT query. This program used the built-in Guid structure in VB 2005 to generate a new Guid. You implement the same code to generate a Guid in the programs that you code in the rest of this book.

To summarize, you should know how to:

- ❑ Code and execute a basic SELECT SQL statement
- ❑ Code and execute a basic INSERT SQL statement
- ❑ Code and execute a basic UPDATE SQL statement
- ❑ Code and execute a basic DELETE SQL statement

In Chapter 5, you explore the OLE DB Data Provider in more detail and learn how to create dynamic database connections. You also learn more about the OleDbDataAdapter and the OleDbDataReader and how to execute the queries that you just built from a VB 2005 program.

Exercises

Exercise 1

Create a SELECT query called **SelectProjectNames** that selects just the ProjectName and SequenceNumber columns from the Projects table. Order the results of the query by ProjectName in descending order.

Exercise 2

Create an UPDATE query called **UpdateProjectDescription** that updates only the ProjectDescription column for a given row of data.

SQL and Queries for Access

In Chapter 4, you created and ran queries from Microsoft Access. That was great for learning how to create queries and learning how Access processed the input parameters to your queries. This chapter takes that a step further by showing you how to execute those queries from a VB 2005 program and how to pass parameters to those queries.

In Chapter 3, you learned about the various data wizards in Visual Studio 2005 and how they take care of generating most of the code for you. In this chapter, you use the OLE DB data classes and write all of your code by hand. This will help you learn more about these data classes and you will gain a deeper understanding about how they work and interact with one another.

In this chapter, you:

❑   Create dynamic database connections using the OleDbConnection class

❑   Execute in-line SQL statements to retrieve data

❑   Execute queries to retrieve data

❑   Use the OleDbDataReader and OleDbDataAdapter classes to read and process data

Dynamic Connections

In Chapter 3, when you used the data wizards to access data from your various data sources, the wizards created a data connection for you based on the database information that you supplied. These data connections can be viewed from the Server Explorer window in Visual Studio 2005 for those of you who are curious.

The major drawback to having the data wizards create data connections for you is that the connection information gets hard coded in your programs, which makes distributing them very difficult. Typically, the connection information is machine-specific, and once compiled in your code, it cannot be changed.

In this section, you explore creating a dynamic connection for an Access database. In future chapters you learn to create dynamic connections for SQL Server and Oracle. The process for creating a dynamic connection includes prompting the user for database information to establish a connection.

In addition, you want to ensure that the connection is successful and determine whether the database is opened or closed. These topics are covered in the subsections that follow, with hands-on exercises.

Building a connection string

Before an OleDbConnection class can be used, you must either provide a connection string when the class is initialized or set the connection string in the ConnectionString property. Either way, a connection string is required so that the OleDbConnection class knows how to connect to your data source.

In Chapter 2, you examined the basic parameters that make up a connection string: the Provider, Data Source, Database, User ID, and Password. A typical connection string is shown in the following code fragment. Of course, because you will be using an Access database and one that is not password protected, the User ID and Password parameters are not required. If the database were password protected, you would be required to supply the User ID and Password parameters.

In the following example, a String variable named strConnectionString has been defined and set using the common parameters mentioned previously. Then a new instance of the OleDbConnection class has been initialized in the variable named objConnection. This is the most typical way of initializing a new instance of the OleDbConnection class.

```
Dim strConnectionString As String = _
    "Provider=Microsoft.Jet.OLEDB.4.0;" & _
    "Data Source=C:\Chapter 5\ProjectTimeTracker.mdb;"
Dim objConnection As New OleDbConnection(strConnectionString)
```

An alternative way of setting the connection string for the OleDbConnection class is to define your connection string in a String variable as in the previous example and then initialize a new instance of the OleDbConnection class without any parameters. Finally, you set the ConnectionString property of the OleDbConnection class using your String variable.

```
Dim strConnectionString As String = _
    "Provider=Microsoft.Jet.OLEDB.4.0;" & _
    "Data Source=C:\Chapter 5\ProjectTimeTracker.mdb;"
Dim objConnection As New OleDbConnection
objConnection.ConnectionString = strConnectionString
```

As you can see, the last example requires one more line of code, which is why the first example shown is the typical way to initialize a new instance of the OleDbConnection class and to set the connection string for that class.

When you build a connection string to access your database, you typically will be prompting the user for the connection information or reading it from an application configuration file or the system registry. These values will then be used to build the complete connection string. You'll see this in action in this chapter and the chapters to come.

Opening, closing, and checking connection state

In Chapter 2, you saw that opening and closing a connection is a straightforward process. To open the connection, you call the `Open` method with the appropriate error-handling code to handle any errors that you might encounter. To close the connection, you call the `Close` method.

You may be wondering how to determine whether the connection is already opened or closed. Well, the `OleDbConnection` class, as do its counterparts, provides a `State` property that you can query. The `State` property returns one of the values from the `ConnectionState` enumeration. Several possible values can be returned, including `Open` and `Closed`.

Using the `State` property is an ideal way to determine the state of your connection, as you may have logic in your code whereby you open and close a connection multiple times and execute multiple queries against the database.

The following code snippet demonstrates how you can determine whether the connection is open. If the `State` property is not equal to `Open`, you call the `OpenDBConnection` procedure, which implements the logic to open the connection.

```
If objConnection.State <> ConnectionState.Open Then
    'Go open the connection
    Call OpenDBConnection()
End If
```

In the following Try It Out, you start building a project that will be used in several more exercises in this chapter. This first part of the project enables you to supply the path and name of your `ProjectTimeTracker` Access database. You then build a dynamic connection to the database and open and close the connection to the database. The connection state will be displayed in a label on your form.

Try It Out   Building Dynamic Connections

To create this project:

1. Start Visual Studio 2005 and start a new project by either clicking the New Project button on the Projects tab of the Start page or by clicking File and selecting New ⇨ Project.

2. In the New Project dialog box, select a Windows Application template and enter a project name of `Access SQL`. Click OK to create this project.

3. Set the following properties for `Form1`:

   ❑   Set `FormBorderStyle` to Fixed Single.

   ❑   Set `MaximizeBox` to False.

   ❑   Set `MinimizeBox` to False.

   ❑   Set `Size` to **472, 384**.

   ❑   Set `StartPosition` to Center Screen.

   ❑   Set `Text` to **Access SQL.**

4. Add a GroupBox control and in the GroupBox control add two Label controls, a TextBox control, and three Button controls to your form and arrange them to look similar to the controls shown on the form in Figure 5-1. Set the following properties of these controls:

    ❑ Set the `Text` property for GroupBox1 to **Dynamic Connection**.

    ❑ Set the `Text` property for Label1 to **Database**.

    ❑ Set the `Name` property for TextBox1 to `txtDatabase`.

    ❑ Set the `Name` property for Button1 to `btnDatabase` and set the `Text` property to . . . .

    ❑ Set the `Name` property for Button2 to `btnOpenConnection` and set the `Text` property to **Open**.

    ❑ Set the `Name` property for Button3 to `btnCloseConnection` and set the `Text` property to **Close**.

    ❑ Set the `Name` property for Label2 to **lblStatus** and set the `Text` property to **Database is not set**.

5. Right-click on Access SQL in the Solution Explorer and choose Add Reference from the context menu. In the Add Reference dialog box, scroll down the list of components in the .NET tab and select `System.Data` and then click OK.

6. Switch to the Code Editor for your form and add the following `Imports` statements at the very top of your class:

```
Imports System.Data
Imports System.Data.OleDb
```

7. Add the following variable declaration after to your `Form` class:

```
Public Class Form1
    'Form level variables
    Private objConnection As OleDbConnection
```

8. In the Class Name combo box at the top of the Code Editor, select `btnDatabase` and in the Method Name combo box select the `Click` event. Add the following code to the `btnDatabase_Click` event handler:

```
Private Sub btnDatabase_Click(ByVal sender As Object, _
    ByVal e As System.EventArgs) Handles btnDatabase.Click

        'Declare OpenFileDialog object
        Dim objOpenFileDialog As New OpenFileDialog

        'Set the OpenFileDialog properties
        With objOpenFileDialog
            .Filter = "Access Database (*.mdb)|*.mdb|All files (*.*)|*.*"
            .FilterIndex = 1
            .Title = "Open Access Database"
        End With

        'Show the dialog
        If objOpenFileDialog.ShowDialog = DialogResult.OK Then
            'If the Open button was clicked, then load the file name selected
```

```
            txtDatabase.Text = objOpenFileDialog.FileName
            'Change the status
            lblStatus.Text = "Database is set"
        End If

        'Cleanup
        objOpenFileDialog.Dispose()
        objOpenFileDialog = Nothing
    End Sub
```

9. Select `btnOpenConnection` in the Class Name combo box and the `Click` event in the Method Name combo box. Add the following code to the `btnOpenConnection_Click` event handler:

```
Private Sub btnOpenConnection_Click(ByVal sender As System.Object, _
    ByVal e As System.EventArgs) Handles btnOpenConnection.Click

        'Initialize a new instance of the OleDbConnection class
        objConnection = New OleDbConnection( _
            "Provider=Microsoft.Jet.OLEDB.4.0;" & _
            "Data Source=" & txtDatabase.Text & ";")

        Try
            'Open the connection
            objConnection.Open()
        Catch OleDbExceptionErr As OleDbException
            'Display the error
            MessageBox.Show(OleDbExceptionErr.Message, "Access SQL")
        Catch InvalidOperationExceptionErr As InvalidOperationException
            'Display the error
            MessageBox.Show(InvalidOperationExceptionErr.Message, "Access SQL")
        End Try

        'Check the state of the connection and report appropriately
        If objConnection.State = ConnectionState.Open Then
            lblStatus.Text = "Database connection is open"
        Else
            lblStatus.Text = "Database connection failed"
        End If
    End Sub
```

10. Select `btnCloseConnection` in the Class Name combo box and the `Click` event in the Method Name combo box and add the following code:

```
Private Sub btnCloseConnection_Click(ByVal sender As System.Object, _
    ByVal e As System.EventArgs) Handles btnCloseConnection.Click

        'Close the connection
        objConnection.Close()
        'Display the status of the connection
        lblStatus.Text = "Database connection is closed"

        'Cleanup
        objConnection.Dispose()
        objConnection = Nothing
    End Sub
```

11. You are ready to test your project. Click Start on the toolbar or click the Debug menu and select Start. When your form displays it should look similar to the one shown in Figure 5-1.

12. Now click the Database button, and in the Open Access Database dialog box, browse to select your `ProjectTimeTracker` Access database. After you select your database, click Open in the dialog box. The path and filename of your database are placed in the text box on your form. The message in the Status label is also updated to read `Database is set`.

13. Now you can test the code that opens and closes the connection to your database. Click the Open button on your form and if the connection opens successfully, the Status label will be updated to read `Database connection is open`.

14. To test closing the database, click the Close button on your form. The database will be closed and the Status label will be updated to read `Database connection is closed`.

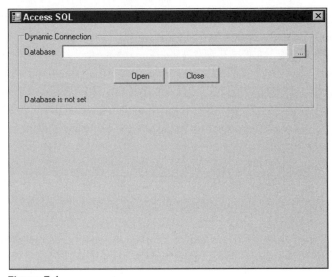

Figure 5-1

How It Works

The first lines of code you add to your project are the `Imports` statements. To access the Data and OLE DB Data classes, you have to import the `Data` and `OleDb` namespaces as shown:

```
Imports System.Data
Imports System.Data.OleDb
```

Next, you define a form-level variable for the `OleDbConnection` class. Because this variable is declared at the form level, it is available to all the procedures in your form class.

```
'Form level variables
Private objConnection As OleDbConnection
```

Next, you add code to the `btnDatabase_Click` procedure, which provides an Open File dialog box that enables you to navigate to the directory in which your database resides and to select it. The first thing that you do in this procedure is declare a variable and set it to a new instance of the `OpenFileDialog` class:

```
Private Sub btnDatabase_Click(ByVal sender As System.Object, _
    ByVal e As System.EventArgs) Handles btnDatabase.Click

    'Declare OpenFileDialog object
    Dim objOpenFileDialog As New OpenFileDialog
```

Now you need to set some properties before calling the `ShowDialog` method. Using the `With...End With` statement, you set multiple properties for the `objOpenFileDialog` variable. When setting multiple properties for an object, using a `With...End With` statement is more efficient than referencing the object several times and setting each property.

The `Filter` property specifies which file types the Open File dialog box supports, enabling the Open File dialog box to show only the files of the type selected in the Files of Type combo box. The `Filter` property is used to load the Files of Type combo box when the dialog box is displayed. You can specify multiple file types in the `Filter` property, as you do here. For each file type you specify, you enter the text to be displayed in the combo box followed by a vertical bar (|), an asterisk followed by a period, and then the file extension. Then you separate each different file type with a vertical bar.

The `FilterIndex` property is a one-based index of the filters that you specified in the `Filter` property. You set the `FilterIndex` property to cause the Open File dialog box to display a specific filter in the Files of Type combo box.

Finally, the `Title` property specifies the title that is displayed in the title bar of the Open File dialog box.

```
    'Set the OpenFileDialog properties
    With objOpenFileDialog
        .Filter = "Access Database (*.mdb)|*.mdb|All files (*.*)|*.*"
        .FilterIndex = 1
        .Title = "Open Access Database"
    End With
```

After you set the properties, you are ready to call the `ShowDialog` method to display the Open File dialog box. The `ShowDialog` method returns a `DialogResult`, which is an enumeration of dialog box result constants. Using an `If...Then` statement along with the `ShowDialog` method, you can display the Open File dialog box, wait for a response, and then proceed if the dialog box result constant returned is OK.

If the dialog box result constant returned is OK, you proceed by displaying the path and filename in the Database text box using the `FileName` property from your `objOpenFileDialog` object. The Open File dialog box does not open a file but merely provides a dialog box with properties that are set if a file is chosen. You can then query those properties to see which file or files were chosen.

Next, you update the `Text` property of the Status label to display a message that the database has been set:

```
    'Show the dialog
    If objOpenFileDialog.ShowDialog = DialogResult.OK Then
        'If the Open button was clicked, then load the file name selected
        txtDatabase.Text = objOpenFileDialog.FileName
        'Change the status
        lblStatus.Text = "Database is set"
    End If
```

Finally, regardless of whether the user clicked the Open or Cancel button in the Open File dialog box, you clean up the resources used in this procedure. You call the `Dispose` method on your `objOpenFileDialog` object so that the object can dispose of any resources that it has used and then you set it to `Nothing` to release your reference to it.

```
    'Cleanup
    objOpenFileDialog.Dispose()
    objOpenFileDialog = Nothing
End Sub
```

The next procedure you add code to is `btnOpenConnection_Click`. This procedure is executed when the Open button is clicked. The first thing you do in this procedure is initialize a new instance of the `OleDbConnection` class in your `objConnection` object.

The connection string that you are passing to the constructor of the `OleDbConnection` class consists of a `String` literal and the value in the `Text` property of the `txtDatabase` text box. Because this is an Access database with no password implemented, you need to provide only the `Provider` and `Data Source` parameters in the connection string. You set the `Provider` parameter to a `String` literal because this will not change, and you provide the database in the `txtDatabase` text box for the `Data Source` parameter.

```
    Private Sub btnOpenConnection_Click(ByVal sender As System.Object, _
        ByVal e As System.EventArgs) Handles btnOpenConnection.Click
        'Initialize a new instance of the OleDbConnection class
        objConnection = New OleDbConnection( _
            "Provider=Microsoft.Jet.OLEDB.4.0;" & _
            "Data Source=" & txtDatabase.Text & ";")
```

Now you open the database connection. If you recall from Chapter 2, several things can go wrong while trying to open a connection to the database. Thus, you have two `Catch` blocks in your `Try...Catch...End Try` block.

The first `Catch` block handles connection-level errors; while the second `Catch` block handles errors that may be returned if you try to open a connection that is already open. When an error occurs, you call the `Show` method of the `MessageBox` class to display a message containing the error. The `Show` method is an overloaded method that accepts several parameters. The following example passes the `Message` property of the error variable for the message and a `String` literal for the caption that will be displayed in the title bar of the MessageBox dialog box.

Next, you display the correct status for the connection by comparing the `State` property of your `objConnection` object against the `Open` constant in the `ConnectionState` enumeration. If they are equal, you display a message in the Status label indicating that the connection is open. Otherwise, you display a message indicating that the connection failed.

```
    Try
        'Open the connection
        objConnection.Open()
    Catch OleDbExceptionErr As OleDbException
        'Display the error
        MessageBox.Show(OleDbExceptionErr.Message, "Access SQL")
    Catch InvalidOperationExceptionErr As InvalidOperationException
        'Display the error
```

```
            MessageBox.Show(InvalidOperationExceptionErr.Message, "Access SQL")
        End Try

        'Check the state of the connection and report appropriately
        If objConnection.State = ConnectionState.Open Then
            lblStatus.Text = "Database connection is open"
        Else
            lblStatus.Text = "Database connection failed"
        End If
    End Sub
```

The last procedure you add code for is btnCloseConnection_Click. This procedure is executed when you click the Close button on your form. Remember that calling the Close method on a connection that is already closed does not produce an error so there's no need to check the current state of the connection. You simply call the Close method and set the appropriate message in the Status label indicating that the connection is closed.

You then call the Dispose method on your objConnection object so that any resources used by that object are released. Then you set the objConnection object to Nothing, releasing your reference to it:

```
    Private Sub btnCloseConnection_Click(ByVal sender As System.Object, _
        ByVal e As System.EventArgs) Handles btnCloseConnection.Click
        'Close the connection
        objConnection.Close()
        'Display the status of the connection
        lblStatus.Text = "Database connection is closed"

        'Cleanup
        objConnection.Dispose()
        objConnection = Nothing
    End Sub
```

At this point, you have a program that can make a dynamic connection to any Access database. However, the program is not complete. All you can do is open and close a connection. In the next few sections, you add code to this project to execute SQL statements against the database that you open.

In-Line SQL

In-line SQL refers to SQL statements defined as String literals in your code. The SQL statements can be SELECT, INSERT, UPDATE, or DELETE statements. Once your project is compiled, these SQL statements become part of your executable and cannot be changed.

The SQL statements that were executed in Chapter 3 were in-line SQL statements. However, because you were using the data wizards, the SQL statements that were generated were added to your code automatically and you didn't see them.

In this section, you explore the OleDbCommand class in a little more detail. This class represents a SQL statement, query, or stored procedure to be executed against your database. If you recall from Chapter 2, you took a look at some of the common constructors for the OleDbCommand class. You apply that knowledge here with hands-on examples.

The `OleDbCommand` class has a `CommandType` property that tells the `OleDbCommand` class what type of command it should execute. This property can be set to three possible values using the `CommandType` enumeration: `StoredProcedure`, `TableDirect`, and `Text`. The `StoredProcedure` constant indicates that the `CommandText` property of the `OleDbCommand` class contains the name of the stored procedure or query to be executed. The `TableDirect` constant indicates that the `CommandText` property contains the name of the table from which data should be retrieved. No SELECT statement is required when the `CommandType` property is set to this constant, only the table name. Finally, the `Text` constant, which is the default for the `CommandType` property, indicates that in-line SQL statements are being executed. It's these last two options that you explore in this section.

Remember that one of the constructors for the `OleDbCommand` class allows you to pass the SQL string to be executed. This is the constructor that you'll be using, as it is the most common constructor. A recap of that constructor is shown in the following code fragment:

```
Dim strSQL As String = _
    "SELECT FirstName, LastName FROM Employees"
Dim objCommand As New OleDbCommand(strSQL, objConnection)
```

The `OleDbCommand` class has several methods for executing SQL statements and stored procedures and you examine those throughout this book. However, the one that you are interested in now is the `ExecuteReader` method.

This method executes commands (SQL statements or stored procedures) that return data. The return value from this method, interestingly enough, is an `OleDbDataReader` object. This works out quite nicely because you want to use an `OleDbDataReader` object to read the data that has been returned.

In Chapter 2, you saw how this was accomplished by setting your object declared as an instance of the `OleDbDataReader` class to the results returned by the `ExecuteReader` method. Again, a recap of that code is shown here for reference:

```
Dim objReader As OleDbDataReader = objCommand.ExecuteReader()
```

In this next Try It Out, you add functionality that enables you to execute in-line SQL statements that you enter in a text box control. You also choose whether to set the `CommandType` property to the `Text` constant or to the `TableDirect` constant. Finally, you execute the `ExecuteReader` method of the `OleDbCommand` object and process the data returned in an `OleDbDataReader` object.

Try It Out   Using the OleDbDataReader

To create this example:

1. Open the `Access SQL` project you created in the previous exercise if it is not already opened.

2. Switch to the Form Designer and add the controls in the following list. Arrange them so they look similar to the controls shown on the form in Figure 5-2:

    ❏   One GroupBox

    ❏   One Label

    ❏   Two RadioButtons

  ❑ One TextBox

  ❑ One Button

3. Set the following properties of these controls:

  ❑ Set the Text property of the GroupBox control to **In-Line SQL.**

  ❑ Set the Text property of the Label to **SQL.**

  ❑ Set the Text property of the first RadioButton to **TableDirect.**

  ❑ Set the Name property of the second RadioButton to **optText**, the Checked property to True, and the Text property to **Text.**

  ❑ Set the Name property of the TextBox to **txtSQL**, the Multiline property to True, the ScrollBars property to Vertical, and the Text property to **SELECT * FROM Projects**. After you set the Multiline property to True, you'll be able to resize the height of the text box control.

  ❑ Set the Name property of the Button to **btnDataReader** and the Text property to **DataReader.**

4. Switch to the Code Editor and add the following procedure:

```
Private Function IsConnectionOpen() As Boolean
    'Is the connection object set to a valid instance
    'of the OleDbConnection class
    If IsNothing(objConnection) Then
        Return False
    End If

    'Is the connection open
    If objConnection.State <> ConnectionState.Open Then
        Return False
    End If

    'If we made it this far return True
    Return True
End Function
```

5. Select btnDataReader in the Class Name combo box at the top of the Code Editor and the Click event in the Method Name combo box. Add the following code to the btnDataReader_Click event handler:

```
Private Sub btnDataReader_Click(ByVal sender As System.Object, _
    ByVal e As System.EventArgs) Handles btnDataReader.Click

    'Validate connection state
    If Not IsConnectionOpen() Then
        Exit Sub
    End If

    'Declare and initialize a new instance of the OleDbCommand class
    Dim objCommand As New OleDbCommand(txtSQL.Text, objConnection)

    'Set the CommandType property
    If optText.Checked Then
```

```
            objCommand.CommandType = CommandType.Text
        Else
            objCommand.CommandType = CommandType.TableDirect
        End If

        'Declare an OleDbDataReader object
        Dim objDataReader As OleDbDataReader

        'Declare a String variable
        Dim strData As String

        Try
            'Execute the SQL text
            objDataReader = objCommand.ExecuteReader()

            'Check to see if we have data
            If objDataReader.HasRows Then

                'Process all rows
                While objDataReader.Read()

                    'Clear the variable
                    strData = String.Empty

                    'Get the data in each column
                    For intIndex As Integer = 0 To objDataReader.FieldCount - 1
                        strData &= objDataReader.Item(intIndex).ToString & ", "
                    Next

                    'Remove the last comma from the string
                    strData = strData.Remove(strData.Length - 2, 2)

                    'Write the data to the TextBox
                    txtSQL.Text &= ControlChars.CrLf & strData

                End While

            End If

            'Close the reader
            objDataReader.Close()

        Catch OleDbExceptionErr As OleDbException
            MessageBox.Show(OleDbExceptionErr.Message, "Access SQL")
        End Try

        'Cleanup
        objCommand.Dispose()
        objCommand = Nothing
        objDataReader = Nothing
    End Sub
```

6. You are ready to test your project, so start it. When your form displays, it should look similar to the one shown in Figure 5-2.

7. Click the `Database` button, navigate to and select the `ProjectTimeTracker` database, and click Open in the Open Access Database dialog box. Then click Open on your form to open the connection to the database.

8. Next, click the DataReader button to execute the SQL statement shown in the text box. You should notice that the results of the SQL statement are processed and written to the text box.

9. Clear the text in the text box and enter the table name of `Projects`. Then select the TableDirect option and click the DataReader button. You should see the same results as before. All data in the Projects table has been read and processed. Click the Close button to close your database connection.

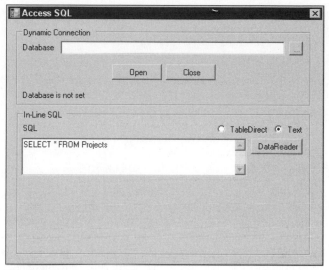

Figure 5-2

10. You can further test your dynamic connection by selecting another Access database, opening it, and selecting all the data from a table. For example, if you have the sample `Northwind` database that is optionally installed with Microsoft Office, you can select that database and then open the connection. Then you can enter the following query:

```
SELECT * FROM Employees
```

When you click the DataReader button, the SQL statement is executed and all the data returned is processed and displayed in the text box on your form.

How It Works

The first thing you add to your project is the `IsConnectionOpen` function, which returns a Boolean value indicating whether the database connection is open. You want to ensure that the `objConnection` object is set to a valid instance of the `OleDbConnection` class. The `IsNothing` function returns a value of `False` if the `objConnection` object is equal to `Nothing` in which case you simply return a value of `False` to the caller of this function. The statement `Return False` in the following code returns a value of `False` and exits the function without executing any additional code:

```
Private Function IsConnectionOpen() As Boolean
    'Is the connection object set to a valid instance
    'of the OleDbConnection class
    If IsNothing(objConnection) Then
        Return False
    End If
```

If the objConnection object has been set to an instance of the OleDbConnection class, you want to ensure that the connection is open by checking the State property against the Open constant in the ConnectionState enumeration. If the State property is not equal to the Open constant, you return with a value of False.

If you make it to the last line of code in this function, the objConnection object has been set to an instance of the OleDbConnection class and the State property of the objConnection object contains a value of Open. At this point you return with a value of True.

```
    'Is the connection open
    If objConnection.State <> ConnectionState.Open Then
        Return False
    End If

    'If we made it this far return True
    Return True
End Function
```

You add code to the btnDataReader_Click procedure next, and this procedure is executed when you click the DataReader button on your form. The first thing that you do in this procedure is ensure that the connection to the database is open. You do this in an If...Then statement, which calls the IsConnectionOpen function. By specifying the Not keyword in the If...Then statement, you are saying that if the value returned from the IsConnectionOpen function is False, then execute the code inside the If...Then statement. The code inside the If...Then statement simply exits the procedure.

```
    Private Sub btnDataReader_Click(ByVal sender As System.Object, _
        ByVal e As System.EventArgs) Handles btnDataReader.Click

        'Validate connection state
        If Not IsConnectionOpen() Then
            Exit Sub
        End If
```

Once you ensure that a valid connection exists to your database and that the connection is open, you declare the objCommand object as a new instance of the OleDbCommand class. Notice that in the constructor for the OleDbCommand class, you are passing the in-line SQL statement from the text box and the objConnection object.

Next, you determine whether Text option is checked, in which case you set the CommandType property to the Text constant in the CommandType enumeration. If the Text option is not checked, you set the CommandType property to a value of TableDirect. Actually, the first statement is not really necessary, as the Text constant from the CommandType enumeration is the default value. It has been specified here for clarity of code.

```
        'Declare and initialize a new instance of the OleDbCommand class
        Dim objCommand As New OleDbCommand(txtSQL.Text, objConnection)
```

```
'Set the CommandType property
If optText.Checked Then
    objCommand.CommandType = CommandType.Text
Else
    objCommand.CommandType = CommandType.TableDirect
End If
```

You need a couple more variables in this procedure: an `OleDbDataReader` object, which is declared in the next line of code, and a `String` variable that can be used to hold the data read from the `objDataReader` object:

```
'Declare a OleDbDataReader object
Dim objDataReader As OleDbDataReader

'Declare a String variable
Dim strData As String
```

You could receive an exception while trying to execute your in-line SQL statement, so you want to include the appropriate error-handling code as shown here. You place your code that executes the `ExecuteReader` method of the `objCommand` object inside a `Try...Catch` block.

First, you execute the `ExecuteReader` method of the `objCommand` object and set the results returned in your `objDataReader` object. Remember that the `ExecuteReader` method of the `OleDbCommand` class returns an `OleDbDataReader`.

Next, you ensure that some data has been returned before continuing. You check the `HasRows` property of the `objDataReader`, which returns a Boolean value indicating whether it contains any rows of data. If the `objDataReader` contains data, you proceed.

You process all rows of data in the `objDataReader` object by setting up a `While...End While` loop in which you execute the `Read` method of the `objDataReader` object.

In this loop, you first clear the `strData` variable of any existing data by setting it to `String.Empty`. The `Empty` field of the `String` class represents a zero-length string. The first time you process the loop, the `strData` variable is empty. The second time, however, this variable contains the data from the previous iteration.

You want to process all columns of data returned as a result of your `SELECT` statement. Because you don't know how many that will be, you set up a `For...Next` loop to process all columns contained in the `FieldCount` property of the `objDataReader` object. You declare an in-line `Integer` variable in the `For...Next` loop and process each column of data.

Remember that most indexes are zero-based, so you start processing at index position zero and process to the value contained in the `FieldCount` property minus one. Remember too that the `FieldCount` property returns the actual number of columns in the `objDataReader` object so you need to specify this property minus one.

Inside this `For...Next` loop, you retrieve the data for each column using the `Item` property of the `objDataReader` object and passing it the index of the column. The `Item` property returns the value in the specified column in its native format. Because the first column in the Projects table is a Guid, this has to be converted to a string in order to add it to the strData variable; thus, you add the ToString method after the Item property. This will convert all data retrieved to a String data type, allowing you to concatenate it to the strData variable.

You want to separate each value retrieved with a comma, so this has been specified as a string literal at the end of the statement.

After you process all columns of data in the For...Next loop, you want to remove the last comma in the strData variable. This is done using the Remove method of the String class. This method expects the starting position within the string to start removing characters and the number of characters to remove from the string. This line of code uses the length of the string minus 2 as the starting position and specifies a value of 2 for the number of characters to remove.

Finally, you want to append the text that you have built in the strData variable to the text box on your form. This is done by first adding a carriage return linefeed character to the text box and then adding the contents of the strData variable. The ControlChars module contains a list of constants that can be used as control characters, such as carriage return line feed, carriage return, line feed, new line, and more. To view the complete list of constants, right-click ControlChars in your code and choose Go To Definition from the context menu. This will take you to this module in the Object Browser where you can view the available constants.

Once you have processed all of the data in the loop, you want to close the objDataReader object, which is done in the last line of code here:

```
Try
    'Execute the SQL text
    objDataReader = objCommand.ExecuteReader()

    'Check to see if we have data
    If objDataReader.HasRows Then

        'Process all rows
        While objDataReader.Read()

            'Clear the variable
            strData = String.Empty

            'Get the data in each column
            For intIndex As Integer = 0 To objDataReader.FieldCount - 1
                strData &= objDataReader.Item(intIndex).ToString & ", "
            Next

            'Remove the last comma from the string
            strData = strData.Remove(strData.Length - 2, 2)

            'Write the data to the TextBox
            txtSQL.Text &= ControlChars.CrLf & strData

        End While

    End If

    'Close the reader
```

```
        objDataReader.Close()
```

If an error occurred during the execution of the `ExecuteReader` method of the `objCommand` object or the reading of the data from the `objDataReader` object, an exception is thrown and you catch it in the following `Catch` block. Then you display the message of the exception using the `Message` property of your error variable and display it in a MessageBox dialog box:

```
        Catch OleDbExceptionErr As OleDbException
            MessageBox.Show(OleDbExceptionErr.Message, "Access SQL")
        End Try
```

Finally, you clean up the resources used in this procedure by calling the `Dispose` method on the `objCommand` object and then setting both the `objCommand` and `objDataReader` objects to `Nothing` to release your reference to them:

```
        'Cleanup
        objCommand.Dispose()
        objCommand = Nothing
        objDataReader = Nothing
    End Sub
```

This example has demonstrated how you can enter SQL statements in a text box on your form and have them execute as in-line SQL statements. The procedure that executes these SQL statements has been designed as a generic procedure to handle the results of any SQL SELECT statement that you enter and will process all columns and rows of data returned and place them in the text box on your form.

In this next Try It Out, you complete the functionality of the Access SQL project by adding a `DataGridView` control to your form and a Button control that will enable you to execute the SQL statement entered in the text box on your form. The procedure for the Button control will populate a `DataTable` object and bind it to the `DataGridView` control. You'll also have the opportunity to programmatically set some styles for the `DataGridView` control to enhance the appearance of this control's interface.

Try It Out   Using the OleDbDataAdapter

To create this example:

1. Open the `Access SQL` project that you modified in the last exercise if it is not already open.

2. Switch to the Form Designer and add the controls in the following list. Arrange them so they look similar to the controls shown on the form in Figure 5-3:
   - ❑ One `DataGridView`
   - ❑ One Button

3. Set the following properties of these controls:
   - ❑ Set the `Name` property of the `DataGridView` control to **grdResults**.
   - ❑ Set the `Name` property of the Button to **btnDataAdapter** and the `Text` property to **DataAdapter**.

4. Double-click the Button and add the following code to the `btnDataAdapter_Click` procedure:

```
Private Sub btnDataAdapter_Click(ByVal sender As System.Object, _
    ByVal e As System.EventArgs) Handles btnDataAdapter.Click

        'Validate connection state
        If Not IsConnectionOpen() Then
            Exit Sub
        End If

        'Declare and initialize a new instance of the OleDbCommand class
        Dim objCommand As New OleDbCommand(txtSQL.Text, objConnection)

        'Set the CommandType property
        If optText.Checked Then
            objCommand.CommandType = CommandType.Text
        Else
            objCommand.CommandType = CommandType.TableDirect
        End If

        'Declare a OleDbDataAdapter object
        Dim objDataAdapter As New OleDbDataAdapter

        'Declare a DataTable object
        Dim objDataTable As New DataTable

        'Set the SelectCommand for the OleDbDataAdapter
        objDataAdapter.SelectCommand = objCommand

        Try
            'Populate the DataTable
            objDataAdapter.Fill(objDataTable)

            'Bind the DataTable to the DataGridView
            grdResults.DataSource = objDataTable

            'Set the AlternatingRowsDefaultCellStyle.BackColor property
            grdResults.AlternatingRowsDefaultCellStyle.BackColor = Color.WhiteSmoke

            'Set the CellBorderStyle property
            grdResults.CellBorderStyle = DataGridViewCellBorderStyle.None

            'Set the SelectionMode property
            grdResults.SelectionMode = DataGridViewSelectionMode.FullRowSelect

        Catch OleDbExceptionErr As OleDbException
            MessageBox.Show(OleDbExceptionErr.Message, "Access SQL")
        End Try

        'Cleanup
        objCommand.Dispose()
        objCommand = Nothing
        objDataAdapter.Dispose()
        objDataAdapter = Nothing
        objDataTable.Dispose()
        objDataTable = Nothing
End Sub
```

5. You are now ready to test your project, so start it. Click the `Database` button and locate and select your `ProjectTimeTracker` database and then click the Open button in the Open Access Database dialog box to have the path and database name placed in the text box on your form. Click the Open button next to open the connection to the database.

6. Click the DataAdapter button and your SQL `SELECT` statement will be executed and the results placed in a `DataTable` and bound to the `DataGridView` on your form. You should see all of the columns and rows from your Projects table listed in the `DataGridView` as shown in Figure 5-3.

7. Now change your SQL `SELECT` statement to only the table name of **Projects.** Select the TableDirect option and then click the DataAdapter button. You'll see the same results as before.

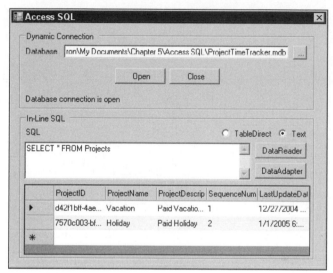

Figure 5-3

How It Works

You start by adding two additional controls to your form, a `DataGridView` that you can bind a `DataTable` to and another Button control to which you add the code to use an `OleDbDataAdapter` to fill a `DataTable` object and to bind the `DataTable` to the `DataGridView`.

The code that you add to the `btnDataAdapter_Click` procedure starts out like the code that you added to the `btnDataReader_Click` procedure in the previous Try It Out. First you use the `IsConnectioOpen` function to determine whether the database connection is open, exiting the procedure if it is not.

Next, you initialize a new instance of the `OleDbCommand` object, passing it the SQL statement to be executed and the `objConnection` object, which contains an open connection to your database. Then you check the `optText` RadioButton and set the `CommandType` property of the `objCommand` object accordingly:

```
Private Sub btnDataAdapter_Click(ByVal sender As System.Object, _
    ByVal e As System.EventArgs) Handles btnDataAdapter.Click

    'Validate connection state
    If Not IsConnectionOpen() Then
```

```
        Exit Sub
    End If

    'Declare and initialize a new instance of the OleDbCommand class
    Dim objCommand As New OleDbCommand(txtSQL.Text, objConnection)

    'Set the CommandType property
    If optText.Checked Then
        objCommand.CommandType = CommandType.Text
    Else
        objCommand.CommandType = CommandType.TableDirect
    End If
```

Next, you declare two objects: one for an `OleDbDataAdapter` and one for a `DataTable`. Then you set the `SelectCommand` property of the `objDataAdapter` object to your `objCommand` object. This provides the `objDataAdapter` object with the SQL SELECT statement to be executed.

```
    'Declare a OleDbDataAdapter object
    Dim objDataAdapter As New OleDbDataAdapter

    'Declare a DataTable object
    Dim objDataTable As New DataTable

    'Set the SelectCommand for the OleDbDataAdapter
    objDataAdapter.SelectCommand = objCommand
```

Again you enclose your critical code in a `Try...Catch` block to trap and handle any database errors that may occur. The first thing that you do inside the `Try` block is fill the `DataTable` with data by calling the `Fill` method on your `objDataAdapter` object and passing it your `objDataTable` object. Then you bind the `DataTable` to the `DataGridView` by setting the `DataSource` property of the `DataGridView` to the `DataTable`.

```
    Try
        'Populate the DataTable
        objDataAdapter.Fill(objDataTable)

        'Bind the DataTable to the DataGridView
        grdResults.DataSource = objDataTable
```

The next section of code sets the styles for the `DataGridView`. The first property being set is `AlternatingRowsDefaultCellStyle.BackColor`. This property controls the color of the odd-numbered rows. Setting this property causes the odd-numbered rows to appear in a different color. You set this property using a `Color` member from the `Color` structure.

The `Color` structure provides a list of properties of named colors in the system, which is what you have used here. It also provides methods that enable you to set the color from red, green, and blue values or by using known or named colors. By far, the easiest means of using the color structure is to use the provided properties that contain an array of colors. You can view a complete list of the color properties by right-clicking `Color` in your code and choosing the Go To Definition menu item in the context menu. This takes you to the Object Browser where you can view the complete list of properties and methods.

The next line of code here sets the `CellBorderStyle` property. By default, the `DataGrid` will display grid lines both horizontally and vertically. Because you have set the `AlternatingRowsDefaultCellStyle.BackColor` property, there is really no need to have the grid lines displayed. The `DataGridViewCellBorderStyle` enumeration is used to set the grid lines to the `None` constant, which effectively turns off the grid lines.

Finally, you set the `SelectionMode` property to control the appearance of a selected row. By default, clicking a cell selects only that cell. Setting the `SelectionMode` property allows you to select the contents of the entire row whenever you click in any cell in a row. This is accomplished using the `FullRowSelect` constant from the `DataGridViewSelectionMode` enumeration.

```
'Set the AlternatingRowsDefaultCellStyle.BackColor property
grdResults.AlternatingRowsDefaultCellStyle.BackColor = Color.WhiteSmoke

'Set the CellBorderStyle property
grdResults.CellBorderStyle = DataGridViewCellBorderStyle.None

'Set the SelectionMode property
grdResults.SelectionMode = DataGridViewSelectionMode.FullRowSelect
```

You now come to the `Catch` block, which, as before, will display a MessageBox dialog box with the error that is contained in the `Message` property of the `OleDbExceptionErr` variable.

Outside of the `Try...Catch` block, you perform the cleanup necessary for this procedure by disposing of the `objCommand`, `objDataAdapter`, and `objDataTable` objects and then setting them to `Nothing`:

```
Catch OleDbExceptionErr As OleDbException
    MessageBox.Show(OleDbExceptionErr.Message, "Access SQL")
End Try

'Cleanup
objCommand.Dispose()
objCommand = Nothing
objDataAdapter.Dispose()
objDataAdapter = Nothing
objDataTable.Dispose()
objDataTable = Nothing
End Sub
```

This exercise has set up a generic procedure that processes in-line SQL statements and populates the results in a `DataTable` using the `OleDbDataAdapter`. The `DataTable` was then bound to a `DataGridView` on your form and the `DataGridView` properties were modified to make it more aesthetically appealing.

You can further test this generic functionality by executing a `SELECT` statement against the Groups table. Of course, the Groups table has no data in it at this point but you'll see the column headers displayed in the `DataGridView`.Access Queries

You've taken a look at how to execute in-line SQL statements, so now it's time to turn your attention to how you execute Access queries from your VB 2005 programs. You can execute Access queries using the `OleDbCommand` object just as you did with your in-line SQL statements.

During the discussion of the `CommandType` property of the `OleDbCommand` class earlier in this chapter, I mentioned that three possible values could be set using the `CommandType` enumeration: `StoredProcedure`, `TableDirect`, and `Text`. You have already explored the last two constants in this enumeration so now it's time to learn about the first constant, `StoredProcedure`.

A query in Access is equivalent to a stored procedure in SQL Server or Oracle when it comes to executing it in a Command object. Chapter 2 provided a brief overview of the `OleDbCommand` class and a code snippet executing a stored procedure, which is shown in the following snippet. The first three properties of the `OleDbCommand` class have already been covered so you should explore the `Parameters` collection in a little more detail before actually using it.

```
Dim objCommand As New OleDbCommand
objCommand.Connection = objConnection
objCommand.CommandText = "SelectEmployee"
objCommand.CommandType = CommandType.StoredProcedure
objCommand.Parameters.Add("EmployeeID", OleDbType.Char, 9).Value = "PTC11962M"
```

The `Parameters` collection contains a collection of `OleDbParameter` objects, with each parameter mapping to an input value in your query or stored procedure. The parameters must be added to the `Parameters` collection in the order in which they are defined in your query or stored procedure.

An `OleDbParameter` object contains many properties that can be set to describe the parameter. A parameter may be defined as input or output to a query or stored procedure or may be defined as both an input and output parameter. It can also be defined as a return value, meaning that the sole purpose of the parameter is to receive a value returned by your query or stored procedure.

Other properties that can be set include properties that set the name of the parameter, the data type that the parameter represents in your query, the size of the data type, and the value that will be passed to your query or stored procedure.

Let's take a look at the `Size` property for a moment. The `Size` property specifies the maximum size for the data type and the value that will be set in the `Value` property. For example, suppose a parameter defined for an Access query expects the project name for a project in the Projects table in your database. The ProjectName field is defined in Access as a text field with a maximum value of 50 characters. Therefore, you must set the `Size` property of your parameter to a value of `50`. This value must be of the same size or smaller than the value specified in your query or stored procedure. If you try to pass a value that is larger than the one defined in your query or stored procedure, you receive a runtime exception when trying to execute that query or stored procedure.

The `Add` method of the `Parameters` collection is an overloaded method providing a lot of flexibility. The `Add` method shown in the preceding code is the most common method used when adding a new `Parameter` to the `Parameters` collection, and it is the method that you'll be using in your exercises.

The parameters to the `Add` method shown in the preceding code are parameter name, OLE DB data type, and OLE DB data type size. The `Value` property of the `Add` method is used to set the value of the parameter. The parameter direction is inferred as the `Direction` property of the `OleDbParameter` class has a default value of `input`. You learn how to override this default value in Chapter 15.

Before you can create a program that executes a parameter query to return data, you need to create a query in Access that accepts a parameter as input and returns only the data requested. This next Try It Out guides you through the steps required to create a query to select a specific project from the Projects table in your `ProjectTimeTracker` database.

Creating Select Project Query

To create this query:

1. Locate your `ProjectTimeTracker` Access database in Windows Explorer and double-click it or start Microsoft Access and open your `ProjectTimeTracker` database.

2. In the navigation bar to the left, click Queries. Then, in the list displayed, double-click Create Query in Design View.

3. The Query Builder is shown in Design View by default and the Show Table dialog box is displayed. You do not want to add any tables, so click the Close button to close the Show Table dialog box.

4. You also do not want to use the Design view to create this query so on the toolbar click the View button or click the View menu and choose the SQL View menu item to switch the Query Builder to the SQL view.

5. Enter the following query:

```
SELECT ProjectID, ProjectName, ProjectDescription, SequenceNumber, LastUpdateDate
FROM Projects
WHERE ProjectID = @ProjectID;
```

6. Click the Save button on the toolbar or click the File menu and choose the Save menu item. In the Save As dialog box, enter a query name of `usp_SelectProject`. Notice that the name is similar to the query `usp_SelectProjects` but is singular, indicating that this query will select a single project only. Once your query has been saved, close the Query Builder window by clicking the X in its upper-right corner.

How It Works

The SELECT query that build here selects only a single project from the Projects table, based on the `ProjectID`. Remember that the `ProjectID` in your Projects table is defined as a primary key; thus, you cannot have duplicate values. Selecting a project in this manner ensures that only a single project is returned.

You specify the `ProjectID` column in the SELECT statement, which is really not necessary, as you already know what the `ProjectID` is because you are using it to specify which project is to be selected. However, this column of data will be used in the last Try It Out in this chapter and it will become evident why it has been included here.

The SELECT query that you build here selects all columns of data in your Projects table. The WHERE clause limits the results to a single project based on the value contained in the input parameter `@ProjectID`.

```
SELECT ProjectID, ProjectName, ProjectDescription, SequenceNumber, LastUpdateDate
FROM Projects
WHERE ProjectID = @ProjectID;
```

Now that you have a SELECT query that accepts an input parameter and returns data, it's time to move right along and create a VB 2005 project that will execute Access queries.

In this Try It Out you create a VB 2005 program that executes an Access query that accepts no parameters and returns all rows of data in the table. Using the `OleDbDataAdapter`, you fill a `DataSet` object with the results of the query and bind that `DataSet` to a `DataGridView` control.

Try It Out   Creating a Non-Parameter Query

To create this project:

1. Start Visual Studio 2005 and start a new project by clicking the New Project button on the Projects tab of the Start page or by selecting File ⇨ New ⇨ Project.

2. In the New Project dialog box, select a Windows Application template and enter a project name of `Access Queries`. Click OK to have this project created.

3. Set the following properties for `Form1`:

   ❑ Set `Size` to **424, 216**.

   ❑ Set `StartPosition` to Center Screen.

   ❑ Set `Text` to **Access Queries**.

4. Add a Button and DataGridView control to your form and arrange them to look similar to the controls shown on the form in Figure 5-4. Set the following properties for these controls:

   ❑ Set the `Name` property for `Button1` to **btnNonParameterQuery**, set the `Anchor` property to Top, Right, and set the `Text` property to **Non-Parameter Query.**

   ❑ Set the `Name` property for `DataGridView1` to **grdResults**, and set the `Anchor` property to Top, Bottom, Left, Right.

5. Right-click Access SQL in the Solution Explorer and choose Add Reference from the context menu. In the Add Reference dialog box, scroll down the list of components in the .NET tab and select System.Data and then click OK.

6. Switch to the Code Editor for your form and add the following `Imports` statement at the very top of your class:

```
Imports System.Data
Imports System.Data.OleDb
```

7. Add the following variable declarations to your `Form` class. You'll need to change the path for the `strConnectionString` variable to point to the correct path for your `ProjectTimeTracker` database:

```
'Form level variables
Private strConnectionString As String = _
    "Provider=Microsoft.Jet.OLEDB.4.0;" & _
    "Data Source=C:\Chapter 5\ProjectTimeTracker.mdb;"

Private objConnection As OleDbConnection
Private objCommand As OleDbCommand
Private objDataAdapter As OleDbDataAdapter
Private objDataSet As DataSet
```

8. You need a procedure to populate the `DataGridView` on your form, so create the `PopulateGrid` procedure and add the following code:

```
Private Sub PopulateGrid()
    'Initialize a new instance of the OleDbDataAdapter class
    objDataAdapter = New OleDbDataAdapter

    'Initialize a new instance of the DataSet class
    objDataSet = New DataSet

    'Set the SelectCommand for the OleDbDataAdapter
    objDataAdapter.SelectCommand = objCommand

    Try
        'Populate the DataSet
        objDataAdapter.Fill(objDataSet, "Projects")

        'Bind the DataSet to the DataGrid
        grdResults.DataSource = objDataSet
        grdResults.DataMember = "Projects"

        'Set the AlternatingRowsDefaultCellStyle.BackColor property
        grdResults.AlternatingRowsDefaultCellStyle.BackColor = Color.WhiteSmoke

        'Set the CellBorderStyle property
        grdResults.CellBorderStyle = DataGridViewCellBorderStyle.None

        'Set the SelectionMode property
        grdResults.SelectionMode = DataGridViewSelectionMode.FullRowSelect

        'Set the AutoSizeColumnsMode property
        grdResults.AutoSizeColumnsMode = _
            DataGridViewAutoSizeColumnsMode.AllCells

        'Right align SequenceNumber column
        grdResults.Columns("SequenceNumber").DefaultCellStyle.Alignment = _
            DataGridViewContentAlignment.MiddleRight

    Catch OleDbException As OleDbException
        MessageBox.Show(OleDbException.Message, "Access Queries")
    End Try

    'Cleanup
    objCommand.Dispose()
    objCommand = Nothing
    objDataAdapter.Dispose()
    objDataAdapter = Nothing
    objDataSet.Dispose()
    objDataSet = Nothing
    objConnection.Dispose()
    objConnection = Nothing
End Sub
```

9. In the Class Name combo box at the top of the Code Editor, select `btnNonParameterQuery` and in the Method Name combo box select the `Click` event. Add the following code to the `btnNonParameterQuery_Click` event handler:

```
Private Sub btnNonParameterQuery_Click(ByVal sender As System.Object, _
    ByVal e As System.EventArgs) Handles btnNonParameterQuery.Click

        'Initialize a new instance of the OleDbConnection class
        objConnection = New OleDbConnection(strConnectionString)

        'Initialize a new instance of the OleDbCommand class
        objCommand = New OleDbCommand

        'Set the objCommand object properties
        objCommand.CommandText = "usp_SelectProjects"
        objCommand.CommandType = CommandType.StoredProcedure
        objCommand.Connection = objConnection

        'Populate the DataGridView
        Call PopulateGrid()
    End Sub
```

10. That's all of the code that you need for this exercise. Run your project and then click the Non-Parameter Query button. When the results of your query are returned and bound to the `DataGridView`, it should look similar to the results shown in Figure 5-4. You will be able to resize your form to see all of the data in the `DataGridView`.

Notice that the Guids displayed in the `DataGrid` in the figure do not contain the brackets around them as you saw in the last chapter when running your query directly in Access. This is because the Data Provider—in this case, OLE DB—has automatically removed them, as they are not needed.

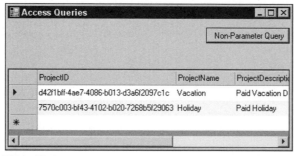

Figure 5-4

How It Works

The first lines of code that you add to your project are the `Imports` statements. This imports the `System.Data` and `System.Data.OleDb` namespaces into your project, making the Data and OLE DB classes available to your code without having to fully qualify the classes.

```
Imports System.Data
Imports System.Data.OleDb
```

Next, you add some variable declarations at the form level. This makes these variables accessible to all procedures in your form class. The first of these variables is the `strConnectionString` variable. This `String` variable contains the connection string needed to connect to your database. You change the path in this variable to match the path in which your `ProjectTimeTracker` database resides.

The next four variables define the objects needed from the `OleDb` namespace to connect to the database, build a command to be executed against the database, execute a command against the database, and fill a `DataSet` with data.

```
'Form level variables
Private strConnectionString As String = _
    "Provider=Microsoft.Jet.OLEDB.4.0;" & _
    "Data Source=C:\Chapter 5\ProjectTimeTracker.mdb;"

Private objConnection As OleDbConnection
Private objCommand As OleDbCommand
Private objDataAdapter As OleDbDataAdapter
Private objDataSet As DataSet
```

The first procedure you add populates the `DataGridView` control on your form. In the next Try It Out, you add more functionality to this project and call this same procedure.

The first thing you do in this procedure is initialize your `objDataAdapter` and `objDataSet` objects. Then you set the `SelectCommand` property of your `objDataAdapter` object to your `objCommand` object. The `objCommand` object will be set in another procedure so when this code executes, the `objCommand` object will already be set with the appropriate properties.

```
Private Sub PopulateGrid()
    'Initialize a new instance of the OleDbDataAdapter class
    objDataAdapter = New OleDbDataAdapter

    'Initialize a new instance of the DataSet class
    objDataSet = New DataSet

    'Set the SelectCommand for the OleDbDataAdapter
    objDataAdapter.SelectCommand = objCommand
```

Anytime you execute code against your database, you want to include some type of error handling to handle any errors that might occur. This is done here in a `Try...Catch` block.

The first thing that you are doing here is executing the `Fill` method of the `objDataAdapter` object to fill the `DataSet`. Remember that the `Fill` method uses the command set in the `SelectCommand` property to execute against the database and to fill the `DataSet`. In this code you are filling your `objDataSet` object and specifying the table name to be used in the `DataSet`.

After the `DataSet` has been populated with data, you want to bind the `DataSet` to the `DataGridView`. You first set the `DataSource` property to your `DataSet` object. Then you set the `DataMember` property to tell the `DataGridView` control which table in the `DataSet` to use. This property has to be set as a `DataSet` may contain multiple `DataTables`.

```
Try
    'Populate the DataSet
    objDataAdapter.Fill(objDataSet, "Projects")

    'Bind the DataSet to the DataGrid
    grdResults.DataSource = objDataSet
    grdResults.DataMember = "Projects"
```

The next section of code sets the various properties of the DataGridView control to customize the look and feel of this control.

The first thing that you do is set the AlternatingRowsDefaultCellStyle.BackColor property to have the odd rows in the DataGridView control set to a different color than the even rows. Then you set the CellBorderStyle property to remove the grid lines around each cell and finally set the SelectionMode so that when a cell is clicked, the entire row is selected. These are the properties that you set in the Access SQL project in the previous exercises:

```
'Set the AlternatingRowsDefaultCellStyle.BackColor property
grdResults.AlternatingRowsDefaultCellStyle.BackColor = Color.WhiteSmoke

'Set the CellBorderStyle property
grdResults.CellBorderStyle = DataGridViewCellBorderStyle.None

'Set the SelectionMode property
grdResults.SelectionMode = DataGridViewSelectionMode.FullRowSelect
```

The new properties that you have not seen before are the AutoSizeColumnsMode and the DefaultCellStyle.Alignment properties. These properties automatically resize the columns in the DataGridView control to fit the data displayed and right align the data in the SequenceNumber column because this column contains numeric data.

The AutoSizeColumnsMode property is set using the AllCells constant from the DataGridViewAutoSizeColumnsMode enumeration. This automatically resizes each cell, including the header columns to fit the widest data placed in the header columns and each cell.

The DefaultCellStyle.Alignment property is set for the SequenceNumber column to right align the numeric data in this column. It is set using the MiddleRight constant from the DataGridViewContentAlignment enumeration:

```
'Set the AutoSizeColumnsMode property
grdResults.AutoSizeColumnsMode = _
    DataGridViewAutoSizeColumnsMode.AllCells

'Right align SequenceNumber column
grdResults.Columns("SequenceNumber").DefaultCellStyle.Alignment = _
    DataGridViewContentAlignment.MiddleRight
```

The Catch block has the appropriate code to display a MessageBox dialog box with the error that was received.

Finally, you clean up the rest of the objects used in this procedure by disposing of them and setting them to Nothing:

```
        Catch OleDbException As OleDbException
            MessageBox.Show(OleDbException.Message, "Access Queries")
        End Try

        'Cleanup
        objCommand.Dispose()
        objCommand = Nothing
        objDataAdapter.Dispose()
        objDataAdapter = Nothing
        objDataSet.Dispose()
        objDataSet = Nothing
        objConnection.Dispose()
        objConnection = Nothing
    End Sub
```

The last procedure in this project is the btnNonParameterQuery_Click procedure. This procedure is executed when the Non-Parameter Query button on your form is clicked.

The first thing that you do in this procedure is initialize a new instance of the OleDbConnection class in your objConnection object, passing it the connection string defined in your strConnectionString variable:

```
    Private Sub btnNonParameterQuery_Click(ByVal sender As System.Object, _
        ByVal e As System.EventArgs) Handles btnNonParameterQuery.Click
        'Initialize a new instance of the OleDbConnection class
        objConnection = New OleDbConnection(strConnectionString)
```

Next, you initialize your objCommand object to a new instance of the OleDbCommand class. Then you set the CommandText property of your objCommand object to the query name that you want to execute.

Remember that the default value for the CommandType property is Text, so you must set this to the StoredProcedure constant from the CommandType enumeration because you are executing a query.

Next, you set the Connection property using your objConnection object.

Finally, you call the PopulateGrid procedure to populate the DataSet with data and bind it to the DataGrid on your form:

```
        'Initialize a new instance of the OleDbCommand class
        objCommand = New OleDbCommand

        'Set the objCommand object properties
        objCommand.CommandText = "usp_SelectProjects"
        objCommand.CommandType = CommandType.StoredProcedure
        objCommand.Connection = objConnection

        'Populate the DataGridView
        Call PopulateGrid()
    End Sub
```

You may have noticed something odd about this project. There is no code to open and close the database connection. This is automatically handled for you by the OleDbDataAdapter object. In the Access SQL project, you specifically performed this operation because an open connection was needed by the OleDbDataReader object.

Because I have already discussed the `OleDbParameter` class and you have built a query that accepts a parameter, you can just jump right in and complete the Access Queries project. In this next Try It Out you add a TextBox and Button control to your form.

The text box will serve as an input field, and the value entered there will become input to your `usp_SelectProject` query. You add code to the button to build an `OleDbCommand` object, set its properties, and append an `OleDbParameter` to the `Parameters` collection.

Try It Out   Passing an Input Field to a Parameter Query

To complete the Access Queries project:

1. Start Visual Studio 2005 if it is not already running and open the `Access Queries` project if it is not already open.

2. Switch to the Form Designer for `Form1` and add a Label, TextBox, and Button control to your form and arrange them to look similar to the controls shown on the form in Figure 5-5. Set the following properties of these controls:

❑ Set the `Text` property for `Label1` to **Project ID**.

❑ Set the `Name` property for `TextBox1` to **txtProjectID**.

❑ Set the `Name` property for `Button1` to **btnParameterQuery** and set the `Text` property to **Parameter Query** and the `Anchor` property to Top, Right.

3. Double-click the Parameter Query button to have the `btnParameterQuery_Click` procedure added. Add the following code to this procedure:

```
Private Sub btnParameterQuery_Click(ByVal sender As System.Object, _
    ByVal e As System.EventArgs) Handles btnParameterQuery.Click
        'Initialize a new instance of the OleDbConnection class
        objConnection = New OleDbConnection(strConnectionString)

        'Initialize a new instance of the OleDbCommand class
        objCommand = New OleDbCommand

        'Set the objCommand object properties
        objCommand.CommandText = "usp_SelectProject"
        objCommand.CommandType = CommandType.StoredProcedure
        objCommand.Connection = objConnection

        'Add the required parameter for the query
        objCommand.Parameters.Add("@ProjectID", OleDbType.Guid, 16).Value = _
            New Guid(txtProjectID.Text)

        'Populate the DataGridView
        Call PopulateGrid()
    End Sub
```

That's all the code that you need to add because the `PopulateGrid` procedure was added in the previous exercise.

4. Run your project and click the Non-Parameter Query button to list all the projects in the Projects table. Next, click a ProjectID in the `DataGridView` and copy it to the Clipboard. Then paste the Guid in the text box on your form and click the Parameter Query button. You should see results similar to those in Figure 5-5.

Notice that you do not have to include the brackets around the Guid that you pasted into the text box or in your code as you did when running queries in Access. Again, the Data Provider takes care of this for you.

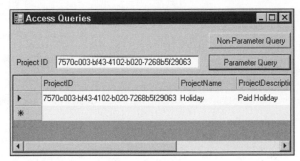

Figure 5-5

How It Works

The code for the `PopulateGrid` procedure was added in the previous exercise and all you need to do is add the code for the `btnParameterQuery_Click` procedure. The code in this procedure is similar to the code in the `btnNonParameterQuery_Click` procedure so it doesn't need to be covered in detail again.

Here are the highlights of what you do. First, you initialize a new `OleDbConnection` object, passing it your connection string. Then you initialize a new instance of the `OleDbCommand` class and set the `CommandText`, `CommandType`, and `Connection` properties.

```
Private Sub btnParameterQuery_Click(ByVal sender As System.Object, _
    ByVal e As System.EventArgs) Handles btnParameterQuery.Click
    'Initialize a new instance of the OleDbConnection class
    objConnection = New OleDbConnection(strConnectionString)

    'Initialize a new instance of the OleDbCommand class
    objCommand = New OleDbCommand

    'Set the objCommand object properties
    objCommand.CommandText = "usp_SelectProject"
    objCommand.CommandType = CommandType.StoredProcedure
    objCommand.Connection = objConnection
```

Here's where things get interesting. First, you need to add a parameter to the `Parameters` collection that represents the input parameter of your query. You do this by executing the `Add` method of the `Parameters` collection. The parameters that you are passing to the `Add` method are the parameter name, data type, and size. Take a look at each of these in turn.

The parameter name represents the name of the parameter in your query or stored procedure. For Access and Oracle, you can put any text string that you want. However, SQL Server requires an exact match to the parameter name specified in the stored procedure.

Once a parameter has been added to the Parameters collection, you can access other properties of that parameter in the collection using the parameter name that you specify here.

The next parameter that you are passing to the Add method is the data type of the parameter in your query or stored procedure. Because the ProjectID field in the Projects table is a Guid known as a Replication ID in Access, you need to specify the Guid constant in the OleDbType enumeration.

The size of a Guid data type in Access, SQL Server, and Oracle is 16 bytes, so you need to pass an Integer value of 16 for the Size parameter of the Add method.

Using the Value property, you set the value of the parameter. Now, because the data type for this parameter is a Guid, you need to convert the string value of the Guid into a Guid structure. You do this by using the constructor for the Guid structure. The Guid structure has an overloaded constructor and the one that you are using here initializes a new instance of the Guid class with the string value of the Guid that it should represent.

After the parameter is added to the Parameters collection, you call the PopulateGrid procedure to execute the objCommand object, load a DataSet, and then bind that DataSet to the DataGridView on your form.

Remember that the PopulateGrid procedure makes reference to the ProjectID column in the grid, which has been bound to a DataSet that also contains this column. Because you want to execute this procedure from multiple places in your code, you need to ensure that any queries you execute return the same columns and in the order that is expected in this procedure. This is why you add the ProjectID column in your SELECT statement for the usp_SelectProject query.

```
        'Add the required parameter for the query
        objCommand.Parameters.Add("@ProjectID", OleDbType.Guid, 16).Value = _
            New Guid(txtProjectID.Text)

        'Populate the DataGridView
        Call PopulateGrid()
    End Sub
```

That wraps up the code for this project. What you have done here is create a VB 2005 program that executes two types of queries in Access. Both queries return results but the first query does not accept any input parameters whereas the second query does.

Summary

This diverse chapter has discussed three main topics related to one another. The chapter started off by discussing dynamic connections using the OleDbConnection class and you saw firsthand how to build and implement a dynamic connection in your VB 2005 programs.

You then moved on to examine how to implement and execute in-line SQL statements in your VB 2005 programs. Using a VB 2005 program that made a dynamic connection to any Access database, you were able to build and execute in-line SQL SELECT statements against any table in any Access database and view the results of the SELECT statement.

You finally moved on to examine how to execute Access queries from your VB 2005 programs. You were able to execute an Access query that did not accept parameters and an Access query that did accept parameters. Both queries returned a result set that was then populated in a DataSet and bound to a DataGridView control.

Throughout this chapter, you have taken a close look at the OleDbConnection, OleDbCommand, OleDbDataReader, and OleDbDataAdapter classes. You should now have a more thorough understanding of these classes and how to use them in your VB 2005 programs.

To summarize, you should know how to:

❑   Use the OleDbConnection class to create a dynamic connection to any Access database

❑   Set the properties of the OleDbCommand class for in-line SQL statements and for queries and stored procedures

❑   Use the OleDbDataReader class to read and process data

❑   Use the OleDbDataAdapter to fill a DataSet and DataTable object

❑   Perform data binding to a DataGridView using two different methods

❑   Set various properties of the DataGridView to customize the look of the control

In Chapter 6, you start building the Time Tracker VB 2005 project that will be used throughout the rest of this book. You'll also implement the SELECT queries that you have built in Access in this project.

Exercises

Exercise 1

Create a Windows application that connects to your ProjectTimeTracker database. Have the application execute a SELECT statement as a SQL string that selects the ProjectID and ProjectName columns for all rows of data from the Projects table. Return the results of the SELECT statement in a DataTable and bind the DataTable to a combo box on your form.

Tip: Set the DropDownStyle property to DropDownList and set the data bindings for the combo box like this:

```
ComboBox1.DataSource = objDataTable.Tables(0)
ComboBox1.DisplayMember = "ProjectName"
ComboBox1.ValueMember = "ProjectID"
```

Exercise 2

Using the application created in Exercise 1 as a base, add a Label and TextBox control to the form. Set the Text property of the label to **Description**.

In the SelectedValueChanged event of the combo box, add code to execute the usp_SelectProject query passing it the ProjectID of the selected project in the combo box. Use a DataReader object to retrieve the results of the query and set the Text property of the text box to the description of the project retrieved.

Tip: When binding the DataTable to the combo box, the SelectedValueChanged event will fire, which is the desired result. Therefore, create a Boolean variable with a default value of True and exit the ComboBox1_SelectedValueChanged procedure when this variable is True. After you have completed the data bindings of the DataTable to the combo box, set this variable to False.

Tip: Use ComboBox1.SelectedValue.ToString to get the Guid of the selected project and to convert it to a string.

Selecting Data in Access

In Chapter 5, you learned how to execute queries in Access from your Visual Basic 2005 program. You were able to successfully execute a query that did not accept parameters and a query that did. Both of these queries returned data, which you processed using `OleDbDataAdapter` and `OleDbDataReader` objects. At this point, you should be quite adept at processing `SELECT` queries in Access.

In this chapter you build and start implementing functionality in the Time Tracker application that you use throughout the rest of this book. You start by implementing code to execute your `SELECT` queries in Access and process that data in this application.

In each of the subsequent chapters up to and including Chapter 12, you add more and more functionality to this application. When you are done, you'll have a functional database application and you'll have learned how to retrieve and manipulate data in various databases. You'll also have learned more about database programming using Visual Basic 2005 and the ADO.NET classes.

In this chapter, you:

- ❑   Build or download the UI for the Time Tracker application
- ❑   Implement functionality in your application to execute and process your `SELECT` queries in Access

Building the Time Tracker Application

The Time Tracker application provides an interface for administrators to be able to select and view, insert, update, and delete data in the various tables in the `ProjectTimeTracker` database. This database contains the core data, such as Groups, Projects, Group Projects, Roles, and Users, needed by the users of the application.

Another interface in the application is provided for the end users of the application and enables them to insert time spent on various projects in a timesheet. They will also be able to view previous timesheets that they have submitted. Along with this interface is a view for managers, who will be able to view and approve timesheets for the employees under their supervision.

The Time Tracker application will ultimately provide a Login dialog box that will direct the user to the appropriate interface based on the role of the login credentials. This is covered later in the book after the Roles and Users tables have been populated.

The Time Tracker application UI is quite involved and contains multiple forms with a lot of controls and common UI code. Figure 6-1 shows the main screen of the Time Tracker application and as you can see, the Outlook 2003–style navigation panel provides a clean look that contains a few controls that will have to be created. The Time Tracker application contains the following forms:

❑ **Admin Form (shown in Figure 6-1):** Used to add, update, and delete administrative data in the application

❑ **TimeSheet Form:** Used by employees to enter their timesheet data and by managers to view and approve timesheets and run reports

❑ **Help Form:** Used to provide help information about the application

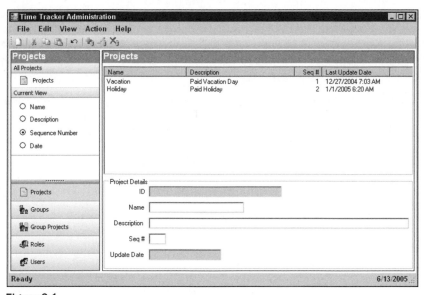

Figure 6-1

The steps required to build this application are listed in Appendix B, which you should now refer to for detailed instructions on building the base UI or for downloading the base UI from the Wrox Web site at www.wrox.com/dynamic/books/download.aspx.

After you have built or downloaded the base UI, return to this chapter to implement your SELECT queries from Access and to get a detailed explanation about some of the code that you implemented in the Time Tracker UI.

Implementing SQL Queries

In Chapter 3, you learned how to load a ListView control using a `DataSet` object. The ListView control merely displayed the data, and no code was added to handle any of the ListView events. In Chapter 5, you learned how to use the `OleDbDataReader` class to load data into a TextBox control. This chapter takes all of that a step further.

In this section, you implement the code to execute the `SELECT` queries from the previous chapter in the Time Tracker application. You use an `OleDbDataReader` object to load the data into a ListView control. You also add code to handle the `Click` event for the ListView control and execute your parameter `SELECT` query to retrieve a specific project. The data retrieved from that query will then be populated in the text fields on your form.

The procedures necessary to execute non-parameter and parameter `SELECT` queries in Access have already been explained and you've already seen the code necessary to perform these tasks. You've also seen firsthand how the `OleDbDataReader` works and how to load data in a ListView control. This next exercise is a good review of that new-found knowledge.

In this next Try It Out, you implement the code in the Time Tracker application to execute the `usp_SelectProjects` query. You use an `OleDbDataReader` to load the data into a ListView control on the Projects screen.

Try It Out Non-Parameter SELECT Query

To complete this exercise:

1. Open the Time Tracker application in Visual Studio 2005 if it is not already open.

2. Switch to the Code Editor for the Admin form. You want to create a procedure called `LoadProjects` whose sole purpose is to execute your `SELECT` query and load the results in the ListView control. Create this procedure and add the following code:

```
Private Sub LoadProjects()
    'Declare variables
    Dim objListViewItem As ListViewItem

    'Initialize a new instance of the data access base class
    Using objData As New WDABase
        Try
            'Get all projects in a DataReader object
            objData.SQL = "usp_SelectProjects"
            objData.InitializeCommand()
            objData.OpenConnection()
            objData.DataReader = objData.Command.ExecuteReader

            'See if any data exists before continuing
            If objData.DataReader.HasRows Then

                'Clear previous list
                lvwProjects.Items.Clear()

                'Process all rows
```

```
                        While objData.DataReader.Read()

                            'Create a new ListViewItem
                            objListViewItem = New ListViewItem

                            'Add the data to the ListViewItem
                            objListViewItem.Text = _
                                objData.DataReader.Item("ProjectName")
                            objListViewItem.Tag = objData.DataReader.Item("ProjectID")

                            'Add the sub items to the listview item
                            objListViewItem.SubItems.Add( _
                                objData.DataReader.Item("ProjectDescription"))
                            objListViewItem.SubItems.Add( _
                                objData.DataReader.Item("SequenceNumber"))
                            objListViewItem.SubItems.Add( _
                                Format(objData.DataReader.Item("LastUpdateDate"), "g"))

                            'Add the ListViewItem to the ListView control
                            lvwProjects.Items.Add(objListViewItem)

                        End While

                    End If

                    objData.DataReader.Close()
                Catch ExceptionErr As Exception
                    MessageBox.Show(ExceptionErr.Message, strAppTitle)
                End Try
            End Using

            'Cleanup
            objListViewItem = Nothing

        End Sub
```

3. The next step is to execute the `LoadProjects` procedure when the form loads. At the bottom of
    the `Admin_Load` procedure, add the following code:

    ```
    'Get the applicataion title
    strAppTitle = My.Application.Info.Title
    ```

    ```
    'Load the projects
    LoadProjects()
    End Sub
    ```

4. Don't forget to verify the path to your `ProjectTimeTracker` Access database by right-clicking
    the project in the Solution Explorer and choosing Properties from the context menu. Then in the
    Property Pages window, click the Settings tab and verify the DataSource setting.

That's all the code you need for this exercise. Run your project, and when the Admin form appears, the
Projects screen will be displayed and the ListView control will be populated with the projects from your
database, as shown in Figure 6-1.

How It Works

The LoadProjects procedure executes your SELECT query and uses an OleDbDataReader object to load the data into a ListView control. The first step in this procedure declares a variable as a ListViewItem. This variable is used to build the row of data to be added to the Items collection in the ListView control. The next step sets up a Using. . .End Using block, which initializes a new instance of the data access base class, WDABase. The New procedure in the WDABase class is the constructor for that class.

A Using...End Using block acquires the resources defined in the block and automatically calls the Dispose procedure on the resource when the End Using statement is encountered. Therefore, any resource specified in a Using. . .End Using block must implement the IDisposable interface and contain a Dispose procedure.

```
Private Sub LoadProjects()
    'Declare variables
    Dim objListViewItem As ListViewItem

    'Initialize a new instance of the data access base class
    Using objData As New WDABase
```

Let's digress for a moment and take a look at that code, which is shown later in this section. In the New procedure, code exists to read the application configuration settings that you specified in the Settings tab of the Property Pages. These settings are used to build the connection string for the OleDbConnection object.

The first thing you do in this procedure is initialize a new instance of the OleDbConnection class in the Connection object. Next, you use the My.Settings class to access the configuration settings that you specified in the Property Pages. The My.Settings class provides access to values that you defined in the applicationSettings section in your configuration file via the Settings tab in the Property Pages.

Notice that the connection string is built and passed to the OleDbConnection class at the same time. In previous chapters, you used a separate String variable to build the connection string and then passed that variable to the constructor for the OleDbConnection class. This is all done in a single step here.

```
Public Sub New()
    'Build the SQL connection string and initialize the Connection object
    Connection = New OleDbConnection( _
    "Provider=" & My.Settings.Provider & ";" & _
    "Data Source=" & My.Settings.DataSource & ";")
End Sub
```

What's important to note here is that the Settings tab of the Property Pages is where you make your changes to the configuration settings while developing your application. When your project is compiled, Visual Studio 2005 creates an application configuration file using the name of your executable file, including the .exe extension, and appends an extension of .config to it.

If you take a look at the bin\Debug folder for your project, you will see a file named Time Tracker.vshost.exe.config. If you open this file in Notepad or any other text editor, you'll see the exact same information that you entered in the Settings tab in the Property Pages in your project.

The configuration file that is automatically generated needs to be distributed with your application and needs to reside in the same directory as your executable. Should you need to change the database connection information after your application has been distributed, all you need to do is change the value for the DataSource key in this configuration file, and the next time your program runs it gets the new information that you entered.

As you can see, this provides a flexible method of specifying database connection information. However, if you need to specify a login name and password for your database, such as those required by SQL Server and Oracle, be sure to encrypt this information in this file so that a casual user cannot read your login name and password. Encryption is covered in Chapter 9, where you encrypt the login name and password for your database.

Let's get back to the code in the LoadProjects procedure; after initializing a new instance of the data access base class, you set up a Try...Catch...Finally block to handle any errors that may be returned from the WDABase class.

The first thing that you do inside the Try block is set the SQL property in the objData object that has been defined as the WDABase class. Then you execute the InitializeCommand method to initialize the OleDbCommand object. Next, you want to open the database connection, so you call the OpenConnection method. Finally you set the DataReader object to the results returned by the ExecuteReader method of the OleDbCommand object.

```
Try
    'Get all projects in a DataReader object
    objData.SQL = "usp_SelectProjects"
    objData.InitializeCommand()
    objData.OpenConnection()
    objData.DataReader = objData.Command.ExecuteReader
```

Let's digress for a moment again and take a look at the methods that you just executed in the WDABase class. The first method was the InitializeCommand method, which is shown in the next code snippet in this section. Before executing any code in this procedure, you ensure that the Command object is set to Nothing, meaning that it is not set to a reference to the OleDbCommand class. This is done for performance reasons. Suppose you were executing the same SQL statement or query in a loop. You wouldn't want to go through the steps to initialize the Command object every time because you would take a performance hit. Using this method is more efficient when executing the same SQL statements or query.

Next, you set up a Try...Catch block so that you can handle and return any errors that you may encounter. Inside the Try block you initialize the Command object to a new instance of the OleDbCommand class, passing it the SQL statement or query as set in the SQL variable and the Connection object as set in the Connection object variable.

Then you want to change the default CommandType value from Text to StoredProcedure if you were executing a stored procedure. You do this by checking the beginning of the SQL variable to ensure that it does not begin with the text of SELECT, INSERT, UPDATE, or DELETE. Using the ToUpper method of the String class, you convert the text in the SQL variable to uppercase and then use the StartsWith method to compare the text in the variable to the text specified, which is also in uppercase. The comparison made with the String class is a case-sensitive comparison, which is why you need to convert it to uppercase and specify the comparison string in uppercase. The extra space included after the text ensures that a query or stored procedure name that starts with SELECT, INSERT, UPDATE, or DELETE is not used and signifies that a SQL statement is being executed.

The `Catch` block here simply passes the error received to the caller of this method. This keeps any code in this class from failing and returns the error to the caller. It is up to the caller to handle the error appropriately.

Using the `Throw` statement, you throw a new `System.Exception`, passing it the parameters needed. The `System.Exception` class provides an overloaded constructor, and the one being used here accepts the message of the error and a reference to the inner exception:

```
Public Sub InitializeCommand()
    If Command Is Nothing Then
        Try
            Command = New OleDbCommand(SQL, Connection)
            'See if this is a stored procedure
            If Not SQL.ToUpper.StartsWith("SELECT ") _
                And Not SQL.ToUpper.StartsWith("INSERT ") _
                And Not SQL.ToUpper.StartsWith("UPDATE ") _
                And Not SQL.ToUpper.StartsWith("DELETE ") Then
                Command.CommandType = CommandType.StoredProcedure
            End If
        Catch OleDbExceptionErr As OleDbException
            Throw New System.Exception(OleDbExceptionErr.Message, _
                OleDbExceptionErr.InnerException)
        End Try
    End If
End Sub
```

The next method in the `WDABase` class that you execute is the `OpenConnection` procedure. The code in this procedure, shown in the following code, should look familiar to you from the Access SQL project that you wrote in the previous chapter. You encapsulate the opening of a database connection in a `Try...Catch` block that contains multiple `Catch` blocks. The first `Catch` block handles any connection-level errors, while the second `Catch` block handles an error received while trying to open a connection that is already opened. Again, in these `Catch` blocks, you throw a new exception, which is then returned to the caller.

```
Public Sub OpenConnection()
    Try
        Connection.Open()
    Catch OleDbExceptionErr As OleDbException
        Throw New System.Exception(OleDbExceptionErr.Message, _
            OleDbExceptionErr.InnerException)
    Catch InvalidOperationExceptionErr As InvalidOperationException
        Throw New System.Exception(InvalidOperationExceptionErr.Message, _
            InvalidOperationExceptionErr.InnerException)
    End Try
End Sub
```

Let's get back to the `LoadProjects` procedure. You want to determine whether the `DataReader` object contains any data before proceeding. The `HasRows` property returns a Boolean value indicating whether the `DataReader` object contains data.

If it does, you set up a `While...End While` loop to process all the data. You use the `Read` method of the `DataReader` object in the `While` statement, which returns a Boolean value indicating whether the `Read` method contains a row of data.

The first thing that you do inside the loop is initialize a new instance of the objListViewItem object. Then you start adding data. First, you set the Text property using the value returned from the Item property of the DataReader object. You access the Item property using the name of the column of data it contains, which is ProjectName. Next, you set the Tag property of the objListViewItem object using the ProjectID from the DataReader object. Remember that the Text property of the ListViewItem class represents the first column of data in the ListView control. The SubItems property represents the rest of the columns in the row of the ListView.

You start adding the SubItems to the objListViewItem object next. Remember that the SubItems property of the objListViewItem object is a collection of SubItems for the ListViewItem class. Using the Add method of the SubItems collection, you add each sub-item in turn.

```
'See if any data exists before continuing
If objData.DataReader.HasRows Then

    'Clear previous list
    lvwProjects.Items.Clear()

    'Process all rows
    While objData.DataReader.Read()

        'Create a new ListViewItem
        objListViewItem = New ListViewItem

        'Add the data to the ListViewItem
        objListViewItem.Text = _
            objData.DataReader.Item("ProjectName")
        objListViewItem.Tag = objData.DataReader.Item("ProjectID")

        'Add the sub items to the listview item
        objListViewItem.SubItems.Add( _
            objData.DataReader.Item("ProjectDescription"))
        objListViewItem.SubItems.Add( _
            objData.DataReader.Item("SequenceNumber"))
```

The last sub-item you add here is the LastUpdateDate. Using the Format function, you format the value of the date before adding it to the SubItems collection. The Format function accepts two parameters: the object to be formatted and the format style to be used as a string. The Format function contains predefined format strings for formatting date and time values. The format string g represents a short date and short time formatted according to the local settings on your computer. It is important to note that the format strings are case-sensitive.

The last line of code in this loop adds the objListViewItem object to the ListView control. After you exit the While...End While loop and the If...Then statement, you close the DataReader object.

```
objListViewItem.SubItems.Add( _
    Format(objData.DataReader.Item("LastUpdateDate"), "g"))

'Add the ListViewItem to the ListView control
```

```
            lvwProjects.Items.Add(objListViewItem)

        End While

    End If

    objData.DataReader.Close()
```

Inside your `Catch` block, you simply display a MessageBox dialog box with the message returned along with the name of your application. You take a look at how the application name is set in the `strAppTitle` variable in just a moment.

After the `End Using` statement, you have the necessary code to dispose of and clean up the objects used in this procedure. The `End Using` statement disposes of your `objData` object, but you need to remove your reference to the `objListViewItem` object by setting it to `Nothing`.

```
        Catch ExceptionErr As Exception
            MessageBox.Show(ExceptionErr.Message, strAppTitle)
        End Try
    End Using

    'Cleanup
    objListViewItem = Nothing
End Sub
```

You may have noticed that you do not include a call to the `CloseConnection` method in your `objData` object to close the database connection. When the `Dispose` method on this object is called by the `End Using` statement, the `Dispose` method takes care of closing the database connection if it is open. The code for the `Dispose` method of the `WDABase` class is listed shortly.

This procedure performs a check on each of the objects that it defined to see if they are `Nothing`, meaning that they were not set to a reference to their OLE DB classes. If they are set to a reference of their OLE DB classes, then they execute the necessary methods and perform the necessary cleanup code to dispose of them and remove a reference to them.

Notice that this procedure automatically closes the `DataReader` and `Connection` objects if they were allocated. It does not matter whether the objects were closed by the caller because the `Close` method is called here to ensure that the objects have been closed before disposing of them. Remember that calling the `Close` method does not return an error if the object is already closed.

```
    Private Overloads Sub Dispose(ByVal disposing As Boolean)
        If Not Me.disposed Then
            If disposing Then
                ' TODO: put code to dispose managed resources
                If Not DataReader Is Nothing Then
                    DataReader.Close()
                    DataReader = Nothing
                End If
                If Not DataAdapter Is Nothing Then
                    DataAdapter.Dispose()
                    DataAdapter = Nothing
```

```
            End If
            If Not Command Is Nothing Then
                Command.Dispose()
                Command = Nothing
            End If
            If Not Connection Is Nothing Then
                Connection.Close()
                Connection.Dispose()
                Connection = Nothing
            End If
        End If


        ' TODO: put code to free unmanaged resources here
    End If
    Me.disposed = True
End Sub
```

Now take a look at the code that sets the title of the application in the `strAppTitle` variable. This code is located in the `Admin_Load` procedure. The `My.Application.Info` class gets the assembly information for your application. Here you want the title information for your application so you use the `Title` property of the `My.Application.Info` class:

```
        'Get the applicataion title
        strAppTitle = My.Application.Info.Title _
```

That wraps up the code for this exercise. You examined the code necessary to execute the `usp_SelectProjects` query and to load the ListView control on your form. You also looked at the code that set the application title in the `strAppTitle` variable.

You've seen the code that was executed in the `WDABase` class, which read the values from your application configuration file and initialized the `Connection` object. You also examined the code that initialized the `Command` object, opened the database connection, and performed the cleanup necessary in the class when the class was disposed.

As you progress through the exercises in this and the next few chapters, you examine more of the code in the WDABase class.

In the next Try It Out, you add the necessary code to execute the `usp_SelectProject` query. Remember that this query accepts a parameter for the `ProjectID` of the project that it should retrieve from the Projects table.

When you click a project in the ListView control on the Projects screen in your application, you want to execute the code necessary to retrieve the project details for the project selected in the ListView control. You then display the project details for the selected project in the Project Details section on the Projects screen.

Parameter SELECT Query

To complete this exercise:

1.   Open the Time Tracker application in Visual Studio 2005 if it is not already open.

2.   Switch to the Code Editor for the Admin form and in the Class Name combo box choose lvwProjects, and in the Method Name combo box choose the Click event. Performing these steps causes the lvwProjects_Click procedure to be inserted into your project. Add the following code to this procedure:

```
Private Sub lvwProjects_Click(ByVal sender As Object, _
    ByVal e As System.EventArgs) Handles lvwProjects.Click

        'Initialize a new instance of the data access base class
        Using objData As New WDABase
            Try
                'Get the specific project selected in the ListView control
                objData.SQL = "usp_SelectProject"
                objData.InitializeCommand()
                objData.AddParameter("@ProjectID", Data.OleDb.OleDbType.Guid, 16, _
                    lvwProjects.SelectedItems.Item(0).Tag)
                objData.OpenConnection()
                objData.DataReader = objData.Command.ExecuteReader

                'See if any data exists before continuing
                If objData.DataReader.HasRows Then

                    'Read the first and only row of data
                    objData.DataReader.Read()

                    'Populate the Project Details section
                    txtProjectID.Text = _
                        objData.DataReader.Item("ProjectID").ToString.ToUpper
                    txtProjectName.Text = _
                        objData.DataReader.Item("ProjectName")
                    txtProjectDescription.Text = _
                        objData.DataReader.Item("ProjectDescription")
                    txtSequenceNumber.Text = _
                        objData.DataReader.Item("SequenceNumber")
                    txtProjectUpdateDate.Text = _
                        Format(objData.DataReader.Item("LastUpdateDate"), "g")

                End If

                objData.DataReader.Close()
            Catch ExceptionErr As Exception
                MessageBox.Show(ExceptionErr.Message, strAppTitle)
            End Try
        End Using
    End Sub
```

3. That's all the code that you need for this exercise. Run your project and then click a project in the ListView control. When you do, the `usp_SelectProject` query runs and the project details are populated in the Project Details section of your form, as shown in Figure 6-2.

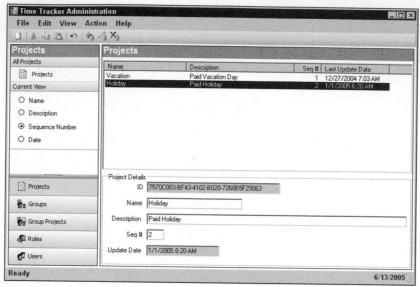

Figure 6-2

How It Works

The first thing that you do in this procedure is initialize a new instance of your `objData` object, which is defined as a `WDABase` class in a `Using...End Using` block. Remember that this class provides all the methods to initialize and open a database connection and to perform the various operations against the database, such as executing queries and retrieving data.

```
Private Sub lvwProjects_Click(ByVal sender As Object, _
    ByVal e As System.EventArgs) Handles lvwProjects.Click

    'Initialize a new instance of the data access base class
    Using objData As New WDABase
```

Then, using a `Try...Catch` block, you execute the `usp_SelectProject` SELECT query. Because you are executing code that accesses the database, you should always use a `Try...Catch` block to handle any unexpected database errors.

The first thing that you do in the `Try` block is set the SQL property in the `objData` object to the query to be executed. Then you call the `InitializeCommand` method to initialize the `Command` object in the `objData` object:

```
Try
    'Get the specific project selected in the ListView control
    objData.SQL = "usp_SelectProject"
    objData.InitializeCommand()
```

The next line of code contains a procedure that you haven't seen before. This code calls the `AddParameter` method in the `objData` object, which adds a new parameter to the `Parameters` collection. Notice that you use the `Tag` property of the selected item in the ListView control. The `Tag` property is an `Object` data type that contains information about the control. This property can be set to anything that you like. In the `LoadProjects` procedure, you set this property to the `ProjectID` when you built the `ListViewItem` and added it to the ListView control. This provides the `ProjectID` of the selected project so that you can use it as input to your query.

```
objData.AddParameter("@ProjectID", Data.OleDb.OleDbType.Guid, 16, _
    lvwProjects.SelectedItems.Item(0).Tag)
```

Let's digress once again and take a quick look at the `AddParameter` procedure in the `WDABase` class, which is shown in the next block of code in this section. Take a look at the input parameters to this procedure. The first parameter is a `String` variable for the name of the parameter and the second parameter is the data type of the parameter to be added, which has been specified as `OleDbType`. This is the `OleDbType` enumeration, so when you start to enter the code for this parameter, you get a drop-down list of constants in this enumeration. Finally, the last two input parameters to this procedure are for the size of the data type being specified and the value of the parameter to be added. Notice that the `Value` input parameter has been defined as an `Object` data type. This is because the `Value` property in the `Parameter` class is defined as an `Object` data type, which allows for any type of input to be used. For example, you can pass a `String` data type for the `Value` property or an `Integer` data type or in this case a `Guid` structure. The `Object` data type is the base class for all other data types; thus, it can represent any data type.

As with the other procedures that you've looked at in this class, this one implements the code inside a `Try...Catch` block and throws any errors received back to the caller of this procedure.

Inside the `Try` block, you add a new parameter to the `Parameters` collection using the `Add` method. The `Add` method provides an overloaded constructor, and the one that you are using here expects the name of the parameter being added, the data type of the parameter, and the size of the parameter. The value for the parameter is set using the `Value` property of the `Parameter` class.

```
Public Sub AddParameter(ByVal Name As String, ByVal Type As OleDbType, _
    ByVal Size As Integer, ByVal Value As Object)
    Try
        Command.Parameters.Add(Name, Type, Size).Value = Value
    Catch OleDbExceptionErr As OleDbException
        Throw New System.Exception(OleDbExceptionErr.Message, _
            OleDbExceptionErr.InnerException)
    End Try
End Sub
```

Back to the code in your `lvwProjects_Click` procedure: the next thing that you do is open the database connection and execute the `ExecuteReader` method of the `Command` object. Then, using the `HasRows` property, you check to see if the `DataReader` object contains any rows of data.

If it does, you read the one and only row of data that it returned by executing the `Read` method of the `DataReader` object:

```
objData.OpenConnection()
objData.DataReader = objData.Command.ExecuteReader

'See if any data exists before continuing
```

```
If objData.DataReader.HasRows Then

    'Read the first and only row of data
    objData.DataReader.Read()
```

Then you populate the text boxes in the Project Details section of your form. Notice that the first line in the following code is converting the ProjectID to a string because the DataReader object will return the data in its native database format. Remember that the ProjectID is defined as a Guid (Replication ID in Access) in the database. To set the Text property of the text box to the ProjectID, it first has to be converted to a string; thus, you execute the ToString method. Then you'll want to display the letters in the Guid in uppercase, so you call the ToUpper method. This is done for aesthetic purposes because a Guid in all uppercase letters is easier to read than one in all lowercase letters.

```
'Populate the Project Details section
txtProjectID.Text = _
    objData.DataReader.Item("ProjectID").ToString.ToUpper
txtProjectName.Text = _
    objData.DataReader.Item("ProjectName")
txtProjectDescription.Text = _
    objData.DataReader.Item("ProjectDescription")
txtSequenceNumber.Text = _
    objData.DataReader.Item("SequenceNumber")
txtProjectUpdateDate.Text = _
    Format(objData.DataReader.Item("LastUpdateDate"), "g")

End If
```

After loading all the fields in the Project Details section of the form, you close the DataReader object.

The Catch block contains the code to display the error message received in a MessageBox dialog box.

The End Using statement disposes of the objData object by calling the Dispose method on that object. Remember that the Dispose method on this object will execute the necessary code to close an open DataReader object, to close an open database Connection, and to clean up the objects that it used.

```
            objData.DataReader.Close()
        Catch ExceptionErr As Exception
            MessageBox.Show(ExceptionErr.Message, strAppTitle)
        End Try
    End Using
End Sub
```

With the implementation of the code in this exercise, you've seen one more procedure in the WDABase class. You look at the other three in Chapter 7. This exercise completed the functionality to display a list of projects and to display the details for a selected project in the ListView control. Your Time Tracker application is now starting to take shape and you add more functionality to it as you progress through the remaining chapters.

Summary

In this chapter, you followed the steps outlined in Appendix B to build the user interface for the Time Tracker application and to add the basic code to that application. You then started implementing database functionality, making it a database-driven application by implementing the two SELECT queries that you created in your ProjectTimeTracker Access database in the last few chapters.

You also took a detailed look at some of the code in the WDABase class. You have seen how this class provides a layer between your user interface code and the database. You did not need to import the System.Data.OleDb namespace in your Admin form class because the WDABase class contains this import statement and handles all of the access to the database. You merely used the properties and objects in that class to access the data needed for your application.

To summarize, you should know:

❑   How to implement and execute a non-parameter and parameter SELECT query

❑   How values are read from your application configuration file

❑   How the application title is extracted from the assembly

In Chapter 7, the pace starts to pick up when you implement code to insert, update, and delete projects. You also write queries to select, insert, update, and delete groups and group projects and to implement the necessary code in your application to execute these queries.

Exercises

Exercise 1

Create a Windows application with a multiline text box and a button. Create two application configuration settings; one called **Provider** with a value of **Microsoft.Jet.OLEDB.4.0** and one called **DataSource** with a value of **C:\Chapter 6\ProjectTimeTracker.mdb**. Change the path to the path where your ProjectTimeTracker database resides.

Add code to the Click event of the button to open the database specified by the configuration settings and to execute a SQL Select statement from the text box that you will provide when running the project. Then use an OleDbDataReader object to populate the text box with the data read from the database. Refer to the Access SQL project from Chapter 5 for that code.

When you ran your project, entered a SQL statement and clicked the button, you should have received results of that query listed in the text box on the form.

Exercise 2

Close Visual Studio 2005 if it is still open and then navigate to the bin\Debug folder of your exercise. Open the application configuration file, which will have a name of Exercise 1.exe.config if you called your project Exercise 1, using Notepad or some other text editor.

Modify the DataSource setting to point to the Northwind.mdb database if it was installed with Microsoft Office. Then save the file and close it. Next, double-click the executable file in this same folder, Exercise 1.exe in this case, to run your project.

When your form displays enter the query SELECT * FROM Customers and then click the button. Your project will open the Northwind.mdb database and execute the query against the Customers table and load that data into the text box.

Inserting, Updating, and Deleting Data in Access

In the last couple of chapters, you saw how to implement code in your VB 2005 programs to execute SELECT queries in Microsoft Access. Now it's time to turn your attention to learning how to execute INSERT, UPDATE, and DELETE queries from your VB 2005 programs. These types of queries do not return data so the code can be less daunting than the code for executing and processing the data from a SELECT query.

In Chapter 4, you examined how to write basic INSERT, UPDATE, and DELETE queries in Access, and you got a chance to execute those queries in Access. In this chapter, you execute the queries that you wrote in Chapter 4 from your VB 2005 program to add more functionality to the Time Tracker application.

During the process of writing code to execute these queries, you have a chance to learn more about the OleDbCommand object and how it can be used to execute queries and stored procedures that insert, update, and delete data.

In this chapter, you:

❑   Write more SELECT, INSERT, UPDATE, and DELETE queries in Access

❑   Implement code to execute SELECT, INSERT, UPDATE, and DELETE queries from VB 2005

❑   Learn more about the OleDbCommand object

OleDbCommand Object

In Chapter 6, you saw firsthand how to add a parameter to the Parameters collection in the OleDbCommand object. The query that you executed returned data; thus you executed the ExecuteReader method of the OleDbCommand object to return the data.

In this chapter, you continue to use the OleDbCommand object and add parameters to the Parameters collection to execute your queries. However, most of the queries that you execute will insert, update, and delete data in your database. Therefore, you cannot use the ExecuteReader method because this method returns an OleDbDataReader and these queries don't return data. The method in the OleDbCommand object that you need to execute is the ExecuteNonQuery method. The NonQuery in the method name means that this method executes a query or stored procedure that does not query the database for information. Rather, it performs an action query, one that inserts, updates, or deletes data.

This method executes a SQL statement (SQL statement, query, or stored procedure) against a connection and returns the number of rows affected by the SQL statement being executed. Therefore, if you execute a query that inserts one row of data, the number of records affected will be one and the number returned by this method will be 1. If you were to execute a query that updated two rows of data, the number returned by this method would be 2.

When using the ExecuteNonQuery method of the OleDbCommand object, you initialize the OleDbCommand object and set the various properties just as you did when executing the ExecuteReader method.

Take a look at the example that follows. This example initializes a new instance of the OleDbCommand class, passing it the query to be executed as the CommandText and the Connection object that represents the OleDbConnection for the database. Then it sets the CommandType property to StoredProcedure and adds a new Parameter to the Parameters collection.

Finally, it executes the ExecuteNonQuery method to have the query executed. Notice that the last line of code that executes this method is setting the intRowsAffected variable to the results of the ExecuteNonQuery method. This method returns an Integer value containing the number of rows affected by the execution of your query or stored procedure. You can then query the intRowsAffected variable to determine whether the results are what you expected.

```
'Initialize a new instance of the OleDbCommand class
Dim objCommand As New OleDbCommand("usp_DeleteProject", objConnection)
'Set the CommandType to be executed
objCommand.CommandType = CommandType.StoredProcedure
'Add the necessary parameters
objCommand.Parameters.Add( _
    "@ProjectID", OleDb.OleDbType.Guid, 16, New Guid(txtProjectID.Text))
'Execute the query
intRowsAffected = objCommand.ExecuteNonQuery
```

As you can see, there's not much to using the ExecuteNonQuery method of the OleDbCommand object. The key here is to receive the number of rows affected by the operation in an Integer variable and then query that variable to ensure that the results are what you expected.

In the following Try It Out, you implement the functionality in your Time Tracker application to execute the INSERT, UPDATE, and DELETE queries in your database that insert, update and delete projects in the Projects table.

You have already implemented a common set of procedures that are executed when the user clicks the Add, Update, and Delete buttons on the toolbar. In this Try It Out, you actually add some working code to call those procedures to execute the ADD, UPDATE, and DELETE queries in your database.

Try It Out   **Implementing Insert, Update, and Delete Queries**

To complete this exercise:

1. Open the Time Tracker application in Visual Studio 2005 if it is not already open.

2. Switch to the Code Editor for the Admin form and add the following variable:

```
Private intIndex As Integer
Private intRowsAffected As Integer

Private strActiveScreen As String = "Projects"
```

3. In the Class Name combo box, choose Admin, and in the Method Name combo box choose ActionAdd. This takes you right to the ActionAdd procedure so you can start entering code. Modify the code in this procedure as follows:

```
Private Sub ActionAdd()
    'Initialize a new instance of the data access base class
    Using objData As New WDABase
        Try
            'Add database row based on the active screen
            Select Case strActiveScreen
                Case "Projects"
                Case "Groups"
                Case "Group Projects"
                Case "Roles"
                Case "Users"
            End Select

            'Display a message that the record was added
            ToolStripStatus.Text = "Record Added"
        Catch ExceptionErr As Exception
            MessageBox.Show(ExceptionErr.Message, strAppTitle)
        End Try
    End Using
End Sub
```

4. In the same procedure, add the following code to the Case "Projects" statement to insert a new project in the database:

```
Case "Projects"
    'Set the SQL string
    objData.SQL = "usp_InsertProject"
    'Initialize the Command object
    objData.InitializeCommand()
    'Add the Parameters to the Parameters collection
    objData.AddParameter("@ProjectID", _
        Data.OleDb.OleDbType.Guid, 16, Guid.NewGuid())
    objData.AddParameter("@ProjectName", _
        Data.OleDb.OleDbType.VarChar, 50, txtProjectName.Text)
    objData.AddParameter("@ProjectDescription", _
        Data.OleDb.OleDbType.LongVarChar, _
        txtProjectDescription.Text.Length, _
        txtProjectDescription.Text)
    objData.AddParameter("@SequenceNumber", _
```

```
                Data.OleDb.OleDbType.UnsignedTinyInt, 1, _
                CType(txtSequenceNumber.Text, Byte))
        'Open the database connection
        objData.OpenConnection()
        'Execute the query
        intRowsAffected = objData.Command.ExecuteNonQuery()
        'Close the database connection
        objData.CloseConnection()
        If intRowsAffected = 0 Then
            Throw New Exception("Insert Project Failed")
        End If
        'Clear the input fields
        txtProjectName.Text = String.Empty
        txtProjectDescription.Text = String.Empty
        txtSequenceNumber.Text = String.Empty
        'Reload the Projects list
        LoadProjects()
```

5. Modify the `ActionUpdate` procedure as follows:

```
Private Sub ActionUpdate()
    'Initialize a new instance of the data access base class
    Using objData As New WDABase
        Try
            'Update database row based on the active screen
            Select Case strActiveScreen
                Case "Projects"
                Case "Groups"
                Case "Group Projects"
                Case "Roles"
                Case "Users"
            End Select

            'Display a message that the record was update
            ToolStripStatus.Text = "Record Updated"
        Catch ExceptionErr As Exception
            MessageBox.Show(ExceptionErr.Message, strAppTitle)
        End Try
    End Using
End Sub
```

6. In the same procedure, add the following code to the `Case "Projects"` statement to update a project in the database:

```
Case "Projects"
    'Set the SQL string
    objData.SQL = "usp_UpdateProject"
    'Initialize the Command object
    objData.InitializeCommand()
    'Add the Parameters to the Parameters collection
    objData.AddParameter("@ProjectName", _
        Data.OleDb.OleDbType.VarChar, 50, txtProjectName.Text)
    objData.AddParameter("@ProjectDescription", _
        Data.OleDb.OleDbType.LongVarChar, _
        txtProjectDescription.Text.Length, _
        txtProjectDescription.Text)
```

```
                    objData.AddParameter("@SequenceNumber", _
                        Data.OleDb.OleDbType.UnsignedTinyInt, 1, _
                        CType(txtSequenceNumber.Text, Byte))
                    objData.AddParameter("@ProjectID", _
                        Data.OleDb.OleDbType.Guid, 16, New Guid(txtProjectID.Text))
                    'Open the database connection
                    objData.OpenConnection()
                    'Execute the query
                    intRowsAffected = objData.Command.ExecuteNonQuery()
                    'Close the database connection
                    objData.CloseConnection()
                    If intRowsAffected = 0 Then
                        Throw New Exception("Update Project Failed")
                    End If
                    'Clear the input fields
                    txtProjectID.Text = String.Empty
                    txtProjectName.Text = String.Empty
                    txtProjectDescription.Text = String.Empty
                    txtSequenceNumber.Text = String.Empty
                    txtProjectUpdateDate.Text = String.Empty
                    'Reload the Projects list
                    LoadProjects()
```

7. Modify the `ActionDelete` procedure as follows:

```
Private Sub ActionDelete()
        'Initialize a new instance of the data access base class
    Using objData As New WDABase
        Try
            'Delete database row based on the active screen
            Select Case strActiveScreen
                Case "Projects"
                Case "Groups"
                Case "Group Projects"
                Case "Roles"
                Case "Users"
            End Select

            'Display a message that the record was deleted
            ToolStripStatus.Text = "Record Deleted"
        Catch ExceptionErr As Exception
            MessageBox.Show(ExceptionErr.Message, strAppTitle)
        End Try
    End Using
End Sub
```

8. In the same procedure, add the following code to the `Case "Projects"` statement to delete a project from the database:

```
            Case "Projects"
                'Set the SQL string
                objData.SQL = "usp_DeleteProject"
                'Initialize the Command object
                objData.InitializeCommand()
                'Add the Parameters to the Parameters collection
```

```
        objData.AddParameter("@ProjectID", _
            Data.OleDb.OleDbType.Guid, 16, New Guid(txtProjectID.Text))
        'Open the database connection
        objData.OpenConnection()
        'Execute the query
        intRowsAffected = objData.Command.ExecuteNonQuery()
        'Close the database connection
        objData.CloseConnection()
        If intRowsAffected = 0 Then
            Throw New Exception("Delete Project Failed")
        End If
        'Clear the input fields
        txtProjectID.Text = String.Empty
        txtProjectName.Text = String.Empty
        txtProjectDescription.Text = String.Empty
        txtSequenceNumber.Text = String.Empty
        txtProjectUpdateDate.Text = String.Empty
        'Reload the Projects list
        LoadProjects()
```

9. That's all the code that you need to execute your INSERT, UPDATE, and DELETE queries. At this point, you want to test your project, so start it up. When the Admin form is displayed, enter a new project in the Project Details section of the form, as shown in Figure 7-1.

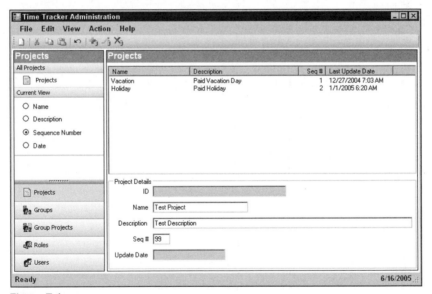

Figure 7-1

10. Click the Action menu and select the Add menu item or click the Add button on the toolbar. Your INSERT query is executed, the project is inserted into the database, and the list of projects on your form is updated to display the new project just added.

Also notice that the fields in the Project Details section of the form were cleared after the new project was added, and the message `Record Added` was displayed in the status bar.

11.   To test the update functionality of your application, click the new project you just added in the Projects list to have the Project Details section of the form populated with the details of the project. Then change the name, description, and/or sequence number for the project. Either click the Action menu and select the Update menu item, or click the Update button on the toolbar.

The project is updated in the database, the Projects list is cleared and populated with fresh data, and the fields in the Project Details section of the form are cleared. The status bar displays the message `Record Updated`.

12.   To test the delete functionality of your application, click the project that you just updated to display the details of that project in the Project Details section of the form. Then click the Action menu and select Delete or click the Delete button on the toolbar.

The project is deleted from the database, the Projects list is cleared and populated with fresh data, and the fields in the Project Details section of the form are cleared. The status bar displays the message Record Deleted.

How It Works

The first thing that you do is add the `intRowsAffected` variable as an Integer data type. Remember that the `ExecuteNonQuery` method of the `OleDbCommand` object returns an Integer value indicating the number of rows affected by the execution of the query or stored procedure.

The variable that you declare is declared at the form level, meaning that it is available to all procedures in the form. This enables you to use this variable in the various procedures to capture the number of rows affected by the execution of the `ExecuteNonQuery` method of the `OleDbCommand` object. You can then query that variable to ensure that the query or stored procedure that you have executed has returned the results that you expected.

```
Private intRowsAffected As Integer
```

Next, you start modifying the `ActionAdd` procedure. This procedure is called whenever the Add menu item is selected or the Add button on the toolbar is clicked. The first thing you do in this procedure is set up a `Using...End Using` block, which initializes a new instance of the `WDABase` class in your `objData` object.

```
Private Sub ActionAdd()
    'Initialize a new instance of the data access base class
    Using objData As New WDABase
```

When executing queries or stored procedures against your database, it is important that you handle any errors that may arise from their execution. This prevents the .NET runtime from displaying a message that may or may not provide the information that you need. It also enables you to control the flow of the code in your program so that your application does not fail because of the error.

To that end, you add a `Try...Catch...Finally` block to your procedure. Inside the `Try` block, you add the code to display a message in the status bar if the Add operation is successful. Inside the `Catch` block, you handle the exception that may be thrown and display a MessageBox dialog box with the error that was received.

The `End Using` statement disposes of your `objData` object by calling the `Dispose` method of the `WDABase` class:

```
        Try
            'Add database row based on the active screen
            Select Case strActiveScreen
                Case "Projects"
                Case "Groups"
                Case "Group Projects"
                Case "Roles"
                Case "Users"
            End Select

            'Display a message that the record was added
            ToolStripStatus.Text = "Record Added"
        Catch ExceptionErr As Exception
            MessageBox.Show(ExceptionErr.Message, strAppTitle)
        End Try
    End Using
End Sub
```

You then add some code to the `Case "Projects"` statement to execute your `INSERT` query. The first thing you do is set the `SQL` property of the `objData` object to the query to be executed, your `INSERT` query. Then you execute the `InitializeCommand` method of the `objData` object. This method was covered in detail in Chapter 6:

```
            Case "Projects"
                'Set the SQL string
                objData.SQL = "usp_InsertProject"
                'Initialize the Command object
                objData.InitializeCommand()
```

You need to supply four input parameters to your `INSERT` query. The first `parameter` that you add is for the `ProjectID` field in your Projects table. This field is defined as a Guid (Replication ID in Access) field so you have to supply a Guid for this parameter.

The `AddParameter` method was also covered in the previous chapter so I won't go into the details of this method again. The parameters that you pass this method are the name, the OLE DB data type, the storage size, and the value of the parameter. The name of the parameter in your Access query is `@ProjectID` so that is what you are passing for the first parameter to the `AddParameter` method.

For the `Type` parameter in the `AddParameter` method, you specify the appropriate constant from the `OleDbType` enumeration, which matches the parameter being added — in this case, a Guid. The storage size for a Guid is 16 bytes in Access, SQL Server, and Oracle so you pass `16` for the `Size` parameter to the `AddParameter` method.

The `Value` parameter for the `AddParameter` method requires a Guid, so you pass a Guid by calling the `NewGuid` method of the `Guid` structure. This generates a new Guid to be passed as input to this parameter.

```
                'Add the Parameters to the Parameters collection
                objData.AddParameter("@ProjectID", _
                    Data.OleDb.OleDbType.Guid, 16, Guid.NewGuid())
```

The next `Parameter` that you add is for the name of the project being added. You pass a parameter name of `@ProjectName` for the `Name` parameter to the `AddParameter` method, an OLE DB data type of `VarChar` for the `Type` parameter to the `AddParameter` method, and a size of `50` for the `Size` parameter as this is the maximum size that the `ProjectName` field in the Projects table can hold. Finally, you pass the name of the project being added by retrieving it from the `Text` property of the `txtProjectName` text box.

```
objData.AddParameter("@ProjectName", _
        Data.OleDb.OleDbType.VarChar, 50, txtProjectName.Text)
```

The third `Parameter` that you add is for the project description. Here you are passing a name of `@ProjectDescription` for the `Name` parameter and an OLE DB data type of `LongVarChar` for the `Type` parameter.

The `ProjectDescription` field in your Projects table in Access is defined as a Memo field, meaning that it can contain variable-length data of up to 65,535 characters. When using this data type in Access, you do not specify the maximum size of the data type for the `Size` parameter of the `AddParameter` method. Instead you pass the maximum size of the data being inserted into this field. To that end, the size is calculated using the `Length` property of the `Text` property of the `txtProjectDescription` text box.

Then, for the `Value` parameter of the `AddParameter` method, you pass the contents of the `txtProjectDescription` text box retrieved from the `Text` property.

```
objData.AddParameter("@ProjectDescription", _
        Data.OleDb.OleDbType.LongVarChar, _
        txtProjectDescription.Text.Length, _
        txtProjectDescription.Text)
```

The final `Parameter` that you add to the `Parameters` collection is the sequence number for the project being added. You pass a name of `@SequenceNumber` for the `Name` parameter of the `AddParameter` method.

The `SequenceNumber` field in the Projects table is defined as a `Byte` data type in Access, with the storage size for this data type being 1 byte, which can contain a value between 0 and 255. To that end, you use the `UnsignedTinyInt` constant from the `OleDbType` enumeration, which represents a `Byte` data type. You also pass a storage size of 1 for the `Size` parameter of the `AddParameter` method.

The `Text` property of the text box represents a string value, so you need to convert the value in the text box to the appropriate data type. This is accomplished with the `CType` function. The `CType` function converts an expression into any legal data type that you specify. A legal data type is defined as one that can be used in the `As` clause of a `Dim` statement. Here you are converting the value contained in the `Text` property of the text box to a `Byte` data type.

If you enter a value greater than 255 in the `txtSequenceNumber` text box and try to convert that value to a `Byte` data type, your error-handling code will trap the error and display a MessageBox dialog box with a message indicating that the arithmetic operation resulted in an overflow:

```
objData.AddParameter("@SequenceNumber", _
        Data.OleDb.OleDbType.UnsignedTinyInt, 1, _
        CType(txtSequenceNumber.Text, Byte))
```

131

After all the parameters are added to the `Parameters` collection, you open the database connection and execute the `ExecuteNonQuery` method of the `Command` object. This executes your `INSERT` query and returns the number of rows affected by your query in the `intRowsAffected` variable.

After you execute your query, you want to close the database connection, so you call the `CloseConnection` method on the `objData` object:

```
'Open the database connection
objData.OpenConnection()
'Execute the query
intRowsAffected = objData.Command.ExecuteNonQuery()
'Close the database connection
objData.CloseConnection()
```

You know that your `INSERT` query should insert one row of data into the Projects table and that the `ExecuteNonQuery` method should return a value of 1. To that end, you check to see whether the value in the `intRowsAffected` variable contains a value of 0. If it does, you throw an exception with a message indicating that the insert failed.

Throwing an exception at this point in your code causes control to be passed to the `Catch` block, where you display a MessageBox dialog box with the message `Insert Project Failed`:

```
If intRowsAffected = 0 Then
    Throw New Exception("Insert Project Failed")
End If
```

If at this point everything is successful, you clear the input fields in the Project Details section of the form by setting the `Text` properties of the text boxes to empty strings. Then you call the `LoadProjects` procedure, which retrieves a new list of projects from the database, clears the Projects list, and then reloads it:

```
'Clear the input fields
txtProjectName.Text = String.Empty
txtProjectDescription.Text = String.Empty
txtSequenceNumber.Text = String.Empty
'Reload the Projects list
LoadProjects()
```

The code in the `ActionUpdate` procedure is similar to the code in the `ActionAdd` procedure, so I'll cover it at a fairly quick pace. You start by modifying the `ActionUpdate` procedure by adding a `Using...End Using` block to initialize a new instance of the `WDABase` class in your `objData` object. Then you add a `Try...Catch` block to handle any update errors that might occur. Within the `Catch` block, you display a MessageBox dialog box with the error that was thrown.

```
Private Sub ActionUpdate()
    'Initialize a new instance of the data access base class
    Using objData As New WDABase
        Try
            'Update database row based on the active screen
            Select Case strActiveScreen
                Case "Projects"
```

```
                    Case "Groups"
                    Case "Group Projects"
                    Case "Roles"
                    Case "Users"
               End Select

                    'Display a message that the record was update
                    ToolStripStatus.Text = "Record Updated"
               Catch ExceptionErr As Exception
                    MessageBox.Show(ExceptionErr.Message, strAppTitle)
               End Try
          End Using
     End Sub
```

You add code to the Case "Projects" statement in this procedure next. This code is similar to the code that you added to the Case "Projects" statement in the ActionAdd procedure. First you set the SQL property of the objData object to your UPDATE query and then you call the InitializeCommand method to initialize the Command object:

```
          Case "Projects"
                'Set the SQL string
                objData.SQL = "usp_UpdateProject"
                'Initialize the Command object
                objData.InitializeCommand()
```

Next, you add the parameters for your UPDATE query to the Parameters collection in the order that they were defined in your query. Notice that the parameter for the @ProjectID is listed last, as it is listed last in your query.

Instead of generating a new Guid as you did for your INSERT query, you need to pass the Guid of the project that you want to update. This parameter expects a Guid structure and the Text property of the txtProjectID text box contains a string representation of the Guid for the project to be updated. Therefore, you have to convert the string representation of the Guid back into a Guid structure.

Using the constructor for the Guid structure, you generate a Guid using the string representation of the Guid to be generated and pass this Guid to the AddParameter method of the objData object:

```
                    'Add the Parameters to the Parameters collection
                    objData.AddParameter("@ProjectName", _
                        Data.OleDb.OleDbType.VarChar, 50, txtProjectName.Text)
                    objData.AddParameter("@ProjectDescription", _
                        Data.OleDb.OleDbType.LongVarChar, _
                        txtProjectDescription.Text.Length, _
                        txtProjectDescription.Text)
                    objData.AddParameter("@SequenceNumber", _
                        Data.OleDb.OleDbType.UnsignedTinyInt, 1, _
                        CType(txtSequenceNumber.Text, Byte))
                    objData.AddParameter("@ProjectID", _
                        Data.OleDb.OleDbType.Guid, 16, _
                        New Guid(txtProjectID.Text))
```

You then open your database connection by calling the OpenConnection method on the objData object and execute your query by calling the ExecuteNonQuery method on the Command object in the objData object. Again, you set the results of this method in the variable, intRowsAffected.

You then close the database connection and query the intRowsAffected variable to ensure that it is not equal to a value of 0. If it is, you throw a new exception with a message indicating that the update failed:

```
'Open the database connection
objData.OpenConnection()
'Execute the query
intRowsAffected = objData.Command.ExecuteNonQuery()
'Close the database connection
objData.CloseConnection()
If intRowsAffected = 0 Then
    Throw New Exception("Update Project Failed")
End If
```

If the update of the project is successful, you clear the text boxes in the Project Details section of the form. Then you call the LoadProjects procedure to clear the Projects list and to reload it with fresh data, which includes the updates that you just made:

```
'Clear the input fields
txtProjectID.Text = String.Empty
txtProjectName.Text = String.Empty
txtProjectDescription.Text = String.Empty
txtSequenceNumber.Text = String.Empty
txtProjectUpdateDate.Text = String.Empty
'Reload the Projects list
LoadProjects()
```

The code that you add to the ActionDelete procedure is also similar to the code added to the ActionAdd and ActionUpdate procedures. You start by modifying the ActionDelete procedure in the same manner in which you modified the ActionAdd and ActionUpdate procedures. You add a Using...End Using block to initialize a new instance of the WDABase class in the objData object.

You then add a Try...Catch block to handle any errors that may occur. Then you add a line of code to the Catch block to display a MessageBox dialog box with the exception that was thrown:

```
Private Sub ActionDelete()
    'Initialize a new instance of the data access base class
    Using objData As New WDABase
        Try
            'Delete database row based on the active screen
            Select Case strActiveScreen
                Case "Projects"
                Case "Groups"
                Case "Group Projects"
                Case "Roles"
                Case "Users"
            End Select

            'Display a message that the record was deleted
```

```
                ToolStripStatus.Text = "Record Deleted"
        Catch ExceptionErr As Exception
                MessageBox.Show(ExceptionErr.Message, strAppTitle)
        End Try
    End Using
End Sub
```

Next, you add some code that is very similar to the code you added below the Case "Projects" statement in the last two procedures, below the Case "Projects" statement in this procedure .You set the SQL property of the objData object to your DELETE query and then call the InitializeCommand method to initialize the Command object.

Only one parameter is needed for your DELETE query, which contains the ProjectID of the project to be deleted. As with the @ProjectID parameter in the ActionUpdate procedure, you need to convert the string representation of the Guid in the text box to a Guid structure. Again, this is done using the constructor of the Guid structure, and you pass the constructor the string representation of the Guid to be converted:

```
            Case "Projects"
                'Set the SQL string
                objData.SQL = "usp_DeleteProject"
                'Initialize the Command object
                objData.InitializeCommand()
                'Add the Parameters to the Parameters collection
                objData.AddParameter("@ProjectID", _
                    Data.OleDb.OleDbType.Guid, 16, _
                    New Guid(txtProjectID.Text))
```

You then open your database connection, execute the query, and close the database connection. Next, you check the intRowsAffected variable to see whether it is equal to a value of 0, indicating no rows were deleted. If it is, you throw a new exception with the appropriate message.

If everything is successful, you clear the text boxes in the Project Details section of your form and then call the LoadProjects procedure to clear and reload the Projects list:

```
                'Open the database connection
                objData.OpenConnection()
                'Execute the query
                intRowsAffected = objData.Command.ExecuteNonQuery()
                'Close the database connection
                objData.CloseConnection()
                If intRowsAffected = 0 Then
                    Throw New Exception("Delete Project Failed")
                End If
                'Clear the input fields
                txtProjectID.Text = String.Empty
                txtProjectName.Text = String.Empty
                txtProjectDescription.Text = String.Empty
                txtSequenceNumber.Text = String.Empty
                txtProjectUpdateDate.Text = String.Empty
                'Reload the Projects list
                LoadProjects()
```

At this point, your Time Tracker application contains the functionality to enable the viewing of a list of projects from the Projects table in your database and the viewing of the details of a specific project. In this exercise, you implemented the functionality to insert, update, and delete projects.

In preparation for the exercises in Chapter 8, add the new projects shown in Figure 7-2 using the functionality you just implemented in your application.

The last two projects in Figure 7-2 and any other projects that you add to the Projects table will contain a sequence number of 99. A sequence number of 99 will be used for actual projects that could be assigned to various groups.

Sequence numbers 1 through 4 are used to indicate common reasons for time off, which will be assigned to all groups. Using sequence numbers in this range causes these common projects to be listed first within each group, which provides consistency throughout your application.

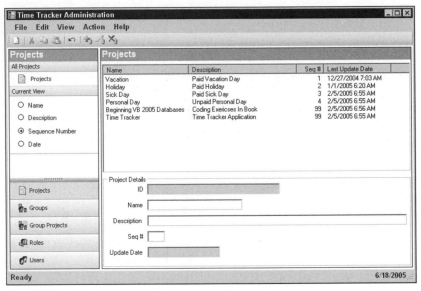

Figure 7-2

Group Queries

In this section, you build the SELECT, INSERT, UPDATE, and DELETE queries in Access for the Groups table in your ProjectTimeTracker database. Because the details of building these queries have already been covered, this section just reiterates the process at a high level.

You need to build a SELECT query that returns all rows of data in the Groups table. This query does not accept any parameters, as you want to return all rows. You also need to build a SELECT query that does accept a parameter and selects a single row of data from the Groups table.

The INSERT query that you build inserts a row of data into the Groups table. Likewise, the UPDATE query updates a row of data in the Groups table, and the DELETE query deletes a row of data from the Groups table.

In this Try It Out, you build two SELECT queries and one INSERT, UPDATE, and DELETE query. These queries operate against the Groups table in your ProjectTimeTracker database.

Try It Out **Building Group Queries**

To create these queries:

1. Locate your ProjectTimeTracker Access database in Windows Explorer and double-click it or start Microsoft Access and open your ProjectTimeTracker database.

2. In the navigation bar to the left, click Queries. Then, in the list displayed, double-click Create Query in Design View.

3. The Query Builder is shown in Design view by default and the Show Table dialog box is displayed. You do not want to add any tables so click the Close button to close the Show Table dialog box.

4. You do not want to use Design view to create this query, so click the View button on the toolbar, or click the View menu and choose the SQL View menu item to switch the Query Builder to the SQL view.

5. Enter the following query to select all rows of data from the Groups table:

```
SELECT GroupID, GroupName, GroupDescription, LastUpdateDate
FROM Groups
ORDER BY GroupName;
```

6. Click the Save button on the toolbar or click the File menu and choose the Save menu item. In the Save As dialog box, enter a query name of usp_SelectGroups. After your query has been saved, close the Query Builder window by clicking the X in its upper-right corner.

7. Double-click Create Query in Design View in the Query list to create another query.

8. Close the Show Table dialog box and then click the View button on the toolbar or click the View menu and choose the SQL View menu item.

9. Enter the following query to select a single group from the Groups table based on the GroupID passed to this query:

```
SELECT GroupID, GroupName, GroupDescription, LastUpdateDate
FROM Groups
WHERE GroupID = @GroupID;
```

10. Click the Save button on the toolbar or click the File menu and choose Save. In the Save As dialog box, enter a query name of usp_SelectGroup. After your query has been saved, close the Query Builder window by clicking the X in its upper-right corner.

11. Double-click Create Query in Design View in the Query list to create another query.

12. Close the Show Table dialog box and then click the View button on the toolbar or click the View menu and choose the SQL View menu item.

13.   Enter the following query to insert a new group in the Groups table:

```
INSERT INTO Groups (GroupID, GroupName, GroupDescription, LastUpdateDate)
VALUES (@GroupID, @GroupName, @GroupDescription, Date()+Time());
```

14.   Click the Save button on the toolbar or click the File menu and choose Save. In the Save As dialog box, enter a query name of usp_InsertGroup. Once your query has been saved, close the Query Builder window by clicking the X in its upper-right corner.

15.   Double-click Create Query in Design View in the Query list to create another query.

16.   Close the Show Table dialog box and then click the View button on the toolbar or click the View menu and choose SQL View.

17.   Enter the following query to update a group in the Groups table:

```
UPDATE Groups
SET GroupName = @GroupName,
GroupDescription = @GroupDescription,
LastUpdateDate = Date()+Time()
WHERE GroupID = @GroupID;
```

18.   Click the Save button on the toolbar or click the File menu and choose Save. In the Save As dialog box, enter a query name of usp_UpdateGroup. Once your query has been saved, close the Query Builder window by clicking the X in its upper-right corner.

19.   Double-click Create Query in Design View in the Query list to create another query.

20.   Close the Show Table dialog box and click the View button on the toolbar, or click the View menu and choose SQL View.

21.   Enter the following query to delete a group in the Groups table:

```
DELETE
FROM Groups
WHERE GroupID = @GroupID;
```

22.   Click the Save button on the toolbar or click the File menu and choose Save. In the Save As dialog box, enter a query name of **usp_DeleteGroup**. After your query has been saved, close the Query Builder window by clicking the X in its upper-right corner.

23.   Close your Access database.

How It Works

You've already seen how to build queries in Access and you've seen how SELECT, INSERT, UPDATE and DELETE queries work, so I'll just summarize what you do in this section.

The first query that you build is the usp_SelectGroups query. This SELECT query does not accept any parameters and selects all rows of data from the Groups table. You specify the columns that you want returned in your results in the select list.

```
SELECT GroupID, GroupName, GroupDescription, LastUpdateDate
FROM Groups
ORDER BY GroupName;
```

The next SELECT query that you build is the usp_SelectGroup query. This is a parameter query, meaning that in order to run, it expects a parameter. This query selects a single group from the Groups table based on the GroupID passed as the parameter to this query.

```
SELECT GroupID, GroupName, GroupDescription, LastUpdateDate
FROM Groups
WHERE GroupID = @GroupID;
```

The INSERT query that you build, usp_InsertGroup, inserts a new row of data into the Groups table. You supply input parameters to this query for the GroupID, GroupName, and GroupDescription columns. The LastUpdateDate column has the current date and time inserted into it using the built-in Access functions Date and Time.

```
INSERT INTO Groups (GroupID, GroupName, GroupDescription, LastUpdateDate)
VALUES (@GroupID, @GroupName, @GroupDescription, Date()+Time());
```

The UPDATE query, usp_UpdateGroup, updates a single group in the Groups table based on the GroupID. Again, you are using the built-in Access functions Date and Time to update the value in the LastUpdateDate column.

```
UPDATE Groups
SET GroupName = @GroupName,
GroupDescription = @GroupDescription,
LastUpdateDate = Date()+Time()
WHERE GroupID = @GroupID;
```

The final query that you build is the usp_DeleteGroup query. This query deletes a single row of data from the Groups table, where the value in the GroupID column matches the value passed in the @GroupID parameter.

```
DELETE
FROM Groups
WHERE GroupID = @GroupID;
```

In this Try It Out, you implement the queries that you just built in your ProjectTimeTracker database in your Time Tracker application. The functionality that you implement in this exercise mirrors the functionality that you implemented for projects in the first exercise in this chapter.

You add code to execute your usp_SelectGroups query to populate the Groups list, and the code to execute your usp_SelectGroup query to select and display the details for a single group. You also add the code necessary to insert, update, and delete a group using your usp_InsertGroup, usp_UpdateGroup, and usp_DeleteGroup queries.

Try It Out   Implementing the Group Queries

To implement this functionality:

1. Open the Time Tracker application in Visual Studio 2005 if it is not already open.

2. Switch to the Code Editor for the Admin form and add the following Imports statement:

```
Imports System.Data
```

```
Public Class Admin
```

3. Now add the following form-level variable declaration:

```
Private objData As WDABase
```

```
Private objGroupsDS As DataSet
```

4. Modify the `Admin_Load` procedure as follows: The IDE displays an error that `LoadGroups` is not declared, as you've not added this procedure yet. Ignore this error for now because you add that procedure in the next step:

```
AddHandler imgUsers.MouseUp, AddressOf NavigationChildControl_MouseUp
```

```
'Display a loading message
ToolStripStatus.Text = "Loading..."
```

```
'Set the current date in the date panel in the status bar
ToolStripDate.Text = Date.Today
```

```
'Get the application title
strAppTitle = My.Application.Info.Title
```

```
'Show the form and refresh it
Me.Show()
Me.Refresh()
```

```
'Load the Projects
LoadProjects()
```

```
'Load the Groups
LoadGroups()
```

```
'Display a ready message
ToolStripStatus.Text = "Ready"
End Sub
```

5. The `LoadGroups` procedure executes your `usp_SelectGroups` query to select all groups in the Groups table. Create the `LoadGroups` procedure and add the following code to it:

```
Private Sub LoadGroups()
    'Declare variables
    Dim objListViewItem As ListViewItem

    'Initialize a new instance of the data access base class
    Using objData As New WDABase
        Try
            'Clear previous data bindings
            cboGroups.DataSource = Nothing
            cboGroups.DisplayMember = String.Empty
            cboGroups.ValueMember = String.Empty

            'Get all Groups in a DataSet object
            objData.SQL = "usp_SelectGroups"
```

```
            objGroupsDS = New DataSet
            objData.FillDataSet(objGroupsDS, "Groups")

            'Clear previous list
            lvwGroups.Items.Clear()

            'Process all rows
            For intIndex = 0 To objGroupsDS.Tables("Groups").Rows.Count - 1

                'Create a new listview item
                objListViewItem = New ListViewItem

                'Add the data to the listview item
                objListViewItem.Text = _
                    objGroupsDS.Tables("Groups").Rows(intIndex).Item( _
                    "GroupName")
                objListViewItem.Tag = _
                    objGroupsDS.Tables("Groups").Rows(intIndex).Item( _
                    "GroupID")

                'Add the sub items to the listview item
                objListViewItem.SubItems.Add( _
                    objGroupsDS.Tables("Groups").Rows(intIndex).Item( _
                    "GroupDescription"))
                objListViewItem.SubItems.Add( _
                    Format(objGroupsDS.Tables("Groups").Rows(intIndex).Item( _
                    "LastUpdateDate"), "g"))

                'Add the listview item to the listview control
                lvwGroups.Items.Add(objListViewItem)

            Next

            'Rebind ComboBox control
            cboGroups.DataSource = objGroupsDS.Tables("Groups")
            cboGroups.DisplayMember = "GroupName"
            cboGroups.ValueMember = "GroupID"

            'Reset the selected index
            cboGroups.SelectedIndex = -1
        Catch ExceptionErr As Exception
            MessageBox.Show(ExceptionErr.Message, strAppTitle)
        End Try
    End Using

    'Cleanup
    objListViewItem = Nothing
End Sub
```

6. The `lvwGroups_Click` procedure executes your `usp_SelectGroup` query to select a single group from the Groups table. In the Class Name combo box, select `lvwGroups`; and in the Method Name combo box, select the `Click` event to add the `lvwGroups_Click` procedure to your project. Add the following code to this procedure:

```
Private Sub lvwGroups_Click(ByVal sender As Object, _
    ByVal e As System.EventArgs) Handles lvwGroups.Click

        'Initialize a new instance of the data access base class
        Using objData As New WDABase
            Try
                'Get the specific Group selected in the ListView control
                objData.SQL = "usp_SelectGroup"
                objData.InitializeCommand()
                objData.AddParameter("@GroupID", Data.OleDb.OleDbType.Guid, 16, _
                    lvwGroups.SelectedItems.Item(0).Tag)
                objData.OpenConnection()
                objData.DataReader = objData.Command.ExecuteReader

                'See if any data exists before continuing
                If objData.DataReader.HasRows Then

                    'Read the first and only row of data
                    objData.DataReader.Read()

                    'Populate the Group Details section
                    txtGroupID.Text = _
                        objData.DataReader.Item("GroupID").ToString.ToUpper
                    txtGroupName.Text = _
                        objData.DataReader.Item("GroupName")
                    txtGroupDescription.Text = _
                        objData.DataReader.Item("GroupDescription")
                    txtGroupUpdateDate.Text = _
                        Format(objData.DataReader.Item("LastUpdateDate"), "g")

                End If

                'Close the DataReader
                objData.DataReader.Close()

                'Close the database connection
                objData.CloseConnection()
            Catch ExceptionErr As Exception
                MessageBox.Show(ExceptionErr.Message, strAppTitle)
            End Try
        End Using
    End Sub
```

7. You want to implement the code to execute your usp_InsertGroup query in the ActionAdd procedure, so modify this procedure as follows:

```
            Case "Groups"
                'Set the SQL string
                objData.SQL = "usp_InsertGroup"
                'Initialize the Command object
                objData.InitializeCommand()
                'Add the Parameters to the Parameters collection
                objData.AddParameter("@GroupID", _
                    Data.OleDb.OleDbType.Guid, 16, Guid.NewGuid())
```

```
objData.AddParameter("@GroupName", _
    Data.OleDb.OleDbType.VarChar, 50, txtGroupName.Text)
objData.AddParameter("@GroupDescription", _
    Data.OleDb.OleDbType.LongVarChar, _
    txtGroupDescription.Text.Length, _
    txtGroupDescription.Text)
'Open the database connection
objData.OpenConnection()
'Execute the query
intRowsAffected = objData.Command.ExecuteNonQuery()
'Close the database connection
objData.CloseConnection()
If intRowsAffected = 0 Then
    Throw New Exception("Insert Group Failed")
End If
'Clear the input fields
txtGroupName.Text = String.Empty
txtGroupDescription.Text = String.Empty
'Reload the Groups list
LoadGroups()
```

8. Next, you need to modify the `ActionUpdate` procedure to execute your `usp_UpdateGroup` query. Modify this procedure as follows:

```
Case "Groups"
    'Set the SQL string
    objData.SQL = "usp_UpdateGroup"
    'Initialize the Command object
    objData.InitializeCommand()
    'Add the Parameters to the Parameters collection
    objData.AddParameter("@GroupName", _
        Data.OleDb.OleDbType.VarChar, 50, txtGroupName.Text)
    objData.AddParameter("@GroupDescription", _
        Data.OleDb.OleDbType.LongVarChar, _
        txtGroupDescription.Text.Length, _
        txtGroupDescription.Text)
    objData.AddParameter("@GroupID", _
        Data.OleDb.OleDbType.Guid, 16, New Guid( _
        txtGroupID.Text))
    'Open the database connection
    objData.OpenConnection()
    'Execute the query
    intRowsAffected = objData.Command.ExecuteNonQuery()
    'Close the database connection
    objData.CloseConnection()
    If intRowsAffected = 0 Then
        Throw New Exception("Update Group Failed")
    End If
    'Clear the input fields
    txtGroupID.Text = String.Empty
    txtGroupName.Text = String.Empty
    txtGroupDescription.Text = String.Empty
    txtGroupUpdateDate.Text = String.Empty
    'Reload the Groups list
    LoadGroups()
```

9. Modify the `ActionDelete` procedure to execute the `usp_DeleteGroup` query. Modify this procedure as follows:

```
Case "Groups"
        'Set the SQL string
        objData.SQL = "usp_DeleteGroup"
        'Initialize the Command object
        objData.InitializeCommand()
        'Add the Parameters to the Parameters collection
        objData.AddParameter("@GroupID", _
            Data.OleDb.OleDbType.Guid, 16, New Guid( _
            txtGroupID.Text))
        'Open the database connection
        objData.OpenConnection()
        'Execute the query
        intRowsAffected = objData.Command.ExecuteNonQuery()
        'Close the database connection
        objData.CloseConnection()
        If intRowsAffected = 0 Then
            Throw New Exception("Delete Group Failed")
        End If
        'Clear the input fields
        txtGroupID.Text = String.Empty
        txtGroupName.Text = String.Empty
        txtGroupDescription.Text = String.Empty
        txtGroupUpdateDate.Text = String.Empty
        'Reload the Groups list
        LoadGroups()
```

10. You are now ready to test the modifications that you have made. Start your project and when the Admin form is displayed, click Groups in the Shortcut navigation pane to display the Groups screen. Of course, no data is displayed, as you have not entered any group data yet.

11. Enter a group name of your choosing in the Name field and a description in the Description field. Click the Add button on the toolbar or click the Action menu and choose Add to have the new group added, as shown in Figure 7-3.

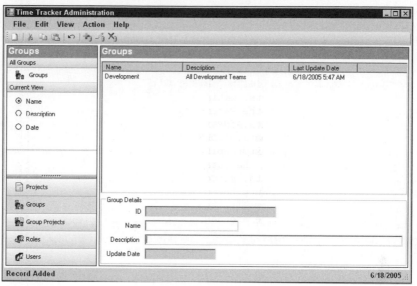

Figure 7-3

Not only will the group be displayed in the Groups list, but it is also added to the ComboBox control on the Group Projects screen. You can click Group Projects in the Shortcuts navigation bar to display the Group Projects screen and then click the Groups ComboBox to see the group listed there.

12. Now you want to test the update functionality by clicking the group you just added in the Groups list and modifying the name and/or description, so navigate back to the Groups screen and click the group to have the group details displayed. Make some modifications to the group name and/or group description. After you have done that, click the Update button on the toolbar or click the Action menu and choose Update. The group is updated and the Groups list is cleared and reloaded with fresh data from the database, displaying your updates to the group.

13. Test the delete functionality, so again click the group in the Groups list to have the group details displayed. Then click the Delete button on the toolbar or click the Action menu and select Delete.

14. When you have finished testing all of the functionality of your application, add three groups of your choosing in preparation for the exercises in the next chapter.

When you were testing your code, you tested one query by simply starting your project: the usp_SelectGroups query. This query was executed in the LoadGroups procedure when the form loaded.

By adding a new group and having it displayed, as shown in Figure 7-3, you tested two queries in two procedures. The first query that you tested was the usp_InsertGroup query in the ActionAdd procedure. This procedure then called the LoadGroups procedure after the group was inserted into the database, which tested the usp_SelectGroups query.

The process of updating and deleting a group tested three queries. First you had to click a group in the list to view the details of the group, which tested the usp_SelectGroup query. This query retrieved the group details from the database and displayed them in the Group Details section of your form. Then, when you clicked the Update or Delete icon on the toolbar, the usp_UpdateGroup or usp_DeleteGroup query was executed and a call was made to the LoadGroups procedure. These actions executed the usp_SelectGroups query. Let's see how this works in detail.

How It Works

The form level DataSet object that you declare is used to load the group data in. This DataSet is then read and used to load the Groups ListView control. It is also used when it is bound to a ComboBox control containing a list of all the groups in your database.

```
Private objGroupsDS As DataSet
```

When you start loading a lot of data from the database when your application starts, you need to do one of two things to let the user know that your application is busy loading. The first option is to display a splash screen, such as the one displayed when Visual Studio 2005 loads, and the second option is to display your empty form with a message that the application is loading data. The second option is the one you implement here.

You implement code in the Admin_Load procedure to set a message in the status bar indicating that the application is loading. Then you display the form by calling the Show method on the form. Notice that you use the Me keyword, which references the current form. Calling the Refresh method on the form after it has been shown forces it to redraw the controls on the form. This ensures that the form controls are properly displayed while the rest of the code in the load procedure executes.

```
'Display a loading message
ToolStripStatus.Text = "Loading..."

. . .

'Show the form and refresh it
Me.Show()
Me.Refresh()

. . .
```

After you call the LoadProjects procedure, you add code to call the LoadGroups procedure. This procedure loads the Groups list and binds a DataSet to the Groups ComboBox control. After control is returned from the LoadGroups procedure, you display a new message in the status bar to indicate to the user that the application is ready for use.

```
'Load the Groups
LoadGroups()

'Display a ready message
ToolStripStatus.Text = "Ready"
```

The LoadGroups procedure is added next. The first thing that you do in this procedure is declare an object as a ListViewItem. This enables you to build a ListView item and add it to the ListView control. Next, you initialize a new instance of the WDABase class in your objData object in a Using...End Using block.

```
Private Sub LoadGroups()
    'Declare variables
    Dim objListViewItem As ListViewItem

    'Initialize a new instance of the data access base class
    Using objData As New WDABase
```

You implement a `Try...Catch` block to handle any errors that may be encountered while loading the `DataSet` with data from the database. The first thing that you do inside the `Try` block is clear the previous bindings of your `cboGroups` ComboBox control by setting the `DataSource` property to `Nothing`. This property is set to the `DataSet` that contains the data to be bound to the control. The `DisplayMember` and `ValueMember` properties are set to an empty string, clearing the String values that get set in these properties. Of course, the first time this procedure is called, the ComboBox control has not yet been bound, but on subsequent executions of this procedure it will have been bound and will need to be cleared.

```
Try
    'Clear previous data bindings
    cboGroups.DataSource = Nothing
    cboGroups.DisplayMember = String.Empty
    cboGroups.ValueMember = String.Empty
```

Next, you set the `SQL` property of the `objData` object to the query that will retrieve a list of all groups in the Groups table. Because you will be binding a `DataSet` to the `cboGroups` ComboBox control and loading the `lvwGroups` ListView control with groups, it is more efficient to populate a `DataSet` with the group data than to use an `OleDbDataReader` object to load the ListView control and then use a `DataSet` that will be bound to a ComboBox control.

After you set the `SQL` property, you then initialize a new instance of the `DataSet` class in your `objGroupsDS` `DataSet` object. Then you call the `FillDataSet` method in your `objData` object to populate your `DataSet` object and set the table name in the `DataSet` to `Groups`.

```
'Get all Groups in a DataSet object
objData.SQL = "usp_SelectGroups"
objGroupsDS = New DataSet
objData.FillDataSet(objGroupsDS, "Groups")
```

Let's digress for a moment and take a look at the `FillDataSet` method in the `WDABase` class because you haven't seen this method in detail yet. This procedure accepts the `DataSet` object that is to be filled with data as the first parameter. The object for this parameter is passed by reference. When you pass an object by reference to a procedure, the procedure that the object is passed to can modify the value of the object in the same manner as the code that called this procedure.

What this means is that you can define the object in one class and modify its value there and when you pass this object by reference to a procedure in another class, it behaves as if the object were declared locally within the called procedure.

The second parameter to the `FillDataSet` method is passed *by value* and is a String value for the table name to be used when the `DataSet` is populated with data. Passing a parameter by value means that you actually pass the value of the parameter and not a reference to it.

Remember that all procedures in the WDABase class encapsulate the code in a Try...Catch block to handle and return any database errors that they may encounter. The first thing accomplished inside the Try block is a call to the InitalizeCommand procedure. You examined this procedure in detail in the previous chapter, and basically it initializes the OleDbCommand object with the SQL string and the OleDbConnection object. It also sets the CommandType property to a StoredProcedure constant if a query or stored procedure is being executed.

A call is made to the InitializeDataAdapter procedure next to initialize an OleDbDataAdapter object. You take a look at that procedure in just a moment. The Fill method of the DataAdapter object is then executed to fill the DataSet with data and set the table name to the table name passed to this procedure.

The Catch block throws a new exception with the error that it received and effectively returns this error to the caller. The Finally block performs the necessary cleanup for this procedure and disposes of the objects used here that are no longer needed:

```
Public Sub FillDataSet(ByRef oDataSet As DataSet, ByVal TableName As String)
    Try
        InitializeCommand()
        InitializeDataAdapter()
        DataAdapter.Fill(oDataSet, TableName)
    Catch OleDbExceptionErr As OleDbException
        Throw New System.Exception(OleDbExceptionErr.Message, _
            OleDbExceptionErr.InnerException)
    Finally
        Command.Dispose()
        Command = Nothing
        DataAdapter.Dispose()
        DataAdapter = Nothing
    End Try
End Sub
```

The FillDataSet procedure calls the InitializeDataAdapter procedure, which follows. This procedure initializes a new instance of the OleDbDataAdapter class in the DataAdapter object and then sets the SelectCommand property of the DataAdapter object to the Command object. This procedure also includes the appropriate error-handling code to return any errors received to the caller.

```
Public Sub InitializeDataAdapter()
    Try
        DataAdapter = New OleDbDataAdapter
        DataAdapter.SelectCommand = Command
    Catch OleDbExceptionErr As OleDbException
        Throw New System.Exception(OleDbExceptionErr.Message, _
        OleDbExceptionErr.InnerException)
    End Try
End Sub
```

When you return to the LoadGroups procedure, the next thing that you do after filling the DataSet with data is clear the previous list of items in the ListView control.

```
'Clear previous list
lvwGroups.Items.Clear()
```

A For...Next loop is set up to process each row of data in the objGroupsDS DataSet and to load that data in the ListView control. Remember that the Count property in a DataSet returns the actual number of rows but the first row of data in a DataSet has an index position of 0, which is why you use Count - 1 in the For statement.

The first thing that you do in this loop is initialize the objListViewItem object to a new instance of the ListViewItem class:

```
'Process all rows
For intIndex = 0 To objGroupsDS.Tables("Groups").Rows.Count - 1

    'Create a new listview item
    objListViewItem = New ListViewItem
```

Next, you set the Text property of the objListViewItem object to the name of the group. You retrieve the group name from the Item property in the DataSet by specifying the column name of GroupName. You set the Tag property next to the GroupID. Remember that the Tag property can contain any object and will be used to retrieve the GroupID of the selected row of data in the ListView control.

You add the sub-items to the objListViewItem object, starting with the group description. Then you add the last update date using the Format function to format the date according to the local settings on your computer.

Finally, you add the new ListViewItem to the Items collection of the ListView control and then repeat the loop:

```
'Add the data to the listview item
objListViewItem.Text = _
    objGroupsDS.Tables("Groups").Rows(intIndex).Item( _
    "GroupName")
objListViewItem.Tag = _
    objGroupsDS.Tables("Groups").Rows(intIndex).Item( _
    "GroupID")

'Add the sub items to the listview item
objListViewItem.SubItems.Add( _
    objGroupsDS.Tables("Groups").Rows(intIndex).Item( _
    "GroupDescription"))
objListViewItem.SubItems.Add( _
    Format(objGroupsDS.Tables("Groups").Rows(intIndex).Item( _
    "LastUpdateDate"), "g"))

'Add the listview item to the listview control
lvwGroups.Items.Add(objListViewItem)

Next
```

After all data in the DataSet is added to the ListView control, it is time to rebind the DataSet to the cboGroups ComboBox control. First you set the DataSource property to the objGroupsDS object and specify which table in the DataSet should be used for binding. Then you set the DisplayMember property to the column name that should be displayed in the ComboBox, which is GroupName. Finally, you set the ValueMember property to the column that should be used to raise the ValueMemberChanged and `SelectedValueChanged` events. When these events are raised, the `SelectedItem` property of the ComboBox control will contain the `GroupID` of the selected group in the ComboBox.

After the ComboBox is rebound to the `DataSet`, set the `SelectedIndex` property to a value of –1. Setting this property to –1 causes no items to be selected. The reasons for setting this property to this value will become evident in Chapter 9 when you add the functionality for the Group Projects screen.

```
'Rebind ComboBox control
cboGroups.DataSource = objGroupsDS.Tables("Groups")
cboGroups.DisplayMember = "GroupName"
cboGroups.ValueMember = "GroupID"

'Reset the selected index
cboGroups.SelectedIndex = -1
```

The `Catch` block contains the standard error-handling code that displays a MessageBox dialog box containing the error received.

After the `End Using` statement, you add the necessary code to clean up the resources used in this procedure:

```
      Catch ExceptionErr As Exception
          MessageBox.Show(ExceptionErr.Message, strAppTitle)
      End Try
   End Using

   'Cleanup
   objListViewItem = Nothing
End Sub
```

The `lvwGroups_Click` procedure is added to handle a `Click` event in the `lvwGroups` ListView control. Whenever you click a row of data in the ListView control, this procedure is executed. This procedure first initializes a new instance of the `WDABase` class in your `objData` object in a `Using...End Using` block.

```
Private Sub lvwGroups_Click(ByVal sender As Object, _
   ByVal e As System.EventArgs) Handles lvwGroups.Click

   'Initialize a new instance of the data access base class
   Using objData As New WDABase
```

Then a `Try...Catch` block is set up, as you'll be executing code that retrieves the selected group from the database. Inside the `Try` block, you set the `SQL` property of your `objData` object to the query to be executed and then call the `InitializeCommand` method on the `objData` object.

Next, you add the one and only parameter expected by the `usp_SelectGroup` query, which is for the `GroupID` of the group that should be retrieved. The value for this parameter is being retrieved from the `Tag` property in the `lvwGroups` ListView control for the selected row of data.

Then you open the database connection by executing the `OpenConnection` method on the `objData` object. The next line of code sets the `DataReader` object in the `objData` object to the results returned from calling the `ExecuteReader` method on the `Command` object:

```
Try
    'Get the specific Group selected in the ListView control
    objData.SQL = "usp_SelectGroup"
    objData.InitializeCommand()
    objData.AddParameter("@GroupID", Data.OleDb.OleDbType.Guid, 16, _
        lvwGroups.SelectedItems.Item(0).Tag)
    objData.OpenConnection()
    objData.DataReader = objData.Command.ExecuteReader
```

Before processing the `DataReader` object, you want to ensure that it contains data. You accomplish this by querying the `HasRows` property, which returns a Boolean value indicating whether it contains data.

After you determine that the `DataReader` object does contain data, you proceed to the code inside the `If...Then` statement. You know that the `usp_SelectGroup` query returns only one row of data so there's no need to set up a loop to process the data. Instead, you call the `Read` method on the `DataReader` object and then proceed to load the data in the text boxes in the Group Details section of your form:

```
    'See if any data exists before continuing
    If objData.DataReader.HasRows Then

        'Read the first and only row of data
        objData.DataReader.Read()

        'Populate the Group Details section
        txtGroupID.Text = _
            objData.DataReader.Item("GroupID").ToString.ToUpper
        txtGroupName.Text = _
            objData.DataReader.Item("GroupName")
        txtGroupDescription.Text = _
            objData.DataReader.Item("GroupDescription")
        txtGroupUpdateDate.Text = _
            Format(objData.DataReader.Item("LastUpdateDate"), "g")

    End If
```

After you process all of the data, you close the `DataReader` object and then close the database connection.

The `Catch` block contains the code necessary to display a MessageBox dialog box with the error that is received.

```
    'Close the DataReader
    objData.DataReader.Close()

    'Close the database connection
    objData.CloseConnection()
Catch ExceptionErr As Exception
    MessageBox.Show(ExceptionErr.Message, strAppTitle)
End Try
    End Using
End Sub
```

You add code to the Case "Groups" statement in the ActionAdd procedure next. This code is executed when you click the Add button on the toolbar to add a new group. The code in this Case statement is similar to the code that you added to the Case "Projects" statement in this same procedure.

The first thing that you do is set the SQL property of the objData object to the query to be executed. Then you call the InitializeCommand method on the objData object to initialize the Command object. You add the parameters for your query next, in the order in which they are defined in your query:

```
Case "Groups"
    'Set the SQL string
    objData.SQL = "usp_InsertGroup"
    'Initialize the Command object
    objData.InitializeCommand()
    'Add the Parameters to the Parameters collection
    objData.AddParameter("@GroupID", _
        Data.OleDb.OleDbType.Guid, 16, Guid.NewGuid())
    objData.AddParameter("@GroupName", _
        Data.OleDb.OleDbType.VarChar, 50, txtGroupName.Text)
    objData.AddParameter("@GroupDescription", _
        Data.OleDb.OleDbType.LongVarChar, _
        txtGroupDescription.Text.Length, _
        txtGroupDescription.Text)
```

After you add all of your parameters, you open the database connection by calling the OpenConnection method on the objData object and then execute your query by calling the ExecuteNonQuery method on the Command object in the objData object. After your query has been executed, you call the CloseConnection method to close the database connection.

The number of rows affected by this query will be returned in the intRowsAffected variable. You check this variable to see whether it contains a value of 0, indicating that no insert was performed. If this is the case, you throw an exception with the appropriate error message and control of your program is transferred to the Catch block in this procedure.

If the intRowsAffected variable contains a value other than 0, the next line of code is executed. These next few lines of code clear the text boxes on the Group Details section of your form. Then you call the LoadGroups procedure, which clears the Groups list and repopulates it with fresh data from your database.

```
'Open the database connection
objData.OpenConnection()
'Execute the query
intRowsAffected = objData.Command.ExecuteNonQuery()
'Close the database connection
objData.CloseConnection()
If intRowsAffected = 0 Then
    Throw New Exception("Insert Group Failed")
End If
'Clear the input fields
txtGroupName.Text = String.Empty
txtGroupDescription.Text = String.Empty
'Reload the Groups list
LoadGroups()
```

The code that you add to the `Case "Groups"` statement in the `ActionUpdate` procedure is similar to the code in the `Case "Projects"` statement in this same procedure. The first thing that you do here is set the `SQL` property of the `objData` object to the query to be executed. Then you call the `InitializeCommand` method to initialize the `Command` object.

You then proceed to add the parameters to the `Parameters` collection in the order in which they are defined in your query. Remember that the `@GroupID` parameter is defined as the last parameter in your query and is listed last here. Again, you use the constructor of the `Guid` structure to return a Guid formatted from the string representation of the Guid that is displayed in the `txtGroupID` text box.

```
Case "Groups"
    'Set the SQL string
    objData.SQL = "usp_UpdateGroup"
    'Initialize the Command object
    objData.InitializeCommand()
    'Add the Parameters to the Parameters collection
    objData.AddParameter("@GroupName", _
        Data.OleDb.OleDbType.VarChar, 50, txtGroupName.Text)
    objData.AddParameter("@GroupDescription", _
        Data.OleDb.OleDbType.LongVarChar, _
        txtGroupDescription.Text.Length, _
        txtGroupDescription.Text)
    objData.AddParameter("@GroupID", _
        Data.OleDb.OleDbType.Guid, 16, New Guid( _
        txtGroupID.Text))
```

After all of your parameters are added to the `Parameters` collection, you open the database connection and execute your query. Then you close the database connection and query the value returned from your query in the `intRowsAffected` variable. Again, a value of `0` in this variable indicates that no rows were updated, and, if this is the case, you throw a new exception with the appropriate error message.

If a row of data was updated, you proceed to the next line of code and clear the text boxes in the Group Details section of your form. Finally, you call the `LoadGroups` procedure to clear the Groups list and reload it with fresh data that will reflect the update just made from the database.

```
'Open the database connection
objData.OpenConnection()
'Execute the query
intRowsAffected = objData.Command.ExecuteNonQuery()
'Close the database connection
objData.CloseConnection()
If intRowsAffected = 0 Then
    Throw New Exception("Update Group Failed")
End If
'Clear the input fields
txtGroupID.Text = String.Empty
txtGroupName.Text = String.Empty
txtGroupDescription.Text = String.Empty
txtGroupUpdateDate.Text = String.Empty
'Reload the Groups list
LoadGroups()
```

The code that you add to the Case "Groups" statement in the ActionDelete procedure mirrors the code for the Case "Projects" statement in this same procedure. You follow the same routine for adding code to this procedure as you did in the last two procedures.

First, you set the SQL property of the objData object to the query to be executed, initialize the Command object, and add your parameter to the Parameters collection. Then you open the database connection, execute the query, and close the database connection.

You query the value in the intRowsAffected variable to ensure it does not contain a value of 0 and proceed to clear the text boxes in the Group Details section of the form. You then call the LoadGroups procedure to clear the Groups list and load it with fresh data from your database:

```
Case "Groups"
    'Set the SQL string
    objData.SQL = "usp_DeleteGroup"
    'Initialize the Command object
    objData.InitializeCommand()
    'Add the Parameters to the Parameters collection
    objData.AddParameter("@GroupID", _
        Data.OleDb.OleDbType.Guid, 16, New Guid( _
        txtGroupID.Text))
    'Open the database connection
    objData.OpenConnection()
    'Execute the query
    intRowsAffected = objData.Command.ExecuteNonQuery()
    'Close the database connection
    objData.CloseConnection()
    If intRowsAffected = 0 Then
        Throw New Exception("Delete Group Failed")
    End If
    'Clear the input fields
    txtGroupID.Text = String.Empty
    txtGroupName.Text = String.Empty
    txtGroupDescription.Text = String.Empty
    txtGroupUpdateDate.Text = String.Empty
    'Reload the Groups list
    LoadGroups()
```

This exercise has implemented the functionality for the Groups screen on the Admin form. You are now able to view a complete list of groups defined in your database, view the details for a single group, and insert, update, and delete groups.

Summary

In this chapter, you explored the OleDbCommand object in more detail. You learned how to use the ExecuteNonQuery method of this object to insert, update, and delete records in your database. Having used the OleDbCommand object extensively throughout the exercises in this chapter, you are now more familiar with the Parameters collection and should be quite comfortable adding parameters to this collection.

You've also created more SELECT, INSERT, UPDATE and DELETE queries in Access and at this point should be quite adept at writing basic SQL statements to create queries that select, insert, update, and delete data in Access. Having used these queries in your Time Tracker application, you should also be quite skilled at using ADO.NET and have a good understanding of how it works.

Throughout the exercises in this chapter, you used both the OleDbDataReader and OleDbDataAdapter to retrieve data from your database. You should be comfortable using the OleDbDataReader and DataSet to load data into the controls on your form.

To summarize, you should know how to:

❑ Use the ExecuteNonQuery method of the OleDbCommand object to execute queries that do not return rows of data

❑ Determine the number of rows affected by the execution of a query or stored procedure when using the ExecuteNonQuery method

❑ Add parameters with different data types to the Parameters collection

❑ Write basic SELECT, INSERT, UPDATE, and DELETE queries in Access

In Chapter 8, you port the data that currently exists in your Access database into either SQL Server or Oracle.

Exercises

Exercise 1

Create a new table in your ProjectTimeTracker.mdb database called **Scores** with the following column definitions:

❑ Column Name = **ScoreID**, Data Type = Number, Field Size = Replication ID, Primary Key

❑ Column Name = **Opposition**, Data Type = Text, Field Size = 50

❑ Column Name = **OurScore**, Data Type = Number, Field Size = Byte

❑ Column Name = **TheirScore**, Data Type = Number, Field Size = Byte

❑ Column Name = **DatePlayed**, Data Type = Date/Time

Write a SELECT query to select all rows of data from this table and a SELECT query to select a specific score base on the ScoreID. Also write an INSERT, UPDATE, and DELETE query for this table.

Exercise 2

Write a simple application that will display a list of scores in a ListView control; contains fields to add, update, and delete scores; and contains three buttons to execute your INSERT, UPDATE, and DELETE queries. Execute your SELECT query that selects all score when the form loads and the SELECT query to select a specific score when you click on an item in the ListView control. Your completed form could look similar to the one shown in Figure 7-4.

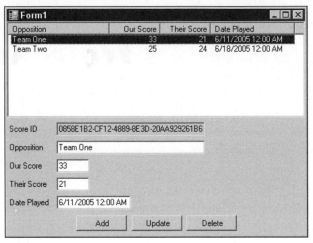

Figure 7-4

Migrating Data from Access

Up until this point, you have been working with Microsoft Access, which is a fine database for working with small groups of users and relatively small amounts of data. However, when you need to work with a large number of users in the hundreds or thousands and large amounts of data, an *enterprise relational database,* such as SQL Server or Oracle, is just the ticket.

From this chapter on, you work with either SQL Server or Oracle, depending on which you have available or need to learn. Of course, you can work with both if you choose and code the exercises to execute against both databases.

Before you can work with one of these enterprise relational databases, you need to migrate the data that currently exists in your Microsoft Access database to the database that you'll be working with. In this chapter, you create an application to perform this data migration.

In this chapter, you:

❑   Learn how to create a dynamic connection to SQL Server and Oracle

❑   Learn about SQL statement parameters

❑   Migrate the data from your Access database to either SQL Server or Oracle, or both if you choose

Dynamic Connections

In Chapter 5, you learned how to create a dynamic connection string to connect to an Access database. You also learned how to check the state of that connection to determine whether that connection was open or closed. You'll expand on that knowledge now and learn how to create a dynamic connection string to connect to both SQL Server and Oracle. Regardless of which database you use from this point forward, learning about and having the knowledge to build connection strings for both databases will serve you well in the future.

The following code fragment is taken from the WDABase class in your Time Tracker application. This code shows how you built the connection string when initializing a new instance of the OleDbConnection class. In this connection string, the only parameters that you had to provide for the connection string were the `Provider` and `Data Source`. The values for these parameters were supplied in and read from your `app.config` file.

```
'Build the SQL connection string and initialize the Connection object
Connection = New OleDbConnection( _
"Provider=" & My.Settings.Provider & ";" & _
"Data Source=" & My.Settings.DataSource & ";")
```

When using the `OleDbConnection` class to build a connection string for SQL Server, there are a few more parameters that you need to supply, as discussed in the "Common constructors" section in Chapter 2. The parameters that you typically supply for a connection to SQL Server include the following:

* Provider
* Data Source
* Database
* User ID
* Password

The driver that you use for the `Provider` parameter is `SQLOLEDB`. The `Data Source` parameter specifies the name of the machine on which your SQL Server database is running, and the `Database` parameter specifies your database name — in this case, `ProjectTimeTracker`. The `User ID` parameter contains the login name that was assigned to you by your database administrator and the `Password` parameter is the password for your login.

Knowing all of the required parameters, you then write a connection string to initialize a new instance of the `OleDbConnection` class. A typical connection string looks like the following code. You substitute the appropriate values for `myServer`, `myLogin`, and `myPassword` with the values that are applicable to your environment:

```
Connection = New OleDbConnection( _
    "Provider=SQLOLEDB;" & _
    "Data Source=myServer;" & _
    "Database=ProjectTimeTracker;" & _
    "User ID=myLogin;" & _
    "Password=myPassword;")
```

When building a connection string to be used to connect to an Oracle database, you use the same parameters as those shown in the preceding code, except for the `Database` parameter. This parameter is not needed when connecting to Oracle because your `tsnames.ora` file contains this information.

Of course, the `Provider` will be different from the previous that of examples because you specify the `MSDAORA` driver to connect to Oracle. Also, the `Data Source` does not specify the machine name on which Oracle is running. Instead, it specifies the system identifier (SID) defined in the `tnsnames.ora` file that was created when you installed and configured the Oracle client on your computer. A sample code fragment for a connection string for Oracle follows. You need to substitute the appropriate values for `mySID`, `myLogin`, and `myPassword` with the values applicable to your environment.

```
Connection = New OleDbConnection( _
    "Provider=MSDAORA;" & _
    "Data Source=mySID;" & _
    "User ID=myLogin;" & _
    "Password=myPassword;")
```

You now have enough information to make a connection to either SQL Server or Oracle. To that end, you jump right in and start creating an application to migrate the data from Access to either SQL Server or Oracle.

In the next Try It Out, you start building a utility application to migrate the data that currently exists in your Access database to either SQL Server or Oracle. This utility is generic and can operate against either a SQL Server or Oracle database.

You build the user interface for this utility in this exercise as well as implement code that builds a dynamic connection string to be used to connect to SQL Server or Oracle. You complete the code for this utility in the next exercise.

Try It Out   Dynamic Connections

To create this utility:

1. Start Visual Studio 2005 and start a new project by either clicking the Project link on the Recent Projects tab of the Start page or by selecting File ➪ New ➪ Project.

2. In the New Project dialog box, select a Windows Application template and enter a project name of DB Migration Utility. Click OK to create this project.

3. Set the following properties for Form1:

   ❑ Set FormBorderStyle to Fixed Single.

   ❑ Set MaximizeBox to False.

   ❑ Set MinimizeBox to False.

   ❑ Set Size to **420, 288**.

   ❑ Set StartPosition to Center Screen.

   ❑ Set Text to **DB Migration Utility**.

4. Add a GroupBox control to the form and set its properties as follows:

   ❑ Set Location to **8, 8**.

   ❑ Set Size to **400, 152**.

   ❑ Set Text to **Database Connection**.

5. Add two RadioButton controls, five Label controls, four TextBox controls, and two Button controls to the GroupBox and arrange them to look similar to the controls shown on the form in Figure 8-1. Set the following properties of these controls:

   ❑ Set the Name property for RadioButton1 to **optSQLServer**, the Checked property to True, and the Text property to **SQL Server**.

   ❑ Set the Name property for RadioButton2 to **optOracle** and the Text property to **Oracle**.

   ❑ Set the Name property for Label1 to **lblServer** and the Text property to **Server**.

   ❑ Set the Name property for TextBox1 to **txtServer**.

   ❑ Set the Name property for Label2 to **lblDatabase** and the Text property to **Database**.

❑ Set the Name property for TextBox2 to **txtDatabase** and the Text property to **ProjectTimeTracker**.

❑ Set the Text property for Label3 to **Login Name**.

❑ Set the Name property for TextBox3 to **txtLoginName**.

❑ Set the Text property for Label4 to **Password**.

❑ Set the Name property for TextBox4 to **txtPassword** and the PasswordChar property to *.

❑ Set the Name property for Label5 to **lblStatus** and the Text property to **Database is not set**.

❑ Set the Name property for Button1 to **btnOpenConnection** and the Text property to **Open**.

❑ Set the Name property for Button2 to **btnCloseConnection** and the Text property to **Close**.

6. Add another GroupBox control to the form and set its properties as follows:

❑ Set Location to **8, 168**.

❑ Set Size to **400, 88**.

❑ Set Text to **Migrations**.

7. To the GroupBox just placed on your form, add two Button controls and two Label controls and arrange them to look similar to the controls shown on the form in Figure 8-1. Set the following properties for these controls:

❑ Set the Name property for Button1 to **btnGroups** and the Text property to **Groups**.

❑ Set the Name property for Label1 to **lblGroups** and the Text property to **Not Migrated**.

❑ Set the Name property for Button2 to **btnProjects** and the Text property to **Projects**.

❑ Set the Name property for Label2 to **lblProjects** and the Text property to **Not Migrated**.

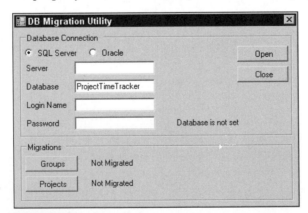

Figure 8-1

8. Right-click the DB Migration Utility project in the Solution Explorer and choose Add Reference from the context menu. In the Add Reference dialog box, scroll down and select the System.Data namespace and then click OK to have this reference added to your project.

9. Now it's time to take advantage of some of the productivity capabilities of Visual Studio 2005 by adding some application configuration settings and a WDABase class to your project just as you've used in your Time Tracker application. However, you don't want to have to recode all of that code or have to open the Time Tracker project and copy the code and paste it into this project. There's no need, as Visual Studio 2005 will do this for you automatically.

Right-click the DB Migration Utility project in Solution Explorer, select Add, and then select Add Existing Item. In the Add Existing Item – DB Migration Utility dialog box, browse to your Time Tracker project. In the Files of Type combo box, select All Files (*) so that you are able to see the app.config file. Then select the app.config file and click Add.

10. Visual Studio 2005 has made a copy of the app.config file from your Time Tracker project and added it to your DB Migration Utility project. You need to modify the section in the app.config file that is for the project name.

In the Solution Explorer, double-click the app.config file and then in the Code Editor under the applicationSettings section, replace all instances of Time_Tracker with DB_Migration_Utility throughout the file.

Now right-click the project in the Solution Explorer and choose Properties from the context menu. When the Property Page for the application is displayed, click the Settings tab on the left side. You receive a message dialog box informing you that Visual Studio 2005 has added the new values from your app.config file.

11. At this point, save your project to have these settings saved. Click the Save All button on the toolbar and then click the Save button in the Save Project dialog box.

12. Now add the WDABase class from your Time Tracker project by repeating the process outlined in the previous steps. When the Add Existing Item – DB Migration Utility dialog box appears, select VB Code Files in the Files of Type combo box so you can see the .vb files. Then select the WDABase.vb file and click Add to add it to your current project.

13. You want the WDABase class to be able to connect to your Access database and to SQL Server and Oracle. Therefore, you need to add an overloaded constructor for this class. Open the WDABase class in the Code Editor and add the following code:

```
Public Sub New(ByVal Provider As String, ByVal Server As String, _
    ByVal Database As String, ByVal Login As String, ByVal Password As String)

    'Build the SQL connection string and initialize the Connection object
    If Provider = "SQL Server" Then
        Connection = New OleDbConnection( _
            "Provider=SQLOLEDB;" & _
            "Data Source=" & Server & ";" & _
            "Database=" & Database & ";" & _
            "User ID=" & Login & ";" & _
            "Password=" & Password & ";")
    Else
        Connection = New OleDbConnection( _
            "Provider=MSDAORA;" & _
            "Data Source=" & Server & ";" & _
            "User ID=" & Login & ";" & _
            "Password=" & Password & ";")
    End If
End Sub
```

14. View the code for `Form1` and add the following form-level variable declarations:

```
'Private variables and objects
Private strProvider As String = "SQL Server"

Private objData As WDABase
Private objAccessDB As WDABase
```

15. Add a procedure that will be executed whenever the SQL Server radio button is clicked. In the Class Name combo box, select optSQLServer and in the Method Name combo box select the `CheckedChanged` event to add the `optSQLServer_CheckedChanged` procedure to your code. Add the following code to this procedure:

```
Private Sub optSQLServer_CheckedChanged(ByVal sender As Object, _
    ByVal e As System.EventArgs) Handles optSQLServer.CheckedChanged

    'Enable Labels and TextBoxes for SQL Server
    strProvider = "SQL Server"
    lblServer.Text = "Server"
    lblDatabase.Enabled = True
    txtDatabase.Enabled = True
    txtServer.Focus()
End Sub
```

16. You want to add the same procedure for the Oracle RadioButton control, so select optOracle in the Class Name combo box and select CheckedChanged in the Method Name combo box. Add the following code to this procedure:

```
Private Sub optOracle_CheckedChanged(ByVal sender As Object, _
    ByVal e As System.EventArgs) Handles optOracle.CheckedChanged

    'Disable Labels and TextBoxes for Oracle
    strProvider = "Oracle"
    lblServer.Text = "SID"
    lblDatabase.Enabled = False
    txtDatabase.Enabled = False
    txtServer.Focus()
End Sub
```

17. Add a procedure to handle the `Click` event for the Open button on your form. Select btnOpenConnection in the Class Name combo box and then select the `Click` event in the Method Name combo box. Add the following code to the `btnOpenConnection_Click` procedure:

```
Private Sub btnOpenConnection_Click(ByVal sender As Object, _
    ByVal e As System.EventArgs) Handles btnOpenConnection.Click

    'Initialize a new instance of the data access base class
    objData = New WDABase(strProvider, txtServer.Text, _
        txtDatabase.Text, txtLoginName.Text, txtPassword.Text)

    Try
        'Open the database connection
        objData.OpenConnection()
        'Set the status message
        lblStatus.Text = "Database opened"
    Catch ExceptionErr As Exception
        'Display the error
```

```
        MessageBox.Show(ExceptionErr.Message)
    End Try
End Sub
```

18. Finally, add a procedure to handle the Click event of the Close button on your form. Select btnCloseConnection in the Class Name combo box and select the `Click` event in the Method Name combo box. Add the following code to the `btnCloseConnection_Click` procedure:

```
Private Sub btnCloseConnection_Click(ByVal sender As Object, _
    ByVal e As System.EventArgs) Handles btnCloseConnection.Click

    'Close the database connection
    objData.CloseConnection()
    'Set the status message
    lblStatus.Text = "Database closed"
    'Cleanup
    objData.Dispose()
    objData = Nothing
End Sub
```

19. Now it's time to run this project to test it out, so start it up. When your form displays, it should look similar to the one shown in Figure 8-1. If you will be developing using SQL Server, enter the server name on which SQL Server is running in the Server field and enter your login credentials for SQL Server in the Login Name and Password fields. Click the Open button and when the database is successfully opened, you'll see the message `Database is not set` change to `Database opened`. Now click the Close button and you will see the message change to `Database closed`.

At this point, you have successfully verified that your dynamic database connection to SQL Server is working correctly, as you were able to open and close the database connection.

20. If you will be developing using an Oracle database, click the Oracle radio button. Notice that the Database Label and TextBox have been disabled, as shown in Figure 8-2. Also notice that the label that read "Server" for SQL Server now reads "SID" for Oracle.

21. Enter the system identifier defined in your `tnsnames.ora` file in the SID field and then enter your login credentials for Oracle in the Login Name and Password fields. Click the Open button and when the database is successfully opened, you see the message `Database is not set` change to `Database opened`. Now click the Close button and you see the message change to `Database closed`.

At this point you have successfully verified that your dynamic database connection to Oracle is working correctly, as you were able to open and close the database connection.

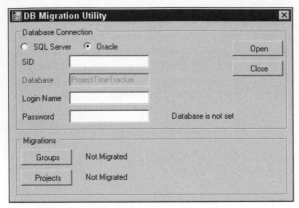

Figure 8-2

How It Works

The first fragment of code that you add is an overloaded constructor for the WDABase class. This procedure is considered an overloaded constructor because you already have a constructor for the WDABase class that does not accept any parameters and is used when connecting to an Access database. This constructor has the same name and accepts parameters, thus making it an overloaded constructor.

When you want to connect to SQL Server or Oracle, you initialize a new instance of the WDABase class using this constructor and pass it the information required to connect to either SQL Server or Oracle.

The first parameter in this procedure is the Provider parameter, which contains a value of either SQL Server or Oracle. The If...Then...Else statement in this procedure uses this information to build the appropriate connection string and initialize a new instance of the OleDbConnection class.

The next parameter for this procedure is the Server parameter, which contains the name of the server on which SQL Server is running or the SID defined in your tnsnames.ora file. The Database parameter contains the database name that exists in the Database name text box on your form, and is always passed. If you are connecting to Oracle, it is simply ignored and not used when building the connection string.

The Login and Password parameters always contain a value, as they are used for both SQL Server and Oracle.

```
Public Sub New(ByVal Provider As String, ByVal Server As String, _
    ByVal Database As String, ByVal Login As String, ByVal Password As String)
```

The If...Then...Else statement first checks the Provider parameter for a value of SQL Server. If the value in this parameter is equal to SQL Server, a dynamic connection string is built for SQL Server and the Connection object is initialized. Notice that the Provider parameter in the connection string is set to a value of SQLOLEDB. This is the provider that must be used when connecting to SQL Server.

If the Provider parameter for this procedure does not contain a value of SQL Server, the code inside the Else statement is executed, a dynamic connection for Oracle is built, and the Connection object is initialized. The `Provider` parameter in the connection string is set to a value of `MSDAORA` and this is the .NET provider that must be used when connecting to Oracle. Also notice that the `Database` parameter in the connection string has been omitted, as it is not needed for Oracle.

```
'Build the SQL connection string and initialize the Connection object
If Provider = "SQL Server" Then
    Connection = New OleDbConnection( _
        "Provider=SQLOLEDB;" & _
        "Data Source=" & Server & ";" & _
        "Database=" & Database & ";" & _
        "User ID=" & Login & ";" & _
        "Password=" & Password & ";")
Else
    Connection = New OleDbConnection( _
        "Provider=MSDAORA;" & _
        "Data Source=" & Server & ";" & _
        "User ID=" & Login & ";" & _
        "Password=" & Password & ";")
End If
End Sub
```

You start adding code to your form next by adding some variable declarations at the form level. These variables will be accessible to all procedures in the form. The first variable is the `strProvider` variable and has a default value set to `SQL Server`. This is the variable that you'll be passing to the overloaded constructor in the `WDABase` class.

This variable is set to a value of `SQL Server` when the SQL Server radio button is selected, and set to a value of `Oracle` when the Oracle radio button is selected. You set a default value for this variable because the form starts up with the SQL Server radio button already in a checked state and this variable would not be set to the appropriate value unless the SQL Server radio button were unchecked and then checked.

The other two variables were defined as objects for the `WDABase` class. The `objData` object will be used to access SQL Server or Oracle and the `objAccessDB` object will be used to access your Access database.

```
Private strProvider As String = "SQL Server"

Private objData As WDABase
Private objAccessDB As WDABase
```

Next, you add some code for the `CheckChanged` event for the SQL Server radio button. This procedure will be executed when the radio button is checked. It should be noted that the SQL Server radio button had the `Checked` property set to `True` at design time and this procedure is not executed when the form loads; hence you must set the `strProvider` variable with a default value.

The first thing that you do in this procedure is set the `strProvider` variable to the appropriate value. Then you set the Server Label to a value of `Server` and enable the label and text box for the database. Finally, you set focus to the Server field so you can start entering data.

```
Private Sub optSQLServer_CheckedChanged(ByVal sender As Object, _
    ByVal e As System.EventArgs) Handles optSQLServer.CheckedChanged

    'Enable Labels and TextBoxes for SQL Server
```

```
        strProvider = "SQL Server"
        lblServer.Text = "Server"
        lblDatabase.Enabled = True
        txtDatabase.Enabled = True
        txtServer.Focus()
End Sub
```

The CheckedChanged event for the Oracle radio button works in a similar manner except that instead of enabling fields, it disables fields. The first thing that you do in this procedure is set the strProvider variable to a value of Oracle. Then you change the Text property for the Server Label to a value of SID. Next you disable the label and text box for the Database field. Finally, you set focus to the Server field, for which you have changed the Text property, so you can start entering data.

```
    Private Sub optOracle_CheckedChanged(ByVal sender As Object, _
        ByVal e As System.EventArgs) Handles optOracle.CheckedChanged

        'Disable Labels and TextBoxes for Oracle
        strProvider = "Oracle"
        lblServer.Text = "SID"
        lblDatabase.Enabled = False
        txtDatabase.Enabled = False
        txtServer.Focus()
End Sub
```

You add code for the Open button next. Here you initialize a new instance of the WDABase class in your objData object, passing the constructor for the WDABase class the required parameters to be used to connect to SQL Server or Oracle.

Then you set up a Try...Catch block to which you add code to call the OpenConnection method on the objData object. Remember that the WDABase class throws an exception if it encounters any problems connecting to a database, so you want to handle those errors using a Try...Catch block.

If the database opens successfully, you change the message displayed on the form to Database opened.

If an error is encountered, you display a MessageBox dialog box with the appropriate error message.

```
    Private Sub btnOpenConnection_Click(ByVal sender As Object, _
        ByVal e As System.EventArgs) Handles btnOpenConnection.Click

        'Initialize a new instance of the data access base class
        objData = New WDABase(strProvider, txtServer.Text, _
            txtDatabase.Text, txtLoginName.Text, txtPassword.Text)

        Try
            'Open the database connection
            objData.OpenConnection()
            'Set the status message
            lblStatus.Text = "Database opened"
        Catch ExceptionErr As Exception
            'Display the error
            MessageBox.Show(ExceptionErr.Message)
        End Try
End Sub
```

The code that you add for the Close button is very simple. You close the database connection by calling the `CloseConnection` method on the `objData` object and then change the message on the form to indicate that the database connection is closed.

Next, you perform the appropriate cleanup by disposing of the `objData` object and setting it to `Nothing`.

```
Private Sub btnCloseConnection_Click(ByVal sender As Object, _
    ByVal e As System.EventArgs) Handles btnCloseConnection.Click

    'Close the database connection
    objData.CloseConnection()
    'Set the status message
    lblStatus.Text = "Database closed"
    'Cleanup
    objData.Dispose()
    objData = Nothing
End Sub
```

At this point, you can make a dynamic connection to both SQL Server and Oracle. You can also see the different parameters required in the connection string for both.

SQL Statement Parameters

Up until this point, you've added parameters to only the `Parameters` collection in the `OleDbCommand` object when executing queries. But did you know you can also use the `Parameters` collection when executing a SQL statement in a string? That's right — you can build a string that contains a SQL statement that accepts parameters and you can add the parameters for the SQL statement to the `Parameters` collection in the `OleDbCommand` object.

The key to this is to use placeholders in your SQL statement. A placeholder is nothing more than a question mark (?) where the actual value in the SQL statement should be. Take a look at the code snippet that follows.

The `INSERT` statement looks normal up until the point where you specify the values. Instead of specifying the actual values, you specify placeholders for the values. The actual values for these placeholders are added to the `Parameters` collection and in the same order that they are expected in the `INSERT` statement. That is, you add a `Parameter` that contains the value to be inserted into column1, then the `Parameter` for column2, followed by the `Parameter` for column3.

```
INSERT INTO myTable
    (column1, column2, column3)
    VALUES(?, ?, ?)
```

You may be wondering why you would want to code a SQL statement in this manner instead of just specifying the values directly in the `VALUE` clause. There are two reasons.

First, when you use a `Parameter` to specify the value, the `Parameter` class correctly handles special characters in the value that you are adding. For example, you know that you typically enclose string values in the VALUE clause with single quotes. But if the value that you are inserting contains a single quote, you must escape it. That is, you must replace all single quotes in your string with two single quotes in order for it to be handled properly by the database. The Add method of the Parameter class will handle this for you automatically.

The second reason is platform independence. Using a SQL statement in the manner described previously allows you to execute this SQL statement against Access, SQL Server, or Oracle without any code changes. One of the problems that you typically run into when inserting data into these databases has to do with the manner in which they handle date values. You can pass a date value to Access or SQL Server as a string and have it inserted properly. However, Oracle requires the date to be passed as a Date data type, which means you need to change your code for Oracle.

When you add the parameters to the Parameters collection, you do so in the manner in which you have become accustomed. The following code snippet shows how you would add the parameters to the Parameters collection for the INSERT statement previously shown using the WDABase class.

```
objCommand.AddParameter("@Column1", OleDbType.VarChar, 50, "value1")
objCommand.AddParameter("@Column2", OleDbType.LongVarChar, 6, "value2")
objCommand.AddParameter("@Column3", OleDbType.Date, 8, Date.Now())
```

In this next Try It Out, you are going to complete the functionality in your DB Migration Utility by reading the data from your Access ProjectTimeTracker database, building INSERT statements that accept parameters, and executing those INSERT statements against your SQL Server or Oracle database.

Try It Out   Executing SQL Statements with Parameters

To complete this exercise:

1. Open the DB Migration Utility project in Visual Studio 2005 if it is not already open.

2. Switch to the Code Editor for your form and select btnGroups in the Class Name combo box and then select the Click event in the Method Name combo box to add the btnGroups_Click procedure. Add the following code to this procedure:

```
Private Sub btnGroups_Click(ByVal sender As Object, _
    ByVal e As System.EventArgs) Handles btnGroups.Click

        'Initialize a new instance of the data access base class
        Using objAccessDB As New WDABase
            Try
                'Get all Groups in a DataReader object
                objAccessDB.SQL = "usp_SelectGroups"
                objAccessDB.InitializeCommand()
                objAccessDB.OpenConnection()
                objAccessDB.DataReader = objAccessDB.Command.ExecuteReader

                'See if any data exists before continuing
                If objAccessDB.DataReader.HasRows Then

                    'Build an INSERT SQL statement
                    objData.SQL = "INSERT INTO Groups " & _
                        "(GroupID, GroupName, GroupDescription, " & _
                        "LastUpdateDate)" & _
```

```
                    "VALUES(?, ?, ?, ?)"

            'Initialize the Command object
            objData.InitializeCommand()

            'Add empty parameters to the Parameters collection
            objData.AddParameter("GroupID", _
                Data.OleDb.OleDbType.Char, 36, Nothing)
            objData.AddParameter("GroupName", _
                Data.OleDb.OleDbType.VarChar, 50, Nothing)
            objData.AddParameter("GroupDescription", _
                Data.OleDb.OleDbType.LongVarChar, 1000, Nothing)
            objData.AddParameter("LastUpdateDate", _
                Data.OleDb.OleDbType.Date, 8, Nothing)

            'Process all rows
            While objAccessDB.DataReader.Read()

                'Set the parameter values
                objData.Command.Parameters("GroupID").Value = _
                    objAccessDB.DataReader.Item("GroupID").ToString
                objData.Command.Parameters("GroupName").Value = _
                    objAccessDB.DataReader.Item("GroupName")
                objData.Command.Parameters("GroupDescription").Size = _
                    objAccessDB.DataReader.Item( _
                    "GroupDescription").ToString.Length
                objData.Command.Parameters("GroupDescription").Value = _
                    objAccessDB.DataReader.Item("GroupDescription")
                objData.Command.Parameters("LastUpdateDate").Value = _
                    objAccessDB.DataReader.Item("LastUpdateDate")

                'Execute the INSERT statement
                objData.Command.ExecuteNonQuery()

            End While

        End If

        'Close the DataReader
        objAccessDB.DataReader.Close()

        'Close the database connection
        objAccessDB.CloseConnection()

        'Set the status message
        lblGroups.Text = "Data successfully migrated"
    Catch ExceptionErr As Exception
        MessageBox.Show(ExceptionErr.Message)
    Finally
        'Cleanup
        objData.Command.Dispose()
        objData.Command = Nothing
    End Try
End Using

End Sub
```

3. Now click the Class Name combo box and select btnProjects, and in the Method Name combo box select the `Click` event. Add the following code to the `btnProjects_Click` procedure:

```
Private Sub btnProjects_Click(ByVal sender As Object, _
    ByVal e As System.EventArgs) Handles btnProjects.Click
```

```
            'Initialize a new instance of the data access base class
            Using objAccessDB As New WDABase
                Try
                    'Get all Projects in a DataReader object
                    objAccessDB.SQL = "usp_SelectProjects"
                    objAccessDB.InitializeCommand()
                    objAccessDB.OpenConnection()
                    objAccessDB.DataReader = objAccessDB.Command.ExecuteReader

                    'See if any data exists before continuing
                    If objAccessDB.DataReader.HasRows Then

                        'Build an INSERT SQL statement
                        objData.SQL = "INSERT INTO Projects " & _
                            "(ProjectID, ProjectName, ProjectDescription, " & _
                            "SequenceNumber, LastUpdateDate) " & _
                            "VALUES(?, ?, ?, ?, ?)"

                        'Initialize the Command object
                        objData.InitializeCommand()

                        'Add empty parameters to the Parameters collection
                        objData.AddParameter("ProjectID", _
                            Data.OleDb.OleDbType.Char, 36, Nothing)
                        objData.AddParameter("ProjectName", _
                            Data.OleDb.OleDbType.VarChar, 50, Nothing)
                        objData.AddParameter("ProjectDescription", _
                            Data.OleDb.OleDbType.LongVarChar, 1000, Nothing)
                        objData.AddParameter("SequenceNumber", _
                            Data.OleDb.OleDbType.UnsignedTinyInt, 1, Nothing)
                        objData.AddParameter("LastUpdateDate", _
                            Data.OleDb.OleDbType.Date, 8, Nothing)

                        'Process all rows
                        While objAccessDB.DataReader.Read()

                            'Set the parameter values
                            objData.Command.Parameters("ProjectID").Value = _
                                objAccessDB.DataReader.Item("ProjectID").ToString
                            objData.Command.Parameters("ProjectName").Value = _
                                objAccessDB.DataReader.Item("ProjectName")
                            objData.Command.Parameters("ProjectDescription").Size = _
                                objAccessDB.DataReader.Item( _
                                "ProjectDescription").ToString.Length
                            objData.Command.Parameters("ProjectDescription").Value = _
                                objAccessDB.DataReader.Item("ProjectDescription")
                            objData.Command.Parameters("SequenceNumber").Value = _
                                objAccessDB.DataReader.Item("SequenceNumber")
                            objData.Command.Parameters("LastUpdateDate").Value = _
```

```
                    objAccessDB.DataReader.Item("LastUpdateDate")

                'Execute the INSERT statement
                objData.Command.ExecuteNonQuery()

            End While

        End If

        'Close the DataReader
        objAccessDB.DataReader.Close()

        'Close the database connection
        objAccessDB.CloseConnection()

        'Set the status message
        lblProjects.Text = "Data successfully migrated"
    Catch ExceptionErr As Exception
        MessageBox.Show(ExceptionErr.Message)
    Finally
        'Cleanup
        objData.Command.Dispose()
        objData.Command = Nothing
    End Try
End Using
End Sub
```

4. This is all the code that you need to begin migrating your data from Access to SQL Server or Oracle. Start your project and when your form displays, enter your database information for SQL Server or Oracle and click Open to open your database connection.

5. After your database connection is open click the Groups button to have the data migrated from Access to SQL Server or Oracle. When all of the data has been processed, you see a message indicating that the data was successfully migrated, as shown in Figure 8-3, which is migrating data to SQL Server.

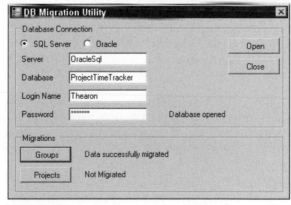

Figure 8-3

6. Now click the Projects button to have the projects data migrated from Access to either SQL Server or Oracle. When this data has been migrated you see a message that the data was successfully migrated, as shown in Figure 8-4, which is migrating data to Oracle.

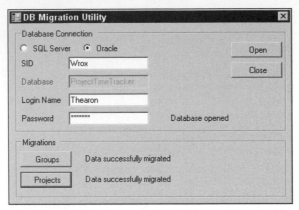

Figure 8-4

7. When you are done, click the Close button to close your database connection to SQL Server or Oracle and then close your form.

How It Works

You need to add only two procedures to complete the functionality for this project. The first procedure that you added was the btnGroups_Click procedure, which executes when you click the Groups button on your form. This procedure migrates the data from the Groups table in Access to the Groups table in SQL Server or Oracle, depending on which database you connected to.

The first thing that you do in this procedure is initialize a new instance of the WDABase class in your objAccessDB object in a Using...End Using block. This object will be used to access the data in your Access database.

```
Private Sub btnGroups_Click(ByVal sender As Object, _
    ByVal e As System.EventArgs) Handles btnGroups.Click

    'Initialize a new instance of the data access base class
    Using objAccessDB As New WDABase
```

Next, you set up a Try...Catch...Finally block to execute your database code in. The first thing that you need to do in the Try block is retrieve all the data from the Groups table in Access. You do this in the same manner as you did in your Time Tracker project, by executing the usp_SelectGroups query. You return your data in an OleDbDataReader object, so you maintain an open connection to two databases: Access and SQL Server or Oracle.

```
    Try
        'Get all Groups in a DataReader object
        objAccessDB.SQL = "usp_SelectGroups"
        objAccessDB.InitializeCommand()
        objAccessDB.OpenConnection()
        objAccessDB.DataReader = objAccessDB.Command.ExecuteReader
```

You know that data exists in the Groups table but it is good coding practice to always check the HasRows property of the DataReader object before continuing, and this is what you do in the next line of code.

If data exists, you set the SQL property of the objData object to the INSERT statement that you built. Notice the placeholders for the values that you'll be inserting using Parameters in the Parameters collection.

After the SQL property is set to your INSERT statement, you initialize the Command object using the InitializeCommand method of the objData object. You do this outside of the loop because you'll be executing the same INSERT statement repeatedly, changing only the values being inserted. Therefore, you need to initialize the Command object only once, saving the extra overhead of disposing of the Command object and initializing it again in every iteration of the loop.

```
'See if any data exists before continuing
If objAccessDB.DataReader.HasRows Then

    'Build an INSERT SQL statement
    objData.SQL = "INSERT INTO Groups " & _
        "(GroupID, GroupName, GroupDescription, " & _
        "LastUpdateDate)" & _
        "VALUES(?, ?, ?, ?)"

    'Initialize the Command object
    objData.InitializeCommand()
```

Because you need to add parameters to the Parameters collection, you also do that outside of the loop and only once. Once inside of the loop, you merely set the value of each Parameter, saving the extra processing of clearing and adding parameters.

The AddParameter method expects a certain number of parameters to be passed to it, with the last parameter being the value that should be set in the Parameter object. Because you don't want to set the value at this point, you are passing the Nothing keyword to the AddParameter method.

Remember that the GroupDescription column in Access was defined as a Memo field and you need to set the length of this Parameter using the actual length of the data being passed. Here you pass a default length of 1000 and set the actual length in the following loop:

```
'Add empty parameters to the Parameters collection
objData.AddParameter("GroupID", _
    Data.OleDb.OleDbType.Char, 36, Nothing)
objData.AddParameter("GroupName", _
    Data.OleDb.OleDbType.VarChar, 50, Nothing)
objData.AddParameter("GroupDescription", _
    Data.OleDb.OleDbType.LongVarChar, 1000, Nothing)
objData.AddParameter("LastUpdateDate", _
    Data.OleDb.OleDbType.Date, 8, Nothing)
```

Next, you set up a While...End While loop to process all of the data in the DataReader object. The first thing that you do here is set the Value property of the various Parameters in the Parameters collection. You do this by accessing the Command object through the objData object and then accessing the Parameters collection. You access each Parameter in the Parameters collection by using the name of the Parameter that you set in the preceding code. Then you set the Value property of the Parameter using the value contained in the DataReader object.

Before you set the `Value` property of the `GroupDescription Parameter`, you need to set the `Size` property to the size of the data actually being passed. You do this in the same manner as you did in your Time Tracker project by using the `Length` property of the `GroupDescription` item in the `DataReader`. Then you set the `Value` property for this `Parameter` to the actual value of the description.

When all parameter values are set, you execute the `INSERT` statement using the `ExecuteNonQuery` method of the `OleDbCommand` object that you learned about in the preceding chapter. Notice, however, that you do not capture the return value from this method to see how many rows are affected by the `INSERT` statement. At this point, you just want to dump the data in; you will verify it later.

```
'Process all rows
While objAccessDB.DataReader.Read()

    'Set the parameter values
    objData.Command.Parameters("GroupID").Value = _
        objAccessDB.DataReader.Item("GroupID").ToString
    objData.Command.Parameters("GroupName").Value = _
        objAccessDB.DataReader.Item("GroupName")
    objData.Command.Parameters("GroupDescription").Size = _
        objAccessDB.DataReader.Item( _
        "GroupDescription").ToString.Length
    objData.Command.Parameters("GroupDescription").Value = _
        objAccessDB.DataReader.Item("GroupDescription")
    objData.Command.Parameters("LastUpdateDate").Value = _
        objAccessDB.DataReader.Item("LastUpdateDate")

    'Execute the INSERT statement
    objData.Command.ExecuteNonQuery()

End While

End If
```

After all the data has been processed, you need to close the `DataReader` object by calling the `Close` method on it and then closing your database connection to Access. You keep your connection to SQL Server or Oracle open, as you open and close that connection using the buttons on your form. Next, you change the text being displayed in the label on your form to indicate that the migration of data was successful.

```
'Close the DataReader
objAccessDB.DataReader.Close()

'Close the database connection
objAccessDB.CloseConnection()

'Set the status message
lblGroups.Text = "Data successfully migrated"
```

Your `Catch` block simply displays a MessageBox dialog box with the error that occurred. The `Finally` block performs the necessary cleanup.

Keep the `objData` object because it has an open connection to SQL Server or Oracle and is used in the `btnProjects_Click` procedure. However, get rid of the `Command` object within the `objData` object. In this procedure, you set the Command object to a specific INSERT statement, add some parameters, and then reuse the Command object repeatedly in a loop. When you use the Command object in the btnProjects_Click procedure, you want to set its CommandText property to a different INSERT statement and add different Parameters to the Parameters collection.

Therefore, you call the Dispose method on the Command object within the objData object and set it to Nothing. You initialize a new instance of the Command object in the btnProjects_Click procedure when it is executed.

```
        Catch ExceptionErr As Exception
            MessageBox.Show(ExceptionErr.Message)
        Finally
            'Cleanup
            objData.Command.Dispose()
            objData.Command = Nothing
        End Try
    End Using
End Sub
```

When you click the Projects button on your form, the btnProjects_Click procedure is executed. This procedure looks exactly like the btnGroups_Click procedure except that it reads the project's data from your Access database and adds that data to your Projects table in SQL Server or Oracle. To that end, I'll just summarize the code in this procedure.

First, you initialize a new instance of the WDABase class in your objAccessDB object in a Using...End Using block. Then you set up a Try...Catch...Finally block. Inside of the Try block, you set the SQL property to the usp_SelectProjects query, initialize the Command object, open your database connection, and then retrieve the project data in a DataReader object.

```
    Private Sub btnProjects_Click(ByVal sender As Object, _
        ByVal e As System.EventArgs) Handles btnProjects.Click

        'Initialize a new instance of the data access base class
        Using objAccessDB As New WDABase
            Try
                'Get all Projects in a DataReader object
                objAccessDB.SQL = "usp_SelectProjects"
                objAccessDB.InitializeCommand()
                objAccessDB.OpenConnection()
                objAccessDB.DataReader = objAccessDB.Command.ExecuteReader
```

You check the HasRows property of the DataReader object and if it contains rows of data, you proceed. First, you set the SQL property of your objData object to the INSERT statement to insert projects in your SQL Server or Oracle database. Again, you are using placeholders in your INSERT statement for the values to be inserted. This indicates that the actual values will come from Parameters in the Parameters collection.

You initialize a new instance of the Command object next by calling the InitializeCommand method in your objData object. Then you proceed to add the required Parameters to the Parameters collection for your INSERT statement.

```
'See if any data exists before continuing
If objAccessDB.DataReader.HasRows Then

    'Build an INSERT SQL statement
    objData.SQL = "INSERT INTO Projects " & _
        "(ProjectID, ProjectName, ProjectDescription, " & _
        "SequenceNumber, LastUpdateDate) " & _
        "VALUES(?, ?, ?, ?, ?)"

    'Initialize the Command object
    objData.InitializeCommand()

    'Add empty parameters to the Parameters collection
    objData.AddParameter("ProjectID", _
        Data.OleDb.OleDbType.Char, 36, Nothing)
    objData.AddParameter("ProjectName", _
        Data.OleDb.OleDbType.VarChar, 50, Nothing)
    objData.AddParameter("ProjectDescription", _
        Data.OleDb.OleDbType.LongVarChar, 1000, Nothing)
    objData.AddParameter("SequenceNumber", _
        Data.OleDb.OleDbType.UnsignedTinyInt, 1, Nothing)
    objData.AddParameter("LastUpdateDate", _
        Data.OleDb.OleDbType.Date, 8, Nothing)
```

Inside of a `While...End While` loop, you process all the data in your `DataReader` object. You set the `Value` properties of your `Parameters` using the values contained in the `Item` property of your `DataReader` object. Then you execute the `INSERT` statement by calling the `ExecuteNonQuery` method on the `Command` object.

```
    'Process all rows
    While objAccessDB.DataReader.Read()

        'Set the parameter values
        objData.Command.Parameters("ProjectID").Value = _
            objAccessDB.DataReader.Item("ProjectID").ToString
        objData.Command.Parameters("ProjectName").Value = _
            objAccessDB.DataReader.Item("ProjectName")
        objData.Command.Parameters("ProjectDescription").Size = _
            objAccessDB.DataReader.Item( _
            "ProjectDescription").ToString.Length
        objData.Command.Parameters("ProjectDescription").Value = _
            objAccessDB.DataReader.Item("ProjectDescription")
        objData.Command.Parameters("SequenceNumber").Value = _
            objAccessDB.DataReader.Item("SequenceNumber")
        objData.Command.Parameters("LastUpdateDate").Value = _
            objAccessDB.DataReader.Item("LastUpdateDate")

        'Execute the INSERT statement
        objData.Command.ExecuteNonQuery()

    End While

End If
```

After you have processed all the data, you close the `DataReader` object and then close the connection to your Access database. Next, you update the label on your form to indicate that the data has been migrated:

```
'Close the DataReader
objAccessDB.DataReader.Close()

'Close the database connection
objAccessDB.CloseConnection()

'Set the status message
lblProjects.Text = "Data successfully migrated"
```

If an error occurs, you catch the error in the `Catch` block and display a MessageBox dialog box with the error received.

In the `Finally` block, you dispose of your `Command` object in your `objData` object:

```
Catch ExceptionErr As Exception
    MessageBox.Show(ExceptionErr.Message)
Finally
    'Cleanup
    objData.Command.Dispose()
    objData.Command = Nothing
End Try
    End Using
End Sub
```

At this point, all of the data in your Access database should be migrated into either your SQL Server or Oracle database.

Summary

In this chapter, you have migrated the existing data in your Access database to either SQL Server or Oracle, depending on which database you chose to use. During the process of migrating the data, you learned how to make a dynamic connection to SQL Server and Oracle. You saw firsthand the parameters required for a connection string for SQL Server and a connection string for Oracle.

During the course of migrating your data, you also learned more about SQL statements and how to use parameters in your SQL string. The placeholders for the parameters in your SQL string were filled with data by adding `Parameters` to the `Parameters` collection. This allowed the `Parameter` object to correctly handle any special characters in your data, such as a single quote. It also allowed for database independence in your code, enabling the use of the same SQL statement to insert data into SQL Server or Oracle.

To summarize, you should know:

❑   What parameters are required for a connection string for SQL Server and Oracle

❑   How to create placeholders in a SQL string for parameters

❑   How to add parameters to the `Parameters` collection for the parameter placeholders in your SQL string

In Chapter 9, you learn how to create and use stored procedures and views for SQL Server and Oracle. You also migrate the queries that exist in your `ProjectTimeTracker` Access database as stored procedures in SQL Server and Oracle.

Exercises

Exercise 1

Create a Windows application to select all Project IDs and Project Names from the Projects table in your SQL Server or Oracle database and display them in a list box. You can populate a `DataTable` with this data and bind it to a list box. Use your `WDABase` class from the DB Migration Utility in your new application. Refer to the Access SQL project from Chapter 5 for a refresher on populating a `DataTable`.

Tip: You'll need to remove the constructor in the `WDABase` class that was used to connect to an Access database.

Exercise 2

Using the application created in Exercise 1, add two labels and two text boxes to your form to display the Sequence Number and Last Update Date. When you click a project in the list, execute a `SELECT` statement with a parameter for the Project ID against your database to retrieve these values for the project selected in the list and display the data in the text boxes. Use a parameter in your `SELECT` statement as you did in the "Executing SQL Statements with Parameters" Try It Out exercise.

Stored Procedures and Views for SQL Server and Oracle

Now that you have data in your SQL Server or Oracle database, it's time to learn how to get more data into those databases and how to get data out of those databases to work with in your application. This is where stored procedures and views come into the picture.

In this chapter, you convert the existing queries in your `ProjectTimeTracker` Access database to stored procedures in SQL Server or Oracle. You learn more about stored procedures and how they relate to and differ from the queries that you wrote in Access. In addition, you write new stored procedures.

You also learn about views and how they can provide alternatives to stored procedures for selecting data. To that end, I cover what views are and how they can be used in your applications.

In this chapter, you:

❑   Learn how to create stored procedures for SQL Server and Oracle using Visual Studio 2005

❑   Learn how to create views for SQL Server and Oracle

❑   Leverage and expand your knowledge of ADO.NET, executing stored procedures and views from your VB 2005 application

❑   Enhance the Time Tracker application to use either a SQL Server or Oracle database

Stored Procedures

If you recall from Chapter 1, a *stored procedure* is a group of SQL statements compiled into an execution plan and stored under a unique name in the database. It is then executed as a unit. Stored procedures in SQL Server and Oracle are similar to queries in Access. However, stored procedures are much more flexible and powerful than queries are, as you discover in later chapters when you start implementing more complex stored procedures.

Each database vendor provides tools that enable you to work with the objects within their databases and to view and create stored procedures. For example, Microsoft provides the SQL Server Management Studio for SQL Server 2005, whereas Oracle provides SQL Plus (Windows application) and iSQL *Plus (Web application) for Oracle 10g.

However, Visual Studio 2005 also provides tools for viewing and creating stored procedures in SQL Server and Oracle. Although these tools are not as robust as the database vendors' tools, they do the job and enable you to develop database applications without having to leave the development environment.

In addition, you'll find that SQL Server is more tightly integrated with the Visual Studio 2005 development environment and provides more features for working with SQL Server than Oracle does. However, Oracle has developed the Oracle Developer Tools for .NET, which provides much improved functionality for working with Oracle databases from within the Visual Studio 2005 development environment. Visit its Web site at www.oracle.com for more information about this tool.

Before you begin using Visual Studio 2005 to develop stored procedures, take a look at the basic syntax for creating stored procedures in SQL Server and Oracle. The following example is a basic stored procedure that inserts group data into the Groups table in SQL Server:

```
CREATE PROCEDURE dbo.usp_InsertGroup
(
    @GroupID            UNIQUEIDENTIFIER,
    @GroupName          VARCHAR(50),
    @GroupDescription   TEXT
)
AS

INSERT INTO Groups
    (GroupID, GroupName, GroupDescription, LastUpdateDate)
    VALUES(@GroupID, @GroupName, @GroupDescription, GETDATE())
```

The INSERT statement for this stored procedure is similar to the INSERT statement that you created for your usp_InsertGroup query in Chapter 7. The only difference is instead of using the built-in Access function to insert a date and time into the LastUpdateDate column, you are using the built-in SQL Server function GETDATE().

When you built your Access query, you didn't need to specify the input parameters to the query or their data types. That is inferred by Access, and Access prompts you for them when running the query within Access. When you ran your query from your VB 2005 program, you knew what parameters to specify and the order in which to specify them based on their use in your INSERT statement. You also knew their data types as specified in the column definition when you created the tables. This is not the case with stored procedures.

You create a stored procedure with a CREATE PROCEDURE statement and then specify the input and/or output parameters to the stored procedure. You also specify the parameter data types as you want them submitted to your stored procedure. A case in point is the example stored procedure listed previously.

Another important point regarding input parameters and variables in general when dealing with SQL Server stored procedures is that the parameters and variables must begin with an at (@) sign as shown in the previous example. This identifies the parameters and variables as variables local to the stored procedure, unlike SQL Server's global variables, which begin with two at signs and are global to all stored procedures. You learn more about global variables in Chapter 11.

Let's examine the syntax of the previous example that creates a stored procedure for SQL Server. You must specify the statement CREATE PROCEDURE to create a new stored procedure in SQL Server. This is followed by the stored procedure name, which can be up to 128 characters in length.

Notice that in the previous example the stored procedure name has been prefixed with dbo. This indicates that this stored procedure is owned by the database owner and not the user who created the stored procedure. If you create a stored procedure without prefixing it with dbo, then the stored procedure is owned by you and will have your prefix assigned to the stored procedure in the database. No other users will be able to execute that stored procedure unless they specify the owner prefix when calling the stored procedure and you have given them permissions to execute that stored procedure.

You then specify the parameters for the stored procedure next and their data types. Enclosing the parameters in a set of parentheses is totally optional in SQL Server but will be done here to be consistent with Oracle, which does require them.

Each parameter begins with an at sign (@) followed by the name of the parameter. Each parameter has the data type of the parameter specified, and if the data type allows a varying number of characters or digits, that must also be specified. For example, the @GroupName parameter in the previous example specifies a data type of VARCHAR. Because this data type allows a varying number of characters, you must also specify the maximum number of characters allowed in the parameter.

After you have specified the CREATE PROCEDURE statement, the stored procedure prefix and name, and the parameters, you specify the AS keyword followed by the body of the stored procedure. The body of the stored procedure will be made up of one or more sets of SQL statements, such as the INSERT statement. The VALUES clause of the INSERT statement shown in the example contains the parameters as the source of input for the INSERT statement.

Now that you've had a look at how to create stored procedures in SQL Server, turn your attention to how a stored procedure is created in Oracle. An example of the usp_InsertGroup stored procedure for Oracle is shown here for reference:

```
CREATE OR REPLACE PROCEDURE usp_InsertGroup
(
    inGroupID            CHAR,
    inGroupName          VARCHAR2,
    inGroupDescription   CLOB
)
AS
BEGIN
INSERT INTO Groups
    (GroupID, GroupName, GroupDescription, LastUpdateDate)
    VALUES(inGroupID, inGroupName, inGroupDescription, SYSDATE);
END;
```

In Oracle, you specify the CREATE OR REPLACE PROCEDURE statement to create a stored procedure, followed by the stored procedure name. You should note that a stored procedure name in Oracle is l imited to 30 characters. Also notice that this stored procedure has no prefix applied because your login in Oracle is assigned to a specific schema (i.e. database) and all stored procedures created by you will be available to all users in that schema.

Next, you must specify the stored procedure parameters inside a set of parentheses. Each parameter is given a name, followed by the data type of the parameter. Note that an at sign (@) is an illegal character in Oracle so the parameters in the previous example have been prefixed with the word in to indicate that these are input parameters. Also note that you do not specify the size of the data type for data types that allow a varying number of characters.

After you have specified the parameters for the stored procedure, you specify the AS keyword and then specify the BEGIN clause. This is followed by the body of the stored procedure, and the BEGIN clause is terminated with a matching END clause and a semicolon.

The body of the stored procedure in this example contains the INSERT statement, which you have become very familiar with. The VALUES clause for this INSERT statement contains the parameters for the stored procedure as the source of input for the INSERT statement. The complete INSERT statement is terminated with a semicolon. It is important to note that every SQL statement in Oracle must be terminated with a semicolon character.

As you can see from the two previous examples, the stored procedure in SQL Server is not all that different from the stored procedure in Oracle. The INSERT statement is the same and uses the parameters for the stored procedure as the source of input for the VALUES clause. There are very minor differences in the syntax for creating a stored procedure in SQL Server and Oracle, as you saw in the previous examples.

Oracle packages

The Oracle stored procedure that you examined previously works well as a stored procedure that inserts data into a table. In fact, stored procedures that insert, update, and delete data in Oracle work in the same manner as they do for SQL Server. You call the stored procedure from your code and pass it the required parameters and the data is inserted, updated, or deleted.

However, the major difference between SQL Server and Oracle becomes apparent when you are using a stored procedure to return data. This is a stored procedure that executes a SQL SELECT statement and returns the results of the SELECT statement back to the caller. Stored procedures that execute SELECT statements in SQL Server behave just like the queries you wrote in Access that execute SELECT statements. However, to have a stored procedure in Oracle return data from a SELECT statement, you must encapsulate the stored procedure in a package.

A *package* in Oracle can be thought of in the same terms as a class in VB 2005. A package, like a class in VB 2005, can contain variables, functions, and procedures. In fact, your package can even contain overloaded stored procedures. That is, multiple stored procedures that are defined with the same name but each stored procedure accepts a different number of parameters.

However, for our discussion here, you examine a simple package that contains a single variable declaration and a single stored procedure. The package itself contains the definition for the stored procedure along with its parameters. However, the stored procedure is created in what is known as the *package body*. Every package contains the definition of the stored procedures within it and the package body contains the actual stored procedures.

Take a look at an example of a package that will perform the same function as your usp_SelectGroups query in Access. The code that follows creates a package that defines a variable named CURSOR_TYPE as a REF CURSOR and a stored procedure definition named usp_SelectGroups. Then the package body is created, and within the package body, the actual stored procedure is created.

A REF CURSOR is a cursor variable in Oracle that can be used by a stored procedure to return data. The stored procedure opens the cursor and populates the cursor with data from the SELECT statement. Then the application that calls the stored procedure fetches the data from the cursor.

```
CREATE OR REPLACE PACKAGE GroupsPackage
AS
   TYPE CURSOR_TYPE IS REF CURSOR;
   PROCEDURE usp_SelectGroups (results_cursor OUT CURSOR_TYPE);
END;
/
CREATE OR REPLACE PACKAGE BODY GroupsPackage
AS
   PROCEDURE usp_SelectGroups (results_cursor OUT CURSOR_TYPE)
   AS
   BEGIN
     OPEN results_cursor FOR
        SELECT GroupID, GroupName, GroupDescription, LastUpdateDate
        FROM Groups
        ORDER BY GroupName;
   END;
END;
/
```

Creating a package is a two-step process. First, you create the package itself using the CREATE OR REPLACE PACKAGE statement followed by the name of the package, which in this example is GroupsPackage. This is followed by the AS keyword and the definition of the package.

The definition of this package contains a variable declaration with a variable named CURSOR_TYPE and is defined as a REF CURSOR. Then the stored procedure definition is specified with the PROCEDURE clause and the name of the stored procedure, along with its parameters, direction, and type. You can distinguish input and output parameters by the inclusion of the OUT keyword. Input parameters can contain the IN keyword but this is the default, and if not specified, the parameter is assumed to be an input parameter. You end the package with the END keyword and a semicolon.

Before you can create the package body, the package itself must be created. You need to signal to Oracle to execute the batch of statements to create the package before creating the package body. You accomplish this by using a forward slash (/). This signals Oracle to execute the preceding batch of statements and to commit them before continuing to the next set of statements, which create the package body.

The package body is created by using the CREATE OR REPLACE PACKAGE BODY statement followed by the package name, which is the package that this package body will belong to. This is followed by the AS keyword and then the statements to create the stored procedures for the package, which in this case is only one stored procedure.

Because the stored procedure is part of a package body, you specify only the PROCEDURE statement to create the stored procedure, followed by the stored procedure name and the parameters for the stored procedure contained in parentheses. Then, the AS keyword is specified, followed by the BEGIN clause.

Next comes the body of the stored procedure. In this example, you must open the cursor using the OPEN statement followed by the cursor name, which is the output parameter to this stored procedure. This is followed by the FOR keyword and then the SELECT statement. The SELECT statement will select all data from the Groups table and place the results of that SELECT statement in the cursor.

The stored procedure is terminated by an END clause and the package body is also terminated by the END clause. Another forward slash has been included so that Oracle will immediately create the package body and commit those statements before it proceeds to the next statement (in this case, there are none.) This is just a good coding habit to get into when executing multiple statements in Oracle to prevent unnecessary errors.

Enough about packages and stored procedures; now it's time to get your feet wet with hands-on exercises.

In this Try It Out, you create stored procedures in SQL Server and stored procedures and packages in Oracle that mirror the functionality of the queries that currently exist in your `ProjectTimeTracker` Access database.

The steps in this exercise and the exercises to come will tell you when something is specific to SQL Server and when something is specific to Oracle. This will enable a single set of instructions to be used by all readers, regardless of the database that you are using.

Try It Out   Creating Stored Procedures and Packages

To create your stored procedures:

1. Start Visual Studio 2005 if it is not started. You do not need a project open to complete this exercise, so you can close any existing project that you may have open.

2. View the Server Explorer window and click the Auto Hide icon on the window to keep it visible.

3. Right-click Data Connections and choose Add Connection from the context menu.

4. In the Add Connection dialog box, click the Change button.

5. In the Change Data Source dialog box, select Microsoft SQL Server if you are working with SQL Server or Oracle Database if you working with Oracle. Then click OK to return to the Add Connection dialog box.

6. If you are working with SQL Server, select the server name in the Server Name combo box where SQL Server is running. If you are using Oracle, then enter the SID defined in your `tnsnames.ora` file.

7. To keep things simple and as consistent as possible, those users who are using SQL Server should use SQL Server Authentication so select the Use SQL Server Authentication option button. All readers should enter their user name and password for the database that they are using and then check the Save my password check box.

8. This step is only for those readers using SQL Server. Select the ProjectTimeTracker database in the Select or enter database name combo box.

9. All readers should now click the Test Connection button to test your connection and you should receive a dialog box informing you that your test connection succeeded. If there were problems, please verify your server name (SID in the case or Oracle) and user credentials. Click OK when you are done.

10. View the Stored Procedures node for your database by expanding your new data connection in the Server Explorer and then click the Stored Procedures node for SQL Server or the Procedures node for Oracle. Of course you have not created any stored procedures yet so there will not be any listed. Future reference to the Stored Procedures node in the following steps and throughout the rest of this book will mean the Procedures node in Oracle.

11. There are ten queries in Access that you need to create as stored procedures in your SQL Server or Oracle database. Readers using SQL Server should right-click the Stored Procedures node and choose Add New Stored Procedure. This causes a stored procedure template to be added to Visual Studio 2005.

Readers using Oracle will need to use their favorite Oracle tool for creating stored procedures such as iSQL *Plus.

Enter the following code:

SQL Server

```
CREATE PROCEDURE usp_DeleteGroup
(
    @GroupID    UNIQUEIDENTIFIER
)
AS
DELETE FROM Groups
WHERE GroupID = @GroupID
```

Click the Save icon on the toolbar to create the stored procedure. You'll see that the `usp_DeleteGroup` stored procedure has been added to the Stored Procedures node in Server Explorer.

Oracle

```
CREATE OR REPLACE PROCEDURE usp_DeleteGroup
(
    inGroupID    CHAR
)
AS
BEGIN
DELETE FROM Groups
WHERE GroupID = inGroupID;
END;
```

Click the Execute button to have the stored procedure created in your database. You'll see that the `usp_DeleteGroup` stored procedure has been added to the Procedures node in Server Explorer.

12. To create the `usp_DeleteProject` stored procedure, SQL Server users should right-click the Stored Procedures node in the Server Explorer and choose Add New Stored Procedure and Oracle users should use their Oracle tool. Enter the following code:

SQL Server

```
CREATE PROCEDURE usp_DeleteProject
(
    @ProjectID    UNIQUEIDENTIFIER
)
AS
DELETE FROM Projects
WHERE ProjectID = @ProjectID
```

185

Click the Save icon on the toolbar to have the stored procedure created in your database.

Oracle

```
CREATE OR REPLACE PROCEDURE usp_DeleteProject
(
    inProjectID    CHAR
)
AS
BEGIN
DELETE FROM Projects
WHERE ProjectID = inProjectID;
END;
```

Click the Execute button to have the stored procedure created in your database.

13. To create the `usp_InsertGroup` stored procedure, SQL Server users should right-click the Stored Procedures node in the Server Explorer and choose Add New Stored Procedure and Oracle users should use their Oracle tool. Enter the following code:

SQL Server

```
CREATE PROCEDURE usp_InsertGroup
(
    @GroupID              UNIQUEIDENTIFIER,
    @GroupName            VARCHAR(50),
    @GroupDescription     TEXT
)
AS
INSERT INTO Groups
    (GroupID, GroupName, GroupDescription, LastUpdateDate)
    VALUES(@GroupID, @GroupName, @GroupDescription, GETDATE())
```

Click the Save icon on the toolbar to have the stored procedure created in your database.

Oracle

```
CREATE OR REPLACE PROCEDURE usp_InsertGroup
(
    inGroupID            CHAR,
    inGroupName          VARCHAR2,
    inGroupDescription   CLOB
)
AS
BEGIN
INSERT INTO Groups
    (GroupID, GroupName, GroupDescription, LastUpdateDate)
    VALUES(inGroupID, inGroupName, inGroupDescription, SYSDATE);
END;
```

Click the Execute button to have the stored procedure created in your database.

14. To create the `usp_InsertProject` stored procedure, SQL Server users should right-click the Stored Procedures node in the Server Explorer and choose Add New Stored Procedure and Oracle users should use their Oracle tool. Enter the following code:

SQL Server

```
CREATE PROCEDURE usp_InsertProject
(
    @ProjectID              UNIQUEIDENTIFIER,
    @ProjectName            VARCHAR(50),
    @ProjectDescription     TEXT,
    @SequenceNumber         TINYINT
)
AS
INSERT INTO Projects
    (ProjectID, ProjectName, ProjectDescription, SequenceNumber,
      LastUpdateDate)
    VALUES(@ProjectID, @ProjectName, @ProjectDescription, @SequenceNumber,
      GETDATE())
```

Click the Save icon on the toolbar to have the stored procedure created in your database.

Oracle

```
CREATE OR REPLACE PROCEDURE usp_InsertProject
(
    inProjectID             CHAR,
    inProjectName           VARCHAR2,
    inProjectDescription    CLOB,
    inSequenceNumber        NUMBER
)
AS
BEGIN
INSERT INTO Projects
    (ProjectID, ProjectName, ProjectDescription, SequenceNumber,
      LastUpdateDate)
    VALUES(inProjectID, inProjectName, inProjectDescription, inSequenceNumber,
      SYSDATE);
END;
```

Click the Execute button to have the stored procedure created in your database.

15. The next stored procedure that you create is the usp SelectGroup stored procedure. Because this stored procedure returns data, readers using Oracle need to create a package, whereas readers using SQL Server just create a stored procedure.

SQL Server

Right-click the Stored Procedures node and choose Add New Stored Procedure from the context menu. Enter the following code:

```
CREATE PROCEDURE usp_SelectGroup
(
    @GroupID    UNIQUEIDENTIFIER
)
AS
SELECT GroupID, GroupName, GroupDescription, LastUpdateDate
FROM Groups
WHERE GroupID = @GroupID
```

Click the Save icon on the toolbar to create the stored procedure in your database.

Oracle

Using your Oracle tool, enter the following code:

```
CREATE OR REPLACE PACKAGE GroupPackage
AS
    TYPE CURSOR_TYPE IS REF CURSOR;
    PROCEDURE usp_SelectGroup (inGroupID IN CHAR,
        results_cursor OUT CURSOR_TYPE);
END;
```

Click the Execute button to have the package created in your database.

Now enter the following code to create the package body:

```
CREATE OR REPLACE PACKAGE BODY GroupPackage
AS
    PROCEDURE usp_SelectGroup (inGroupID IN CHAR,
        results_cursor OUT CURSOR_TYPE)
    AS
    BEGIN
    OPEN results_cursor FOR
    SELECT GroupID, GroupName, GroupDescription, LastUpdateDate
    FROM Groups
    WHERE GroupID = inGroupID;
    END;
END;
```

Click the Execute button to have the package body created in your database.

16. The `usp_SelectGroups` stored procedure also returns data so readers using SQL Server just create a stored procedure, whereas readers using Oracle need to create a package.

SQL Server

Right-click the Stored Procedures node and choose Add New Stored Procedure from the context menu. Enter the following code:

```
CREATE PROCEDURE usp_SelectGroups
AS
SELECT GroupID, GroupName, GroupDescription, LastUpdateDate
FROM Groups
ORDER BY GroupName
```

Click the Save icon on the toolbar to create the stored procedure in your database.

Oracle

Using your Oracle tool, enter the following code:

```
CREATE OR REPLACE PACKAGE GroupsPackage
AS
    TYPE CURSOR_TYPE IS REF CURSOR;
    PROCEDURE usp_SelectGroups (results_cursor OUT CURSOR_TYPE);
END;
```

Click the Execute button to have the package created in your database.

Now enter the following code to create the package body:

```
CREATE OR REPLACE PACKAGE BODY GroupsPackage
AS
    PROCEDURE usp_SelectGroups (results_cursor OUT CURSOR_TYPE)
    AS
    BEGIN
    OPEN results_cursor FOR
    SELECT GroupID, GroupName, GroupDescription, LastUpdateDate
    FROM Groups
    ORDER BY GroupName;
    END;
END;
```

Click the Execute button to have the package body created in your database.

17. The `usp_SelectProject` stored procedure requires a stored procedure in SQL Server and a package in Oracle.

SQL Server

Right-click the Stored Procedures node and choose Add New Stored Procedure from the context menu. Enter the following code:

```
CREATE PROCEDURE usp_SelectProject
(
    @ProjectID    UNIQUEIDENTIFIER
)
AS
SELECT ProjectID, ProjectName, ProjectDescription, SequenceNumber, LastUpdateDate
FROM Projects
WHERE ProjectID = @ProjectID
```

Click the Save icon on the toolbar to create the stored procedure in your database.

Oracle

Using your Oracle tool, enter the following code:

```
CREATE OR REPLACE PACKAGE ProjectPackage
AS
    TYPE CURSOR_TYPE IS REF CURSOR;
    PROCEDURE usp_SelectProject (inProjectID IN CHAR,
        results_cursor OUT CURSOR_TYPE);
END;
```

Click the Execute button to have the package created in your database.

Now enter the following code to create the package body:

```
CREATE OR REPLACE PACKAGE BODY ProjectPackage
AS
    PROCEDURE usp_SelectProject (inProjectID IN CHAR,
        results_cursor OUT CURSOR_TYPE)
    AS
    BEGIN
```

```
    OPEN results_cursor FOR
    SELECT ProjectID, ProjectName, ProjectDescription, SequenceNumber,
      LastUpdateDate
    FROM Projects
    WHERE ProjectID = inProjectID;
    END;
END;
```

Click the Execute button to have the package body created in your database.

18. The last stored procedure that returns data is the `usp_SelectProjects` stored procedure. This will be a stored procedure in SQL Server and a package in Oracle.

SQL Server

Right-click the Stored Procedures node and choose Add New Stored Procedure. Enter the following code:

```
CREATE PROCEDURE usp_SelectProjects
AS
SELECT ProjectID, ProjectName, ProjectDescription, SequenceNumber, LastUpdateDate
FROM Projects
ORDER BY SequenceNumber
```

Click the Save icon on the toolbar to create the stored procedure in your database.

Oracle

Using your Oracle tool, enter the following code:

```
CREATE OR REPLACE PACKAGE ProjectsPackage
AS
    TYPE CURSOR_TYPE IS REF CURSOR;
    PROCEDURE usp_SelectProjects (results_cursor OUT CURSOR_TYPE);
END;
```

Click the Execute button to have the package created in your database.

Now enter the following code to create the package body:

```
CREATE OR REPLACE PACKAGE BODY ProjectsPackage
AS
    PROCEDURE usp_SelectProjects (results_cursor OUT CURSOR_TYPE)
    AS
    BEGIN
    OPEN results_cursor FOR
    SELECT ProjectID, ProjectName, ProjectDescription, SequenceNumber,
      LastUpdateDate
    FROM Projects
    ORDER BY SequenceNumber;
    END;
END;
```

Click the Execute button to have the package body created in your database.

19. To create the `usp_UpdateGroup` stored procedure, SQL Server users should right-click the Stored Procedures node in the Server Explorer and choose Add New Stored Procedure and Oracle users should use their Oracle tool. Enter the following code:

SQL Server

```
CREATE PROCEDURE usp_UpdateGroup
(
    @GroupName          VARCHAR(50),
    @GroupDescription   TEXT,
    @GroupID            UNIQUEIDENTIFIER
)
AS
UPDATE Groups
SET GroupName = @GroupName,
    GroupDescription = @GroupDescription,
    LastUpdateDate = GETDATE()
WHERE GroupID = @GroupID
```

Click the Save icon on the toolbar to have the stored procedure created in your database.

Oracle

```
CREATE OR REPLACE PROCEDURE usp_UpdateGroup
(
    inGroupName         VARCHAR2,
    inGroupDescription  CLOB,
    inGroupID           CHAR
)
AS
BEGIN
UPDATE Groups
SET GroupName = inGroupName,
    GroupDescription = inGroupDescription,
    LastUpdateDate = SYSDATE
WHERE GroupID = inGroupID;
END;
```

Click the Execute button to have the stored procedure created in your database.

20. The final stored procedure that needs to be created is the usp_UpdateProject stored procedure. SQL Server users should right-click the Stored Procedures node in the Server Explorer and choose Add New Stored Procedure and Oracle users should use their Oracle tool. Enter the following code:

SQL Server

```
CREATE PROCEDURE usp_UpdateProject
(
    @ProjectName         VARCHAR(50),
    @ProjectDescription  TEXT,
    @SequenceNumber      TINYINT,
    @ProjectID           UNIQUEIDENTIFIER
)
AS
UPDATE Projects
SET ProjectName = @ProjectName,
    ProjectDescription = @ProjectDescription,
    SequenceNumber = @SequenceNumber,
    LastUpdateDate = GETDATE()
WHERE ProjectID = @ProjectID
```

Click the Save icon on the toolbar to have the stored procedure created in your database.

Oracle

```
CREATE OR REPLACE PROCEDURE usp_UpdateProject
(
    inProjectName           VARCHAR2,
    inProjectDescription    CLOB,
    inSequenceNumber        NUMBER,
    inProjectID             CHAR
)
AS
BEGIN
UPDATE Projects
SET ProjectName = inProjectName,
    ProjectDescription = inProjectDescription,
    SequenceNumber = inSequenceNumber,
    LastUpdateDate = SYSDATE
WHERE ProjectID = inProjectID;
END;
```

Click the Execute button to have the stored procedure created in your database.

How It Works

Because there are so many stored procedures and packages, I won't cover them all, as you already know how basic SQL statements work. This section describes how a few stored procedures and packages are created.

The first thing that you do is view the Server Explorer window, which enables you to connect to and view the objects in your database. After you create your database connection, you are then able to expand the nodes in your database and view and create stored procedures.

The first stored procedure that I want to cover is the usp_DeleteGroup stored procedure. When you create this stored procedure for SQL Server, you specify the CREATE PROCEDURE statement followed by the stored procedure name. Then you include the input parameter for this stored procedure in parentheses and specify the input parameter name followed by the data type. Remember that parameters and local variable names in SQL Server must begin with an at (@) sign.

You specify the AS keyword next and then specify the body of your stored procedure, which is the same SQL statement that you saw when you created the corresponding query in Access:

```
CREATE PROCEDURE usp_DeleteGroup
(
    @GroupID    UNIQUEIDENTIFIER
)
AS
DELETE FROM Groups
WHERE GroupID = @GroupID
```

Readers using Oracle create a stored procedure that is very similar to SQL Server's. First you specify the CREATE OR REPLACE PROCEDURE statement followed by the stored procedure name. Then you enclose the input parameter to this stored procedure in parentheses. Because the at (@) sign is an illegal character in

Oracle, you prefix the input parameter name with the word in. The data type for the GroupID column in Oracle is defined as a CHAR(36) data type, so you specify the CHAR data type for the input parameter. Remember that you do not specify the number of characters in a data type in your input parameters.

You then specify the AS keyword and enclose the body of your stored procedure in the BEGIN...END statement. Also note that you terminate your statements with a semicolon.

```
CREATE OR REPLACE PROCEDURE usp_DeleteGroup
(
    inGroupID    CHAR
)
AS
BEGIN
DELETE FROM Groups
WHERE GroupID = inGroupID;
END;
```

Note to all readers: The different data types and how they map between Access, SQL Server, and Oracle are covered in Appendix A.

The last stored procedure that I want to cover here is the usp_SelectProject stored procedure. This is a stored procedure in SQL Server and created within a package in Oracle.

Take a look at the stored procedure in SQL Server first: You create this stored procedure in the same manner as you do all other stored procedures in SQL Server. The reason behind this is that stored procedures in SQL Server can return data natively without any special processing, unlike Oracle. This will not only be evident here when creating this stored procedure but also in your code when executing it.

This stored procedure requires a single input parameter and will select a specific row of data from the Groups table based on the Group ID specified in the input parameter.

```
CREATE PROCEDURE usp_SelectGroup
(
    @GroupID    UNIQUEIDENTIFIER
)
AS
SELECT GroupID, GroupName, GroupDescription, LastUpdateDate
FROM Groups
WHERE GroupID = @GroupID
```

To create this stored procedure in Oracle, you have to encapsulate it within a package because this stored procedure returns data, and to have the stored procedure return data, you must open and use a REF CURSOR to return the data to the caller.

When using Visual Studio 2005 to create a package and package body, you must create each one separately. They cannot be created together as they were in the example shown earlier in the discussion on Oracle packages. The example shown earlier will work when creating a package and package body using your Oracle tools, such as iSQL *Plus or SQL Plus.

To create the GroupPackage in Oracle, you specify the CREATE OR REPLACE PACKAGE statement, followed by the package name. You follow this with the AS keyword and then specify a variable declaration for your REF CURSOR and the definition for your stored procedure, along with its parameters.

The usp_SelectGroup stored procedure is slightly different from the usp_SelectGroups stored procedure described in our discussion on Oracle packages. This stored procedure not only returns data, it also accepts an input parameter to limit the amount of data that it will return. This is evident by the presence of the input parameter inGroupID.

```
CREATE OR REPLACE PACKAGE GroupPackage
AS
    TYPE CURSOR_TYPE IS REF CURSOR;
    PROCEDURE usp_SelectGroup (inGroupID IN CHAR,
        results_cursor OUT CURSOR_TYPE);
END;
```

After the package is created, you have to create the package body separately. This is done using the CREATE OR REPLACE PACKAGE BODY statement, followed by the package name and the AS keyword.

You then create the usp_SelectGroup stored procedure within the package body by specifying the PROCEDURE statement followed by the stored procedure name and its parameters, both input and output. Notice that you specify both the IN and OUT keywords for your parameters. While it is not necessary to specify the IN keyword for input parameters, it does help document your parameters when your stored procedure contains both input and output parameters.

The input parameter is defined as a CHAR data type, while the output parameter is defined as a CURSOR_TYPE parameter, which is the variable defined in your package as a REF CURSOR. The SQL statements in the package body are enclosed around the BEGIN...END statement.

```
CREATE OR REPLACE PACKAGE BODY GroupPackage
AS
    PROCEDURE usp_SelectGroup (inGroupID IN CHAR,
        results_cursor OUT CURSOR_TYPE)
    AS
    BEGIN
    OPEN results_cursor FOR
    SELECT GroupID, GroupName, GroupDescription, LastUpdateDate
    FROM Groups
    WHERE GroupID = inGroupID;
    END;
END;
```

The GroupsPackage package and package body that you create are the same as the ones shown in the example for the discussion on Oracle packages. The ProjectPackage is similar to the GroupPackage discussed previously, and the ProjectsPackage is similar to the GroupsPackage.

At this point, you have all of the stored procedures that existed in your ProjectTimeTracker Access database in your SQL Server or Oracle database. The database has also been populated with the data that existed in your Access database so you are ready to modify your Time Tracker application to use either your SQL Server or Oracle database.

In this Try It Out, you modify your Time Tracker application to access either SQL Server or Oracle. If you want to follow along and use both databases, then you need to make a copy of your Time Tracker application so one copy can access SQL Server and one copy can access Oracle.

Try It Out   Accessing SQL Server or Oracle

To modify your application:

1. Open your Time Tracker application in Visual Studio 2005.

2. Right-click the project in the Solution Explorer and choose Properties from the context menu. When the Property Page is displayed, click the Settings tab on the left. Make the following modifications:

- ❑ Set `Provider` to **Nothing**.
- ❑ Set `DataSource` to *myServer*.
- ❑ Set `InitialCatalog` to **ProjectTimeTracker**.
- ❑ Set `UserID` to *myUserID*.
- ❑ Set `Password` to *myPassword*.

In the previous list, change the value of `myServer` to the server name on which SQL Server is running (if you are using SQL Server). If you are running an instance of SQL Server, this will be your server name followed by a backslash and the instance name—for example: `myServer\myInstance`. If you are using Oracle, the value of `myServer` will be the system identifier (SID) defined in your `tnsnames.ora` file.

The InitialCatalog key can be set to the value shown previously for Oracle or to a value of Nothing. This parameter is ignored for Oracle when building the connection string.

Change the value of *myUserID* to the User ID used to log into your database and change the value of *myPassword* to your password.

3. Now you need to make some modifications to the `WDABase` class, so view the code for it and modify the `Imports` statements as follows:

SQL Server

```
Imports System.Data
Imports System.Data.SqlClient
```

Oracle

Right-click the project in Solution Explorer and choose Add Reference from the context menu.

In the Add Reference dialog box, scroll down the list on the .NET tab until you see `System.Data.OracleClient` and then select it. Then click OK to add this reference to your project.

Now modify your `Imports` statements as follows:

```
Imports System.Data  ,
Imports System.Data.OracleClient
```

4. Modify the following `Public` variables in your class:

SQL Server

```
Public Connection As SqlConnection
Public Command As SqlCommand
Public DataAdapter As SqlDataAdapter
Public DataReader As SqlDataReader
```

Oracle

```
Public Connection As OracleConnection
Public Command As OracleCommand
Public DataAdapter As OracleDataAdapter
Public DataReader As OracleDataReader
```

5. Modify the constructor for your Connection object in the New procedure as follows. Note that the Database parameter is not needed for Oracle:

SQL Server

```
Connection = New SqlConnection( _
    "Data Source=" & My.Settings.DataSource & ";" & _
    "Database=" & My.Settings.InitialCatalog & ";" & _
    "User ID=" & My.Settings.UserID & ";" & _
    "Password=" & My.Settings.Password & ";")
```

Oracle

```
Connection = New OracleConnection( _
    "Data Source=" & My.Settings.DataSource & ";" & _
    "User ID=" & My.Settings.UserID & ";" & _
    "Password=" & My.Settings.Password & ";")
```

6. Modify the rest of the procedures in your class, making the following changes:

SQL Server

❑ Replace OleDbCommand with **SqlCommand**.

❑ Replace OleDbException with **SqlException**.

❑ Replace OleDbType with **SqlDbType**.

❑ Replace OleDbDataAdapter with **SqlDataAdapter**.

Oracle

❑ Replace OleDbCommand with **OracleCommand**.

❑ Replace OleDbException with **OracleException**.

❑ Replace OleDbType with **OracleType**.

❑ Replace OleDbDataAdapter with **OracleDataAdapter**.

7. For Oracle readers only, add the following overloaded AddParameter method to your WDABase class:

```
Public Sub AddParameter(ByVal Name As String, ByVal Type As OracleType, _
    ByVal Direction As ParameterDirection)
    Try
        Command.Parameters.Add(Name, Type).Direction = Direction
```

```
        Catch OracleExceptionErr As OracleException
            Throw New System.Exception(OracleExceptionErr.Message, _
                OracleExceptionErr.InnerException)
        End Try
    End Sub
```

8. View the code for the Admin form next and make the following modifications to the `ActionAdd` procedure:

SQL Server

Modify the parameters in the `Case "Projects"` code as follows:

```
objData.AddParameter("@ProjectID", _
    Data.SqlDbType.UniqueIdentifier, 16, Guid.NewGuid())
objData.AddParameter("@ProjectName", _
    Data.SqlDbType.VarChar, 50, txtProjectName.Text)
objData.AddParameter("@ProjectDescription", _
    Data.SqlDbType.Text, _
    txtProjectDescription.Text.Length, _
    txtProjectDescription.Text)
objData.AddParameter("@SequenceNumber", _
    Data.SqlDbType.TinyInt, 1, _
    CType(txtSequenceNumber.Text, Byte))
```

Modify the parameters in the `Case "Groups"` code as follows:

```
objData.AddParameter("@GroupID", _
    Data.SqlDbType.UniqueIdentifier, 16, Guid.NewGuid())
objData.AddParameter("@GroupName", _
    Data.SqlDbType.VarChar, 50, txtGroupName.Text)
objData.AddParameter("@GroupDescription", _
    Data.SqlDbType.Text, _
    txtGroupDescription.Text.Length, _
    txtGroupDescription.Text)
```

Oracle

Modify the parameters in the `Case "Projects"` code as follows:

```
objData.AddParameter("inProjectID", _
    Data.OracleClient.OracleType.Char, 36, _
    Guid.NewGuid.ToString.ToUpper)
objData.AddParameter("inProjectName", _
    Data.OracleClient.OracleType.VarChar, 50, _
    txtProjectName.Text)
objData.AddParameter("inProjectDescription", _
    Data.OracleClient.OracleType.Clob, _
    txtProjectDescription.Text.Length, _
    txtProjectDescription.Text)
objData.AddParameter("inSequenceNumber", _
    Data.OracleClient.OracleType.Number, 1, _
    CType(txtSequenceNumber.Text, Byte))
```

Modify the parameters in the Case "Groups" code as follows:

```
objData.AddParameter("inGroupID", _
    Data.OracleClient.OracleType.Char, 36, _
    Guid.NewGuid.ToString.ToUpper)
objData.AddParameter("inGroupName", _
    Data.OracleClient.OracleType.VarChar, 50, _
    txtGroupName.Text)
objData.AddParameter("inGroupDescription", _
    Data.OracleClient.OracleType.Clob, _
    txtGroupDescription.Text.Length, _
    txtGroupDescription.Text)
```

9. Modify the code in the ActionUpdate procedure as follows:

SQL Server

Modify the parameters in the Case "Projects" code as follows:

```
objData.AddParameter("@ProjectName", _
    Data.SqlDbType.VarChar, 50, txtProjectName.Text)
objData.AddParameter("@ProjectDescription", _
    Data.SqlDbType.Text, _
    txtProjectDescription.Text.Length, _
    txtProjectDescription.Text)
objData.AddParameter("@SequenceNumber", _
    Data.SqlDbType.TinyInt, 1, _
    CType(txtSequenceNumber.Text, Byte))
objData.AddParameter("@ProjectID", _
    Data.SqlDbType.UniqueIdentifier, 16, _
    New Guid(txtProjectID.Text))
```

Modify the parameters in the Case "Groups" code as follows:

```
objData.AddParameter("@GroupName", _
    Data.SqlDbType.VarChar, 50, txtGroupName.Text)
objData.AddParameter("@GroupDescription", _
    Data.SqlDbType.Text, _
    txtGroupDescription.Text.Length, _
    txtGroupDescription.Text)
objData.AddParameter("@GroupID", _
    Data.SqlDbType.UniqueIdentifier, 16, _
    New Guid(txtGroupID.Text))
```

Oracle

Modify the parameters in the Case "Projects" code as follows:

```
objData.AddParameter("inProjectName", _
    Data.OracleClient.OracleType.VarChar, 50, _
    txtProjectName.Text)
objData.AddParameter("inProjectDescription", _
    Data.OracleClient.OracleType.Clob, _
    txtProjectDescription.Text.Length, _
    txtProjectDescription.Text)
objData.AddParameter("inSequenceNumber", _
    Data.OracleClient.OracleType.Number, 1, _
    CType(txtSequenceNumber.Text, Byte))
```

```
                        objData.AddParameter("inProjectID", _
                            Data.OracleClient.OracleType.Char, 36, _
                            txtProjectID.Text)
```

Modify the parameters in the `Case "Groups"` code as follows:

```
                        objData.AddParameter("inGroupName", _
                            Data.OracleClient.OracleType.VarChar, 50, _
                            txtGroupName.Text)
                        objData.AddParameter("inGroupDescription", _
                            Data.OracleClient.OracleType.Clob, _
                            txtGroupDescription.Text.Length, _
                            txtGroupDescription.Text)
                        objData.AddParameter("inGroupID", _
                            Data.OracleClient.OracleType.Char, 36, _
                            txtGroupID.Text)
```

10. Modify the code in the `ActionDelete` procedure as follows:

SQL Server

Modify the parameters in the `Case "Projects"` code as follows:

```
                        objData.AddParameter("@ProjectID", _
                            Data.SqlDbType.UniqueIdentifier, 16, _
                            New Guid(txtProjectID.Text))
```

Modify the parameters in the `Case "Groups"` code as follows:

```
                        objData.AddParameter("@GroupID", _
                            Data.SqlDbType.UniqueIdentifier, 16, _
                            New Guid(txtGroupID.Text))
```

Oracle

Modify the parameters in the `Case "Projects"` code as follows:

```
                        objData.AddParameter("inProjectID", _
                            Data.OracleClient.OracleType.Char, 36, _
                            txtProjectID.Text)
```

Modify the parameters in the `Case "Groups"` code as follows:

```
                        objData.AddParameter("inGroupID", _
                            Data.OracleClient.OracleType.Char, 36, _
                            txtGroupID.Text)
```

11. Modify the `LoadProjects` procedure as follows:

SQL Server

No modifications needed.

Oracle

Modify the `SQL` property to prefix the stored procedure with the package name and add the new parameter:

```
objData.SQL = "ProjectsPackage.usp_SelectProjects"
objData.InitializeCommand()
objData.AddParameter("results_cursor", _
    Data.OracleClient.OracleType.Cursor, _
    Data.ParameterDirection.Output)
```

12. Modify the `lvwProjects_Click` procedure as follows:

SQL Server

```
objData.SQL = "usp_SelectProject"
objData.InitializeCommand()
objData.AddParameter("@ProjectID", _
    Data.SqlDbType.UniqueIdentifier, _
    16, lvwProjects.SelectedItems.Item(0).Tag)
```

Oracle

Modify the SQL property to prefix the stored procedure with the package name, modify the existing parameter, and add the new parameter:

```
objData.SQL = "ProjectPackage.usp_SelectProject"
objData.InitializeCommand()
objData.AddParameter("inProjectID", _
    Data.OracleClient.OracleType.Char, _
    36, lvwProjects.SelectedItems.Item(0).Tag)
objData.AddParameter("results_cursor", _
    Data.OracleClient.OracleType.Cursor, _
    Data.ParameterDirection.Output)
```

13. Modify the `LoadGroups` procedure as follows:

SQL Server

No modifications needed.

Oracle

Modify the SQL property to prefix the stored procedure with the package name, add the line of code to call the `InitializeCommand` method, and add the new parameter:

```
objData.SQL = "GroupsPackage.usp_SelectGroups"
objData.InitializeCommand()
objData.AddParameter("results_cursor", _
    Data.OracleClient.OracleType.Cursor, _
    Data.ParameterDirection.Output)
objGroupsDS = New DataSet
```

14. Modify the `lvwGroups_Click` procedure as follows:

SQL Server

```
objData.SQL = "usp_SelectGroup"
objData.InitializeCommand()
objData.AddParameter("@GroupID", _
    Data.SqlDbType.UniqueIdentifier, _
    16, lvwGroups.SelectedItems.Item(0).Tag)
```

Oracle

Modify the SQL property to prefix the stored procedure with the package name, modify the existing parameter, and add the new parameter:

```
objData.SQL = "GroupPackage.usp_SelectGroup"
objData.InitializeCommand()
objData.AddParameter("inGroupID", _
    Data.OracleClient.OracleType.Char, _
    36, lvwGroups.SelectedItems.Item(0).Tag)
objData.AddParameter("results_cursor", _
    Data.OracleClient.OracleType.Cursor, _
    Data.ParameterDirection.Output)
```

Those are all the changes that you need to make to your application. You are now ready to test your changes, so start your project. When your form displays, it should look similar to the one shown in Figure 9-1. Congratulations, you are now using a SQL Server or Oracle database! If your application had errors, go back and check the code changes required for your database.

You can test the functionality of your application by clicking a project to view the project details as shown in Figure 9-1 and you can insert, update, and delete projects. You can also view the details of a group and insert, update, and delete a group.

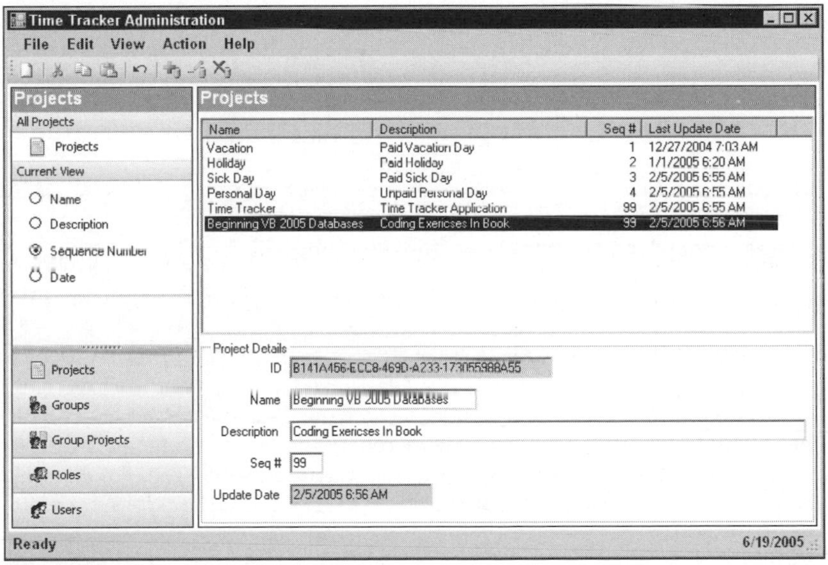

Figure 9-1

How It Works

The modifications to your Time Tracker application are minor and reflect the changes made to the WDABase class. Let's start with the changes to your app.config file first. You modify the values for the keys in your app.config file via the Property Pages for your application so that it points to either your SQL Server or Oracle database. There is nothing drastic about that and it is a simple change.

You set the `DataSource` key to the server name where your SQL Server is running if using SQL Server or the system identifier (SID) defined in your `tnsnames.ora` file if you are using Oracle. The `InitialCatalog` key is set to the `ProjectTimeTracker` database for SQL Server and to a value of `Nothing` for Oracle. The `UserID` and `Password` keys are set to your database credentials.

You modify your `WDABase` class next, changing the `Imports` statement to import the appropriate namespace for the database that you are using. Readers using SQL Server import the `System.Data.SqlClient` namespace as follows:

```
Imports System.Data.SqlClient
```

Readers using Oracle have to set a reference to the `System.Data.OracleClient` namespace before importing the `System.Data.OracleClient` namespace:

```
Imports System.Data.OracleClient
```

The modifications to the connection string are also minor. Because you have to implement the appropriate namespace for your database, you do not need the `Provider` parameter in the connection string so it has been omitted. You do, however, need the `Data Source` parameter, which will point to the server on which SQL Server is running or to your system identifier as defined in your `tnsnames.ora` file for Oracle. The following code is for SQL Server and specifies the database to connect to in the `Database` parameter:

```
Connection = New SqlConnection( _
    "Data Source=" & My.Settings.DataSource & ";" & _
    "Database=" & My.Settings.InitialCatalog & ";" & _
    "User ID=" & My.Settings.UserID & ";" & _
    "Password=" & My.Settings.Password & ";")
```

The following code example is the code for the Oracle connection string. It has the `Database` parameter omitted from the connection string, as it not needed for Oracle. Both code examples have parameters for `User ID` and `Password`, which are being read from your `app.config` file:

```
Connection = New OracleConnection( _
    "Data Source=" & My.Settings.DataSource & ";" & _
    "User ID=" & My.Settings.UserID & ";" & _
    "Password=" & My.Settings.Password & ";")
```

The rest of the changes to the `WDABase` class are merely changing the prefix on the objects and classes that you are using to point to the appropriate provider being implemented. For example, instead of `OleDbCommand`, you use `SqlCommand` for SQL Server, or `OracleCommand` for Oracle.

Oracle readers had to implement an overloaded version of the `AddParameter` method to support working with packages. Remember that your stored procedures that return data in Oracle require a cursor in order to return the data. Therefore, you need an overloaded version of the `AddParameter` method to support adding a parameter as a cursor and specifying the direction of the parameter.

```
Public Sub AddParameter(ByVal Name As String, ByVal Type As OracleType, _
    ByVal Direction As ParameterDirection)
    Try
        Command.Parameters.Add(Name, Type).Direction = Direction
    Catch OracleExceptionErr As OracleException
```

```
                    Throw New System.Exception(OracleExceptionErr.Message, _
                          OracleExceptionErr.InnerException)
            End Try
        End Sub
```

The changes that you make to the code in the Admin form are also minor and reflect the changes needed for the specific provider that you are using. Starting with the changes to the `ActionAdd` procedure for SQL Server, you'll notice that you modify the data type being used in the `AddParameter` method to reflect the appropriate data type used in SQL Server.

It is also important to note that the parameter names used here match the parameter names in your stored procedures. This is a requirement when using the `System.Data.SqlClient` namespace.

SQL Server

Case `"Projects"` code:

```
                        objData.AddParameter("@ProjectID", _
                            Data.SqlDbType.UniqueIdentifier, 16, Guid.NewGuid())
                        objData.AddParameter("@ProjectName", _
                            Data.SqlDbType.VarChar, 50, txtProjectName.Text)
                        objData.AddParameter("@ProjectDescription", _
                            Data.SqlDbType.Text, _
                            txtProjectDescription.Text.Length, _
                            txtProjectDescription.Text)
                        objData.AddParameter("@SequenceNumber", _
                            Data.SqlDbType.TinyInt, 1, _
                            CType(txtSequenceNumber.Text, Byte))
```

Case `"Groups"` code:

```
                        objData.AddParameter("@GroupID", _
                            Data.SqlDbType.UniqueIdentifier, 16, Guid.NewGuid())
                        objData.AddParameter("@GroupName", _
                            Data.SqlDbType.VarChar, 50, txtGroupName.Text)
                        objData.AddParameter("@GroupDescription", _
                            Data.SqlDbType.Text, _
                            txtGroupDescription.Text.Length, _
                            txtGroupDescription.Text)
```

The changes that you make for Oracle reflect the data types being used in Oracle and include alterations to the parameter names to match the parameter names used in your stored procedure, as this is also a requirement of the `System.Data.OracleClient` namespace.

Oracle

Case `"Projects"` code:

```
                        objData.AddParameter("inProjectID", _
                            Data.OracleClient.OracleType.Char, 36, _
                            Guid.NewGuid.ToString.ToUpper)
                        objData.AddParameter("inProjectName", _
```

```
                        Data.OracleClient.OracleType.VarChar, 50, _
                        txtProjectName.Text)
                objData.AddParameter("inProjectDescription", _
                        Data.OracleClient.OracleType.Clob, _
                        txtProjectDescription.Text.Length, _
                        txtProjectDescription.Text)
                objData.AddParameter("inSequenceNumber", _
                        Data.OracleClient.OracleType.Number, 1, _
                        CType(txtSequenceNumber.Text, Byte))
```

Case "Groups" code:

```
                objData.AddParameter("inGroupID", _
                        Data.OracleClient.OracleType.Char, 36, _
                        Guid.NewGuid.ToString.ToUpper)
                objData.AddParameter("inGroupName", _
                        Data.OracleClient.OracleType.VarChar, 50, _
                        txtGroupName.Text)
                objData.AddParameter("inGroupDescription", _
                        Data.OracleClient.OracleType.Clob, _
                        txtGroupDescription.Text.Length, _
                        txtGroupDescription.Text)
```

The changes that you make to the ActionUpdate and ActionDelete procedures are similar in nature to the changes mentioned previously. To that end, there's no need to list the code for those procedures here.

The LoadProjects procedure does not require any changes for those readers using SQL Server because a SQL Server stored procedure returns data natively. However, readers using Oracle have to make some minor modifications to execute the usp_SelectProjects stored procedure in the ProjectsPackage package. This is evident in the following code because you have to prefix your stored procedure name with the package name in which this stored procedure exists.

You then have to add an output parameter to receive the data that the stored procedure returns. This output parameter is added using the new overloaded version of AddParameter method that you added in the WDABase class. Here you pass the parameter name, the data type, and the direction of the parameter.

The parameter name that has been specified here must match the parameter name defined in your stored procedure, and the data type chosen is a Cursor, which also matches the data type defined in your stored procedure. Because the cursor returns data, you specify a direction of Output.

The rest of the code in the LoadProjects procedure remains the same and the output from this stored procedure will be returned in the DataReader object:

```
                objData.SQL = "ProjectsPackage.usp_SelectProjects"
                objData.InitializeCommand()
                objData.AddParameter("results_cursor", _
                    Data.OracleClient.OracleType.Cursor, _
                    Data.ParameterDirection.Output)
```

The changes required for the lvwProjects_Click procedure are minor. For SQL Server, they involve changing the data type being used to match the data type being used in SQL Server:

```
objData.SQL = "usp_SelectProject"
objData.InitializeCommand()
objData.AddParameter("@ProjectID", _
    Data.SqlDbType.UniqueIdentifier, _
    16, lvwProjects.SelectedItems.Item(0).Tag)
```

For Oracle, the changes are similar to the changes made for SQL Server and the changes that were made in the LoadProjects procedure. First, you have to prefix your stored procedure name with the package name in which the stored procedure exists. Then you modify the input parameter to this stored procedure to reflect the input parameter name of inProjectID and modify the data type for this parameter to match the data type specified in the stored procedure.

Finally, you add an output parameter to receive the data that this stored procedure returns, just as you did in the LoadProjects procedure, ensuring that the parameter name and data type match the parameter name and data type used in the stored procedure:

```
objData.SQL = "ProjectPackage.usp_SelectProject"
objData.InitializeCommand()
objData.AddParameter("inProjectID", _
    Data.OracleClient.OracleType.Char, _
    36, lvwProjects.SelectedItems.Item(0).Tag)
objData.AddParameter("results_cursor", _
    Data.OracleClient.OracleType.Cursor, _
    Data.ParameterDirection.Output)
```

The changes made to the LoadGroups and lvwGroups_Click procedures reflect the same types of changes made to the LoadProjects and lvwProjects_Click procedures. Therefore, the code will not be listed again.

To summarize the changes: You make changes to your app.config file via the Property Pages to point to the database to which you want to connect. You then modify the WDABase class to use the appropriate provider for your database. The changes you make to the code in the Admin form reflect the data type changes made in the WDABase class. Readers using Oracle add an overloaded version of the AddParameter method in the WDABase class and add an additional parameter to receive the data being returned by the stored procedures.

Views

I talked briefly about views in Chapter 1 and said that a view is like a virtual table containing data from one or more tables. A view is stored in the database as the actual SQL statements that are contained in the view, much like a stored procedure. When the view is referenced, the virtual table is created using the SQL statements that are contained in the view. In a nutshell, this is exactly what a view is: a SELECT query saved in your database.

However, one major restriction is placed on you by a view: You cannot supply a view with input parameters. Remember that the usp_SelectProject stored procedure accepted an input parameter to limit the results returned by the SELECT statement in that stored procedure to a specific row of data. Because a view does not allow you to specify input parameters, you must select all rows of data in the view or find an alternative way around this restriction, which is what you will learn about next.

First, let's assume that you created a view containing the following SELECT statement. When you execute your view, all rows of data are returned by the view in the virtual table that the database creates:

```
CREATE VIEW vw_SelectProjects
AS
SELECT ProjectID, ProjectName, ProjectDescription, SequenceNumber, LastUpdateDate
FROM Projects
```

However, to retrieve data from a view, you have to create a query that selects data from the view itself because the view is a virtual table. For example, the following query selects just two columns from the view and orders the results by ProjectName. You can see that the view itself is treated just like a table, which in fact it is; it's just virtual:

```
SELECT ProjectID, ProjectName
FROM vw_SelectProjects
ORDER BY ProjectName
```

Now take a look at how you can select a specific row of data from the view, just as your usp_SelectProject stored procedure does. You build your SELECT statement just as though you were selecting data from a table, and specify a WHERE clause to limit the results of your SELECT statement to only the row of data in the view in which you are interested:

```
SELECT ProjectID, ProjectName
FROM vw_SelectProjects
WHERE ProjectID = 'D4F0369A-F41B-4BCB-8D1C-629C7B77BB36'
```

Views work the same way in SQL Server as they do in Oracle, and you create the same code in your VB 2005 program to retrieve data from a view for both SQL Server and Oracle. This makes views sound like great things, and they are when used appropriately.

If you want to return all rows of data from a table, then using a view can be less code-intensive in your database and VB 2005 code for Oracle. Rather than creating a package and the extra code in your VB 2005 program to deal with Oracle stored procedures that return data, a view might sound like an appropriate alternative. However, this is not the case.

Using a view requires you to hard-code the SELECT statement in your code, like the example shown previously, and it then becomes part of your compiled program. Sure, you can use a variable to substitute the appropriate ProjectID needed in the WHERE clause, but look at the SQL that gets compiled in your code. What happens if a major change is made to the view and the columns that you have coded in your SELECT statement are no longer available or have been renamed? You must modify your application, recompile it, and then redistribute it to your users.

There's also the network to consider. Sending large amounts of data, such as the SELECT statement shown previously, causes more traffic on your network. This doesn't look like much data, but consider what would happen if you had hundreds of users using your application concurrently and you used numerous SELECT statements in your code. That's a lot of extra data unnecessarily being sent across the network when the use of a stored procedure would have been a better alternative.

Where do views really shine? They are great in restricting users to specific columns or even rows of data in a table. Assume you have two clerks working in the Human Resources department. One clerk is responsible for maintaining current phone number and location information within the company and the other clerk is responsible for maintaining salary information. Just for argument's sake, assume that all that information is available in one table. Using two different views, you can provide the appropriate data to both clerks, giving each of them only the information needed to perform his or her job.

Views are also really great when used to join the data from multiple tables and present the data as if it came from one table. Using the previous example, assume that the employee data is spread out in multiple tables, just as it typically would be in the real world. Using views, you can create a SELECT statement that selects the appropriate data from the multiple tables and returns it as if it came from one table.

Finally, views are great for performing multiple or complex calculations and computations on data and returning the results of those calculations and computations in columns and rows. This shields the end user from the actual data and the source of the data, and provides only the results that the user needs.

Creating a view

The first example shown in the previous section was the complete syntax for creating a view for SQL Server. You specify the CREATE VIEW statement followed by the name of the view. This is followed by the AS keyword and the SELECT statements that make up the view.

An example of a view for Oracle follows. To create a view in Oracle, you specify the CREATE OR REPLACE VIEW statement followed by the view name. This is followed by the AS keyword and then the SELECT statements that make up the view. Don't forget that you must terminate each SQL statement with a semicolon in Oracle.

```
CREATE OR REPLACE VIEW vw_SelectProjects
AS
SELECT ProjectID, ProjectName, ProjectDescription, SequenceNumber, LastUpdateDate
FROM Projects;
```

The same rules that apply to stored procedures also apply to view names for SQL Server and Oracle. A view name in SQL Server can be up to 128 characters in length, whereas a view name in Oracle can be up to 30 characters in length.

In this Try It Out, you create a view to return all data from the GroupProjects table in your database. While this is not the ideal use of a view, it demonstrates how to effectively use a view from your application. You also create a stored procedure to insert data into the GroupProjects table and a stored procedure to delete data from the GroupProjects table.

Try It Out   Creating Views and Stored Procedures

To complete this exercise:

1. Start Visual Studio 2005 if it is not already started.
2. View the Server Explorer window and click the Auto Hide icon on the window to keep it visible.
3. Expand your data connection and view the Views node for your database to create the view.

   SQL Server
   a. Right-click the Views node and select Add New View from the context menu.
   b. The Query Builder that you saw in Chapter 3 appears and the Add Table dialog box appears. Add the GroupProjects table, the Groups table, and the Projects table. Then close the Add Table dialog box.

c. Notice that the joins between the tables have automatically been made for you, as shown in Figure 9-2.

d. Select the GroupProjectID, GroupID, and ProjectID columns in the GroupProjects table.

e. Select the GroupName column in the Groups table.

f. Select the ProjectName and SequenceNumber columns in the Projects table.

g. At this point, the SELECT statement for the view has been built and all that is left to do is to save the view.

h. Click the Save button on the toolbar and you are prompted with the Save New View dialog box. Enter a view name of **vw_SelectGroupProjects** and click OK to save the view.

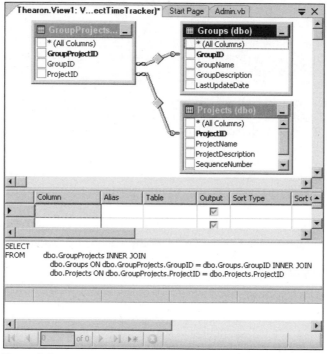

Figure 9-2

Oracle

Visual Studio 2005 does not support creating views in an Oracle database, so you need to create your view using your favorite Oracle tool for creating database objects, such as iSQL *Plus or SQL Plus. Enter the following code and execute it to create the view. After you have created your view you can refresh the Views node in the Server Explorer in Visual Studio 2005 to see your view listed:

```
CREATE OR REPLACE VIEW vw_SelectGroupProjects
AS
SELECT GroupProjects.GroupProjectID, GroupProjects.GroupID,
GroupProjects.ProjectID,
   Groups.GroupName, Projects.ProjectName, Projects.SequenceNumber
```

```
FROM GroupProjects
INNER JOIN Groups ON GroupProjects.GroupID = Groups.GroupID
INNER JOIN Projects ON GroupProjects.ProjectID = Projects.ProjectID;
```

4. Create the stored procedure that will insert group projects into the GroupProjects table next. SQL Server users should right-click the Stored Procedures node in the Server Explorer and choose Add New Stored Procedure and Oracle users should use their Oracle tool. Enter the following code:

SQL Server

```
CREATE PROCEDURE usp_InsertGroupProject
(
    @GroupProjectID    UNIQUEIDENTIFIER,
    @GroupID           UNIQUEIDENTIFIER,
    @ProjectID         UNIQUEIDENTIFIER
)
AS
INSERT INTO GroupProjects
    (GroupProjectID, GroupID, ProjectID)
    VALUES(@GroupProjectID, @GroupID, @ProjectID)
```

Click the Save icon on the toolbar to have the stored procedure created in your database.

Oracle

```
CREATE OR REPLACE PROCEDURE usp_InsertGroupProject
(
    inGroupProjectID    CHAR,
    inGroupID           CHAR,
    inProjectID         CHAR
)
AS
BEGIN
INSERT INTO GroupProjects
    (GroupProjectID, GroupID, ProjectID)
    VALUES(inGroupProjectID, inGroupID, inProjectID),
END;
```

Click the Execute button to have the stored procedure created in your database.

5. You need to create the stored procedure that will delete group projects from the GroupProjects table next. SQL Server users should right-click the Stored Procedures node in the Server Explorer and choose Add New Stored Procedure and Oracle users should use their Oracle tool. Enter the following code:

SQL Server

```
CREATE PROCEDURE usp_DeleteGroupProjects
(
    @GroupID    UNIQUEIDENTIFIER
)
AS
DELETE
FROM GroupProjects
WHERE GroupID = @GroupID
```

Click the Save icon on the toolbar to have the stored procedure created in your database.

Oracle

```
CREATE OR REPLACE PROCEDURE usp_DeleteGroupProjects
(
    inGroupID    CHAR
)
AS
BEGIN
DELETE
FROM GroupProjects
WHERE GroupID = inGroupID;
END;
```

Click the Execute button to have the stored procedure created in your database.

How It Works

You start this exercise by creating a view to select group projects from the GroupProjects table. In the process of creating this view, several joins are made to get the relevant information for both groups and projects.

Readers using SQL Server are able to create this view using the Query Builder in Visual Studio 2005. Having used the Query Builder extensively in Chapter 3, you should be quite familiar with it. What is different here is that you add three tables for this query, and Visual Studio 2005 automatically joins the tables based on the primary and foreign keys defined in the tables. You then merely select the columns from each table that you want in your view. The results of those selections are shown in the next block of code, which has been slightly reformatted for easier viewing in this book

Notice that Visual Studio 2005 prefixes each column and each table with the owner of the table. This is typically not necessary and can be removed if you so desire. Notice that the SELECT statement is generated to prefix each column name with the table name that it comes from. This is not necessary for the columns that are selected from the table in the FROM clause, but is necessary for the columns in the tables listed in the JOIN clauses. However, it is good coding practice to always prefix each column with the table name when using joins because it helps document your code, and you'll know exactly what table the column belongs to.

The SELECT list contains all columns from the GroupProjects table and the GroupName column from the Groups table as well as the ProjectName and SequenceNumber columns from the Projects table. The FROM clause specifies the primary table that you want to select data from. Because you are interested in group projects, you specify the GroupProjects table in the FROM clause.

The next clause that you see is an INNER JOIN clause. Briefly, an INNER JOIN returns all rows of data from the joined table whose values in the joined column match the values in the column of the table to which it is joined. I explain more about joins in Chapter 12.

The first INNER JOIN clause joins the Groups table on values in the GroupID column, which causes all rows of data in the Groups table to be joined to the GroupProjects table where a GroupID exists in the GroupProjects table and the Groups table.

The next `INNER JOIN` clause joins the Projects table on values in the ProjectID column and causes all rows of data in the Projects table to be joined to the GroupProjects table where a ProjectID exists in the GroupProjects table and the Projects table.

```
SELECT dbo.GroupProjects.GroupProjectID, dbo.GroupProjects.GroupID,
    dbo.GroupProjects.ProjectID, dbo.Groups.GroupName, dbo.Projects.ProjectName,
    dbo.Projects.SequenceNumber
FROM         dbo.GroupProjects
INNER JOIN dbo.Groups ON dbo.GroupProjects.GroupID = dbo.Groups.GroupID
INNER JOIN dbo.Projects ON dbo.GroupProjects.ProjectID = dbo.Projects.ProjectID
```

Readers using Oracle have to use their favorite tool for creating views and stored procedures, as Visual Studio 2005 does not support creating views in Oracle from within the development environment.

You start by specifying the `CREATE OR REPLACE VIEW` statement followed by the view name. Notice that you prefix the view name with the letters vw followed by an underscore. This helps provide a consistent naming standard for database objects and is not required. You then specify the `AS` keyword followed by the body of the view.

The body of the view consists of the same SQL statements that were shown previously for the SQL Server example and will not be explained again. The only difference in this SQL is that the columns and tables are not prefixed with the database owner of the objects. Also note that, as with your stored procedures, you must terminate your SQL statements with a semicolon, which has been done here.

```
CREATE OR REPLACE VIEW vw_SelectGroupProjects
AS
SELECT GroupProjects.GroupProjectID, GroupProjects.GroupID,
GroupProjects.ProjectID,
    Groups.GroupName, Projects.ProjectName, Projects.SequenceNumber
FROM GroupProjects
INNER JOIN Groups ON GroupProjects.GroupID = Groups.GroupID
INNER JOIN Projects ON GroupProjects.ProjectID = Projects.ProjectID;
```

You create the `usp_InsertGroupProject` stored procedure next. This stored procedure inserts a new group project into the GroupProjects table. Group projects consist of a single group and multiple projects assigned to that group, and the whole purpose of the GroupProjects table is to provide a one-to-many relationship between a single group and multiple projects.

The SQL Server version of this stored procedure contains three input parameters, all defined as a `UNIQUEIDENTIFIER` data type: one for the primary key, one for the Group ID, and one for the Project ID:

```
CREATE PROCEDURE usp_InsertGroupProject
(
    @GroupProjectID    UNIQUEIDENTIFIER,
    @GroupID           UNIQUEIDENTIFIER,
    @ProjectID         UNIQUEIDENTIFIER
)
AS
INSERT INTO GroupProjects
    (GroupProjectID, GroupID, ProjectID)
    VALUES(@GroupProjectID, @GroupID, @ProjectID)
```

For Oracle, this stored procedure also contains the same three input parameters. However, their data type has been defined as CHAR, as the Guids for these parameters are stored in a column in Oracle defined as a CHAR(36) data type:

```
CREATE OR REPLACE PROCEDURE usp_InsertGroupProject
(
    inGroupProjectID    CHAR,
    inGroupID           CHAR,
    inProjectID         CHAR
)
AS
BEGIN
INSERT INTO GroupProjects
    (GroupProjectID, GroupID, ProjectID)
    VALUES(inGroupProjectID, inGroupID, inProjectID);
END;
```

The last stored procedure that you create in this exercise is the usp_DeleteGroupProjects stored procedure. You may have noticed two things. First, there is no stored procedure to update a group project. Second, the delete stored procedure deletes all group projects in the GroupProjects table. This is by design and provides the most efficient processing in your application and the database.

When you make a group project assignment, you provide a ListBox control containing all projects that should be assigned to a group. Initially, you add all of the projects in the ListBox control to the GroupProjects table. When an update to the ListBox control occurs, you need to determine which projects are preexisting projects, which projects are new, and which projects have been removed. Therefore, it is much simpler and requires less processing to delete all existing projects for the group and then insert all the projects in the ListBox control again.

To that end, the usp_DeleteGroupProjects stored procedure deletes all rows of data in the GroupProjects table based on the GroupID column. Remember that this column provides a one-to-many relationship, which means there is one GroupID in this table and many different ProjectIDs.

The SQL Server version of this stored procedure accepts one input parameter for the GroupID and is defined as a UNIQUEIDENTIFIER data type:

```
CREATE PROCEDURE usp_DeleteGroupProjects
(
    @GroupID    UNIQUEIDENTIFIER
)
AS
DELETE
FROM GroupProjects
WHERE GroupID = @GroupID
```

The Oracle version of this stored procedure also accepts the GroupID as an input parameter and the data type here is defined as a CHAR data type. Also note that the SQL statements are terminated with semicolons:

```
CREATE OR REPLACE PROCEDURE usp_DeleteGroupProjects
(
    inGroupID    CHAR
)
```

```
AS
BEGIN
DELETE
FROM GroupProjects
WHERE GroupID = inGroupID;
END;
```

At this point, you have all of the views and stored procedures needed to insert, display, and delete group projects in your Time Tracker application. All that is left to do is to modify your application to implement these views and stored procedures.

In the next Try It Out, you implement the code to select data from the vw_SelectGroupProjects view to display all projects for a specific group. You also implement the code to insert, update, and delete group projects in the GroupProjects table.

In addition, you implement drag-and-drop functionality into your application. A complete list of available projects will be displayed in one ListBox control from which you drag the projects and drop them into another ListBox to be added to a group.

Try It Out   Implementing Views and Stored Procedures in VB 2005

To implement this functionality:

1.   Open your Time Tracker project in Visual Studio 2005 and view the code for the Admin form.

2.   Add the following variable declarations at the top of your form class:

```
Private blnLoading As Boolean

Private objGroupsDS As DataSet
Private objProjectsDS As DataSet
Private objGroupProjectsDS As DataSet
```

3.   Edit the ActionAdd procedure and add the following code to the Case "Group Projects" statement:

SQL Server and Oracle

```
Case "Group Projects"
        'Turn the loading flag on so no items are processed
        blnLoading = True
        'Delete any previous projects
        Call ActionDelete()
        'Turn the loading flag off
        blnLoading = False
        'Set the SQL string
        objData.SQL = "usp_InsertGroupProject"
        'Open the database connection
        objData.OpenConnection()
        'Initialize the Command object
        objData.InitializeCommand()
        For intIndex = 0 To _
            objGroupProjectsDS.Tables( _
            "GroupProjects").Rows.Count - 1
```

SQL Server

```
'Add the Parameters to the Parameters collection
objData.AddParameter("@GroupProjectID", _
    Data.SqlDbType.UniqueIdentifier, 16, _
    Guid.NewGuid())
objData.AddParameter("@GroupID", _
    Data.SqlDbType.UniqueIdentifier, 16, _
    cboGroups.SelectedItem.Item("GroupID"))
objData.AddParameter("@ProjectID", _
    Data.SqlDbType.UniqueIdentifier, 16, _
    objGroupProjectsDS.Tables( _
    "GroupProjects").Rows(intIndex).Item("ProjectID"))
```

Oracle

```
'Add the Parameters to the Parameters collection
objData.AddParameter("inGroupProjectID", _
    Data.OracleClient.OracleType.Char, 36, _
    Guid.NewGuid.ToString.ToUpper)
objData.AddParameter("inGroupID", _
    Data.OracleClient.OracleType.Char, 36, _
    cboGroups.SelectedItem.Item("GroupID"))
objData.AddParameter("inProjectID", _
    Data.OracleClient.OracleType.Char, 36, _
    objGroupProjectsDS.Tables( _
    "GroupProjects").Rows(intIndex).Item("ProjectID"))
```

SQL Server and Oracle

```
            'Execute the stored procedure
            objData.Command.ExecuteNonQuery()
            'Clear the Parameters collection for the next insert
            objData.Command.Parameters.Clear()
        Next
        'Close the database connection
        objData.CloseConnection()
        'Clear previous bindings
        lstGroupProjects.DataSource = Nothing
        lstGroupProjects.DisplayMember = String.Empty
        lstGroupProjects.ValueMember = String.Empty
        lstGroupProjects.Items.Clear()
        'Turn the loading flag on so no items are processed
        blnLoading = True
        cboGroups.SelectedIndex = -1
        'Turn the loading flag off
        blnLoading = False
```

4. Edit the `ActionUpdate` procedure and add the following code to the `Case "Group Projects"` statement:

```
    Case "Group Projects"
        'Turn the loading flag on so no items are processed
        blnLoading = True
        Call ActionAdd()
```

5. Edit the `ActionDelete` procedure and add the following code to the `Case "Group Projects"` statement:

SQL Server and Oracle

```
            Case "Group Projects"
                'Set the SQL string
                objData.SQL = "usp_DeleteGroupProjects"
                'Initialize the Command object
                objData.InitializeCommand()
```

SQL Server

```
                'Add the Parameters to the Parameters collection
                objData.AddParameter("@GroupID", _
                    Data.SqlDbType.UniqueIdentifier, _
                    16, cboGroups.SelectedItem.Item("GroupID"))
```

Oracle

```
                'Add the Parameters to the Parameters collection
                objData.AddParameter("inGroupID", _
                    Data.OracleClient.OracleType.Char, _
                    36, cboGroups.SelectedItem.Item("GroupID"))
```

SQL Server and Oracle

```
                'Open the database connection
                objData.OpenConnection()
                'Execute the stored procedure
                objData.Command.ExecuteNonQuery()
                'Close the database connection
                objData.CloseConnection()
                'Clear previous bindings
                If Not blnLoading Then
                    lstGroupProjects.DataSource = Nothing
                    lstGroupProjects.DisplayMember = String.Empty
                    lstGroupProjects.ValueMember = String.Empty
                    lstGroupProjects.Items.Clear()
                    blnLoading = True
                    cboGroups.SelectedIndex = -1
                    blnLoading = False
                End If
```

6. Modify the `LoadProjects` procedure as follows:

SQL Server and Oracle

```
        Try
            'Clear previous bindings
            lstProjects.DataSource = Nothing
            lstProjects.DisplayMember = String.Empty
            lstProjects.ValueMember = String.Empty
```

SQL Server

```
'Get all Projects in a DataSet
objData.SQL = "usp_SelectProjects"
objProjectsDS = New Data.DataSet
Call objData.FillDataSet(objProjectsDS, "Projects")
```

Oracle

```
'Get all Projects in a DataSet
objData.SQL = "ProjectsPackage.usp_SelectProjects"
objData.InitializeCommand()
objData.AddParameter("results_cursor", _
    Data.OracleClient.OracleType.Cursor, _
    Data.ParameterDirection.Output)
objProjectsDS = New Data.DataSet
Call objData.FillDataSet(objProjectsDS, "Projects")
```

SQL Server and Oracle

```
'Clear previous list
lvwProjects.Items.Clear()

'Process all rows
For intIndex = 0 To objProjectsDS.Tables("Projects").Rows.Count - 1
    'Create a new listview item
    objListViewItem = New ListViewItem
    'Add the data to the listview item
    objListViewItem.Text = objProjectsDS.Tables( _
        "Projects").Rows(intIndex).Item("ProjectName")
    objListViewItem.Tag = objProjectsDS.Tables( _
        "Projects").Rows(intIndex).Item("ProjectID")
    'Add the sub items to the listview item
    objListViewItem.SubItems.Add(objProjectsDS.Tables( _
        "Projects").Rows(intIndex).Item("ProjectDescription"))
    objListViewItem.SubItems.Add(objProjectsDS.Tables( _
        "Projects").Rows(intIndex).Item("SequenceNumber"))
    objListViewItem.SubItems.Add(Format(objProjectsDS.Tables( _
        "Projects").Rows(intIndex).Item("LastUpdateDate"), "g"))
    'Add the listview item to the listview control
    lvwProjects.Items.Add(objListViewItem)
Next

'Rebind ListBox control
lstProjects.DataSource = objProjectsDS.Tables("Projects")
lstProjects.DisplayMember = "ProjectName"
lstProjects.ValueMember = "ProjectID"
```

SQL Server and Oracle

```
Catch ExceptionErr As Exception
```

7. Modify the LoadGroups procedure as follows:

SQL Server and Oracle

```
Private Sub LoadGroups()
    'Declare variables
    Dim objListViewItem As ListViewItem

    'Turn the loading flag on so no items are processed
    blnLoading = True

    'Initialize a new instance of the data access base class
    Using objData As New WDABase
    .
    .
    .
    'Turn off loading switch
    blnLoading = False
End Sub
```

8. You need to add a procedure for the cboGroups ComboBox control to handle the SelectedIndexChanged event. Click the Method Name combo box at the top of the Code Editor and select cboGroups; and in the Class Name combo box, select the SelectedIndexChanged event. Enter the following code in the cboGroups_SelectedIndexChanged procedure:

SQL Server and Oracle

```
Private Sub cboGroups_SelectedIndexChanged(ByVal sender As Object, _
    ByVal e As System.EventArgs) Handles cboGroups.SelectedIndexChanged

    'Don't process if the ComboBox is being loaded
    If blnLoading Then
        Exit Sub
    End If

    Using objData As New WDABase
        Try
            'Clear previous bindings
            lstGroupProjects.DataSource = Nothing
            lstGroupProjects.DisplayMember = String.Empty
            lstGroupProjects.ValueMember = String.Empty
```

SQL Server

```
            'Get the specific Group Projects selected in the ComboBox control
            objData.SQL = "SELECT ProjectID, ProjectName " & _
                "FROM vw_SelectGroupProjects " & _
                "WHERE GroupID = @GroupID " & _
                "ORDER BY SequenceNumber"
            objData.InitializeCommand()
            objData.AddParameter("@GroupID", Data.SqlDbType.UniqueIdentifier, _
                16, cboGroups.SelectedItem.Item("GroupID"))
```

Oracle

```
            'Get the specific Group Projects selected in the ComboBox control
            objData.SQL = "SELECT ProjectID, ProjectName " & _
                "FROM vw_SelectGroupProjects " & _
                "WHERE GroupID = :inGroupID " & _
```

```
                        "ORDER BY SequenceNumber"
                objData.InitializeCommand()
                objData.AddParameter("inGroupID", _
                    Data.OracleClient.OracleType.Char, _
                    36, cboGroups.SelectedItem.Item("GroupID"))
```

SQL Server and Oracle

```
                objGroupProjectsDS = New Data.DataSet
                Call objData.FillDataSet(objGroupProjectsDS, "GroupProjects")

                'Rebind ListBox control
                lstGroupProjects.DataSource = _
                    objGroupProjectsDS.Tables("GroupProjects")
                lstGroupProjects.DisplayMember = "ProjectName"
                lstGroupProjects.ValueMember = "ProjectID"
            Catch ExceptionErr As Exception
                MessageBox.Show(ExceptionErr.Message, strAppTitle)
            End Try
        End Using
    End Sub
```

9. To implement drag-and-drop functionality, you need to implement some event procedures for
    the lstProjects and lstGroupProjects ListBox controls. Click the Class Name combo box
    in the Code Editor and select lstProjects, and in the Method Name combo box, select the
    MouseDown event. Add the following code to the lstProjects_MouseDown procedure:

```
Private Sub lstProjects_MouseDown(ByVal sender As Object, _
    ByVal e As System.Windows.Forms.MouseEventArgs) _
    Handles lstProjects.MouseDown

    If e.Button = MouseButtons.Left Then
        lstProjects.DoDragDrop(objProjectsDS.Tables("Projects").Rows( _
            lstProjects.SelectedIndex)("ProjectID").ToString, _
            DragDropEffects.Copy)
    End If
End Sub
```

10. Now click the Class Name combo box and select lstGroupProjects, and in the Method Name combo
    box, select the DragEnter event. Add the following code to the lstGroupProjects_DragEnter
    procedure:

```
Private Sub lstGroupProjects_DragEnter(ByVal sender As Object, _
    ByVal e As System.Windows.Forms.DragEventArgs) _
    Handles lstGroupProjects.DragEnter

    'Exit if nothing has been selected in the cboGroups ComboBox
    If cboGroups.SelectedIndex = -1 Then
        Exit Sub
    End If

    'Now ensure that the drag content is the correct type for this control
    If (e.Data.GetDataPresent(DataFormats.Text)) Then
        'If the item does not already exist then allow the copy
        Dim objDataView As Data.DataView = New _
```

```
                    Data.DataView(objGroupProjectsDS.Tables("GroupProjects"))
                objDataView.Sort = "ProjectID"
                intIndex = objDataView.Find(e.Data.GetData(DataFormats.Text))
                If intIndex = -1 Then
                    e.Effect = DragDropEffects.Copy
                Else
                    e.Effect = DragDropEffects.None
                End If
            Else
                e.Effect = DragDropEffects.None
            End If
    End Sub
```

11. Click the Class Name combo box and select lstGroupProjects again, and in the Method Name combo, select the DragDrop event. Enter the following code in the lstGroupProjects_DragDrop procedure:

```
Private Sub lstGroupProjects_DragDrop(ByVal sender As Object, _
    ByVal e As System.Windows.Forms.DragEventArgs) _
    Handles lstGroupProjects.DragDrop
```

```
        Dim objDataRow As Data.DataRow
        Dim objDataView As Data.DataView = New _
            Data.DataView(objProjectsDS.Tables("Projects"))
        objDataView.Sort = "ProjectID"
        intIndex = objDataView.Find(e.Data.GetData(DataFormats.Text))
        objDataRow = objGroupProjectsDS.Tables("GroupProjects").NewRow
        objDataRow.Item("ProjectID") = New _
            Guid(e.Data.GetData(DataFormats.Text).ToString)
        objDataRow.Item("ProjectName") = _
            objDataView.Item(intIndex).Item("ProjectName")
        objGroupProjectsDS.Tables("GroupProjects").Rows.Add(objDataRow)
        objGroupProjectsDS.AcceptChanges()
    End Sub
```

12. To be able to delete unwanted projects in the lstGroupProjects ListBox, you need to add code to handle the Delete key. Once again click the Class Name combo box and select lstGroupProjects, and in the Method Name combo box, select the KeyUp event. Add the following code to the lstGroupProjects_KeyUp procedure:

```
Private Sub lstGroupProjects_KeyUp(ByVal sender As Object, _
    ByVal e As System.Windows.Forms.KeyEventArgs) _
    Handles lstGroupProjects.KeyUp
```

```
        If e.KeyCode = Keys.Delete Then
            objGroupProjectsDS.Tables("GroupProjects").Rows.RemoveAt( _
                lstGroupProjects.SelectedIndex)
            objGroupProjectsDS.AcceptChanges()
        End If
    End Sub
```

That's all the code you need to implement the new view and two new stored procedures. Start your project so you can test your changes. When your form displays, click Group Projects in the Navigation pane or navigate to the Group Projects screen.

Select a group in the Groups combo box and then drag a project from the Available Projects list and drop it in the Group Projects list. Repeat this process for a few projects as shown in Figure 9-3. This will test the drag-and-drop functionality. To test the delete functionality of the Group Projects ListBox control, click a project in the Group Projects list and press the Delete key. The selected project will be deleted from the list box.

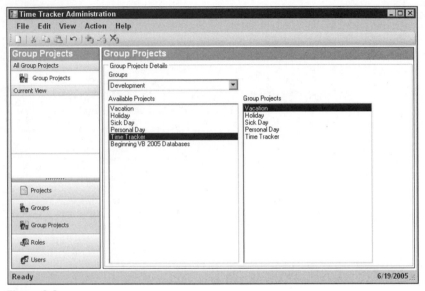

Figure 9-3

To test the add functionality, click the Add button on the toolbar or click the Action menu and choose Add. The group projects are added to the selected group, the Groups combo box is cleared, the Group Projects list is cleared, and the message Record Added is displayed in the status bar. This test has exercised your usp_InsertGroupProject stored procedure.

To exercise your vw_SelectGroupProjects view and to verify that the projects were added to the group, select the group name in the Groups combo box and the Group Projects list will be populated with the groups just added. Select another group name in the Groups combo box and the Group Projects list will be empty.

To test your usp_DeleteGroupProject stored procedure, click the group name in the Groups combo box that contains group projects. Now add some more projects to the list, delete some projects, or do both. Then click the Update button on the toolbar or click the Action menu and choose Update. Remember that the code for an update will call the ActionDelete procedure, which executes the usp_DeleteGroupProjects stored procedure and then calls the ActionAdd procedure, which executes the usp_InsertGroupProject stored procedure.

Finally, if you want to test the delete functionality, click the group name in the Groups combo box that contains group projects. When the group projects are displayed, click the Delete button on the toolbar or click the Action menu and choose Delete.

Before you move on, populate a couple of groups with group projects in preparation for future exercises.

How It Works

You add three variables at the form level for this exercise. The first variable, blnLoading, is used when loading group data and prevents the combo box event procedure from executing when data is being loaded into the combo box. You saw this variable used in the various procedures that you added for this exercise.

The next two variables are defined as a DataSet to hold the project and group project data retrieved from the database.

```
Private blnLoading As Boolean

Private objProjectsDS As DataSet
Private objGroupProjectsDS As DataSet
```

The first procedure that you modify is ActionAdd. You modified the Case "Group Projects" statement, adding the necessary code to add group projects. The first thing that you do in this procedure is set the blnLoading flag to True.

I talked a little about this earlier but want to cover it again. Because you are dealing with a one-to-many relationship between a group and many projects, it is more efficient to simply delete any previously existing group projects and to add them again than to try to determine which projects exist, which projects need to be deleted, and which projects need to be added.

Because this procedure is called from the ActionUpdate procedure, you have included a call to the ActionDelete procedure before adding any new group projects. Therefore, the next thing that you do is delete any existing group projects by calling the ActionDelete procedure. Then you can turn the loading flag off as it is not needed anymore:

SQL Server and Oracle

```
Case "Group Projects"
    'Turn the loading flag on so no items are processed
    blnLoading = True
    'Delete any previous projects
    Call ActionDelete()
    'Turn the loading flag off
    blnLoading = False
```

Next, you set the SQL property to your usp_InsertGroupProject stored procedure. Then you open the database connection by calling the OpenConnection method on your objData object and initialize the Command object by calling the InitializeCommand method:

```
'Set the SQL string
objData.SQL = "usp_InsertGroupProject"
'Open the database connection
objData.OpenConnection()
```

221

```
'Initialize the Command object
objData.InitializeCommand()
```

You set up a For...Next loop to process all data in the objGroupProjectsDS DataSet. The objGroupProjectsDS DataSet will be populated in two ways. First, when you select a group, the DataSet will be populated with any existing projects in that group. Then, when you drag and drop a project in the Group Projects list, the project will be added to the DataSet. The For...Next loop uses the Count property of the Rows property to determine how many iterations it needs to process:

```
For intIndex = 0 To _
    objGroupProjectsDS.Tables( _
    "GroupProjects").Rows.Count - 1
```

Inside the loop for SQL Server, you add the parameters required by the usp_InsertGroupProject stored procedure. Three parameters are needed: a new GroupProjectID, the GroupID of an existing group, and the ProjectID of the project being added to this group. Because all of these parameters are defined as a UNIQUEIDENTIFIER data type in the stored procedure, you specify this data type in the AddParameter method. The data for the @GroupProjectID is set using the NewGuid method of the Guid structure, whereas the data for the @GroupID is retrieved from the selected group in the cboGroups combo box and the @ProjectID parameters are retrieved from the DataSet.

SQL Server

```
'Add the Parameters to the Parameters collection
objData.AddParameter("@GroupProjectID", _
    Data.SqlDbType.UniqueIdentifier, 16, _
    Guid.NewGuid())
objData.AddParameter("@GroupID", _
    Data.SqlDbType.UniqueIdentifier, 16, _
    cboGroups.SelectedItem.Item("GroupID"))
objData.AddParameter("@ProjectID", _
    Data.SqlDbType.UniqueIdentifier, 16, _
    objGroupProjectsDS.Tables( _
    "GroupProjects").Rows(intIndex).Item("ProjectID"))
```

The same parameters apply for the Oracle version of this stored procedure except that the parameters for Oracle are defined as a CHAR data type. Also, the parameter names are prefixed with the word in as opposed to an at (@) sign for SQL Server.

Oracle

```
'Add the Parameters to the Parameters collection
objData.AddParameter("inGroupProjectID", _
    Data.OracleClient.OracleType.Char, 36, _
    Guid.NewGuid.ToString.ToUpper)
objData.AddParameter("inGroupID", _
    Data.OracleClient.OracleType.Char, 36, _
    cboGroups.SelectedItem.Item("GroupID"))
objData.AddParameter("inProjectID", _
    Data.OracleClient.OracleType.Char, 36, _
    objGroupProjectsDS.Tables( _
    "GroupProjects").Rows(intIndex).Item("ProjectID"))
```

After the parameters have been added to the `Parameters` collection, you execute the stored procedure and then clear the `Parameters` collection for the next iteration of the loop. Remember that you initialize the `Command` object outside of the loop for performance reasons because you will be executing the same stored procedure repeatedly. You could also add the parameters outside of the loop and then merely set their values inside of the loop. However, I demonstrated that method in Chapter 8. I wanted to show you an alternative method in which you add the parameters to the `Parameters` collection inside of the loop and then clear the `Parameters` collection after you execute your stored procedure.

SQL Server and Oracle

```
'Execute the stored procedure
objData.Command.ExecuteNonQuery()
'Clear the Parameters collection for the next insert
objData.Command.Parameters.Clear()
Next
```

After you have finished processing all the data, you close your database connection and clear the previous bindings for the `lstGroupProjects` list box. Turn on the loading flag again and then set the `SelectedIndex` of the `cboGroups` combo box to a value of –1, which indicates that no items are selected in the combo box. Setting the `SelectedIndex` property of the combo box causes the `SelectedIndexChanged` event to be fired, which means the code inside the `cboGroups_SelectedIndexChanged` procedure will be executed. Finally, you turn off the loading flag.

```
'Close the database connection
objData.CloseConnection()
'Clear previous bindings
lstGroupProjects.DataSource = Nothing
lstGroupProjects.DisplayMember = String.Empty
lstGroupProjects.ValueMember = String.Empty
lstGroupProjects.Items.Clear()
'Turn the loading flag on so no items are processed
blnLoading = True
cboGroups.SelectedIndex = -1
'Turn the loading flag off
blnLoading = False
```

The next procedure that you modify is `ActionUpdate`. Here you modify the `Case "Group Projects"` statement, adding the necessary code to perform an update for group projects. All you do here is turn on the loading flag and call the `ActionAdd` procedure to add the new group projects. Remember that the `ActionAdd` procedure will make a call to the `ActionDelete` procedure to delete any existing group projects before attempting to add new ones.

```
Case "Group Projects"
    'Turn the loading flag on so no items are processed
    blnLoading = True
    Call ActionAdd()
```

You modify the `Case "Group Projects"` statement in the `ActionDelete` procedure next, adding new code to delete group projects. The first thing that you do in this procedure is set the `SQL` property to the stored procedure to be executed and then initialize the `Command` object.

SQL Server and Oracle

```
Case "Group Projects"
    'Set the SQL string
    objData.SQL = "usp_DeleteGroupProjects"
    'Initialize the Command object
    objData.InitializeCommand()
```

For SQL Server, you add the one parameter needed, which is the `@GroupID Parameter`, and you set its value using the `GroupID` of the selected group in the `cboGroups` combo box.

SQL Server

```
'Add the Parameters to the Parameters collection
objData.AddParameter("@GroupID", _
    Data.SqlDbType.UniqueIdentifier, _
    16, cboGroups.SelectedItem.Item("GroupID"))
```

You set the one parameter needed for the stored procedure for Oracle in the same manner as you do for SQL Server, except you use the CHAR data type for Oracle and a parameter name prefixed with the word in.

Oracle

```
'Add the Parameters to the Parameters collection
objData.AddParameter("inGroupID", _
    Data.OracleClient.OracleType.Char, _
    36, cboGroups.SelectedItem.Item("GroupID"))
```

After the one and only parameter has been set, you open the database connection, execute the stored procedure, and then close the database connection. Remember that the `usp_DeleteGroupProjects` stored procedure will delete all projects in the GroupProjects table by using the GroupID of the group.

SQL Server and Oracle

```
'Open the database connection
objData.OpenConnection()
'Execute the stored procedure
objData.Command.ExecuteNonQuery()
'Close the database connection
objData.CloseConnection()
```

If the loading flag is not turned on, you clear the data bindings for the Group Projects list and set the `SelectedIndex` property on the `cboGroups` combo box to a value of -1 to clear any selected item:

```
'Clear previous bindings
If Not blnLoading Then
    lstGroupProjects.DataSource = Nothing
    lstGroupProjects.DisplayMember = String.Empty
    lstGroupProjects.ValueMember = String.Empty
    lstGroupProjects.Items.Clear()
    blnLoading = True
    cboGroups.SelectedIndex = -1
    blnLoading = False
End If
```

Given that you want to load a list of projects in the Available Projects list, it makes sense to modify the LoadProjects procedure to fill a DataSet with data and use it to load the lvwProjects list and then to bind the DataSet to the lstProjects list box.

To that end, you modify this procedure by adding code to clear the previous data bindings for the lstProjects ListBox. Then, instead of getting the project data in a DataReader object, you fill a DataSet with the project data.

```
Try
    'Clear previous bindings
    lstProjects.DataSource = Nothing
    lstProjects.DisplayMember = String.Empty
    lstProjects.ValueMember = String.Empty
```

SQL Server

```
    'Get all Projects in a DataSet
    objData.SQL = "usp_SelectProjects"
    objProjectsDS = New Data.DataSet
    Call objData.FillDataSet(objProjectsDS, "Projects")
```

Oracle

```
    'Get all Projects in a DataSet
    objData.SQL = "ProjectsPackage.usp_SelectProjects"
    objData.InitializeCommand()
    objData.AddParameter("results_cursor", _
        Data.OracleClient.OracleType.Cursor, _
        Data.ParameterDirection.Output)
    objProjectsDS = New Data.DataSet
    Call objData.FillDataSet(objProjectsDS, "Projects")
```

Next, you change the loop to load the lvwProjects ListView control to process the data from a DataSet instead of a DataReader object. Because I've already explained how to process data from a DataSet, I won't repeat it again.

SQL Server and Oracle

```
    'Clear previous list
    lvwProjects.Items.Clear()

    'Process all rows
    For intIndex = 0 To objProjectsDS.Tables("Projects").Rows.Count - 1
        'Create a new listview item
        objListViewItem = New ListViewItem
        'Add the data to the listview item
        objListViewItem.Text = objProjectsDS.Tables( _
            "Projects").Rows(intIndex).Item("ProjectName")
        objListViewItem.Tag = objProjectsDS.Tables( _
            "Projects").Rows(intIndex).Item("ProjectID")
        'Add the sub items to the listview item
        objListViewItem.SubItems.Add(objProjectsDS.Tables( _
            "Projects").Rows(intIndex).Item("ProjectDescription"))
        objListViewItem.SubItems.Add(objProjectsDS.Tables( _
```

```
                  "Projects").Rows(intIndex).Item("SequenceNumber"))
              objListViewItem.SubItems.Add(Format(objProjectsDS.Tables( _
                  "Projects").Rows(intIndex).Item("LastUpdateDate"), "g"))
              'Add the listview item to the listview control
              lvwProjects.Items.Add(objListViewItem)
          Next
```

After the `lvwProjects` ListView control has been reloaded, bind the `lstProjects` ListBox control using the `objProjectsDS` DataSet.

```
          'Rebind ListBox control
          lstProjects.DataSource = objProjectsDS.Tables("Projects")
          lstProjects.DisplayMember = "ProjectName"
          lstProjects.ValueMember = "ProjectID"
```

The next procedure that you modify is `LoadGroups`. The modifications to this procedure include adding the `blnLoading` flag to the beginning of the procedure and then turning the flag on and adding the flag to the end of the procedure and turning it off. The code modifications to this procedure are not listed here.

The first new procedure that you add is `cboGroups_SelectedIndexChanged`. This procedure is executed when you select an entry in the `cboGroups` ComboBox control, which is located on the Group Projects screen.

The first thing that you do in this procedure is check the `blnLoading` flag that you've been turning on and off in the previous procedures. If the flag is on, the program is loading data into this combo box. You do not want to execute any code in this procedure, so you exit the procedure.

If the flag is off, you proceed, and the first line of code that you execute is the code to initialize a new instance of the `WDABase` class in your `objData` object. Then you proceed to clear the previous data bindings to the Group Projects list.

SQL Server and Oracle

```
      Private Sub cboGroups_SelectedIndexChanged(ByVal sender As Object, _
          ByVal e As System.EventArgs) Handles cboGroups.SelectedIndexChanged

          'Don't process if the ComboBox is being loaded
          If blnLoading Then
              Exit Sub
          End If

          Using objData As New WDABase
              Try
                  'Clear previous bindings
                  lstGroupProjects.DataSource = Nothing
                  lstGroupProjects.DisplayMember = String.Empty
                  lstGroupProjects.ValueMember = String.Empty
```

This is the procedure where you have implemented the code to execute the view that you created in the previous exercise. The SELECT statement shown later in this section for SQL Server selects only the columns from the view that are needed by your application and only the projects that belong to a particular group.

As you can see, this is a long SQL string to be executing and sending across the network. This is why I'm not a particular fan of using views in this manner. But I have demonstrated this here so that you can see the pros and cons of using views and stored procedures to return data.

You could shorten the SELECT statement by omitting the column names and including only an asterisk but that is not a good idea because you really want to select only the columns from the view your application needs. The view can be modified at any time to include more columns, which means that if you use an asterisk to select all columns, you are retrieving more data than is needed and causing more unnecessary network traffic.

Notice that the FROM clause has specified the view name. Remember that a view is a virtual table in the database; thus, you are selecting data from the virtual table that the database generates for this view. The WHERE clause limits the amount of data returned to only those rows of data that match the GroupID that you specify.

Notice also that you have specified a parameter for the GroupID, which has been named @GroupID. You could have simply supplied the GroupID as part of the SQL string but I wanted to demonstrate how to pass a parameter to a SQL string using SQL Server and Oracle, which is shown next.

Finally, the ORDER BY clause in the SQL statement orders the results by the SequenceNumber column so that all of the projects are displayed in the correct order. Even though the SequenceNumber column does not appear in the SELECT list, it does appear in the columns returned by the view; thus, you are able to use it in the ORDER BY clause.

The next statement that is executed is the method to initialize the Command object. Then you add the Parameter for the GroupID to the Parameters collection. Notice that you have specified this Parameter as if you were executing a stored procedure and that the parameter name in your SELECT statement is specified as if it were used in a stored procedure.

SQL Server

```
'Get the specific Group Projects selected in the ComboBox control
objData.SQL = "SELECT ProjectID, ProjectName " & _
    "FROM vw_SelectGroupProjects " & _
    "WHERE GroupID = @GroupID " & _
    "ORDER BY SequenceNumber"
objData.InitializeCommand()
objData.AddParameter("@GroupID", Data.SqlDbType.UniqueIdentifier, _
    16, cboGroups.SelectedItem.Item("GroupID"))
```

The SELECT statement for Oracle is basically the same as for SQL Server with one minor difference: the parameter name in the WHERE clause. A parameter name that is specified in your SQL statement outside of a stored procedure must be prefixed with a colon.

Next, you initialize the Command object and then add the Parameter to the Parameters collection in the same manner as you did for your Oracle stored procedures.

Oracle

```
'Get the specific Group Projects selected in the ComboBox control
objData.SQL = "SELECT ProjectID, ProjectName " & _
    "FROM vw_SelectGroupProjects " & _
```

```
                "WHERE GroupID = :inGroupID " & _
                "ORDER BY SequenceNumber"
            objData.InitializeCommand()
            objData.AddParameter("inGroupID", _
                Data.OracleClient.OracleType.Char, _
                36, cboGroups.SelectedItem.Item("GroupID"))
```

Next, you set your `objGroupsProjectDS` object to a new instance of the `DataSet` class and then call the `FillDataSet` method to fill the `DataSet`. You pass the appropriate parameters to this method, which includes the `DataSet` object and the name that you want set as the table name in your `DataSet`.

After the `DataSet` object has been populated with data, you want to rebind the `DataSet` to the `lstGroupProjects` list box.

SQL Server and Oracle

```
            objGroupProjectsDS = New Data.DataSet
            Call objData.FillDataSet(objGroupProjectsDS, "GroupProjects")

            'Rebind ListBox control
            lstGroupProjects.DataSource = _
                objGroupProjectsDS.Tables("GroupProjects")
            lstGroupProjects.DisplayMember = "ProjectName"
            lstGroupProjects.ValueMember = "ProjectID"
```

The procedure ends like most others in this project. You have the `Catch` block that handles and displays any errors that may have occurred.

SQL Server and Oracle

```
        Catch ExceptionErr As Exception
            MessageBox.Show(ExceptionErr.Message, strAppTitle)
        End Try
    End Using
End Sub
```

The next procedure that you add is `lstProjects_MouseDown`, which is the first of three procedures required to implement drag-and-drop functionality in your ListBox controls. You may have noticed that you are using two different `DataSets` bound to the ListBox controls and may be thinking, Why not simply populate the ListBox controls with data instead of binding them to a `DataSet`?

Loading a ListBox control with data from a `DataReader` object or a `DataSet` is a very simple procedure and it is even easier to implement drag-and-drop functionality using this method. However, you have bought this book to learn how to write database applications using VB 2005 and I would be remiss if I didn't teach you as much as possible about VB 2005, ADO.NET, and processing and accessing data in your databases.

I have chosen to use bound ListBox controls because this gives you the opportunity to learn even more about `DataSet` objects and how to add new rows to a `DataSet` object and then later process the added rows of data. It also gives you a chance to explore the process of searching a `DataSet` object for a specific row of data.

When you click a mouse button on an item in the lstProjects ListBox, the lstProjects_MouseDown procedure is executed. The first thing that this procedure does is ensure that the left mouse button has been pressed. If it was not the left mouse button, no code in this procedure will be executed.

If the left mouse button is pressed, the DoDragDrop method is called with the appropriate parameters. This method begins a drag-and-drop operation and the second parameter determines how the drag operation will be performed.

Let's back up for a moment and look at the first parameter to the DoDragDrop method. The first parameter is the data that the DoDragDrop method will operate with and is passed to this method as an object. You are retrieving the ProjectID of the selected project in the list box from the objProjectsDS DataSet. Because the ProjectID is a Guid, you must convert it to a string value for it to be handled properly in the lstGroupProjects_DragEnter procedure.

So how do you know which ProjectID to retrieve from the DataSet? You use the SelectedIndex property of the ListBox. This property returns a zero-based index of the item selected in the list box, which corresponds exactly to the zero-based index of the Rows property in the DataSet. You then retrieve the value in the ProjectID column for that row in the DataSet and convert it to a string using the ToString method.

The second parameter to the DoDragDrop method is one of the constants from the DragDropEffects enumeration. There are several possible values to choose from, but what you want to do is to copy the data, not physically move it. This way, all of the projects remain in the Available Projects list and you simply copy the project that should be added to the Group Projects list.

```
Private Sub lstProjects_MouseDown(ByVal sender As Object, _
    ByVal e As System.Windows.Forms.MouseEventArgs) _
    Handles lstProjects.MouseDown

    If e.Button = MouseButtons.Left Then
        lstProjects.DoDragDrop(objProjectsDS.Tables("Projects").Rows( _
            lstProjects.SelectedIndex)("ProjectID").ToString, _
            DragDropEffects.Copy)
    End If
End Sub
```

The lstGroupProjects_DragEnter procedure is the next procedure that you add to support the drag-and-drop operation and it's a little more involved. This procedure is executed when you attempt to drag an item into the Group Projects list box.

Before even attempting to add a project to the Group Projects list, ensure that a group has been selected in the Groups combo box. You do this by checking the SelectedIndex property of the cboGroups combo box. A value of –1 indicates that no group has been selected so you exit this procedure, effectively canceling the drag-and-drop operation.

```
Private Sub lstGroupProjects_DragEnter(ByVal sender As Object, _
    ByVal e As System.Windows.Forms.DragEventArgs) _
    Handles lstGroupProjects.DragEnter

    'Exit if nothing has been selected in the cboGroups ComboBox
    If cboGroups.SelectedIndex = -1 Then
        Exit Sub
    End If
```

If a group has been selected in the Groups combo box, ensure that the item being dragged is in the correct format. You do this by calling the GetDataPresent method on the DragEventArgs class that has been passed as a parameter to this procedure. The DragEventArgs class provides data for the DragDrop, DragEnter, and DragOver events. The GetDataPresent method of the Data property determines whether the data being dragged is in the format that you specify. The DataFormats class provides several public fields that can be used to test for the appropriate data type being passed. Here you are checking to ensure that the object being dragged is a Text data type.

```
'Now ensure that the drag content is the correct type for this control
If (e.Data.GetDataPresent(DataFormats.Text)) Then
```

Now determine whether the item being dragged already exists in the objGroupProjectsDS DataSet. Remember that this DataSet is bound to the list box into which you are dragging the data. To determine whether the item exists in the DataSet, you need to create a DataView object of the DataSet. The DataView object provides a customized view of a table in your DataSet and allows you to sort, filter, and search the data in the DataView.

First, you declare an object as a DataView and then initialize a new instance of it using an overloaded constructor, passing it the GroupProjects table from your objGroupProjectsDS DataSet. To execute the Find method on the DataView, you must first set the column to be used in the Find method. This is done by setting the Sort property to the column that you want to search on in the Find method.

Next, you execute the Find method, passing it the value being dragged from the DragEventArgs class. The Find method will return a value of -1 if it does not find the item in the DataView or return the row number of the item in the DataView. The results of the Find method are set in the intIndex variable.

Now query the intIndex variable to determine whether a matching row was found. If the value is -1, no matching row was found and you set the Effect property of the DragEventArgs class to the Copy constant of the DragDropEffects enumeration. This indicates that a drag-and-drop copy operation will be allowed in the list box. If the value in the intIndex variable is not -1, then you set the Effect property to the None constant in the DragDropEffects enumeration, meaning no drag-and-drop operation is allowed in the list box.

The last Else statement here will also set the Effect property to the None constant in the DragDropEffects enumeration if the data type being dragged is not a Text data type:

```
'If the item does not already exist then allow the copy
Dim objDataView As DataView = New _
    DataView(objGroupProjectsDS.Tables("GroupProjects"))
objDataView.Sort = "ProjectID"
intIndex = objDataView.Find(e.Data.GetData(DataFormats.Text))
If intIndex = -1 Then
    e.Effect = DragDropEffects.Copy
Else
    e.Effect = DragDropEffects.None
End If
Else
    e.Effect = DragDropEffects.None
End If
End Sub
```

The last procedure in the drag-and-drop operation is lstGroupProjects_DragDrop, which performs the actual work of receiving the item being dragged and dropped into the lstGroupProjects ListBox.

The item being dragged and dropped into the Group Projects list will be added to the objGroupProjectsDS DataSet object. To that end, you need to declare a DataRow object that will be used to build the new row to be added to the objGroupProjectsDS DataSet.

Because you will be retrieving the project name from the objProjectsDS DataSet, you need to declare a DataView object and set it to the Projects table in the objProjectsDS DataSet. Then you set the Sort property to the ProjectID column in the DataView and then execute the Find method to find the ProjectID of the project that has been dropped into the list box, setting the row number of the project in the intIndex variable:

```
Private Sub lstGroupProjects_DragDrop(ByVal sender As Object, _
    ByVal e As System.Windows.Forms.DragEventArgs) _
    Handles lstGroupProjects.DragDrop

    Dim objDataRow As DataRow
    Dim objDataView As DataView = New _
        DataView(objProjectsDS.Tables("Projects"))
    objDataView.Sort = "ProjectID"
    intIndex = objDataView.Find(e.Data.GetData(DataFormats.Text))
```

Now it's time to start building the new DataRow to be added to the objGroupProjectsDS DataSet. You initialize the objDataRow object by calling the NewRow method on the table in your DataSet. This initializes the DataRow object using the same schema defined in the table. This means that the DataRow object will have the same columns, data types, and constraints that exist in the table in your DataSet.

The first item that you add in the DataRow object is the ProjectID of the project being dropped into the list. You get the ProjectID from the DragEventArgs class and convert it to a string. The ProjectName is retrieved from the objDataView object using the intIndex variable, which points to the row of data in which the ProjectID was found.

Then you add this DataRow to the GroupProjects table in the objGroupProjectsDS DataSet. You use the Add method of the Rows property, passing it your DataRow object. Finally, for the changes to become visible in the list box, you must accept the changes to the DataSet. You use the AcceptChanges method on the DataSet object:

```
    objDataRow = objGroupProjectsDS.Tables("GroupProjects").NewRow
    objDataRow.Item("ProjectID") = New _
        Guid(e.Data.GetData(DataFormats.Text).ToString)
    objDataRow.Item("ProjectName") = _
        objDataView.Item(intIndex).Item("ProjectName")
    objGroupProjectsDS.Tables("GroupProjects").Rows.Add(objDataRow)
    objGroupProjectsDS.AcceptChanges()
End Sub
```

The final procedure in this exercise is lstGroupProjects_KeyUp. This procedure is called whenever you press and release a key on a selected item in the Group Projects list box. The intent here is to check to see if the Delete key was pressed and released and to delete the selected item.

The KeyEventArgs class provides access to the key that has been pressed and released. You check the key released by comparing the KeyCode property of the KeyEventArgs class to the Delete constant in the Keys enumeration. If this was the key that was released, you delete the selected item.

The Rows property provides the RemoveAt method, which accepts the index of the row to be removed from the table. The SelectedIndex property of the Group Projects ListBox provides the index of the selected item and is used as input to the RemoveAt method.

Again, for the changes to become visible in the list box, you must accept the changes made to the DataSet in which the list box is bound.

```
Private Sub lstGroupProjects_KeyUp(ByVal sender As Object, _
    ByVal e As System.Windows.Forms.KeyEventArgs) _
    Handles lstGroupProjects.KeyUp

    If e.KeyCode = Keys.Delete Then
        objGroupProjectsDS.Tables("GroupProjects").Rows.RemoveAt( _
            lstGroupProjects.SelectedIndex)
        objGroupProjectsDS.AcceptChanges()
    End If
End Sub
```

That wraps up the code for this exercise, in which you have learned how to implement code to execute a view in your database, how to perform a drag-and-drop operation between two list boxes, and how to add and remove rows of data in a DataSet. You also learned how to work with a DataView object to find a specific row of data. So, all in all, this exercise has proven to be a good learning experience for you and has covered a wide variety of topics.

Summary

This has been a fairly long chapter but it has covered a lot of ground with regard to stored procedures and views for SQL Server and Oracle. You have seen firsthand how to execute stored procedures that not only insert, update, and delete data but also return data. Regardless of which back-end database you are using, you have had the opportunity to see the different ways each database handles stored procedures that return data.

If you are using an Oracle database, you also had a chance to create stored procedures in a package, which allowed you to return data from those stored procedures. You also had a chance to implement the functionality in your program to retrieve and process the data returned from those stored procedures.

In your examination of views, you learned how a view is constructed in both SQL Server and Oracle and how you execute a view from your VB 2005 code. Fortunately, both databases handle views in the same manner, and selecting data from a view in your code is handled in the same manner, by specifying a SELECT statement.

In the implementation of the drag-and-drop functionality, you had the opportunity to become more familiar with DataSet objects. You were exposed to the DataView and DataRow objects and should now be familiar with how to search for data contained in a DataSet and how to add and remove rows of data in a DataSet.

To summarize, you should know how to:

❑ Create a stored procedure in your database using Visual Studio 2005

❑ Return data from a stored procedure using either SQL Server or Oracle

❑ Execute a stored procedure in your VB 2005 programs

❑ Create and select data from views

❑ Use a `DataView` object to find data in a `DataSet`

❑ Use a `DataRow` object to add a new row of data to a `DataSet`

In Chapter 10, you build middle-tier components, which include a business logic component to handle business logic and a data access component. These components will shield your application from the complexities of the business logic needed to implement the business rules around your processes and to access your back-end database.

Exercises

Exercise 1

Create a view to select the ProjectID, ProjectName, and ProjectDescription columns for all rows of data from the Projects table. Name the view **vw_SelectProjects**. Then create a Windows application that selects the ProjectID and ProjectName from the view, and populate a DataTable with the data. Bind the data to a list box control on the form to display all project names. Use your `app.config` file and `WDABase` class from your Time Tracker application in this exercise.

Exercise 2

Using the application created in Exercise 1, add a text box to the form to display the project description. When you click a project in the ListBox control, execute the code to select the corresponding project description from the vw_SelectProjects view and display it in the text box.

Tip: The `WHERE` clause in your SQL statement should look like this for SQL Server:

```
WHERE ProjectID = @ProjectID
```

and like this for Oracle:

```
WHERE ProjectID = :inProjectID
```

Building Business Logic and Data Access Components

Information technology is changing at a rapid pace and your company makes changes to keep up with the shifting landscape, not just in information technology but in the way your company does business. These changes often have a cascading effect on the applications that you write — as the business plan for your company changes, your applications may also change. Changes to your database and business logic can be shielded from your application through the use of *components,* which can minimize, if not eliminate, the impact of these changes to your applications.

In real-world applications, you typically put your business logic and data access logic in separate components to shield your application from these complexities. This enables your application to concentrate on the user interface (UI) that deals with the presentation of data and the how the end user interacts with that data.

In this chapter, you see firsthand how the use of business components and data access components can help eliminate changes in your front-end application as you design and build components to be used by your Time Tracker application. Any changes occurring in the database or business logic will be shielded from your application.

In this chapter, you:

- ❑ Explore the design goals of business logic and data access components
- ❑ Learn how to encrypt and decrypt data and how to hash data
- ❑ Learn how to read and write data in the registry
- ❑ Build a data access component
- ❑ Build a business logic component
- ❑ Modify your Time Tracker application to use these components

Distributed Application Architecture

A distributed application architecture is made up of a client interface and multiple components that employ business logic and data access logic. Figure 10-1 shows what a typical distributed application architecture might look. The components in this architecture typically run on different servers but can sometimes run on the same server while the database itself resides on a different server. When it is said that you have a distributed application, this means that your application runs on the client and the components run on one or more separate servers.

One benefit of using distributed applications is that you create loosely coupled applications that are independent of the database and that separate the presentation logic from the business logic. Security is also a major benefit and can be included at all levels of the design, not just for the database. Performance and scalability are other benefits of a well-designed distributed application architecture.

Loosely coupled applications take advantage of technologies such as Web Services and message queuing. Although you don't see many applications developed today using message queuing, they have been around for a while. Today's hottest technology is Web Services and an application uses a Web Service to pass and receive data. The internals of a Web Service encapsulate the logic needed to process a request and to respond to the caller with the appropriate information. This shields the application from any business logic and enables multiple applications to use a single Web Service. A single Web Service can also be accessed from Windows applications as well as Web applications.

Business logic can and should be separated from the presentation logic in an application through the use of business logic components and/or Web Services. These components encapsulate the logic required to follow a given workflow for a business process. For example, suppose you have a business component that maintains checking and savings account balances. When you transfer money from one account to another, you need to encapsulate the logic needed to debit one account and credit another account in the workflow. This workflow ensures that the money to be transferred actually exists in the account, that one account is debited, and that the other account is credited. Most importantly, the workflow ensures atomicity.

Atomicity means that all transactions are completed as a group. If the debit of the first account succeeds and the credit of the second account fails, you want to roll back the debit to the first account. This ensures atomicity and maintains the integrity of your data.

Business logic components deal with workflows and business logic and have no knowledge of the presentation of the data or how the data is stored or accessed in the database. Accessing the data in your database is the job of your data access components.

Your data access components know what database to use, how to connect to that database, and which stored procedures and views to execute to return the information needed by a business logic component. Data access components are typically designed as stateless. This means that no state is held between calls to the various methods in your data access components. To make multiple calls to a data access component to insert data into multiple tables, you implement transactions in the workflows of your business logic components. The job of a data access component is to shield the business logic components from the knowledge of and complexities of the database.

Before you design a distributed application, you need to research the available technologies and determine which technology is best suited for your business needs. The MSDN Library that is installed with

Visual Studio 2005 has a wealth of information about architecture and design patterns for distributed applications. You would be wise to spend some time reviewing this material before implementing a production design.

Design Goals of the Wrox Components

The design goal of the business logic and data access components that you'll be building in this chapter is to illustrate the separation of presentation, business logic, and data access logic. These components will be designed to run on a single machine, but with a little work you can easily adapt them to run on separate machines.

When designing your components, you must determine a logical starting point for your design. This would be the actual data that you'll be dealing with and you need to design a method to get data into and out of the database. To that end, you start your design process with the data access component.

Designing the data access component

Several factors must be considered when designing your data access component. The first is how the data access component learns which database to connect to and how it gets the required credentials to establish that connection. You've already seen how to use an application configuration file to pass database information to your application so you'll want to explore something a little different here.

Components are typically created as dynamic link libraries (DLLs) and are installed on the servers where they run. Registry entries are usually created to provide the DLLs with the information they need to run. For example, you could create registry entries for your data access component to read to get the database information that it needs to connect to the appropriate database. This is the route that you take when building your data access component.

Using the registry provides a little more security than using an app.config file but is still vulnerable to prying eyes. You do not want unauthorized personnel to be able to view your database credentials in the registry and then to be able to use those credentials to connect to your database. Therefore, you need to encrypt the information before storing it in the registry. Your data access component must be able to encrypt and decrypt data.

Your data access component should implement classes that pertain to particular data-related functions. For example, a Projects screen in your Time Tracker application lets you view, insert, update, and delete projects. The Groups screen allows you to view, insert, update, and delete groups. Therefore, you should provide a logical separation of these processes in your data access component through the use of different classes and implement functions in each class related to those processes.

Taking the Projects screen as an example, you would implement a class for projects that would provide functions to select all project data; select a specific project; and insert, update, and delete projects. These functions would then execute the appropriate stored procedures in your database to perform the task at hand.

A base class that provides access to the core database functions is also needed and you have already designed and used that class in your existing Time Tracker application. The WDABase class will be used in your data access component to provide the necessary functions to retrieve data and to insert, update, and delete data in the database.

Designing the business logic component

The design of your business logic component will follow a design similar to that of your data access component by providing separate classes for each business process. Therefore, you implement a class to provide the business logic required to select all projects, select a single project, and insert, update, and delete projects. Of course, the logic in your business logic component will provide the business logic required to perform these tasks and then call the appropriate functions in your data access component to have the data retrieved or entered in the database.

For example, a class to handle the business logic for projects would include logic to ensure that the data to insert a new project is complete and that the values for the various fields fall in the range required. For example, to insert a new project, your business component could first ensure that all required data for a project is present. Then it would ensure that the values do not fall outside of the range of the field definitions in the database. A project name can be a maximum of 50 characters in length so your business component could validate that the project name does not exceed this length. It could also validate such items as the sequence number to ensure that it falls in a valid range of 1 through 255.

Your business logic component could also provide your presentation logic with the necessary schema for a new project, and this is what you will be implementing in this design. Your business logic component will build a DataSet that contains the necessary fields for a new project and the data type for those fields. It will also contain constraint information about each field indicating which fields are required.

Design overview

Now that you have an idea of what will be required for your data access component and your business logic component, take a look at the big picture before proceeding to build these components. Figure 10-1 illustrates the separation of the different layers in your design and the components required in each layer.

The presentation layer is where your Time Tracker application runs and this is the project that you have been working with up until this point. The application running in the presentation layer is responsible for presenting the user interface that the user will work with and for interacting with the business logic layer to retrieve and send data.

The business logic layer contains the Wrox Business Logic Component and is responsible for applying the appropriate workflows for your business logic. This includes ensuring that data to be inserted is validated and that the entire workflow is successful or backed out. This business logic component interacts with the presentation layer and the data access layer. The component does not know about stored procedures or any processes that may happen in the data access component; it merely knows that functions exists to select, insert, update, and delete data.

The business logic component is broken down into individual classes that relate to the major functions of your application. Each class contains the functions to provide the application with the data necessary for that area and any necessary workflows for inserting, updating, and deleting data.

The data access layer contains the Wrox Data Access component, which is responsible for retrieving data from the database as well as inserting, updating, and deleting data in the database. The data access component has a base class that all the other classes in the data access component inherit. This is the same base class that you've been working with up until this point and provides the base functions needed to perform the database operations.

Like the business logic component, the data access component is broken down into individual classes that relate to the major areas of your application. These classes select, insert, update, and delete data for those major areas in your application.

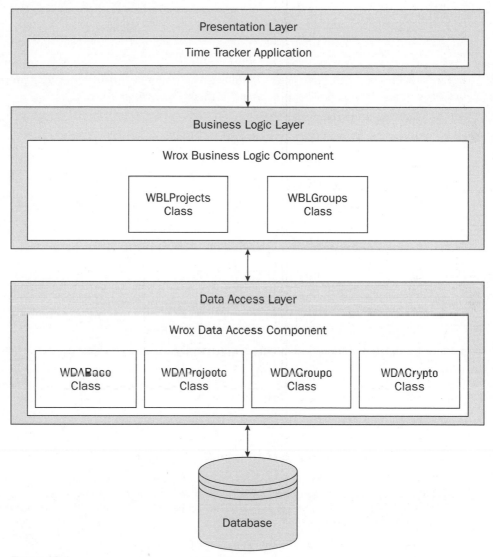

Figure 10-1

Before you build the components shown in Figure 10-1, you need to create some registry keys to be used in the data access component. This next Try It Out guides you through the process of creating registry keys and setting their values.

In this exercise, you create the encryption class to be used in your data access component and a small Windows application to create the registry keys. The data access component doesn't create registry keys; it merely reads the values from the registry to discover which database it should connect to.

Try It Out   Creating Registry Keys

To create this application:

1. Start Visual Studio 2005 and start a new project by clicking the Create Project link on the Recent Projects tab of the Start page or by selecting File ⇨ New ⇨ Project.

2. In the New Project dialog box, select a Windows Application template and enter a project name of **Create Registry Keys**. Click OK to have this project created.

3. Set the following properties for Form1:

   ❑ Set FormBorderStyle to FixedSingle.

   ❑ Set MaximizeBox to False.

   ❑ Set MinimizeBox to False.

   ❑ Set Size to **360, 200**.

   ❑ Set StartPosition to CenterScreen.

   ❑ Set Text to **Create Registry Keys**.

4. Add six labels, six text boxes, and one button to the form and arrange them to look similar to the controls shown on the form in Figure 10-2. Set the following properties for these controls:

   ❑ Set the Name property of TextBox1 to **txtCompany**.

   ❑ Set the Name property of TextBox2 to **txtApplication**.

   ❑ Set the Name property of TextBox3 to **txtDBServer**.

   ❑ Set the Name property of TextBox4 to **txtDBName**.

   ❑ Set the Name property of TextBox5 to **txtLogin**.

   ❑ Set the Name property of TextBox6 to **txtPassword**, and set the PasswordChar property to *.

   ❑ Set the Name property of Button1 to **btnCreate** and set the Text property to **Create.**

5. Add the encryption class for this project. Right-click the project in Solution Explorer and choose Add; then choose the Class submenu item. In the Add New Item – Create Registry Keys dialog box, enter a class name of **WDACrypto.vb** in the Name field. Then click the Add button to have this class added to your project.

6. Add the following Imports statements at the top of your class:

```
Imports System.IO
Imports System.Text
Imports System.Security.Cryptography
```

7. Add the following `Implements` statement to your class. When you finish typing the complete `Implements` statement and press Enter, the `Dispose` procedure is automatically added:

```
Public Class WDACrypto
    Implements IDisposable

End Class
```

8. Add the following variable declarations at the top of your class:

```
Implements IDisposable

'Private variables and objects
Private bytKey() As Byte
Private bytIV() As Byte
Private bytInput() As Byte

Private objTripleDES As TripleDESCryptoServiceProvider
Private objOutputStream As MemoryStream
```

9. Add the following constructor to this class:

```
Public Sub New(ByVal Key() As Byte, ByVal IV() As Byte)
    'Initialize the security key and initialization vector
    bytKey = Key
    bytIV = IV

    'Instantiate a new instance of the TripleDESCryptoServiceProvider class
    objTripleDES = New TripleDESCryptoServiceProvider
End Sub
```

10. Add the following code to the `Dispose` procedure:

```
Private Overloads Sub Dispose(ByVal disposing As Boolean)
    If Not Me.disposed Then
        If disposing Then
            ' TODO: put code to dispose managed resources
        End If

        'Clean up
        objTripleDES = Nothing
    End If
    Me.disposed = True
End Sub
```

11. Add the following function to encrypt a string and to return the encrypted string to the caller:

```
Public Function Encrypt(ByVal strToEncrypt As String) As String
    Try
        'Convert the input string to a byte array
        Dim bytInput() As Byte = Encoding.UTF8.GetBytes(strToEncrypt)

        'Instantiate a new instance of the MemoryStream class
        Using objOutputStream As New MemoryStream
            'Encrypt the byte array
            Dim objCryptoStream As New CryptoStream(objOutputStream, _
```

```
                    objTripleDES.CreateEncryptor(bytKey, bytIV), _
                    CryptoStreamMode.Write)
                objCryptoStream.Write(bytInput, 0, bytInput.Length)
                objCryptoStream.FlushFinalBlock()

                'Return the byte array as a Base64 string
                Encrypt = Convert.ToBase64String(objOutputStream.ToArray())
            End Using

        Catch ExceptionErr As Exception
            Throw New System.Exception(ExceptionErr.Message, _
                ExceptionErr.InnerException)
        End Try
    End Function
```

12. Add the following function to decrypt a string and return the decrypted string to the caller:

```
Public Function Decrypt(ByVal strToDecrypt As String) As String
    Try
        'Convert the input string to a byte array
        Dim inputByteArray() As Byte = Convert.FromBase64String(strToDecrypt)

        'Instantiate a new instance of the MemoryStream class
        Using objOutputStream As New MemoryStream
            'Decrypt the byte array
            Dim objCryptoStream As New CryptoStream(objOutputStream, _
                objTripleDES.CreateDecryptor(bytKey, bytIV), _
                CryptoStreamMode.Write)
            objCryptoStream.Write(inputByteArray, 0, inputByteArray.Length)
            objCryptoStream.FlushFinalBlock()

            'Return the byte array as a string
            Decrypt = Encoding.UTF8.GetString(objOutputStream.ToArray())
        End Using

    Catch ExceptionErr As Exception
        Throw New System.Exception(ExceptionErr.Message, _
            ExceptionErr.InnerException)
    End Try
End Function
```

13. View the code for your form and add the following `Imports` statement:

```
Imports Microsoft.Win32
```

14. Click the Class Name combo box and select btnCreate. In the Method Name combo box select the Click event. Add the following code to the `btnCreate_Click` procedure:

```
Private Sub btnCreate_Click(ByVal sender As Object, _
    ByVal e As System.EventArgs) Handles btnCreate.Click

    'Declare variables
    Dim objReg As RegistryKey

    'Key size must be 128 bits to 192 bits in increments of 64 bits
    Dim bytKey() As Byte = System.Text.Encoding.UTF8.GetBytes( _
```

```
                    "G~v!x@Z#c$a%C^b&h*K(e)K_")
        Dim bytIV() As Byte = System.Text.Encoding.UTF8.GetBytes( _
            "rgY^p$b%")

        Using objCrypto As New WDACrypto(bytKey, bytIV)
            Try
                'Try to open the key with write permissions
                objReg = Registry.LocalMachine.OpenSubKey( _
                    "SOFTWARE\" & txtCompany.Text & "\" & _
                    txtApplication.Text & "\Database", True)

                If objReg Is Nothing Then
                    'Create the registry key
                    objReg = Registry.LocalMachine.CreateSubKey( _
                        "SOFTWARE\" & txtCompany.Text & "\" & _
                        txtApplication.Text & "\Database")
                End If

                'Set the registry key values
                objReg.SetValue("Server", txtDBServer.Text)
                objReg.SetValue("Database", txtDBName.Text)
                objReg.SetValue("Login", objCrypto.Encrypt(txtLogin.Text))
                objReg.SetValue("Password", objCrypto.Encrypt(txtPassword.Text))

                'Close the registry key
                objReg.Close()

                'Display a message that the key was created
                MessageBox.Show("Registry key successfully created.")
            Catch SecurityExceptionErr As Security.SecurityException
                MessageBox.Show(SecurityExceptionErr.Message)
            Finally
                'Clean up
                objReg = Nothing
            End Try
        End Using
    End Sub
```

That's all the code you need. You are ready to test your project so start it up. When your form displays, enter the information shown in Figure 10-2. Replace the value of myServer with the name of the server running your SQL Server; or if you are running an instance of SQL Server, the server name followed by a backslash and the instance name. If you are running Oracle, enter the name of the SID that you have been using.

For both SQL Server and Oracle readers, replace the value of myLogin with your database login and enter your password in the Password field.

Click the Create button to have the registry key created. When the registry key has been created, you receive a confirmation dialog box; click OK to close this dialog box.

You can verify this registry key by running the Registry Editor program. Click the Start button and click Run. In the Run dialog box, enter **regedit** in the Open combo box and then click OK. When the Registry

Editor appears, navigate to the following key in the registry to view the values that were created for this registry key: HKEY_LOCAL_MACHINE\SOFTWARE\Wrox\Time Tracker\Database.

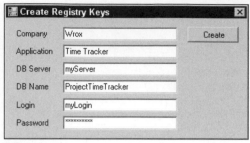

Figure 10-2

How It Works

The first code that you write for this exercise is in a class for encrypting and decrypting data. The .NET Framework provides many options for encrypting and decrypting data and different classes that support various types of encryption. The type of encryption chosen for this exercise was the Triple Data Encryption Standard, which is implemented in the TripleDESCryptoServiceProvider class.

I chose this method of encryption because the TripleDESCryptoServiceProvider class is very easy to work with. Another reason is that it supports encryption key lengths from 128 to 192 bits, providing a higher level of security for your data.

All encryption classes are derived from the System.Security.Cryptography namespace, which was one of the namespaces that you imported into the WDACrypto class, as shown here:

```
Imports System.IO
Imports System.Text
Imports System.Security.Cryptography
```

Like the WDABase class that you created in Chapter 6, you want this class to implement the IDisposable interface so you code the Implements statement in your class. When you press Enter, the Dispose procedure is automatically added to your class.

```
Implements IDisposable
```

Defined at the class level are the variables and objects needed in this class. These variables and objects will be accessible to all procedures in this class.

```
'Private variables and objects
Private bytKey() As Byte
Private bytIV() As Byte
Private bytInput() As Byte

Private objTripleDES As TripleDESCryptoServiceProvider
Private objOutputStream As MemoryStream
```

The constructor for this class accepts the key and initialization vector as input and sets the variables for this class with the data being passed here. Requiring these parameters in the constructor ensures that anyone wanting to use this class passes the appropriate data that the class needs and helps to add a bit more security to this class by not storing the security key and initialization vector in the class. Next you instantiate a new instance of the `TripleDESCryptoServiceProvider` class.

```
Public Sub New(ByVal Key() As Byte, ByVal IV() As Byte)
    'Initialize the security key and initialization vector
    bytKey = Key
    bytIV = IV

    'Instantiate a new instance of the TripleDESCryptoServiceProvider class
    objTripleDES = New TripleDESCryptoServiceProvider
End Sub
```

The Dispose procedure provides the code to set your objTripleDes object to Nothing, releasing your reference to it.

```
Private Overloads Sub Dispose(ByVal disposing As Boolean)
    If Not Me.disposed Then
        If disposing Then
            ' TODO: put code to dispose managed resources
        End If

        'Clean up
        objTripleDES = Nothing
    End If
    Me.disposed = True
End Sub
```

There are two main functions in this class, a function to encrypt data and a function to decrypt data. The `Encrypt` function accepts the string to be encrypted and returns the encrypted string as output. A `Try...Catch` block handles any errors that might occur when attempting to encrypt data.

The first thing that you need to do in this procedure is to convert the input string into a byte array, which is done using the `Encoding` class. The `Encoding` class is used to encode data in the various character formats.

The `UTF8` property of this class represents data encoding in the UCS Transformation Format 8-bit (UTF-8) format, which is the most widely used method of encoding data. This format handles Unicode characters so it can be used on any language to provide international support in your applications. The `GetBytes` method encodes the string supplied as input into a byte array of UTF-8 characters.

```
Public Function Encrypt(ByVal strToEncrypt As String) As String
    Try
        'Convert the input string to a byte array
        Dim bytInput() As Byte = Encoding.UTF8.GetBytes(strToEncrypt)
```

The `CryptoStream` class performs the actual encryption using the cryptographic algorithm that you specified; in this case, it will be the TripleDES algorithm. The constructor for the `CryptoStream` class expects an output stream to write the encrypted results to the cryptographic transformation algorithm to be used and to the mode that should be used.

The output from the `CryptoStream` class is written to a `MemoryStream` object so you initialized the `objOutputStream` object in a `Using...End Using` block. Then you declare and initialize an object for the `CryptoStream` class, passing the constructor the required parameters.

Notice the cryptographic transformation parameter to the `CryptoStream` class. You are calling the `CreateEncryptor` method on the `objTripleDes` object and are passing it the key and initialization vector. This returns a `TripleDes` encryptor object to be used for the cryptographic transformation.

```
'Instantiate a new instance of the MemoryStream class
Using objOutputStream As New MemoryStream
    'Encrypt the byte array
    Dim objCryptoStream As New CryptoStream(objOutputStream, _
        objTripleDES.CreateEncryptor(bytKey, bytIV), _
        CryptoStreamMode.Write)
```

Now you want to write the encrypted output to the `objOutputStream` object and you do so by using the `Write` method from the `CryptoStream` class. Here you are specifying the byte array that contains the input, the offset within that byte array, and the number of bytes to be written. Because you want to write the entire contents to the output buffer, you use the `Length` property of the byte array to determine how many bytes should be written. Next, you flush the buffer, signifying that the write operation is complete.

```
objCryptoStream.Write(bytInput, 0, bytInput.Length)
objCryptoStream.FlushFinalBlock()
```

You need to transform the byte array back into a complete string to be returned by this function. You could use the `Encoding.UTF8.GetString` method to return the string because you used the opposite function to convert the string into a byte array. However, if you want to use the encoded string in XML, you should use something that can be written to and read from XML without any problems. The `GetString` method returns an encrypted string with all kinds of special characters that could cause problems when used in XML.

The `Convert` class converts one base data type into another. The following code uses the `ToBase64String` method to convert an array of bytes into a complete string. The input to this method is a byte array so you use the `ToArray` function to convert the individual bytes in the `objOutputStream` object to a byte array.

```
'Return the byte array as a Base64 string
Encrypt = Convert.ToBase64String(objOutputStream.ToArray())
End Using
```

The encrypted value for the login, sa, *is returned as* ☐$/ *using the* `Encoding.UTF8.GetString` *method and is returned as* iJ6/25EkpS8= *using the* `Convert.ToBase64String` *method. You can see that the last method will return normal characters that do not need any special encoding when used in an XML document.*

The `Catch` block handles an exception if thrown and then throws a new exception to the caller when an error occurs:

```
Catch ExceptionErr As Exception
    Throw New System.Exception(ExceptionErr.Message, _
        ExceptionErr.InnerException)
    End Try
End Function
```

The Decrypt function that you coded works in the same manner as the Encrypt function except in reverse. You convert your encrypted string into a byte array. Notice that you are using the Convert function for this and the FromBase64String method.

```
Public Function Decrypt(ByVal strToDecrypt As String) As String
    Try
        'Convert the input string to a byte array
        Dim inputByteArray() As Byte = Convert.FromBase64String(strToDecrypt)
```

Next, you initialize a new instance of the MemoryStream class followed by the CryptoStream class, passing it the required parameters to decrypt the string. Using the Write method of your objCryptoStream object, you write the decrypted value into a byte array and then flush the memory stream.

```
        'Instantiate a new instance of the MemoryStream class
        Using objOutputStream As New MemoryStream
            'Decrypt the byte array
            Dim objCryptoStream As New CryptoStream(objOutputStream, _
                objTripleDES.CreateDecryptor(bytKey, bytIV), _
                CryptoStreamMode.Write)
            objCryptoStream.Write(inputByteArray, 0, inputByteArray.Length)
            objCryptoStream.FlushFinalBlock()
```

You want to return the decrypted string back to the caller in UTF-8 format so you use the Encoding class with the UTF8 property to get the decrypted string from the byte array.

The Catch block handles any errors that occur and throws a new exception that will be returned to the caller:

```
            'Return the byte array as a string
            Decrypt = Encoding.UTF8.GetString(objOutputStream.ToArray())
        End Using

    Catch ExceptionErr As Exception
        Throw New System.Exception(ExceptionErr.Message, _
            ExceptionErr.InnerException)
    End Try
End Function
```

Switching now to the code that you add to your form: The first thing that you do is add the appropriate Imports statement. The Microsoft.Win32 namespace provides access to the registry classes that will be used to read and write keys and values in the registry.

```
Imports Microsoft.Win32
```

The btnCreate_Click procedure is executed when you click the button on your form. It encrypts some of the values from your form, and then creates and writes the registry keys and values. The first thing that you do in this procedure is declare and initialize some variables.

The first variable that you declare is an object for the RegistryKey class that provides access to registry keys. Then you declare a byte array for the key and initialization vector for your WDACrypto class and set their values.

```
Private Sub btnCreate_Click(ByVal sender As Object, _
    ByVal e As System.EventArgs) Handles btnCreate.Click

    'Declare variables
    Dim objReg As RegistryKey

    'Key size must be 128 bits to 192 bits in increments of 64 bits
    Dim bytKey() As Byte = System.Text.Encoding.UTF8.GetBytes( _
        "G~v!x@Z#c$a%C^b&h*K(e)K_")
    Dim bytIV() As Byte = System.Text.Encoding.UTF8.GetBytes( _
        "rgY^p$b%")
```

You instantiate a new instance of the WDACrypto class, passing it the required parameters in a Using...
End Using block. Then you set up a Try...Catch...Finally block to handle any exceptions that
might be thrown. The first thing that you do in the Try block is open the registry key with write permissions. If the registry subkey does not exist, the objReg object is Nothing and you know that you need to
create the subkey in the registry. If the subkey does exist, the objReg object is set to the subkey and you
can overwrite the values in the subkey.

The Registry class contains fields that provide access to the root keys found in the registry. The following code accesses the LocalMachine root key and attempts to open a subkey under this root key:

```
Using objCrypto As New WDACrypto(bytKey, bytIV)
    Try
        'Try to open the key with write permissions
        objReg = Registry.LocalMachine.OpenSubKey( _
            "SOFTWARE\" & txtCompany.Text & "\" & _
            txtApplication.Text & "\Database", True)

        If objReg Is Nothing Then
            'Create the registry key
            objReg = Registry.LocalMachine.CreateSubKey( _
                "SOFTWARE\" & txtCompany.Text & "\" & _
                txtApplication.Text & "\Database")
        End If
```

After you have opened or created the subkey, the objReg object is set to the subkey, allowing you to
read and write the values for that subkey. You merely want to set the values so you use the SetValue
method. The SetValue method accepts two parameters: the name of the value and the data to store in
the value.

The first value that you set is the server, followed by the database. The data for these values is retrieved
from the text boxes on your form. The values for login and password are also retrieved from your form
but are encrypted before being set.

You may be wondering why I chose to encrypt both the login and password. This just provides an extra
level of security and keeps prying eyes from determining at a glance whose login is being used.

```
'Set the registry key values
objReg.SetValue("Server", txtDBServer.Text)
objReg.SetValue("Database", txtDBName.Text)
objReg.SetValue("Login", objCrypto.Encrypt(txtLogin.Text))
objReg.SetValue("Password", objCrypto.Encrypt(txtPassword.Text))
```

After you have set the values in the registry, you close the registry subkey. Finally, you display a MessageBox dialog box to indicate that the registry keys were set:

```
'Close the registry key
objReg.Close()

'Display a message that the key was created
MessageBox.Show("Registry key successfully created.")
```

The `Catch` block provides the appropriate error-handling code to display a message reporting any errors that may have occurred. The `Finally` block contains the necessary code to clean up the resources used in this procedure:

```
        Catch SecurityExceptionErr As Security.SecurityException
            MessageBox.Show(SecurityExceptionErr.Message)
        Finally
            'Clean up
            objReg = Nothing
        End Try
    End Using
End Sub
```

At this point, your project creates registry keys and writes values in the registry. In addition, you can encrypt the data being written to the registry. You can use this program as a guide to write other applications that create registry keys and write values in the registry.

In this next Try It Out, you create the Wrox Data Access Component and leverage your existing classes. You use the `WDACrypto` class that you wrote in the previous exercise and the `WDABase` class that you've been using in your Time Tracker application. This significantly reduces the amount of code you have to write.

You update this component in subsequent chapters to enhance the functionality that you build in the Time Tracker application. To facilitate these enhancements, you create this component as part of the Time Tracker solution.

Try It Out   Wrox Data Access Component

To create this component:

1.   Open your Time Tracker project in Visual Studio 2005.

2.   Right click the Time Tracker solution in Solution Explorer, and then select Add ➪ New Project from the context menu.

3.   In the Add New Project dialog box, select Class Library in the Templates pane, and enter a project name of **WroxDataAccess** in the Name field. Click OK to have this project created and added to the Time Tracker solution.

4.   Right-click the WroxDataAccess project in Solution Explorer and select Properties. In the Property Pages, click the Compile tab and then click the Advanced Compile Options button.

5.   The DLL base address that is displayed has a default value of &H00400000, which is the default value of all class libraries that are created. Enter a new value of **&H113A0000** and then click OK to close this dialog box and then close the Property Pages window.

6. You want to delete the default class that was added so right-click `Class1.vb` in Solution Explorer and select Delete. You'll be prompted with a confirmation dialog box; click OK to delete this class.

7. You need to add the `WDACrypto.vb` class from the Create Registry Keys project, so right-click the WroxDataAccess project in Solution Explorer, select Add from the context menu, and then select Add Existing Item. In the Add Existing Item – WroxDataAccess dialog box, navigate to your Create Registry Keys project and select the `WDACrypto.vb` class. Then click Add to add this class to your project.

8. Expand your Time Tracker project in Solution Explorer if it is not already expanded. Click the `WDABase.vb` class in the Time Tracker project and drag it to the WroxDataAcess project and drop it. This copies the `WDABase.vb` class from your Time Tracker project to the WroxDataAccess project.

9. You want to delete the `WDABase.vb` class left in your Time Tracker project, so right-click the `WDABase.vb` class in Solution Explorer and choose Delete. You'll be prompted with a confirmation dialog box; click OK to delete this class.

10. You'll need to set a reference to the `System.Data` namespace in the WroxDataAccess project so right-click this project in the Solution Explorer and choose Add Reference from the context menu. Select the `System.Data` namespace in the list and then click OK to have this reference added to your project.

11. Readers using Oracle will also need to set a reference to the `System.Data.OracleClient` namespace so repeat the previous step and select the `System.Data.OracleClient` namespace.

12. Add the following `Imports` statements in the WDABase class:

```
Imports Microsoft.Win32
Imports System.Data
```

13. Modify the constructor for the class as follows.

Caution: The key and initialization vector byte arrays must be the same ones used in your Create Registry Keys project.

SQL Server and Oracle

```
Public Sub New(ByVal Company As String, ByVal Application As String)
    'Declare variables
    Dim objReg As RegistryKey

    'Key size must be 128 bits to 192 bits in increments of 64 bits
    Dim bytKey() As Byte = System.Text.Encoding.UTF8.GetBytes( _
        "G~v!x@Z#c$a%C^b&h*K(e)K_")
    Dim bytIV() As Byte = System.Text.Encoding.UTF8.GetBytes( _
        "rgY^p$b%")

    Using objCrypto As New WDACrypto(bytKey, bytIV)
        Try
            'Open the registry key
            objReg = Registry.LocalMachine.OpenSubKey("SOFTWARE\" & _
                Company & "\" & Application & "\Database", False)
```

SQL Server without Integrated Security

```
'Build the SQL connection string from the registry values
'and initialize the Connection object
Connection = New SqlConnection( _
    "Data Source=" & objReg.GetValue("Server") & ";" & _
    "Database=" & objReg.GetValue("Database") & ";" & _
    "User ID=" & objCrypto.Decrypt( _
        objReg.GetValue("Login")) & ";" & _
    "Password=" & objCrypto.Decrypt( _
        objReg.GetValue("Password")) & ";")
```

SQL Server with Integrated Security

```
'Build the SQL connection string from the registry values
'and initialize the Connection object
Connection = New SqlConnection( _
    "Data Source=" & objReg.GetValue("Server") & ";" & _
    "Database=" & objReg.GetValue("Database") & ";" & _
    "Integrated Security=SSPI;")
```

Oracle

```
'Build the SQL connection string from the registry values
'and initialize the Connection object
Connection = New OracleConnection( _
    "Data Source=" & objReg.GetValue("Server") & ";" & _
    "User ID=" & objCrypto.Decrypt( _
        objReg.GetValue("Login")) & ";" & _
    "Password=" & objCrypto.Decrypt( _
        objReg.GetValue("Password")) & ";")
```

SQL Server and Oracle

```
        Catch ExceptionErr As Exception
            Throw New System.Exception(ExceptionErr.Message, _
                ExceptionErr.InnerException)
        Finally
            'Clean up
            objReg = Nothing
        End Try
    End Using
End Sub
```

14. Now you need to add a class to support the functions required to retrieve, insert, update, and delete group data in your database. Right-click the WroxDataAccess project, select Add, and then select Class. In the Add New Item – WroxDataAccess dialog box, enter a class name of **WDAGroups.vb** in the Name field and click the Add button to add this class to your project.

15. Now it's time to implement a little inheritance in your project. The WDAGroups class inherits the WDABase class, which causes the WDABase class to expose all public properties, procedures, and functions to the WDAGroups class. Add the following Inherits statement to your class:

```
Public Class WDAGroups
    Inherits WDABase
```

16. The WDABase class constructor requires parameters to be passed to it, so the WDAGroups class also needs a constructor that accepts the same parameters. When the constructor for this class is called, it calls the constructor in the base class, passing it the required parameters. Add the following constructor to the WDAGroups class:

```
Public Sub New(ByVal Company As String, ByVal Application As String)
    MyBase.New(Company, Application)
End Sub
```

17. You need to implement a Dispose procedure to call the Dispose procedure in the base class to clean up all used resources. Add the following procedure to your class:

```
Public Shadows Sub Dispose()
    MyBase.Dispose()
End Sub
```

18. Add a function for each stored procedure that is executed for group data. The first function to add is the GetGroups function. Add the following procedure and code to your class:

SQL Server

```
Public Function GetGroups() As DataSet
    Try
        GetGroups = New DataSet
        MyBase.SQL = "usp_SelectGroups"
        'Fill the DataSet
        MyBase.FillDataSet(GetGroups, "Groups")
    Catch ExceptionErr As Exception
        Throw New System.Exception(ExceptionErr.Message, _
        ExceptionErr.InnerException)
    End Try
End Function
```

Oracle

```
Public Function GetGroups() As DataSet
    Try
        GetGroups = New DataSet
        MyBase.SQL = "GroupsPackage.usp_SelectGroups"
        'Initialize the Command object
        MyBase.InitializeCommand()
        'Add a Parameter to the Parameters collection
        MyBase.AddParameter("results_cursor", _
            OracleClient.OracleType.Cursor, ParameterDirection.Output)
        'Fill the DataSet
        MyBase.FillDataSet(GetGroups, "Groups")
    Catch ExceptionErr As Exception
        Throw New System.Exception(ExceptionErr.Message, _
        ExceptionErr.InnerException)
    End Try
End Function
```

19. The next function to add is a function to get a specific group. Add the following code to your class:

SQL Server

```
Public Function GetGroup(ByVal GroupID As Guid) As DataSet
    Try
        GetGroup = New DataSet
```

```
        MyBase.SQL = "usp_SelectGroup"
        'Initialize the Command object
        MyBase.InitializeCommand()
        'Add a Parameter to the Parameters collection
        MyBase.AddParameter("@GroupID", SqlDbType.UniqueIdentifier, _
            16, GroupID)
        'Fill the DataSet
        MyBase.FillDataSet(GetGroup, "Group")
    Catch ExceptionErr As Exception
        Throw New System.Exception(ExceptionErr.Message, _
        ExceptionErr.InnerException)
    End Try
End Function
```

Oracle

```
Public Function GetGroup(ByVal GroupID As Guid) As DataSet
    Try
        GetGroup = New DataSet
        MyBase.SQL = "GroupPackage.usp_SelectGroup"
        'Initialize the Command object
        MyBase.InitializeCommand()
        'Add a Parameter to the Parameters collection
        MyBase.AddParameter("inGroupID", OracleClient.OracleType.Char, _
            36, GroupID.ToString)
        MyBase.AddParameter("results_cursor", _
            OracleClient.OracleType.Cursor, ParameterDirection.Output)
        'Fill the DataSet
        MyBase.FillDataSet(GetGroup, "Group")
    Catch ExceptionErr As Exception
        Throw New System.Exception(ExceptionErr.Message, _
        ExceptionErr.InnerException)
    End Try
End Function
```

20. Add the AddGroup function to add a new group to the database using the following code:

SQL Server

```
Public Function AddGroup(ByVal Group As DataSet) As Boolean
    Try
        MyBase.SQL = "usp_InsertGroup"
        'Initialize the Command object
        MyBase.InitializeCommand()
        'Add the Parameters to the Parameters collection
        MyBase.AddParameter("@GroupID", _
            SqlDbType.UniqueIdentifier, 16, _
            Group.Tables("Group").Rows(0).Item("GroupID"))
        MyBase.AddParameter("@GroupName", _
            SqlDbType.VarChar, 50, _
            Group.Tables("Group").Rows(0).Item("GroupName"))
        MyBase.AddParameter("@GroupDescription", _
            SqlDbType.Text, _
            Group.Tables("Group").Rows(0).Item( _
            "GroupDescription").ToString.Length, _
            Group.Tables("Group").Rows(0).Item("GroupDescription"))
```

```
                    'Execute the stored procedure
                    AddGroup = ExecuteStoredProcedure()
            Catch ExceptionErr As Exception
                    Throw New System.Exception(ExceptionErr.Message, _
                    ExceptionErr.InnerException)
            End Try
    End Function
```

Oracle

```
Public Function AddGroup(ByVal Group As DataSet) As Boolean
        Try
            MyBase.SQL = "usp_InsertGroup"
            'Initialize the Command object
            MyBase.InitializeCommand()
            'Add the Parameters to the Parameters collection
            MyBase.AddParameter("inGroupID", _
                OracleClient.OracleType.Char, 36, _
                Group.Tables("Group").Rows(0).Item("GroupID").ToString)
            MyBase.AddParameter("inGroupName", _
                OracleClient.OracleType.VarChar, 50, _
                Group.Tables("Group").Rows(0).Item("GroupName"))
            MyBase.AddParameter("inGroupDescription", _
                OracleClient.OracleType.Clob, _
                Group.Tables("Group").Rows(0).Item( _
                "GroupDescription").ToString.Length, _
                Group.Tables("Group").Rows(0).Item("GroupDescription"))
            'Execute the stored procedure
            AddGroup = ExecuteStoredProcedure()
        Catch ExceptionErr As Exception
            Throw New System.Exception(ExceptionErr.Message, _
                ExceptionErr.InnerException)
        End Try
End Function
```

21. The `UpdateGroup` function is next, so add the following code to the class:

SQL Server

```
Public Function UpdateGroup(ByVal Group As DataSet) As Boolean
        Try
            MyBase.SQL = "usp_UpdateGroup"
            'Initialize the Command object
            MyBase.InitializeCommand()
            'Add the Parameters to the Parameters collection
            MyBase.AddParameter("@GroupName", _
                SqlDbType.VarChar, 50, _
                Group.Tables("Group").Rows(0).Item("GroupName"))
            MyBase.AddParameter("@GroupDescription", _
                SqlDbType.Text, _
                Group.Tables("Group").Rows(0).Item( _
                "GroupDescription").ToString.Length, _
                Group.Tables("Group").Rows(0).Item("GroupDescription"))
            MyBase.AddParameter("@GroupID", _
                SqlDbType.UniqueIdentifier, 16, _
```

```
            Group.Tables("Group").Rows(0).Item("GroupID"))
        'Execute the stored procedure
        UpdateGroup = ExecuteStoredProcedure()
    Catch ExceptionErr As Exception
        Throw New System.Exception(ExceptionErr.Message, _
            ExceptionErr.InnerException)
    End Try
End Function
```

Oracle

```
Public Function UpdateGroup(ByVal Group As DataSet) As Boolean
    Try
        MyBase.SQL = "usp_UpdateGroup"
        'Initialize the Command object
        MyBase.InitializeCommand()
        'Add the Parameters to the Parameters collection
        MyBase.AddParameter("inGroupName", _
            OracleClient.OracleType.VarChar, 50, _
            Group.Tables("Group").Rows(0).Item("GroupName"))
        MyBase.AddParameter("inGroupDescription", _
            OracleClient.OracleType.Clob, _
            Group.Tables("Group").Rows(0).Item( _
            "GroupDescription").ToString.Length, _
            Group.Tables("Group").Rows(0).Item("GroupDescription"))
        MyBase.AddParameter("inGroupID", _
            OracleClient.OracleType.Char, 36, _
            Group.Tables("Group").Rows(0).Item("GroupID").ToString)
        'Execute the stored procedure
        UpdateGroup = ExecuteStoredProcedure()
    Catch ExceptionErr As Exception
        Throw New System.Exception(ExceptionErr.Message, _
            ExceptionErr.InnerException)
    End Try
End Function
```

22. The last group function that you need is the `DeleteGroup` function. Add this code to your class:

SQL Server

```
Public Function DeleteGroup(ByVal GroupID As Guid) As Boolean
    Try
        MyBase.SQL = "usp_DeleteGroup"
        'Initialize the Command object
        MyBase.InitializeCommand()
        'Add a Parameter to the Parameters collection
        MyBase.AddParameter("@GroupID", _
            SqlDbType.UniqueIdentifier, 16, GroupID)
        'Execute the stored procedure
        DeleteGroup = ExecuteStoredProcedure()
    Catch ExceptionErr As Exception
        Throw New System.Exception(ExceptionErr.Message, _
            ExceptionErr.InnerException)
    End Try
End Function
```

Oracle

```
Public Function DeleteGroup(ByVal GroupID As Guid) As Boolean
    Try
        MyBase.SQL = "usp_DeleteGroup"
        'Initialize the Command object
        MyBase.InitializeCommand()
        'Add a Parameter to the Parameters collection
        MyBase.AddParameter("inGroupID", _
            OracleClient.OracleType.Char, 36, GroupID.ToString)
        'Execute the stored procedure
        DeleteGroup = ExecuteStoredProcedure()
    Catch ExceptionErr As Exception
        Throw New System.Exception(ExceptionErr.Message, _
            ExceptionErr.InnerException)
    End Try
End Function
```

23. Group Projects are related to groups and projects and there are a minimal number of stored procedures and views to be executed. Therefore, the functions for Group Projects will also be added to the WDAGroups class. Add the following code to create the GetGroupProjects function:

SQL Server

```
Public Function GetGroupProjects(ByVal GroupID As Guid) As DataSet
    Try
        GetGroupProjects = New DataSet
        MyBase.SQL = "SELECT ProjectID, ProjectName " & _
            "FROM vw_SelectGroupProjects " & _
            "WHERE GroupID = @GroupID " & _
            "ORDER BY SequenceNumber"
        'Initialize the Command object
        MyBase.InitializeCommand()
        'Add a Parameter to the Parameters collection
        MyBase.AddParameter("@GroupID", _
            SqlDbType.UniqueIdentifier, 16, GroupID)
        'Fill the DataSet
        MyBase.FillDataSet(GetGroupProjects, "GroupProjects")
    Catch ExceptionErr As Exception
        Throw New System.Exception(ExceptionErr.Message, _
            ExceptionErr.InnerException)
    End Try
End Function
```

Oracle

```
Public Function GetGroupProjects(ByVal GroupID As Guid) As DataSet
    Try
        GetGroupProjects = New DataSet
        MyBase.SQL = "SELECT ProjectID, ProjectName " & _
            "FROM vw_SelectGroupProjects " & _
            "WHERE GroupID = :inGroupID " & _
            "ORDER BY SequenceNumber"
        'Initialize the Command object
        MyBase.InitializeCommand()
        'Add a Parameter to the Parameters collection
        MyBase.AddParameter("inGroupID", _
            OracleClient.OracleType.Char, 36, GroupID.ToString)
```

```
            'Fill the DataSet
            MyBase.FillDataSet(GetGroupProjects, "GroupProjects")
        Catch ExceptionErr As Exception
            Throw New System.Exception(ExceptionErr.Message, _
                ExceptionErr.InnerException)
        End Try
    End Function
```

24. You create the `AddGroupProjects` function next, so add the following code:

SQL Server

```
Public Function AddGroupProjects(ByVal GroupProjects As DataSet) As Boolean
    Try
        MyBase.SQL = "usp_InsertGroupProject"
        'Initialize the Command object
        MyBase.InitializeCommand()
        'Add the Parameters to the Parameters collection
        MyBase.AddParameter("@GroupProjectID", _
            SqlDbType.UniqueIdentifier, 16, Nothing)
        MyBase.AddParameter("@GroupID", _
            SqlDbType.UniqueIdentifier, 16, Nothing)
        MyBase.AddParameter("@ProjectID", _
            SqlDbType.UniqueIdentifier, 16, Nothing)
        'Process all rows in the table
        For intIndex As Integer = 0 To _
            GroupProjects.Tables("GroupProjects").Rows.Count - 1
            MyBase.Command.Parameters.Item("@GroupProjectID").Value = _
                GroupProjects.Tables("GroupProjects").Rows(intIndex).Item( _
                "GroupProjectID")
            MyBase.Command.Parameters.Item("@GroupID").Value = _
                GroupProjects.Tables("GroupProjects").Rows(intIndex).Item( _
                "GroupID")
            MyBase.Command.Parameters.Item("@ProjectID").Value = _
                GroupProjects.Tables("GroupProjects").Rows(intIndex).Item( _
                "ProjectID")
            'Execute the stored procedure
            AddGroupProjects = ExecuteStoredProcedure()
        Next
    Catch ExceptionErr As Exception
        Throw New System.Exception(ExceptionErr.Message, _
            ExceptionErr.InnerException)
    End Try
End Function
```

Oracle

```
Public Function AddGroupProjects(ByVal GroupProjects As DataSet) As Boolean
    Try
        MyBase.SQL = "usp_InsertGroupProject"
        'Initialize the Command object
        MyBase.InitializeCommand()
        'Add the Parameters to the Parameters collection
        MyBase.AddParameter("inGroupProjectID", _
            OracleClient.OracleType.Char, 36, Nothing)
        MyBase.AddParameter("inGroupID", _
            OracleClient.OracleType.Char, 36, Nothing)
```

```
        MyBase.AddParameter("inProjectID", _
            OracleClient.OracleType.Char, 36, Nothing)
        'Process all rows in the table
        For intIndex As Integer = 0 To _
            GroupProjects.Tables("GroupProjects").Rows.Count - 1
            MyBase.Command.Parameters.Item("inGroupProjectID").Value = _
                GroupProjects.Tables("GroupProjects").Rows(intIndex).Item( _
                "GroupProjectID").ToString
            MyBase.Command.Parameters.Item("inGroupID").Value = _
                GroupProjects.Tables("GroupProjects").Rows(intIndex).Item( _
                "GroupID").ToString
            MyBase.Command.Parameters.Item("inProjectID").Value = _
                GroupProjects.Tables("GroupProjects").Rows(intIndex).Item( _
                "ProjectID").ToString
            'Execute the stored procedure
            AddGroupProjects = ExecuteStoredProcedure()
        Next
    Catch ExceptionErr As Exception
        Throw New System.Exception(ExceptionErr.Message, _
            ExceptionErr.InnerException)
    End Try
End Function
```

25. The final function needed for Group Projects is `DeleteGroupProjects`. Add the following code to create this function:

SQL Server

```
Public Function DeleteGroupProjects(ByVal GroupID As Guid) As Boolean
    Try
        MyBase.SQL = "usp_DeleteGroupProjects"
        'Initialize the Command object
        MyBase.InitializeCommand()
        'Add a Parameter to the Parameters collection
        MyBase.AddParameter("@GroupID", _
            SqlDbType.UniqueIdentifier, 16, GroupID)
        'Execute the stored procedure
        DeleteGroupProjects = ExecuteStoredProcedure()
    Catch ExceptionErr As Exception
        Throw New System.Exception(ExceptionErr.Message, _
            ExceptionErr.InnerException)
    End Try
End Function
```

Oracle

```
Public Function DeleteGroupProjects(ByVal GroupID As Guid) As Boolean
    Try
        MyBase.SQL = "usp_DeleteGroupProjects"
        'Initialize the Command object
        MyBase.InitializeCommand()
        MyBase.Command.CommandType = CommandType.StoredProcedure
        'Add a Parameter to the Parameters collection
        MyBase.AddParameter("inGroupID", _
            OracleClient.OracleType.Char, 36, GroupID.ToString)
        'Execute the stored procedure
        DeleteGroupProjects = ExecuteStoredProcedure()
```

```
            Catch ExceptionErr As Exception
                Throw New System.Exception(ExceptionErr.Message, _
                    ExceptionErr.InnerException)
            End Try
    End Function
```

26. Now it's time to add a class to provide functions for the stored procedures related to Projects. Right-click the WroxDataAccess project, select Add, and then select Class. In the Add New Item – WroxDataAccess dialog box, enter a class name of **WDAProjects.vb** in the Name field and then click the Add button to add this class to your project.

27. You also want this class to inherit the base class so add the following Inherits statement to this class:

```
Public Class WDAProjects
    Inherits WDABase
```

28. You need to modify the constructor for this class so that it matches and calls the constructor in the base class. Add the following constructor to this class:

```
Public Sub New(ByVal Company As String, ByVal Application As String)
    MyBase.New(Company, Application)
End Sub
```

29. Implement the Dispose function next by adding the following code:

```
Public Shadows Sub Dispose()
    MyBase.Dispose()
End Sub
```

30. Now you're ready to start adding functions to support the stored procedures related to Projects. You want to add a function to return all projects so add the following code:

SQL Server

```
Public Function GetProjects() As DataSet
    Try
        GetProjects = New DataSet
        MyBase.SQL = "usp_SelectProjects"
        'Fill the DataSet
        MyBase.FillDataSet(GetProjects, "Projects")
    Catch ExceptionErr As Exception
        Throw New System.Exception(ExceptionErr.Message, _
        ExceptionErr.InnerException)
    End Try
End Function
```

Oracle

```
Public Function GetProjects() As DataSet
    Try
        GetProjects = New DataSet
        MyBase.SQL = "ProjectsPackage.usp_SelectProjects"
        'Initialize the Command object
        MyBase.InitializeCommand()
        'Add a Parameter to the Parameters collection
        MyBase.AddParameter("results_cursor", _
```

```
            OracleClient.OracleType.Cursor, ParameterDirection.Output)
            'Fill the DataSet
            MyBase.FillDataSet(GetProjects, "Projects")
        Catch ExceptionErr As Exception
            Throw New System.Exception(ExceptionErr.Message, _
            ExceptionErr.InnerException)
        End Try
End Function
```

31. The next function to be added selects a project based on the ProjectID passed. Add the following code:

SQL Server

```
Public Function GetProject(ByVal ProjectID As Guid) As DataSet
    Try
        GetProject = New DataSet
        MyBase.SQL = "usp_SelectProject"
        'Initialize the Command object
        MyBase.InitializeCommand()
        'Add a Parameter to the Parameters collection
        MyBase.AddParameter("@ProjectID", _
            SqlDbType.UniqueIdentifier, 16, ProjectID)
        'Fill the DataSet
        MyBase.FillDataSet(GetProject, "Project")
    Catch ExceptionErr As Exception
        Throw New System.Exception(ExceptionErr.Message, _
        ExceptionErr.InnerException)
    End Try
End Function
```

Oracle

```
Public Function GetProject(ByVal ProjectID As Guid) As DataSet
    Try
        GetProject = New DataSet
        MyBase.SQL = "ProjectPackage.usp_SelectProject"
        'Initialize the Command object
        MyBase.InitializeCommand()
        'Add the Parameters to the Parameters collection
        MyBase.AddParameter("inProjectID", _
            OracleClient.OracleType.Char, 36, ProjectID.ToString)
        MyBase.AddParameter("results_cursor", _
            OracleClient.OracleType.Cursor, ParameterDirection.Output)
        'Fill the DataSet
        MyBase.FillDataSet(GetProject, "Project")
    Catch ExceptionErr As Exception
        Throw New System.Exception(ExceptionErr.Message, _
        ExceptionErr.InnerException)
    End Try
End Function
```

32. The next function to be added is the AddProject function, which adds a new project to the database. Add the following code for this function:

SQL Server

```vbnet
Public Function AddProject(ByVal Project As DataSet) As Boolean
    Try
        MyBase.SQL = "usp_InsertProject"
        'Initialize the Command object
        MyBase.InitializeCommand()
        'Add the Parameters to the Parameters collection
        MyBase.AddParameter("@ProjectID", _
            SqlDbType.UniqueIdentifier, 16, _
            Project.Tables("Project").Rows(0).Item("ProjectID"))
        MyBase.AddParameter("@ProjectName", _
            SqlDbType.VarChar, 50, _
            Project.Tables("Project").Rows(0).Item("ProjectName"))
        MyBase.AddParameter("@ProjectDescription", _
            SqlDbType.Text, _
            Project.Tables("Project").Rows(0).Item( _
            "ProjectDescription").ToString.Length, _
            Project.Tables("Project").Rows(0).Item("ProjectDescription"))
        MyBase.AddParameter("@SequenceNumber", _
            SqlDbType.TinyInt, 1, _
            Project.Tables("Project").Rows(0).Item("SequenceNumber"))
        'Execute the stored procedure
        AddProject = ExecuteStoredProcedure
    Catch ExceptionErr As Exception
        Throw New System.Exception(ExceptionErr.Message, _
        ExceptionErr.InnerException)
    End Try
End Function
```

Oracle

```vbnet
Public Function AddProject(ByVal Project As DataSet) As Boolean
    Try
        MyBase.SQL = "usp InsertProject"
        'Initialize the Command object
        MyBase.InitializeCommand()
        'Add the Parameters to the Parameters collection
        MyBase.AddParameter("inProjectID", _
            OracleClient.OracleType.Char, 36, _
            Project.Tables("Project").Rows(0).Item("ProjectID").ToString)
        MyBase.AddParameter("inProjectName", _
            OracleClient.OracleType.VarChar, 50, _
            Project.Tables("Project").Rows(0).Item("ProjectName"))
        MyBase.AddParameter("inProjectDescription", _
            OracleClient.OracleType.Clob, _
            Project.Tables("Project").Rows(0).Item( _
            "ProjectDescription").ToString.Length, _
            Project.Tables("Project").Rows(0).Item("ProjectDescription"))
        MyBase.AddParameter("inSequenceNumber", _
            OracleClient.OracleType.Number, 1, _
            Project.Tables("Project").Rows(0).Item("SequenceNumber"))
        'Execute the stored procedure
        AddProject = ExecuteStoredProcedure
    Catch ExceptionErr As Exception
        Throw New System.Exception(ExceptionErr.Message, _
```

```
            ExceptionErr.InnerException)
        End Try
End Function
```

33.   A function to update a project is next so add the following code:

SQL Server

```
Public Function UpdateProject(ByVal Project As DataSet) As Boolean
    Try
        MyBase.SQL = "usp_UpdateProject"
        'Initialize the Command object
        MyBase.InitializeCommand()
        'Add the Parameters to the Parameters collection
        MyBase.AddParameter("@ProjectName", _
            SqlDbType.VarChar, 50, _
            Project.Tables("Project").Rows(0).Item("ProjectName"))
        MyBase.AddParameter("@ProjectDescription", _
            SqlDbType.Text, _
            Project.Tables("Project").Rows(0).Item( _
            "ProjectDescription").ToString.Length, _
            Project.Tables("Project").Rows(0).Item("ProjectDescription"))
        MyBase.AddParameter("@SequenceNumber", _
            SqlDbType.TinyInt, 1, _
            Project.Tables("Project").Rows(0).Item("SequenceNumber"))
        MyBase.AddParameter("@ProjectID", _
            SqlDbType.UniqueIdentifier, 16, _
            Project.Tables("Project").Rows(0).Item("ProjectID"))
        'Execute the stored procedure
        UpdateProject = ExecuteStoredProcedure
    Catch ExceptionErr As Exception
        Throw New System.Exception(ExceptionErr.Message, _
        ExceptionErr.InnerException)
    End Try
End Function
```

Oracle

```
Public Function UpdateProject(ByVal Project As DataSet) As Boolean
    Try
        MyBase.SQL = "usp_UpdateProject"
        'Initialize the Command object
        MyBase.InitializeCommand()
        'Add the Parameters to the Parameters collection
        MyBase.AddParameter("inProjectName", _
            OracleClient.OracleType.VarChar, 50, _
            Project.Tables("Project").Rows(0).Item("ProjectName"))
        MyBase.AddParameter("inProjectDescription", _
            OracleClient.OracleType.Clob, _
            Project.Tables("Project").Rows(0).Item( _
            "ProjectDescription").ToString.Length, _
            Project.Tables("Project").Rows(0).Item("ProjectDescription"))
        MyBase.AddParameter("inSequenceNumber", _
            OracleClient.OracleType.Number, 1, _
            Project.Tables("Project").Rows(0).Item("SequenceNumber"))
        MyBase.AddParameter("inProjectID", _
```

```
                    OracleClient.OracleType.Char, 36, _
                    Project.Tables("Project").Rows(0).Item("ProjectID").ToString)
                'Execute the stored procedure
                UpdateProject = ExecuteStoredProcedure
            Catch ExceptionErr As Exception
                Throw New System.Exception(ExceptionErr.Message, _
                ExceptionErr.InnerException)
            End Try
        End Function
```

34. The final function to add to the `WDAProjects` class and the final code for the `WroxDataAccess` component is the `DeleteProject` function. Add the following code to this class:

SQL Server

```
Public Function DeleteProject(ByVal ProjectID As Guid) As Boolean
    Try
        MyBase.SQL = "usp_DeleteProject"
        'Initialize the Command object
        MyBase.InitializeCommand()
        'Add a Parameter to the Parameters collection
        MyBase.AddParameter("@ProjectID", _
            SqlDbType.UniqueIdentifier, 16, ProjectID)
        'Execute the stored procedure
        DeleteProject = ExecuteStoredProcedure
    Catch ExceptionErr As Exception
        Throw New System.Exception(ExceptionErr.Message, _
        ExceptionErr.InnerException)
    End Try
End Function
```

Oracle

```
Public Function DeleteProject(ByVal ProjectID As Guid) As Boolean
    Try
        MyBase.SQL = "usp_DeleteProject"
        'Initialize the Command object
        MyBase.InitializeCommand()
        'Add a Parameter to the Parameters collection
        MyBase.AddParameter("inProjectID", _
            OracleClient.OracleType.Char, 36, ProjectID.ToString)
        'Execute the stored procedure
        DeleteProject = ExecuteStoredProcedure
    Catch ExceptionErr As Exception
        Throw New System.Exception(ExceptionErr.Message, _
        ExceptionErr.InnerException)
    End Try
End Function
```

That's all the code that you need for the data access component. At this point, it would be a good idea to save your entire solution by clicking Save All on the toolbar.

How It Works

In this exercise, after you add the WroxDataAccess project to your solution, you modify the default base address for the DLL that will be generated when this project is compiled. Let me take a minute to explain why you do this.

When the operating system loads a DLL, it tries to load it in memory at its base address, the address specified in the DLL. If the memory address already contains another component, the system must go through a fix-up process, which involves searching the computer's memory for another free address space in which to place your DLL. It then performs the necessary steps to place it there. This process slows the loading of your component and is repeated every time it is loaded.

To avoid this fix-up process, you assign a unique base address to your component. To ensure your address is unique, you must keep track of the addresses of all your components, a topic beyond the scope of this book.

The range of addresses available for VB.NET components is from &H00400000 to &H80000000. These addresses are on 64K boundaries and even if your component is less than 64K in size, the entire address space is reserved for your component. Likewise, if your component is 65K in size, your component reserves two consecutive address spaces.

After changing the base address for your component, you add the WDACrypto class to your project. This was the class that you created in the previous exercise and will be used by the data access component to decrypt the registry values for the database login and password.

Next, you reuse more code by copying the WDABase class from your Time Tracker project to the WroxDataAccess project. The modifications required to this class were minor and implemented the functionality to read the database connection information from the registry, rather than an application configuration file.

You start by importing the Microsoft.Win32 namespace to gain access to the registry classes used to read from and write to the registry:

```
Imports Microsoft.Win32
```

Next, you modify the constructor for this class by adding two parameters: one for the company name and one for the application name. These parameters will be used in this constructor to read the appropriate registry key. You could have specified these parameters in your application configuration file, but I wanted to show you how to pass parameters from your application to the business component and on through to the data access component.

The constructor has four variables defined. The first variable is an object that represents a registry key. The next two variables are byte arrays that contain the key and initialization vector to be passed to the crypto component to decrypt your database login and password. The final variable is an object that represents your encryption class and is used in a Using...End Using block.

As usual, you enclose your code in a Try...Catch...Finally block to handle any errors that may occur. The first thing that you do in the Try block is open the registry key using the company name and application name passed to this constructor.

SQL Server and Oracle

```
Public Sub New(ByVal Company As String, ByVal Application As String)
    'Declare variables
    Dim objReg As RegistryKey

    'Key size must be 128 bits to 192 bits in increments of 64 bits
    Dim bytKey() As Byte = System.Text.Encoding.UTF8.GetBytes( _
        "G~v!x@Z#c$a%C^b&h*K(e)K_")
```

```
Dim bytIV() As Byte = System.Text.Encoding.UTF8.GetBytes( _
    "rgY^p$b%")

Using objCrypto As New WDACrypto(bytKey, bytIV)
    Try
        'Open the registry key
        objReg = Registry.LocalMachine.OpenSubKey("SOFTWARE\" & _
            Company & "\" & Application & "\Database", False)
```

After the registry key is open, you build the connection string appropriate for the database that you are using. For SQL Server, this includes building a connection string using the `Data Source`, `Database`, `User ID`, and `Password` parameters without integrated security. When using integrated security, you omit the `User ID` and `Password` parameters and specify the `Integrated Security` parameter with a value of `SSPI`, which indicates that your Windows user account information is used to validate you in SQL Server. For Oracle, this includes building a connection string using the same parameters as SQL Server except for the `Database` parameter.

The values for the parameters mentioned are read from the registry and the values for the `User ID` and `Password` parameters are passed to your `objCrypto` object to be decrypted.

SQL Server

```
'Build the SQL connection string from the registry values
'and initialize the Connection object
Connection = New SqlConnection( _
    "Data Source=" & objReg.GetValue("Server") & ";" & _
    "Database=" & objReg.GetValue("Database") & ";" & _
    "User ID=" & objCrypto.Decrypt( _
        objReg.GetValue("Login")) & ";" & _
    "Password=" & objCrypto.Decrypt( _
        objReg.GetValue("Password")) & ";")
```

Oracle

```
'Build the SQL connection string from the registry values
'and initialize the Connection object
Connection = New OracleConnection( _
    "Data Source=" & objReg.GetValue("Server") & ";" & _
    "User ID=" & objCrypto.Decrypt( _
        objReg.GetValue("Login")) & ";" & _
    "Password=" & objCrypto.Decrypt( _
        objReg.GetValue("Password")) & ";")
```

The `Catch` block contains the necessary code to throw an exception if an error occurs. The `Finally` block contains the code to clean up the resources used in this constructor.

SQL Server and Oracle

```
Catch ExceptionErr As Exception
    Throw New System.Exception(ExceptionErr.Message, _
        ExceptionErr.InnerException)
Finally
    'Clean up
    objReg = Nothing
End Try
End Using
End Sub
```

In the next step in this exercise, you add a new class to this project to support group functions, functions that retrieve, insert, update, and delete group data in the database. The WDAGroups class was added and inherited the WDABase class, as shown in the Inherits statement that follows.

When a class inherits another class it gains access to all properties, methods, events, and constants in the base class. The class that does the inheriting can then choose to use those properties, methods, events, and constants or extend them by overriding them with its own. In this exercise, you just use the properties and methods in the base class, but it is useful to know that you could override them with properties and methods of your own.

```
Inherits WDABase
```

The constructor for this class accepts the same parameters expected in the base class and then initializes the base class by calling its constructor, passing it the parameters that it received. Notice how the constructor is called in the base class. Whenever you want to refer to properties, methods, and constants in the base class, you simply prefix them with the MyBase keyword. The MyBase keyword works in a similar fashion to the Me keyword except that it refers to the class that is inherited.

```
Public Sub New(ByVal Company As String, ByVal Application As String)
    MyBase.New(Company, Application)
End Sub
```

When the Dispose method is called on this class, you need to clean up the resources used in the base class by calling the Dispose method in the base class. Again, you refer to this method in the base class by prefixing it with the MyBase keyword.

```
Public Shadows Sub Dispose()
    MyBase.Dispose()
End Sub
```

The first function that you added to this class was the GetGroups function, which retrieves all groups in the database and returns them in a DataSet. Notice the use of the properties and methods in the base class. When you set the SQL string property to the stored procedure to be executed, you are setting it directly in the base class, and this is indicated through the use of the MyBase keyword. Likewise, when you call the method to fill the DataSet, you have prefixed it with the MyBase keyword indicating that this method exists in the base class.

There's one important point that I want to bring to your attention here regarding the use of the MyBase keyword. It is not required in this context because there are no properties or methods in this class called SQL or FillDataSet; they exist only in the base class. Therefore, you could simply omit the MyBase keyword.

However, there are two distinct advantages to using the MyBase keyword here. First, using the MyBase keyword followed by a period causes Visual Studio 2005's IntelliSense to kick in and provide a drop-down list of all properties and methods in the base class, as you've already discovered. Second, it helps you self-document your code, as you can look at this code and quickly determine that the SQL property and FillDataSet method exist in the base class and not in this class.

SQL Server

```
Public Function GetGroups() As DataSet
    Try
```

```
            GetGroups = New DataSet
            MyBase.SQL = "usp_SelectGroups"
            'Fill the DataSet
            MyBase.FillDataSet(GetGroups, "Groups")
        Catch ExceptionErr As Exception
            Throw New System.Exception(ExceptionErr.Message, _
            ExceptionErr.InnerException)
        End Try
    End Function
```

In the GetGroups function, you enclose your code in a Try...Catch block to trap and handle any errors that may occur. If an error is returned from the base class, you trap it here and then pass it back to the caller of this function.

The difference between the SQL Server version of this function and the Oracle version is that the Oracle version must use a package to return data from a stored procedure, as you discovered in the last chapter. To save space, I simply show the SQL Server version of the code in the rest of the How It Works sections and mention the difference between SQL Server and Oracle.

Oracle

```
Public Function GetGroups() As DataSet
    Try
            GetGroups = New DataSet
            MyBase.SQL = "GroupsPackage.usp_SelectGroups"
            'Initialize the Command object
            MyBase.InitializeCommand()
            'Add a Parameter to the Parameters collection
            MyBase.AddParameter("results_cursor", _
                OracleClient.OracleType.Cursor, ParameterDirection.Output)
            'Fill the DataSet
            MyBase.FillDataSet(GetGroups, "Groups")
        Catch ExceptionErr As Exception
            Throw New System.Exception(ExceptionErr.Message, _
            ExceptionErr.InnerException)
        End Try
    End Function
```

The next function that you add is GetGroup, which accepts the GroupID as the only input parameter to this function. Again, you are returning the data in a DataSet to be consistent in your implementation regarding how data is returned to the caller.

The GroupID is passed to this function as a Guid, which provides a consistent interface for the business logic component. However, the implementation of this differs between SQL Server and Oracle. The Oracle version has the GroupID defined as a CHAR data type in the database. Therefore, the Oracle version of this function must convert the Guid to a string when it adds it to the Parameters collection.

```
        Public Function GetGroup(ByVal GroupID As Guid) As DataSet
            Try
                GetGroup = New DataSet
                MyBase.SQL = "usp_SelectGroup"
                'Initialize the Command object
                MyBase.InitializeCommand()
                'Add a Parameter to the Parameters collection
```

```
            MyBase.AddParameter("@GroupID", SqlDbType.UniqueIdentifier, _
                16, GroupID)
            'Fill the DataSet
            MyBase.FillDataSet(GetGroup, "Group")
        Catch ExceptionErr As Exception
            Throw New System.Exception(ExceptionErr.Message, _
            ExceptionErr.InnerException)
        End Try
    End Function
```

The AddGroup function accepts a DataSet as its input parameter and executes the stored procedure to add a new group to the database. Because only a single group is expected to be passed in the DataSet, there has been no loop set up to process the DataSet. Instead, the columns are accessed in the DataSet for row 0 only. The only difference between the versions of this function for SQL Server and Oracle are the data types used in the databases.

```
    Public Function AddGroup(ByVal Group As DataSet) As Boolean
        Try
            MyBase.SQL = "usp_InsertGroup"
            'Initialize the Command object
            MyBase.InitializeCommand()
            'Add the Parameters to the Parameters collection
            MyBase.AddParameter("@GroupID", _
                SqlDbType.UniqueIdentifier, 16, _
                Group.Tables("Group").Rows(0).Item("GroupID"))
            MyBase.AddParameter("@GroupName", _
                SqlDbType.VarChar, 50, _
                Group.Tables("Group").Rows(0).Item("GroupName"))
            MyBase.AddParameter("@GroupDescription", _
                SqlDbType.Text, _
                Group.Tables("Group").Rows(0).Item( _
                "GroupDescription").ToString.Length, _
                Group.Tables("Group").Rows(0).Item("GroupDescription"))
            'Execute the stored procedure
            AddGroup = ExecuteStoredProcedure()
        Catch ExceptionErr As Exception
            Throw New System.Exception(ExceptionErr.Message, _
            ExceptionErr.InnerException)
        End Try
    End Function
```

The UpdateGroup function was added next and like the AddGroup function it accepts a DataSet as its input parameter. The processing of the DataSet in this function is identical to the AddGroup function in that you are processing only a single row from the DataSet. The only differences between the SQL Server and Oracle versions of this function are the data types used in the stored procedure.

```
    Public Function UpdateGroup(ByVal Group As DataSet) As Boolean
        Try
            MyBase.SQL = "usp_UpdateGroup"
            'Initialize the Command object
            MyBase.InitializeCommand()
            'Add the Parameters to the Parameters collection
            MyBase.AddParameter("@GroupName", _
```

```
                SqlDbType.VarChar, 50, _
                Group.Tables("Group").Rows(0).Item("GroupName"))
            MyBase.AddParameter("@GroupDescription", _
                SqlDbType.Text, _
                Group.Tables("Group").Rows(0).Item( _
                "GroupDescription").ToString.Length, _
                Group.Tables("Group").Rows(0).Item("GroupDescription"))
            MyBase.AddParameter("@GroupID", _
                SqlDbType.UniqueIdentifier, 16, _
                Group.Tables("Group").Rows(0).Item("GroupID"))
            'Execute the stored procedure
            UpdateGroup = ExecuteStoredProcedure()
        Catch ExceptionErr As Exception
            Throw New System.Exception(ExceptionErr.Message, _
                ExceptionErr.InnerException)
        End Try
    End Function
```

The final group function that you create is `DeleteGroup`. Because the stored procedure to delete a group expects only the GroupID as its input parameter, this is the input parameter passed to this function. Again, the data types used in SQL Server and Oracle differ, so the Oracle version of this function needs to convert the Guid to a string when it adds it to the `Parameters` collection.

```
    Public Function DeleteGroup(ByVal GroupID As Guid) As Boolean
        Try
            MyBase.SQL = "usp_DeleteGroup"
            'Initialize the Command object
            MyBase.InitializeCommand()
            'Add a Parameter to the Parameters collection
            MyBase.AddParameter("@GroupID", _
                SqlDbType.UniqueIdentifier, 16, GroupID)
            'Execute the stored procedure
            DeleteGroup = ExecuteStoredProcedure()
        Catch ExceptionErr As Exception
            Throw New System.Exception(ExceptionErr.Message, _
                ExceptionErr.InnerException)
        End Try
    End Function
```

Because group projects are so closely related to groups, you also add the necessary functions to support retrieving, inserting, and deleting group projects to the WDAGroups class. The first function that you add is the GetGroupProjects function.

The code in this function should look familiar from the previous chapter as it is very similar. The only difference is that you prefixed the properties and methods with MyBase instead of objData, as in the last chapter.

Again, the only differences in the implementation of this function between SQL Server and Oracle are the data types used and how they are implemented in the databases that they support.

```
    Public Function GetGroupProjects(ByVal GroupID As Guid) As DataSet
        Try
            GetGroupProjects = New DataSet
```

```
        MyBase.SQL = "SELECT ProjectID, ProjectName " & _
            "FROM vw_SelectGroupProjects " & _
            "WHERE GroupID = @GroupID " & _
            "ORDER BY SequenceNumber"
        'Initialize the Command object
        MyBase.InitializeCommand()
        'Add a Parameter to the Parameters collection
        MyBase.AddParameter("@GroupID", _
            SqlDbType.UniqueIdentifier, 16, GroupID)
        'Fill the DataSet
        MyBase.FillDataSet(GetGroupProjects, "GroupProjects")
    Catch ExceptionErr As Exception
        Throw New System.Exception(ExceptionErr.Message, _
            ExceptionErr.InnerException)
    End Try
End Function
```

The AddGroupProjects function is implemented a little differently from the other functions in this class that insert data. Remember that you'll typically be adding multiple group projects to the GroupProjects table and it really doesn't make sense to call this function repetitively in a loop. Instead, all of the group projects to be added are added to the DataSet by the client and passed to this function as input. This function processes all rows of data in the DataSet in a loop.

The first thing that you do in this function is set the SQL property in the base class to the stored procedure to be executed and then call the InitializeCommand method to initialize the Command object. Then you call the AddParameter method to add all the required Parameters to the Parameters collection. Notice that you are passing a value of Nothing as the value to be set for each Parameter. All you want to do at this point is populate the Parameters collection with the required Parameters.

```
    Public Function AddGroupProjects(ByVal GroupProjects As DataSet) As Boolean
        Try
            MyBase.SQL = "usp_InsertGroupProject"
            'Initialize the Command object
            MyBase.InitializeCommand()
            'Add the Parameters to the Parameters collection
            MyBase.AddParameter("@GroupProjectID", _
                SqlDbType.UniqueIdentifier, 16, Nothing)
            MyBase.AddParameter("@GroupID", _
                SqlDbType.UniqueIdentifier, 16, Nothing)
            MyBase.AddParameter("@ProjectID", _
                SqlDbType.UniqueIdentifier, 16, Nothing)
```

Next, you set up a loop to process all rows in the DataSet. You determine the number of rows to process using the Count property minus 1. Remember that the Count property returns the actual number of rows that exist and that you access each row using a zero-based index; thus, you use Count − 1 in your loop.

Because you've already added the Parameters to the Parameters collection, all you need to do in the loop is set the value of each Parameter to the value contained in the DataSet. Then you execute the stored procedure and repeat the loop until all rows have been processed.

The only difference between the implementation of this function in SQL Server and Oracle is the data types used. The Oracle version uses a CHAR data type; thus, you have to convert the Guid to a string when adding it to the parameters.

```
                    'Process all rows in the table
                    For intIndex As Integer = 0 To _
                        GroupProjects.Tables("GroupProjects").Rows.Count - 1
                        MyBase.Command.Parameters.Item("@GroupProjectID").Value = _
                            GroupProjects.Tables("GroupProjects").Rows(intIndex).Item( _
                            "GroupProjectID")
                        MyBase.Command.Parameters.Item("@GroupID").Value = _
                            GroupProjects.Tables("GroupProjects").Rows(intIndex).Item( _
                            "GroupID")
                        MyBase.Command.Parameters.Item("@ProjectID").Value = _
                            GroupProjects.Tables("GroupProjects").Rows(intIndex).Item( _
                            "ProjectID")
                        'Execute the stored procedure
                        AddGroupProjects = ExecuteStoredProcedure()
                    Next
                Catch ExceptionErr As Exception
                    Throw New System.Exception(ExceptionErr.Message, _
                        ExceptionErr.InnerException)
                End Try
            End Function
```

The final function that you added to the WDAGroups class is DeleteGroupProjects. This function deletes all group projects related to a specific group. As such, it accepts the GroupID as a Guid structure as its input parameter, as that is all that is required for the stored procedure.

Again, the implementation of this function for Oracle differs in the data type used in the stored procedure and the fact that the Guid must be converted to a string as it is added to the Parameter.

```
            Public Function DeleteGroupProjects(ByVal GroupID As Guid) As Boolean
                Try
                    MyBase.SQL = "usp_DeleteGroupProjects"
                    'Initialize the Command object
                    MyBase.InitializeCommand()
                    'Add a Parameter to the Parameters collection
                    MyBase.AddParameter("@GroupID", _
                        SqlDbType.UniqueIdentifier, 16, GroupID)
                    'Execute the stored procedure
                    DeleteGroupProjects = ExecuteStoredProcedure()
                Catch ExceptionErr As Exception
                    Throw New System.Exception(ExceptionErr.Message, _
                        ExceptionErr.InnerException)
                End Try
            End Function
```

The next class that you add to your data access component is WDAProjects. This class supports the necessary functions to retrieve, insert, update, and delete projects in the Projects table in your database. Like the WDAGroups class, this class must also inherit the base class, as shown in the following code. This provides this class with access to all of the core data functions to retrieve, insert, update, and delete data in your database.

```
Inherits WDABase
```

The constructor for this class mirrors the constructor for the WDAGroups class in that it accepts the same parameters as the constructor in the base class and then calls the constructor in the base class, as shown in the following code:

```
Public Sub New(ByVal Company As String, ByVal Application As String)
    MyBase.New(Company, Application)
End Sub
```

The Dispose function calls the Dispose function in the base class to clean up all resources that the base class used:

```
Public Shadows Sub Dispose()
    MyBase.Dispose()
End Sub
```

The first function that you add in this class is the GetProjects function. This function returns a list of all projects in a DataSet object. This is straightforward code that you implemented in the Time Tracker application.

The difference between the SQL Server and Oracle versions of this function is that the Oracle version executes the stored procedure in a package. Thus, the Oracle version must use an output Parameter to retrieve the data from the database.

```
Public Function GetProjects() As DataSet
    Try
        GetProjects = New DataSet
        MyBase.SQL = "usp_SelectProjects"
        'Fill the DataSet
        MyBase.FillDataSet(GetProjects, "Projects")
    Catch ExceptionErr As Exception
        Throw New System.Exception(ExceptionErr.Message, _
        ExceptionErr.InnerException)
    End Try
End Function
```

The next function that you add is the GetProject function. The code for this function is similar to the code that you implemented in the Time Tracker application. You pass the ProjectID to this function as a Guid and then retrieve the specific project based on the Guid.

The Oracle version of this function has to convert the Guid to a string for the input Parameter to the stored procedure. Additionally, because this stored procedure returns data, the stored procedure is created as part of a package, and an output parameter has to be defined in this function.

```
Public Function GetProject(ByVal ProjectID As Guid) As DataSet
    Try
        GetProject = New DataSet
        MyBase.SQL = "usp_SelectProject"
```

```
                    'Initialize the Command object
                    MyBase.InitializeCommand()
                    'Add a Parameter to the Parameters collection
                    MyBase.AddParameter("@ProjectID", _
                        SqlDbType.UniqueIdentifier, 16, ProjectID)
                    'Fill the DataSet
                    MyBase.FillDataSet(GetProject, "Project")
            Catch ExceptionErr As Exception
                    Throw New System.Exception(ExceptionErr.Message, _
                    ExceptionErr.InnerException)
            End Try
        End Function
```

The `AddProject` function is created next and accepts a `DataSet` as input. This function adds a new project and should look similar to the code implemented in the Time Tracker application in the previous chapter.

Because you are expecting only a single project, you do not set up a loop to process the rows in the `DataSet`. You process only the one row you are expecting by specifying row 0 in the `Rows` property.

The only difference between the SQL Server version of this function and the Oracle version is the data types used in the database.

```
        Public Function AddProject(ByVal Project As DataSet) As Boolean
            Try
                    MyBase.SQL = "usp_InsertProject"
                    'Initialize the Command object
                    MyBase.InitializeCommand()
                    'Add the Parameters to the Parameters collection
                    MyBase.AddParameter("@ProjectID", _
                        SqlDbType.UniqueIdentifier, 16, _
                        Project.Tables("Project").Rows(0).Item("ProjectID"))
                    MyBase.AddParameter("@ProjectName", _
                        SqlDbType.VarChar, 50, _
                        Project.Tables("Project").Rows(0).Item("ProjectName"))
                    MyBase.AddParameter("@ProjectDescription",
                        SqlDbType.Text, _
                        Project.Tables("Project").Rows(0).Item( _
                        "ProjectDescription").ToString.Length, _
                        Project.Tables("Project").Rows(0).Item("ProjectDescription"))
                    MyBase.AddParameter("@SequenceNumber", _
                        SqlDbType.TinyInt, 1, _
                        Project.Tables("Project").Rows(0).Item("SequenceNumber"))
                    'Execute the stored procedure
                    AddProject = ExecuteStoredProcedure
            Catch ExceptionErr As Exception
                    Throw New System.Exception(ExceptionErr.Message, _
                    ExceptionErr.InnerException)
            End Try
        End Function
```

The `UpdateProject` function is added next and updates an existing project. Like the `AddProject` function, this function also accepts a `DataSet` as an input parameter. The data to be updated is contained in this `DataSet` and again you are expecting only a single row in the `DataSet`.

The data types used in this function are the only difference between the SQL Server and Oracle versions of this function.

```
Public Function UpdateProject(ByVal Project As DataSet) As Boolean
    Try
        MyBase.SQL = "usp_UpdateProject"
        'Initialize the Command object
        MyBase.InitializeCommand()
        'Add the Parameters to the Parameters collection
        MyBase.AddParameter("@ProjectName", _
            SqlDbType.VarChar, 50, _
            Project.Tables("Project").Rows(0).Item("ProjectName"))
        MyBase.AddParameter("@ProjectDescription", _
            SqlDbType.Text, _
            Project.Tables("Project").Rows(0).Item( _
            "ProjectDescription").ToString.Length, _
            Project.Tables("Project").Rows(0).Item("ProjectDescription"))
        MyBase.AddParameter("@SequenceNumber", _
            SqlDbType.TinyInt, 1, _
            Project.Tables("Project").Rows(0).Item("SequenceNumber"))
        MyBase.AddParameter("@ProjectID", _
            SqlDbType.UniqueIdentifier, 16, _
            Project.Tables("Project").Rows(0).Item("ProjectID"))
        'Execute the stored procedure
        UpdateProject = ExecuteStoredProcedure
    Catch ExceptionErr As Exception
        Throw New System.Exception(ExceptionErr.Message, _
        ExceptionErr.InnerException)
    End Try
End Function
```

The final function you add to the WDAProjects class is the DeleteProject function, which deletes a specific project from the database and accepts the ProjectID as a Guid for input.

Because the input parameter to this function is a Guid, the Oracle version of this function converts the Guid to a string when adding it to the input parameter of the stored procedure.

```
Public Function DeleteProject(ByVal ProjectID As Guid) As Boolean
    Try
        MyBase.SQL = "usp_DeleteProject"
        'Initialize the Command object
        MyBase.InitializeCommand()
        'Add a Parameter to the Parameters collection
        MyBase.AddParameter("@ProjectID", _
            SqlDbType.UniqueIdentifier, 16, ProjectID)
        'Execute the stored procedure
        DeleteProject = ExecuteStoredProcedure
    Catch ExceptionErr As Exception
        Throw New System.Exception(ExceptionErr.Message, _
        ExceptionErr.InnerException)
    End Try
End Function
```

In this next Try It Out, you create the Wrox Business Logic component. This component interacts with both the presentation layer (the Time Tracker application) and the data access layer (the WroxDataAccess component).

At this point, you don't actually implement any business logic, as that comes in the next chapter. Here you create this component implementing the functions necessary to perform the required tasks for selecting, inserting, updating, and deleting groups, projects, and group projects.

Try It Out   Wrox Business Logic Component

To create this component:

1. Right click the Time Tracker solution in Solution Explorer and select Add ➪ New Project. In the Add New Project dialog box, select Class Library in the Templates pane and enter a project name of **WroxBusinessLogic** in the Name field. Click OK to create this project and add it to the Time Tracker solution.

2. You'll want to change the DLL base address, so right-click the WroxBusinessLogic project in Solution Explorer and select Properties. In the Property Pages, click the Compile tab and then click the Advanced Compile Options button. Enter a new DLL base address of **&H11280000** and then click OK.

3. Right-click `Class1.vb` in Solution Explorer and select Delete from the context menu. You're prompted with a confirmation dialog box. Click OK to have this class deleted.

4. Right-click the WroxBusinessLogic project, select Add, and then select Class. In the Add New Item – WroxBusinessLogic dialog box, enter a class name of **WBLGroups.vb** in the Name field and then click Add to add this class to your project.

5. You want this class to implement a disposable interface so that it can clean up all used resources. Add the following `Implements` statement to your class. When you press the Enter key, a `Dispose` procedure is added to your project:

```
Public Class WBLGroups
    Implements IDisposable
```

6. You now need to set a reference to the WroxDataAccess component. Right-click the WroxBusinessLogic project in the Solution Explorer and choose Add Reference from the context menu. In the Add Reference dialog box, click the Projects tab and then select the WroxDataAccess component in the list. Click OK to add this reference and close the Add Reference dialog box.

7. Because the business component will be interacting with the data access component, you need to declare an object at the class level for the data access component. Add the following variable declaration:

```
    Implements IDisposable

    'Private variables and objects
    Private objWDAGroups As WroxDataAccess.WDAGroups
```

8. The constructor for this class should initialize a new instance of the `WDAGroups` class in the `objWDAGroups` object. Add the following code to this class:

```
Public Sub New(ByVal Company As String, ByVal Application As String)
    objWDAGroups = New WroxDataAccess.WDAGroups(Company, Application)
End Sub
```

9. You now want to modify the `Dispose` procedure to clean up the used resources in this class. Modify this procedure as shown:

```
Private Overloads Sub Dispose(ByVal disposing As Boolean)
    If Not Me.disposed Then
        If disposing Then
            ' TODO: put code to dispose managed resources
        End If

        objWDAGroups.Dispose()
        objWDAGroups = Nothing
    End If
    Me.disposed = True
End Sub
```

10. Now it's time to start adding some functions that support the business processes for selecting, adding, updating, and deleting groups. The first function that you want to add is the `GetGroups` function. This function calls the corresponding function in the data access component to retrieve all groups. Add the following code to your class:

```
Public Function GetGroups() As DataSet
    Try
        'Call the data component to get all groups
        GetGroups = objWDAGroups.GetGroups
    Catch ExceptionErr As Exception
        Throw New System.Exception(ExceptionErr.Message, _
            ExceptionErr.InnerException)
    End Try
End Function
```

11. The next function to be added is a function to retrieve a specific group. Add the following code to your class:

```
Public Function GetGroup(ByVal GroupID As Guid) As DataSet
    Try
        'Call the data component to get a specific group
        GetGroup = objWDAGroups.GetGroup(GroupID)
    Catch ExceptionErr As Exception
        Throw New System.Exception(ExceptionErr.Message, _
            ExceptionErr.InnerException)
    End Try
End Function
```

12. Before the client can add a new group it must call the business component to get a `DataSet` for a group. The `GetNewGroupDS` function builds and returns a `DataSet` for Groups. Add the following code to your class:

```
Public Function GetNewGroupDS() As DataSet
    Try
        'Instantiate a new DataSet object
```

```
            GetNewGroupDS = New DataSet

            'Create a DataTable object
            Dim objDataTable As DataTable = GetNewGroupDS.Tables.Add("Group")

            'Create a DataColumn object
            Dim objDataColumn As DataColumn

            'Instantiate a new DataColumn and set its properties
            objDataColumn = New DataColumn("GroupID", _
                Type.GetType("System.Guid"))
            objDataColumn.AllowDBNull = False

            'Add the column to the table
            objDataTable.Columns.Add(objDataColumn)

            'Instantiate a new DataColumn and set its properties
            objDataColumn = New DataColumn("GroupName", _
                Type.GetType("System.String"))
            objDataColumn.AllowDBNull = False
            objDataColumn.MaxLength = 50

            'Add the column to the table
            objDataTable.Columns.Add(objDataColumn)

            'Instantiate a new DataColumn and set its properties
            objDataColumn = New DataColumn("GroupDescription", _
                Type.GetType("System.String"))

            'Add the column to the table
            objDataTable.Columns.Add(objDataColumn)

        Catch ExceptionErr As Exception
            Throw New System.Exception(ExceptionErr.Message, _
                ExceptionErr.InnerException)
        End Try
    End Function
```

13. The client calls the AddGroup function to add a new group and passes it a populated DataSet with group data. Add the following code for the AddGroup function to your class:

```
Public Function AddGroup(ByVal Group As DataSet) As Boolean
    Try
        'Call the data component to add the new group
        Return objWDAGroups.AddGroup(Group)
    Catch ExceptionErr As Exception
        Throw New System.Exception(ExceptionErr.Message, _
            ExceptionErr.InnerException)
    End Try
End Function
```

14. The UpdateGroup function also accepts a populated DataSet as input and updates a group. Add the following code to your class:

```
Public Function UpdateGroup(ByVal Group As DataSet) As Boolean
    Try
```

```
            'Call the data component to update the group
            Return objWDAGroups.UpdateGroup(Group)
        Catch ExceptionErr As Exception
            Throw New System.Exception(ExceptionErr.Message, _
                ExceptionErr.InnerException)
        End Try
    End Function
```

15. The `DeleteGroup` function accepts only the GroupID of the group to be deleted as input. Add this function to your class:

```
Public Function DeleteGroup(ByVal GroupID As Guid) As Boolean
    Try
            'Call the data component to delete the group
            Return objWDAGroups.DeleteGroup(GroupID)
        Catch ExceptionErr As Exception
            Throw New System.Exception(ExceptionErr.Message, _
                ExceptionErr.InnerException)
        End Try
    End Function
```

16. Like the `WDAGroups` class in the data access component, the `WBLGroups` class will also contain the necessary functions to support group projects. The first function that you want to add is the `GetGroupProjects` function. This function returns all group projects in a specific group. Add the following code to your class:

```
Public Function GetGroupProjects(ByVal GroupID As Guid) As DataSet
    Try
            'Call the data component to get all group projects
            GetGroupProjects = objWDAGroups.GetGroupProjects(GroupID)
        Catch ExceptionErr As Exception
            Throw New System.Exception(ExceptionErr.Message, _
                ExceptionErr.InnerException)
        End Try
    End Function
```

17. Before new group projects can be added, the client needs to get a `DataSet` for group projects to populate. The `GetNewGroupProjectsDS` function builds and returns a `DataSet` to the caller. Add the following code to your class:

```
Public Function GetNewGroupProjectsDS() As DataSet
    Try
        'Instantiate a new DataSet object
        GetNewGroupProjectsDS = New DataSet

        'Create a DataTable object
        Dim objDataTable As DataTable = _
            GetNewGroupProjectsDS.Tables.Add("GroupProjects")

        'Create a DataColumn object
        Dim objDataColumn As DataColumn

        'Instantiate a new DataColumn and set its properties
        objDataColumn = New DataColumn("GroupProjectID", _
            Type.GetType("System.Guid"))
```

```
                objDataColumn.AllowDBNull = False

                'Add the column to the table
                objDataTable.Columns.Add(objDataColumn)

                'Instantiate a new DataColumn and set its properties
                objDataColumn = New DataColumn("GroupID", _
                    Type.GetType("System.Guid"))
                objDataColumn.AllowDBNull = False

                'Add the column to the table
                objDataTable.Columns.Add(objDataColumn)

                'Instantiate a new DataColumn and set its properties
                objDataColumn = New DataColumn("ProjectID", _
                    Type.GetType("System.Guid"))
                objDataColumn.AllowDBNull = False

                'Add the column to the table
                objDataTable.Columns.Add(objDataColumn)
        Catch ExceptionErr As Exception
            Throw New System.Exception(ExceptionErr.Message, _
                ExceptionErr.InnerException)
        End Try
    End Function
```

18. The `AddGroupProjects` function accepts a `DataSet` as input that contains all of the group projects to be added. Add this function to your class:

```
Public Function AddGroupProjects(ByVal GroupProjects As DataSet) As Boolean
    Try
            'Call the data component to add the group projects
            Return objWDAGroups.AddGroupProjects(GroupProjects)
    Catch ExceptionErr As Exception
        Throw New System.Exception(ExceptionErr.Message, _
            ExceptionErr.InnerException)
    End Try
End Function
```

19. The `DeleteGroupProjects` function deletes all group projects for a specified group. Add the following code to your class:

```
Public Function DeleteGroupProjects(ByVal GroupID As Guid) As Boolean
    Try
            'Call the data component to delete the group projects
            Return objWDAGroups.DeleteGroupProjects(GroupID)
    Catch ExceptionErr As Exception
        Throw New System.Exception(ExceptionErr.Message, _
            ExceptionErr.InnerException)
    End Try
End Function
```

20. You now want to add a class to support the functions related to selecting, inserting, updating and deleting projects. Right-click the WroxBusinessLogic project, select Add, and then select Class. In the Add New Item – WroxBusinessLogic dialog box, enter a class name of **WBLProjects.vb** in the Name field and click the Add button to add this class to your project.

21. This class should also implement a disposable interface so add the following `Implements` statement to this class:

```
Public Class WBLProjects
    Implements IDisposable
```

22. You need to add a variable declaration to this class so that the functions in this class have access to the `WDAProjects` class in the data access component. Add the following declaration:

```
Implements IDisposable

'Private variables and objects
Private objWDAProject As WroxDataAccess.WDAProjects
```

23. The constructor for this class should mirror the constructor that you added for the `WBLGroups` class. Add the following constructor to this class:

```
Public Sub New(ByVal Company As String, ByVal Application As String)
    objWDAProject = New WroxDataAccess.WDAProjects(Company, Application)
End Sub
```

24. You want to modify the `Dispose` procedure next to clean up the resources used in this class. Make the following modifications to this procedure:

```
Private Overloads Sub Dispose(ByVal disposing As Boolean)
    If Not Me.disposed Then
        If disposing Then
            ' TODO: put code to dispose managed resources
        End If

        objWDAProject.Dispose()
        objWDAProject = Nothing
    End If
    Me.disposed = True
End Sub
```

25. You're now ready to start adding functions to support selecting, inserting, updating, and deleting projects. The first function you add is the `GetProjects` function, which returns a `DataSet` of all projects in the Projects table. Add the following code to your class:

```
Public Function GetProjects() As DataSet
    Try
        'Call the data component to get all projects
        GetProjects = objWDAProject.GetProjects
    Catch ExceptionErr As Exception
        Throw New System.Exception(ExceptionErr.Message, _
            ExceptionErr.InnerException)
    End Try
End Function
```

26. The next function to be added is a function to return a specific project. Add the following `GetProject` function to your class:

```
Public Function GetProject(ByVal ProjectID As Guid) As DataSet
    Try
        'Call the data component to get a specific project
```

```
            GetProject = objWDAProject.GetProject(ProjectID)
        Catch ExceptionErr As Exception
            Throw New System.Exception(ExceptionErr.Message, _
                ExceptionErr.InnerException)
        End Try
    End Function
```

27. You want to create a function that returns a `DataSet` for Projects so add the following code to your class:

```
Public Function GetNewProjectDS() As DataSet
    Try
        'Instantiate a new DataSet object
        GetNewProjectDS = New DataSet

        'Create a DataTable object
        Dim objDataTable As DataTable = GetNewProjectDS.Tables.Add("Project")

        'Create a DataColumn object
        Dim objDataColumn As DataColumn

        'Instantiate a new DataColumn and set its properties
        objDataColumn = New DataColumn("ProjectID", _
            Type.GetType("System.Guid"))
        objDataColumn.AllowDBNull = False

        'Add the column to the table
        objDataTable.Columns.Add(objDataColumn)

        'Instantiate a new DataColumn and set its properties
        objDataColumn = New DataColumn("ProjectName", _
            Type.GetType("System.String"))
        objDataColumn.AllowDBNull = False
        objDataColumn.MaxLength = 50

        'Add the column to the table
        objDataTable.Columns.Add(objDataColumn)

        'Instantiate a new DataColumn and set its properties
        objDataColumn = New DataColumn("ProjectDescription", _
            Type.GetType("System.String"))

        'Add the column to the table
        objDataTable.Columns.Add(objDataColumn)

        'Instantiate a new DataColumn and set its properties
        objDataColumn = New DataColumn("SequenceNumber", _
            Type.GetType("System.Byte"))
        objDataColumn.AllowDBNull = False

        'Add the column to the table
        objDataTable.Columns.Add(objDataColumn)
    Catch ExceptionErr As Exception
        Throw New System.Exception(ExceptionErr.Message, _
```

```
            ExceptionErr.InnerException)
        End Try
    End Function
```

28.   The `AddProject` function accepts a `DataSet` as input and calls the corresponding function in the data access component to add a new project. Add the following code for the `AddProject` function to your class:

```
Public Function AddProject(ByVal Project As DataSet) As Boolean
    Try
        'Call the data component to add the project
        Return objWDAProject.AddProject(Project)
    Catch ExceptionErr As Exception
        Throw New System.Exception(ExceptionErr.Message, _
            ExceptionErr.InnerException)
    End Try
End Function
```

29.   The `UpdateProject` function provides the functionality to update an existing project. Add this function to your class:

```
Public Function UpdateProject(ByVal Project As DataSet) As Boolean
    Try
        'Call the data component to update the project
        Return objWDAProject.UpdateProject(Project)
    Catch ExceptionErr As Exception
        Throw New System.Exception(ExceptionErr.Message, _
            ExceptionErr.InnerException)
    End Try
End Function
```

30.   The last function to be added to this class is the `DeleteProject` function. Add the following code to your class:

```
Public Function DeleteProject(ByVal ProjectID As Guid) As Boolean
    Try
        'Call the data component to delete the project
        Return objWDAProject.DeleteProject(ProjectID)
    Catch ExceptionErr As Exception
        Throw New System.Exception(ExceptionErr.Message, _
            ExceptionErr.InnerException)
    End Try
End Function
```

That completes the code needed for the business logic component. At this point it would be a good idea to save your entire solution again, so click the Save All button on the toolbar.

How It Works

The business logic component does not know about any specific database; it only knows to call the functions in the data access component to perform the work. The business logic component is the component that you start implementing the business logic in when you read Chapter 11. In this chapter, you merely get this component created and implement the functions necessary to retrieve, insert, update, and delete groups, group projects, and projects.

The first thing that you do after creating this component is change the base address for the DLL to a unique value, as you did in the data access component. This enables this component to load as fast as possible without any conflicts in the memory that it uses.

The next step in the creation of the business logic component is to create the WBLGroups class. This class handles all functions necessary to retrieve, insert, update, and delete groups and group projects. This class interacts with the WDAGroups class in the data access component, so you add a reference to the WroxDataAccess component next.

This class implements the IDisposable interface, which provides your class with the Dispose method, which can be called by the client. You can and do implement code in the Dispose method to clean up the resources used in the class. To that end, you add the following code to implement the disposable interface:

```
Implements IDisposable
```

The constructor that you create for this class mirrors the constructor for the WDAGroups class. This constructor accepts the company name and application name as input parameters and then calls the constructor in the WDAGroups class, passing it these parameters.

```
Public Sub New(ByVal Company As String, ByVal Application As String)
    objWDAGroups = New WroxDataAccess.WDAGroups(Company, Application)
End Sub
```

The Dispose method in this class cleans up the resources it used by calling the Dispose method in the WDAGroups class so that class can clean up the resources it used. You can see how the Dispose method comes in very handy and can have a chained event.

```
Private Overloads Sub Dispose(ByVal disposing As Boolean)
    If Not Me.disposed Then
        If disposing Then
            ' TODO: put code to dispose managed resources
        End If

        objWDAProject.Dispose()
        objWDAProject = Nothing
    End If
    Me.disposed = True
End Sub
```

The functions in this class are simple and merely call the same named functions in the data access component. This keeps the design of your business logic component simple because the function names, parameters, and return data types match their corresponding counterparts in the data access component. The real job of the business logic component is to validate data and control the workflows necessary to perform any given task. Thus far, the workflows used in the Time Tracker application are simple.

The GetGroups function calls the same named function in the data access component and returns a DataSet containing all groups in the database. The appropriate error-handling has been included so that if the GetGroups function in the data access throws an exception, this function receives it and then throws the same exception to the client that called this function.

This allows the code in the data access component and the business logic component to complete and return the appropriate error to the client. It is the client's responsibility to appropriately handle any and all errors returned.

```
Public Function GetGroups() As DataSet
    Try
        'Call the data component to get all groups
        GetGroups = objWDAGroups.GetGroups
    Catch ExceptionErr As Exception
        Throw New System.Exception(ExceptionErr.Message, _
            ExceptionErr.InnerException)
    End Try
End Function
```

Because the majority of the functions created in the WBLGroups class are all simple I won't list all of the code here again. Likewise, they need no further explanation as they merely accept the appropriate input parameters if required and then call their corresponding functions in the data access component.

The one function that I do want to cover is the GetNewGroupDS function. This function actually builds a DataSet that gets returned to the caller. The first step here is to create a new instance of the DataSet class. Because this function returns a DataSet it acts like a DataSet and can be used to instantiate a new instance of the DataSet class.

Next, you create a new DataTable object and add it to the DataSet specifying a table name of Project. Then you declare an object for the DataColumn class.

```
Public Function GetNewGroupDS() As DataSet
    Try
        'Instantiate a new DataSet object
        GetNewGroupDS = New DataSet

        'Create a DataTable object
        Dim objDataTable As DataTable = GetNewGroupDS.Tables.Add("Group")

        'Create a DataColumn object
        Dim objDataColumn As DataColumn
```

You instantiate a new instance of the DataColumn class next, passing the column name and data type to the constructor of the DataColumn class. Then you set the AllowDBNull property to False indicating that this column requires data. Then you add the new column to the DataTable Columns collection using the Add method.

This process is repeated for each column in the DataTable. The GroupName column is a String data type that allows a maximum of only 50 characters so the MaxLength property of the DataColumn has been set to a value of 50. The GroupDescription column is also a String data type and is virtually unlimited in the amount of data that it can accept so you do not set the MaxLength property for this column.

```
'Instantiate a new DataColumn and set its properties
objDataColumn = New DataColumn("GroupID", _
    Type.GetType("System.Guid"))
objDataColumn.AllowDBNull = False

'Add the column to the table
```

```
        objDataTable.Columns.Add(objDataColumn)

        'Instantiate a new DataColumn and set its properties
        objDataColumn = New DataColumn("GroupName", _
            Type.GetType("System.String"))
        objDataColumn.AllowDBNull = False
        objDataColumn.MaxLength = 50

        'Add the column to the table
        objDataTable.Columns.Add(objDataColumn)

        'Instantiate a new DataColumn and set its properties
        objDataColumn = New DataColumn("GroupDescription", _
            Type.GetType("System.String"))

        'Add the column to the table
        objDataTable.Columns.Add(objDataColumn)
```

The rest of the code in this function is the standard error handling that you've seen before and needs no further explanation.

```
        Catch ExceptionErr As Exception
            Throw New System.Exception(ExceptionErr.Message, _
                ExceptionErr.InnerException)
        End Try
    End Function
```

After you create all the required functions in the WBLGroups class, you create a new class to support retrieving, inserting, updating, and deleting project data. The WBLProjects class was built in the same manner as the WBLGroups class.

It implements the IDisposable interface and contains a constructor that will accept the required parameters for the data access component. This constructor calls the constructor in the WDAProjects class, passing it the required parameters.

```
        Public Sub New(ByVal Company As String, ByVal Application As String)
            objWDAProject = New WroxDataAccess.WDAProjects(Company, Application)
        End Sub
```

Likewise, the Dispose method in this class cleans up its used resources by calling the Dispose method in the WDAProjects class in the data access component, to let that component clean up its used resources.

```
        Private Overloads Sub Dispose(ByVal disposing As Boolean)
            If Not Me.disposed Then
                If disposing Then
                    ' TODO: put code to dispose managed resources
                End If

                objWDAProject.Dispose()
                objWDAProject = Nothing
            End If
            Me.disposed = True
        End Sub
```

The functions in this class are similar to the functions created in the WBLGroups class. Each function has a corresponding function in the WDAProjects class and accepts the same input parameters if required and returns the same data types.

These functions call their counterparts in the data access component and then return the appropriate data back to the caller. The error-handling code in these functions handles any errors that are returned from the data access component and then passes the error on to the client so that the client can appropriately handle the errors.

```
Public Function GetProjects() As DataSet
    Try
        'Call the data component to get all projects
        GetProjects = objWDAProject.GetProjects
    Catch ExceptionErr As Exception
        Throw New System.Exception(ExceptionErr.Message, _
            ExceptionErr.InnerException)
    End Try
End Function
```

Again, because the functions in the WBLProjects class are so simple and merely call their counterparts in the data access component, there is no need to list each function again.

In this next Try It Out, you modify the Time Tracker project to use the functions in the business logic component to select, insert, update, and delete data. This requires adapting your Time Tracker project to work exclusively with DataSet objects, as this has been the design chosen for your business logic component and data access component.

Try It Out   Modifying the Time Tracker Project

To modify the Time Tracker project:

1. In Solution Explorer, right-click References for the Time Tracker project and choose Add Reference. In the Add Reference dialog box, click the Projects tab and select the WroxBusinessLogic component. Click OK to add the reference to your project.

2. View the code for the Admin form and make the following variable declaration changes:

```
Private strAppTitle As String
Private strCompany As String = "Wrox"
Private strApplication As String = "Time Tracker"

Private objGroups As WroxBusinessLogic.WBLGroups
Private objProjects As WroxBusinessLogic.WBLProjects

Private objDataSet As Data.DataSet
Private objGroupsDS As Data.DataSet
Private objProjectsDS As Data.DataSet
Private objGroupProjectsDS As Data.DataSet
```

3. You modify the ActionAdd procedure next. Start by removing the Using...End Using block that initializes a new instance of the WDABase class in the objData object so that the beginning of your procedure now looks like this:

```
Private Sub ActionAdd()
    Try
        'Add database row based on the active screen
        Select Case strActiveScreen
```

4. The `ActionAdd` procedure contains three `Case` statements that need to be modified. First, modify the code under the `Case "Projects"` statement with the code shown here:

```
Case "Projects"
        'Initialize a new instance of the business logic component
        Using objProjects As New WroxBusinessLogic.WBLProjects( _
            strCompany, strApplication)
            'Get a new Project DataSet
            objDataSet = objProjects.GetNewProjectDS()
            'Initialize a datarow object from the Project DataSet
            Dim objDataRow As Data.DataRow = _
                objDataSet.Tables("Project").NewRow
            'Set the values in the DataRow
            objDataRow.Item("ProjectID") = Guid.NewGuid()
            objDataRow.Item("ProjectName") = txtProjectName.Text
            objDataRow.Item("ProjectDescription") = _
                txtProjectDescription.Text
            objDataRow.Item("SequenceNumber") = _
                CType(txtSequenceNumber.Text, Byte)
            'Add the DataRow to the DataSet
            objDataSet.Tables("Project").Rows.Add(objDataRow)
            'Add the Project
            If Not objProjects.AddProject(objDataSet) Then
                Throw New Exception("Insert Project Failed")
            End If
        End Using

        'Clear the input fields
```

5. Now modify the code under the `Case "Groups"` statement in the same procedure with the following code:

```
Case "Groups"
        'Initialize a new instance of the business logic component
        Using objGroups As New WroxBusinessLogic.WBLGroups( _
            strCompany, strApplication)
            'Get a new Group DataSet
            objDataSet = objGroups.GetNewGroupDS()
            'Initialize a datarow object from the Group DataSet
            Dim objDataRow As Data.DataRow = _
                objDataSet.Tables("Group").NewRow
            'Set the values in the DataRow
            objDataRow.Item("GroupID") = Guid.NewGuid()
            objDataRow.Item("GroupName") = txtGroupName.Text
            objDataRow.Item("GroupDescription") = _
                txtGroupDescription.Text
            'Add the DataRow to the DataSet
            objDataSet.Tables("Group").Rows.Add(objDataRow)
            'Add the Groups to the database
            If Not objGroups.AddGroup(objDataSet) Then
```

```
                    Throw New Exception("Insert Group Failed")
            End If
        End Using


        'Clear the input fields
```

6. Modify the code under the `Case "Group Projects"` as follows:

```
Case "Group Projects"
    'Turn the loading flag on so no items are processed
    blnLoading = True
    'Delete any previous projects
    Call ActionDelete()
    'Turn the loading flag off
    blnLoading = False

    'Initialize a new instance of the business logic component
    Using objGroups As New WroxBusinessLogic.WBLGroups( _
        strCompany, strApplication)
        'Get a new GroupProjects DataSet
        objDataSet = objGroups.GetNewGroupProjectsDS()
        For intIndex = 0 To objGroupProjectsDS.Tables( _
            "GroupProjects").Rows.Count - 1
            'Initialize a datarow object from the
            'GroupProjects(DataSet)
            Dim objDataRow As Data.DataRow = _
                objDataSet.Tables("GroupProjects").NewRow
            'Set the values in the DataRow
            objDataRow.Item("GroupProjectID") = Guid.NewGuid()
            objDataRow.Item("GroupID") = _
                cboGroups.SelectedItem.Item("GroupID")
            objDataRow.Item("ProjectID") = _
                objGroupProjectsDS.Tables( _
                "GroupProjects").Rows(intIndex).Item("ProjectID")
            'Add the DataRow to the DataSet
            objDataSet.Tables("GroupProjects").Rows.Add(objDataRow)
        Next
        'Add the GroupProjects to the database
        If Not objGroups.AddGroupProjects(objDataSet) Then
            Throw New Exception("Insert Group Failed")
        End If
    End Using

    'Clear previous bindings
```

7. Modify the code in the `ActionUpdate` procedure. Starting at the top of this procedure, modify it as shown by removing the `Using...End Using` block that initializes a new instance of the `WDABase` class in the `objData` object:

```
Private Sub ActionUpdate()
    Try
        'Update database row based on the active screen
        Select Case strActiveScreen
```

8. Now modify the code under the `Case "Projects"` statement in the `ActionUpdate` procedure as shown:

```
Case "Projects"
        'Initialize a new instance of the business logic component
        Using objProjects As New WroxBusinessLogic.WBLProjects( _
            strCompany, strApplication)
            'Get a new Project DataSet
            objDataSet = objProjects.GetNewProjectDS()
            'Initialize a datarow object from the Project DataSet
            Dim objDataRow As Data.DataRow = _
                objDataSet.Tables("Project").NewRow
            'Set the values in the DataRow
            objDataRow.Item("ProjectID") = New Guid(txtProjectID.Text)
            objDataRow.Item("ProjectName") = txtProjectName.Text
            objDataRow.Item("ProjectDescription") = _
                txtProjectDescription.Text
            objDataRow.Item("SequenceNumber") = _
                CType(txtSequenceNumber.Text, Integer)
            'Add the DataRow to the DataSet
            objDataSet.Tables("Project").Rows.Add(objDataRow)
            'Update the Project in the database
            If Not objProjects.UpdateProject(objDataSet) Then
                Throw New Exception("Update Project Failed")
            End If
        End Using

        'Clear the input fields
```

9. Modify the code under the `Case "Groups"` statement as shown:

```
Case "Groups"
        'Initialize a new instance of the business logic component
        Using objGroups As New WroxBusinessLogic.WBLGroups( _
            strCompany, strApplication)
            'Get a new Group DataSet
            objDataSet = objGroups.GetNewGroupDS()
            'Initialize a datarow object from the Group DataSet
            Dim objDataRow As Data.DataRow = _
                objDataSet.Tables("Group").NewRow
            'Set the values in the DataRow
            objDataRow.Item("GroupID") = New Guid(txtGroupID.Text)
            objDataRow.Item("GroupName") = txtGroupName.Text
            objDataRow.Item("GroupDescription") = _
                txtGroupDescription.Text
            'Add the DataRow to the DataSet
            objDataSet.Tables("Group").Rows.Add(objDataRow)
            'Add the Group to the database
            If Not objGroups.UpdateGroup(objDataSet) Then
                Throw New Exception("Update Group Failed")
            End If
        End Using

        'Clear the input fields
```

10. No modifications are necessary for the code under the `Case "Group Projects"` statement.

11. The next procedure to be modified is the `ActionDelete` procedure. Again, starting at the top, remove the `Using...End Using` block that initializes a new instance of the `WDABase` class in the `objData` object. Your modifications should now look like the following:

```
Private Sub ActionDelete()
    Try
        'Delete database row based on the active screen
        Select Case strActiveScreen
```

12. Now modify the code under the `Case "Projects"` statement in the `ActionDelete` procedure as shown:

```
Case "Projects"
    'Initialize a new instance of the business logic component
    Using objProjects As New WroxBusinessLogic.WBLProjects( _
        strCompany, strApplication)
        'Delete the project
        If Not objProjects.DeleteProject( _
            New Guid(txtProjectID.Text)) Then
            Throw New Exception("Delete Project Failed")
        End If
    End Using

    'Clear the input fields
```

13. Modify the code under the `Case "Groups"` statement as indicated:

```
Case "Groups"
    'Initialize a new instance of the business logic component
    Using objGroups As New WroxBusinessLogic.WBLGroups( _
        strCompany, strApplication)
        'Delete the group
        If Not objGroups.DeleteGroup( _
            New Guid(txtGroupID.Text)) Then
            Throw New Exception("Delete Group Failed")
        End If
    End Using

    'Clear the input fields
```

14. Modify the code under the `Case "Group Projects"` statement as shown:

```
Case "Group Projects"
    'Initialize a new instance of the business logic component
    Using objGroups As New WroxBusinessLogic.WBLGroups( _
        strCompany, strApplication)
        'Delete the group projects
        objGroups.DeleteGroupProjects( _
            New Guid( _
            cboGroups.SelectedItem.Item("GroupID").ToString))
    End Using

    'Clear previous bindings
```

15. Now it's time to move on to the `LoadProjects` procedure. Modify the code in this procedure as follows. The entire procedure is not shown, only the relevant parts:

```
Private Sub LoadProjects()
    'Declare variables
    Dim objListViewItem As ListViewItem

        'Initialize a new instance of the business logic component
        Using objProjects As New WroxBusinessLogic.WBLProjects( _
            strCompany, strApplication)

        Try
            .
            .
            .

                'Get all projects in a DataSet object
                objProjectsDS = objProjects.GetProjects()

                'Clear previous list
                lvwProjects.Items.Clear()
```

16. The next procedure that needs to be modified is the `lvwProjects_Click` procedure. This procedure requires a lot of modifications as you'll be getting rid of the code that uses the `DataReader`. Modify this procedure as follows:

```
Private Sub lvwProjects_Click(ByVal sender As Object, _
    ByVal e As System.EventArgs) Handles lvwProjects.Click

        'Initialize a new instance of the business logic component
        Using objProjects As New WroxBusinessLogic.WBLProjects( _
            strCompany, strApplication)

        Try
                'Get the specific project selected in the ListView control
                objDataSet = objProjects.GetProject( _
                    New Guid(lvwProjects.SelectedItems.Item(0).Tag.ToString))

                'Populate the Project Details section
                txtProjectID.Text = _
                    objDataSet.Tables("Project").Rows(0).Item( _
                    "ProjectID").ToString.ToUpper
                txtProjectName.Text = _
                    objDataSet.Tables("Project").Rows(0).Item("ProjectName")
                txtProjectDescription.Text = _
                    objDataSet.Tables("Project").Rows(0).Item( _
                    "ProjectDescription")
                txtSequenceNumber.Text = _
                    objDataSet.Tables("Project").Rows(0).Item("SequenceNumber")
                txtProjectUpdateDate.Text = _
                    objDataSet.Tables("Project").Rows(0).Item("LastUpdateDate")

        Catch ExceptionErr As Exception
            MessageBox.Show(ExceptionErr.Message, strAppTitle)
        End Try
    End Using
End Sub
```

17. You'll need to modify some group procedures next. Starting with the LoadGroups procedure, make the following modifications. The entire procedure is not listed here, only the relevant sections that you need to modify:

```
'Turn the loading flag on so no items are processed
blnLoading = True
```

```
'Initialize a new instance of the business logic component
Using objGroups As New WroxBusinessLogic.WBLGroups( _
    strCompany, strApplication)
```

```
        Try
    .
    .
    .
```

```
            'Get all groups in a DataSet object
            objGroupsDS = objGroups.GetGroups()
```

```
            'Clear previous list
            lvwGroups.Items.Clear()
```

18. The lvwGroups_Click procedure is next; replace the code that uses a DataReader with code that uses a DataSet:

```
Private Sub lvwGroups_Click(ByVal sender As Object, _
    ByVal e As System.EventArgs) Handles lvwGroups.Click
```

```
        'Initialize a new instance of the business logic component
    Using objGroups As New WroxBusinessLogic.WBLGroups( _
        strCompany, strApplication)
```

```
        Try
            'Get the specific Group selected in the ListView control
            objDataSet = objGroups.GetGroup( _
                New Guid(lvwGroups.SelectedItems.Item(0).Tag.ToString))

            'Populate the Group Details section
            txtGroupID.Text = _
                objDataSet.Tables("Group").Rows(0).Item( _
                "GroupID").ToString.ToUpper
            txtGroupName.Text = _
                objDataSet.Tables("Group").Rows(0).Item("GroupName")
            txtGroupDescription.Text = _
                objDataSet.Tables("Group").Rows(0).Item("GroupDescription")
            txtGroupUpdateDate.Text = _
                objDataSet.Tables("Group").Rows(0).Item("LastUpdateDate")
        Catch ExceptionErr As Exception
            MessageBox.Show(ExceptionErr.Message, strAppTitle)
        End Try
    End Using
End Sub
```

19. The last procedure to modify is the cboGroups_SelectedIndexChanged procedure. Make the following modifications to this procedure:

```vb
Private Sub cboGroups_SelectedIndexChanged(ByVal sender As Object, _
    ByVal e As System.EventArgs) Handles cboGroups.SelectedIndexChanged

    'Don't process if the ComboBox is being loaded
    If blnLoading Then
        Exit Sub
    End If

    'Initialize a new instance of the business logic component
    Using objGroups As New WroxBusinessLogic.WBLGroups( _
        strCompany, strApplication)

        Try
            'Clear previous bindings
            lstGroupProjects.DataSource = Nothing
            lstGroupProjects.DisplayMember = String.Empty
            lstGroupProjects.ValueMember = String.Empty

            'Get the Group Projects
            objGroupProjectsDS = objGroups.GetGroupProjects( _
                New Guid(cboGroups.SelectedItem.Item("GroupID").ToString))

            'Rebind ListBox control
            lstGroupProjects.DataSource = _
                objGroupProjectsDS.Tables("GroupProjects")
            lstGroupProjects.DisplayMember = "ProjectName"
            lstGroupProjects.ValueMember = "ProjectID"

        Catch ExceptionErr As Exception
            MessageBox.Show(ExceptionErr.Message, strAppTitle)
        End Try
    End Using
End Sub
```

20. Build your project to ensure that there are no errors in your code. Click the Build menu and select the Build Solution.

At this point, your Time Tracker application is using the business logic component and data access component and should be fully functional. Run your application and the functionality should be the same as it was in Chapter 9.

How It Works

To have your Time Tracker application use the business logic component, you have to set a reference to it as the first step in modifying your application. You then declare some variables that will be needed by both your business logic component and your application.

The strCompany and strApplication variables are used by the data access component to read the appropriate key values from the registry. This is fed to the data access component from the business logic component through their constructors. You defined these variables at the class level for your form and set their values.

The next variables that you define are objects that represent the WBLGroups and WBLProjects classes in the business logic component. You'll instantiate these objects as needed and then dispose of them when you are done using them.

The last variable that you define at the class level is an object for a DataSet. This DataSet object is used to receive data that will be used to populate the various ListView controls and detail sections on your form. This is a catch-all DataSet and is repeatedly used to receive data from the business logic component.

```
Private strCompany As String = "Wrox"
Private strApplication As String = "Time Tracker"

Private objGroups As WroxBusinessLogic.WBLGroups
Private objProjects As WroxBusinessLogic.WBLProjects

Private objDataSet As DataSet
```

The first procedure that you modify in the Admin form is the ActionAdd procedure. The first modification that you make is to remove the reference to the WDABase class as it no longer exists in your project.

Next, you modify the code under the Case "Projects" statement to use the business logic component. The first step is to initialize a new instance of the WBLProjects class in the business logic component, passing the constructor the required parameters for company and application. Then you call the GetNewProjectDS function, which returns an empty DataSet with the appropriate schema for a project. This DataSet contains the columns that need to be populated as well as their appropriate data types and constraints, such as whether the column can contain NULL values or not.

After you get a new DataSet for a project in the objDataSet object, you need to declare a DataRow object. A DataRow represents a new row of data in a DataSet and is initialized using the NewRow method of the table in the DataSet. This sets the DataRow object with the appropriate columns and constraints for the DataSet.

```
Case "Projects"
    'Initialize a new instance of the business logic component
    Using objProjects As New WroxBusinessLogic.WBLProjects( _
        strCompany, strApplication)
        'Get a new Project DataSet
        objDataSet = objProjects.GetNewProjectDS()
        'Initialize a datarow object from the Project DataSet
        Dim objDataRow As Data.DataRow = _
            objDataSet.Tables("Project").NewRow
```

The next step is to start adding the values to the columns in the DataRow object. You add the values to the DataRow object using the Item property, which gets or sets the data value stored in a specific column. You can access the Item property by using a zero-based index or by specifying the name of the column. The latter method has been chosen as it helps to self-document your code and makes maintenance a lot easier, as you know exactly what column is being set.

After you have set the value for each column in the DataRow object, you must add the DataRow object to the DataSet. This is done using the Add method of the Rows property and passing it the DataRow object to be added.

```
'Set the values in the DataRow
objDataRow.Item("ProjectID") = Guid.NewGuid()
objDataRow.Item("ProjectName") = txtProjectName.Text
objDataRow.Item("ProjectDescription") = _
    txtProjectDescription.Text
objDataRow.Item("SequenceNumber") = _
    CType(txtSequenceNumber.Text, Byte)
'Add the DataRow to the DataSet
objDataSet.Tables("Project").Rows.Add(objDataRow)
```

At this point, your objDataSet object contains a row of data to be added. You then call the AddProject method in the business logic component, passing it the DataSet object containing your data. The AddProject method returns a Boolean value indicating whether a row of data was added.

You call this method in an If...Then...End If statement to determine whether the project was added. If the project was not added, you throw an exception with the appropriate message and your error-handling code for this procedure catches and displays the error.

```
'Add the Project
If Not objProjects.AddProject(objDataSet) Then
    Throw New Exception("Insert Project Failed")
End If
End Using
```

The code under the Case "Groups" statement works in the same manner except that it accesses the WBLGroups class in the business logic component and works with the Group DataSet. Therefore, the code for this Case statement is not listed here again.

The code under the Case "Group Projects" statement works a little differently so let me explain it in detail. You start in the same manner as you did in the Case "Projects" statement by initializing a new instance of the business logic component except that you are working with the WBLGroups class in this section of code. You then get a new DataSet for Group Projects in the objDataSet object by calling the GetNewGroupProjectsDS method.

```
'Initialize a new instance of the business logic component
Using objGroups As New WroxBusinessLogic.WBLGroups( _
    strCompany, strApplication)
    'Get a new GroupProjects DataSet
    objDataSet = objGroups.GetNewGroupProjectsDS()
```

Because you will typically be adding multiple group projects at one time, you set up a loop to process all projects in the objGroupProjectsDS DataSet. For each iteration of the loop, you declare and initialize a new DataRow object and then add the appropriate project.

The DataRow object contains three columns, all of which are defined as Guid structures. The first column is the GroupProjectID, which is set to a new Guid that you generate. The second column is the Guid for the GroupID, which is retrieved from the selected group in the cboGroups combo box. The final column is the ProjectID, which is retrieved from the objGroupProjectsDS DataSet. Remember that this DataSet is bound to the Group Projects ListBox and contains a list of selected projects.

After the DataRow object has been populated with the required data, you add the DataRow object to the DataSet. Then you repeat the loop again until all data in the objGroupProjectsDS has been processed.

```
For intIndex = 0 To objGroupProjectsDS.Tables( _
    "GroupProjects").Rows.Count - 1
    'Initialize a datarow object from the
    'GroupProjects(DataSet)
    Dim objDataRow As Data.DataRow = _
        objDataSet.Tables("GroupProjects").NewRow
    'Set the values in the DataRow
    objDataRow.Item("GroupProjectID") = Guid.NewGuid()
    objDataRow.Item("GroupID") = _
        cboGroups.SelectedItem.Item("GroupID")
    objDataRow.Item("ProjectID") = _
        objGroupProjectsDS.Tables( _
        "GroupProjects").Rows(intIndex).Item("ProjectID")
    'Add the DataRow to the DataSet
    objDataSet.Tables("GroupProjects").Rows.Add(objDataRow)
Next
```

When the `DataSet` has been populated with all rows of data, you call the `AddGroupProjects` method in the business logic component, passing it the `DataSet` containing all group projects. This method calls the same named function in the data access component and adds each group project to the GroupProjects table in the database.

You've included the call to the `AddGroupProjects` method in an `If...Then...End If` statement to test whether the call was successful, and throw an exception with the appropriate error message if it was not.

```
'Add the GroupProjects to the database
If Not objGroups.AddGroupProjects(objDataSet) Then
    Throw New Exception("Insert Group Failed")
End If
End Using
```

The changes made to the `ActionUpdate` procedure mirror the changes made to the `ActionAdd` procedure, so the code is not listed here again.

The `ActionDelete` procedure requires few changes and starts out like the `ActionAdd` procedure. You modify the code under the `Case "Projects"` statement to initialize a new instance of the business logic component, accessing the appropriate class in that component. Next, you make a call to the `DeleteProject` method, passing it the Guid of the project to be deleted.

Again, you have included this call in an `If...Then...End If` statement to test whether the call was successful. If the call was not successful, you throw an exception with the appropriate error message.

```
'Initialize a new instance of the business logic component
Using objProjects As New WroxBusinessLogic.WBLProjects( _
    strCompany, strApplication)
    'Delete the project
    If Not objProjects.DeleteProject( _
        New Guid(txtProjectID.Text)) Then
        Throw New Exception("Delete Project Failed")
    End If
End Using
```

The code under the `Case "Groups"` and `Case "Group Projects"` statements works in a similar manner and is not repeated here.

The `LoadProjects` procedure already processed data from a `DataSet` so the modifications you make to this procedure are relatively minor. All you have to do in this procedure is modify the code to retrieve the projects in a `DataSet` from the business component by calling the `GetProjects` method:

```
'Get all projects in a DataSet object
objProjectsDS = objProjects.GetProjects()
```

The `lvwProjects_Click` procedure requires a little more work than the previous procedure because this procedure used a `DataReader` object to process data. Because the business component returns only data in a `DataSet`, you have to modify this procedure to process the data from a `DataSet` object.

You start by initializing a new instance of the business logic component. Then you get the data for the selected project in a `DataSet` object by calling the `GetProject` method, passing it the ProjectID of the selected project:

```
Private Sub lvwProjects_Click(ByVal sender As Object, _
    ByVal e As System.EventArgs) Handles lvwProjects.Click

    'Initialize a new instance of the business logic component
    Using objProjects As New WroxBusinessLogic.WBLProjects( _
        strCompany, strApplication)

    Try
        'Get the specific project selected in the ListView control
        objDataSet = objProjects.GetProject( _
            New Guid(lvwProjects.SelectedItems.Item(0).Tag.ToString))
```

Because you know that only a single row of data will be returned, you do not need to process the data from the `DataSet` in a loop. You populate the project detail section of the form using the first row of data from the `DataSet`.

```
'Populate the Project Details section
txtProjectID.Text = _
    objDataSet.Tables("Project").Rows(0).Item( _
    "ProjectID").ToString.ToUpper
txtProjectName.Text = _
    objDataSet.Tables("Project").Rows(0).Item("ProjectName")
txtProjectDescription.Text = _
    objDataSet.Tables("Project").Rows(0).Item( _
    "ProjectDescription")
txtSequenceNumber.Text = _
    objDataSet.Tables("Project").Rows(0).Item("SequenceNumber")
txtProjectUpdateDate.Text = _
    objDataSet.Tables("Project").Rows(0).Item("LastUpdateDate")
```

The `LoadGroups` procedure is modified next, and the modifications to this procedure mirror the changes that you made to the `LoadProjects` procedure. Instead of executing a stored procedure to populate a `DataSet` with group data, you call the `GetGroups` method in the business logic component to get a `DataSet` containing all the groups in the database.

The changes that you make to the `lvwGroups_Click` procedure mirror the changes made to the `lvwProjects_Click` procedure. You retrofit this procedure to process data from a `DataSet`, rather than a `DataReader` object. Because the changes mirror the changes made in the `lvwProjects_Click` procedure, the code for the `lvwGroups_Click` procedure is not listed again.

The last procedure that has to be modified is the `cboGroups_SelectedIndexChanged` procedure. Again, the changes required are minor and require getting the list of group projects for the selected group from the business component. This procedure already used a `DataSet` for the group projects, so no changes are needed there.

```
'Get the Group Projects
objGroupProjectsDS = objGroups.GetGroupProjects( _
    New Guid(cboGroups.SelectedItem.Item("GroupID").ToString))
```

After all the changes are made to the Time Tracker application, your application uses the business logic component to retrieve, insert, update, and delete data. This provides several benefits, the first of which is that now your application can concentrate on the presentation logic and does not need to know anything about any databases.

Likewise, the business logic component does not know about any databases and can concentrate on the business logic and workflows needed to process data. You'll be implementing business logic in the WroxBusinessLogic component in the next chapter.

The data access component can concentrate on the task of working with data in the specific database. You could have designed a generic data access component that used the `System.Data.OleDb` namespace instead of a data access component that is tied to a specific database. However, I wanted to demonstrate the use of the `System.Data.SqlClient` and `System.Data.OracleClient` namespaces and the advantages that they provide when working with their own databases.

Summary

This has been quite a busy chapter and has covered a lot of ground. You have spent most of your time building new components and modifying your Time Tracker application to use the components that you built.

However, the key information that you should walk away with is the importance of separating the presentation logic from the business logic and the data access logic. When setting out to design a distributed application architecture for your real-world applications, you know that you have a lot of options and many things to consider in the design of your components. Designing a distributed application architecture requires research on your part to determine which options are available and which option will best suit your business requirements and physical architecture.

You need to consider how data will be marshaled between the components in your architecture, the security of your components, and the performance of your components. Although the design of the components for your Time Tracker application is simple, they demonstrate the separation of layers in your architecture.

To summarize, you should know:

❑ The benefits of using a distributed application architecture

❑ A distributed application architecture consists of a presentation layer, a business logic layer, and a data access layer

❑ How to read from and write to the registry

❑ How to create components and use those components in your application

In Chapter 11, you enhance the business logic component that you built in this chapter by actually adding some business logic. You also explore stored procedures that insert data in more depth and learn how to perform error-checking in your stored procedures.

Exercise

Using Exercise 2 from Chapter 9 as a base, modify that application to use the Wrox Business Logic component that you built in this chapter. You need only to set a reference to the `WroxBusinessLogic.dll` in this project and not actually add the `WroxBusinessLogic` project to your solution.

Inserting Data

The insert stored procedures that you've been working with up until this point have been straightforward; they insert data into the database. No data validation has been performed on the data passed to the stored procedures or on any data that exists in database tables. This can be a bad thing, and as the old adage says, "Garbage in, garbage out."

Data validation can be performed at four levels: in the client application, in the business logic component, in the data access component, and in the database. In this chapter, you touch on data validation in the client application, but your main focus is on data validation in the business logic component and in the stored procedures that execute in the database. Placing data validation logic in the data access component isn't really a good fit with your design, as the stored procedures can perform all of the data validation necessary in the database and with greater efficiency.

In this chapter, you learn how to:

- ❑ Validate data in the business logic component to handle empty strings and NULL values
- ❑ Validate phone numbers, e-mail addresses, and passwords
- ❑ Write stored procedures that use variables, perform error checking, and use logic to control the execution of code in the stored procedure
- ❑ Write stored procedures that incorporate transactions and insert data into multiple tables

Validating Data in the Business Logic Component

Business logic components do more than define and control the workflows to accomplish a business process; they also perform data validation. Data validation involves more than ensuring that the data is of the correct data type and that the values are valid. It also includes how to properly format the data being passed so that it is stored in the database in a consistent format. Another function of data validation is to ensure that empty strings and NULL values are handled properly.

In this section, I describe how your business logic component can and should validate data. I explain how to check for and handle empty strings, and string validation.

Handling empty strings and NULL values

The design of your business logic component calls for creating a DataSet that contains certain constraints such as columns that can and cannot contain null values and columns of different data types. When the DataSet is passed back to the client application, the client application has certain restrictions placed on it by the DataSet. These include ensuring that the data added to the DataSet is of the correct data type and that any column requiring data contains data. Therefore, your business logic component does not need to validate data types or check for empty columns that require data.

However, empty strings or strings with one or more spaces can be inserted into the columns of the DataSet. This may be valid in some cases but not in others. You need to validate the length of the data in each column in the DataSet to ensure that actual data is present where required and to remove the spaces in columns that do not contain data.

You want to remove the spaces from columns where no data is required because inserting a blank space into the database wastes space. A column in a database table that has a blank space requires storage space in the database. Why use up that extra storage space when it is not necessary?

The next example code shows how you can validate that data exists in a DataSet column. The example takes the value in the RoleName column in the Role DataSet and converts it to a string using the ToString method. Then it uses the Trim method to remove the leading and trailing spaces, if any, and the Length property to check for the length. The length of the data is determined after all leading and trailing spaces are removed so if a user entered a space in the input field, it is removed before the length is calculated.

If the length of the data in this column is zero, you throw an exception that is passed back to the caller. This prevents a user from entering a space as input when an actual value is required.

```
'Validate the Name exists
If Role.Tables("Role").Rows(0).Item("RoleName").ToString.Trim.Length = 0 Then
    Throw New System.Exception("Role Name is a required field.")
End If
```

In addition to checking for a zero-length string, it is also good to remove any leading or trailing spaces before the data is passed to the data access component. Again, a user could have entered a space before or after the role name, intentionally or not. If you do not remove the leading and trailing spaces, they are inserted into the database, wasting space.

The following code shows how to remove the leading and trailing spaces in the DataSet column. Again, you must convert the value to a string by using the ToString method and call the Trim method to remove the leading and trailing space. Basically, you are setting the value in the column to itself minus any spaces:

```
'Trim spaces
Role.Tables("Role").Rows(0).Item("RoleName") = _
    Role.Tables("Role").Rows(0).Item("RoleName").ToString.Trim
```

A NULL value should be inserted into columns in the DataSet that do not contain any data and that allow NULL values. This allows a NULL value to be inserted into the database instead of a blank space or empty string, thereby reducing the storage space required for this data.

The following code snippet demonstrates how to check columns in a DataSet that do not require any data. First you want to ensure that the column does not already contain a NULL value by using the IsDBNull function. This function returns a True/False value indicating whether the column contains a NULL value. If you don't perform this check first and the column already contains a NULL value, comparing the value of the column to String.Empty throws an exception.

Basically, this code first determines whether the column contains a NULL value. If it does not, it determines whether the column contains an empty string value or a zero-length string after trimming the spaces from the column. If it does, it sets the value in the column to a DBNull.Value.

If the column does not contain an empty string or zero-length string, you trim the spaces from the column. Just as a side note, an empty string is equivalent to a zero-length string. However, to determine whether the column contains a zero-length string, you must first use the Trim function to remove any spaces from the column:

```
'Validate Description value
If Not IsDBNull(Role.Tables("Role").Rows(0).Item("RoleDescription")) Then
    If Role.Tables("Role").Rows(0).Item("RoleDescription") = String.Empty Or _
        Role.Tables("Role").Rows(0).Item( _
        "RoleDescription").ToString.Trim.Length = 0 Then
        'Set it to a null value
        Role.Tables("Role").Rows(0).Item("RoleDescription") = DBNull.Value
    Else
        'Trim spaces
        Role.Tables("Role").Rows(0).Item("RoleDescription") = _
            Role.Tables("Role").Rows(0).Item( _
            "RoleDescription").ToString.Trim
    End If
End If
```

Validating string data

Validating string data is the process of ensuring that the data in a column meets the minimum required length and/or contains the appropriate values according to your organization's business rules.

For example, the Time Tracker application enables an administrator to enter phone numbers. Suppose numerous administrators entered phone numbers in different formats—for example, (123) 456-7890 or 123-456-7890 or 123 456-7890 or 123.456.7890). All the phone numbers listed are valid U.S. phone numbers that include the area code. However, the format in which they are entered is inconsistent.

Consistent entry of data can be controlled in several ways. First, the client application could force the user to enter the phone number in a specific format, which would provide consistent data but isn't very user-friendly. Second, the business logic component could accept the phone numbers in the various formats and then validate the phone numbers to ensure that they all contain the correct number of digits for a U.S. phone number. This would allow the users of your application to enter the phone number in the format to which they are accustomed.

However, the mere validation of a phone number does not stop here. You still want to ensure that the phone numbers are stored in the database in a consistent format. This enables the client application or applications to retrieve the phone numbers and have them all in the same format. Therefore, the business logic component would not only be responsible for validating that the phone numbers are valid, but it would also be responsible for formatting the phone numbers in the same manner according to the business rules of your organization.

E-mail addresses and passwords are other examples of information for which the business logic component should validate the data. E-mail addresses can be validated to ensure that they are in the proper format (for example, someone@somewhere.com).

Passwords can and should be validated according to the business rules of your organization. Validation would include validating that passwords are of the minimum length as specified by your business rules, that they contain the appropriate characters (uppercase and lowercase), and that they contain numbers and special characters if required.

All these validations can and should be performed in your business logic component before the data is passed to the data access component to be inserted or updated in the database.

In this Try It Out, you add data validation to the business logic components for projects and groups. You want to validate data when a project or group is added or updated and add the appropriate code for such validations.

Try It Out   Validating Projects and Groups

To implement this functionality:

1. Open your Time Tracker application in Visual Studio 2005.

2. View the code for the WBLProjects class in the WroxBusinessLogic project.

3. Add the following code to the GetProjects method:

```
'Call the data component to get all projects
GetProjects = objWDAProject.GetProjects
```

```
'Loop through the DataSet and convert all DBNull values
'to empty strings
For intindex As Integer = 0 To _
    GetProjects.Tables("Projects").Rows.Count - 1

    'If the column contains a null value...
    If IsDBNull(GetProjects.Tables("Projects").Rows( _
        intindex).Item("ProjectDescription")) Then

        'Convert it to an empty string
        GetProjects.Tables("Projects").Rows( _
            intindex).Item("ProjectDescription") = String.Empty
    End If
Next
Catch ExceptionErr As Exception
```

4. Now add the following code to the `GetProject` method:

```
'Call the data component to get a specific project
GetProject = objWDAProject.GetProject(ProjectID)


        'If the column contains a null value...
        If IsDBNull(GetProject.Tables("Project").Rows(0).Item( _
            "ProjectDescription")) Then
            'Convert it to an empty string
            GetProject.Tables("Project").Rows(0).Item( _
                "ProjectDescription") = String.Empty
        End If
    Catch ExceptionErr As Exception
```

5. Add the following procedure to validate project data:

```
Private Sub ValidateProjectData(ByRef Project As DataSet)
    'Validate the Name exists
    If Project.Tables("Project").Rows(0).Item( _
        "ProjectName").ToString.Trim.Length = 0 Then
        Throw New System.Exception( _
            "Project Name is a required field.")
    End If

    'Validate Description value
    If Not IsDBNull(Project.Tables("Project").Rows(0).Item( _
        "ProjectDescription")) Then
        If Project.Tables("Project").Rows(0).Item( _
            "ProjectDescription") = String.Empty Or _
            Project.Tables("Project").Rows(0).Item( _
            "ProjectDescription").ToString.Trim.Length = 0 Then
            'Set it to a null value
            Project.Tables("Project").Rows(0).Item( _
                "ProjectDescription") = DBNull.Value
        Else
            'Trim spaces
            Project.Tables("Project").Rows(0).Item("ProjectDescription") = _
                Project.Tables("Project").Rows(0).Item( _
                "ProjectDescription").ToString.Trim
        End If
    End If

    'Validate the Sequence Number
    If Project.Tables("Project").Rows(0).Item( _
        "SequenceNumber") = 0 Then
        Throw New System.Exception( _
            "Sequence Number must contain a value between 1 and 255.")
    End If

    'Trim spaces
    Project.Tables("Project").Rows(0).Item("ProjectName") = _
        Project.Tables("Project").Rows(0).Item("ProjectName").ToString.Trim
End Sub
```

6. Add the following code to the `AddProject` method:

```
Try
        'Validate project data
        ValidateProjectData(Project)

        'Call the data component to add the project
        Return objWDAProject.AddProject(Project)
```

7. Add the following code to the `UpdateProject` method:

```
Try
        'Validate project data
        ValidateProjectData(Project)

        'Call the data component to update the project
        Return objWDAProject.UpdateProject(Project)
```

8. View the code for the `WBLGroups` class in the WroxBusinessLogic project.

9. Add the following code to the `GetGroups` method:

```
        'Call the data component to get all groups
        GetGroups = objWDAGroups.GetGroups

        'Loop through the DataSet and convert all DBNull values
        'to empty strings
        For intindex As Integer = 0 To _
            GetGroups.Tables("Groups").Rows.Count - 1

            'If the column contains a null value...
            If IsDBNull(GetGroups.Tables("Groups").Rows( _
                intindex).Item("GroupDescription")) Then

                'Convert it to an empty string
                GetGroups.Tables("Groups").Rows( _
                    intindex).Item("GroupDescription") = String.Empty
            End If
        Next
Catch ExceptionErr As Exception
```

10. Add the following code to the `GetGroup` method:

```
        'Call the data component to get a specific group
        GetGroup = objWDAGroups.GetGroup(GroupID)

        'If the column contains a null value...
        If IsDBNull(GetGroup.Tables("Group").Rows(0).Item( _
            "GroupDescription")) Then
            'Convert it to an empty string
            GetGroup.Tables("Group").Rows(0).Item( _
                "GroupDescription") = String.Empty
        End If
Catch ExceptionErr As Exception
```

11. Add the following procedure to validate group data:

```
Private Sub ValidateGroupData(ByRef Group As DataSet)
    'Validate the Name exists
    If Group.Tables("Group").Rows(0).Item( _
        "GroupName").ToString.Trim.Length = 0 Then
        Throw New System.Exception( _
            "Group Name is a required field.")
    End If

    'Validate Description value
    If Not IsDBNull(Group.Tables("Group").Rows(0).Item( _
        "GroupDescription")) Then
        If Group.Tables("Group").Rows(0).Item( _
            "GroupDescription") = String.Empty Or _
            Group.Tables("Group").Rows(0).Item( _
            "GroupDescription").ToString.Trim.Length = 0 Then
            'Set it to a null value
            Group.Tables("Group").Rows(0).Item( _
                "GroupDescription") = DBNull.Value
        Else
            'Trim spaces
            Group.Tables("Group").Rows(0).Item("GroupDescription") = _
                Group.Tables("Group").Rows(0).Item( _
                "GroupDescription").ToString.Trim
        End If
    End If

    'Trim spaces
    Group.Tables("Group").Rows(0).Item("GroupName") = _
        Group.Tables("Group").Rows(0).Item("GroupName").ToString.Trim
End Sub
```

12. Add the following code to the AddGroup method:

```
Try
    'Validate group data
    ValidateGroupData(Group)

    'Call the data component to add the new group
    Return objWDAGroups.AddGroup(Group)
```

13. Add the following code to the UpdateGroup method:

```
Try
    'Validate group data
    ValidateGroupData(Group)

    'Call the data component to update the group
    Return objWDAGroups.UpdateGroup(Group)
```

14. That's all the code you need. Start your project and when the Project screen is displayed, enter a sequence number of **0** and click the Add button on the toolbar. You receive a message that the project name is a required field.

15. Now enter a project name and click the Add button on the toolbar. You receive a message that the sequence number must be between 1 and 255.

16. Enter a valid sequence number and click the Add button on the toolbar. The project is added without a description and the ProjectDescription field in the database will contain a `Null` value.

17. Click the project just added and clear the Project Name field on the form and enter a sequence number of **0** in the Sequence Number field. Now click the Update button on the toolbar. You receive a message that the project name is a required field.

18. Now enter a project name and click the Update button on the toolbar. Now you receive a message that the sequence number must be between 1 and 255.

19. Enter a valid sequence number and click the Update button on the toolbar. The project is updated without a description and the ProjectDescription field in the database will contain a `Null` value.

20. Repeat the same process for the Groups screen to test your validation code for a required group name.

How It Works

You start this exercise by adding code to the `GetProjects` method to loop through the `DataSet` and set the `ProjectDescription` column to an empty string when that column contained a `Null` value. This prevents the client from receiving an error when dealing with a column that contains a `Null` value:

```
'Loop through the DataSet and convert all DBNull values
'to empty strings
For intindex As Integer = 0 To _
    GetProjects.Tables("Projects").Rows.Count - 1

    'If the column contains a null value...
    If IsDBNull(GetProjects.Tables("Projects").Rows( _
        intindex).Item("ProjectDescription")) Then

        'Convert it to an empty string
        GetProjects.Tables("Projects").Rows( _
            intindex).Item("ProjectDescription") = String.Empty
    End If
Next
```

You perform the same operation in the `GetProject` method except that this method returns a `DataSet` with only one row of data so there is no loop here:

```
'If the column contains a null value...
If IsDBNull(GetProject.Tables("Project").Rows(0).Item( _
    "ProjectDescription")) Then
    'Convert it to an empty string
    GetProject.Tables("Project").Rows(0).Item( _
        "ProjectDescription") = String.Empty
End If
```

The procedure to validate project data gets its input by reference. This means you pass a pointer to the `DataSet` to this procedure and this procedure can update the `DataSet`. You first check to ensure a project name exists. If it does not then an exception is thrown which gets passed back to the caller of this procedure and then passed back to the client application:

```
Private Sub ValidateProjectData(ByRef Project As DataSet)
    'Validate the Name exists
    If Project.Tables("Project").Rows(0).Item( _
        "ProjectName").ToString.Trim.Length = 0 Then
        Throw New System.Exception( _
            "Project Name is a required field.")
    End If
```

Next, you check the project description for a `Null` value and if it does not contain a null value you then proceed to see if the description contains an empty string. Remember that you want to trim all the spaces from the column before you check the length to see if the column contained a space. If the column does not contain any data, you set it to a `Null` value using the Value field of the `DBNull` class. This causes a `Null` value to be inserted into the database instead of a blank or empty string.

If the description does contain data, you set the column equal to itself minus any leading or trailing spaces by calling the `Trim` method of the `String` class:

```
'Validate Description value
If Not IsDBNull(Project.Tables("Project").Rows(0).Item( _
    "ProjectDescription")) Then
    If Project.Tables("Project").Rows(0).Item( _
        "ProjectDescription") = String.Empty Or _
        Project.Tables("Project").Rows(0).Item( _
        "ProjectDescription").ToString.Trim.Length = 0 Then
        'Set it to a null value
        Project.Tables("Project").Rows(0).Item( _
            "ProjectDescription") = DBNull.Value
    Else
        'Trim spaces
        Project.Tables("Project").Rows(0).Item("ProjectDescription") = _
            Project.Tables("Project").Rows(0).Item( _
            "ProjectDescription").ToString.Trim
    End If
End If
```

Next, you validate that the sequence number passed is not equal to 0. The SequenceNumber column in the `DataSet` is defined as a Byte data type; thus it allows values only between 0 and 255 so there's no need to check for a value greater than 255 as that error would be trapped by the client. You do however, need to check for and disallow a value of 0, which is what this code does:

```
'Validate the Sequence Number
If Project.Tables("Project").Rows(0).Item( _
    "SequenceNumber") = 0 Then
    Throw New System.Exception( _
        "Sequence Number must contain a value between 1 and 255.")
End If
```

Finally, if all of the validations have passed, you trim any leading or trailing spaces from the project name in the ProjectName column.

```
'Trim spaces
Project.Tables("Project").Rows(0).Item("ProjectName") = _
    Project.Tables("Project").Rows(0).Item("ProjectName").ToString.Trim
End Sub
```

You modified the `AddProject` and `UpdateProject` methods to call the validation function to validate the data before adding it or updating it.

```
'Validate project data
ValidateProjectData(Project)
```

The modifications made to the WBLGroups class were similar in nature and that code will not be listed here again.

In this next Try It Out, you create a stored procedure to insert data into the Roles table and a stored procedure to insert data into the Users table. You also add the necessary functions to the business logic component to support inserting this data as well as functions to validate and format data.

Try It Out Validating Roles

To implement this functionality:

1. Open your Time Tracker application in Visual Studio 2005 if it is not already open.

2. Readers using SQL Server should view the Server Explorer window and click the Auto Hide icon on the window to keep it visible. Then expand your data connection for the `ProjectTimeTracker` database and expand the Stored Procedures node. Readers using Oracle will need to use their favorite Oracle tool for creating stored procedures.

3. The first stored procedure you want to create is a stored procedure to insert a new role. Enter the following code:

SQL Server

```
CREATE PROCEDURE usp_InsertRole
(
    @RoleID             UNIQUEIDENTIFIER,
    @RoleName           VARCHAR(50),
    @RoleDescription    TEXT,
    @Ranking            TINYINT
)
AS
INSERT INTO Roles
    (RoleID, RoleName, RoleDescription, Ranking, LastUpdateDate)
    VALUES(@RoleID, @RoleName, @RoleDescription, @Ranking, GETDATE())
```

Oracle

```
CREATE OR REPLACE PROCEDURE usp_InsertRole
(
    inRoleID            CHAR,
    inRoleName          VARCHAR2,
    inRoleDescription   CLOB,
    inRanking           NUMBER
)
AS
BEGIN
```

```
INSERT INTO Roles
    (RoleID, RoleName, RoleDescription, Ranking, LastUpdateDate)
    VALUES(inRoleID, inRoleName, inRoleDescription, inRanking, SYSDATE);
END;
```

Click the Save button on the toolbar in Visual Studio 2005 or click Execute in iSQL *Plus to have the stored procedure created.

4. The next stored procedure that you want to create is the stored procedure to insert a user. Enter the following code in this template:

SQL Server

```
CREATE  PROCEDURE usp_InsertUser
(
    @UserID        UNIQUEIDENTIFIER,
    @LoginName     VARCHAR(15),
    @Password      VARCHAR(30),
    @FirstName     VARCHAR(15),
    @LastName      VARCHAR(15),
    @Email         VARCHAR(50),
    @Phone         VARCHAR(20),
    @Status        BIT,
    @GroupID       UNIQUEIDENTIFIER,
    @RoleID        UNIQUEIDENTIFIER,
    @ManagerID     UNIQUEIDENTIFIER
)
AS
INSERT INTO Users
    (UserID, LoginName, Password, FirstName, LastName, Email,
    Phone, Status, GroupID, RoleID, ManagerID, LastUpdateDate)
    VALUES(@UserID, @LoginName, @Password, @FirstName, @LastName, @Email,
    @Phone, @Status, @GroupID, @RoleID, @ManagerID, GETDATE())
```

Oracle

```
CREATE OR REPLACE PROCEDURE usp_InsertUser
(
    inUserID       CHAR,
    inLoginName    VARCHAR2,
    inPassword     VARCHAR2,
    inFirstName    VARCHAR2,
    inLastName     VARCHAR2,
    inEmail        VARCHAR2,
    inPhone        VARCHAR2,
    inStatus       NUMBER,
    inGroupID      CHAR,
    inRoleID       CHAR,
    inManagerID    CHAR
)
AS
BEGIN
INSERT INTO Users
    (UserID, LoginName, Password, FirstName, LastName, Email,
```

```
      Phone, Status, GroupID, RoleID, ManagerID,  LastUpdateDate)
      VALUES(inUserID, inLoginName, inPassword, inFirstName, inLastName, inEmail,
      inPhone, inStatus, inGroupID, inRoleID, inManagerID, SYSDATE);
   END;
```

Click the Save button on the toolbar in Visual Studio 2005 or click Execute in iSQL *Plus to have the stored procedure created.

5. Modify the WroxDataAccess component next by adding classes to support Roles and Users. Starting with Roles, right-click the WroxDataAccess project in Solution Explorer, select Add, and then select Class. In the Add New Item – WroxDataAccess dialog box, enter a class name of **WDARoles.vb** and click the Add button to create the class.

6. Like the other classes that you've added to the WroxDataAccess component, this class needs to inherit the base class. Add the following code to this class:

```
Public Class WDARoles
    Inherits WDABase
```

7. Add the constructor for this class next, followed by the `Dispose` procedure. Add the following code to this class:

```
Public Sub New(ByVal Company As String, ByVal Application As String)
    MyBase.New(Company, Application)
End Sub

Public Shadows Sub Dispose()
    MyBase.Dispose()
End Sub
```

8. The `AddRole` function adds a new role to the Roles table in the database. Add the following code to create this function:

SQL Server

```
Public Function AddRole(ByVal Role As DataSet) As Boolean
    Try
        MyBase.SQL = "usp_InsertRole"
        'Initialize the Command object
        MyBase.InitializeCommand()
        'Add the Parameters to the Parameters collection
        MyBase.AddParameter("@RoleID", _
            SqlDbType.UniqueIdentifier, 16, _
            Role.Tables("Role").Rows(0).Item("RoleID"))
        MyBase.AddParameter("@RoleName", _
            SqlDbType.VarChar, 50, _
            Role.Tables("Role").Rows(0).Item("RoleName"))
        MyBase.AddParameter("@RoleDescription", _
            SqlDbType.Text, _
            Role.Tables("Role").Rows(0).Item( _
            "RoleDescription").ToString.Length, _
            Role.Tables("Role").Rows(0).Item("RoleDescription"))
        MyBase.AddParameter("@Ranking", _
            SqlDbType.TinyInt, 1, _
            Role.Tables("Role").Rows(0).Item("Ranking"))
```

```
        'Execute the stored procedure
        AddRole = ExecuteStoredProcedure()
    Catch ExceptionErr As Exception
        Throw New System.Exception(ExceptionErr.Message, _
        ExceptionErr.InnerException)
    End Try
End Function
```

Oracle

```
Public Function AddRole(ByVal Role As DataSet) As Boolean
    Try
        MyBase.SQL = "usp_InsertRole"
        'Initialize the Command object
        MyBase.InitializeCommand()
        'Add the Parameters to the Parameters collection
        MyBase.AddParameter("inRoleID", _
            OracleClient.OracleType.Char, 36, _
            Role.Tables("Role").Rows(0).Item("RoleID").ToString)
        MyBase.AddParameter("inRoleName", _
            OracleClient.OracleType.VarChar, 50, _
            Role.Tables("Role").Rows(0).Item("RoleName"))
        MyBase.AddParameter("inRoleDescription", _
            OracleClient.OracleType.Clob, _
            Role.Tables("Role").Rows(0).Item( _
            "RoleDescription").ToString.Length, _
            Role.Tables("Role").Rows(0).Item("RoleDescription"))
        MyBase.AddParameter("inRanking", _
            OracleClient.OracleType.Number, 1, _
            Role.Tables("Role").Rows(0).Item("Ranking"))
        'Execute the stored procedure
        AddRole = ExecuteStoredProcedure()
    Catch ExceptionErr As Exception
        Throw New System.Exception(ExceptionErr.Message, _
        ExceptionErr.InnerException)
    End Try
End Function
```

9. The next class to be added to the WroxDataAccess component is the Users class. Right-click the WroxDataAccess project, select the Add menu item from the context menu, and then select the Class submenu item. In the Add New Item – WroxDataAccess dialog box, enter a class name of **WDAUsers.vb** and then click the Add button to have the class created.

10. This class also needs to inherit the base class. Add the following code to this class:

```
Public Class WDAUsers
    Inherits WDABase
```

11. Add the constructor for this class next, followed by the Dispose procedure, using the following code:

```
Public Sub New(ByVal Company As String, ByVal Application As String)
    MyBase.New(Company, Application)
End Sub
```

```
Public Shadows Sub Dispose()
    MyBase.Dispose()
End Sub
```

12. The AddUser function adds a new user. Add the following code to the WDAUsers class:

SQL Server

```
Public Function AddUser(ByVal User As DataSet) As Boolean
    Try
        MyBase.SQL = "usp_InsertUser"
        'Initialize the Command object
        MyBase.InitializeCommand()
        'Add the Parameters to the Parameters collection
        MyBase.AddParameter("@UserID", _
            SqlDbType.UniqueIdentifier, 16, _
            User.Tables("User").Rows(0).Item("UserID"))
        MyBase.AddParameter("@LoginName", _
            SqlDbType.VarChar, 15, _
            User.Tables("User").Rows(0).Item("LoginName"))
        MyBase.AddParameter("@Password", _
            SqlDbType.VarChar, 30, _
            User.Tables("User").Rows(0).Item("Password"))
        MyBase.AddParameter("@FirstName", _
            SqlDbType.VarChar, 30, _
            User.Tables("User").Rows(0).Item("FirstName"))
        MyBase.AddParameter("@LastName", _
            SqlDbType.VarChar, 30, _
            User.Tables("User").Rows(0).Item("LastName"))
        MyBase.AddParameter("@Email", _
            SqlDbType.VarChar, 50, _
            User.Tables("User").Rows(0).Item("Email"))
        MyBase.AddParameter("@Phone", _
            SqlDbType.VarChar, 20, _
            User.Tables("User").Rows(0).Item("Phone"))
        MyBase.AddParameter("@Status", _
            SqlDbType.Bit, 1, _
            User.Tables("User").Rows(0).Item("Status"))
        MyBase.AddParameter("@GroupID", _
            SqlDbType.UniqueIdentifier, 16, _
            User.Tables("User").Rows(0).Item("GroupID"))
        MyBase.AddParameter("@RoleID", _
            SqlDbType.UniqueIdentifier, 16, _
            User.Tables("User").Rows(0).Item("RoleID"))
        MyBase.AddParameter("@ManagerID", _
            SqlDbType.UniqueIdentifier, 16, _
            User.Tables("User").Rows(0).Item("ManagerID"))
        'Execute the stored procedure
        AddUser = ExecuteStoredProcedure()
    Catch ExceptionErr As Exception
        Throw New System.Exception(ExceptionErr.Message, _
        ExceptionErr.InnerException)
    End Try
End Function
```

Oracle

```
Public Function AddUser(ByVal User As DataSet) As Boolean
    Try
        MyBase.SQL = "usp_InsertUser"
        'Initialize the Command object
        MyBase.InitializeCommand()
        'Add the Parameters to the Parameters collection
        MyBase.AddParameter("inUserID", _
            OracleClient.OracleType.Char, 36, _
            User.Tables("User").Rows(0).Item("UserID").ToString)
        MyBase.AddParameter("inLoginName", _
            OracleClient.OracleType.VarChar, 15, _
            User.Tables("User").Rows(0).Item("LoginName"))
        MyBase.AddParameter("inPassword", _
            OracleClient.OracleType.VarChar, 30, _
            User.Tables("User").Rows(0).Item("Password"))
        MyBase.AddParameter("inFirstName", _
            OracleClient.OracleType.VarChar, 30, _
            User.Tables("User").Rows(0).Item("FirstName"))
        MyBase.AddParameter("inLastName", _
            OracleClient.OracleType.VarChar, 30, _
            User.Tables("User").Rows(0).Item("LastName"))
        MyBase.AddParameter("inEmail", _
            OracleClient.OracleType.VarChar, 50, _
            User.Tables("User").Rows(0).Item("Email"))
        MyBase.AddParameter("inPhone", _
            OracleClient.OracleType.VarChar, 20, _
            User.Tables("User").Rows(0).Item("Phone"))
        MyBase.AddParameter("inStatus", _
            OracleClient.OracleType.Number, 1, _
            User.Tables("User").Rows(0).Item("Status"))
        MyBase.AddParameter("inGroupID", _
            OracleClient.OracleType.Char, 36, _
            User.Tables("User").Rows(0).Item("GroupID").ToString)
        MyBase.AddParameter("inRoleID", _
            OracleClient.OracleType.Char, 36, _
            User.Tables("User").Rows(0).Item("RoleID").ToString)
        MyBase.AddParameter("inManagerID", _
            OracleClient.OracleType.Char, 36, _
            User.Tables("User").Rows(0).Item("ManagerID").ToString)
        'Execute the stored procedure
        AddUser = ExecuteStoredProcedure()
    Catch ExceptionErr As Exception
        Throw New System.Exception(ExceptionErr.Message, _
        ExceptionErr.InnerException)
    End Try
End Function
```

At this point, you have created the new stored procedures to support adding a new role and user to your database. You have also added the appropriate functions to your data access component to execute these stored procedures.

The next step in the process will be to add the corresponding functions in your business logic component:

1. Right-click the WroxBusinessLogic project in Solution Explorer, select Add, and then select the Class. In the Add New Item – WroxBusinessLogic dialog box, enter a class name of **WBLRoles.vb** in the Name field and then click the Add button to add this class to your project.

2. This class needs to implement the IDisposable interface so add the following Implements statement to your class. When you press Enter, the Dispose procedure is automatically added to your project:

```
Public Class WBLRoles
    Implements IDisposable
```

3. You need an object declaration for the WDARoles class in the WroxDataAccess component that is global to your class. Add the following declaration to your class:

```
'Private variables and objects
Private objWDARoles As WroxDataAccess.WDARoles
```

4. Like the other classes in the business logic component, you need a constructor that matches the constructor in the corresponding class in the data access component. Add the following constructor to this class:

```
Public Sub New(ByVal Company As String, ByVal Application As String)
    objWDARoles = New WroxDataAccess.WDARoles(Company, Application)
End Sub
```

5. Modify the Dispose procedure by adding the following code to clean up the resources being used in this class:

```
Private Overloads Sub Dispose(ByVal disposing As Boolean)
    If Not Me.disposed Then
        If disposing Then
            ' TODO: put code to dispose managed resources
        End If

        objWDARoles.Dispose()
        objWDARoles = Nothing
    End If
    Me.disposed = True
End Sub
```

6. You need a function to create a DataSet for a Role and return it to the client. Add the GetNewRoleDS function:

```
Public Function GetNewRoleDS() As DataSet
    Try
        'Instantiate a new DataSet object
        GetNewRoleDS = New DataSet

        'Create a DataTable object
        Dim objDataTable As DataTable = GetNewRoleDS.Tables.Add("Role")

        'Create a DataColumn object
```

```
                Dim objDataColumn As DataColumn

                'Instantiate a new DataColumn and set its properties
                objDataColumn = New DataColumn("RoleID", _
                    Type.GetType("System.Guid"))
                objDataColumn.AllowDBNull = False

                'Add the column to the table
                objDataTable.Columns.Add(objDataColumn)

                'Instantiate a new DataColumn and set its properties
                objDataColumn = New DataColumn("RoleName", _
                    Type.GetType("System.String"))
                objDataColumn.AllowDBNull = False
                objDataColumn.MaxLength = 50

                'Add the column to the table
                objDataTable.Columns.Add(objDataColumn)

                'Instantiate a new DataColumn and set its properties
                objDataColumn = New DataColumn("RoleDescription", _
                    Type.GetType("System.String"))

                'Add the column to the table
                objDataTable.Columns.Add(objDataColumn)

                'Instantiate a new DataColumn and set its properties
                objDataColumn = New DataColumn("Ranking", _
                    Type.GetType("System.Byte"))
                objDataColumn.AllowDBNull = False

                'Add the column to the table
                objDataTable.Columns.Add(objDataColumn)
            Catch ExceptionErr As Exception
                Throw New System.Exception(ExceptionErr.Message, _
                    ExceptionErr.InnerException)
            End Try
        End Function
```

7. You need a procedure to validate role data, so add the following procedure:

```
Private Sub ValidateRoleData(ByRef Role As DataSet)
    'Validate the Name exists
    If Role.Tables("Role").Rows(0).Item( _
        "RoleName").ToString.Trim.Length = 0 Then
        Throw New System.Exception( _
            "Role Name is a required field.")
    End If

    'Validate Description value
    If Not IsDBNull(Role.Tables("Role").Rows(0).Item( _
        "RoleDescription")) Then
        If Role.Tables("Role").Rows(0).Item( _
            "RoleDescription") = String.Empty Or _
            Role.Tables("Role").Rows(0).Item( _
```

```
                    "RoleDescription").ToString.Trim.Length = 0 Then
                    'Set it to a null value
                    Role.Tables("Role").Rows(0).Item( _
                        "RoleDescription") = DBNull.Value
            Else
                    'Trim spaces
                    Role.Tables("Role").Rows(0).Item("RoleDescription") = _
                        Role.Tables("Role").Rows(0).Item( _
                        "RoleDescription").ToString.Trim
            End If
        End If

        'Validate the Ranking
        If Role.Tables("Role").Rows(0).Item( _
            "Ranking") = 0 Then
            Throw New System.Exception( _
                "Ranking must contain a value between 1 and 255.")
        End If

        'Trim spaces
        Role.Tables("Role").Rows(0).Item("RoleName") = _
            Role.Tables("Role").Rows(0).Item("RoleName").ToString.Trim
    End Sub
```

8. Now it's time to add the `AddRole` function. This function performs the necessary data validation before calling the data access component to add a new role. Add the following code to your class:

```
Public Function AddRole(ByVal Role As DataSet) As Boolean
    Try
        'Validate role data
        ValidateRoleData(Role)

        'Call the data component to add the new group
        Return objWDARoles.AddRole(Role)
    Catch ExceptionErr As Exception
        Throw New System.Exception(ExceptionErr.Message, _
            ExceptionErr.InnerException)
    End Try
End Function
```

9. Now it's time to implement the code to support validating and adding users. You need to create some validation functions to validate a user's password, phone number, and e-mail address. Because you may add other validation functions later and may want to share these validation functions with other classes in the business logic component, you should implement them in such a way that they are accessible to the other classes in the WroxBusinessLogic project. This can be done by adding a module to the WroxBusinessLogic project. Right-click the WroxBusinessLogic project, select Add, and then select Module. In the Add New Item – WroxBusinessLogic dialog box, enter a name of **ValidationFunctions.vb** in the Name field and then click Add to add this module to your project.

10. You'll be using regular expressions to perform your validations so import the following namespace in your module:

```
Imports System.Text.RegularExpressions

Module ValidationFunctions
```

11. You need to add some private variable declarations to this module, which means that they are accessible only to this module. Add the following variable declarations:

```
'Private variables
Private bytMinimumPasswordLength As Byte = 6
Private bytMaximumPasswordLength As Byte = 9
Private strPasswordSpecialCharacters As String = "!@#$%^&*()"
```

12. Any errors that occur during validation are set in a public variable that will be accessible to the classes that call the functions in this module. Add the following public variable declaration:

```
'Public variables
Public strErrorMessage As String = String.Empty
```

13. All the validation functions return Boolean values indicating whether the data was successfully validated. Any errors that occur during the validation are set in the aforementioned variable declaration. The first validation function to be added is a function to validate phone numbers. Add the following code to this module:

```
Public Function IsValidPhoneNumber(ByVal strPhoneNumber As String) As Boolean
    'Rules: phone number must be in one of the following formats
    '        123 456-7890
    '        (123) 456-7890
    '        123-456-7890
    IsValidPhoneNumber = Regex.IsMatch(strPhoneNumber, ( _
        "((\(\d{3}\) ?)|(\d{3}-))?\d{3}-\d{4}"))
    If IsValidPhoneNumber Then
        'Clear the error message
        strErrorMessage = String.Empty
    Else
        'Set the new error message
        strErrorMessage = "The phone number entered is invalid." & _
            ControlChars.CrLf & ControlChars.CrLf & _
            "Phone numbers must be in one of the following formats:" & _
            ControlChars.CrLf & _
            "   123 456-7890" & ControlChars.CrLf & _
            "   (123) 456-7890" & ControlChars.CrLf & _
            "   123-456-7890"""
    End If
End Function
```

14. The next validation function to add is a function to validate e-mail addresses. Add the following code to your module:

```
Public Function IsValidEmail(ByVal strEmail As String) As Boolean
    'Pattern:    name@domain.type
    'Rules:      name - any character, digit, or special character;
    '                any number of characters
    '            domain - any alpha character or digit;
    '                special characters of - or _ only;
    '                must contain at least one character or digit
```

```
'                    after a - or _
'              type - any domain type (alpha characters only)
'                  between 2 and 4 characters in length
    IsValidEmail = Regex.IsMatch(strEmail, _
        ("\w+((-\w+)|(\.\w+))*\@[A-Za-z0-9]+((\.|-|_)" & _
        "[A-Za-z0-9]+)*\.([A-Za-z]{2,4})$"))
    If IsValidEmail Then
        'Clear the error message
        strErrorMessage = String.Empty
    Else
        strErrorMessage = "The email entered is invalid." & _
            ControlChars.CrLf & ControlChars.CrLf & _
            "Email addresses must be in the format of: someone@domain.type"
    End If
End Function
```

15. The final validation function to add is a function to validate passwords. This function validates the password length and that the password contains uppercase and lowercase characters as well as numbers and special characters if required. Add the following code to your module:

```
Public Function IsValidPassword(ByVal strPassword As String) As Boolean
    'Rules: must contain at least one upper case character
'           must contain at least one lower case character
'           must contain at least one numeric digit
'           must contain at least one special character
'               (defined in strPasswordSpecialCharacters variable)
'           must be between the minimum and maximum length
'               (defined in the bytMinimumPasswordLength and
'               bytMaximumPasswordLength variables)
    IsValidPassword = Regex.IsMatch(strPassword, _
        ("^(?=.*\d)(?=.*[A-Z])(?=.*[a-z])" & _
        "(?=.*[" & strPasswordSpecialCharacters & "]).{" & _
        bytMinimumPasswordLength & "," & _
        bytMaximumPasswordLength & "}$"))
    If IsValidPassword Then
        'Clear the error message
        strErrorMessage = String.Empty
    Else
        strErrorMessage = "The password entered is not strongly typed." & _
            ControlChars.CrLf & ControlChars.CrLf & _
            "Passwords must be between " & _
            bytMinimumPasswordLength.ToString & _
            " and " & bytMaximumPasswordLength.ToString & _
            " characters in length and" & ControlChars.CrLf & _
            "contain at least one upper case letter, " & _
            "one lower case letter," & ControlChars.CrLf & _
            "one numeric digit, and one special character." & _
            ControlChars.CrLf & _
            "Valid special characters are: " & strPasswordSpecialCharacters
    End If
End Function
```

16. There's one final function that you add to this module. If a phone number is valid, you want to ensure that all phone numbers inserted into the Users table are consistent. Add the `FormatPhoneNumber` function to this module:

```
Public Function FormatPhoneNumber(ByVal strPhoneNumber As String) As String
    'Remove all special characters (e.g. ( ) - and spaces)
    strPhoneNumber = strPhoneNumber.Replace("(", "").Replace( _
        ")", "").Replace("-", "").Replace(Chr(34), "")

    'Now format the phone number for storage in the database
    FormatPhoneNumber = strPhoneNumber.Substring(0, 3) & "-" & _
        strPhoneNumber.Substring(3, 3) & "-" & _
        strPhoneNumber.Substring(6, 4)
End Function
```

17. You want to add a class to support users, so right-click the WroxBusinessLogic project, select Add, and then select Class. In the Add New Item – WroxBusinessLogic dialog box, enter a class name of **WBLUsers.vb** in the Name field and click Add.

18. You'll be hashing a user's password before it is added to the database so add the following `Imports` statements to support hashing:

```
Imports System.Text
Imports System.Security.Cryptography
```

19. You need to add the `IDisposable` interface next, so add the following `Implements` statement:

```
Public Class WBLUsers
    Implements IDisposable
```

20. Add the following class-level variable declaration to your class to reference the data access component:

```
'Private variables and objects
Private objWDAUsers As WroxDataAccess.WDAUsers
```

21. Now add the following constructor, which matches the constructor in the corresponding class in the data access component:

```
Public Sub New(ByVal Company As String, ByVal Application As String)
    objWDAUsers = New WroxDataAccess.WDAUsers(Company, Application)
End Sub
```

22. Modify the `Dispose` procedure as follows to clean up the resources used in this class:

```
Private Overloads Sub Dispose(ByVal disposing As Boolean)
    If Not Me.disposed Then
        If disposing Then
            ' TODO: put code to dispose managed resources
        End If

        objWDAUsers.Dispose()
        objWDAUsers = Nothing
    End If
    Me.disposed = True
End Sub
```

23. Now add the `GetNewUserDS` function to create a `DataSet` that will be used for adding a new user:

```
Public Function GetNewUserDS() As DataSet
    Try
        'Instantiate a new DataSet object
        GetNewUserDS = New DataSet

        'Create a DataTable object
        Dim objDataTable As DataTable = GetNewUserDS.Tables.Add("User")

        'Create a DataColumn object
        Dim objDataColumn As DataColumn

        'Instantiate a new DataColumn and set its properties
        objDataColumn = New DataColumn("UserID", _
            Type.GetType("System.Guid"))
        objDataColumn.AllowDBNull = False

        'Add the column to the table
        objDataTable.Columns.Add(objDataColumn)

        'Instantiate a new DataColumn and set its properties
        objDataColumn = New DataColumn("LoginName", _
            Type.GetType("System.String"))
        objDataColumn.AllowDBNull = False
        objDataColumn.MaxLength = 15

        'Add the column to the table
        objDataTable.Columns.Add(objDataColumn)

        'Instantiate a new DataColumn and set its properties
        objDataColumn = New DataColumn("Password", _
            Type.GetType("System.String"))
        objDataColumn.AllowDBNull = True
        objDataColumn.MaxLength = 30

        'Add the column to the table
        objDataTable.Columns.Add(objDataColumn)

        'Instantiate a new DataColumn and set its properties
        objDataColumn = New DataColumn("FirstName", _
            Type.GetType("System.String"))
        objDataColumn.AllowDBNull = False
        objDataColumn.MaxLength = 30

        'Add the column to the table
        objDataTable.Columns.Add(objDataColumn)

        'Instantiate a new DataColumn and set its properties
        objDataColumn = New DataColumn("LastName", _
            Type.GetType("System.String"))
        objDataColumn.AllowDBNull = False
        objDataColumn.MaxLength = 30

        'Add the column to the table
```

```
        objDataTable.Columns.Add(objDataColumn)

        'Instantiate a new DataColumn and set its properties
        objDataColumn = New DataColumn("Email", _
            Type.GetType("System.String"))
        objDataColumn.AllowDBNull = False
        objDataColumn.MaxLength = 50

        'Add the column to the table
        objDataTable.Columns.Add(objDataColumn)

        'Instantiate a new DataColumn and set its properties
        objDataColumn = New DataColumn("Phone", _
            Type.GetType("System.String"))
        objDataColumn.AllowDBNull = False
        objDataColumn.MaxLength = 20

        'Add the column to the table
        objDataTable.Columns.Add(objDataColumn)

        'Instantiate a new DataColumn and set its properties
        objDataColumn = New DataColumn("Status", _
            Type.GetType("System.Boolean"))
        objDataColumn.AllowDBNull = False

        'Add the column to the table
        objDataTable.Columns.Add(objDataColumn)

        'Instantiate a new DataColumn and set its properties
        objDataColumn = New DataColumn("GroupID", _
            Type.GetType("System.Guid"))
        objDataColumn.AllowDBNull = False

        'Add the column to the table
        objDataTable.Columns.Add(objDataColumn)

        'Instantiate a new DataColumn and set its properties
        objDataColumn = New DataColumn("RoleID", _
            Type.GetType("System.Guid"))
        objDataColumn.AllowDBNull = False

        'Add the column to the table
        objDataTable.Columns.Add(objDataColumn)

        'Instantiate a new DataColumn and set its properties
        objDataColumn = New DataColumn("ManagerID", _
            Type.GetType("System.Guid"))
        objDataColumn.AllowDBNull = True

        'Add the column to the table
        objDataTable.Columns.Add(objDataColumn)
    Catch ExceptionErr As Exception
        Throw New System.Exception(ExceptionErr.Message, _
            ExceptionErr.InnerException)
    End Try
End Function
```

24. Now add the following function to hash a user's password:

```
Private Function HashPassword(ByVal strPassword As String) As String
    Try
        'Declare local variables
        Dim bytPasswordIn() As Byte
        Dim bytPasswordOut() As Byte

        Using objHashAlgorithm As New SHA1CryptoServiceProvider
            'Convert the input password to an array of bytes
            bytPasswordIn = Encoding.UTF8.GetBytes(strPassword)

            'Compute the Hash (returns an array of bytes)
            bytPasswordOut = objHashAlgorithm.ComputeHash(bytPasswordIn)

            'Return a base 64 encoded string of the hashed password
            HashPassword = Convert.ToBase64String(bytPasswordOut)
        End Using
    Catch ExceptionErr As Exception
        Throw New System.Exception(ExceptionErr.Message, _
            ExceptionErr.InnerException)
    End Try
End Function
```

25. Now add the following function to validate user data:

```
Private Sub ValidateUserData(ByRef User As DataSet)
    'Validate the Login Name exists
    If User.Tables("User").Rows(0).Item( _
        "LoginName").ToString.Trim.Length = 0 Then
        Throw New System.Exception("Login Name is a required field.")
    End If

    'Validate the First Name exists
    If User.Tables("User").Rows(0).Item( _
        "FirstName").ToString.Trim.Length = 0 Then
        Throw New System.Exception("First Name is a required field.")
    End If

    'Validate the Last Name exists
    If User.Tables("User").Rows(0).Item( _
        "LastName").ToString.Trim.Length = 0 Then
        Throw New System.Exception("Last Name is a required field.")
    End If

    'Validate the password
    If Not IsValidPassword(User.Tables( _
        "User").Rows(0).Item("Password")) Then
        Throw New System.Exception(strErrorMessage)
    End If

    'Validate the email address
    If Not IsValidEmail(User.Tables( _
        "User").Rows(0).Item("Email")) Then
        Throw New System.Exception(strErrorMessage)
```

```
        End If

        'Validate the phone number
        If Not IsValidPhoneNumber(User.Tables( _
            "User").Rows(0).Item("Phone")) Then
            Throw New System.Exception(strErrorMessage)
        End If

        'Validate manager
        If Not IsDBNull(User.Tables("User").Rows(0).Item("ManagerID")) Then
            If Not TypeOf User.Tables("User").Rows(0).Item("ManagerID") _
                Is Guid Then
                If User.Tables("User").Rows(0).Item("ManagerID") = _
                    String.Empty Then
                    'Set it to a null value
                    User.Tables("User").Rows(0).Item("ManagerID") = _
                        DBNull.Value
                End If
            End If
        End If

        'Trim spaces
        User.Tables("User").Rows(0).Item("LoginName") = _
            User.Tables("User").Rows(0).Item("LoginName").ToString.Trim
        User.Tables("User").Rows(0).Item("Password") = _
            User.Tables("User").Rows(0).Item("Password").ToString.Trim
        User.Tables("User").Rows(0).Item("FirstName") = _
            User.Tables("User").Rows(0).Item("FirstName").ToString.Trim
        User.Tables("User").Rows(0).Item("LastName") = _
            User.Tables("User").Rows(0).Item("LastName").ToString.Trim
        User.Tables("User").Rows(0).Item("Email") = _
            User.Tables("User").Rows(0).Item("Email").ToString.Trim

        'Hash the password
        User.Tables("User").Rows(0).Item("Password") = _
            HashPassword(User.Tables("User").Rows(0).Item("Password"))

        'Format the phone number
        User.Tables("User").Rows(0).Item("Phone") = _
            FormatPhoneNumber(User.Tables("User").Rows(0).Item("Phone"))
    End Sub
```

26. Now create the AddUser function, which validates the user data, formats the phone number, and hashes the user's password. Add the following code to your class:

```
Public Function AddUser(ByVal User As DataSet) As Boolean
    Try
        'Validate user data
        ValidateUserData(User)

        'Call the data component to add the new user
        Return objWDAUsers.AddUser(User)
    Catch ExceptionErr As Exception
```

```
            Throw New System.Exception(ExceptionErr.Message, _
                ExceptionErr.InnerException)
        End Try
    End Function
```

At this point, you have added to your business logic component the functions necessary to generate a Role and User DataSet along with some validation functions and functions to insert a new role and user.

The following steps will add support in your Admin form to insert new roles and users:

1. You need to modify the Admin form in the Time Tracker project to support adding roles and users. Switch to the code in the Admin form and add the following two variable declarations:

```
Private objGroups As WroxBusinessLogic.WBLGroups
Private objProjects As WroxBusinessLogic.WBLProjects
Private objRoles As WroxBusinessLogic.WBLRoles
Private objUsers As WroxBusinessLogic.WBLUsers
```

2. Modify the `ActionAdd` procedure next, adding code under the `Case "Roles"` statement to call the business logic component to add a new role. Add the following code under this statement:

```
            Case "Roles"
                'Initialize a new instance of the business logic component
                Using objRoles As New WroxBusinessLogic.WBLRoles( _
                    strCompany, strApplication)
                    'Get a new Role DataSet
                    objDataSet = objRoles.GetNewRoleDS()
                    'Initialize a datarow object from the Role DataSet
                    Dim objDataRow As Data.DataRow = _
                        objDataSet.Tables("Role").NewRow
                    'Set the values in the DataRow
                    objDataRow.Item("RoleID") = Guid.NewGuid
                    objDataRow.Item("RoleName") = txtRoleName.Text
                    objDataRow.Item("RoleDescription") = _
                        txtRoleDescription.Text
                    If IsNumeric(txtRanking.Text) Then
                        objDataRow.Item("Ranking") = _
                            CType(txtRanking.Text, Byte)
                    Else
                        Throw New Exception( _
                            "Ranking must contain a numeric value.")
                    End If
                    'Add the DataRow to the DataSet
                    objDataSet.Tables("Role").Rows.Add(objDataRow)
                    'Add the Role to the database
                    If Not objRoles.AddRole(objDataSet) Then
                        Throw New Exception("Insert Role Failed")
                    End If
                End Using

                'Clear the input fields
                txtRoleID.Text = String.Empty
                txtRoleName.Text = String.Empty
                txtRoleDescription.Text = String.Empty
                txtRanking.Text = String.Empty
                txtRoleUpdateDate.Text = String.Empty
```

3. Now add some code under the `Case "Users"` statement in this same procedure. Add the following code to add a new user:

```
Case "Users"
            'Initialize a new instance of the business logic component
            Using objUsers As New WroxBusinessLogic.WBLUsers( _
                strCompany, strApplication)
                'Get a new User DataSet
                objDataSet = objUsers.GetNewUserDS()
                'Initialize a datarow object from the User DataSet
                Dim objDataRow As Data.DataRow = _
                    objDataSet.Tables("User").NewRow
                'Set the values in the DataRow
                objDataRow.Item("UserID") = Guid.NewGuid
                objDataRow.Item("LoginName") = txtLogin.Text
                objDataRow.Item("Password") = txtPassword.Text
                objDataRow.Item("FirstName") = txtFirstName.Text
                objDataRow.Item("LastName") = txtLastName.Text
                objDataRow.Item("Email") = txtEmail.Text
                objDataRow.Item("Phone") = txtPhone.Text
                objDataRow.Item("Status") = optStatusActive.Checked
                objDataRow.Item("GroupID") = _
                    cboUserGroup.SelectedItem.Item("GroupID")
                objDataRow.Item("RoleID") = _
                    cboUserRole.SelectedItem.Item("RoleID")
                If cboUserManager.SelectedIndex <> -1 Then
                    objDataRow.Item("ManagerID") = _
                        cboUserManager.SelectedItem.item("ManagerID")
                End If
                'Add the DataRow to the DataSet
                objDataSet.Tables("User").Rows.Add(objDataRow)
                'Add the User to the database
                If Not objUsers.AddUser(objDataSet) Then
                    Throw New Exception("Insert User Failed")
                End If
            End Using

            'Clear the input fields
            txtUserID.Text = String.Empty
            txtLogin.Text = String.Empty
            txtPassword.Text = String.Empty
            txtFirstName.Text = String.Empty
            txtLastName.Text = String.Empty
            txtEmail.Text = String.Empty
            txtPhone.Text = String.Empty
            optStatusActive.Checked = True
            cboUserGroup.SelectedIndex = -1
            cboUserRole.SelectedIndex = -1
            cboUserManager.SelectedIndex = -1
            txtUserUpdateDate.Text = String.Empty
```

You're ready to run your project to test your changes. Start your project and click the Roles icon in the navigation pane. On the Roles screen, enter a role name of **User** in the Name field and add any description that you like.

The role ranking indicates the level of permissions that a user has. The higher the ranking the more permission a user has. The User role will have the lowest ranking of all, so enter a value of **1** in the Ranking field, as shown in Figure 11-1. Then click Add on the toolbar or click the Action menu and select Add.

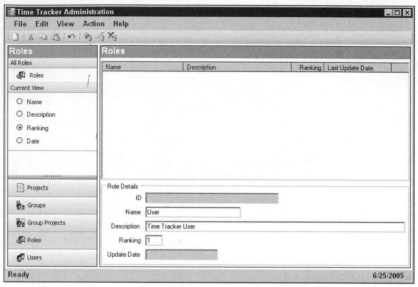

Figure 11-1

After the record has been added, you see the Record Added message in the status bar. However, because you've not implemented any stored procedures to retrieve the roles from the database, the application will not display the role added.

There is a way, however, to view the roles in the database. Close the Admin form so you are returned to the Visual Studio 2005 development environment. Expand the Server Explorer window and navigate to your database using the procedures outlined in this exercise. Then expand the Tables node, right-click the Roles table, and select Show Table Data from the context menu. The data is retrieved and displayed in Visual Studio 2005.

1. Now run your project again and add a role for a manager. Enter **Manager** in the Name field and enter **5** in the Ranking field. You can enter any description you like. After that role is added, add a role for the administrator. Enter **Admin** in the Name field and enter **99** in the Ranking field. Again, you can enter any description that you want.

2. Stop your project and you are returned to the development environment. You should still see the query results from the Roles table displayed. Now click the Execute SQL icon on the toolbar to refresh the display of data so that you see the two new roles that you just added.

3. You're going to need a Guid from the Roles table as well as a Guid from the Groups table when adding a new user. View the data in the Groups table. Then set a breakpoint on the following line of code under the `Case "Users"` statement in the `ActionAdd` procedure in the Admin form. Then start your project and navigate to the Users screen.

```
objDataRow.Item("GroupID") = _
    cboUserGroup.SelectedItem.Item("GroupID")
```

4. Enter the information for a new user, similar to the information shown in Figure 11-2. Remember that the password must be between six and nine characters in length, contain uppercase and lowercase letters, and have at least one special character (e.g., !@#$%^&*()) and a number. When you have entered all of your information for a user, click Add on the toolbar or click the Action menu and select Add.

5. When you encounter the breakpoint in your code, view the Command Window – Immediate window, which should be visible at the bottom of your development environment. If it is not, select View ⇨ Other Windows ⇨ Command Window.

    *If the Command Window does not have the word Immediate in the title and displays a greater than (>) sign, you are not in immediate mode. Type **immed** at the prompt and press Enter to be taken to immediate mode.*

6. In the Command Window – Immediate window, enter the following code, replacing the Guid for a group with a Guid that exists in your database. Also replace the Guid for a role using the Guid for the user role from your database:

```
objDataRow.Item("GroupID") = New Guid("DC7AA81E-7487-40FF-B12F-5C423F9D94B9")
objDataRow.Item("RoleID") = New Guid("38E118D8-86BD-4993-A26E-B459891B4A99")
```

7. Now drag the yellow arrow in the breakpoint margin to the following line of code and then click Continue on the toolbar:

```
objDataSet.Tables("User").Rows.Add(objDataRow)
```

The rest of the code executes and the user is added. Repeat the process, adding a user with the Manager role and a user with the Admin role. It does not matter what groups these users are assigned to. Take note of the login names and passwords that you assign, as you need them in Chapter 12.

Figure 11-2

At this point, you should have three new roles in the Roles table: User, Manager, and Admin. You should also have three new users, each with one of the roles just mentioned. You can view the data in the Users table using the same procedures outlined previously. Notice that the passwords have been hashed, which provides another level of security for your data.

Now you want to add one more user and assign that user to the manager that you just added. Repeat the process to add a user and after you set the Guid for the GroupID and RoleID, set the Guid for the ManagerID using the Guid of your manager, as shown in the following code:

```
objDataRow.Item("ManagerID") = New Guid("B27560AB-FD4C-4E68-9462-2A3147E0C598")
```

How It Works

You start this exercise by creating two stored procedures: one to insert a role and another to insert a user. These are simple insert stored procedures that you've seen before so there's no need to show the code again or explain them any further.

The next step in this exercise is to add a new class for roles to the data access component and again this was straightforward code that you've seen before. You added a class to the data access component for users next, which was also simple code that you've implemented numerous times.

Things start to get interesting after you create the WBLRoles class in the business logic component and add the ValidateRoleData procedure. Here you start to implement some business logic by validating the data that is required.

As with the other validation procedures that you created in the other classes in the business logic component, this procedure also accepts a DataSet as input by reference. This allows this procedure to modify the contents of the DataSet during validation, trimming blank spaces and setting empty fields to Null.

The first thing that you do in this procedure is validate that a role name exists. This is the same type of validation code that you implemented in the WBLGroups and WBLProjects classes.

```
Private Sub ValidateRoleData(ByRef Role As DataSet)
    'Validate the Name exists
    If Role.Tables("Role").Rows(0).Item( _
        "RoleName").ToString.Trim.Length = 0 Then
        Throw New System.Exception( _
            "Role Name is a required field.")
    End If
```

Next, you validate the role description and if it does not exist, then you set the field in the DataSet to a Null value. Again, this is the same type of code that you implemented in the WBLGroups and WBLProjects classes.

```
        'Validate Description value
    If Not IsDBNull(Role.Tables("Role").Rows(0).Item( _
        "RoleDescription")) Then
        If Role.Tables("Role").Rows(0).Item( _
            "RoleDescription") = String.Empty Or _
            Role.Tables("Role").Rows(0).Item( _
            "RoleDescription").ToString.Trim.Length = 0 Then
```

```
                   'Set it to a null value
                   Role.Tables("Role").Rows(0).Item( _
                       "RoleDescription") = DBNull.Value
               Else
                   'Trim spaces
                   Role.Tables("Role").Rows(0).Item("RoleDescription") = _
                       Role.Tables("Role").Rows(0).Item( _
                       "RoleDescription").ToString.Trim
               End If
           End If
```

You validate the role ranking next and ensure that the rank contains a value between 1 and 255, throwing an error if it does not. Finally, you trim the spaces in the RoleName field in the DataSet.

```
           'Validate the Ranking
           If Role.Tables("Role").Rows(0).Item( _
               "Ranking") = 0 Then
               Throw New System.Exception( _
                   "Ranking must contain a value between 1 and 255.")
           End If

           'Trim spaces
           Role.Tables("Role").Rows(0).Item("RoleName") = _
               Role.Tables("Role").Rows(0).Item("RoleName").ToString.Trim
       End Sub
```

The AddRole function is added next and mirrors the code that you implemented in the WBLGroups and WBLProjects classes:

```
       Public Function AddRole(ByVal Role As DataSet) As Boolean
           Try
               'Validate role data
               ValidateRoleData(Role)

               'Call the data component to add the new group
               Return objWDARoles.AddRole(Role)
           Catch ExceptionErr As Exception
               Throw New System.Exception(ExceptionErr.Message, _
                   ExceptionErr.InnerException)
           End Try
       End Function
```

You create the ValidationFunctions module next and add the appropriate validation functions to validate and format data. Because this module uses regular expressions to validate data, you first import the System.Text.RegularExpressions namespace.

```
   Imports System.Text.RegularExpressions
```

The private variables that you add to this module are accessible by only the functions in this module and can be adjusted to suit your business needs. These variables are used for password validation. The first variable here defines the minimum length that a password needs to be and it can be adjusted to suit your business needs. The next variable defines the maximum length that a password can be and again it can be adjusted. The `strPasswordSpecialCharacters` variable contains a value specifying the available special characters that can be contained in a password and it can also be adjusted to suit your business needs:

```
'Private variables
Private bytMinimumPasswordLength As Byte = 6
Private bytMaximumPasswordLength As Byte = 9
Private strPasswordSpecialCharacters As String = "!@#$%^&*()"
```

There is one public variable in this module that will contain the error message that should be available to the client in the event that one of the validation functions fails. The class that invokes the validation functions here can access this variable if the validation function fails and then return that message to the client application:

```
Public strErrorMessage As String = String.Empty
```

The `IsValidPhoneNumber` function accepts the phone number to be validated as input and returns a Boolean value indicating whether the phone number is valid. The `Regex` class is used to perform regular expression validations, matching, and replacing characters in strings. You use this class to validate that a phone matches a set regular expression pattern.

Regular expression patterns can be quite complex, so I'll just cover the basics here as a detailed discussion of the topic is beyond the scope of this book. The pattern that you are using here is looking for the area code of a U.S. phone number as three numeric digits contained in a set of parentheses or followed by a space, `(\(\d{3}\) ?)`, or three numeric digits followed by a dash, `(\d{3}-)`. Next, it looks for the three-digit prefix of the phone number followed by a dash and then the last four digits of the phone number, `\d{3}-\d{4}`.

The `IsMatch` function will return a `Boolean` value indicating whether the phone number matches the pattern and the result is set in the function name because it also returns a `Boolean` value.

```
Public Function IsValidPhoneNumber(ByVal strPhoneNumber As String) As Boolean
    'Rules: phone number must be in one of the following formats
    '       123 456-7890
    '       (123) 456-7890
    '       123-456-7890
    IsValidPhoneNumber = Regex.IsMatch(strPhoneNumber, ( _
        "((\(\d{3}\) ?)|(\d{3}-))?\d{3}-\d{4}"))
```

Next, you query the function name to determine if it has been set to a value of `True` and if so you clear the error message variable just in case it has been set to an error message from a previous function. If the function name contains a value of `False`, you set the appropriate error message in the error message variable and then the function returns to the caller.

```
If IsValidPhoneNumber Then
    'Clear the error message
    strErrorMessage = String.Empty
Else
    'Set the new error message
    strErrorMessage = "The phone number entered is invalid." & _
        ControlChars.CrLf & ControlChars.CrLf & _
        "Phone numbers must be in one of the following formats:" & _
```

```
                ControlChars.CrLf & _
                "    123 456-7890" & ControlChars.CrLf & _
                "    (123) 456-7890" & ControlChars.CrLf & _
                "    123-456-7890""")
        End If
    End Function
```

The `IsValidEmail` function was added next; it accepts the e-mail address as input and returns a Boolean value indicating whether the e-mail address is valid. There are several parts to an e-mail address: the user's e-mail name, the address domain, and the domain type (for example com, net, org, etc.).

Again you use a regular expression to validate the data. The regular expression pattern starts by validating the user's e-mail name using a pattern of `\w+((-\w+)|(\.\w+))*`. Then the domain name is validated using a pattern of `@[A-Za-z0-9]+((\.|-|_)[A-Za-z0-9]+)*\`. Finally, the domain type is validated using the pattern `.([A-Za-z]{2,4})$`.

```
    Public Function IsValidEmail(ByVal strEmail As String) As Boolean
        'Pattern:    name@domain.type
        'Rules:      name - any character, digit, or special character;
        '                 any number of characters
        '            domain - any alpha character or digit;
        '                 special characters of - or _ only;
        '                 must contain at least one character or digit
        '                 after a - or _
        '            type - any domain type (alpha characters only)
        '                 between 2 and 4 characters in length
        IsValidEmail = Regex.IsMatch(strEmail, _
            ("\w+((-\w+)|(\.\w+))*\@[A-Za-z0-9]+((\.|-|_)" & _
            "[A-Za-z0-9]+)*\.([A-Za-z]{2,4})$"))
```

If the validation returned a value of `True`, you clear the error message variable in case it was set to an error from another function call. If the validation returned a value of `False`, you set the error message variable to the appropriate error message:

```
        If IsValidEmail Then
            'Clear the error message
            strErrorMessage = String.Empty
        Else
            strErrorMessage = "The email entered is invalid." & _
                ControlChars.CrLf & ControlChars.CrLf & _
                "Email addresses must be in the format of: someone@domain.type"
        End If
    End Function
```

The `IsValidPassword` function uses a regular expression to validate that a password contains at least one upper- and one lowercase character, one numeric digit, and one special character. In addition to these validations, it also validates that the password is of the minimum length and does not exceed the maximum length defined in your class level variables.

The regular expression pattern starts off by validating that the password contains at least one numeric digit using the pattern of `^(?=.*\d)`. Then it validates that at least one uppercase character is specified in the password using a pattern of `(?=.*[A-Z])`. To validate that at least one lowercase character is specified the pattern of `(?=.*[a-z])` is used.

The pattern used to validate special characters is built using the `strPasswordSpecialCharacters` variable that you defined at the top of your class. This allows you to easily change the special characters that are valid in a password as your business needs dictate. The regular expression pattern for validating special characters is defined as `(?=.*[" & strPasswordSpecialCharacters & "])`.

The pattern for validating the minimum and maximum length of the password is contained in the code below following the pattern portion for validating special characters. Again you see that you are using the class level variables that you defined at the top of this class for the minimum and maximum length of a password. This allows you to easily change these values as needed.

```
Public Function IsValidPassword(ByVal strPassword As String) As Boolean
    'Rules: must contain at least one upper case character
    '       must contain at least one lower case character
    '       must contain at least one numeric digit
    '       must contain at least one special character
    '           (defined in strPasswordSpecialCharacters variable)
    '       must be between the minimum and maximum length
    '           (defined in the bytMinimumPasswordLength and
    '           bytMaximumPasswordLength variables)
    IsValidPassword = Regex.IsMatch(strPassword, _
        ("^(?=.*\d)(?=.*[A-Z])(?=.*[a-z])" & _
        "(?=.*[" & strPasswordSpecialCharacters & "]).{" & _
        bytMinimumPasswordLength & "," & _
        bytMaximumPasswordLength & "}$"))
```

If the validation returns a value of `True`, you clear the error message variable in case it was set to an error from another function call. If the validation returns a value of `False`, you set the error message variable to the appropriate error message:

```
    If IsValidPassword Then
        'Clear the error message
        strErrorMessage = String.Empty
    Else
        strErrorMessage = "The password entered is not strongly typed." & _
            ControlChars.CrLf & ControlChars.CrLf & _
            "Passwords must be between " & _
            bytMinimumPasswordLength.ToString & _
            " and " & bytMaximumPasswordLength.ToString & _
            " characters in length and" & ControlChars.CrLf & _
            "contain at least one upper case letter, " & _
            "one lower case letter," & ControlChars.CrLf & _
            "one numeric digit, and one special character." & _
            ControlChars.CrLf & _
            "Valid special characters are: " & strPasswordSpecialCharacters
    End If
End Function
```

The final function in the `ValidationFunctions` module does not validate data but rather formats data so that all phones numbers are in a consistent format. The `FormatPhoneNumber` function accepts the phone number to be formatted as input and returns the formatted phone number as output.

The first thing you do in this function is replace all the special characters in a phone number with a blank space. This effectively removes the special characters from the phone number.

After all of the special characters have been replaced, you are left with the phone number with all numeric data. Now you use the Substring method of the String class to extract the pieces of the phone number and build the formatted phone number to be returned. You set the formatted phone number in the function name because this function returns a string. When you complete the last line of code, the function exits with the formatted phone number:

```
Public Function FormatPhoneNumber(ByVal strPhoneNumber As String) As String
    'Remove all special characters (e.g. ( ) - and spaces)
    strPhoneNumber = strPhoneNumber.Replace("(", "").Replace( _
        ")", "").Replace("-", "").Replace(Chr(34), "")

    'Now format the phone number for storage in the database
    FormatPhoneNumber = strPhoneNumber.Substring(0, 3) & "-" & _
        strPhoneNumber.Substring(3, 3) & "-" & _
        strPhoneNumber.Substring(6, 4)
End Function
```

When you add the WBLUsers class to the business logic component you start out by importing two namespaces that are required when hashing and encoding hashed passwords.

```
Imports System.Text
Imports System.Security.Cryptography
```

Next, you add the necessary code to add an object to represent the WDAUsers class in the data access component and then add a constructor and modify the Dispose procedure to clean up the resources used in this class. You then add a procedure to return a User DataSet. Because this is all straightforward code that you've seen before there is no need to list it again.

The function to hash a password was added next. You will not be storing the user's password in the database. Instead you hash the password and store the hashed value in the database. When a user logs in to the application, you hash the password entered and then compare the hashed value of that password against the hashed value that is stored in the database. This provides a great level of security as hashing is one-way. That is, you can hash a password but cannot un-hash it.

This function starts by accepting the password to be hashed as an input parameter to this function and returns the hashed value as output. Next, you declare a couple of Byte arrays that will be used to store the password to be hashed and return the hashed password.

Then you instantiate a new instance of the SHA1CryptoServiceProvider class in a Using...End Using block. This class is used to compute an SHA1 hash value.

You must convert the password passed to this function into a byte array so you use the GetBytes method of the UTF8 property of the Encoding class. This is the same code that you saw when encrypting data in the last chapter.

After the password has been converted into a Byte array, you call the ComputeHash method to hash the password. The output from this method is a Byte array containing the hashed password. You need to convert the `Byte` array back into a string before returning it to the caller so you use the `ToBase64String` method of the `Convert` class. Again, this is the same code that you used in the last chapter when encrypting data.

All of the code is in a `Try...Catch` block to handle any errors that may occur, and the `Catch` block simply throws the error that it receives so the error gets returned to the caller of this function.

```
Private Function HashPassword(ByVal strPassword As String) As String
    Try
        'Declare local variables
        Dim bytPasswordIn() As Byte
        Dim bytPasswordOut() As Byte

        Using objHashAlgorithm As New SHA1CryptoServiceProvider
            'Convert the input password to an array of bytes
            bytPasswordIn = Encoding.UTF8.GetBytes(strPassword)

            'Compute the Hash (returns an array of bytes)
            bytPasswordOut = objHashAlgorithm.ComputeHash(bytPasswordIn)

            'Return a base 64 encoded string of the hashed password
            HashPassword = Convert.ToBase64String(bytPasswordOut)
        End Using
    Catch ExceptionErr As Exception
        Throw New System.Exception(ExceptionErr.Message, _
            ExceptionErr.InnerException)
    End Try
End Function
```

The `ValidateUserData` procedure was added next and this procedure contains the same standard validation code that you've already seen so there's no need to list that procedure again. However, I do want to point out that this procedure calls the `HashPassword` function to hash the user's password in the `DataSet` and also calls the `FormatPhoneNumber` function to format the user's phone number. You add the `AddUser` function next and again this is the same standard code that you've seen before so it will not be listed again.

Two objects were added to the Admin form code to represent the classes for roles and users in the business logic component:

```
Private objRoles As WroxBusinessLogic.WBLRoles
Private objUsers As WroxBusinessLogic.WBLUsers
```

Next, you modify the `ActionAdd` procedure to add new code to insert a role and you add this code under the `Case "Roles"` statement. The first thing you do here is set the `objRoles` object to a new instance of the `WBLRoles` class in the business logic component in a `Using...End Using` block. Then you call the `GetNewRoleDS` function in the business logic component to get a new `DataSet` for `Roles` in the `objDataSet` object:

```
Case "Roles"
    'Initialize a new instance of the business logic component
    Using objRoles As New WroxBusinessLogic.WBLRoles( _
        strCompany, strApplication)
```

```
'Get a new Role DataSet
objDataSet = objRoles.GetNewRoleDS()
```

After you have a new DataSet, you proceed by initializing a new DataRow in the objDataRow object. Next, you set the values in the appropriate columns in the objDataRow object using the input fields from the Roles screen in the Admin form.

Notice you are checking the value in the txtRanking text box to ensure that a numeric value was entered. While this isn't necessary, I wanted to demonstrate how this type of data validation could be performed in the application layer. The reason why it is not necessary is because the constraints of the DataSet force the value you add to this column to be numeric and in a valid range for the data type, which is from 0 to 255.

After all the values have been set in the columns in the DataRow object, you add the new DataRow to the DataSet. Then you call the AddRole method in the objRoles object, passing it the DataSet:

```
'Initialize a datarow object from the Role DataSet
Dim objDataRow As Data.DataRow = _
    objDataSet.Tables("Role").NewRow
'Set the values in the DataRow
objDataRow.Item("RoleID") = Guid.NewGuid
objDataRow.Item("RoleName") = txtRoleName.Text
objDataRow.Item("RoleDescription") = _
    txtRoleDescription.Text
If IsNumeric(txtRanking.Text) Then
    objDataRow.Item("Ranking") =
        CType(txtRanking.Text, Byte)
Else
    Throw New Exception( _
        "Ranking must contain a numeric value.")
End If
'Add the DataRow to the DataSet
objDataSet.Tables("Role").Rows.Add(objDataRow)
'Add the Role to the database
If Not objRoles.AddRole(objDataSet) Then
    Throw New Exception("Insert Role Failed")
End If
End Using
```

After the new role is added, you clear the input fields as you did in the previous code in this procedure:

```
'Clear the input fields
txtRoleID.Text = String.Empty
txtRoleName.Text = String.Empty
txtRoleDescription.Text = String.Empty
txtRanking.Text = String.Empty
txtRoleUpdateDate.Text = String.Empty
```

The code you add under the Case "Users" statement adds a new user to the database. You start in the same manner as the code you just looked at by initializing the objUsers object to a new instance of the WBLUsers class in the business logic component.

Then you get a new `User DataSet` by calling the `GetNewUserDS` method in the business logic component. After you have a new `User DataSet`, you initialize the `objDataRow` object to a new row of data from the `User DataSet`:

```
Case "Users"
        'Initialize a new instance of the business logic component
        Using objUsers As New WroxBusinessLogic.WBLUsers( _
            strCompany, strApplication)
        'Get a new User DataSet
        objDataSet = objUsers.GetNewUserDS()
        'Initialize a datarow object from the User DataSet
        Dim objDataRow As Data.DataRow = _
            objDataSet.Tables("User").NewRow
```

You set the values for the various columns in the `DataSet` next by using the input fields from the Users screen on the Admin form:

```
'Set the values in the DataRow
objDataRow.Item("UserID") = Guid.NewGuid
objDataRow.Item("LoginName") = txtLogin.Text
objDataRow.Item("Password") = txtPassword.Text
objDataRow.Item("FirstName") = txtFirstName.Text
objDataRow.Item("LastName") = txtLastName.Text
objDataRow.Item("Email") = txtEmail.Text
objDataRow.Item("Phone") = txtPhone.Text
objDataRow.Item("Status") = optStatusActive.Checked
```

The `GroupID`, `RoleID`, and `ManagerID` columns are eventually set using data from the combo boxes on the User screen but you have not written any code to populate those combo boxes yet, which is why you set a breakpoint here and manually add the values for `GroupID` and `RoleID`.

Notice that you check the `cboUserManager` combo box to see if any data was selected before attempting to set the value in the `ManagerID` column of the `DataSet` because the `ManagerID` column is not a required column and you want to leave it set to a `DBNull` value if no manager was selected. Just as a side note, all columns in the `DataRow` are set to a `DBNull` value when the `DataRow` is initialized.

```
objDataRow.Item("GroupID") = _
    cboUserGroup.SelectedItem.Item("GroupID")
objDataRow.Item("RoleID") = _
    cboUserRole.SelectedItem.Item("RoleID")
If cboUserManager.SelectedIndex <> -1 Then
    objDataRow.Item("ManagerID") = _
        cboUserManager.SelectedItem.item("ManagerID")
End If
```

After the values for all columns are set, you add the `DataRow` object to the `DataSet`. Then you call the `AddUser` method in the business logic component, passing it the `DataSet`. You throw an exception if the `AddUser` method returned a value of `False`:

```
'Add the DataRow to the DataSet
objDataSet.Tables("User").Rows.Add(objDataRow)
'Add the User to the database
If Not objUsers.AddUser(objDataSet) Then
```

```
                    Throw New Exception("Insert User Failed")
            End If
    End Using
```

After the user is added, you clear the input fields on the Users screen and set the `SelectedIndex` property on the combo boxes to a value of `-1`, which deselects any selected items in those combo boxes:

```
'Clear the input fields
txtUserID.Text = String.Empty
txtLogin.Text = String.Empty
txtPassword.Text = String.Empty
txtFirstName.Text = String.Empty
txtLastName.Text = String.Empty
txtEmail.Text = String.Empty
txtPhone.Text = String.Empty
optStatusActive.Checked = True
cboUserGroup.SelectedIndex = -1
cboUserRole.SelectedIndex = -1
cboUserManager.SelectedIndex = -1
txtUserUpdateDate.Text = String.Empty
```

Stored Procedures That Insert Data

Sometimes client-side validation is not enough or is not the most efficient means of validating data. At times you'll need to perform some validation in the stored procedures that you write and execute. This could be the validation of the input data to the stored procedure or validation of existing rows of data in one or more tables.

In this section, you examine stored procedures that perform validation, error checking, and conditional processing logic (for example, using an `If` statement). You also examine stored procedures that perform inserts into multiple tables and incorporate transactional support.

Local variables

The term "local variables" refers to variables that are declared in your stored procedures other than the input parameters used to pass data to your stored procedures. These variables can have data inserted into them by `SELECT` statements and can be used in the same manner that you use variables in your VB 2005 applications.

Local variables in SQL Server are always prefixed with an at (@) sign, whereas Oracle does not require any special prefixes for variables. The following code snippet shows a variable declaration for both SQL Server and Oracle:

```
-- SQL Server variable declaration
DECLARE @TimeSheetDate DATETIME

-- Oracle variable declaration
varTimeSheetDate DATE;
```

Notice that in SQL Server you must use the DECLARE statement followed by the variable name, prefixed with an at (@) sign, followed by the data type that the variable represents. In Oracle, you simply define the variable name followed by the data type and end it with a semicolon. Note that the two dashes in the code snippet signify a comment in both SQL Server and Oracle stored procedures. Anything following the two dashes is treated as a comment and not code.

A variable can be populated with data in one of two ways: You can set the data in a variable or you can select data into a variable from a table. The following code snippet shows how to set the variable defined previously to the current date:

```
-- SQL Server variable
SET @TimeSheetDate = GETDATE()

-- Oracle variable
varTimeSheetDate := SYSDATE;
```

Notice that in SQL Server you must use the SET statement to set a value in the variable; whereas Oracle requires a colon before the equal sign.

To populate a variable with data from a table, you must use the SELECT statement. The following code fragment demonstrates how this is performed in the two databases. In the first part of this code, you can see that you specify the variable first, followed by the value that should be set in the variable in the SELECT statement for SQL Server. For Oracle, you select the data into the variable using the INTO keyword.

```
-- SQL Server SELECT
SELECT @TimeSheetDate = LastUpdateDate

-- Oracle SELECT
SELECT LastUpdateDate INTO varTimeSheetDate
```

Error checking and raising errors

Error handling is an important part of any code that you write and this applies to your stored procedures as well. Both SQL Server and Oracle provide support for checking and handling errors that may occur in your stored procedures. Although both database vendors implement error handling in different ways, it is important that you use it.

Because error handling is implemented in totally different ways by the database vendors, I want you to look at each of these implementations separately. The following code fragment demonstrates how error handling is performed in SQL Server.

The code for your INSERT statement is enclosed inside of a TRY block and your error handling code is contained inside of a CATCH block. This is very similar to a VB 2005 Try...Catch block except that SQL Server requires the BEGIN and END keywords for each block. Another important point to note here is that this error handling technique is supported only in SQL Server 2005 and is not backward compatible with earlier versions of SQL Server.

In the following code, if an error occurs in the TRY block, control is passed to the CATCH block. You then execute the appropriate error handling inside of your CATCH block. Here you are using the RAISERROR statement, which raises a user-defined error message that will be returned to the caller. This statement accepts a number of parameters but in its simplest form, as shown in the following code, it accepts the error message to be set, the severity level, and the state. The error message is a string value that should describe the error, while the severity level determines the severity of the error. User-defined severity levels can be in the range of 0 through 18. A severity of 15 or less is not considered critical and will not cause your stored procedure to stop executing, whereas a severity level of 16 through 18 will. However, it's always a good idea to include the RETURN statement after raising an error so that your stored procedure will stop executing and return to the caller with the error message that you defined. The state parameter is an arbitrary number from 1 through 127 that represents information about the state of the error and is typically set to a value of 1.

```
BEGIN TRY
   INSERT INTO sometable
   ...
END TRY
BEGIN CATCH
   RAISERROR('Insert into sometable failed.',18,1)
   RETURN
END CATCH
```

Oracle has a similar approach to error handling. You enclose the SQL statements in a BEGIN...END block as shown in the code and then execute your INSERT statement. Immediately following the INSERT statement you include the EXCEPTION statement and provide the exceptions that you want to handle. Numerous exception types can be specified but the more common ones are OTHERS, NO_DATA_FOUND, TOO_MANY_ROWS, and DUP_VAL_ON_INDEX. You precede each exception that you specify with the WHEN keyword and follow it with the THEN keyword, as shown in the following code.

In the following example, you insert the data into the table and then use the OTHERS exception statement to handle the exception when the insert fails. You then use the RAISE_APPLICATION_ERROR statement to raise a user-defined error message.

The RAISE_APPLICATION_ERROR statement accepts two parameters: the error number of the message as an Integer data type and the error message as a string. User-defined error numbers can be in the range of –20,000 to –20,999 and have no significance to the severity of the error.

After raising an error, you exit the stored procedure by including the RETURN statement, which causes the stored procedure to immediately return with the error raised and no further code will be executed.

```
BEGIN
   INSERT INTO sometable
   ...
   EXCEPTION
      WHEN OTHERS THEN
      RAISE_APPLICATION_ERROR (-20999,'Insert into sometable failed.');
      RETURN;
END;
```

Conditional logic

Stored procedures also provide a means to perform conditional processing, just as your VB 2005 applications do. Both SQL Server and Oracle support the IF and IF...ELSE statements, which allow you to perform conditional processing in your stored procedures, but you should note some minor differences between the implementations of these statements.

SQL Server implements the IF and IF...ELSE statements without a THEN or END IF statement. It is important that you understand how the SQL statements are treated in these IF...ELSE blocks. SQL Server executes only a single SQL statement in an IF...ELSE statement regardless of the number of statements you include, as shown in the first part of the example that follows.

If you need to execute multiple SQL statements, you enclose the SQL statements in a *statement block*, which is defined through the use of the BEGIN...END statements. This ensures that all code in this statement block is executed. The second part of the following code example shows how this is done.

It's important to note that the first method is valid if it contains only a single SQL statement to be executed. However, using the second method shown here is a good coding practice to get into because you may modify a stored procedure to add more SQL statements and if they aren't originally enclosed in the statement block, you may forget and wonder why your stored procedure is not producing the expected results.

```
-- Single SQL Statement
IF somecondition
    -- this SQL statement will be executed
    SELECT some data
    -- this SQL statement will NOT be executed
    SELECT some data
ELSE
    -- this SQL statement will be executed
    SELECT some data
    -- this SQL statement will NOT be executed
    SELECT some data


-- Multiple SQL Statements
IF somecondition
    BEGIN
    -- this SQL statement will be executed
    SELECT some data
    -- this SQL statement will be executed
    SELECT some data
    END
ELSE
    BEGIN
    -- this SQL statement will be executed
    SELECT some data
    -- this SQL statement will be executed
    SELECT some data
    END
```

Oracle takes a more formal and less confusing approach to IF and IF...ELSE statements by providing the use of the THEN and END IF statements. As you would expect, all SQL statements inside the IF or ELSE block are executed as shown in the following code:

```
IF somecondition THEN
    -- this SQL statement will be executed
    SELECT some data;
    -- this SQL statement will be executed
    SELECT some data;
ELSE
    -- this SQL statement will be executed
```

```
    SELECT some data;
    -- this SQL statement will be executed
    SELECT some data;
END IF;
```

Both database vendors support nested IF statements, meaning that you can nest one IF statement inside another just as you would in VB 2005. While there is no physical limit to the number of IF statements that can be implemented, common sense and code readability place a practical limit on this just as in VB 2005.

Transactions

A transaction is a single unit of work that typically consists of multiple SQL statements. When all SQL statements in the transaction are executed successfully, the transaction is committed and all the work that the SQL statements performed is made a permanent part of the database. When one or more of the SQL statements fail, the transaction is rolled back, meaning that the changes made by the successful SQL statements are undone.

Both database vendors implement automatic transactions for a single SQL statement. For example, the insert stored procedures that you have been creating up until this point use a single INSERT statement and the database will automatically create a transaction around that SQL statement.

However, the use of explicit transactions enables you to control when the work should be committed or when it should be rolled back by specifying the TRANSACTION keyword, which is applicable only in SQL Server. Oracle automatically implements transactions regardless of the number of SQL statements the stored procedure contains.

Both database vendors, however, allow you to control when to commit or roll back a transaction through the use of the COMMIT and ROLLBACK statements. This provides fine-grain control over the work being performed, as some data modifications may be permissible even if the transaction fails.

The following example shows how transactions are implemented in SQL Server. Notice that you specify the BEGIN TRANSACTION statement to explicitly start a transaction. SQL Server allows you to optionally name a transaction but limits the name to 32 characters.

In this example, the transaction is started and an INSERT statement is executed. Your error-handling code will catch an error if one occurred and you roll back the transaction using the ROLLBACK TRANSACTION statement. If the insert was successful, you commit the transaction using the COMMIT TRANSACTION statement.

While this is a simplistic example, it does demonstrate the use of transactions in SQL Server.

```
BEGIN TRANSACTION
BEGIN TRY
    INSERT INTO sometable
    ...
END TRY
BEGIN CATCH
    ROLLBACK TRANSACTION
    RAISERROR('Insert into sometable failed.',18,1)
    RETURN
END CATCH
COMMIT TRANSACTION
```

As I mentioned earlier, Oracle automatically begins a transaction with the first SQL statement that modifies data. If you want fine-grain control over the transaction instead of letting the database decide what to do, you can use the COMMIT and ROLLBACK statements to either commit or roll back the transaction.

In this example, you implement your error-handling code and if the INSERT statement was successful, you commit the transaction by specifying the COMMIT statement. If an error did occur, you roll back the transaction by issuing the ROLLBACK statement.

```
BEGIN
  INSERT INTO sometable;
     COMMIT;
  EXCEPTION
     WHEN OTHERS THEN
       ROLLBACK;
       RETURN;
END;
```

Cursors

When you execute a SQL SELECT statement, a result set is formed that will be returned to the caller of the stored procedure, which only applies to SQL Server. Remember that Oracle requires a REF CURSOR to be defined to return data from a stored procedure. Sometimes it is necessary to select multiple rows of data from a table and operate on those rows of data inside the stored procedure without returning the results of that SELECT statement to the client.

A cursor is a mechanism that allows you to select and process data in a stored procedure without having the result set of the SELECT statement returned to the client. Instead, the result set of the SELECT statement is returned to the cursor.

SQL Server and Oracle implement cursors in pretty much the same manner with only minor differences in how you work with them. Each database requires you to declare a cursor variable with the appropriate SELECT statement defining the data that should be returned in the cursor. Then, before you can use the cursor, you must open it and fetch data from the cursor to be processed. Only a single row of data is returned from the cursor, so you must call the FETCH statement to get a new row of data from the cursor. When you are done with the cursor, you must close it.

The minor differences occur in the loop that processes a cursor. In SQL Server, you set up a WHILE loop and check the @@FETCH_STATUS variable to determine whether data was returned from the cursor. Oracle uses the LOOP statement to process the cursor in a loop and provides a more formal approach in determining when no data has been returned from the cursor. It provides the NOTFOUND condition when no more data exists for the SELECT statement of the cursor.

Data in a cursor is processed one row at a time and you do not access the data directly in the cursor. Instead, you fetch the data that exists in the cursor into local variables and then work with the data in the local variables. You see how this works in the examples that follow.

In the following example for SQL Server, you first declare a cursor by giving it a name — in this case, Project_Cursor. Then you specify the CURSOR FOR statement and specify the SELECT statement that will be used to populate the cursor with data. Next, you open the cursor and fetch the first row of data from the cursor into a local variable. You use the FETCH NEXT FROM statement to fetch data from the cursor and then specify the cursor name. You fetch the data into one or more local variables by specifying the INTO keyword followed by a comma-delimited list of variable names, as shown in the example that follows.

After you have fetched the first row of data, you set up a WHILE loop and process the data while the @@FETCH_STATUS variable is equal to a value of 0, which indicates that a row of data was fetched from the cursor. Inside the WHILE loop you enclose the SQL statements being executed in a statement block, as you saw in the previous SQL Server examples. At the end of the statement block, you fetch the next row of data from the cursor into your local variables and start the loop over if the @@FETCH_STATUS variable is equal to a value of 0.

After all data has been processed from the cursor, you close it using the CLOSE statement. Then you deallocate the cursor by executing the DEALLOCATE statement. This last step is not necessary, as SQL Server automatically deallocates the cursor when it goes out of scope, meaning when your stored procedure has finished processing. However, specifying this SQL statement is a good practice to adopt because it immediately frees up the resources held by the cursor. You should not hold onto resources any longer than necessary in a stored procedure, or in any programming language for that matter.

```
-- Declare the cursor
DECLARE Project_Cursor CURSOR FOR SELECT some data

-- Open the cursor
OPEN Project_Cursor

-- Get the first row of data from the cursor
FETCH NEXT FROM Project_Cursor INTO @ProjectID, @ProjectName

-- Process all data in a loop
WHILE @@FETCH_STATUS = 0
    BEGIN
    -- Process the data from the cursor
    some SQL statements
    -- Get the next row of data from the cursor
    FETCH NEXT FROM Project_Cursor INTO @ProjectID, @ProjectName
    END

-- Close the cursor
CLOSE Project_Cursor

-- Deallocate cursor
DEALLOCATE Project_Cursor
```

In the Oracle example shown next, you follow the same pattern as with SQL Server. First you declare your cursor using the CURSOR statement, followed by the cursor name, the IS keyword, and then the SELECT statement that will be used to populate the cursor. Then you open the cursor to populate it.

Processing the cursor in a loop in Oracle is a lot easier and cleaner as you do not have to fetch the first row of data before entering the loop because Oracle implements the NOTFOUND condition, which provides a more structured loop. The loop in Oracle is implemented with the LOOP . . . END LOOP SQL statements.

Once inside the loop you fetch the data from the cursor into your local variables as shown in the following example. The second statement handles the NOTFOUND condition that is thrown when the FETCH statement fails to return a row of data and causes processing to exit the loop. As you can see, this is much more structured than the loop processing done in SQL Server. After you have the data in your local variables you provide the SQL statements to process the data.

After processing has exited the loop, you close your cursor by specifying the CLOSE statement followed by the cursor name.

```
-- Declare the cursor
CURSOR Project_Cursor IS SELECT some data;

-- Open the cursor
OPEN Project_Cursor;

-- Process all data in a loop
LOOP
    -- Get the next row of data from the cursor
    FETCH Project_Cursor INTO varProjectID, varProjectName;
    -- Exit when no more data
    EXIT WHEN Project_Cursor%NOTFOUND;
    -- Process the data from the cursor
    some SQL statements;
END LOOP;

-- Close the cursor
CLOSE Project_Cursor;
```

In this next Try It Out, you modify the usp_InsertRole stored procedure to perform some data validation before inserting a new role and creating a stored procedure to insert a new timesheet along with the appropriate timesheet items. This last stored procedure will implement all of the stored procedure topics that were just discussed.

After your stored procedures have been modified and created, you implement the necessary code in your Time Tracker application to execute the new stored procedure.

Try It Out   Inserting Stored Procedures

To modify and create the stored procedures:

1. Open your Time Tracker application in Visual Studio 2005 if it is not already open.

2. Navigate to the stored procedures for your database using the steps outlined in the previous Try It Out in this chapter.

3. Modify the usp_InsertRole stored procedure to perform some data validation. Readers using SQL Server should locate this stored procedure and right-click it and choose Open from the context menu to have this stored procedure displayed in Visual Studio 2005. Readers using Oracle can locate the stored procedure and open it and then copy the code and paste it in your favorite Oracle tool such as iSQL *Plus.

4. Make the following modifications to this stored procedure:

SQL Server

```
ALTER PROCEDURE usp_InsertRole
(
    @RoleID             UNIQUEIDENTIFIER,
    @RoleName           VARCHAR(50),
    @RoleDescription    TEXT,
    @Ranking            TINYINT
)
AS
IF EXISTS (SELECT Ranking FROM Roles WHERE Ranking = @Ranking)
    BEGIN
    RAISERROR('Ranking already exists and cannot be duplicated',18,1)
    END
ELSE
    BEGIN
    INSERT INTO Roles
        (RoleID, RoleName, RoleDescription, Ranking, LastUpdateDate)
        VALUES(@RoleID, @RoleName, @RoleDescription, @Ranking, GETDATE())
    END
```

Oracle

```
CREATE OR REPLACE PROCEDURE usp_InsertRole
(
inRoleID            CHAR,
inRoleName          VARCHAR2,
inRoleDescription   CLOB,
inRanking           NUMBER
)
AS

RankAvailable number(3,0);

BEGIN
    BEGIN
        SELECT Ranking INTO RankAvailable
        FROM Roles
        WHERE Ranking = inRanking;
        RAISE_APPLICATION_ERROR (-20999,
            'Ranking already exists and cannot be duplicated');
    EXCEPTION
        WHEN NO_DATA_FOUND THEN
        INSERT INTO Roles
            (RoleID, RoleName, RoleDescription, Ranking, LastUpdateDate)
            VALUES(inRoleID, inRoleName, inRoleDescription, inRanking, SYSDATE);
    END;
END;
```

Readers using SQL Server should click Save to update the stored procedure in their database and readers using Oracle should click Execute in their Oracle tool.

5. Create the stored procedure to insert a new timesheet. SQL Server users should right-click the Stored Procedures node in the Database Explorer and choose Add New Stored Procedure and Oracle users should use their Oracle tool. Enter the following code:

SQL Server

```
CREATE  PROCEDURE usp_InsertTimeSheet
(
    @TimeSheetID       UNIQUEIDENTIFIER,
    @UserID            UNIQUEIDENTIFIER,
    @WeekEndingDate    DATETIME
)
AS

DECLARE @GroupID UNIQUEIDENTIFIER,
        @ProjectID UNIQUEIDENTIFIER,
        @TimeSheetDate DATETIME,
        @i TINYINT

-- Get the GroupID that the user belongs to
SELECT @GroupID = GroupID FROM Users WHERE UserID = @UserID

DECLARE Project_Cursor CURSOR FOR SELECT ProjectID
    FROM GroupProjects WHERE GroupID = @GroupID

BEGIN TRANSACTION
    BEGIN TRY
        -- Insert the time sheet
        INSERT INTO TimeSheets
            (TimeSheetID, UserID, WeekEndingDate, Submitted, ApprovalDate,
            ManagerID, LastUpdateDate)
            VALUES(@TimeSheetID, @UserID, @WeekEndingDate, 0, NULL,
            NULL, GETDATE())
    END TRY
    BEGIN CATCH
        ROLLBACK TRANSACTION
        RAISERROR('Insert into TimeSheets failed.',18,1)
        RETURN
    END CATCH

    -- Set the initial time sheet date to the beginning of the week
    SET @TimeSheetDate = @WeekEndingDate - 4

    -- Set up a loop to insert time sheet items for 5 days
    SET @i = 1
    WHILE (@i < 6)

        BEGIN
        -- Open the cursor
        OPEN Project_Cursor

        -- Get the first row of data from the cursor into our variable
        FETCH NEXT FROM Project_Cursor INTO @ProjectID

        WHILE @@FETCH_STATUS = 0
            BEGIN
```

```
            BEGIN TRY
                -- Insert the time sheet item
                INSERT INTO TimeSheetItems
                (TimeSheetItemID, TimeSheetID, ProjectID, Hours, TimeSheetDate)
                    VALUES(NEWID(), @TimeSheetID, @ProjectID, 0, @TimeSheetDate)
            END TRY
            BEGIN CATCH
                ROLLBACK TRANSACTION
                RAISERROR('Insert into TimeSheetItems failed.',18,1)
                RETURN
            END CATCH
            -- Get the next row of data from the cursor into our variable
            FETCH NEXT FROM Project_Cursor INTO @ProjectID
            END

        CLOSE Project_Cursor

        -- Increment the date by one day
        SET @TimeSheetDate = @TimeSheetDate + 1
        -- Increment the loop counter by one
        SET @i = @i + 1
        END

-- Deallocate cursor
DEALLOCATE Project_Cursor

-- Commit all inserts
COMMIT TRANSACTION
```

Oracle

```
CREATE OR REPLACE PROCEDURE usp_InsertTimeSheet
(
    inTimeSheetID       CHAR,
    inUserID            CHAR,
    inWeekEndingDate    DATE
)
AS

varGroupID CHAR(36);
CURSOR Project_Cursor IS SELECT ProjectID
    FROM GroupProjects WHERE GroupID = varGroupID;
varProjectID CHAR(36);
varGuid CHAR(32);
varTimeSheetItemID CHAR(36);
varTimeSheetDate DATE;

BEGIN
    -- Get the GroupID that the user belongs to
    SELECT GroupID INTO varGroupID FROM Users WHERE UserID = inUserID;

    BEGIN
        -- Insert the time sheet
```

```
      INSERT INTO TimeSheets
         (TimeSheetID, UserID, WeekEndingDate, Submitted, ApprovalDate,
         ManagerID, LastUpdateDate)
         VALUES(inTimeSheetID, inUserID, inWeekEndingDate, 0, NULL,
         NULL, SYSDATE);
      EXCEPTION
         WHEN OTHERS THEN
         ROLLBACK;
         RAISE_APPLICATION_ERROR( -20999,'Insert into TimeSheets failed.');
         RETURN;
END;

BEGIN
   -- Set the initial time sheet date to the beginning of the week
   varTimeSheetDate := inWeekEndingDate - 4;

   -- Set up a loop to insert time sheet items for 5 days
   FOR i IN 1 .. 5

      LOOP
      -- Open the cursor
      OPEN Project_Cursor;

         LOOP
         -- Fetch a row of data from the cursor into our variable
         FETCH Project_Cursor INTO varProjectID;
         -- Exit when no more data
         EXIT WHEN Project_Cursor%NOTFOUND;
         -- Get a Guid
         SELECT SYS_GUID() INTO varGuid FROM DUAL;
         -- Format the Guid with dashes in our variable
         varTimeSheetItemID := SUBSTR(varGuid,1,8) || '-' ||
            SUBSTR(varGuid,9,4) || '-' ||
            SUBSTR(varGuid,13,4) || '-' ||
            SUBSTR(varGuid,17,4) || '-' ||
            SUBSTR(varGuid,21,12);
         BEGIN
            -- Insert the time sheet item
            INSERT INTO TimeSheetItems
               (TimeSheetItemID, TimeSheetID, ProjectID, Hours,
               TimeSheetDate)
               VALUES(varTimeSheetItemID, inTimeSheetID, varProjectID, 0,
               varTimeSheetDate);
            EXCEPTION
               WHEN OTHERS THEN
               ROLLBACK;
               RAISE_APPLICATION_ERROR( -20999,
                   'Insert into TimeSheetItems failed.');
               RETURN;
            END;
         END LOOP;

      CLOSE Project_Cursor;

      -- Increment the date by one day
```

```
              varTimeSheetDate := varTimeSheetDate + 1;
              END LOOP;
        END;

    -- Commit all inserts
    COMMIT;
END;
```

Readers using SQL Server should click Save to create the stored procedure and readers using Oracle should click Execute in their Oracle tool.

6. Now that your stored procedures have been modified and created, implement the necessary code to execute the usp_InsertTimeSheet stored procedure. No code changes are necessary for the modified usp_InsertRole stored procedure. The first task will be to add a new class to the data access component for timesheets. Right-click the WroxDataAccess project in Solution Explorer, select Add, and then select Class. In the Add New Item – WroxDataAccess dialog box, enter a class name of **WDATimeSheets.vb** in the Name field and click Add to add this class to your project.

7. Like the other classes in this project, you want this class to inherit the base class. Add the following Inherits statement to your class:

```
Public Class WDATimeSheets
    Inherits WDABase
```

8. You need to create the constructor for this class next and add the Dispose procedure. Add the following code to this class:

```
Public Sub New(ByVal Company As String, ByVal Application As String)
    MyBase.New(Company, Application)
End Sub

Public Shadows Sub Dispose()
    MyBase.Dispose()
End Sub
```

9. At this point, you need to add only one function to this class — the AddTimeSheet function — to execute the usp_InsertTimeSheet stored procedure. Add the following code to this class:

SQL Server

```
Public Function AddTimeSheet(ByVal TimeSheet As DataSet) As Boolean
    Try
        'Clear previous Command just in case it has been set
        MyBase.Command = Nothing
        MyBase.SQL = "usp_InsertTimeSheet"
        'Initialize the Command object
        MyBase.InitializeCommand()
        'Add the Parameters to the Parameters collection
        MyBase.AddParameter("@TimeSheetID", _
            SqlDbType.UniqueIdentifier, 16, _
            TimeSheet.Tables("TimeSheet").Rows(0).Item("TimeSheetID"))
        MyBase.AddParameter("@UserID", _
            SqlDbType.UniqueIdentifier, 16, _
            TimeSheet.Tables("TimeSheet").Rows(0).Item("UserID"))
        MyBase.AddParameter("@WeekEndingDate", _
```

```
             SqlDbType.DateTime, 8, _
             TimeSheet.Tables("TimeSheet").Rows(0).Item("WeekEndingDate"))
          'Execute the stored procedure
          AddTimeSheet = ExecuteStoredProcedure()
      Catch ExceptionErr As Exception
          Throw New System.Exception(ExceptionErr.Message, _
          ExceptionErr.InnerException)
      End Try
  End Function
```

Oracle

```
Public Function AddTimeSheet(ByVal TimeSheet As DataSet) As Boolean
    Try
        'Clear previous Command just in case it has been set
        MyBase.Command = Nothing
        MyBase.SQL = "usp_InsertTimeSheet"
        'Initialize the Command object
        MyBase.InitializeCommand()
        'Add the Parameters to the Parameters collection
        MyBase.AddParameter("inTimeSheetID", _
            OracleClient.OracleType.Char, 36, _
            TimeSheet.Tables("TimeSheet").Rows(0).Item("TimeSheetID"))
        MyBase.AddParameter("inUserID", _
            OracleClient.OracleType.Char, 36, _
            TimeSheet.Tables("TimeSheet").Rows(0).Item("UserID"))
        MyBase.AddParameter("inWeekEndingDate", _
            OracleClient.OracleType.DateTime, 8, _
            TimeSheet.Tables("TimeSheet").Rows(0).Item("WeekEndingDate"))
        'Execute the stored procedure
        AddTimeSheet = ExecuteStoredProcedure()
    Catch ExceptionErr As Exception
        Throw New System.Exception(ExceptionErr.Message, _
        ExceptionErr.InnerException)
    End Try
End Function
```

10. The next step is to add a class to your business logic component to support timesheets although you will not be adding any timesheet functions at this point. Right-click the WroxBusinessLogic project in Solution Explorer, select Add, and then select Class. In the Add New Item – WroxBusinessLogic dialog box, enter a class name of **WBLTimeSheets.vb** in the Name field and click Add to add this class to your project.

11. You want to implement the IDisposable interface in this class, so add the following Implements statement to this class:

```
Public Class WBLTimeSheets
    Implements IDisposable
```

12. You need an object at the class level that represents the corresponding class in the data access component. Add the following variable declaration to this class:

```
    'Private variables and objects
    Private objWDATimeSheets As WroxDataAccess.WDATimeSheets
```

13. Now add a constructor for this class:

```
Public Sub New(ByVal Company As String, ByVal Application As String)
    objWDATimeSheets = New WroxDataAccess.WDATimeSheets(Company, Application)
End Sub
```

14. Modify the `Dispose` procedure to clean up the resources used in this class by adding the following code to it:

```
Private Overloads Sub Dispose(ByVal disposing As Boolean)
    If Not Me.disposed Then
        If disposing Then
            ' TODO: put code to dispose managed resources
        End If

        objWDATimeSheets.Dispose()
        objWDATimeSheets = Nothing
    End If
    Me.disposed = True
End Sub
```

At this point, you have not implemented any code in the TimeSheet form to support adding a new timesheet. Therefore, you will not be able to test the `usp_InsertTimeSheet` stored procedure in this chapter.

You will, however, be able to test the modifications to the `usp_InsertRole` stored procedure, which is what you want to do now. Start your project and navigate to the Roles screen. Enter any role name and description that you want but make sure that you enter a ranking of **1,** as shown in Figure 11-3.

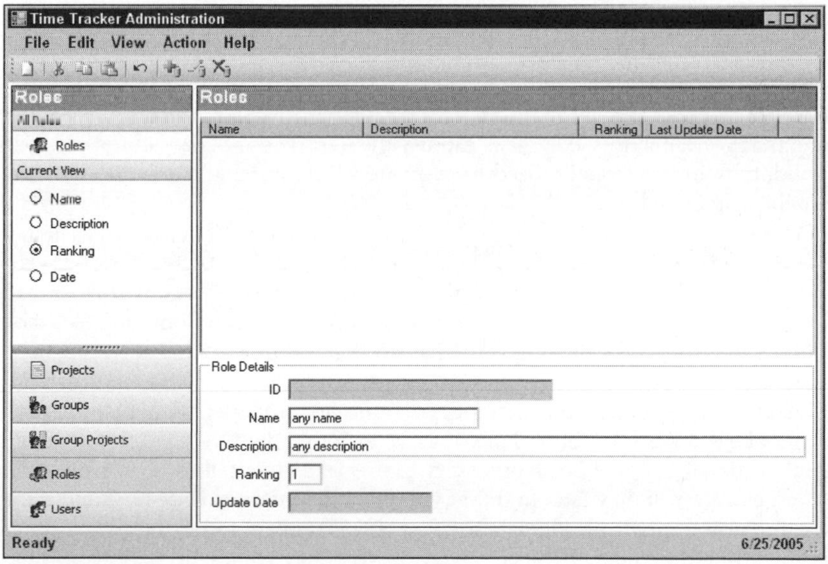

Figure 11-3

Now click the Add button or click the Action menu and select Add. When your stored procedure is executed, it performs the data validation that you added to the stored procedure and determines that a role already exists with a ranking of 1, returning the error shown in Figure 11-4 for SQL Server and the error shown in Figure 11-5 for Oracle.

Notice that SQL Server and Oracle returned the same message, which is the message that you set in the stored procedure. However, Oracle has also returned the error number that you set as part of the message and indicates where the error occurred in the stored procedure. If you prefer not to display the entire error message with the error numbers to the client, you can extract the actual message from the string returned and display that as shown in Figure 11-4.

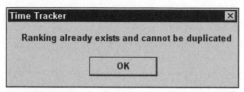

Figure 11-4

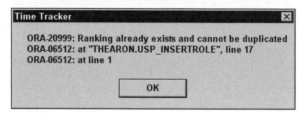

Figure 11-5

How It Works

The first thing that you do in this exercise is modify the usp_InsertRole stored procedure to implement some data validation. In this stored procedure, you are validating that a role does not already exist with the same ranking you are adding.

You do this in SQL Server by using an IF...ELSE statement and the EXISTS keyword. The EXISTS keyword executes a subquery and returns a Boolean value indicating whether any rows of data exist. The subquery you execute is a SELECT statement selecting the Ranking column from the Roles table, where the existing ranking value equals the ranking value passed in the @Ranking input parameter.

If a row of data already exists with this ranking, you raise an error specifying that the ranking already exists and cannot be duplicated. Notice that you have included the RAISERROR statement in a statement block. Remember that although it is not necessary to use a statement block for a single SQL statement, it is a good habit to get into. You may later find that you want to add more code here and if the statement block does not exist and you forgot to add it, only the first SQL statement following the IF statement would be executed. By including the statement block now, you won't have that worry about adding it later.

If the ranking did not exist, the logic would flow to the SQL statements in the ELSE block. Again, only one SQL statement is being executed, but you have enclosed it in a statement block. Here you have your original code, which is the INSERT statement to insert this new role:

SQL Server

```
IF EXISTS (SELECT Ranking FROM Roles WHERE Ranking = @Ranking)
    BEGIN
    RAISERROR('Ranking already exists and cannot be duplicated',18,1)
    END
ELSE
    BEGIN
    INSERT INTO Roles
        (RoleID, RoleName, RoleDescription, Ranking, LastUpdateDate)
        VALUES(@RoleID, @RoleName, @RoleDescription, @Ranking, GETDATE())
    END
```

Oracle does not support the EXISTS statement for comparisons. In Oracle, you declare a local variable, which is done in the first line of code of the partial listing that follows. Because the Ranking column is defined as a Number(3,0) data type, you must declare your variable with the same data type.

Then you set up a BEGIN. . .END block and select the value in the Ranking column into the RankAvailable variable, where the value in the Ranking column is equal to the inRanking input parameter.

If the SELECT statement is successful in finding a matching row of data, no error is thrown so you raise an application error using the RAISE_APPLICATION_ERROR statement, specifying that the ranking already exists and cannot be duplicated.

If the SELECT statement is not successful in finding a row of data that matched the ranking passed in the input parameter, you proceed with your INSERT statement and insert the new row of data.

Oracle

```
RankAvailable number(3,0);

BEGIN
    BEGIN
        SELECT Ranking INTO RankAvailable
        FROM Roles
        WHERE Ranking = inRanking;
        RAISE_APPLICATION_ERROR (-20999,
            'Ranking already exists and cannot be duplicated'),
    EXCEPTION
        WHEN NO_DATA_FOUND THEN
        INSERT INTO Roles
            (RoleID, RoleName, RoleDescription, Ranking, LastUpdateDate)
            VALUES(inRoleID, inRoleName, inRoleDescription, inRanking, SYSDATE);
    END;
```

You create the usp_InsertTimeSheet stored procedure next. This stored procedure may seem a little overwhelming at first but if you follow the logic it is quite simple. This stored procedure inserts a new timesheet for a given user for a specified week ending date. It also inserts all the timesheet items into the TimeSheetItems table. A timesheet item is inserted for each project in the group that this user belongs to as well as for each business day for that project. For example, every group has the Vacation project assigned so five timesheet items are inserted for the Vacation project, one for Monday, one for Tuesday, and so on.

You'll want to examine the SQL Server version of this stored procedure first, followed by the Oracle version. In the SQL Server version, you start by declaring your input parameters to this stored procedure. This includes an input parameter for a new TimeSheetID, the UserID that this timesheet is for, and the week ending date that this timesheet is for.

Some local variables will also be needed by this stored procedure. You need a local variable to store the GroupID of the group to which the user belongs. You need a local variable to retrieve the ProjectID of the various projects in the group, and a variable that contains the date for the timesheet item being inserted into the TimeSheetItems table. The final variable declaration is a counter that is used in a loop to process all timesheet items.

SQL Server

```
CREATE   PROCEDURE usp_InsertTimeSheet
(
    @TimeSheetID        UNIQUEIDENTIFIER,
    @UserID             UNIQUEIDENTIFIER,
    @WeekEndingDate     DATETIME
)
AS

DECLARE @GroupID UNIQUEIDENTIFIER,
        @ProjectID UNIQUEIDENTIFIER,
        @TimeSheetDate DATETIME,
        @i TINYINT
```

Now you want to populate the @GroupID variable with the GroupID of the group to which the user belongs. The easiest way to get this information is to select the GroupID for the user from the Users table, which is what is being done in the next SQL statement.

After you have the GroupID of the group to which the user belongs, you need to declare a cursor. This is done in the next statement. The SELECT statement for the cursor retrieves only a single column, ProjectID, from the GroupProjects table for the specified group.

You use this cursor in a loop to insert a timesheet item for each project that exists in the GroupProjects table.

```
-- Get the GroupID that the user belongs to
SELECT @GroupID = GroupID FROM Users WHERE UserID = @UserID

DECLARE Project_Cursor CURSOR FOR SELECT ProjectID
    FROM GroupProjects WHERE GroupID = @GroupID
```

Transactions are expensive resources in that they place locks on rows and tables, preventing other users from accessing that data. Therefore, you should never begin a transaction until absolutely necessary, which is why you select the GroupID and declare your cursor before beginning the transaction in the next statement.

To handle any errors that might occur, you use a BEGIN TRY . . . END TRY and a BEGIN CATCH . . . END CATCH block. Inside of the BEGIN TRY . . . END TRY block you insert a new timesheet for the specified user into the TimeSheets table. If an error occurs, processing will fall through to your BEGIN CATCH . . . END CATCH block where you roll back the transaction, raise an error, and exit this stored procedure by using the RETURN statement:

```
BEGIN TRANSACTION
    BEGIN TRY
        -- Insert the time sheet
        INSERT INTO TimeSheets
            (TimeSheetID, UserID, WeekEndingDate, Submitted, ApprovalDate,
            ManagerID, LastUpdateDate)
            VALUES(@TimeSheetID, @UserID, @WeekEndingDate, 0, NULL,
            NULL, GETDATE())
    END TRY
    BEGIN CATCH
        ROLLBACK TRANSACTION
        RAISERROR('Insert into TimeSheets failed.',18,1)
        RETURN
    END CATCH
```

Now you set up and prepare to process a loop. The first thing that you do is set the `@TimeSheetDate` local variable to Monday's date for the week that this timesheet is for by subtracting 4 from the date in the `@WeekEndingDate` input parameter. You could have used the `DATEADD` function to do this by passing it a negative number but SQL Server enables you to subtract days from a date using arithmetic operations, which simplifies things.

Every time you iterate through the loop, you add 1 to the date and then insert a timesheet item for the next date until you have inserted a timesheet item for each project for each business day of the week.

```
-- Set the initial time sheet date to the beginning of the week
SET @TimeSheetDate = @WeekEndingDate - 4
```

Next, you set your `@i` variable to an initial value of 1 using the `SET` statement. Then you start processing your loop. SQL Server uses the `WHILE` statement to process loops and you set the condition for the `WHILE` statement, which determines when the loop should stop processing. In this instance, you want to process the loop while the `@i` local variable contains a value that is less than 6, which means that the loop will process five times.

Because SQL Server does not implement an `END WHILE` statement, you must enclose the SQL statements for the loop inside a statement block, which you do by using the `BEGIN` and `END` statements:

```
-- Set up a loop to insert time sheet items for 5 days
SET @i = 1
WHILE (@i < 6)

    BEGIN
```

Inside the `WHILE` loop you want to open the cursor first. Then you fetch the first row of data from the cursor into the `@ProjectID` local variable. Then you enter another `WHILE` loop to process all the data from the cursor. The condition on this `WHILE` loop processes while the `FETCH` statement returns a `@@FETCH_STATUS` of 0 indicating that a row of data was fetched:

```
-- Open the cursor
OPEN Project_Cursor

-- Get the first row of data from the cursor into our variable
FETCH NEXT FROM Project_Cursor INTO @ProjectID

WHILE @@FETCH_STATUS = 0
```

The actual work is done inside this inner WHILE loop, and again you have enclosed all the SQL statements in a statement block by including the BEGIN and END statements. Here you use the ProjectID fetched from the cursor to insert a new timesheet item into the TimeSheetItems table. The INSERT statement in the next line of code does just that.

A new Guid is needed for the TimeSheetItemID column in the TimeSheetItems table and this was previously generated from VB 2005 and passed to the stored procedure. However, because you have no idea how many Guids may be needed by this stored procedure, it doesn't make sense to pass them as input parameters. Instead, you let SQL Server take care of generating those Guids for you. The NEWID() function creates a new Guid in the appropriate format for the TimeSheetItemID column.

Your BEGIN CATCH. . .END CATCH block will handle any errors that occur and you roll back the transaction, which causes all data inserted into the TimeSheetItems table and the data inserted into the TimeSheets table in the previous INSERT statement in this stored procedure to be rolled back. Then you raise an error and return from this stored procedure.

```
BEGIN
BEGIN TRY
    -- Insert the time sheet item
    INSERT INTO TimeSheetItems
    (TimeSheetItemID, TimeSheetID, ProjectID, Hours, TimeSheetDate)
        VALUES(NEWID(), @TimeSheetID, @ProjectID, 0, @TimeSheetDate)
END TRY
BEGIN CATCH
    ROLLBACK TRANSACTION
    RAISERROR('Insert into TimeSheetItems failed.',18,1)
    RETURN
END CATCH
-- Get the next row of data from the cursor into our variable
FETCH NEXT FROM Project_Cursor INTO @ProjectID
END
```

After all data has been processed from the cursor in the inner WHILE loop, you get to the next line of code in the outer WHILE loop where you close the cursor. Then you increment the timesheet date in the @TimeSheetDate local variable and increment the counter for the outer WHILE loop. Then you start the outer WHILE loop over again.

```
CLOSE Project_Cursor

-- Increment the date by one day
SET @TimeSheetDate = @TimeSheetDate + 1
-- Increment the loop counter by one
SET @i = @i + 1
END
```

After you exit the outer WHILE loop, you come to the next line of code in which you deallocate your cursor variable, causing the resources held by the cursor to be released. While this statement is not necessary, it is a good coding habit because you want to release held resources in your stored procedures as soon as possible to prevent blocking those resources from other users. If you do not include this statement, SQL Server deallocates the cursor when your stored procedure goes out of scope — that is, when your stored procedure ends.

The last statement in your stored procedure commits the work done in the transaction, which makes it a permanent part of the database.

```
-- Deallocate cursor
DEALLOCATE Project_Cursor

-- Commit all inserts
COMMIT TRANSACTION
```

Now it's time for you to take a look at the Oracle version of this stored procedure. The biggest difference between the SQL Server and Oracle version of this stored procedure is the way that Oracle handles processing loops and errors. Both are much more structured and even if you aren't an Oracle fan, you have to appreciate the structured approach that Oracle takes here.

You start this stored procedure by declaring the input parameters needed for a TimeSheetID, UserID, and the week ending date. Then you declare your local variables for this stored procedure. You have a local variable to hold the GroupID that the user belongs to, a cursor variable to select the ProjectID of each project in the group that the user belongs to, and a variable that contains the ProjectID returned from your cursor. The last three variables are used to hold a raw Guid that is generated in this stored procedure, a formatted Guid, and the timesheet item date.

Oracle

```
CREATE OR REPLACE PROCEDURE usp_InsertTimeSheet
(
    inTimeSheetID       CHAR,
    inUserID            CHAR,
    inWeekEndingDate    DATE
)
AS

varGroupID CHAR(36);
CURSOR Project_Cursor IS SELECT ProjectID
    FROM GroupProjects WHERE GroupID = varGroupID;
varProjectID CHAR(36);
varGuid CHAR(32);
varTimeSheetItemID CHAR(36);
varTimeSheetDate DATE;
```

You start this stored procedure like the SQL Server version by getting the GroupID of the group to which the user belongs by selecting the GroupID into the `varGroupID` variable from the Users table.

Then you insert a new timesheet into the TimeSheets table. Using Oracle's error-handling method, you handle any exceptions that may be thrown, roll back the transaction, raise an error, and return from this stored procedure.

```
BEGIN
    -- Get the GroupID that the user belongs to
    SELECT GroupID INTO varGroupID FROM Users WHERE UserID = inUserID;

    BEGIN
        -- Insert the time sheet
      INSERT INTO TimeSheets
```

```
        (TimeSheetID, UserID, WeekEndingDate, Submitted, ApprovalDate,
        ManagerID, LastUpdateDate)
        VALUES(inTimeSheetID, inUserID, inWeekEndingDate, 0, NULL,
        NULL, SYSDATE);
    EXCEPTION
        WHEN OTHERS THEN
        ROLLBACK;
        RAISE_APPLICATION_ERROR( -20999,'Insert into TimeSheets failed.');
        RETURN;
    END;
```

Now you set the `varTimeSheetDate` local variable to Monday's date for the week that this timesheet is for by subtracting 4 from the date in the `inWeekEndingDate` input parameter. Subtracting and adding to date variables using arithmetic operations is the only way to get new date values incremented by days in Oracle, as Oracle does not implement a `DATEADD` function like SQL Server does.

Next, you set up the outer loop using the `FOR` statement in a similar manner as you do in VB 2005. In Oracle, you do not need to declare the variable i that the `FOR` statement uses as it is declared in-line with the `FOR` statement. Here you are specifying that the code following the `FOR` statement should be processed five times by indicating the `1 . . 5` enumerator.

Following the `FOR` statement, you specify the `LOOP. . .END LOOP` statements to actually define the outer loop. The `FOR` statement above the `LOOP` statement is merely an enumerator for the outer loop, specifying how many enumerations the loop should make. Once inside the outer loop, you open the cursor to have it retrieve the data.

```
    BEGIN
        -- Set the initial time sheet date to the beginning of the week
        varTimeSheetDate := inWeekEndingDate - 4;

        -- Set up a loop to insert time sheet items for 5 days
        FOR i IN 1 .. 5

            LOOP
            -- Open the cursor
            OPEN Project_Cursor;
```

Now you set up the inner loop by specifying the `LOOP. . .END LOOP` statements. Inside the inner loop you fetch a row of data from the cursor into the `varProjectID` local variable. The `FETCH` statement throws a `NOTFOUND` condition when no more data exists so you handle this with the next statement, which is the `EXIT WHEN` statement. Here you specify the cursor name followed by a percent (%) sign and the condition that you are checking for, which is the `NOTFOUND` condition.

In Chapter 1, I mentioned that Oracle does support generating Guids but not in the format that you see in VB 2005 or SQL Server or Access. Oracle generates a raw Guid that is not formatted with the dashes. Therefore, you need to have Oracle generate a Guid for you and then format the Guid in the format that you want.

Using the `SYS_GUID` function, you select the data into your local `varGuid` variable. Notice that this `SELECT` statement is selecting data from the DUAL table. The DUAL table is a special one-row, one-column table that is part of the data dictionary in Oracle and does not actually return any rows or data. Earlier, I demonstrated how to set a value in a variable using the colon equal sign (:=), and this time I want to demonstrate how to use the SELECT statement to set a value in a variable. Every SELECT statement must include the FROM clause, and using DUAL in the FROM clause causes Oracle to recognize it as a special table and not attempt to return any data from it.

After you have the raw Guid in the varGuid variable, you need to format the Guid into the xxxxxxxx-xxxx-xxxx-xxxx-xxxxxxxxxxxx format. Using the SUBSTR function you can extract the portions of the Guid and build a formatted Guid in the varTimeSheetItemID variable. The SUBSTR function accepts the variable containing the data to extract, the starting position in that variable to start extracting data, and the number of characters to extract. It then returns the number of characters specified. To concatenate the data, you use the two consecutive pipe (|) characters and specify the dashes in single quotes ('):

```
LOOP
-- Fetch a row of data from the cursor into our variable
FETCH Project_Cursor INTO varProjectID;
-- Exit when no more data
EXIT WHEN Project_Cursor%NOTFOUND;
-- Get a Guid
SELECT SYS_GUID() INTO varGuid FROM DUAL;
-- Format the Guid with dashes in our variable
varTimeSheetItemID := SUBSTR(varGuid,1,8) || '-' ||
    SUBSTR(varGuid,9,4) || '-' ||
    SUBSTR(varGuid,13,4) || '-' ||
    SUBSTR(varGuid,17,4) || '-' ||
    SUBSTR(varGuid,21,12);
```

After you have the formatted the Guid, you are ready to insert a new timesheet item in the TimeSheetItems table. The INSERT statement uses the formatted Guid in the varTimeSheetItemID variable for the TimeSheetItemID column.

You include your error-handling code to handle any exceptions that might be thrown by the INSERT statement. If an error does occur, you roll back the transaction, raise an error, and return from the stored procedure. A rollback at this point rolls back any inserts that have been made in the TimeSheetItems table as well as the insert that was made in the TimeSheets table earlier.

```
BEGIN
    -- Insert the time sheet item
    INSERT INTO TimeSheetItems
        (TimeSheetItemID, TimeSheetID, ProjectID, Hours,
        TimeSheetDate)
        VALUES(varTimeSheetItemID, inTimeSheetID, varProjectID, 0,
        varTimeSheetDate);
    EXCEPTION
        WHEN OTHERS THEN
        ROLLBACK;
        RAISE_APPLICATION_ERROR( -20999,
            'Insert into TimeSheetItems failed.');
        RETURN;
        END;
END LOOP;
```

At the end of the outer loop, you close your cursor and increment the date in the varTimeSheetDate variable by one day and then start the outer loop over:

```
        CLOSE Project_Cursor;

        -- Increment the date by one day
        varTimeSheetDate := varTimeSheetDate + 1;
        END LOOP;
    END;
```

When the outer loop completes, you commit all the inserts. Notice that you do not need to deallocate your cursor in Oracle as it handles this for you.

```
    -- Commit all inserts
    COMMIT;
  END;
```

You add the WDATimeSheets class to your data access component next to support adding a new time sheet. This class starts the same way as the other classes that you added to the data access component, by inheriting the base class and adding the appropriate constructor and Dispose procedure, which is not shown here.

Next you add the AddTimeSheet function, which accepts the timesheet to be added as a DataSet and returns a Boolean value indicating success or failure. The code for the SQL Server version is shown in the following code and the only difference between the SQL Server version and the Oracle version is the data types used in the parameters.

Inside this function you include the appropriate error handling through the implementation of the TRY...CATCH block.

In Chapter 12, you will call this procedure from another procedure in this class and the Command object may have been set. To that end, you want to set the Command object to Nothing in case it has already been used. You set the SQL property in the base class to the stored procedure to be executed and then initialize the Command object. Then you add the parameters to the Parameters collection. Adding the parameters is performed in the same manner as in the other functions in the data access component so there's no need to go into any detail here.

```
Public Function AddTimeSheet(ByVal TimeSheet As DataSet) As Boolean
    Try
        'Clear previous Command just in case it has been set
        MyBase.Command = Nothing
        MyBase.SQL = "usp_InsertTimeSheet"
        'Initialize the Command object
        MyBase.InitializeCommand()
        'Add the Parameters to the Parameters collection
        MyBase.AddParameter("@TimeSheetID", _
            SqlDbType.UniqueIdentifier, 16, _
            TimeSheet.Tables("TimeSheet").Rows(0).Item("TimeSheetID"))
        MyBase.AddParameter("@UserID", _
            SqlDbType.UniqueIdentifier, 16, _
            TimeSheet.Tables("TimeSheet").Rows(0).Item("UserID"))
        MyBase.AddParameter("@WeekEndingDate", _
            SqlDbType.DateTime, 8, _
            TimeSheet.Tables("TimeSheet").Rows(0).Item("WeekEndingDate"))
```

After all the parameters have been added to the `Parameters` collection, you call the `ExecuteStoredProcedure` method in the base class to execute the stored procedure and set the results of that call to this function.

The `CATCH` block handles any exceptions that may be thrown and returns the exception to the caller:

```
            'Execute the stored procedure
            AddTimeSheet = ExecuteStoredProcedure()
        Catch ExceptionErr As Exception
            Throw New System.Exception(ExceptionErr.Message, _
            ExceptionErr.InnerException)
        End Try
    End Function
```

The `WBLTimeSheets` class is added next to the business logic component and implements the `IDisposable` interface just as the other classes in this component do. You add a private variable to represent the corresponding class in the data access component, create the constructor, and modify the `Dispose` procedure. Refer to the Try It Out exercise to review that. You'll be adding functions to this class in the next chapter when you start writing more complex `SELECT` statements in your stored procedures.

Summary

This chapter has taken a close look at data validation on all fronts. You did a little data validation in the client application when you validated that the ranking for a role was a numeric value. This demonstrated how you could perform data validation in the client application. You also did some data validation in the `usp_InsertRole` stored procedure, which demonstrated how to perform data validation in a stored procedure, which was more efficient than executing a separate stored procedure to determine if a ranking already existed before calling the stored procedure to insert data.

The bulk of the data validation, however, was performed where it should be, in the business logic component. Here you not only validate data to ensure that it conforms to the business rules, but you also massage the data to remove blank spaces from it and set empty strings to `NULL` values. This increases the efficiency of your data storage in the database because there's no need to store blank spaces when they are not needed.

You also took a more detailed look at insert stored procedures, but you have only scratched the surface of the real power of stored procedures. You learned that you could perform conditional processing and error handling, and execute transactions in your stored procedures. This knowledge will serve you well in the future and I cannot stress enough the importance of error handling in your VB 2005 code as well as in your stored procedures.

To summarize, you should know:

❑ How to remove unwanted leading and trailing spaces from your data

❑ How to use regular expressions to validate data

❑ How to declare and use local variables in your stored procedures

❑   How to perform error handling in your stored procedures

❑   How to use conditional logic and transactions in your stored procedures

❑   How to use cursors in your stored procedures

In Chapter 12, you will write a lot of SELECT stored procedures to select data, and implement code to display the Login and TimeSheet forms.

Exercises

Exercise 1

Using Exercise 1 from the last chapter as a base, modify the ListBox1_Click procedure to validate the ProjectDescription column in the Project table before setting the Text property of the txtProjectDescription text box. If the column contains an empty string then set the Text property of the txtProjectDescription text box to "No Data Available." Run your TimeTracker application and insert a project with no description.

Exercise 2

Modify your usp_InsertRole stored procedure to include the appropriate error handling code for your database.

Selecting Data

Up until this point, the SELECT stored procedures that you have written have been simple and have selected data from a single table. The functionality that you implement in your Time Tracker application in this chapter requires more complex SELECT stored procedures.

Sometimes, selecting data from a single table does not produce the desired results. Often, you want to calculate or summarize the results of the data in a column. Your application's business requirements may also dictate that you select data from multiple columns and have it returned as a single column in your result set. It may also be desirable to select data from multiple rows in a table and have it returned as a single row of data in the result set. Other business requirements of your application may dictate that you select data from multiple tables in a single stored procedure to process the data in your application efficiently.

These are the situations that you will be examining in this chapter as you learn how to write more complex SELECT stored procedures. The topics covered in this chapter lay the groundwork for writing more effective stored procedures and will serve you well in the future.

In this chapter, you:

- ❑ Learn about column aliases
- ❑ Learn about table aliases
- ❑ Learn about join fundamentals
- ❑ Learn how to use like comparisons when selecting data
- ❑ Learn how to select data from multiple rows and return the results as a single row in the result set

Column Aliases

A *column alias* is an alternate name for a column of data or the name for an expression in your SELECT statement. You can use column aliases to shorten the column name in the result set or to assign a name to an unnamed expression in the result set. You can also use a column alias to provide a more descriptive name for a column in a result set.

The following SQL SELECT statement selects the minimum and maximum values from the SequenceNumber column in the Projects table:

```
SELECT MIN(SequenceNumber), MAX(SequenceNumber)
FROM Projects
```

When the results are returned in a DataSet in your VB 2005 program, you see some unexpected column names. In SQL Server, the column names are returned as Column1 and Column2, whereas Oracle returns the column names as MIN(SEQUENCENUMBER) and MAX(SEQUENCENUMBER). Such results can be confusing. Using a column alias for the expressions in your query causes the results to be returned with the column name that you specify.

Now consider the following modifications to the previous query. Here you specify the AS keyword followed by the column alias that should be assigned to your expression. The use of the AS keyword is optional when specifying a column alias but it helps to make your SQL statements more readable.

```
SELECT MIN(SequenceNumber) AS MinSeq, MAX(SequenceNumber) AS MaxSeq
FROM Projects
```

When this query is executed, the column names are returned in the DataSet as MinSeq and MaxSeq by both SQL Server and Oracle. As expected, Oracle returns the column names in uppercase characters but they can be accessed in the DataSet using mixed case.

Assigning a column alias to an expression is not the limit of column aliases. You can also assign a column alias to an existing column name to shorten it in the query results, as shown in the following example:

```
SELECT SequenceNumber AS SeqNum
FROM Projects
```

In this case, you are selecting the data from the SequenceNumber column in the Projects table. However, the column name in the results will be displayed as SeqNum rather than the original column name of SequenceNumber. Because you assigned a column alias to the column, you shortened the column name in your result set, reducing the amount of typing needed in your programs.

This can also work in reverse by allowing you to provide a more descriptive column name in your results set for a column in the database that is somewhat cryptic.

Table Aliases

A *table alias* is similar to a column alias in that it allows you to assign a new name to a table in your query. You may want to do this for several reasons but the most common reason is that it may be necessary to use the same table twice in a query. That is, you may want to join the same table to itself to produce the required results. You'll see an example of this shortly.

A table alias works the same in SQL Server and Oracle. You specify the table name to which you assign an alias and follow that up with the table alias. Oracle does not support the AS keyword when assigning a table alias; however, SQL Server does. I provide the examples in a format that works with both databases.

In the following example, you are selecting two columns from the same table. However, they are treated as different tables in the query because you joined the tables and assigned a table alias to the second table. The FROM clause specifies the Users table as the primary table to select data from. The INNER JOIN statement joins the Users table to the Users table as the Managers table because you specified a table alias of Managers. The condition of the join is specified following the ON keyword. Here you specify that the Managers table is joined such that the ManagerID column in the Users table is equal to the UserID in the Managers table. Remember that the ManagerID column in the Users table is a circular reference to the UserID of the manager in the Users table. You see more on joins shortly.

```
SELECT Users.LoginName, Managers.LoginName AS ManagerLogin
FROM Users
INNER JOIN Users Managers ON Users.ManagerID = Managers.UserID
```

When you specify a table alias for a table, all references to columns in that table are made with the table alias that you specify. It is not always necessary to prefix the column names in the SELECT list with the table name, but it is required in this example to prevent an ambiguous column name error, as you are selecting the LoginName column from both tables. Notice also that a column alias has been assigned to the LoginName column from the Managers table so that it is obvious what this column represents.

Concatenation

Sometimes you want to concatenate the results of two or more columns into a single column. For example, you may want to display a person's first and last name as a single string in your program. You could select the first name and last name columns from your table and join the two columns in your program. However, it is more efficient to have the database do this for you and simply return the results of the two columns as one column in your result set.

Concatenation is performed the same way in SQL Server and Oracle, but each database uses a different concatenation character. SQL Server uses a single plus (+) sign to concatenate two columns. Oracle uses two consecutive pipe characters (||), as examples in this section demonstrate.

This first example demonstrates how concatenation is performed in SQL Server. You can see that you are concatenating the FirstName and LastName columns from the Users table. You specify the FirstName column in the SELECT statement followed by the concatenation character of a plus sign. Because you want a space to appear between the first and last names, you include this space between single quote marks as a string literal and then use another concatenation character followed by the LastName column. Concatenated columns will be displayed without a column name so you use a column alias to assign a name to the concatenated results.

```
SELECT FirstName + ' ' + LastName AS UserName
FROM Users
```

This next example demonstrates how concatenation is performed in Oracle. As you can see, the only difference is in the use of the concatenation character, which is two consecutive pipe characters:

```
SELECT FirstName || ' ' || LastName AS UserName
FROM Users
```

Joins

A *join* is a logical relationship between two tables that enables you to select data from both tables. Joins are based on a logical relationship between the tables, such as the primary and foreign keys. This enables two tables to be joined on the common value of the primary key in one table and a foreign key in another table.

Joins do not have to join tables using a primary and foreign key relationship. Any column in the tables being joined that contain the same values can be used. For example, you could join two tables on a column that contains a date value. However, using the primary and foreign key is the typical choice for joins as they provide the logical relationship between the tables. The primary and foreign key columns are also indexed, which greatly improves the efficiency of the join.

Several different types of joins are available in both SQL Server and Oracle. As space is limited, I don't cover each different join in both databases. What I cover are the types of joins that you use in your stored procedures for the Time Tracker application.

Inner or natural join

The default join in SQL Server is referred to as an INNER JOIN, whereas the default join in Oracle is referred to as a *natural* JOIN. The join in both databases operates the same and the SQL statements for the join are the same in both databases. This type of join displays only the rows of data that match the primary and foreign keys in both tables. Because an INNER JOIN or natural JOIN is the default join type for both databases, you can specify this type of join in several ways in both databases.

In the following example, the Roles table is joined to the Users table based on the primary and foreign keys specified in the WHERE clause. The join in this SELECT statement is not very obvious at first glance because you do not see the JOIN clause.

```
SELECT LoginName, RoleName
FROM Users, Roles
WHERE Users.RoleID = Roles.RoleID
```

In this next example, the JOIN clause is specified and the condition of the join is made a part of the JOIN clause. A join in this SQL statement is more obvious with the inclusion of the JOIN clause.

```
SELECT LoginName, RoleName
FROM Users
JOIN Roles ON Users.RoleID = Roles.RoleID
```

In this final example, the full JOIN clause is specified as INNER JOIN, which leaves no doubt as to what type of join is being used. Again, the condition of the join is specified in the JOIN clause.

```
SELECT LoginName, RoleName
FROM Users
INNER JOIN Roles ON Users.RoleID = Roles.RoleID
```

All of the previous examples produce the same results: They select the data from the Users table and all matching rows from the Roles table based on the RoleID in both tables.

LEFT OUTER JOIN

A LEFT OUTER JOIN returns all rows of data from the left table even when there are no matching rows of data in the joined table. This ensures that all rows of data are returned from the primary table and any data that does not match in the joined table is returned as a NULL value. The LEFT OUTER JOIN has the same syntax and works the same way in both SQL Server and Oracle.

Consider the following example, which returns the login name of each user in the Users table as well as the login name of the manager assigned to that user. A NULL value is returned where a manager has not been assigned to a user. This ensures that you get a complete list of all users in the Users table even when no manager has been assigned to that user.

```
SELECT Users.LoginName, Managers.LoginName AS ManagerLogin
FROM Users
LEFT OUTER JOIN Users Managers ON Users.ManagerID = Managers.UserID
```

To give you an idea of the results that you can expect from an LEFT OUTER JOIN, the results of this query are listed here. As you can see, a NULL value is returned where no manager has been assigned to a user and all users in the Users table are listed in the results.

```
LoginName        ManagerLogin
---------------  ---------------
admin            NULL
zmanager         NULL
zuser1           zmanager
zuser2           NULL
```

In this Try It Out, you implement the functionality in your Time Tracker application to display all users and roles in the Admin form. You also create the stored procedures required to display all roles as well as a single role, and all users as well as a single user. Because users can have a manager assigned, you also need a stored procedure to select all managers so they can be displayed in the combo box on the Users screen in the Admin form.

Try It Out   Stored Procedures, Joins, Concatenation, and Column Aliases

To implement this functionality:

1. Open your Time Tracker application in Visual Studio 2005.

2. View the Server Explorer window and click the Auto Hide icon on the window to keep it visible and then view the Stored Procedures node for your database.

3. Readers using SQL Server should right-click the Stored Procedures and choose Add New Stored Procedure from the context menu. Readers using Oracle should use their favorite Oracle tool such as iSQL *Plus to create the stored procedures. Enter the code for the following stored procedure:

SQL Server

```
CREATE PROCEDURE usp_SelectRoles
AS
SELECT RoleID, RoleName, RoleDescription, Ranking, LastUpdateDate
FROM ROLES
ORDER BY Ranking, RoleName
```

Click the Save icon on the toolbar to create the stored procedure.

Oracle

```
CREATE OR REPLACE PACKAGE RolesPackage
AS
    TYPE CURSOR_TYPE IS REF CURSOR;
    PROCEDURE usp_SelectRoles (results_cursor OUT CURSOR_TYPE);
END;
```

Click the Execute button to create the package in your database and then enter the following code to create the package body:

```
CREATE OR REPLACE PACKAGE BODY RolesPackage
AS
    PROCEDURE usp_SelectRoles (results_cursor OUT CURSOR_TYPE)
    AS
    BEGIN
       OPEN results_cursor FOR
       SELECT RoleID, RoleName, RoleDescription, Ranking, LastUpdateDate
       FROM ROLES
       ORDER BY Ranking, RoleName;
    END;
END;
```

Click the Execute button to have the package body created in your database.

4. The next stored procedure that you want to create is the `usp_SelectRole` stored procedure, which selects a single role from the database. SQL Server users should right-click the Stored Procedures node in the Server Explorer and choose Add New Stored Procedure and Oracle users should use their Oracle tool. Enter the following code:

SQL Server

```
CREATE PROCEDURE usp_SelectRole
(
    @RoleID    UNIQUEIDENTIFIER
)
AS
SELECT RoleID, RoleName, RoleDescription, Ranking, LastUpdateDate
FROM ROLES
WHERE RoleID = @RoleID
```

Click the Save icon on the toolbar to have the stored procedure created in your database.

Oracle

Enter the following code to create the package:

```
CREATE OR REPLACE PACKAGE RolePackage
AS
    TYPE  CURSOR_TYPE IS REF CURSOR;
    PROCEDURE usp_SelectRole (inRoleID IN CHAR, results_cursor OUT CURSOR_TYPE);
END;
```

Click the Execute button to create the package in your database and then enter the following code to create the package body:

```
CREATE OR REPLACE PACKAGE BODY RolePackage
AS
    PROCEDURE usp_SelectRole (inRoleID IN CHAR, results_cursor OUT CURSOR_TYPE)
    AS
    BEGIN
        OPEN results_cursor FOR
        SELECT RoleID, RoleName, RoleDescription, Ranking, LastUpdateDate
        FROM ROLES
        WHERE RoleID = inRoleID;
    END;
END;
```

Click the Execute button to have the package body created in your database.

5. The next stored procedure to create is the `usp_SelectUsers` stored procedure, which returns all users in the Users table. SQL Server users should right-click the Stored Procedures node in the Server Explorer and choose Add New Stored Procedure and Oracle users should use their Oracle tool. Enter the following code:

SQL Server

```
CREATE PROCEDURE usp_SelectUsers
AS
SELECT UserID, LoginName, FirstName + ' ' + LastName AS UserName,
    Email, Phone, Status
FROM Users
ORDER BY UserName
```

Click the Save icon on the toolbar to have the stored procedure created in your database.

Oracle

Enter the following code to create the package:

```
CREATE OR REPLACE PACKAGE UsersPackage
AS
    TYPE CURSOR_TYPE IS REF CURSOR;
    PROCEDURE usp_SelectUsers (results_cursor OUT CURSOR_TYPE),
END;
```

Click the Execute button to create the package in your database and then enter the following code to create the package body:

```
CREATE OR REPLACE PACKAGE BODY UsersPackage
AS
    PROCEDURE usp_SelectUsers (results_cursor OUT CURSOR_TYPE)
    AS
    BEGIN
        OPEN results_cursor FOR
        SELECT UserID, LoginName, FirstName || ' ' || LastName AS UserName,
            Email, Phone, Status
        FROM Users
        ORDER BY UserName;
    END;
END;
```

Click the Execute button to have the package body created in your database.

6. Now you create the `usp_SelectUser` stored procedure to select the details for a single user from the Users table. SQL Server users should right-click the Stored Procedures node in the Server Explorer and choose Add New Stored Procedure and Oracle users should use their Oracle tool. Enter the following code:

SQL Server

```
CREATE PROCEDURE usp_SelectUser
(
    @UserID    UNIQUEIDENTIFIER
)
AS
SELECT UserID, LoginName, FirstName, LastName,
    Email, Phone, Status, GroupID, RoleID, ManagerID, LastUpdateDate
FROM Users
WHERE UserID = @UserID
```

Click the Save icon on the toolbar to have the stored procedure created in your database.

Oracle

Enter the following code to create the package:

```
CREATE OR REPLACE PACKAGE UserPackage
AS
    TYPE  CURSOR_TYPE IS REF CURSOR;
    PROCEDURE usp_SelectUser (inUserID IN CHAR, results_cursor OUT CURSOR_TYPE);
END;
```

Click the Execute button to create the package in your database and then enter the following code to create the package body:

```
CREATE OR REPLACE PACKAGE BODY UserPackage
AS
    PROCEDURE usp_SelectUser (inUserID IN CHAR, results_cursor OUT CURSOR_TYPE)
    AS
    BEGIN
       OPEN results_cursor FOR
       SELECT UserID, LoginName, FirstName, LastName,
          Email, Phone, Status, GroupID, RoleID, ManagerID, LastUpdateDate
       FROM Users
       WHERE UserID = inUserID;
    END;
END;
```

Click the Execute button to have the package body created in your database.

7. The final stored procedure for this exercise is the `usp_SelectManagers` stored procedure. This stored procedure returns all managers in the Users table. SQL Server users should right-click the Stored Procedures node in the Server Explorer and choose Add New Stored Procedure and Oracle users should use their Oracle tool. Enter the following code:

SQL Server

```
CREATE PROCEDURE usp_SelectManagers
AS
SELECT UserID AS ManagerID, FirstName + ' ' + LastName AS ManagerName
FROM Users
JOIN Roles ON Users.RoleID = Roles.RoleID
WHERE UPPER(RoleName) LIKE '%MANAGER%'
```

Click the Save icon on the toolbar to have the stored procedure created in your database.

Oracle

Enter the following code to create the package:

```
CREATE OR REPLACE PACKAGE ManagersPackage
AS
    TYPE CURSOR_TYPE IS REF CURSOR;
    PROCEDURE usp_SelectManagers (results_cursor OUT CURSOR_TYPE);
END;
```

Click the Execute button to create the package in your database and then enter the following code to create the package body:

```
CREATE OR REPLACE PACKAGE BODY ManagersPackage
AS
    PROCEDURE usp_SelectManagers (results_cursor OUT CURSOR_TYPE)
    AS
    BEGIN
        OPEN results_cursor FOR
        SELECT UserID AS ManagerID, FirstName || ' ' || LastName AS ManagerName
        FROM Users
        JOIN Roles ON Users.RoleID = Roles.RoleID
        WHERE UPPER(RoleName) LIKE '%MANAGER%';
    END;
END;
```

Click the Execute button to have the package body created in your database.

8. Now it's time to modify your data access component to execute these stored procedures. View the code for the WDARoles class and add the following function to return all roles:

SQL Server

```
Public Function GetRoles() As DataSet
    Try
        GetRoles = New DataSet
        MyBase.SQL = "usp_SelectRoles"
        'Fill the DataSet
        MyBase.FillDataSet(GetRoles, "Roles")
    Catch ExceptionErr As Exception
        Throw New System.Exception(ExceptionErr.Message, _
        ExceptionErr.InnerException)
    End Try
End Function
```

Oracle

```
Public Function GetRoles() As DataSet
    Try
        GetRoles = New DataSet
        MyBase.SQL = "RolesPackage.usp_SelectRoles"
        'Initialize the Command object
        MyBase.InitializeCommand()
        'Add a Parameter to the Parameters collection
        MyBase.AddParameter("results_cursor", _
            OracleClient.OracleType.Cursor, ParameterDirection.Output)
        'Fill the DataSet
        MyBase.FillDataSet(GetRoles, "Roles")
    Catch ExceptionErr As Exception
        Throw New System.Exception(ExceptionErr.Message, _
        ExceptionErr.InnerException)
    End Try
End Function
```

9. The GetRole function is next and returns the details for a single role in the Roles table. Add the following function to the WDARoles class:

SQL Server

```
Public Function GetRole(ByVal RoleID As Guid) As DataSet
    Try
        GetRole = New DataSet
        MyBase.SQL = "usp_SelectRole"
        'Initialize the Command object
        MyBase.InitializeCommand()
        'Add a Parameter to the Parameters collection
        MyBase.AddParameter("@RoleID", SqlDbType.UniqueIdentifier, _
            16, RoleID)
        'Fill the DataSet
        MyBase.FillDataSet(GetRole, "Role")
    Catch ExceptionErr As Exception
        Throw New System.Exception(ExceptionErr.Message, _
        ExceptionErr.InnerException)
    End Try
End Function
```

Oracle

```
Public Function GetRole(ByVal RoleID As Guid) As DataSet
    Try
        GetRole = New DataSet
        MyBase.SQL = "RolePackage.usp_SelectRole"
        'Initialize the Command object
        MyBase.InitializeCommand()
        'Add a Parameter to the Parameters collection
        MyBase.AddParameter("inRoleID", OracleClient.OracleType.Char, _
            36, RoleID.ToString)
        MyBase.AddParameter("results_cursor", _
            OracleClient.OracleType.Cursor, ParameterDirection.Output)
        'Fill the DataSet
        MyBase.FillDataSet(GetRole, "Role")
```

```
        Catch ExceptionErr As Exception
            Throw New System.Exception(ExceptionErr.Message, _
            ExceptionErr.InnerException)
        End Try
    End Function
```

10. Now view the code for the WDAUsers class and add the following code for the GetUsers function, which will return all users in the Users table:

SQL Server

```
Public Function GetUsers() As DataSet
    Try
        GetUsers = New DataSet
        MyBase.SQL = "usp_SelectUsers"
        'Fill the DataSet
        MyBase.FillDataSet(GetUsers, "Users")
    Catch ExceptionErr As Exception
        Throw New System.Exception(ExceptionErr.Message, _
        ExceptionErr.InnerException)
    End Try
End Function
```

Oracle

```
Public Function GetUsers() As DataSet
    Try
        GetUsers = New DataSet
        MyBase.SQL = "UsersPackage.usp_SelectUsers"
        'Initialize the Command object
        MyBase.InitializeCommand()
        'Add a Parameter to the Parameters collection
        MyBase.AddParameter("results_cursor", _
            OracleClient.OracleType.Cursor, ParameterDirection.Output)
        'Fill the DataSet
        MyBase.FillDataSet(GetUsers, "Users")
    Catch ExceptionErr As Exception
        Throw New System.Exception(ExceptionErr.Message, _
        ExceptionErr.InnerException)
    End Try
End Function
```

11. The GetUser function is next and returns the details for a single user from the Users table. Add the following code to your class:

SQL Server

```
Public Function GetUser(ByVal UserID As Guid) As DataSet
    Try
        GetUser = New DataSet
        MyBase.SQL = "usp_SelectUser"
        'Initialize the Command object
        MyBase.InitializeCommand()
        'Add a Parameter to the Parameters collection
        MyBase.AddParameter("@UserID", SqlDbType.UniqueIdentifier, _
            16, UserID)
```

```
          'Fill the DataSet
          MyBase.FillDataSet(GetUser, "User")
     Catch ExceptionErr As Exception
          Throw New System.Exception(ExceptionErr.Message, _
          ExceptionErr.InnerException)
     End Try
End Function
```

Oracle

```
Public Function GetUser(ByVal UserID As Guid) As DataSet
     Try
          GetUser = New DataSet
          MyBase.SQL = "UserPackage.usp_SelectUser"
          'Initialize the Command object
          MyBase.InitializeCommand()
          'Add a Parameter to the Parameters collection
          MyBase.AddParameter("inUserID", OracleClient.OracleType.Char, _
               36, UserID.ToString)
          MyBase.AddParameter("results_cursor", _
               OracleClient.OracleType.Cursor, ParameterDirection.Output)
          'Fill the DataSet
          MyBase.FillDataSet(GetUser, "User")
     Catch ExceptionErr As Exception
          Throw New System.Exception(ExceptionErr.Message, _
          ExceptionErr.InnerException)
     End Try
End Function
```

12.   The final function to add to the WDAUsers class is the GetManagers function. This function returns a DataSet of all managers in the Users table. Add the following code:

SQL Server

```
Public Function GetManagers() As DataSet
     Try
          GetManagers = New DataSet
          MyBase.SQL = "usp_SelectManagers"
          'Fill the DataSet
          MyBase.FillDataSet(GetManagers, "Managers")
     Catch ExceptionErr As Exception
          Throw New System.Exception(ExceptionErr.Message, _
          ExceptionErr.InnerException)
     End Try
End Function
```

Oracle

```
Public Function GetManagers() As DataSet
     Try
          GetManagers = New DataSet
          MyBase.SQL = "ManagersPackage.usp_SelectManagers"
          'Initialize the Command object
          MyBase.InitializeCommand()
          'Add a Parameter to the Parameters collection
          MyBase.AddParameter("results_cursor", _
```

```
                OracleClient.OracleType.Cursor, ParameterDirection.Output)
            'Fill the DataSet
            MyBase.FillDataSet(GetManagers, "Managers")
        Catch ExceptionErr As Exception
            Throw New System.Exception(ExceptionErr.Message, _
            ExceptionErr.InnerException)
        End Try
    End Function
```

13. Now you want to switch to your business logic component and add the necessary functions to call the corresponding functions in the data access component. View the code for the WBLRoles class first and add the following function:

```
Public Function GetRoles() As DataSet
    Try
        'Call the data component to get all roles
        GetRoles = objWDARoles.GetRoles
    Catch ExceptionErr As Exception
        Throw New System.Exception(ExceptionErr.Message, _
            ExceptionErr.InnerException)
    End Try
End Function
```

14. The GetRole function is next and returns the details for a single role. Add this function to your class:

```
Public Function GetRole(ByVal RoleID As Guid) As DataSet
    Try
        'Call the data component to get a specific role
        GetRole = objWDARoles.GetRole(RoleID)
    Catch ExceptionErr As Exception
        Throw New System.Exception(ExceptionErr.Message, _
            ExceptionErr.InnerException)
    End Try
End Function
```

15. You want to view the code in the WBLUsers class next and add the GetUsers function listed here:

```
Public Function GetUsers() As DataSet
    Try
        'Call the data component to get all user
        GetUsers = objWDAUsers.GetUsers
    Catch ExceptionErr As Exception
        Throw New System.Exception(ExceptionErr.Message, _
            ExceptionErr.InnerException)
    End Try
End Function
```

16. The GetUser function is next and returns the details for a single user. Add this function to your class:

```
Public Function GetUser(ByVal UserID As Guid) As DataSet
    Try
        'Call the data component to get a specific user
        GetUser = objWDAUsers.GetUser(UserID)
```

```
        Catch ExceptionErr As Exception
            Throw New System.Exception(ExceptionErr.Message, _
                ExceptionErr.InnerException)
        End Try
    End Function
```

17. The final function to add to the WBLUsers class is the GetManagers function. Add the following code to this class:

```
Public Function GetManagers() As DataSet
    Try
        'Call the data component to get all user
        GetManagers = objWDAUsers.GetManagers
    Catch ExceptionErr As Exception
        Throw New System.Exception(ExceptionErr.Message, _
            ExceptionErr.InnerException)
    End Try
End Function
```

18. Now you want to view the code for the Admin form in the Time Tracker project and make the necessary modifications to get the roles, users, and managers. First you add some variable declarations for the DataSets to hold the roles, users, and managers. Add these declarations as shown:

```
Private objGroupProjectsDS As Data.DataSet
Private objRolesDS As Data.DataSet
Private objUsersDS As Data.DataSet
Private objManagersDS As Data.DataSet
```

19. The LoadRoles procedure is added next to load the list of roles in the ListView control and bind it to the combo box on the Users screen. Add the following code:

```
Private Sub LoadRoles()
    'Declare variables
    Dim objListViewItem As ListViewItem

    'Turn the loading flag on so no items are processed
    blnLoading = True

    'Initialize a new instance of the business logic component
    Using objRoles As New WroxBusinessLogic.WBLRoles( _
        strCompany, strApplication)

        Try
            'Clear previous data bindings
            cboUserRole.DataSource = Nothing
            cboUserRole.DisplayMember = String.Empty
            cboUserRole.ValueMember = String.Empty

            'Get all roles in a DataSet object
            objRolesDS = objRoles.GetRoles()

            'Clear previous list
            lvwRoles.Items.Clear()

            'Process all rows
```

```
                For intIndex = 0 To objRolesDS.Tables("Roles").Rows.Count - 1
                    'Create a new listview item
                    objListViewItem = New ListViewItem
                    'Add the data to the listview item
                    objListViewItem.Text = _
                        objRolesDS.Tables("Roles").Rows(intIndex).Item("RoleName")
                    objListViewItem.Tag = _
                        objRolesDS.Tables("Roles").Rows(intIndex).Item("RoleID")
                    'Add the sub items to the listview item
                    objListViewItem.SubItems.Add( _
                        objRolesDS.Tables("Roles").Rows(intIndex).Item( _
                        "RoleDescription"))
                    objListViewItem.SubItems.Add( _
                        objRolesDS.Tables("Roles").Rows(intIndex).Item("Ranking"))
                    objListViewItem.SubItems.Add( _
                        Format(objRolesDS.Tables("Roles").Rows( _
                        intIndex).Item("LastUpdateDate"), "g"))
                    'Add the listview item to the listview control
                    lvwRoles.Items.Add(objListViewItem)
                Next

                'Rebind ComboBox control
                cboUserRole.DataSource = objRolesDS.Tables("Roles")
                cboUserRole.DisplayMember = "RoleName"
                cboUserRole.ValueMember = "RoleID"

                'Reset the selected index
                cboUserRole.SelectedIndex = -1
            Catch ExceptionErr As Exception
                MessageBox.Show(ExceptionErr.Message, strAppTitle)
            Finally
                'Cleanup
                objListViewItem = Nothing
            End Try
        End Using

        'Turn off loading switch
        blnLoading = False
End Sub
```

20. When you click a role in the ListView control, you want the details of that role displayed in the detail section of the Roles screen. In the Class Name combo box at the top of the Code Editor, select lvwRoles and in the Method Name combo box, select the Click event. Add the following code to this procedure:

```
Private Sub lvwRoles_Click(ByVal sender As Object, _
    ByVal e As System.EventArgs) Handles lvwRoles.Click

        'Initialize a new instance of the business logic component
        Using objRoles As New WroxBusinessLogic.WBLRoles( _
            strCompany, strApplication)

            Try
                'Get the specific role selected in the ListView control
                objDataSet = objRoles.GetRole( _
```

```
                    New Guid(lvwRoles.SelectedItems.Item(0).Tag.ToString))

            'Populate the Role Details section
            txtRoleID.Text = _
                objDataSet.Tables("Role").Rows(0).Item( _
                "RoleID").ToString.ToUpper
            txtRoleName.Text = _
                objDataSet.Tables("Role").Rows(0).Item("RoleName")
            txtRoleDescription.Text = _
                objDataSet.Tables("Role").Rows(0).Item( _
                "RoleDescription")
            txtRanking.Text = _
                objDataSet.Tables("Role").Rows(0).Item("Ranking")
            txtRoleUpdateDate.Text = _
                objDataSet.Tables("Role").Rows(0).Item("LastUpdateDate")

        Catch ExceptionErr As Exception
            MessageBox.Show(ExceptionErr.Message, strAppTitle)
        End Try
    End Using
End Sub
```

21. The `LoadUsers` procedure is next and loads the ListView control on the Users screen with all the users. Add the following code to your project:

```
Private Sub LoadUsers()
    'Declare variables
    Dim objListViewItem As ListViewItem

    'Initialize a new instance of the business logic component
    Using objUsers As New WroxBusinessLogic.WBLUsers( _
        strCompany, strApplication)

        Try
            'Get all users in a DataSet object
            objUsersDS = objUsers.GetUsers()

            'Clear previous list
            lvwUsers.Items.Clear()

            'Process all rows
            For intIndex = 0 To objUsersDS.Tables("Users").Rows.Count - 1
                'Create a new listview item
                objListViewItem = New ListViewItem
                'Add the data to the listview item
                objListViewItem.Text = _
                    objUsersDS.Tables("Users").Rows(intIndex).Item( _
                    "LoginName")
                objListViewItem.Tag = _
                    objUsersDS.Tables("Users").Rows(intIndex).Item( _
                    "UserID")
                'Add the sub items to the listview item
                objListViewItem.SubItems.Add( _
                    objUsersDS.Tables("Users").Rows(intIndex).Item( _
                    "UserName"))
```

```
                    objListViewItem.SubItems.Add( _
                        objUsersDS.Tables("Users").Rows(intIndex).Item( _
                        "Email"))
                    objListViewItem.SubItems.Add( _
                        objUsersDS.Tables("Users").Rows(intIndex).Item( _
                        "Phone"))
                    If objUsersDS.Tables("Users").Rows(intIndex).Item( _
                        "Status") Then
                        objListViewItem.SubItems.Add("Active")
                    Else
                        objListViewItem.SubItems.Add("Suspended")
                    End If
                    'Add the listview item to the listview control
                    lvwUsers.Items.Add(objListViewItem)
                Next

        Catch ExceptionErr As Exception
            MessageBox.Show(ExceptionErr.Message, strAppTitle)
        Finally
            'Cleanup
            objListViewItem = Nothing
        End Try
    End Using
End Sub
```

22. When you click a user in the ListView control, you want the details of that user displayed. To add the appropriate event handler to your code, click the Class Name combo box, select lvwUsers, and in the Method Name combo box select the Click event. Add the following code to the lvwUsers_Click procedure:

```
Private Sub lvwUsers_Click(ByVal sender As Object, _
    ByVal e As System.EventArgs) Handles lvwUsers.Click

        'Initialize a new instance of the business logic component
        Using objUsers As New WroxBusinessLogic.WBLUsers( _
            strCompany, strApplication)

            Try
                'Get the specific user selected in the ListView control
                objDataSet = objUsers.GetUser( _
                    New Guid(lvwUsers.SelectedItems.Item(0).Tag.ToString))

                'Populate the User Details section
                txtUserID.Text = _
                    objDataSet.Tables("User").Rows(0).Item( _
                    "UserID").ToString.ToUpper
                If objDataSet.Tables("User").Rows(0).Item("Status") Then
                    optStatusActive.Checked = True
                Else
                    optStatusSuspended.Checked = True
                End If
                txtLogin.Text = _
                    objDataSet.Tables("User").Rows(0).Item("LoginName")
                txtPassword.Text = String.Empty
                txtFirstName.Text = _
```

```
                      objDataSet.Tables("User").Rows(0).Item("FirstName")
            txtLastName.Text = _
                      objDataSet.Tables("User").Rows(0).Item("LastName")
            txtEmail.Text = _
                      objDataSet.Tables("User").Rows(0).Item("Email")
            txtPhone.Text = _
                      objDataSet.Tables("User").Rows(0).Item("Phone")
            For intIndex = 0 To objGroupsDS.Tables("Groups").Rows.Count - 1
                If objGroupsDS.Tables("Groups").Rows(intIndex).Item( _
                      "GroupID").ToString = _
                      objDataSet.Tables("User").Rows(0).Item( _
                          "GroupID").ToString Then
                    cboUserGroup.SelectedIndex = intIndex
                    Exit For
                End If
            Next
            For intIndex = 0 To objRolesDS.Tables("Roles").Rows.Count - 1
                If objRolesDS.Tables("Roles").Rows(intIndex).Item( _
                      "RoleID").ToString = _
                      objDataSet.Tables("User").Rows(0).Item( _
                      "RoleID").ToString Then
                    cboUserRole.SelectedIndex = intIndex
                    Exit For
                End If
            Next
            If Not IsDBNull(objDataSet.Tables("User").Rows(0).Item( _
                  "ManagerID")) Then
                For intIndex = 0 To objManagersDS.Tables( _
                      "Managers").Rows.Count - 1
                    If objManagersDS.Tables("Managers").Rows(intIndex).Item( _
                          "ManagerID").ToString = _
                          objDataSet.Tables("User").Rows(0).Item( _
                          "ManagerID").ToString Then
                        cboUserManager.SelectedIndex = intIndex
                        Exit For
                    End If
                Next
            Else
                cboUserManager.SelectedIndex = -1
            End If
            txtUserUpdateDate.Text = _
                      objDataSet.Tables("User").Rows(0).Item("LastUpdateDate")

        Catch ExceptionErr As Exception
            MessageBox.Show(ExceptionErr.Message, strAppTitle)
        End Try
    End Using
End Sub
```

23. The last procedure to be added loads the managers in the combo box on the Users screen. Add the following code:

```
Private Sub LoadManagers()
    'Initialize a new instance of the business logic component
    Using objUsers As New WroxBusinessLogic.WBLUsers( _
```

```
            strCompany, strApplication)

        Try
            'Clear previous data bindings
            cboUserManager.DataSource = Nothing
            cboUserManager.DisplayMember = String.Empty
            cboUserManager.ValueMember = String.Empty

            'Get all manager in a DataSet object
            objManagersDS = objUsers.GetManagers()

            'Rebind ComboBox control
            cboUserManager.DataSource = objManagersDS.Tables("Managers")
            cboUserManager.DisplayMember = "ManagerName"
            cboUserManager.ValueMember = "ManagerID"

            'Reset the selected index
            cboUserManager.SelectedIndex = -1
        Catch ExceptionErr As Exception
            MessageBox.Show(ExceptionErr.Message, strAppTitle)
        End Try
    End Using
End Sub
```

24. You want the roles, users, and managers loaded when the Admin form starts up. To that end, modify the code in the `Admin_Load` event next. Add the following code at the end of this procedure:

```
'Load the Groups
Call LoadGroups()

'Load the Roles
Call LoadRoles()

'Load the Users
Call LoadUsers()

'Load the Managers
Call LoadManagers()

'Display a ready message
ToolStripStatus.Text = "Ready"
```

25. The next step is to modify the `LoadGroups` procedure to bind the `objGroupsDS DataSet` to the Groups combo box on the Users screen. Modify the relevant sections of this procedure as shown here:

```
'Clear previous data bindings
cboGroups.DataSource = Nothing
cboGroups.DisplayMember = String.Empty
cboGroups.ValueMember = String.Empty
cboUserGroup.DataSource = Nothing
cboUserGroup.DisplayMember = String.Empty
```

```
cboUserGroup.ValueMember = String.Empty

  .
  .
  .

'Rebind ComboBox control
cboGroups.DataSource = objGroupsDS.Tables("Groups")
cboGroups.DisplayMember = "GroupName"
cboGroups.ValueMember = "GroupID"
cboUserGroup.DataSource = objGroupsDS.Tables("Groups")
cboUserGroup.DisplayMember = "GroupName"
cboUserGroup.ValueMember = "GroupID"

'Reset the selected index
cboGroups.SelectedIndex = -1
cboUserGroup.SelectedIndex = -1
```

26. The next step is to modify the code under the `Case Roles` statement in the `ActionAdd` procedure to reload the list of roles. Modify the relevant sections of this procedure as shown here:

```
'Clear the input fields
txtRoleID.Text = String.Empty
txtRoleName.Text = String.Empty
txtRoleDescription.Text = String.Empty
txtRanking.Text = String.Empty
txtRoleUpdateDate.Text = String.Empty

'Reload the Roles list
LoadRoles()
```

27. The final step is to modify the code under the `Case Users` statement in the `ActionAdd` procedure to reload the list of users. Modify the relevant sections of this procedure as shown here:

```
'Clear the input fields
txtUserID.Text = String.Empty
txtLogin.Text = String.Empty
txtPassword.Text = String.Empty
txtFirstName.Text = String.Empty
txtLastName.Text = String.Empty
txtEmail.Text = String.Empty
txtPhone.Text = String.Empty
optStatusActive.Checked = True
cboUserGroup.SelectedIndex = -1
cboUserRole.SelectedIndex = -1
cboUserManager.SelectedIndex = -1
txtUserUpdateDate.Text = String.Empty

'Reload the Users list
LoadUsers()
```

You're ready to test your modifications. Start your project and when the Admin form displays, navigate to the Roles screen. You'll see a list of roles displayed. Click a role to view the details of that role, as shown in Figure 12-1.

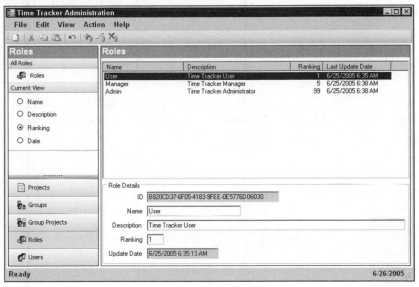

Figure 12-1

Navigate to the Users screen and you see a complete list of users. The combo boxes in the details section of the screen are populated with the appropriate data. Clicking a user in the ListView control causes the details for that user to be displayed, as shown in Figure 12-2.

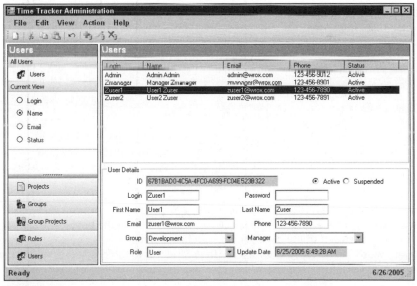

Figure 12-2

How It Works

You start this exercise by creating the `usp_SelectRoles` stored procedure. Readers using Oracle have to create a package for this stored procedure before creating the stored procedure in the package body. This is a simple stored procedure that returns all roles in the Roles table. As this is simple code that you've seen before there is no need to list the code again.

The `usp_SelectRole` stored procedure is next and selects the details for a single role based on the RoleID passed to this stored procedure. Again, it's a simple stored procedure and the code will not be listed again.

The `usp_SelectUsers` stored procedure is created next and implements concatenation and a column alias, which you read about earlier in this chapter. The SELECT statement from this stored procedure is listed next for both SQL Server and Oracle.

In the SQL Server version of this stored procedure, you can see that you are concatenating the first and last name of the user to return the entire user name as a single field in the result set. You specify the FirstName column followed by the plus sign and follow that with a literal string that contains a space. You concatenate the last name to the first name and space by specifying another plus sign and the LastName column. Additionally, you assign a column alias to the results of the concatenation of UserName.

SQL Server

```
SELECT UserID, LoginName, FirstName + ' ' + LastName AS UserName,
    Email, Phone, Status
FROM Users
ORDER BY UserName
```

The Oracle version is the same as the SQL Server version except for the concatenation character used. In Oracle you must use two consecutive pipe characters, as shown in the following code:

Oracle

```
SELECT UserID, LoginName, FirstName || ' ' || LastName AS UserName,
    Email, Phone, Status
FROM Users
ORDER BY UserName;
```

The `usp_SelectUser` stored procedure was next and this stored procedure selects the details for a specific user as specified by the UserID passed to this stored procedure. Because this is simple code that you've seen before there is no need to list it again.

There is one note to make about this stored procedure. You may have noticed that you did not select the password for the user. This is because the password was hashed in the business logic component and the hashed value was stored in the database. Remember that hashing is one-way so there is no need to retrieve the password because you cannot unhash it. Updates to the password will be handled in the stored procedure to update a user, which you create in the next chapter.

The `usp_SelectManagers` stored procedure is created next and in addition to implementing concatenation and a column alias it has a unique WHERE clause. The SELECT statement for this stored procedure is listed here for SQL Server only, as the WHERE clause is the same for both SQL Server and Oracle.

The join used in this stored procedure is an INNER JOIN and joins only the rows in the Roles table where the RoleID in the Users table matches the RoleID in the Roles table. Thus, only the rows of data in the Roles table that exist in the Users table will be returned.

Selecting the managers from the Users table presents a unique challenge because the role names are not fixed and can be added, updated, and deleted. To determine whether a user is a manager you must join the Roles table to the Users table to query the role name to determine whether the user is a manager. The role name could contain the word "manager" in addition to other words and could be in all lowercase, all uppercase, or in mixed case.

The WHERE clause compensates for this by converting the data selected from the RoleName column to all uppercase and uses the LIKE keyword to compare the data in the RoleName column to the fixed string value of %MANAGER%. The LIKE keyword determines whether a string matches a given pattern. The percent (%) signs in the string to be compared against are used as wildcard characters, and by including the percent sign at the beginning and end of the word MANAGER, you are specifying that any role name that contains the word MANAGER is considered a match.

```
SELECT UserID AS ManagerID, FirstName + ' ' + LastName AS ManagerName
FROM Users
JOIN Roles ON Users.RoleID = Roles.RoleID
WHERE UPPER(RoleName) LIKE '%MANAGER%'
```

You modify the WDARoles and WDAUsers classes next in your data access component to implement the functions necessary to execute these stored procedures. These are simple functions that you've coded in the previous chapters and there's no need to list the code again.

The modifications you make to the WBLRoles and WBLUsers classes in the business logic component are also simple and include adding the appropriate functions to call the new functions in the data access component to execute these stored procedures. The code is not listed again for these functions.

You start modifying the Admin form by adding three variable declarations to hold the roles, users, and managers. These DataSets will load the ListView controls for the roles and users and will populate the combo boxes on the Users screen.

```
Private objRolesDS As Data.DataSet
Private objUsersDS As Data.DataSet
Private objManagersDS As Data.DataSet
```

You create the LoadRoles procedure next and this is all very straightforward code that you've seen before. Therefore, I only briefly explain this code. You start this procedure by declaring the variables that will be local to this procedure, which is a variable for the ListViewItem class. Then you turn on the loading flag to prevent code from executing when you load the Roles combo box on the Users screen. Then you initialize a new instance of the business logic component in a Using...End Using block.

```
Private Sub LoadRoles()
    'Declare variables
    Dim objListViewItem As ListViewItem

    'Turn the loading flag on so no items are processed
    blnLoading = True

    'Initialize a new instance of the business logic component
```

```
Using objRoles As New WroxBusinessLogic.WBLRoles( _
    strCompany, strApplication)
```

You implement a `Try...Catch...Finally` block to handle any errors that might occur and to clean up the resources used in this procedure. Inside the `Try` block you clear the previous data bindings in the Roles combo box on the Users screen. Then you call the `GetRoles` method to populate the `objRolesDS` `DataSet`. Next, you clear the ListView control of any previous roles:

```
Try
    'Clear previous data bindings
    cboUserRole.DataSource = Nothing
    cboUserRole.DisplayMember = String.Empty
    cboUserRole.ValueMember = String.Empty

    'Get all roles in a DataSet object
    objRolesDS = objRoles.GetRoles()

    'Clear previous list
    lvwRoles.Items.Clear()
```

You set up a `For...Next` loop to process all rows of data in the `objRolesDS` `DataSet` to load the ListView control with the roles. After the ListView control is loaded, you rebind the `cboUserRole` combo box on the Users screen with the `objRolesDS` `DataSet`:

```
    'Process all rows
    For intIndex = 0 To objRolesDS.Tables("Roles").Rows.Count - 1
        'Create a new listview item
        objListViewItem = New ListViewItem
        'Add the data to the listview item
        objListViewItem.Text = _
            objRolesDS.Tables("Roles").Rows(intIndex).Item("RoleName")
        objListViewItem.Tag = _
            objRolesDS.Tables("Roles").Rows(intIndex).Item("RoleID")
        'Add the sub items to the listview item
        objListViewItem.SubItems.Add( _
            objRolesDS.Tables("Roles").Rows(intIndex).Item( _
            "RoleDescription"))
        objListViewItem.SubItems.Add( _
            objRolesDS.Tables("Roles").Rows(intIndex).Item("Ranking"))
        objListViewItem.SubItems.Add( _
            Format(objRolesDS.Tables("Roles").Rows( _
            intIndex).Item("LastUpdateDate"), "g"))
        'Add the listview item to the listview control
        lvwRoles.Items.Add(objListViewItem)
    Next

    'Rebind ComboBox control
    cboUserRole.DataSource = objRolesDS.Tables("Roles")
    cboUserRole.DisplayMember = "RoleName"
    cboUserRole.ValueMember = "RoleID"

    'Reset the selected index
    cboUserRole.SelectedIndex = -1
```

The final part of this procedure contains the Catch block to handle any errors that might occur, and the Finally block, which contains the necessary code to clean up the resources used in this procedure:

```
        Catch ExceptionErr As Exception
            MessageBox.Show(ExceptionErr.Message, strAppTitle)
        Finally
            'Cleanup
            objListViewItem = Nothing
        End Try
    End Using

    'Turn off loading switch
    blnLoading = False
End Sub
```

The lvwRoles_Click procedure is created next and contains the necessary code to get the details for a specific role and display those details in the details section of the Roles screen. You start this procedure by adding the code to initialize a new instance of the business logic component. Then you set up a Try...Catch block to process the data and handle any errors that might occur.

Inside the Try block, you get the details of a specific role in the objDataSet DataSet and process that data, populating the text boxes on the Roles screen. The Catch block contains the code to display an error if one should occur.

```
    Private Sub lvwRoles_Click(ByVal sender As Object, _
        ByVal e As System.EventArgs) Handles lvwRoles.Click

        'Initialize a new instance of the business logic component
        Using objRoles As New WroxBusinessLogic.WBLRoles( _
            strCompany, strApplication)

            Try
                'Get the specific role selected in the ListView control
                objDataSet = objRoles.GetRole( _
                    New Guid(lvwRoles.SelectedItems.Item(0).Tag.ToString))

                'Populate the Role Details section
                txtRoleID.Text = _
                    objDataSet.Tables("Role").Rows(0).Item( _
                    "RoleID").ToString.ToUpper
                txtRoleName.Text = _
                    objDataSet.Tables("Role").Rows(0).Item("RoleName")
                txtRoleDescription.Text = _
                    objDataSet.Tables("Role").Rows(0).Item( _
                    "RoleDescription")
                txtRanking.Text = _
                    objDataSet.Tables("Role").Rows(0).Item("Ranking")
                txtRoleUpdateDate.Text = _
                    objDataSet.Tables("Role").Rows(0).Item("LastUpdateDate")

            Catch ExceptionErr As Exception
                MessageBox.Show(ExceptionErr.Message, strAppTitle)
            End Try
        End Using
    End Sub
```

The LoadUsers procedure is added next to populate the ListView control on the Users screen. The first thing you do in this procedure is declare a variable for the ListViewItem class. Then you initialize a new instance of the business logic component. Again, you incorporate a Try...Catch...Finally block to handle any errors and to execute your cleanup code:

```
Private Sub LoadUsers()
    'Declare variables
    Dim objListViewItem As ListViewItem

    'Initialize a new instance of the business logic component
    Using objUsers As New WroxBusinessLogic.WBLUsers( _
        strCompany, strApplication)
```

Inside the Try block, you call the GetUsers method in the business logic component to return a list of users in the objUsersDS DataSet. Then you clear the ListView control on the Users screen of any previous list of users.

Next, you set up a For...Next loop to process all users in the objUsersDS DataSet, adding them to the ListView control. Notice that when adding the user's name to the objListViewItem object, you access the data in the DataSet using the column alias of UserName that you assigned in your usp_SelectUsers stored procedure.

The Status column in the Users table contains a value of 0 or 1, with 1 being an active user. That works nicely for you because a Boolean is returned in the Status column of the DataSet. To that end, you are able to use the Status column in the DataSet as a Boolean variable to determine whether a user is active or suspended and can display the appropriate text in the ListView control using an If...Then statement to test the value in the Status column:

```
Try
    'Get all users in a DataSet object
    objUsersDS = objUsers.GetUsers()

    'Clear previous list
    lvwUsers.Items.Clear()

    'Process all rows
    For intIndex = 0 To objUsersDS.Tables("Users").Rows.Count - 1
        'Create a new listview item
        objListViewItem = New ListViewItem
        'Add the data to the listview item
        objListViewItem.Text = _
            objUsersDS.Tables("Users").Rows(intIndex).Item( _
            "LoginName")
        objListViewItem.Tag = _
            objUsersDS.Tables("Users").Rows(intIndex).Item( _
            "UserID")
        'Add the sub items to the listview item
        objListViewItem.SubItems.Add( _
            objUsersDS.Tables("Users").Rows(intIndex).Item( _
            "UserName"))
        objListViewItem.SubItems.Add( _
            objUsersDS.Tables("Users").Rows(intIndex).Item( _
            "Email"))
```

```
                objListViewItem.SubItems.Add( _
                    objUsersDS.Tables("Users").Rows(intIndex).Item( _
                    "Phone"))
                If objUsersDS.Tables("Users").Rows(intIndex).Item( _
                    "Status") Then
                    objListViewItem.SubItems.Add("Active")
                Else
                    objListViewItem.SubItems.Add("Suspended")
                End If
                'Add the listview item to the listview control
                lvwUsers.Items.Add(objListViewItem)
            Next
```

The final part of this procedure contains the Catch and Finally blocks to handle errors and clean up the resources used in this procedure:

```
            Catch ExceptionErr As Exception
                MessageBox.Show(ExceptionErr.Message, strAppTitle)
            Finally
                'Cleanup
                objListViewItem = Nothing
            End Try
        End Using
    End Sub
```

The lvwUsers_Click procedure is created next and contains a bit of logic so you can select the appropriate entries in the combo boxes displayed in the details section of the Users screen. You start this procedure by initializing a new instance of the business logic component. Then you set up a Try...Catch block to process your data and handle any errors that might occur:

```
    Private Sub lvwUsers_Click(ByVal sender As Object, _
        ByVal e As System.EventArgs) Handles lvwUsers.Click

        'Initialize a new instance of the business logic component
        Using objUsers As New WroxBusinessLogic.WBLUsers( _
            strCompany, strApplication)
```

Inside the Try block, you get the details of a specific user by calling the GetUser method in your business logic component and have those details returned in the objDataSet DataSet. You then populate the fields in the details section of the Users screen:

```
        Try
            'Get the specific user selected in the ListView control
            objDataSet = objUsers.GetUser( _
                New Guid(lvwUsers.SelectedItems.Item(0).Tag.ToString))

            'Populate the User Details section
            txtUserID.Text = _
                objDataSet.Tables("User").Rows(0).Item( _
                "UserID").ToString.ToUpper
            If objDataSet.Tables("User").Rows(0).Item("Status") Then
                optStatusActive.Checked = True
            Else
                optStatusSuspended.Checked = True
```

```
       End If
       txtLogin.Text = _
           objDataSet.Tables("User").Rows(0).Item("LoginName")
       txtPassword.Text = String.Empty
       txtFirstName.Text = _
           objDataSet.Tables("User").Rows(0).Item("FirstName")
       txtLastName.Text = _
           objDataSet.Tables("User").Rows(0).Item("LastName")
       txtEmail.Text = _
           objDataSet.Tables("User").Rows(0).Item("Email")
       txtPhone.Text = _
           objDataSet.Tables("User").Rows(0).Item("Phone")
```

To select the appropriate group that this user belongs to, you must set up a loop to process all the groups in the objGroupsDS DataSet. You compare the GroupID in the objGroupsDS DataSet to the GroupID in the objDataSet DataSet, which contains the selected user. After a match is found, you set the SelectedIndex property of the cboUserGroup combo box using the intIndex variable and exit the For loop, as no further processing needs to be done.

You repeat the same procedure to determine and set the appropriate SelectedIndex for the cboUserRole combo box.

Because a user may not have a manager assigned, you must determine whether the ManagerID in the DataSet contains a DBNull value. You do this by using the IsDBNull function, which returns a True/False value indicating whether the data in this column of the DataSet is null. If the ManagerID exists, you perform the previous process to select the appropriate manager in the combo box.

If the ManagerID column in the DataSet does contain a DBNull value you set the SelectedIndex property of the combo box to a value of -1, which deselects any selected entry:

```
       For intIndex = 0 To objGroupsDS.Tables("Groups").Rows.Count - 1
           If objGroupsDS.Tables("Groups").Rows(intIndex).Item( _
               "GroupID").ToString = _
               objDataSet.Tables("User").Rows(0).Item( _
                   "GroupID").ToString Then
               cboUserGroup.SelectedIndex = intIndex
               Exit For
           End If
       Next
       For intIndex = 0 To objRolesDS.Tables("Roles").Rows.Count - 1
           If objRolesDS.Tables("Roles").Rows(intIndex).Item( _
               "RoleID").ToString = _
               objDataSet.Tables("User").Rows(0).Item( _
               "RoleID").ToString Then
               cboUserRole.SelectedIndex = intIndex
               Exit For
           End If
       Next
       If Not IsDBNull(objDataSet.Tables("User").Rows(0).Item( _
           "ManagerID")) Then
           For intIndex = 0 To objManagersDS.Tables( _
               "Managers").Rows.Count - 1
               If objManagersDS.Tables("Managers").Rows(intIndex).Item( _
                   "ManagerID").ToString = _
```

```
                         objDataSet.Tables("User").Rows(0).Item( _
                         "ManagerID").ToString Then
                         cboUserManager.SelectedIndex = intIndex
                         Exit For
                 End If
            Next
        Else
            cboUserManager.SelectedIndex = -1
        End If
        txtUserUpdateDate.Text = _
             objDataSet.Tables("User").Rows(0).Item("LastUpdateDate")
```

The final part of this procedure handles any exceptions that are thrown:

```
        Catch ExceptionErr As Exception
            MessageBox.Show(ExceptionErr.Message, strAppTitle)
        End Try
    End Using
End Sub
```

The LoadManagers procedure is added next and clears any previous bindings from the cboUserManager combo box on the Users screen, gets a new list of managers in the objManagersDS DataSet, and rebinds the combo box:

```
Private Sub LoadManagers()
    'Initialize a new instance of the business logic component
    Using objUsers As New WroxBusinessLogic.WBLUsers( _
        strCompany, strApplication)

        Try
            'Clear previous data bindings
            cboUserManager.DataSource = Nothing
            cboUserManager.DisplayMember = String.Empty
            cboUserManager.ValueMember = String.Empty

            'Get all manager in a DataSet object
            objManagersDS = objUsers.GetManagers()

            'Rebind ComboBox control
            cboUserManager.DataSource = objManagersDS.Tables("Managers")
            cboUserManager.DisplayMember = "ManagerName"
            cboUserManager.ValueMember = "ManagerID"

            'Reset the selected index
            cboUserManager.SelectedIndex = -1
        Catch ExceptionErr As Exception
            MessageBox.Show(ExceptionErr.Message, strAppTitle)
        End Try
    End Using
End Sub
```

You modify the Admin_Load load event next to call the procedures to load the ListView and ComboBox controls in the Admin form with roles, users, and managers when the form loads:

```
'Load the Roles
Call LoadRoles()

'Load the Users
Call LoadUsers()

'Load the Managers
Call LoadManagers()
```

The next step in your code modifications to the Admin form is to modify the `LoadGroups` procedure to include the `cboUserGroup` combo box on the Users screen when the groups are loaded:

```
cboUserGroup.DataSource = Nothing
cboUserGroup.DisplayMember = String.Empty
cboUserGroup.ValueMember = String.Empty

.
.
.

cboUserGroup.DataSource = objGroupsDS.Tables("Groups")
cboUserGroup.DisplayMember = "GroupName"
cboUserGroup.ValueMember = "GroupID"

.
.
.

cboUserGroup.SelectedIndex = -1
```

The final step in your code modifications to the Admin form is to modify the `ActionAdd` procedure to call the `LoadRoles` and `LoadUsers` procedures after adding a new role or new user. The code is not shown here.

In this next Try It Out, you create the stored procedures necessary to implement some functionality in the TimeSheet and Login forms. You also modify the code in the Main module to call the Login form, and based on who is logging in, you display the Admin form or the TimeSheet form.

Try It Out   Implementing Login and TimeSheet Functionality

To implement this functionality:

1. Open your Time Tracker application in Visual Studio 2005.

2. View the Server Explorer window and click the Auto Hide icon on the window to keep it visible.

3. The first stored procedure to create is `usp_SelectTimeSheet`, which selects the timesheet for a specific week ending date for a specific user. This stored procedure may look daunting at first but it is really simple and will be thoroughly explained in the How It Works section. Readers using SQL Server should right-click the Stored Procedures and choose Add New Stored Procedure from the context menu. Readers using Oracle should use their favorite Oracle tool, such as iSQL *Plus, to create the stored procedures. Enter the code for the following stored procedure:

SQL Server

```
CREATE PROCEDURE usp_SelectTimeSheet
(
    @UserID          UNIQUEIDENTIFIER,
    @WeekEndingDate  DATETIME
)
AS
-- Select the TimeSheetID, Submitted, ProjectID and ProjectName
SELECT TimeSheets.TimeSheetID, Submitted, Projects.ProjectID, ProjectName,
    -- Select the TimeSheetItemID and Hours for Monday
    Monday.TimeSheetItemID AS MondayTimeSheetItemID,
    Monday.Hours AS MondayHours,
    -- Select the TimeSheetItemID and Hours for Tuesday
    Tuesday.TimeSheetItemID AS TuesdayTimeSheetItemID,
    Tuesday.Hours AS TuesdayHours,
    -- Select the TimeSheetItemID and Hours for Wednesday
    Wednesday.TimeSheetItemID AS WednesdayTimeSheetItemID,
    Wednesday.Hours AS WednesdayHours,
    -- Select the TimeSheetItemID and Hours for Thursday
    Thursday.TimeSheetItemID AS ThursdayTimeSheetItemID,
    Thursday.Hours AS ThursdayHours,
    -- Select the TimeSheetItemID and Hours for Friday
    Friday.TimeSheetItemID AS FridayTimeSheetItemID,
    Friday.Hours AS FridayHours
-- TimeSheets is the main table
FROM TimeSheets
-- Join TimeSheetItems table for Monday's data
LEFT OUTER JOIN TimeSheetItems Monday ON
    TimeSheets.TimeSheetID = Monday.TimeSheetID
    AND Monday.TimeSheetDate = DATEADD(day,-4,@WeekEndingDate)
-- Join Projects table for Project names
LEFT OUTER JOIN Projects ON
    Monday.ProjectID = Projects.ProjectID
-- Join TimeSheetItems table for Tuesday's data
LEFT OUTER JOIN TimeSheetItems Tuesday ON
    TimeSheets.TimeSheetID = Tuesday.TimeSheetID
    AND Tuesday.ProjectID = Monday.ProjectID
    AND Tuesday.TimeSheetDate = DATEADD(day,-3,@WeekEndingDate)
-- Join TimeSheetItems table for Wednesday's data
LEFT OUTER JOIN TimeSheetItems Wednesday ON
    TimeSheets.TimeSheetID = Wednesday.TimeSheetID
    AND Wednesday.ProjectID = Monday.ProjectID
    AND Wednesday.TimeSheetDate = DATEADD(day,-2,@WeekEndingDate)
-- Join TimeSheetItems table for Thursday's data
LEFT OUTER JOIN TimeSheetItems Thursday
    ON TimeSheets.TimeSheetID = Thursday.TimeSheetID
    AND Thursday.ProjectID = Monday.ProjectID
    AND Thursday.TimeSheetDate = DATEADD(day,-1,@WeekEndingDate)
-- Join TimeSheetItems table for Friday's data
LEFT OUTER JOIN TimeSheetItems Friday ON
    TimeSheets.TimeSheetID = Friday.TimeSheetID
    AND Friday.ProjectID = Monday.ProjectID
    AND Friday.TimeSheetDate = @WeekEndingDate
-- Search criteria is the WeekEndingDate and UserID
```

```
WHERE WeekEndingDate = @WeekEndingDate
   AND UserID = @UserID
-- Order the results by the SequenceNumber of the projects
ORDER BY SequenceNumber
```

Click the Save icon on the toolbar to create the stored procedure.

Oracle

```
CREATE OR REPLACE PACKAGE TimeSheetPackage
AS
   TYPE CURSOR_TYPE IS REF CURSOR;
   PROCEDURE usp_SelectTimeSheet (inUserID IN CHAR,
      inWeekEndingDate IN DATE, results_cursor OUT CURSOR_TYPE);
END;
```

Click the Execute button to create the package in your database and then enter the following code to create the package body:

```
CREATE OR REPLACE PACKAGE BODY TimeSheetPackage
AS
   PROCEDURE usp_SelectTimeSheet (inUserID IN CHAR,
      inWeekEndingDate IN DATE, results_cursor OUT CURSOR_TYPE)
  AS
  BEGIN
   OPEN results_cursor FOR
   -- Select the TimeSheetID, Submitted, ProjectID and ProjectName
   SELECT TimeSheets.TimeSheetID, Submitted, Projects.ProjectID, ProjectName,
      -- Select the TimeSheetItemID and Hours for Monday
      Monday.TimeSheetItemID AS MondayTimeSheetItemID,
      Monday.Hours AS MondayHours,
      -- Select the TimeSheetItemID and Hours for Tuesday
      Tuesday.TimeSheetItemID AS TuesdayTimeSheetItemID,
      Tuesday.Hours AS TuesdayHours,
      -- Select the TimeSheetItemID and Hours for Wednesday
      Wednesday.TimeSheetItemID AS WednesdayTimeSheetItemID,
      Wednesday.Hours AS WednesdayHours,
      -- Select the TimeSheetItemID and Hours for Thursday
      Thursday.TimeSheetItemID AS ThursdayTimeSheetItemID,
      Thursday.Hours AS ThursdayHours,
      -- Select the TimeSheetItemID and Hours for Friday
      Friday.TimeSheetItemID AS FridayTimeSheetItemID,
      Friday.Hours AS FridayHours
   -- TimeSheets is the main table
   FROM TimeSheets
   -- Join TimeSheetItems table for Monday's data
   LEFT OUTER JOIN TimeSheetItems Monday ON
      TimeSheets.TimeSheetID = Monday.TimeSheetID
      AND Monday.TimeSheetDate = inWeekEndingDate - 4
   -- Join Projects table for Project names
   LEFT OUTER JOIN Projects ON
      Monday.ProjectID = Projects.ProjectID
   -- Join TimeSheetItems table for Tuesday's data
   LEFT OUTER JOIN TimeSheetItems Tuesday ON
      TimeSheets.TimeSheetID = Tuesday.TimeSheetID
```

```
        AND Tuesday.ProjectID = Monday.ProjectID
        AND Tuesday.TimeSheetDate = inWeekEndingDate - 3
    -- Join TimeSheetItems table for Wednesday's data
    LEFT OUTER JOIN TimeSheetItems Wednesday ON
        TimeSheets.TimeSheetID = Wednesday.TimeSheetID
        AND Wednesday.ProjectID = Monday.ProjectID
        AND Wednesday.TimeSheetDate = inWeekEndingDate - 2
    -- Join TimeSheetItems table for Thursday's data
    LEFT OUTER JOIN TimeSheetItems Thursday
        ON TimeSheets.TimeSheetID = Thursday.TimeSheetID
        AND Thursday.ProjectID = Monday.ProjectID
        AND Thursday.TimeSheetDate = inWeekEndingDate - 1
    -- Join TimeSheetItems table for Friday's data
    LEFT OUTER JOIN TimeSheetItems Friday ON
        TimeSheets.TimeSheetID = Friday.TimeSheetID
        AND Friday.ProjectID = Monday.ProjectID
        AND Friday.TimeSheetDate = inWeekEndingDate
    -- Search criteria is the WeekEndingDate and UserID
    WHERE WeekEndingDate = inWeekEndingDate
        AND UserID = inUserID
    -- Order the results by the SequenceNumber of the projects
    ORDER BY SequenceNumber;
    END;
END;
```

Click the Execute button to have the package body created in your database.

4. The next stored procedure to create is the usp_SelectManagerEmployees stored procedure, which selects all employees for a specific manager. SQL Server users should right-click the Stored Procedures node in the Server Explorer and choose Add New Stored Procedure and Oracle users should use their Oracle tool. Enter the following code:

SQL Server

```
CREATE PROCEDURE usp_SelectManagerEmployees
(
    @ManagerID   UNIQUEIDENTIFIER
)
AS
SELECT UserID, FirstName + ' ' + LastName AS EmployeeName
FROM Users
Where ManagerID = @ManagerID
ORDER BY EmployeeName
```

Click the Save icon on the toolbar to have the stored procedure created in your database.

Oracle

Enter the following code to create the package:

```
CREATE OR REPLACE PACKAGE ManagerEmployeesPackage
AS
    TYPE CURSOR_TYPE IS REF CURSOR;
    PROCEDURE usp_SelectManagerEmployees (inManagerID IN CHAR,
        results_cursor OUT CURSOR_TYPE);
END;
```

Click the Execute button to create the package in your database and then enter the following code to create the package body:

```
CREATE OR REPLACE PACKAGE BODY ManagerEmployeesPackage
AS
    PROCEDURE usp_SelectManagerEmployees (inManagerID IN CHAR,
        results_cursor OUT CURSOR_TYPE)
    AS
    BEGIN
        OPEN results_cursor FOR
        SELECT UserID, FirstName || ' ' || LastName AS EmployeeName
        FROM Users
        Where ManagerID = inManagerID
        ORDER BY EmployeeName;
    END;
END;
```

Click the Execute button to have the package body created in your database.

5. The final stored procedure to create for this exercise is usp_ValidateLogin, which validates a user's login and returns the RoleID, UserID, and username, if they were validated, as well as the user's status. SQL Server users should right-click the Stored Procedures node in the Server Explorer and choose Add New Stored Procedure and Oracle users should use their Oracle tool. Enter the following code:

SQL Server

```
CREATE PROCEDURE usp_ValidateLogin
(
    @LoginName    VARCHAR(15),
    @Password     VARCHAR(30)
)
AS
SELECT RoleName, UserID, FirstName + ' ' + LastName AS UserName, Status
FROM Users
JOIN Roles ON Users.RoleID = Roles.RoleID
WHERE UPPER(LoginName) = UPPER(@LoginName) AND Password = @Password
```

Click the Save icon on the toolbar to have the stored procedure created in your database.

Oracle

Enter the following code to create the package:

```
CREATE OR REPLACE PACKAGE ValidateLoginPackage
AS
    TYPE CURSOR_TYPE IS REF CURSOR;
    PROCEDURE usp_ValidateLogin (inLoginName IN CHAR, inPassword IN CHAR,
        results_cursor OUT CURSOR_TYPE);
END;
```

Click the Execute button to create the package in your database and then enter the following code to create the package body:

```
CREATE OR REPLACE PACKAGE BODY ValidateLoginPackage
AS
    PROCEDURE usp_ValidateLogin (inLoginName IN CHAR, inPassword IN CHAR,
```

```
        results_cursor OUT CURSOR_TYPE)
    AS
    BEGIN
        OPEN results_cursor FOR
        SELECT RoleName, UserID, FirstName || ' ' || LastName AS UserName, Status
        FROM Users
        JOIN Roles ON Users.RoleID = Roles.RoleID
        WHERE UPPER(LoginName) = UPPER(inLoginName) AND Password = inPassword;
    END;
END;
```

Click the Execute button to have the package body created in your database.

6. Now you want to start adding code to the WDATimeSheets class in your data access component. The first function to add to this class is the GetTimeSheet function to return a timesheet for a user. View the code for this class and add the following function:

SQL Server

```
Public Function GetTimeSheet(ByVal UserID As Guid, _
    ByVal WeekEndingDate As Date) As DataSet
    Try
        GetTimeSheet = New DataSet
        MyBase.SQL = "usp_SelectTimeSheet"
        'Clear previous Command just in case it has been set
        MyBase.Command = Nothing
        'Initialize the Command object
        MyBase.InitializeCommand()
        'Add the Parameters to the Parameters collection
        MyBase.AddParameter("@UserID", _
            SqlDbType.UniqueIdentifier, 16, UserID)
        MyBase.AddParameter("@WeekEndingDate", _
            SqlDbType.DateTime, 8, WeekEndingDate)
        'Fill the DataSet
        MyBase.FillDataSet(GetTimeSheet, "TimeSheet")
        'Check the DataSet for 0 rows and create a new timesheet
        'if necessary
        If GetTimeSheet.Tables("TimeSheet").Rows.Count = 0 Then
            'Create a now TimeSheet DataSet
            Dim objDataSet As New DataSet
            'Create a DataTable
            Dim objDataTable As DataTable = objDataSet.Tables.Add("TimeSheet")
            'Add the DataColumns to the table
            objDataTable.Columns.Add( _
                "TimeSheetID", Type.GetType("System.Guid"))
            objDataTable.Columns.Add( _
                "UserID", Type.GetType("System.Guid"))
            objDataTable.Columns.Add( _
                "WeekEndingDate", Type.GetType("System.DateTime"))
            'Initialize a datarow object from the TimeSheet DataSet
            Dim objDataRow As DataRow = objDataSet.Tables("TimeSheet").NewRow
            'Set the values in the DataRow
            objDataRow.Item("TimeSheetID") = Guid.NewGuid
            objDataRow.Item("UserID") = UserID
            objDataRow.Item("WeekEndingDate") = WeekEndingDate
            'Add the DataRow to the DataSet
```

```
                    objDataSet.Tables("TimeSheet").Rows.Add(objDataRow)
                    'Add the TimeSheet to the database
                    If Not AddTimeSheet(objDataSet) Then
                        Throw New Exception("Insert TimeSheet Failed")
                    End If
                    'Now perform a recursive call to this procedure
                    Return GetTimeSheet(UserID, WeekEndingDate)
                End If
        Catch ExceptionErr As Exception
            Throw New System.Exception(ExceptionErr.Message, _
            ExceptionErr.InnerException)
        End Try
    End Function
```

Oracle

```
Public Function GetTimeSheet(ByVal UserID As Guid, _
    ByVal WeekEndingDate As Date) As DataSet
    Try
        GetTimeSheet = New DataSet
        MyBase.SQL = "TimeSheetPackage.usp_SelectTimeSheet"
        'Clear previous Command just in case it has been set
        MyBase.Command = Nothing
        'Initialize the Command object
        MyBase.InitializeCommand()
        'Add the Parameters to the Parameters collection
        MyBase.AddParameter("inUserID", _
            OracleClient.OracleType.Char, 36, UserID.ToString)
        MyBase.AddParameter("inWeekEndingDate", _
            OracleClient.OracleType.DateTime, 8, WeekEndingDate)
        MyBase.AddParameter("results_cursor", _
            OracleClient.OracleType.Cursor, ParameterDirection.Output)
        'Fill the DataSet
        MyBase.FillDataSet(GetTimeSheet, "TimeSheet")
        'Check the DataSet for 0 rows and create a new timesheet
        'if necessary
        If GetTimeSheet.Tables("TimeSheet").Rows.Count = 0 Then
            'Create a new TimeSheet DataSet
            Dim objDataSet As New DataSet
            'Create a DataTable
            Dim objDataTable As DataTable = objDataSet.Tables.Add("TimeSheet")
            'Add the DataColumns to the table
            objDataTable.Columns.Add( _
                "TimeSheetID", Type.GetType("System.String"))
            objDataTable.Columns.Add( _
                "UserID", Type.GetType("System.String"))
            objDataTable.Columns.Add( _
                "WeekEndingDate", Type.GetType("System.DateTime"))
            'Initialize a datarow object from the TimeSheet DataSet
            Dim objDataRow As DataRow = objDataSet.Tables("TimeSheet").NewRow
            'Set the values in the DataRow
            objDataRow.Item("TimeSheetID") = Guid.NewGuid.ToString
            objDataRow.Item("UserID") = UserID.ToString
            objDataRow.Item("WeekEndingDate") = WeekEndingDate
            'Add the DataRow to the DataSet
            objDataSet.Tables("TimeSheet").Rows.Add(objDataRow)
```

```
                  'Add the TimeSheet to the database
                  If Not AddTimeSheet(objDataSet) Then
                      Throw New Exception("Insert TimeSheet Failed")
                  End If
                  'Now perform a recursive call to this procedure
                  Return GetTimeSheet(UserID, WeekEndingDate)
              End If
          Catch ExceptionErr As Exception
              Throw New System.Exception(ExceptionErr.Message, _
              ExceptionErr.InnerException)
          End Try
      End Function
```

7. The next function to create is the GetManagerEmployees function. Because this function relates to users, it is created in the WDAUsers class in your data access component. View the code for this class and add the following function:

SQL Server

```
Public Function GetManagerEmployees(ByVal ManagerID As Guid) As DataSet
    Try
        GetManagerEmployees - New DataSet
        MyBase.SQL = "usp_SelectManagerEmployees"
        'Initialize the Command object
        MyBase.InitializeCommand()
        'Add a Parameter to the Parameters collection
        MyBase.AddParameter("@ManagerID", SqlDbType.UniqueIdentifier, _
            16, ManagerID)
        'Fill the DataSet
        MyBase.FillDataSet(GetManagerEmployees, "Employees")
    Catch ExceptionErr As Exception
        Throw New System.Exception(ExceptionErr.Message, _
        ExceptionErr.InnerException)
    End Try
End Function
```

Oracle

```
Public Function GetManagerEmployees(ByVal ManagerID As Guid) As DataSet
    Try
        GetManagerEmployees = New DataSet
        MyBase.SQL = "ManagerEmployeesPackage.usp_SelectManagerEmployees"
        'Initialize the Command object
        MyBase.InitializeCommand()
        'Add a Parameter to the Parameters collection
        MyBase.AddParameter("inManagerID", OracleClient.OracleType.Char, _
            36, ManagerID.ToString)
        MyBase.AddParameter("results_cursor", _
            OracleClient.OracleType.Cursor, ParameterDirection.Output)
        'Fill the DataSet
        MyBase.FillDataSet(GetManagerEmployees, "Employees")
    Catch ExceptionErr As Exception
        Throw New System.Exception(ExceptionErr.Message, _
        ExceptionErr.InnerException)
    End Try
End Function
```

8. The final function to create in the WDAUsers class is the ValidateLogin function. Add the following code to this class:

SQL Server

```
Public Function ValidateLogin(ByVal LoginName As String, _
    ByVal Password As String) As DataSet

    Try
        ValidateLogin = New DataSet
        MyBase.SQL = "usp_ValidateLogin"
        'Initialize the Command object
        MyBase.InitializeCommand()
        'Add the Parameters to the Parameters collection
        MyBase.AddParameter("@LoginName", SqlDbType.VarChar, _
            15, LoginName)
        MyBase.AddParameter("@Password", SqlDbType.VarChar, _
            30, Password)
        'Fill the DataSet
        MyBase.FillDataSet(ValidateLogin, "User")
    Catch ExceptionErr As Exception
        Throw New System.Exception(ExceptionErr.Message, _
        ExceptionErr.InnerException)
    End Try
End Function
```

Oracle

```
Public Function ValidateLogin(ByVal LoginName As String, _
    ByVal Password As String) As DataSet

    Try
        'Initialize a new instance of the Crypto class
        ValidateLogin = New DataSet
        MyBase.SQL = "ValidateLoginPackage.usp_ValidateLogin"
        'Initialize the Command object
        MyBase.InitializeCommand()
        'Add the Parameters to the Parameters collection
        MyBase.AddParameter("inLoginName", OracleClient.OracleType.VarChar, _
            15, LoginName)
        MyBase.AddParameter("inPassword", OracleClient.OracleType.VarChar, _
            30, Password)
        MyBase.AddParameter("results_cursor", _
            OracleClient.OracleType.Cursor, ParameterDirection.Output)
        'Fill the DataSet
        MyBase.FillDataSet(ValidateLogin, "User")
    Catch ExceptionErr As Exception
        Throw New System.Exception(ExceptionErr.Message, _
        ExceptionErr.InnerException)
    End Try
End Function
```

9. Now you need to add the corresponding functions for the data access functions in your business logic component. View the code for the WBLTimeSheets class first and then add the following code:

```
Public Function GetTimeSheet(ByVal UserID As Guid, _
    ByVal WeekEndingDate As Date) As DataSet

    Try
        'Call the data component to get a user timesheet
        GetTimeSheet = objWDATimeSheets.GetTimeSheet(UserID, WeekEndingDate)
    Catch ExceptionErr As Exception
        Throw New System.Exception(ExceptionErr.Message, _
            ExceptionErr.InnerException)
    End Try
End Function
```

10. Now view the code for the WBLUsers class in your business logic component and add the following code:

```
Public Function GetManagerEmployees(ByVal ManagerID As Guid) As DataSet
    Try
        'Call the data component to get the manager's employees
        GetManagerEmployees = objWDAUsers.GetManagerEmployees(ManagerID)
    Catch ExceptionErr As Exception
        Throw New System.Exception(ExceptionErr.Message, _
            ExceptionErr.InnerException)
    End Try
End Function
```

11. The final function to add to the WBLUsers class is the ValidateLogin function. Add the following code to this class:

```
Public Function ValidateLogin(ByVal LoginName As String, _
    ByVal Password As String) As DataSet

    Try
        'Call the data component to get a specific user
        ValidateLogin = objWDAUsers.ValidateLogin(LoginName, _
            HashPassword(Password))
    Catch ExceptionErr As Exception
        Throw New System.Exception(ExceptionErr.Message, _
            ExceptionErr.InnerException)
    End Try
End Function
```

12. You need to add a module to your project that will contain some public variables that will be shared among various forms in your project. Right-click the Time Tracker project in the Solution Explorer and select Add from the context menu and then select Module. In the Add New Item – Time Tracker dialog box, enter a name of **GlobalVariables.vb** and then click the Add button.

13. Add the following global variable declarations to the top of the module:

```
Module GlobalVariables
    'Global variables
    Public g_strUserRole As String = String.Empty
    Public g_strUserID As String
    Public g_strUserName As String
```

14. You modify the `MainEntry` class next so view the code for this class. Modify the `Main` procedure as follows:

```
Sub Main()
        Dim objLogin As New Login
        objLogin.ShowDialog()
        objLogin.Dispose()
        objLogin = Nothing

        If g_strUserRole.Trim.Length > 0 Then
            If g_strUserRole.ToLower Like "admin" Then
                Dim objAdmin As New Admin
                objAdmin.ShowDialog()
                objAdmin.Dispose()
                objAdmin = Nothing
        Else
                Dim objTimeSheet As New TimeSheet
                objTimeSheet.ShowDialog()
                objTimeSheet.Dispose()
                objTimeSheet = Nothing
            End If
        End If
End Sub
```

15. You need to add some logic to the Login form next, so view the code for the Login form. You want to allow a user only three attempts to log in before canceling the login process and closing the Login form. To that end, declare some private variables at the form level by adding the following code:

```
'Declare variables
Private intAttemptCount As Integer = 0
Private blnAllowClosing As Boolean = False
```

16. Create the event handler procedure for the `Click` event of the OK button. In the Class Name combo box at the top of the Code Editor, select `btnOK` and in the Method Name combo box, select the `Click` event. Add the following code to the `btnOK_Click` procedure:

```
Private Sub btnOK_Click(ByVal sender As System.Object, _
    ByVal e As System.EventArgs) Handles btnOK.Click

        'Initialize a new instance of the business logic component
        Using objUsers As New WroxBusinessLogic.WBLUsers("Wrox", "Time Tracker")

            'Validate the user and get their role
            Dim objDataSet As Data.DataSet = objUsers.ValidateLogin( _
                txtLoginName.Text, txtPassword.Text)

            If objDataSet.Tables("User").Rows.Count > 0 Then
                If objDataSet.Tables("User").Rows(0).Item("Status") Then
                    g_strUserRole = objDataSet.Tables("User").Rows(0).Item( _
                        "RoleName")
                    g_strUserID = objDataSet.Tables("User").Rows(0).Item( _
                        "UserID").ToString
                    g_strUserName = objDataSet.Tables("User").Rows(0).Item( _
                        "UserName").ToString
```

```
            Else
                MessageBox.Show("Your account has been suspended." & _
                    ControlChars.CrLf & "Please contact your administrator.", _
                    "Time Tracker", MessageBoxButtons.OK, MessageBoxIcon.Error)
            End If
            blnAllowClosing = True
        Else
            MessageBox.Show("Your credentials were not validated.", _
                "Time Tracker", MessageBoxButtons.OK, MessageBoxIcon.Error)
        End If

        'Clean up
        objDataSet.Dispose()
        objDataSet = Nothing

        'Increment attempt count
        intAttemptCount += 1
    End Using
End Sub
```

17. You want to create the event handler procedure for the Cancel button next. Click the Class Name combo box and select btnCancel and in the Method Name combo box, select the Click event. Add the following code to the btnCancel_Click procedure:

```
Private Sub btnCancel_Click(ByVal sender As System.Object, _
    ByVal e As System.EventArgs) Handles btnCancel.Click
```

```
    blnAllowClosing = True
    Me.Close()
End Sub
```

18. Because the Login form is displayed as a dialog box from the Main procedure, you want to control when the form is closed. To that end, you need to add code to the FormClosing event of the form. In the Class Name combo box, select (Login Events) and in the Method Name combo box select the FormClosing event. Add the following code to the Login_FormClosing event procedure:

```
Private Sub Login_FormClosing(ByVal sender As Object, _
    ByVal e As System.Windows.Forms.FormClosingEventArgs) _
    Handles Me.FormClosing
```

```
    If Not blnAllowClosing Then
        If intAttemptCount < 3 Then
            e.Cancel = True
        End If
    End If
End Sub
```

19. After users enter a password, they can press the Enter key to submit their data, rather than click OK. To handle this, you need to add code to the KeyUp event of the Password text box. Click the Class Name combo box and select txtPassword, and in the Method Name combo box select the KeyUp event. Add the following code to this procedure:

```
Private Sub txtPassword_KeyUp(ByVal sender As Object, _
    ByVal e As System.Windows.Forms.KeyEventArgs) Handles txtPassword.KeyUp
```

```
        If e.KeyCode = Keys.Enter Then
            Call btnOK_Click(sender, e)
        End If
        If blnAllowClosing Then
            Me.Close()
        End If
    End Sub
```

At this point, it would be a good idea to save your project and test the functionality of the Login form. After starting your project, the first form that should be displayed is the Login form shown in Figure 12-3. Click the Cancel button and your project should end.

Start your project again, enter an invalid username and password, and click OK. You'll receive a Message Box dialog box indicating that your credentials were not validated. Click OK in the message box and then click OK on the Login form. Repeat the process two more times and after the third attempt your project will end.

Start your project again and when the Login form displays, enter the Admin username and password and press Enter while in the password field. Your credentials will be validated and the Admin form will be displayed. Close the Admin form and your project will end.

The final test to perform is to validate a user and have the TimeSheet form displayed. Start your project and enter a valid username and password. Once validated, the TimeSheet form will be displayed. Of course, because you have not implemented any code in the TimeSheet form it will be displayed with empty fields. Close the TimeSheet form so that your project ends.

Figure 12-3

Now you complete this exercise by implementing the necessary code in the TimeSheet form to make it functional, so view the code for the TimeSheet form.

1. The first step is to add some variable declarations. Add the following variable declarations at the top of your class:

```
Private intIndex As Integer
Private intTotal As Integer

Private blnEmployeeDisplay As Boolean = True
Private blnLoading As Boolean = True

Private strAppTitle As String
Private strCompany As String = "Wrox"
Private strApplication As String = "Time Tracker"
```

```
Private strUserID As String
Private strManagerID As String

Private objTimeSheets As WroxBusinessLogic.WBLTimeSheets
Private objUsers As WroxBusinessLogic.WBLUsers

Private objDataSet As Data.DataSet
Private objTimeSheetDS As Data.DataSet
Private objEmployees As Data.DataSet

Private objTimeSheetDV As Data.DataView
```

2. Modify the `TimeSheet_Load` procedure as follows. You'll receive an error that the `LoadEmployees`, `GetPreviousWeekEndingDate`, and `GetCurrentWeekEndingDate` procedures are not defined. You can ignore these errors as you create those procedures next:

```
Private Sub TimeSheet_Load(ByVal sender As Object, _
    ByVal e As System.EventArgs) Handles Me.Load

    'Set the current date in the date panel in the status bar
    ToolStripDate.Text = Date.Today

    'Get the process title from the executable name
    strAppTitle = My.Application.Info.Title

    'Hide the managers menu option for regular users
    If g_strUserRole.ToLower Like "user" Then
        EmployeeTimeSheetsToolStripMenuItem.Visible = False
        blnEmployeeDisplay = True
        strUserID = g_strUserID
    Else
        blnEmployeeDisplay = False
        Call EmployeeTimeSheetsToolStripMenuItem_Click(Nothing, Nothing)
        strManagerID = g_strUserID
        Call LoadEmployees()
    End If

    'Display the users name
    lblEmployee.Text &= " " & g_strUserName

    'Load the week ending date combo boxes
    cboWeekEnding.Items.Add(GetPreviousWeekEndingDate)
    cboEmployeeWeekEnding.Items.Add(GetPreviousWeekEndingDate)
    cboWeekEnding.Items.Add(GetCurrentWeekEndingDate)
    cboEmployeeWeekEnding.Items.Add(GetCurrentWeekEndingDate)

    If g_strUserRole.ToLower Like "user" Then
        cboWeekEnding.SelectedIndex = 1
    Else
        cboWeekEnding.SelectedIndex = -1
    End If

    'Turn off the loading flag
    blnLoading = False
End Sub
```

3. Add the `GetCurrentWeekEndingDate` procedure next with the code shown here:

```
Private Function GetCurrentWeekEndingDate() As String
    GetCurrentWeekEndingDate = DateSerial( _
        Year(Now), Month(Now), DateAndTime.Day(Now) - _
        DatePart("w", Now, FirstDayOfWeek.Sunday) + 6)
End Function
```

4. Add the procedure to return the previous week ending date as follows:

```
Private Function GetPreviousWeekEndingDate() As String
    GetPreviousWeekEndingDate = DateSerial( _
        Year(Now), Month(Now), DateAndTime.Day(Now) - _
        DatePart("w", Now, FirstDayOfWeek.Sunday) - 1)
End Function
```

5. Next is the procedure to load the employees, so add the following code. Readers using Oracle need to ensure that the string values for the `DisplayMember` and `ValueMember` properties are in uppercase characters:

```
Private Sub LoadEmployees()
    'Clear previous bindings
    cboEmployee.DataSource = Nothing
    cboEmployee.DisplayMember = String.Empty
    cboEmployee.ValueMember = String.Empty

    'Initialize a new instance of the business logic component
    Using objUsers As New WroxBusinessLogic.WBLUsers( _
        strCompany, strApplication)

        'Get the timesheet for the user
        objEmployees = objUsers.GetManagerEmployees(New Guid(strManagerID))

        'Rebind ComboBox control
        cboEmployee.DataSource = objEmployees.Tables("Employees")
        cboEmployee.DisplayMember = "EmployeeName"
        cboEmployee.ValueMember = "UserID"
    End Using
End Sub
```

6. Add the `LoadTimeSheet` procedure next, which loads the timesheet for the specified user and week ending date. Add the following code:

```
Private Sub LoadTimeSheet(ByVal WeekEndingDate As ComboBox)
    'Clear previous bindings
    grdTimeSheet.DataSource = Nothing
    grdTimeSheet.DataMember = String.Empty
    grdTimeSheet.Columns.Clear()

    'Initialize a new instance of the business logic component
    Using objTimeSheets As New WroxBusinessLogic.WBLTimeSheets( _
        strCompany, strApplication)

        'Get the timesheet for the user
        objTimeSheetDS = objTimeSheets.GetTimeSheet( _
```

```
                New Guid(strUserID), WeekEndingDate.SelectedItem)

'Set the DataView object with the data from the DataSet
objTimeSheetDV = New Data.DataView(objTimeSheetDS.Tables("TimeSheet"))

'Initialize a new DataRowView object
Dim objDataRowView As Data.DataRowView = objTimeSheetDV.AddNew

'Set the values in the columns
objDataRowView("ProjectName") = "Total Hours"

'Calculate and set the total hours for Monday
intTotal = 0
For intIndex = 0 To objTimeSheetDS.Tables("TimeSheet").Rows.Count - 1
    intTotal += objTimeSheetDS.Tables( _
        "TimeSheet").Rows(intIndex).Item("MondayHours")
Next
objDataRowView("MondayHours") = intTotal

'Calculate and set the total hours for Tuesday
intTotal = 0
For intIndex = 0 To objTimeSheetDS.Tables("TimeSheet").Rows.Count - 1
    intTotal += objTimeSheetDS.Tables( _
        "TimeSheet").Rows(intIndex).Item("TuesdayHours")
Next
objDataRowView("TuesdayHours") = intTotal

'Calculate and set the total hours for Wednesday
intTotal = 0
For intIndex = 0 To objTimeSheetDS.Tables("TimeSheet").Rows.Count - 1
    intTotal += objTimeSheetDS.Tables( _
        "TimeSheet").Rows(intIndex).Item("WednesdayHours")
Next
objDataRowView("WednesdayHours") = intTotal

'Calculate and set the total hours for Thursday
intTotal = 0
For intIndex = 0 To objTimeSheetDS.Tables("TimeSheet").Rows.Count - 1
    intTotal += objTimeSheetDS.Tables( _
        "TimeSheet").Rows(intIndex).Item("ThursdayHours")
Next
objDataRowView("ThursdayHours") = intTotal

'Calculate and set the total hours for Friday
intTotal = 0
For intIndex = 0 To objTimeSheetDS.Tables("TimeSheet").Rows.Count - 1
    intTotal += objTimeSheetDS.Tables( _
        "TimeSheet").Rows(intIndex).Item("FridayHours")
Next
objDataRowView("FridayHours") = intTotal

'Commit the changes to the row
objDataRowView.EndEdit()

'Disallow new records
```

```
            objTimeSheetDV.AllowNew = False

            'Bind the DataView to the DataGridView
            grdTimeSheet.AutoGenerateColumns = False
            grdTimeSheet.DataSource = objTimeSheetDV

            'Set the DataGridView properties
            grdTimeSheet.AlternatingRowsDefaultCellStyle.BackColor = _
                Color.WhiteSmoke

            'Create and add DataGridView text box columns
            Dim objColumn As New DataGridViewTextBoxColumn
            With objColumn
                .HeaderText = "Project Name"
                .DataPropertyName = "ProjectName"
                .ReadOnly = True
                .Width = 225
            End With
            grdTimeSheet.Columns.Add(objColumn)

            objColumn = New DataGridViewTextBoxColumn
            With objColumn
                .HeaderText = "Monday"
                .DataPropertyName = "MondayHours"
                .Width = 70
                If objTimeSheetDS.Tables("TimeSheet").Rows(0).Item("Submitted") _
                    Or Not blnEmployeeDisplay Then
                    .ReadOnly = True
                End If
            End With
            grdTimeSheet.Columns.Add(objColumn)

            objColumn = New DataGridViewTextBoxColumn
            With objColumn
                .HeaderText = "Tuesday"
                .DataPropertyName = "TuesdayHours"
                .Width = 70
                If objTimeSheetDS.Tables("TimeSheet").Rows(0).Item("Submitted") _
                    Or Not blnEmployeeDisplay Then
                    .ReadOnly = True
                End If
            End With
            grdTimeSheet.Columns.Add(objColumn)

            objColumn = New DataGridViewTextBoxColumn
            With objColumn
                .HeaderText = "Wednesday"
                .DataPropertyName = "WednesdayHours"
                .Width = 70
                If objTimeSheetDS.Tables("TimeSheet").Rows(0).Item("Submitted") _
                    Or Not blnEmployeeDisplay Then
                    .ReadOnly = True
                End If
            End With
```

```
                    grdTimeSheet.Columns.Add(objColumn)

                    objColumn = New DataGridViewTextBoxColumn
                    With objColumn
                        .HeaderText = "Thursday"
                        .DataPropertyName = "ThursdayHours"
                        .Width = 70
                        If objTimeSheetDS.Tables("TimeSheet").Rows(0).Item("Submitted") _
                            Or Not blnEmployeeDisplay Then
                            .ReadOnly = True
                        End If
                    End With
                    grdTimeSheet.Columns.Add(objColumn)

                    objColumn = New DataGridViewTextBoxColumn
                    With objColumn
                        .HeaderText = "Friday"
                        .DataPropertyName = "FridayHours"
                        .Width = 70
                        If objTimeSheetDS.Tables("TimeSheet").Rows(0).Item("Submitted") _
                            Or Not blnEmployeeDisplay Then
                            .ReadOnly = True
                        End If
                    End With
                    grdTimeSheet.Columns.Add(objColumn)

                    'Change the locked icon if the timesheet is readonly
                    If objTimeSheetDS.Tables("TimeSheet").Rows(0).Item("Submitted") _
                        Or Not blnEmployeeDisplay Then
                        imgStatus.Image = ImageList1.Images(1)
                    Else
                        imgStatus.Image = ImageList1.Images(0)
                    End If
                End Using
        End Sub
```

7. When an employee chooses a new week ending date in the combo box on the TimeSheet form, you want to display the timesheet for the selected week ending date. Click the Class Name combo box and select cboWeekEnding, and in the Method Name combo box select the SelectedIndexChanged event. Add the following code to the cboWeekEnding_SelectedIndexChanged procedure:

```
Private Sub cboWeekEnding_SelectedIndexChanged(ByVal sender As Object, _
    ByVal e As System.EventArgs) Handles cboWeekEnding.SelectedIndexChanged
```

```
    If Not blnEmployeeDisplay And blnLoading Then
        Exit Sub
    End If

    'Load the timesheet
    Call LoadTimeSheet(cboWeekEnding)
End Sub
```

8. The timesheet displays a total row that contains the total number of hours for each day. This total is recalculated every time the user enters a new value in a cell and tabs out of the cell. Click the Class Name combo box and select grdTimeSheet, and in the Method Name combo box select the CurrentCellChanged event. Add the following code to the grdTimeSheet_CurrentCellChanged procedure:

```
Private Sub grdTimeSheet_CurrentCellChanged(ByVal sender As Object, _
    ByVal e As System.EventArgs) Handles grdTimeSheet.CurrentCellChanged
```

```
        'Declare variables
        Dim objDataRowView As Data.DataRowView
        Dim objDataRowTotal As Data.DataRowView

        'Get the total row so we can update the totals
        objDataRowTotal = objTimeSheetDV.Item(objTimeSheetDV.Count - 1)

        'Recalculate Monday's total
        intTotal = 0
        For intIndex As Integer = 0 To objTimeSheetDV.Count - 2
            objDataRowView = objTimeSheetDV.Item(intIndex)
            intTotal += objDataRowView.Item("MondayHours")
        Next
        'Update Monday's total
        objDataRowTotal.Item("MondayHours") = intTotal

        'Recalculate Tuesday's total
        intTotal = 0
        For intIndex As Integer = 0 To objTimeSheetDV.Count - 2
            objDataRowView = objTimeSheetDV.Item(intIndex)
            intTotal += objDataRowView.Item("TuesdayHours")
        Next
        'Update Tuesday's total
        objDataRowTotal.Item("TuesdayHours") = intTotal

        'Recalculate Wednesday's total
        intTotal = 0
        For intIndex As Integer = 0 To objTimeSheetDV.Count - 2
            objDataRowView = objTimeSheetDV.Item(intIndex)
            intTotal += objDataRowView.Item("WednesdayHours")
        Next
        'Update Wednesday's total
        objDataRowTotal.Item("WednesdayHours") = intTotal

        'Recalculate Thursday's total
        intTotal = 0
        For intIndex As Integer = 0 To objTimeSheetDV.Count - 2
            objDataRowView = objTimeSheetDV.Item(intIndex)
            intTotal += objDataRowView.Item("ThursdayHours")
        Next
        'Update Thursday's total
        objDataRowTotal.Item("ThursdayHours") = intTotal

        'Recalculate Friday's total
```

```
        intTotal = 0
        For intIndex As Integer = 0 To objTimeSheetDV.Count - 2
            objDataRowView = objTimeSheetDV.Item(intIndex)
            intTotal += objDataRowView.Item("FridayHours")
        Next
        'Update Friday's total
        objDataRowTotal.Item("FridayHours") = intTotal

        'Commit the changes to the total row
        objDataRowTotal.EndEdit()
    End Sub
```

9. When a manager selects an employee from the `cboEmployee` ComboBox, you want to save the UserID of the selected employee. Click the Class Name combo box and select `cboEmployee`, and in the Method Name combo box select the `SelectedIndexChanged` event. Add the following code to the `cboEmployee_SelectedIndexChanged` procedure:

```
Private Sub cboEmployee_SelectedIndexChanged(ByVal sender As Object, _
    ByVal e As System.EventArgs) Handles cboEmployee.SelectedIndexChanged
```

```
        strUserID = objEmployees.Tables("Employees").Rows( _
            cboEmployee.SelectedIndex).Item("UserID").ToString
    End Sub
```

10. When the manager selects a new week ending date, you want to retrieve the timesheet for the specified employee and week ending date. Click the Class Name combo box and select `cboEmployeeWeekEndingDate`, and in the Method Name combo box select the `SelectedIndexChanged` event. Add the following code to the `cboEmployeeWeekEnding_SelectedIndexChanged` procedure:

```
Private Sub cboEmployeeWeekEnding_SelectedIndexChanged( _
    ByVal sender As Object, ByVal e As System.EventArgs) _
    Handles cboEmployeeWeekEnding.SelectedIndexChanged
```

```
        If blnLoading Then
            Exit Sub
        End If

        'Load the timesheet
        Call LoadTimeSheet(cboEmployeeWeekEnding)
    End Sub
```

That's all the code needed to implement the functionality in the TimeSheet form to display timesheets. You're now ready to test your project, so save it and then start it up. When the Login form is displayed, enter a user who has been assigned to the User role. When the TimeSheet form displays, it automatically displays a timesheet for the current week ending date as shown in Figure 12-4.

Note that this application has been designed to accept input only for Monday through Friday and that the week ending date is always on a Friday. You can test the functionality that was added to recalculate the total hours by entering time in a cell and tabbing to the next cell.

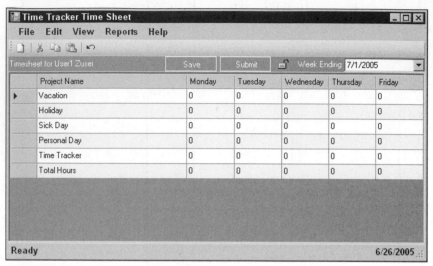

Figure 12-4

To test the functionality for a manager, stop the application and then start it again. When the Login form is displayed, enter a user who has been assigned the Manager role. When the TimeSheet form is displayed, the Employee combo box contains a list of employees, with the first employee automatically selected. The combo box for Week Ending will not have an entry selected so select a week ending date and the grid will be populated with the timesheet for the selected employee and week ending date, as shown in Figure 12-5.

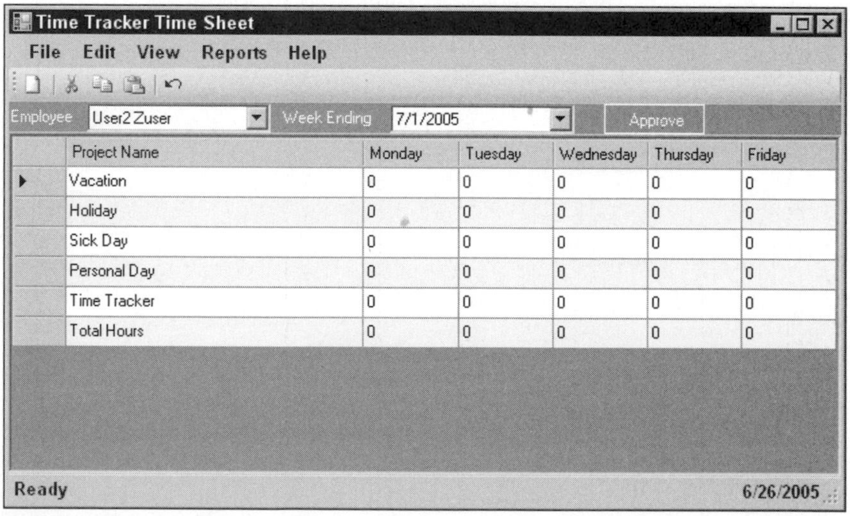

Figure 12-5

How It Works

The first stored procedure that you create is the usp_SelectTimeSheet stored procedure. The data for a timesheet is stored in a relational format in multiple tables and the hours for each project for each day are stored as separate rows of data in a single table. However, you want to display the data in a grid or spreadsheet-style format as shown in Figures 12-4 and 12-5. This is where the power of stored procedures really shines. You can create a stored procedure to select the data in the format needed by using joins, and column and table aliases, and the built-in functions of the database to manipulate date values.

Because this stored procedure is large and there are some subtle differences between SQL Server and Oracle, I go through each stored procedure, starting with the SQL Server version. This stored procedure returns a complete timesheet for a specific user and week ending date. Therefore, there are two input parameters, the UserID and the week ending date.

SQL Server

```
CREATE PROCEDURE usp_SelectTimeSheet
(
    @UserID             UNIQUEIDENTIFIER,
    @WeekEndingDate     DATETIME
)
AS
```

There are a couple of columns of data that you need in every row of data returned by this stored procedure. These are listed in the first line of the SELECT statement. Notice the use of comments throughout this stored procedure. This helps document the code and simplifies maintenance later.

```
-- Select the TimeSheetID, Submitted, ProjectID and ProjectName
SELECT TimeSheets.TimeSheetID, Submitted, Projects.ProjectID, ProjectName,
```

You want to return the hours for each business day of the week for each project in a single row in the result set. This is accomplished by using a LEFT OUTER JOIN and table alias. Then you use the table alias to access each table, selecting the same columns and giving them a new name in the result set using a column alias.

As you can see in the following code, you are selecting the TimeSheetItemID and Hours columns from the Monday table, which is actually the TimeSheetItems table. You then assign a new column name to each by using a column alias of MondayTimeSheetItemID and MondayHours. You repeat this process for each business day of the week so that the hours for each day are listed in a single row for the given project:

```
-- Select the TimeSheetItemID and Hours for Monday
Monday.TimeSheetItemID AS MondayTimeSheetItemID,
Monday.Hours AS MondayHours,
-- Select the TimeSheetItemID and Hours for Tuesday
Tuesday.TimeSheetItemID AS TuesdayTimeSheetItemID,
Tuesday.Hours AS TuesdayHours,
-- Select the TimeSheetItemID and Hours for Wednesday
Wednesday.TimeSheetItemID AS WednesdayTimeSheetItemID,
Wednesday.Hours AS WednesdayHours,
-- Select the TimeSheetItemID and Hours for Thursday
Thursday.TimeSheetItemID AS ThursdayTimeSheetItemID,
Thursday.Hours AS ThursdayHours,
-- Select the TimeSheetItemID and Hours for Friday
Friday.TimeSheetItemID AS FridayTimeSheetItemID,
Friday.Hours AS FridayHours
```

415

The main table you are selecting data from is the TimeSheets table. If you recall from the schema from Chapter 1, the TimeSheets table contains the UserID and week ending date for a timesheet. The TimeSheetItems table contains the details for a timesheet, such as the hours of each project and the date for which the hours are entered.

```
-- TimeSheets is the main table
FROM TimeSheets
```

Next you join the TimeSheetItems table using a LEFT OUTER JOIN to ensure that you are getting only the data that you need, and that if no row exists, a NULL value is returned. You assign a table alias of Monday to this table and specify two criteria for the join. The first criterion is that the TimeSheetID in the TimeSheets table must match the TimeSheetID in the Monday (TimeSheetItems) table. This ensures that you are selecting only the timesheet items for a given user. Next, you specify a criterion for the date in the Monday table, which is calculated to be Monday's date for the week ending date passed to this stored procedure.

The DATEADD function is used to add or subtract from a date and accepts multiple parameters. The first parameter is the date part and has been specified here as day. This instructs the DATEADD function to either subtract or add days to the date that you pass. The next parameter is the number of days to be added or subtracted. If you want to add days, then you specify a positive number; and if you want to subtract days, you specify a negative number, as shown in this example. Finally, you pass the date that you want to use for either adding or subtracting days, which is the date in the input parameter to this stored procedure.

The next table that you join is the Projects table. Again, you are using a LEFT OUTER JOIN to get only the projects that apply to this timesheet. The criterion for the join is the ProjectID in the Monday (TimeSheetItems) table and the ProjectID in the Projects table. This ensures that you get only the projects for which there are timesheet items.

```
-- Join TimeSheetItems table for Monday's data
LEFT OUTER JOIN TimeSheetItems Monday ON
    TimeSheets.TimeSheetID = Monday.TimeSheetID
    AND Monday.TimeSheetDate = DATEADD(day,-4,@WeekEndingDate)
-- Join Projects table for Project names
LEFT OUTER JOIN Projects ON
    Monday.ProjectID = Projects.ProjectID
```

You repeat the process of joining the TimeSheetItems table, assigning a table alias for each business day of the week and incrementing the number of days used in the DATEADD function until you reach the date for Friday, which is the actual week ending date:

```
-- Join TimeSheetItems table for Tuesday's data
LEFT OUTER JOIN TimeSheetItems Tuesday ON
    TimeSheets.TimeSheetID = Tuesday.TimeSheetID
    AND Tuesday.ProjectID = Monday.ProjectID
    AND Tuesday.TimeSheetDate = DATEADD(day,-3,@WeekEndingDate)
    - Join TimeSheetItems table for Wednesday's data
LEFT OUTER JOIN TimeSheetItems Wednesday ON
    TimeSheets.TimeSheetID = Wednesday.TimeSheetID
    AND Wednesday.ProjectID = Monday.ProjectID
    AND Wednesday.TimeSheetDate = DATEADD(day,-2,@WeekEndingDate)
-- Join TimeSheetItems table for Thursday's data
LEFT OUTER JOIN TimeSheetItems Thursday
```

```
        ON TimeSheets.TimeSheetID = Thursday.TimeSheetID
        AND Thursday.ProjectID = Monday.ProjectID
        AND Thursday.TimeSheetDate = DATEADD(day,-1,@WeekEndingDate)
-- Join TimeSheetItems table for Friday's data
LEFT OUTER JOIN TimeSheetItems Friday ON
        TimeSheets.TimeSheetID = Friday.TimeSheetID
        AND Friday.ProjectID = Monday.ProjectID
        AND Friday.TimeSheetDate = @WeekEndingDate
```

The WHERE clause for this stored procedure uses the week ending date and UserID that were passed to this stored procedure as input parameters. The ORDER BY clause orders the results using the SequenceNumber column in the Projects table to ensure that the projects are listed in a consistent manner:

```
-- Search criteria is the WeekEndingDate and UserID
WHERE WeekEndingDate = @WeekEndingDate
    AND UserID = @UserID
-- Order the results by the SequenceNumber of the projects
ORDER BY SequenceNumber
```

The Oracle version of this stored procedure operates in a similar manner. However, because you are returning data from this stored procedure, you must create a package and package body as you have done with your other Oracle stored procedures that return data. Following is the code for the package. It defines the cursor to be used to return the results from the stored procedure and lists the stored procedure and its parameters, which will be defined in the package body.

Oracle

```
CREATE OR REPLACE PACKAGE TimeSheetPackage
AS
    TYPE CURSOR_TYPE IS REF CURSOR;
    PROCEDURE usp_SelectTimeSheet (inUserID IN CHAR,
        inWeekEndingDate IN DATE, results_cursor OUT CURSOR_TYPE);
END;
```

The actual stored procedure is defined in the package body. It accepts the same input parameters as its SQL Server counterpart, with the addition of the cursor to be used to return data. You begin this stored procedure by first opening the cursor to be used to return the data from this stored procedure.

```
CREATE OR REPLACE PACKAGE BODY TimeSheetPackage
AS
    PROCEDURE usp_SelectTimeSheet (inUserID IN CHAR,
        inWeekEndingDate IN DATE, results_cursor OUT CURSOR_TYPE)
    AS
    BEGIN
      OPEN results_cursor FOR
```

The first part of this stored procedure is the same as its SQL Server counterpart and uses column aliases to assign new column names in the result set:

```
-- Select the TimeSheetID, Submitted, ProjectID and ProjectName
SELECT TimeSheets.TimeSheetID, Submitted, Projects.ProjectID, ProjectName,
    -- Select the TimeSheetItemID and Hours for Monday
    Monday.TimeSheetItemID AS MondayTimeSheetItemID,
    Monday.Hours AS MondayHours,
```

```
    -- Select the TimeSheetItemID and Hours for Tuesday
    Tuesday.TimeSheetItemID AS TuesdayTimeSheetItemID,
    Tuesday.Hours AS TuesdayHours,
    -- Select the TimeSheetItemID and Hours for Wednesday
    Wednesday.TimeSheetItemID AS WednesdayTimeSheetItemID,
    Wednesday.Hours AS WednesdayHours,
    -- Select the TimeSheetItemID and Hours for Thursday
    Thursday.TimeSheetItemID AS ThursdayTimeSheetItemID,
    Thursday.Hours AS ThursdayHours,
    -- Select the TimeSheetItemID and Hours for Friday
    Friday.TimeSheetItemID AS FridayTimeSheetItemID,
    Friday.Hours AS FridayHours
```

The subtle differences in this stored procedure are reflected in the way date values are calculated. Oracle does not have a DATEADD function but instead relies on regular arithmetic operations to add and subtract days from a date. As you can see in the following code, you calculate a new date by merely subtracting the number of days from the date specified in the input parameter. The rest of the code is the same as SQL Server and is not explained again.

```
    -- TimeSheets is the main table
    FROM TimeSheets
    -- Join TimeSheetItems table for Monday's data
    LEFT OUTER JOIN TimeSheetItems Monday ON
        TimeSheets.TimeSheetID = Monday.TimeSheetID
        AND Monday.TimeSheetDate = inWeekEndingDate - 4
    -- Join Projects table for Project names
    LEFT OUTER JOIN Projects ON
        Monday.ProjectID = Projects.ProjectID
    -- Join TimeSheetItems table for Tuesday's data
    LEFT OUTER JOIN TimeSheetItems Tuesday ON
        TimeSheets.TimeSheetID = Tuesday.TimeSheetID
        AND Tuesday.ProjectID = Monday.ProjectID
        AND Tuesday.TimeSheetDate = inWeekEndingDate - 3
    -- Join TimeSheetItems table for Wednesday's data
    LEFT OUTER JOIN TimeSheetItems Wednesday ON
        TimeSheets.TimeSheetID = Wednesday.TimeSheetID
        AND Wednesday.ProjectID = Monday.ProjectID
        AND Wednesday.TimeSheetDate = inWeekEndingDate - 2
    -- Join TimeSheetItems table for Thursday's data
    LEFT OUTER JOIN TimeSheetItems Thursday
        ON TimeSheets.TimeSheetID = Thursday.TimeSheetID
        AND Thursday.ProjectID = Monday.ProjectID
        AND Thursday.TimeSheetDate = inWeekEndingDate - 1
    -- Join TimeSheetItems table for Friday's data
    LEFT OUTER JOIN TimeSheetItems Friday ON
        TimeSheets.TimeSheetID = Friday.TimeSheetID
        AND Friday.ProjectID = Monday.ProjectID
        AND Friday.TimeSheetDate = inWeekEndingDate
    -- Search criteria is the WeekEndingDate and UserID
    WHERE WeekEndingDate = inWeekEndingDate
        AND UserID = inUserID
    -- Order the results by the SequenceNumber of the projects
    ORDER BY SequenceNumber;
    END;
END;
```

The next stored procedure created was the usp_SelectManagerEmployees stored procedure. This stored procedure selects all employees assigned to a specific manager, returning their UserIDs and their first and last names as EmployeeName, as shown in the following SELECT statement of the SQL Server version of this stored procedure. The entire stored procedure is not listed to conserve space. The only difference between the SQL Server version and the Oracle version is the concatenation character used. In SQL Server it is a plus (+) sign, as shown in the following code, whereas in Oracle it is two consecutive pipe (||) characters.

```
SELECT UserID, FirstName + ' ' + LastName AS EmployeeName
FROM Users
Where ManagerID = @ManagerID
ORDER BY EmployeeName
```

The final stored procedure that you create in this exercise is the usp_ValidateLogin stored procedure. To conserve space, only the SELECT statement for the SQL Server version is shown here. When a user logs on, certain information is needed to determine which form to display. This information is returned from this stored procedure if the credentials that the user supplied are validated.

You can see that the SELECT statement will return the RoleName for the role that this user has been assigned to as well as the UserID and username. The Status is also returned so you can determine whether the user account is active or suspended. You are selecting data from the Users table and joining the Roles table to get the role name.

The WHERE clause is where things are interesting in this stored procedure. A user might not enter his or her login name in the same upper and lower case characters that it was entered in the Admin form when the user was added, and it shouldn't matter. You really shouldn't validate the case of the login name for a user so this stored procedure converts the LoginName in the WHERE clause to all uppercase characters and converts the login name passed in the input parameter to all uppercase characters when doing the comparison. This allows a user to enter the login name in any manner — all lowercase, all uppercase, or mixed case — and a match will always be made if the login name is found.

The password, however, should be verified in a case-sensitive manner; and as you can see, there is no conversion of the case for a password. If the login name and password passed to this stored procedure as input parameters match the login name and password in the Users table, this stored procedure will return the data listed in the SELECT statement. If they do not match, then this stored procedure returns zero rows of data.

```
SELECT RoleName, UserID, FirstName + ' ' + LastName AS UserName, Status
FROM Users
JOIN Roles ON Users.RoleID = Roles.RoleID
WHERE UPPER(LoginName) = UPPER(@LoginName) AND Password = @Password
```

You start adding code to the WDATimeSheets class next by adding the GetTimeSheet function. The code for the SQL Server version follows; the only difference between this version and the Oracle version is the addition of the parameter for the cursor and the database data types used in the parameters.

This function is unique in that it will first execute the usp_SelectTimeSheet stored procedure and then check for zero rows returned. If no data was returned, it means that a timesheet has not yet been entered for this user, and this function will make a call to the AddTimeSheet function to add the timesheet and then make a recursive call to itself to get the timesheet just added.

This function accepts the UserID and week ending date as input parameters and encapsulates the code in a Try...Catch block. The first thing you do in this function is set the SQL property in the base class to the stored procedure being executed. You clear the Command object in the base class just in case you are making a recursive call to this function; then you initialize the Command object by calling the InitializeCommand method in the base class.

Next, you add the Parameters to the Parameters collection and call the FillDataSet method in the base class to get a DataSet filled with the timesheet data:

```
Public Function GetTimeSheet(ByVal UserID As Guid, _
    ByVal WeekEndingDate As Date) As DataSet
    Try
        GetTimeSheet = New DataSet
        MyBase.SQL = "usp_SelectTimeSheet"
        'Clear previous Command just in case it has been set
        MyBase.Command = Nothing
        'Initialize the Command object
        MyBase.InitializeCommand()
        'Add the Parameters to the Parameters collection
        MyBase.AddParameter("@UserID", _
            SqlDbType.UniqueIdentifier, 16, UserID)
        MyBase.AddParameter("@WeekEndingDate", _
            SqlDbType.DateTime, 8, WeekEndingDate)
        'Fill the DataSet
        MyBase.FillDataSet(GetTimeSheet, "TimeSheet")
```

After the stored procedure executes, you want to check the row count in the DataSet to determine whether a timesheet was found and returned. This is done by querying the Count property of the Rows property. If no rows were found, you create a new DataSet object and populate it in preparation for calling the AddTimeSheet function.

The first thing that you do here is create a new DataSet object and then a DataTable object. You set the DataTable object to a new DataTable by calling the Add method of the Tables collection in the DataSet, passing it the name that you want for the DataTable, which in this case is TimeSheet:

```
'Check the DataSet for 0 rows and create a new timesheet
'if necessary
If GetTimeSheet.Tables("TimeSheet").Rows.Count = 0 Then
    'Create a new TimeSheet DataSet
    Dim objDataSet As New DataSet
    'Create a DataTable
    Dim objDataTable As DataTable = objDataSet.Tables.Add("TimeSheet")
```

After the DataTable is created, you need to add the columns to the DataTable by calling the Add method of the Columns collection. The Add method is an overloaded method and the method that you are using here accepts the column name to be assigned and the data type for the column as input. The column name is passed as a String constant and the data type is returned by the GetType method of the Type class.

The Type class represents the data types in the .NET Framework and the GetType method returns the data type with the specified name. You pass the data type as a String value to the GetType method as follows. After the GetType method executes, it returns the data type you specified to the Add method of the Columns collection:

```
'Add the DataColumns to the table
objDataTable.Columns.Add( _
    "TimeSheetID", Type.GetType("System.Guid"))
objDataTable.Columns.Add( _
    "UserID", Type.GetType("System.Guid"))
objDataTable.Columns.Add( _
    "WeekEndingDate", Type.GetType("System.DateTime"))
```

After the columns are defined in the `DataTable`, you can create a `DataRow` object from the `DataTable` by calling the `NewRow` method of the `Tables` collection. Then you can add the values to the columns in the `DataRow`. The first value that you are adding is a new Guid for the timesheet, followed by the UserID that this timesheet is for and the week ending date for the timesheet.

After the values are added to the `DataRow` object, you need to add the `DataRow` object to the table in the `DataSet`, by calling the `Add` method of the `Rows` collection for the `Tables` collection:

```
'Initialize a datarow object from the TimeSheet DataSet
Dim objDataRow As DataRow = objDataSet.Tables("TimeSheet").NewRow
'Set the values in the DataRow
objDataRow.Item("TimeSheetID") = Guid.NewGuid
objDataRow.Item("UserID") = UserID
objDataRow.Item("WeekEndingDate") = WeekEndingDate
'Add the DataRow to the DataSet
objDataSet.Tables("TimeSheet").Rows.Add(objDataRow)
```

Now that you have a `DataSet` object with the details needed to add a timesheet, you call the `AddTimeSheet` function, passing it the `DataSet`. You encapsulate this call in an `If...Then` statement to handle any errors and throw the exception that was thrown by the `AddTimeSheet` function.

If all was successful, you perform a recursive call to this function, which then returns the timesheet just inserted, and then you return that timesheet to the caller of this function. The `Catch` block contains the standard error-handling code that you've seen before:

```
'Add the TimeSheet to the database
If Not AddTimeSheet(objDataSet) Then
    Throw New Exception("Insert TimeSheet Failed")
End If
'Now perform a recursive call to this procedure
Return GetTimeSheet(UserID, WeekEndingDate)
        End If
    Catch ExceptionErr As Exception
        Throw New System.Exception(ExceptionErr.Message, _
        ExceptionErr.InnerException)
    End Try
End Function
```

The next step is to add the `GetManagerEmployees` function. Because this is a simple function that you've seen before, the code is not listed here. This function accepts the ManagerID as input and calls the `usp_SelectManagerEmployees` stored procedure, returning a `DataSet` with all employees assigned to the specified manager.

The ValidateLogin function is added next and again it's a simple function with code that you've seen before so the code is not listed again. This function calls the usp_ValidateLogin stored procedure passing it the login name and password of the user attempting to log on and returns a dataset with that user's information if he or she was validated in the database.

The next step is to add the corresponding functions in the business logic component for the GetTimeSheet, GetManagerEmployees, and ValidateLogin functions. Most of this is straightforward code that you've seen before so there is no need to list it all again. I do, however, want to cover the ValidateLogin function briefly.

Because the business logic component is responsible for business logic and workflows, the ValidateLogin function performs some manipulation of data before calling the corresponding function in the data access component.

As you can see in the following code, you hash the password as you call the corresponding function in the data access component. This causes the hashed password to be passed to the ValidateLogin function in the data access component so that the hashed value of the password that the user entered is used in the usp_ValidateLogin stored procedure to compare against the hashed password stored in the database.

```
Public Function ValidateLogin(ByVal LoginName As String, _
    ByVal Password As String) As DataSet

    Try
        'Call the data component to get a specific user
        ValidateLogin = objWDAUsers.ValidateLogin(LoginName, _
            HashPassword(Password))
    Catch ExceptionErr As Exception
        Throw New System.Exception(ExceptionErr.Message, _
            ExceptionErr.InnerException)
    End Try
End Function
```

You need to share some common variables between the various forms in your project. The easiest way to do this is to create a module and declare these variables as Public. This is done when you create the GlobalVariables module and add the following declarations:

```
'Global variables
Public g_strUserRole As String = String.Empty
Public g_strUserID As String
Public g_strUserName As String
```

You modify the Main procedure in the MainEntry class next so that the Login form is always shown first. This allows users to enter their credentials and have them validated. After the login form is closed, control is returned to this procedure for further processing.

Next, you determine whether the length of the g_strUserRole variable is greater than 0. If it is, the user's credentials have been validated and you continue. If the length of the g_strUserRole variable is equal to 0, then the user canceled the Login form or used up three attempts trying to log in and you want to end the program.

If the length of the g_strUserRole variable is greater than 0, you check to see what role the user has by using the Like operator to determine whether the role name contains the characters admin. If the role name contains the characters admin, you display the Admin form. Otherwise, you display the TimeSheet form for users and managers.

```
Sub Main()
    Dim objLogin As New Login
    objLogin.ShowDialog()
    objLogin.Dispose()
    objLogin = Nothing

    If g_strUserRole.Trim.Length > 0 Then
        If g_strUserRole.ToLower Like "admin" Then
            Dim objAdmin As New Admin
            objAdmin.ShowDialog()
            objAdmin.Dispose()
            objAdmin = Nothing
        Else
            Dim objTimeSheet As New TimeSheet
            objTimeSheet.ShowDialog()
            objTimeSheet.Dispose()
            objTimeSheet = Nothing
        End If
    End If
End Sub
```

The next step is to add some logic to the Login form to validate a user's credentials. You start by adding two variables at the form level so that these variables are accessible to all procedures in this form. The intAttemptCount variable keeps track of the number of attempts the user makes to log in, while the blnAllowClosing variable is used to control whether the Login form can be closed.

```
Private intAttemptCount As Integer = 0
Private blnAllowClosing As Boolean = False
```

The first procedure that you add is the btnOK_Click procedure. This procedure is called when the user clicks OK or presses the Enter key in the password field. The first thing that you do in this procedure is initialize a new instance of the business logic component. Then you call the ValidateLogin method, passing it the login name and password entered, retrieving the results of that call in a DataSet object.

```
Private Sub btnOK_Click(ByVal sender As System.Object, _
    ByVal e As System.EventArgs) Handles btnOK.Click

    'Initialize a new instance of the business logic component
    Using objUsers As New WroxBusinessLogic.WBLUsers("Wrox", "Time Tracker")

        'Validate the user and get their role
        Dim objDataSet As Data.DataSet = objUsers.ValidateLogin( _
            txtLoginName.Text, txtPassword.Text)
```

Now you want to see if the DataSet contains any rows. If the Count property is greater than 0, you know that the user has been validated. You test the value in the Status column of the DataSet to see if the user account has been suspended. Remember that if the account is active, the Status column in the database contains a value of 1, and if the account is suspended, the Status column contains a value of 0.

This works out nicely for you, as a Boolean value is returned in the DataSet, enabling you to use the Status column in the DataSet to test for a True/False value.

You use the Status column in the DataSet in your If...Then statement. If it is True, you set the global variables defined in the GlobalVariables module to the values contained in the DataSet. If the value in the Status column is equal to False, you display a Message Box dialog box indicating that the account has been suspended.

Whether the account is active or suspended, you also set the blnAllowClosing variable to True so that when this function ends, the form can be closed, as the Login_FormClosing procedure will be called next.

This procedure is automatically called because this form has been displayed as a dialog box and the OK and Cancel buttons were set to automatically fire the events associated with a dialog box.

If the DataSet does not contain a row of data, you want to display the appropriate message in a Message Box dialog box, indicating that the credentials were not validated. Then you implement the necessary code to clean up the resources used in this procedure and increment the attempt count:

```
            If objDataSet.Tables("User").Rows.Count > 0 Then
                If objDataSet.Tables("User").Rows(0).Item("Status") Then
                    g_strUserRole = objDataSet.Tables("User").Rows(0).Item( _
                        "RoleName")
                    g_strUserID = objDataSet.Tables("User").Rows(0).Item( _
                        "UserID").ToString
                    g_strUserName = objDataSet.Tables("User").Rows(0).Item( _
                        "UserName").ToString
                Else
                    MessageBox.Show("Your account has been suspended." & _
                        ControlChars.CrLf & "Please contact your administrator.", _
                        "Time Tracker", MessageBoxButtons.OK, MessageBoxIcon.Error)
                End If
                blnAllowClosing = True
            Else
                MessageBox.Show("Your credentials were not validated.", _
                    "Time Tracker", MessageBoxButtons.OK, MessageBoxIcon.Error)
            End If

            'Clean up
            objDataSet.Dispose()
            objDataSet = Nothing

            'Increment attempt count
            intAttemptCount += 1
        End Using
    End Sub
```

The code for the Cancel button is added next, and here you set the blnAllowClosing variable to True so that the form will be allowed to close, and then you call the Close method on the form using the Me keyword, which refers to the current form:

```
Private Sub btnCancel_Click(ByVal sender As System.Object, _
    ByVal e As System.EventArgs) Handles btnCancel.Click

    blnAllowClosing = True
    Me.Close()
End Sub
```

The `FormClosing` event fires when the form is closing and allows you to cancel the closing of the form. You first check to see whether you want to allow the form to close by querying the `blnAllowClosing` variable. If this variable is not set to `True`, you query the `intAttemptCount` variable and if it contains a value of less than 3, you cancel the `Closing` event by setting the `Cancel` property of the `CancelEventArgs` class to `True`. The `CancelEventArgs` class provides data for a cancelable event, which in this case is the `FormClosing` event of the form.

```
Private Sub Login_FormClosing(ByVal sender As Object, _
    ByVal e As System.Windows.Forms.FormClosingEventArgs) _
    Handles Me.FormClosing

    If Not blnAllowClosing Then
        If intAttemptCount < 3 Then
            e.Cancel = True
        End If
    End If
End Sub
```

You do not want to require users to click OK to validate their credentials. It would be nice if they could enter their login name and password and press Enter. This is what the code in the `txtPassword_KeyUp` procedure does for you. It enables a user to press Enter while in the password field and then it calls the `btnOK_Click` procedure.

The first thing that you do in this procedure is query the `KeyCode` from the `KeyEventArgs` class against the `Enter` constant of the `Keys` enumeration. If they are equal, you call the `btnOK_Click` procedure, passing it the values passed to this procedure.

After control is returned from the `btnOK_Click` procedure, you want to see if this form is allowed to be closed. If so, you call the `Close` event on the form.

```
Private Sub txtPassword_KeyUp(ByVal sender As Object, _
    ByVal e As System.Windows.Forms.KeyEventArgs) Handles txtPassword.KeyUp

    If e.KeyCode = Keys.Enter Then
        Call btnOK_Click(sender, e)
    End If
    If blnAllowClosing Then
        Me.Close()
    End If
End Sub
```

After testing the functionality that you added up to this point, you add the necessary functionality to make the TimeSheet form work. You start by adding some variables that are local to the form and that will be used throughout the procedures in this form.

You modify the `TimeSheet_Load` procedure next, adding the following code. First, you see if the user belongs to the User role or the Manager role by using the `Like` operator and comparing the role name in the global `g_strUserRole` variable to a value of `user`. If the user belongs to the User role, you hide the manager's menu option from the user by setting the `Visible` property of the `Employee-TimeSheetsToolStripMenuItem` menu item to `False`. Then you set the `blnEmployeeDisplay` variable to `True`, indicating that this is a user and not a manager. You also save the user's UserID in the `strUserID` variable.

If the user is a manager, you set the `blnEmployeeDisplay` variable to `False` and call the `EmployeeTimeSheetsToolStripMenuItem_Click` procedure, passing it a value of `Nothing` for the required parameters for this procedure. Then you set the `strManagerID` variable using the global `g_strUserID` variable, and finally call the `LoadEmployees` procedure to populate the Employee combo box:

```
'Hide the managers menu option for regular users
If g_strUserRole.ToLower Like "user" Then
    EmployeeTimeSheetsToolStripMenuItem.Visible = False
    blnEmployeeDisplay = True
    strUserID = g_strUserID
Else
    blnEmployeeDisplay = False
    Call EmployeeTimeSheetsToolStripMenuItem_Click(Nothing, Nothing)
    strManagerID = g_strUserID
    Call LoadEmployees()
End If
```

Next you display the employee's name in the text field on the TimeSheet form and load the Week Ending combo boxes on the form with the previous week ending date and the current week ending date:

```
'Display the users name
lblEmployee.Text &= " " & g_strUserName

'Load the week ending date combo boxes
cboWeekEnding.Items.Add(GetPreviousWeekEndingDate)
cboEmployeeWeekEnding.Items.Add(GetPreviousWeekEndingDate)
cboWeekEnding.Items.Add(GetCurrentWeekEndingDate)
cboEmployeeWeekEnding.Items.Add(GetCurrentWeekEndingDate)
```

Again, you determine whether the user belongs to the User role or the Manager role and set the `SelectedIndex` of the `cboWeekEnding` combo box appropriately. Setting the `SelectedIndex` property to a value of greater than –1 causes the `SelectedIndexChanged` event to fire, which causes the timesheet for the current week ending date to be loaded. Finally, you turn off the loading flag by setting it to a value of `False`.

```
If g_strUserRole.ToLower Like "user" Then
    cboWeekEnding.SelectedIndex = 1
Else
    cboWeekEnding.SelectedIndex = -1
End If

'Turn off the loading flag
blnLoading = False
```

You add the `GetCurrentWeekEndingDate` function next, which calculates the current week ending date and returns it as a string to be loaded in the combo boxes on the form. The `DateSerial` function returns a `DateTime` data type for the year, month, and day that you pass it. You use the `Year` function to extract the year and pass it a parameter of `Now`, which returns the year from the `Now` property. The `Now` property represents the current date and time. You use the `Month` function, passing it the `Now` property to return the current month. Finally, for the day parameter to the `DateSerial` function, you extract the day using the `DateAndTime` module and using the `Day` property and pass it the `Now` property.

Because you want to calculate the date for Friday of the current week, you subtract the first day of the week from the day and add 6 to it by using the `DatePart` function, which returns the specified component of the date specified. You specify the weekday by passing it a value of `w`, which causes the `DatePart` function to return a value of 1 through 7 representing the current day of the week. The second parameter to the `DatePart` function is the date value that should be used in the calculation and you have specified the current date using the `Now` property. Finally, you specify what the first day of the week is using the `Sunday` constant from the `FirstDayofWeek` enumeration. After you subtract the first day of the week from the current day, you add 6 to it to get the date for Friday of the current week.

```
Private Function GetCurrentWeekEndingDate() As String
    GetCurrentWeekEndingDate = DateSerial( _
        Year(Now), Month(Now), DateAndTime.Day(Now) - _
        DatePart("w", Now, FirstDayOfWeek.Sunday) + 6)
End Function
```

The `GetPreviousWeekEndingDate` function is added next and operates on the same principle as the `GetCurrentWeekEndingDate` function. However, instead of adding 6 to the day returned from the current day minus the first day of the week, you subtract 1 from it to give you the previous Friday's date.

```
Private Function GetPreviousWeekEndingDate() As String
    GetPreviousWeekEndingDate = DateSerial( _
        Year(Now), Month(Now), DateAndTime.Day(Now) - _
        DatePart("w", Now, FirstDayOfWeek.Sunday) - 1)
End Function
```

The next code you add is the `LoadEmployees` procedure to load all the employees assigned to a manager. Here you clear the previous bindings from the `cboEmployee` combo box, initialize a new instance of the business logic component, and call the `GetManagerEmployees` function to get the employees in a `DataSet`.

The final step is to rebind the `DataSet` to the `cboEmployee` combo box.

```
Private Sub LoadEmployees()
    'Clear previous bindings
    cboEmployee.DataSource = Nothing
    cboEmployee.DisplayMember = String.Empty
    cboEmployee.ValueMember = String.Empty

    'Initialize a new instance of the business logic component
    Using objUsers As New WroxBusinessLogic.WBLUsers( _
        strCompany, strApplication)

        'Get the timesheet for the user
```

```
              objEmployees = objUsers.GetManagerEmployees(New Guid(strManagerID))

              'Rebind ComboBox control
              cboEmployee.DataSource = objEmployees.Tables("Employees")
              cboEmployee.DisplayMember = "EmployeeName"
              cboEmployee.ValueMember = "UserID"
        End Using
    End Sub
```

Loading a timesheet in the `DataGridView` control on the form presents a unique challenge. You cannot simply bind the `DataSet` containing the timesheet to the `DataGridView` because that would allow a user to add new rows to the `DataSet` via the `DataGridView`. Additionally, you want to add a total row to automatically calculate the totals for each day as the user enters data and you do not want this row of data to be editable by the user. Thus you use a `DataView` object and bind that object to the `DataGridView`.

This procedure accepts the week ending date selected as a combo box as this procedure could be called automatically for a user when the `SelectedIndex` property on the `cboWeekEnding` is set for a user. Or, it could be called when the manager selects a week ending date in the `cboEmployeeWeekEnding` combo box. Passing the combo box as an input parameter provides you with a method to extract the selected week ending date from a combo box without using an `If...Then...Else` statement to determine which combo box was used.

In this procedure, you first clear the previous bindings from the `DataGridView` on the form. Then you initialize a new instance of the business logic component and call the `GetTimeSheet` method to return the timesheet in a `DataSet` object. You use the UserID stored in the `strUserID` variable and the `SelectedItem` property of the combo box passed to this procedure as input to the `GetTimeSheet` method.

```
    Private Sub LoadTimeSheet(ByVal WeekEndingDate As ComboBox)
        'Clear previous bindings
        grdTimeSheet.DataSource = Nothing
        grdTimeSheet.DataMember = String.Empty
        grdTimeSheet.Columns.Clear()

        'Initialize a new instance of the business logic component
        Using objTimeSheets As New WroxBusinessLogic.WBLTimeSheets( _
            strCompany, strApplication)

            'Get the timesheet for the user
            objTimeSheetDS = objTimeSheets.GetTimeSheet( _
                New Guid(strUserID), WeekEndingDate.SelectedItem)
```

After you have a timesheet in the `DataSet` object, you create a new `DataView` from the `DataSet` by calling the constructor of the `DataView` class, passing it the table in the `DataSet` object. Next, you create a total row in the `DataView` object that will contain a total for the hours entered for each project for a given day. You do this by calling the `AddNew` method on the `objTimeSheetDV` object to create a new `DataRowView` object.

You set the value in the `ProjectName` column to `Total Hours` and then start calculating the total hours for each day of the week starting with Monday. You want to loop through each row of the `DataSet` for each day of the week, and this is done by setting up a `For` loop. You use the `Count` property of the `Rows` property to determine the maximum number of iterations that the `For` loop should perform. Remember that you need to subtract 1 from the Count property, as the Count property returns the actual number of rows in the DataSet, but you access each row using a zero-based index.

You extract the hours in the MondayHours column and add them to the intTotal variable. After you complete processing of all the rows in the DataSet, you set the value in the MondayHours column in the DataView row to the value contained in the intTotal variable.

You repeat the process for each day of the week.

```
'Set the DataView object with the data from the DataSet
objTimeSheetDV = New Data.DataView(objTimeSheetDS.Tables("TimeSheet"))

'Initialize a new DataRowView object
Dim objDataRowView As Data.DataRowView = objTimeSheetDV.AddNew

'Set the values in the columns
objDataRowView("ProjectName") = "Total Hours"

'Calculate and set the total hours for Monday
intTotal = 0
For intIndex = 0 To objTimeSheetDS.Tables("TimeSheet").Rows.Count - 1
    intTotal += objTimeSheetDS.Tables( _
        "TimeSheet").Rows(intIndex).Item("MondayHours")
Next
objDataRowView("MondayHours") = intTotal

'Calculate and set the total hours for Tuesday
intTotal = 0
For intIndex = 0 To objTimeSheetDS.Tables("TimeSheet").Rows.Count - 1
    intTotal += objTimeSheetDS.Tables( _
        "TimeSheet").Rows(intIndex).Item("TuesdayHours")
Next
objDataRowView("TuesdayHours") = intTotal

'Calculate and set the total hours for Wednesday
intTotal = 0
For intIndex = 0 To objTimeSheetDS.Tables("TimeSheet").Rows.Count - 1
    intTotal += objTimeSheetDS.Tables( _
        "TimeSheet").Rows(intIndex).Item("WednesdayHours")
Next
objDataRowView("WednesdayHours") = intTotal

'Calculate and set the total hours for Thursday
intTotal = 0
For intIndex = 0 To objTimeSheetDS.Tables("TimeSheet").Rows.Count - 1
    intTotal += objTimeSheetDS.Tables( _
        "TimeSheet").Rows(intIndex).Item("ThursdayHours")
Next
objDataRowView("ThursdayHours") = intTotal

'Calculate and set the total hours for Friday
intTotal = 0
For intIndex = 0 To objTimeSheetDS.Tables("TimeSheet").Rows.Count - 1
    intTotal += objTimeSheetDS.Tables( _
```

```
                     "TimeSheet").Rows(intIndex).Item("FridayHours")
            Next
            objDataRowView("FridayHours") = intTotal
```

After the new `DataRowView` object is populated, you want to commit the changes by calling the `EndEdit` method on the object. Then, to prevent the user from adding new rows to the `DataView` object, you set the `AllowNew` property to `False`. Finally, you set the `AutoGenerateColumns` property of the `DataGridView` to `False`, which prevents this control from automatically generating columns from the `DataView` object when you bind the `DataView` object to the `DataGridView`, which is done in the next line of code.

The final line of code here sets the background color of the cells in the odd rows to whitesmoke, which helps provide a more aesthetically pleasing user interface.

```
            'Commit the changes to the row
            objDataRowView.EndEdit()

            'Disallow new records
            objTimeSheetDV.AllowNew = False

            'Bind the DataView to the DataGridView
            grdTimeSheet.AutoGenerateColumns = False
            grdTimeSheet.DataSource = objTimeSheetDV

            'Set the DataGridView properties
            grdTimeSheet.AlternatingRowsDefaultCellStyle.BackColor = _
                Color.WhiteSmoke
```

Next, you declare a `DataGridViewTextBoxColumn` object and set the `HeaderText` property to the value that should be displayed in the `DataGridView`, and set the `DataPropertyName` property to the value that should be mapped to the column in the `DataView` object. You set the `ReadOnly` property to `True` so that this column cannot be edited and then set the width of the column. Finally, you add the new column to the `DataGridView`.

```
            'Create and add DataGridView text box columns
            Dim objColumn As New DataGridViewTextBoxColumn
            With objColumn
                .HeaderText = "Project Name"
                .DataPropertyName = "ProjectName"
                .ReadOnly = True
                .Width = 225
            End With
            grdTimeSheet.Columns.Add(objColumn)
```

Now you create a new instance of the `DataGridViewTextBoxColumn` class and set the `HeaderText` property to `Monday` and the `DataPropertyName` property to `MondayHours` so that it maps to the MondayHours column in the `DataView` object. Then you set the width of the column as it should appear in the `DataGridView`. You want to determine if this timesheet should be displayed as read-only. Because this procedure could be called by either a manager or an employee, you want to check the value in the Submitted column of the `DataSet` and the `blnEmployeeDisplay` variable to determine whether this timesheet should be displayed as read-only. If it should, you set the `ReadOnly` property to `True`. You repeat this process for each day of the week.

```
objColumn = New DataGridViewTextBoxColumn
With objColumn
    .HeaderText = "Monday"
    .DataPropertyName = "MondayHours"
    .Width = 70
    If objTimeSheetDS.Tables("TimeSheet").Rows(0).Item("Submitted") _
        Or Not blnEmployeeDisplay Then
        .ReadOnly = True
    End If
End With
grdTimeSheet.Columns.Add(objColumn)

objColumn = New DataGridViewTextBoxColumn
With objColumn
    .HeaderText = "Tuesday"
    .DataPropertyName = "TuesdayHours"
    .Width = 70
    If objTimeSheetDS.Tables("TimeSheet").Rows(0).Item("Submitted") _
        Or Not blnEmployeeDisplay Then
        .ReadOnly = True
    End If
End With
grdTimeSheet.Columns.Add(objColumn)

objColumn = New DataGridViewTextBoxColumn
With objColumn
    .HeaderText = "Wednesday"
    .DataPropertyName = "WednesdayHours"
    .Width = 70
    If objTimeSheetDS.Tables("TimeSheet").Rows(0).Item("Submitted") _
        Or Not blnEmployeeDisplay Then
        .ReadOnly = True
    End If
End With
grdTimeSheet.Columns.Add(objColumn)

objColumn = New DataGridViewTextBoxColumn
With objColumn
    .HeaderText = "Thursday"
    .DataPropertyName = "ThursdayHours"
    .Width = 70
    If objTimeSheetDS.Tables("TimeSheet").Rows(0).Item("Submitted") _
        Or Not blnEmployeeDisplay Then
        .ReadOnly = True
    End If
End With
grdTimeSheet.Columns.Add(objColumn)

objColumn = New DataGridViewTextBoxColumn
With objColumn
    .HeaderText = "Friday"
    .DataPropertyName = "FridayHours"
    .Width = 70
    If objTimeSheetDS.Tables("TimeSheet").Rows(0).Item("Submitted") _
        Or Not blnEmployeeDisplay Then
        .ReadOnly = True
```

```
                          End If
                  End With
                  grdTimeSheet.Columns.Add(objColumn)
```

To wrap things up in this procedure, you determine whether the timesheet has been displayed as read-only and set the appropriate lock icon on the form.

```
                  'Change the locked icon if the timesheet is readonly
                  If objTimeSheetDS.Tables("TimeSheet").Rows(0).Item("Submitted") _
                      Or Not blnEmployeeDisplay Then
                      imgStatus.Image = ImageList1.Images(1)
                  Else
                      imgStatus.Image = ImageList1.Images(0)
                  End If
              End Using
          End Sub
```

When an employee selects a new week ending date in the cboWeekEnding combo box, you want to load the appropriate timesheet for that date. This procedure is also fired from the form's Load event when the SelectedIndex value is changed. To that end, the first thing that you do here is determine whether this is a manager and whether the form is loading by querying the blnEmployeeDisplay and blnLoading flags, respectively. If this is a manager and the form is loading, you exit the procedure.

If this is a user or the form is not loading, you call the LoadTimeSheet procedure, passing it the cboWeekEnding combo box as its input parameter.

```
      Private Sub cboWeekEnding_SelectedIndexChanged(ByVal sender As Object, _
          ByVal e As System.EventArgs) Handles cboWeekEnding.SelectedIndexChanged

          If Not blnEmployeeDisplay And blnLoading Then
              Exit Sub
          End If

          'Load the timesheet
          Call LoadTimeSheet(cboWeekEnding)
      End Sub
```

As a user navigates from one cell to the next in the DataGridView, you want to recalculate the total hours displayed. This is done by adding code to the CurrentCellChanged event for the DataGridView. The first thing you do in this procedure is declare a couple of local objects in the DataRowView class. The first object is used to access each row in the DataView minus the last row, and the second object is used to access the total row in the DataView.

You set the objDataRowTotal object to the total row in the DataView so that you can update the totals for each day of the week:

```
      Private Sub grdTimeSheet_CurrentCellChanged(ByVal sender As Object, _
          ByVal e As System.EventArgs) Handles grdTimeSheet.CurrentCellChanged

          'Declare variables
          Dim objDataRowView As Data.DataRowView
```

```
Dim objDataRowTotal As Data.DataRowView

'Get the total row so we can update the totals
objDataRowTotal = objTimeSheetDV.Item(objTimeSheetDV.Count - 1)
```

Next, you start recalculating the total for each day much as you did in the LoadTimeSheet procedure. However, instead of accessing the rows in the DataSet, here you access the rows in the DataView.

You perform the process of calculating the new total for each day of the week and then set the new total in the objDataRowTotal object. After all the totals have been recalculated, you call the EndEdit method on the objDataRowTotal object, which refreshes the DataView object with the new totals for each day.

```
'Recalculate Monday's total
intTotal = 0
For intIndex As Integer = 0 To objTimeSheetDV.Count - 2
    objDataRowView = objTimeSheetDV.Item(intIndex)
    intTotal += objDataRowView.Item("MondayHours")
Next
'Update Monday's total
objDataRowTotal.Item("MondayHours") = intTotal

'Recalculate Tuesday's total
intTotal = 0
For intIndex As Integer = 0 To objTimeSheetDV.Count - 2
    objDataRowView - objTimeSheetDV.Item(intIndex)
    intTotal += objDataRowView.Item("TuesdayHours")
Next
'Update Tuesday's total
objDataRowTotal.Item("TuesdayHours") = intTotal

'Recalculate Wednesday's total
intTotal = 0
For intIndex As Integer - 0 To objTimeSheetDV.Count - 2
    objDataRowView = objTimeSheetDV.Item(intIndex)
    intTotal += objDataRowView.Item("WednesdayHours")
Next
'Update Wednesday's total
objDataRowTotal.Item("WednesdayHours") = intTotal

'Recalculate Thursday's total
intTotal = 0
For intIndex As Integer = 0 To objTimeSheetDV.Count - 2
    objDataRowView = objTimeSheetDV.Item(intIndex)
    intTotal += objDataRowView.Item("ThursdayHours")
Next
'Update Thursday's total
objDataRowTotal.Item("ThursdayHours") = intTotal

'Recalculate Friday's total
intTotal = 0
For intIndex As Integer = 0 To objTimeSheetDV.Count - 2
    objDataRowView = objTimeSheetDV.Item(intIndex)
```

```
            intTotal += objDataRowView.Item("FridayHours")
        Next
        'Update Friday's total
        objDataRowTotal.Item("FridayHours") = intTotal

        'Commit the changes to the total row
        objDataRowTotal.EndEdit()
    End Sub
```

When a manager selects an employee in the cboEmployee combo box, you need to save the UserID of that employee in the strUserID variable that you declared at the form level. Remember that this variable is used in the LoadTimeSheet procedure when calling the GetTimeSheet method in the business logic component.

```
    Private Sub cboEmployee_SelectedIndexChanged(ByVal sender As Object, _
        ByVal e As System.EventArgs) Handles cboEmployee.SelectedIndexChanged

        strUserID = objEmployees.Tables("Employees").Rows( _
            cboEmployee.SelectedIndex).Item("UserID").ToString
    End Sub
```

The last bit of code you add is the cboEmployeeWeekEnding_SelectedIndexChanged procedure. This procedure is executed when a manager selects a new week ending date in the cboEmployeeWeekEnding combo box.

First, this procedure determines whether the TimeSheet form is loading by querying the blnLoading variable. If it is, you exit this procedure without executing any other code. If the form is not loading, you call the LoadTimeSheet procedure, passing it the cboEmployeeWeekEnding combo box as input.

```
    Private Sub cboEmployeeWeekEnding_SelectedIndexChanged( _
        ByVal sender As Object, ByVal e As System.EventArgs) _
        Handles cboEmployeeWeekEnding.SelectedIndexChanged

        If blnLoading Then
            Exit Sub
        End If

        'Load the timesheet
        Call LoadTimeSheet(cboEmployeeWeekEnding)
    End Sub
```

After adding this last bit of code, you test your project again, logging in as a user to view the behavior of the TimeSheet form for a user, and then logging in as a manager to view the behavior of the TimeSheet form for a manager.

Summary

This chapter has taken a more detailed look at stored procedures and I hope you have gained a deeper appreciation of their power. Using concatenation and column aliases, you were able to combine the results of multiple columns and return the results under a new name. You saw firsthand how using joins and table aliases increases the efficiency of your stored procedures, allows you to return results in a gridlike format, and enables you to join the same table to itself to produce the required results.

You also learned a little more about some of the functions and features of stored procedures, such as functions that perform date manipulation in SQL Server and arithmetic operations in Oracle. You saw how using the LIKE keyword enables you to select data that matches a certain pattern.

In addition to learning more about stored procedures, you also had a chance to learn more about the DataSet and DataView classes. In the second exercise in this chapter, you implemented the code to create a DataSet from scratch; create the DataTable, DataColumns, and DataRows; and load data into the DataSet for processing. You also had the chance to work more with the DataView class and learned how to add a new DataRowView object to the DataView and populate it with data.

In working with the DataView class, you had a chance to work more with the DataGridView class and saw how to implement styles that affect how the DataGrid formats and displays the data in the DataGridView. Using the DataGridViewTextBoxColumn class, you were able to control which columns were displayed in the DataGridView as well as which columns were marked as read-only.

To summarize, you should know how to:

❑ Concatenate data in a SELECT statement and assign a column alias to the results

❑ Use an INNER JOIN and LEFT OUTER JOIN to join tables

❑ Use a table alias when joining tables

❑ Create a DataSet, DataTable, DataColumn, and DataRow

❑ Customize the appearance of a DataGridView

In Chapter 13, you take a closer look at stored procedures that update data, and complete the functionality in the Admin and TimeSheet forms.

Exercises

Exercise 1

Create a stored procedure named **usp_Chapter12Ex1** that will select all usernames and their corresponding role. The stored procedure should concatenate the user's first and last name and return that name in a column called **UserName**. Order the results returned by UserName.

Readers using Oracle will need to create a package and package body. You can name your package **Chapter12Ex1Package**.

Exercise 2

Create a Windows application that executes your stored procedure and fills a DataSet and then displays the results in a DataGridView control. Create your own columns in the DataGridView control much as you did in the TimeSheet form.

Updating Data

Now that you can insert and select data for roles, users, and timesheets, you can focus your attention on updating this data. This chapter takes you through the process of updating roles and users, which completes the functionality in the Admin form. Additionally, you'll be implementing the functionality for updating, submitting, and approving timesheets in the TimeSheet form.

Although the update stored procedures that you create in this chapter are relatively simple, the logic involved in when and how each should be called is more complex. There will also be some repetitive processing of a stored procedure to update timesheets.

In this chapter, you:

- ❏ Implement logic in stored procedures
- ❏ Implement error handling in stored procedures
- ❏ Complete the functionality in the Admin form
- ❏ Add more functionality in the TimeSheet form

Stored Procedure Logic

In Chapter 11 you implemented functionality in the usp_InsertRole stored procedure to verify that an existing role did not exist with a specified ranking before inserting the new role. This ensured that each role added had a unique ranking.

When updating a role, you want to perform the same check. However, there is a caveat to this process. The ranking that exists could belong to the role being updated, so you need to examine the RoleID of the role that was found with the existing ranking against the RoleID of the role being updated. If they are the same, you perform the update of the role. If they are not the same, you want to raise an error in your stored procedure and exit the stored procedure without updating the role. You see the details of this implementation in the usp_UpdateRole stored procedure created in the exercise that follows.

The logic that you implement in the usp_UpdateRole stored procedure in the next Try It Out involves the use of IF statements, variables, and the implementation of error handling. You saw these SQL statements in action in the various INSERT stored procedures that you wrote in Chapter 11.

Try It Out   Admin Form Stored Procedures

To complete this exercise:

1. Open your Time Tracker application in Visual Studio 2005.

2. View the Server Explorer window and click the Auto Hide icon on the window to keep it visible and then view the Stored Procedures node for your database.

3. The first stored procedure to be created is the usp_UpdateRole stored procedure. This stored procedure updates a single role in the Roles table. Readers using SQL Server should right-click the Stored Procedures and choose Add New Stored Procedure from the context menu. Readers using Oracle should use their favorite Oracle tool such as iSQL *Plus to create the stored procedures. Enter the code for the following stored procedure:

    SQL Server

```
CREATE PROCEDURE usp_UpdateRole
(
    @RoleID             UNIQUEIDENTIFIER,
    @RoleName           VARCHAR(50),
    @RoleDescription    TEXT,
    @Ranking            TINYINT
)
AS
-- Declare local variables
DECLARE @ID    UNIQUEIDENTIFIER

-- See if the ranking exists
SELECT @ID = RoleID FROM Roles WHERE Ranking = @Ranking
    BEGIN
    IF @ID IS NOT NULL
        BEGIN
        -- The ranking exists, now verify it doesn't belong to the
        -- role you are updating
        IF @RoleID <> @ID
            BEGIN
            RAISERROR('Ranking already exists and cannot be duplicated.',18,1)
            RETURN
            END
        END
    END

-- Either the ranking does not exist or it belongs to the role being updated
BEGIN TRY
    UPDATE Roles
        Set RoleName = @RoleName,
        RoleDescription = @RoleDescription,
        Ranking = @Ranking,
        LastUpdateDate = GETDATE()
        WHERE RoleID = @RoleID
END TRY
```

```
BEGIN CATCH
    BEGIN
    RAISERROR('Update role failed.',18,1)
    RETURN
    END
END CATCH
```

Click the Save icon on the toolbar to create the stored procedure.

Oracle

```
CREATE OR REPLACE PROCEDURE usp_UpdateRole
(
    inRoleID            CHAR,
    inRoleName          VARCHAR2,
    inRoleDescription   CLOB,
    inRanking           NUMBER
)
AS

-- Declare local variables
varID CHAR(36);

BEGIN
    BEGIN
        -- See if the ranking exists
        SELECT RoleID INTO varID
        FROM Roles
        WHERE Ranking = inRanking;
        -- The ranking exists, now verify it doesn't belong to the
        -- role you are updating
        IF inRoleID <> varID THEN
            RAISE_APPLICATION_ERROR (-20999,
            'Ranking already exists and cannot be duplicated.');
            RETURN;
        END IF;
        EXCEPTION
            WHEN NO_DATA_FOUND THEN
            -- Handle the error but perform no processing
            NULL;
    END;
    BEGIN
        -- Either the ranking does not exist or it belongs
        -- to the role being updated
        UPDATE Roles
            Set RoleName = inRoleName,
            RoleDescription = inRoleDescription,
            Ranking = inRanking,
            LastUpdateDate = SYSDATE
            WHERE RoleID = inRoleID;
        EXCEPTION
            WHEN OTHERS THEN
            RAISE_APPLICATION_ERROR( -20999,'Update role failed.');
            RETURN;
    END;
END;
```

Click the Execute button to have the stored procedure created in your database.

4. The next stored procedure that you create is the usp_UpdateUser stored procedure, which updates a user in the Users table. SQL Server users should right-click the Stored Procedures node in the Server Explorer and choose Add New Stored Procedure and Oracle users should use their Oracle tool. Enter the following code:

SQL Server

```
CREATE PROCEDURE usp_UpdateUser
(
    @UserID       UNIQUEIDENTIFIER,
    @LoginName    VARCHAR(15),
    @Password     VARCHAR(30),
    @FirstName    VARCHAR(15),
    @LastName     VARCHAR(15),
    @Email        VARCHAR(50),
    @Phone        VARCHAR(20),
    @Status       BIT,
    @GroupID      UNIQUEIDENTIFIER,
    @RoleID       UNIQUEIDENTIFIER,
    @ManagerID    UNIQUEIDENTIFIER
)
AS

-- Check to see if the password is blank
-- (no updates to the password)
IF LEN(@Password) = 0
    BEGIN
    -- Get the current password
    SELECT @Password = Password
    FROM Users
    WHERE UserID = @UserID
    END

-- Update the user
BEGIN TRY
    UPDATE Users
        SET LoginName = @LoginName,
        Password = @Password,
        FirstName = @FirstName,
        LastName = @LastName,
        Email = @Email,
        Phone = @Phone,
        Status = @Status,
        GroupID = @GroupID,
        RoleID = @RoleID,
        ManagerID = @ManagerID,
        LastUpdateDate = GETDATE()
        WHERE UserID = @UserID
END TRY
BEGIN CATCH
    BEGIN
    RAISERROR('Update user failed.',18,1)
    RETURN
    END
END CATCH
```

Click the Save icon on the toolbar to have the stored procedure created in your database.

Oracle

```
CREATE OR REPLACE PROCEDURE usp_UpdateUser
(
    inUserID      CHAR,
    inLoginName   VARCHAR2,
    inPassword    VARCHAR2,
    inFirstName   VARCHAR2,
    inLastName    VARCHAR2,
    inEmail       VARCHAR2,
    inPhone       VARCHAR2,
    inStatus      NUMBER,
    inGroupID     CHAR,
    inRoleID      CHAR,
    inManagerID   CHAR
)
AS

-- Declare local variables
varPassword VARCHAR2(30);

BEGIN
    BEGIN
        -- Check to see if the password is null
        -- (no updates to the password)
        IF inPassword IS NULL THEN
            -- Get the current password
            SELECT Password INTO varPassword
            FROM Users
            WHERE UserID = inUserID;
        ELSE
            varPassword := inPassword;
        END IF;
    END;

    BEGIN
        -- Update the user
        UPDATE Users
            SET LoginName = inLoginName,
            Password = varPassword,
            FirstName = inFirstName,
            LastName = inLastName,
            Email = inEmail,
            Phone = inPhone,
            Status = inStatus,
            GroupID = inGroupID,
            RoleID = inRoleID,
            ManagerID = inManagerID,
            LastUpdateDate = SYSDATE
            WHERE UserID = inUserID;
        EXCEPTION
            WHEN OTHERS THEN
            RAISE_APPLICATION_ERROR (-20999,'Update Users failed.');
```

```
          RETURN;
    END;
END;
```

Click the Execute button to have the stored procedure created in your database.

5. Add some code to your data access component to execute these stored procedures. Starting with the WDARoles class, you add a function to update a role. Add the UpdateRole function to this class:

SQL Server

```
Public Function UpdateRole(ByVal Role As DataSet) As Boolean
    Try
        MyBase.SQL = "usp_UpdateRole"
        'Initialize the Command object
        MyBase.InitializeCommand()
        'Add the Parameters to the Parameters collection
        MyBase.AddParameter("@RoleID", _
         SqlDbType.UniqueIdentifier, 16, _
         Role.Tables("Role").Rows(0).Item("RoleID"))
        MyBase.AddParameter("@RoleName", _
         SqlDbType.VarChar, 50, _
         Role.Tables("Role").Rows(0).Item("RoleName"))
        MyBase.AddParameter("@RoleDescription", _
         SqlDbType.Text, _
         Role.Tables("Role").Rows(0).Item( _
         "RoleDescription").ToString.Length, _
         Role.Tables("Role").Rows(0).Item("RoleDescription"))
        MyBase.AddParameter("@Ranking", _
         SqlDbType.TinyInt, 1, _
         Role.Tables("Role").Rows(0).Item("Ranking"))
        'Execute the stored procedure
        UpdateRole = ExecuteStoredProcedure()
    Catch ExceptionErr As Exception
        Throw New System.Exception(ExceptionErr.Message, _
        ExceptionErr.InnerException)
    End Try
End Function
```

Oracle

```
Public Function UpdateRole(ByVal Role As DataSet) As Boolean
    Try
        MyBase.SQL = "usp_UpdateRole"
        'Initialize the Command object
        MyBase.InitializeCommand()
        'Add the Parameters to the Parameters collection
        MyBase.AddParameter("inRoleID", _
         OracleClient.OracleType.Char, 36, _
         Role.Tables("Role").Rows(0).Item("RoleID").ToString)
        MyBase.AddParameter("inRoleName", _
         OracleClient.OracleType.VarChar, 50, _
         Role.Tables("Role").Rows(0).Item("RoleName"))
        MyBase.AddParameter("inRoleDescription", _
         OracleClient.OracleType.Clob, _
         Role.Tables("Role").Rows(0).Item( _
```

```
        "RoleDescription").ToString.Length, _
        Role.Tables("Role").Rows(0).Item("RoleDescription"))
      MyBase.AddParameter("inRanking", _
      OracleClient.OracleType.Number, 1, _
      Role.Tables("Role").Rows(0).Item("Ranking"))
      'Execute the stored procedure
      UpdateRole = ExecuteStoredProcedure()
    Catch ExceptionErr As Exception
      Throw New System.Exception(ExceptionErr.Message, _
      ExceptionErr.InnerException)
    End Try
End Function
```

6. Add the `UpdateUser` function, which is in the `WDAUsers` class. View the code for that class and add the following function:

SQL Server

```
Public Function UpdateUser(ByVal User As DataSet) As Boolean
    Try
      MyBase.SQL = "usp_UpdateUser"
      'Initialize the Command object
      MyBase.InitializeCommand()
      'Add the Parameters to the Parameters collection
      MyBase.AddParameter("@UserID", _
          SqlDbType.UniqueIdentifier, 16, _
          User.Tables("User").Rows(0).Item("UserID"))
      MyBase.AddParameter("@LoginName", _
          SqlDbType.VarChar, 15, _
          User.Tables("User").Rows(0).Item("LoginName"))
      MyBase.AddParameter("@Password", _
          SqlDbType.VarChar, 30, _
          User.Tables("User").Rows(0).Item("Password"))
      MyBase.AddParameter("@FirstName", _
          SqlDbType.VarChar, 30, _
          User.Tables("User").Rows(0).Item("FirstName"))
      MyBase.AddParameter("@LastName", _
          SqlDbType.VarChar, 30, _
          User.Tables("User").Rows(0).Item("LastName"))
      MyBase.AddParameter("@Email", _
          SqlDbType.VarChar, 50, _
          User.Tables("User").Rows(0).Item("Email"))
      MyBase.AddParameter("@Phone", _
          SqlDbType.VarChar, 20, _
          User.Tables("User").Rows(0).Item("Phone"))
      MyBase.AddParameter("@Status", _
          SqlDbType.Bit, 1, _
          User.Tables("User").Rows(0).Item("Status"))
      MyBase.AddParameter("@GroupID", _
          SqlDbType.UniqueIdentifier, 16, _
          User.Tables("User").Rows(0).Item("GroupID"))
      MyBase.AddParameter("@RoleID", _
          SqlDbType.UniqueIdentifier, 16, _
          User.Tables("User").Rows(0).Item("RoleID"))
      MyBase.AddParameter("@ManagerID", _
          SqlDbType.UniqueIdentifier, 16, _
          User.Tables("User").Rows(0).Item("ManagerID"))
```

```
            'Execute the stored procedure
            UpdateUser = ExecuteStoredProcedure()
        Catch ExceptionErr As Exception
            Throw New System.Exception(ExceptionErr.Message, _
            ExceptionErr.InnerException)
        End Try
    End Function
```

Oracle

```
Public Function UpdateUser(ByVal User As DataSet) As Boolean
    Try
        MyBase.SQL = "usp_UpdateUser"
        'Initialize the Command object
        MyBase.InitializeCommand()
        'Add the Parameters to the Parameters collection
        MyBase.AddParameter("inUserID", _
            OracleClient.OracleType.Char, 36, _
            User.Tables("User").Rows(0).Item("UserID").ToString)
        MyBase.AddParameter("inLoginName", _
            OracleClient.OracleType.VarChar, 15, _
            User.Tables("User").Rows(0).Item("LoginName"))
        MyBase.AddParameter("inPassword", _
            OracleClient.OracleType.VarChar, 30, _
            User.Tables("User").Rows(0).Item("Password"))
        MyBase.AddParameter("inFirstName", _
            OracleClient.OracleType.VarChar, 30, _
            User.Tables("User").Rows(0).Item("FirstName"))
        MyBase.AddParameter("inLastName", _
            OracleClient.OracleType.VarChar, 30, _
            User.Tables("User").Rows(0).Item("LastName"))
        MyBase.AddParameter("inEmail", _
            OracleClient.OracleType.VarChar, 50, _
            User.Tables("User").Rows(0).Item("Email"))
        MyBase.AddParameter("inPhone", _
            OracleClient.OracleType.VarChar, 20, _
            User.Tables("User").Rows(0).Item("Phone"))
        MyBase.AddParameter("inStatus", _
            OracleClient.OracleType.Number, 1, _
            User.Tables("User").Rows(0).Item("Status"))
        MyBase.AddParameter("inGroupID", _
            OracleClient.OracleType.Char, 36, _
            User.Tables("User").Rows(0).Item("GroupID").ToString)
        MyBase.AddParameter("inRoleID", _
            OracleClient.OracleType.Char, 36, _
            User.Tables("User").Rows(0).Item("RoleID").ToString)
        MyBase.AddParameter("inManagerID", _
            OracleClient.OracleType.Char, 36, _
            User.Tables("User").Rows(0).Item("ManagerID").ToString)
        'Execute the stored procedure
        UpdateUser = ExecuteStoredProcedure()
    Catch ExceptionErr As Exception
        Throw New System.Exception(ExceptionErr.Message, _
        ExceptionErr.InnerException)
    End Try
End Function
```

7. Now you add code in your business logic component to support the functions just added in your data access component. View the code for the WBLRoles class and add the following function to update a role:

```
Public Function UpdateRole(ByVal Role As DataSet) As Boolean
    Try
        'Validate role data
        ValidateRoleData(Role)

        'Call the data component to update the role
        Return objWDARoles.UpdateRole(Role)
    Catch ExceptionErr As Exception
        Throw New System.Exception(ExceptionErr.Message, _
          ExceptionErr.InnerException)
    End Try
End Function
```

8. Now view the code for the WBLUsers class and add the UpdateUser function:

```
Public Function UpdateUser(ByVal User As DataSet) As Boolean
    Try
        'Validate the Login Name exists
        If User.Tables("User").Rows(0).Item( _
            "LoginName").ToString.Trim.Length = 0 Then
            Throw New System.Exception("Login Name is a required field.")
        End If

        'Validate the First Name exists
        If User.Tables("User").Rows(0).Item( _
            "FirstName").ToString.Trim.Length = 0 Then
            Throw New System.Exception("First Name is a required field.")
        End If

        'Validate the Last Name exists
        If User.Tables("User").Rows(0).Item( _
            "LastName").ToString.Trim.Length = 0 Then
            Throw New System.Exception("Last Name is a required field.")
        End If

        'Validate the password
        If User.Tables("User").Rows(0).Item( _
            "Password").ToString.Trim.Length = 0 Then
            'The old password is not being updated so set it to Null
            User.Tables("User").Rows(0).Item("Password") = DBNull.Value
        Else
            'A new password has been supplied
            If Not IsValidPassword(User.Tables( _
                "User").Rows(0).Item("Password")) Then
                Throw New System.Exception(strErrorMessage)
            Else
                'Hash the password
                User.Tables("User").Rows(0).Item("Password") = _
                    HashPassword(User.Tables("User").Rows(0).Item( _
                    "Password"))
            End If
```

```
            End If

            'Validate the email
            If Not IsValidEmail(User.Tables( _
                "User").Rows(0).Item("Email")) Then
                Throw New System.Exception(strErrorMessage)
            End If

            'Validate the phone number
            If Not IsValidPhoneNumber(User.Tables( _
                "User").Rows(0).Item("Phone")) Then
                Throw New System.Exception(strErrorMessage)
            End If

            'Validate manager
            If Not IsDBNull(User.Tables("User").Rows(0).Item("ManagerID")) Then
                If Not TypeOf User.Tables("User").Rows(0).Item("ManagerID") _
                    Is Guid Then
                    If User.Tables("User").Rows(0).Item("ManagerID") = _
                        String.Empty Then
                        'Set it to a null value
                        User.Tables("User").Rows(0).Item("ManagerID") = _
                            DBNull.Value
                    End If
                End If
            End If

            'Trim spaces
            User.Tables("User").Rows(0).Item("LoginName") = _
                User.Tables("User").Rows(0).Item("LoginName").ToString.Trim
            User.Tables("User").Rows(0).Item("Password") = _
                User.Tables("User").Rows(0).Item("Password").ToString.Trim
            User.Tables("User").Rows(0).Item("FirstName") = _
                User.Tables("User").Rows(0).Item("FirstName").ToString.Trim
            User.Tables("User").Rows(0).Item("LastName") = _
                User.Tables("User").Rows(0).Item("LastName").ToString.Trim
            User.Tables("User").Rows(0).Item("Email") = _
                User.Tables("User").Rows(0).Item("Email").ToString.Trim

            'Format the phone number
            User.Tables("User").Rows(0).Item("Phone") = _
                FormatPhoneNumber(User.Tables("User").Rows(0).Item("Phone"))

            'Call the data component to update the user
            Return objWDAUsers.UpdateUser(User)
        Catch ExceptionErr As Exception
            Throw New System.Exception(ExceptionErr.Message, _
             ExceptionErr.InnerException)
        End Try
    End Function
```

9. Switch to the code in the Admin form and update it to execute the functions you added in your business logic component. View the code for the ActionUpdate procedure and add the following code under the Case "Roles" statement:

```
        Case "Roles"
            'Initialize a new instance of the business logic component
            Using objRoles As New WroxBusinessLogic.WBLRoles( _
                strCompany, strApplication)
                'Get a new Role DataSet
                objDataSet = objRoles.GetNewRoleDS()
                'Initialize a datarow object from the Role DataSet
                Dim objDataRow As Data.DataRow = _
                    objDataSet.Tables("Role").NewRow
                'Set the values in the DataRow
                objDataRow.Item("RoleID") = New Guid(txtRoleID.Text)
                objDataRow.Item("RoleName") = txtRoleName.Text
                objDataRow.Item("RoleDescription") = _
                    txtRoleDescription.Text
                objDataRow.Item("Ranking") = _
                    CType(txtRanking.Text, Byte)
                'Add the DataRow to the DataSet
                objDataSet.Tables("Role").Rows.Add(objDataRow)
                'Update the Role in the database
                If Not objRoles.UpdateRole(objDataSet) Then
                    Throw New Exception("Update Role Failed")
                End If
            End Using

            'Clear the input fields
            txtRoleID.Text = String.Empty
            txtRoleName.Text = String.Empty
            txtRoleDescription.Text = String.Empty
            txtRanking.Text = String.Empty
            txtRoleUpdateDate.Text = String.Empty

            'Reload the Roles list
            Call LoadRoles()
```

10. Now add the following code under the `Case "Users"` statement in the same procedure:

```
        Case "Users"
            'Initialize a new instance of the business logic component
            Using objUsers As New WroxBusinessLogic.WBLUsers( _
                strCompany, strApplication)
                'Get a new User DataSet
                objDataSet = objUsers.GetNewUserDS()
                'Initialize a datarow object from the Role DataSet
                Dim objDataRow As Data.DataRow = _
                    objDataSet.Tables("User").NewRow
                'Set the values in the DataRow
                objDataRow.Item("UserID") = New Guid(txtUserID.Text)
                objDataRow.Item("LoginName") = txtLogin.Text
                objDataRow.Item("Password") = txtPassword.Text
                objDataRow.Item("FirstName") = txtFirstName.Text
                objDataRow.Item("LastName") = txtLastName.Text
                objDataRow.Item("Email") = txtEmail.Text
                objDataRow.Item("Phone") = txtPhone.Text
                objDataRow.Item("Status") = optStatusActive.Checked
```

```
                        objDataRow.Item("GroupID") = _
                            cboUserGroup.SelectedItem.Item("GroupID")
                        objDataRow.Item("RoleID") = _
                            cboUserRole.SelectedItem.Item("RoleID")
                        If cboUserManager.SelectedIndex <> -1 Then
                            objDataRow.Item("ManagerID") = _
                                cboUserManager.SelectedItem.item("ManagerID")
                        End If
                        'Add the DataRow to the DataSet
                        objDataSet.Tables("User").Rows.Add(objDataRow)
                        'Update the User in the database
                        If Not objUsers.UpdateUser(objDataSet) Then
                            Throw New Exception("Update User Failed")
                        End If
                End Using

                'Clear the input fields
                txtUserID.Text = String.Empty
                txtLogin.Text = String.Empty
                txtPassword.Text = String.Empty
                txtFirstName.Text = String.Empty
                txtLastName.Text = String.Empty
                txtEmail.Text = String.Empty
                txtPhone.Text = String.Empty
                optStatusActive.Checked = True
                txtUserUpdateDate.Text = String.Empty


                'Reload the Managers combo box
                Call LoadManagers()

                'Reload the Users list
                Call LoadUsers()
                cboUserGroup.SelectedIndex = -1
                cboUserRole.SelectedIndex = -1
                cboUserManager.SelectedIndex = -1
```

To test these changes, start your project. When the Login form is displayed, enter the admin user and password that you created in your database. When the Admin form is displayed, navigate to the Roles screen.

Click a role and change the ranking for that role to one that is not used. Then click the Update button on the toolbar or click the Action menu and select Update. The role will be updated as shown in Figure 13-1.

Click the same role again and update the ranking to one being used by one of the other roles. When you attempt to update the role in the database, you receive a message dialog box informing you that the ranking already exists and cannot be duplicated. The role will not be updated and the information displayed in the details section of the screen remains, enabling you to correct the problem and try again.

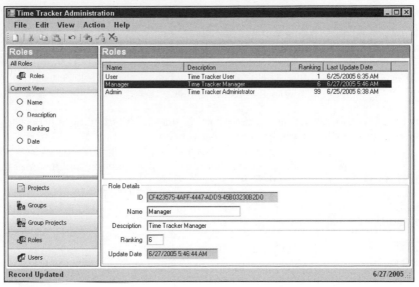

Figure 13-1

You can test updating the other fields in the User Details section of the screen and test changing the status of the user to suspended and then back to active.

Navigate to the Users screen and select a user who does not have a manager assigned. In the details section of the screen, select a manager and then click the Update button on the toolbar to update that user, as shown in Figure 13-2.

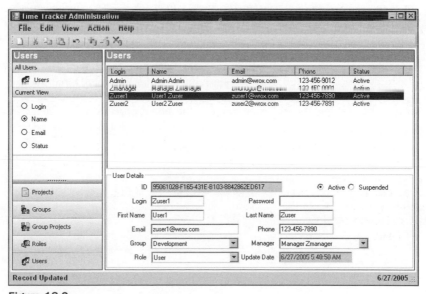

Figure 13-2

How It Works

The first stored procedure you create in this exercise is the `usp_UpdateRole` stored procedure. This stored procedure checks the Roles table for an existing ranking equal to the one passed to this stored procedure. It then compares the RoleID of that ranking, if found, against the RoleID being passed to this stored procedure to determine whether the ranking belongs to the role being updated. If the ranking does not belong to the role being updated, an error is raised and the update is cancelled.

Because the Oracle version of this stored procedure differs slightly from the SQL Server version, I explain both versions, starting with the SQL Server version.

The first part of this stored procedure defines the stored procedure name and its input parameters. This is all standard stuff that you've seen time and again.

SQL Server
```
CREATE PROCEDURE usp_UpdateRole
(
    @RoleID             UNIQUEIDENTIFIER,
    @RoleName           VARCHAR(50),
    @RoleDescription    TEXT,
    @Ranking            TINYINT
)
AS
```

You need to retrieve the RoleID from the Roles table if an existing ranking is found that matches the ranking passed to this stored procedure. This enables you to compare the RoleID in the Roles table against the RoleID passed as input to this stored procedure. To that end, you must declare a local variable in your stored procedure for the RoleID, which is what has been done in the next line of code.

Next, you set the `@ID` variable by selecting the RoleID into it where the Ranking column contains the same ranking as the `@Ranking` input parameter. Next, you check the `@ID` variable to see if it is not null in the `IF` statement that follows the `SELECT` statement. This determines whether a row of data was selected.

If the `@ID` variable is not null, a row of data exists in the Roles table with the same ranking as the one passed to this stored procedure. You want to determine whether the RoleID that was set in the `@ID` variable is not equal to the RoleID passed in the `@RoleID` input parameter. If the values are not equal, you raise an error that the ranking already exists and exit the stored procedure via the `RETURN` statement.

```
-- Declare local variables
DECLARE @ID    UNIQUEIDENTIFIER

-- See if the ranking exists
SELECT @ID = RoleID FROM Roles WHERE Ranking = @Ranking
    BEGIN
    IF @ID IS NOT NULL
        BEGIN
        -- The ranking exists, now verify it doesn't belong to the
        -- role you are updating
        IF @RoleID <> @ID
            BEGIN
```

```
                RAISERROR('Ranking already exists and cannot be duplicated.',18,1)
                RETURN
                END
            END
        END
```

If you've gotten this far, the ranking does not already exist or it belongs to the role being updated. Therefore, you proceed with the UPDATE statement to update the role. If an error occurred during the processing of the UPDATE statement, control will be passed to your BEGIN CATCH...END CATCH block where you raise an error that the update failed.

```
    -- Either the ranking does not exist or it belongs to the role being updated
    BEGIN TRY
        UPDATE Roles
            Set RoleName = @RoleName,
            RoleDescription = @RoleDescription,
            Ranking = @Ranking,
            LastUpdateDate = GETDATE()
            WHERE RoleID = @RoleID
    END TRY
    BEGIN CATCH
        BEGIN
        RAISERROR('Update role failed.',18,1)
        RETURN
        END
    END CATCH
```

The Oracle version of this stored procedure starts the same as the SQL Server version. You define the stored procedure name and its input parameters.

Oracle
```
CREATE OR REPLACE PROCEDURE usp_UpdateRole
(
    inRoleID            CHAR,
    inRoleName          VARCHAR2,
    inRoleDescription   CLOB,
    inRanking           NUMBER
)
AS
```

You also need to declare a local variable to hold the RoleID that will be selected from the Roles table, and that it done in the next statement. Then you begin the stored procedure with the BEGIN...END block and you have two separate blocks of logic: both are enclosed in a BEGIN...END block.

You select the RoleID into the varID local variable where the Ranking column in the Roles table matches the value in the inRanking input parameter. Oracle throws an exception if no data is found so you have code to handle that exception. Immediately following the SELECT statement you compare the RoleID in the inRoleID input parameter against the RoleID in the varID variable to see if they are not equal. If they are not equal, you raise an error that the ranking already exists and exit the stored procedure via the RETURN statement.

If the NO_DATA_FOUND exception was thrown, you know that the ranking did not already exist and you do not want to do anything. However, you have to have the code in your stored procedure to handle the NO_DATA_FOUND exception and you must include some code in that block. Because you do not want to do anything, you specify a NULL statement, which satisfies Oracle's compiler that the NO_DATA_FOUND exception block contains some code.

```
-- Declare local variables
varID CHAR(36);

BEGIN
    BEGIN
        -- See if the ranking exists
        SELECT RoleID INTO varID
        FROM Roles
        WHERE Ranking = inRanking;
        -- The ranking exists, now verify it doesn't belong to the
        -- role you are updating
        IF inRoleID <> varID THEN
            RAISE_APPLICATION_ERROR (-20999,
            'Ranking already exists and cannot be duplicated.');
            RETURN;
        END IF;
        EXCEPTION
            WHEN NO_DATA_FOUND THEN
            -- Handle the error but perform no processing
            NULL;
    END;
```

At this point, you know that the ranking did not already exist or that it belongs to the role being updated. Now you can update the role in the Roles table using the following UPDATE statement. You've included the appropriate error handling to handle any errors that may occur from the UPDATE statement.

```
    BEGIN
        -- Either the ranking does not exist or it belongs
        -- to the role being updated
        UPDATE Roles
            Set RoleName = inRoleName,
            RoleDescription = inRoleDescription,
            Ranking = inRanking,
            LastUpdateDate = SYSDATE
            WHERE RoleID = inRoleID;
        EXCEPTION
            WHEN OTHERS THEN
            RAISE_APPLICATION_ERROR( -20999,'Update role failed.');
            RETURN;
    END;
END;
```

The next stored procedure you create is the usp_UpdateUser stored procedure. This stored procedure is a fairly simple UPDATE stored procedure that you've seen before; therefore, the entire code will not be listed again. The one thing that is different about this stored procedure is that it checks to see whether a password has been passed to this stored procedure.

The SQL Server version of this stored procedure checks the length of the @Password input parameter using the LEN function. This function returns the number of characters in the expression being evaluated. If the length of the @Password input parameter is equal to zero, you select the current user's password into this parameter, which will be used in the UPDATE statement.

```
-- Check to see if the password is blank
-- (no updates to the password)
IF LEN(@Password) = 0
    BEGIN
    -- Get the current password
    SELECT @Password = Password
    FROM Users
    WHERE UserID = @UserID
    END
```

The Oracle version of this stored procedure requires that you declare a local variable first as you cannot alter the contents of the input parameters to the stored procedure. Then you check to see whether the inPassword parameter is null by using the IS NULL statement. If it is null, you select the user's current password into the varPassword variable; otherwise you set the password in the inPassword parameter in the varPassword variable. This variable will then be used in your UPDATE statement to update the user's password.

```
-- Declare local variables
varPassword VARCHAR2(30);

BEGIN
    BEGIN
        -- Check to see if the password is null
        -- (no updates to the password)
        IF inPassword IS NULL THEN
            -- Get the current password
            SELECT Password INTO varPassword
            FROM Users
            WHERE UserID = inUserID;
        ELSE
            varPassword := inPassword;
        END IF;
    END;
```

You add the UpdateRole function to the WDARoles class in the data access component next. The SQL Server version of this function is listed next in this section and the only differences between the SQL Server and Oracle versions are the data types used in the Parameters collection.

You encapsulate the code in this function in a Try...Catch block to handle any errors that may be thrown from the execution of the usp_UpdateRole stored procedure. The first thing that you do in the Try block is set the SQL property in the base class to the stored procedure being executed. Then you call the InitializeCommand method in the base class to initialize the Command object. You then proceed by adding the appropriate parameters to the Parameters collection, passing the values for the parameters using the data from the Role DataSet that was passed as input to this function. Finally, you execute the stored procedure by calling the ExecuteStoredProcedure method in the base class.

The Catch block contains the appropriate error-handling code to throw a new exception back to the caller of this function, passing it the exception that this function received.

```
Public Function UpdateRole(ByVal Role As DataSet) As Boolean
    Try
        MyBase.SQL = "usp_UpdateRole"
        'Initialize the Command object
        MyBase.InitializeCommand()
        'Add the Parameters to the Parameters collection
        MyBase.AddParameter("@RoleID", _
         SqlDbType.UniqueIdentifier, 16, _
         Role.Tables("Role").Rows(0).Item("RoleID"))
        MyBase.AddParameter("@RoleName", _
         SqlDbType.VarChar, 50, _
         Role.Tables("Role").Rows(0).Item("RoleName"))
        MyBase.AddParameter("@RoleDescription", _
         SqlDbType.Text, _
         Role.Tables("Role").Rows(0).Item( _
         "RoleDescription").ToString.Length, _
         Role.Tables("Role").Rows(0).Item("RoleDescription"))
        MyBase.AddParameter("@Ranking", _
         SqlDbType.TinyInt, 1, _
         Role.Tables("Role").Rows(0).Item("Ranking"))
        'Execute the stored procedure
        UpdateRole = ExecuteStoredProcedure()
    Catch ExceptionErr As Exception
        Throw New System.Exception(ExceptionErr.Message, _
        ExceptionErr.InnerException)
    End Try
End Function
```

The next function that you add to your data access component is the UpdateUser function. Again, only the SQL Server version is listed and the only differences between this version and the Oracle version are the data types used in the Parameters collection.

You set the SQL property in the base class to the stored procedure being executed and call the InitializeCommand method in the base class to initialize the Command object. You then add the parameters to the Parameters collection and pass the appropriate values using the data in the User DataSet.

```
Public Function UpdateUser(ByVal User As DataSet) As Boolean
    Try
        MyBase.SQL = "usp_UpdateUser"
        'Initialize the Command object
        MyBase.InitializeCommand()
        'Add the Parameters to the Parameters collection
        MyBase.AddParameter("@UserID", _
            SqlDbType.UniqueIdentifier, 16, _
            User.Tables("User").Rows(0).Item("UserID"))
        MyBase.AddParameter("@LoginName", _
            SqlDbType.VarChar, 15, _
            User.Tables("User").Rows(0).Item("LoginName"))
        MyBase.AddParameter("@Password", _
            SqlDbType.VarChar, 30, _
```

```
            User.Tables("User").Rows(0).Item("Password"))
        MyBase.AddParameter("@FirstName", _
            SqlDbType.VarChar, 30, _
            User.Tables("User").Rows(0).Item("FirstName"))
        MyBase.AddParameter("@LastName", _
            SqlDbType.VarChar, 30, _
            User.Tables("User").Rows(0).Item("LastName"))
        MyBase.AddParameter("@Email", _
            SqlDbType.VarChar, 50, _
            User.Tables("User").Rows(0).Item("Email"))
        MyBase.AddParameter("@Phone", _
            SqlDbType.VarChar, 20, _
            User.Tables("User").Rows(0).Item("Phone"))
        MyBase.AddParameter("@Status", _
            SqlDbType.Bit, 1, _
            User.Tables("User").Rows(0).Item("Status"))
        MyBase.AddParameter("@GroupID", _
            SqlDbType.UniqueIdentifier, 16, _
            User.Tables("User").Rows(0).Item("GroupID"))
        MyBase.AddParameter("@RoleID", _
            SqlDbType.UniqueIdentifier, 16, _
            User.Tables("User").Rows(0).Item("RoleID"))
        MyBase.AddParameter("@ManagerID", _
            SqlDbType.UniqueIdentifier, 16, _
            User.Tables("User").Rows(0).Item("ManagerID"))
```

After all the parameters are added to the `Parameters` collection, you execute the stored procedure by calling the `ExecuteStoredProcedure` method in the base class. You handle any errors that may occur in the `Catch` block.

```
        'Execute the stored procedure
        UpdateUser = ExecuteStoredProcedure()
    Catch ExceptionErr As Exception
        Throw New System.Exception(ExceptionErr.Message, _
        ExceptionErr.InnerException)
    End Try
End Function
```

The next step is to add the appropriate functions to the business logic component. You add the `UpdateRole` function in the `WBLRoles` class next. The code for this function is not listed here but essentially mirrors the code that you added in the `AddRole` function in Chapter 11.

You then add the `UpdateUser` function in the `WBLUsers` class. Because the password may or may not be updated, you cannot use the `ValidateUserData` function to validate the data. Instead, your `UpdateUser` function contains the code to validate the data. The only major difference in this function from the other functions that you've added is the way you handle validating the password. To that end, only the code for the password validation will be listed here.

First, you need to determine whether a password exists in the `DataSet`. This is done by converting the column to a string using the `ToString` method, trimming any blanks spaces using the `Trim` method, and finally checking the length using the `Length` function. If the password is blank, you set it to a `DBNull` value using the `DBNull` function.

If the password is not blank, you validate the password using the IsValidPassword function and then hash the password using the HashPassword function:

```
'Validate the password
If User.Tables("User").Rows(0).Item( _
    "Password").ToString.Trim.Length = 0 Then
    'The old password is not being updated so set it to Null
    User.Tables("User").Rows(0).Item("Password") = DBNull.Value
Else
    'A new password has been supplied
    If Not IsValidPassword(User.Tables( _
        "User").Rows(0).Item("Password")) Then
        Throw New System.Exception(strErrorMessage)
    Else
        'Hash the password
        User.Tables("User").Rows(0).Item("Password") = _
            HashPassword(User.Tables("User").Rows(0).Item( _
            "Password"))
    End If
End If
```

You add code to the ActionUpdate procedure in the Admin form next. You add the appropriate code to update a role under the Case "Roles" statement as follows. First, this code initializes a new instance of the business logic component. Then you get a new Role DataSet in the objDataSet object and initialize a new DataRow object.

```
Case "Roles"
    'Initialize a new instance of the business logic component
    Using objRoles As New WroxBusinessLogic.WBLRoles( _
        strCompany, strApplication)
        'Get a new Role DataSet
        objDataSet = objRoles.GetNewRoleDS()
        'Initialize a datarow object from the Role DataSet
        Dim objDataRow As Data.DataRow = _
            objDataSet.Tables("Role").NewRow
```

You then set the values in the DataRow object using the input fields from the Role Details section of the Roles screen. After the DataRow object is populated with the appropriate data, you add the DataRow object to the DataSet.

The call to the UpdateRole method in the business logic component is encapsulated in an If...Then statement to handle any errors that might be thrown.

```
'Set the values in the DataRow
objDataRow.Item("RoleID") = New Guid(txtRoleID.Text)
objDataRow.Item("RoleName") = txtRoleName.Text
objDataRow.Item("RoleDescription") = _
    txtRoleDescription.Text
objDataRow.Item("Ranking") = _
    CType(txtRanking.Text, Byte)
'Add the DataRow to the DataSet
objDataSet.Tables("Role").Rows.Add(objDataRow)
'Update the Role in the database
```

```
                    If Not objRoles.UpdateRole(objDataSet) Then
                        Throw New Exception("Update Role Failed")
                    End If
            End Using
```

After the role is successfully updated, you clear the fields in the Role Details section of the Roles screen by setting the Text property of the text boxes to an empty string. Then you call the LoadRoles procedure to update the list of roles to reflect the changes just made.

```
                'Clear the input fields
                txtRoleID.Text = String.Empty
                txtRoleName.Text = String.Empty
                txtRoleDescription.Text = String.Empty
                txtRanking.Text = String.Empty
                txtRoleUpdateDate.Text = String.Empty
                'Reload the Roles list
                Call LoadRoles()
```

You add code for the Case "Users" statement next to update a user. Again, you start by initializing a new instance of the business logic component and then you get a User DataSet. You initialize a new DataRow object next and set the values in the DataRow using the fields from the User Details section of the Users screen.

```
            Case "Users"
                'Initialize a new instance of the business logic component
                Using objUsers As New WroxBusinessLogic.WBLUsers( _
                    strCompany, strApplication)
                    'Get a new User DataSet
                    objDataSet = objUsers.GetNewUserDS()
                    'Initialize a datarow object from the Role DataSet
                    Dim objDataRow As Data.DataRow = _
                        objDataSet.Tables("User").NewRow
                    'Set the values in the DataRow
                    objDataRow.Item("UserID") = New Guid(txtUserID.Text)
                    objDataRow.Item("LoginName") = txtLogin.Text
                    objDataRow.Item("Password") = txtPassword.Text
                    objDataRow.Item("FirstName") = txtFirstName.Text
                    objDataRow.Item("LastName") = txtLastName.Text
                    objDataRow.Item("Email") = txtEmail.Text
                    objDataRow.Item("Phone") = txtPhone.Text
                    objDataRow.Item("Status") = optStatusActive.Checked
                    objDataRow.Item("GroupID") = _
                        cboUserGroup.SelectedItem.Item("GroupID")
                    objDataRow.Item("RoleID") = _
                        cboUserRole.SelectedItem.Item("RoleID")
                    If cboUserManager.SelectedIndex <> -1 Then
                        objDataRow.Item("ManagerID") = _
                            cboUserManager.SelectedItem.item("ManagerID")
                    End If
```

After all the values are set in the DataRow object, you add the DataRow object to the DataSet. Then you call the UpdateUser method in the business logic component and encapsulate that call in an If...Then statement to handle any errors that might be thrown from that call.

If all was successful, you clear the Text property of the text boxes in the User Details section of the Users screen by setting them to an empty string.

Next, you call the LoadManagers and LoadUsers procedures to reload the list of managers in the cboUserManager combo box and the list of users in the Users screen. You then set the SelectedIndex property of the combo boxes to a value of -1, which causes no entries to be selected.

```
                    'Add the DataRow to the DataSet
                    objDataSet.Tables("User").Rows.Add(objDataRow)
                    'Update the User in the database
                    If Not objUsers.UpdateUser(objDataSet) Then
                        Throw New Exception("Update User Failed")
                    End If
            End Using

            'Clear the input fields
            txtUserID.Text = String.Empty
            txtLogin.Text = String.Empty
            txtPassword.Text = String.Empty
            txtFirstName.Text = String.Empty
            txtLastName.Text = String.Empty
            txtEmail.Text = String.Empty
            txtPhone.Text = String.Empty
            optStatusActive.Checked = True
            txtUserUpdateDate.Text = String.Empty

            'Reload the Managers combo box
            Call LoadManagers()
            'Reload the Users list
            Call LoadUsers()
            cboUserGroup.SelectedIndex = -1
            cboUserRole.SelectedIndex = -1
            cboUserManager.SelectedIndex = -1
```

This completes the code for the Admin form and you are now able to update roles and users as you saw when you tested your changes. The only functionality that has not been implemented for roles and users is delete functionality.

Updating Timesheets

The way that a timesheet is displayed in the TimeSheet form and the way that it is stored in the database are totally different, as you saw when you built the usp_SelectTimeSheet stored procedure in the last chapter. When a user saves a timesheet, you update the hours for each project for each day of the week in the TimeSheetItems table.

This actually simplifies the update process, as you have the TimeSheetItemID and the hours to be updated in the TimeSheet DataSet. All you need to do is iterate through each row in the DataSet and perform a call to the update stored procedure for a timesheet to update the hours for each day and each project.

Remember that the `TimeSheet DataSet` contains one project per row in the `DataSet` and a column for each business day of the week for that project. You will be calling the update stored procedure for each day of the week in each row. Therefore, you basically call the update stored procedure five times for each row of data in the `DataSet`. You see how this is implemented in the `SaveTimeSheet` function in the data access component in the next exercise.

In this Try It Out, you add to the TimeSheet form the functionality for a user to update and submit his or her timesheet, as well as the functionality for a manager to approve a timesheet.

Try It Out   Completing the TimeSheet Form

To complete this exercise:

1. Open your Time Tracker application in Visual Studio 2005 if it is not still open.

2. View the Server Explorer window and click the Auto Hide icon on the window to keep it visible and then view the Stored Procedures node for your database.

3. Create the `usp_UpdateTimeSheetItem` stored procedure first. This stored procedure updates a single timesheet item in a timesheet for a user. Readers using SQL Server should right-click the Stored Procedures and choose Add New Stored Procedure from the context menu. Readers using Oracle should use their favorite Oracle tool such as iSQL *Plus to create the stored procedures. Enter the code for the following stored procedure:

   SQL Server

```
CREATE PROCEDURE usp_UpdateTimeSheetItem
(
    @TimeSheetItemID    UNIQUEIDENTIFIER,
    @Hours              TINYINT
)
AS

BEGIN TRY
    UPDATE TimeSheetItems
        SET Hours = @Hours
        WHERE TimeSheetItemID = @TimeSheetItemID
END TRY
BEGIN CATCH
    BEGIN
    RAISERROR('Update timesheet item failed.',18,1)
    RETURN
    END
END CATCH
```

   Click the Save icon on the toolbar to create the stored procedure.

   Oracle

```
CREATE OR REPLACE PROCEDURE usp_UpdateTimeSheetItem
(
    inTimeSheetItemID    CHAR,
    inHours              NUMBER
)
AS
BEGIN
```

```
      UPDATE TimeSheetItems
         SET Hours = inHours
         WHERE TimeSheetItemID = inTimeSheetItemID;
      EXCEPTION
         WHEN OTHERS THEN
         RAISE_APPLICATION_ERROR( -20999,'Update timesheet item failed.');
         RETURN;
   END;
```

Click the Execute button to have the stored procedure created in your database.

4. Create the `usp_SubmitTimeSheet` stored procedure next. This stored procedure updates a timesheet, marking it as submitted and preventing the user from editing the contents. SQL Server users should right-click the Stored Procedures node in the Server Explorer and choose Add New Stored Procedure and Oracle users should use their Oracle tool. Enter the following code:

SQL Server

```
CREATE PROCEDURE usp_SubmitTimeSheet
(
   @TimeSheetID   UNIQUEIDENTIFIER
)
AS

BEGIN TRY
   UPDATE TimeSheets
      SET Submitted = 1
      WHERE TimeSheetID = @TimeSheetID
END TRY
BEGIN CATCH
   BEGIN
   RAISERROR('Submit timesheet failed.',18,1)
   RETURN
   END
END CATCH
```

Click the Save icon on the toolbar to have the stored procedure created in your database.

Oracle

```
CREATE OR REPLACE PROCEDURE usp_SubmitTimeSheet
(
   inTimeSheetID   CHAR
)
AS

BEGIN
   UPDATE TimeSheets
      SET Submitted = 1
      WHERE TimeSheetID = inTimeSheetID;
   EXCEPTION
      WHEN OTHERS THEN
      RAISE_APPLICATION_ERROR( -20999,'Submit timesheet failed.');
      RETURN;
END;
```

Click the Execute button to have the stored procedure created in your database.

5. The final stored procedure to create is the usp_ApproveTimeSheet stored procedure. This stored procedure updates the status of a timesheet, marking it as approved by a manager. SQL Server users should right-click the Stored Procedures node in the Server Explorer and choose Add New Stored Procedure and Oracle users should use their Oracle tool. Enter the following code:

SQL Server

```
CREATE PROCEDURE usp_ApproveTimeSheet
(
    @TimeSheetID    UNIQUEIDENTIFIER,
    @ManagerID      UNIQUEIDENTIFIER
)
AS

BEGIN TRY
    UPDATE TimeSheets
        SET ApprovalDate = GETDATE(),
        ManagerID = @ManagerID
        WHERE TimeSheetID = @TimeSheetID
END TRY
BEGIN CATCH
    BEGIN
    RAISERROR('Approve timesheet failed.',18,1)
    RETURN
    END
END CATCH
```

Click the Save icon on the toolbar to have the stored procedure created in your database.

Oracle

```
CREATE OR REPLACE PROCEDURE usp_ApproveTimeSheet
(
    inTimeSheetID    CHAR,
    inManagerID      CHAR
)
AS

BEGIN
    UPDATE TimeSheets
        SET ApprovalDate = SYSDATE,
        ManagerID = inManagerID
        WHERE TimeSheetID = inTimeSheetID;
    EXCEPTION
        WHEN OTHERS THEN
        RAISE_APPLICATION_ERROR( -20999,'Approve timesheet failed.');
        RETURN;
END;
```

Click the Execute button to have the stored procedure created in your database.

6. View the code in the WDATimeSheets class in your data access component. The first function to add in this class is the SaveTimeSheet function. Add the following code to this class:

SQL Server

```
Public Function SaveTimeSheet(ByVal TimeSheet As DataSet) As Boolean
    Try
        MyBase.SQL = "usp_UpdateTimeSheetItem"
        'Initialize the Command object
        MyBase.InitializeCommand()
        'Add the Parameters to the Parameters collection
        MyBase.AddParameter("@TimeSheetItemID", _
         SqlDbType.UniqueIdentifier, 16, Nothing)
        MyBase.AddParameter("@Hours", _
         SqlDbType.TinyInt, 1, Nothing)
        'Process all rows in the table
        For intIndex As Integer = 0 To _
            TimeSheet.Tables("TimeSheet").Rows.Count - 2
            'Update Monday's Hours
            MyBase.Command.Parameters.Item("@TimeSheetItemID").Value = _
                TimeSheet.Tables("TimeSheet").Rows(intIndex).Item( _
                "MondayTimeSheetItemID")
            MyBase.Command.Parameters.Item("@Hours").Value = _
                TimeSheet.Tables("TimeSheet").Rows(intIndex).Item( _
                "MondayHours")
            SaveTimeSheet = ExecuteStoredProcedure()
            'Update Tuesday's Hours
            MyBase.Command.Parameters.Item("@TimeSheetItemID").Value = _
                TimeSheet.Tables("TimeSheet").Rows(intIndex).Item( _
                "TuesdayTimeSheetItemID")
            MyBase.Command.Parameters.Item("@Hours").Value = _
                TimeSheet.Tables("TimeSheet").Rows(intIndex).Item( _
                "TuesdayHours")
            SaveTimeSheet = ExecuteStoredProcedure()
            'Update Wednesday's Hours
            MyBase.Command.Parameters.Item("@TimeSheetItemID").Value = _
                TimeSheet.Tables("TimeSheet").Rows(intIndex).Item( _
                "WednesdayTimeSheetItemID")
            MyBase.Command.Parameters.Item("@Hours").Value = _
                TimeSheet.Tables("TimeSheet").Rows(intIndex).Item( _
                "WednesdayHours")
            SaveTimeSheet = ExecuteStoredProcedure()
            'Update Thursday's Hours
            MyBase.Command.Parameters.Item("@TimeSheetItemID").Value = _
                TimeSheet.Tables("TimeSheet").Rows(intIndex).Item( _
                "ThursdayTimeSheetItemID")
            MyBase.Command.Parameters.Item("@Hours").Value = _
                TimeSheet.Tables("TimeSheet").Rows(intIndex).Item( _
                "ThursdayHours")
            SaveTimeSheet = ExecuteStoredProcedure()
            'Update Friday's Hours
            MyBase.Command.Parameters.Item("@TimeSheetItemID").Value = _
                TimeSheet.Tables("TimeSheet").Rows(intIndex).Item( _
                "FridayTimeSheetItemID")
            MyBase.Command.Parameters.Item("@Hours").Value = _
                TimeSheet.Tables("TimeSheet").Rows(intIndex).Item( _
                "FridayHours")
```

```
            SaveTimeSheet = ExecuteStoredProcedure()
        Next
    Catch ExceptionErr As Exception
        Throw New System.Exception(ExceptionErr.Message, _
        ExceptionErr.InnerException)
    End Try
End Function
```

Oracle

```
Public Function SaveTimeSheet(ByVal TimeSheet As DataSet) As Boolean
    Try
        MyBase.SQL = "usp_UpdateTimeSheetItem"
        'Initialize the Command object
        MyBase.InitializeCommand()
        'Add the Parameters to the Parameters collection
        MyBase.AddParameter("inTimeSheetItemID", _
         OracleClient.OracleType.Char, 36, Nothing)
        MyBase.AddParameter("inHours", _
         OracleClient.OracleType.Number, 3, Nothing)
        'Process all rows in the table
        For intIndex As Integer = 0 To _
            TimeSheet.Tables("TimeSheet").Rows.Count - 2
            'Update Monday's Hours
            MyBase.Command.Parameters.Item("inTimeSheetItemID").Value = _
                TimeSheet.Tables("TimeSheet").Rows(intIndex).Item( _
                "MondayTimeSheetItemID").ToString
            MyBase.Command.Parameters.Item("inHours").Value = _
                TimeSheet.Tables("TimeSheet").Rows(intIndex).Item( _
                "MondayHours")
            SaveTimeSheet = ExecuteStoredProcedure()
            'Update Tuesday's Hours
            MyBase.Command.Parameters.Item("inTimeSheetItemID").Value = _
                TimeSheet.Tables("TimeSheet").Rows(intIndex).Item( _
                "TuesdayTimeSheetItemID").ToString
            MyBase.Command.Parameters.Item("inHours").Value = _
                TimeSheet.Tables("TimeSheet").Rows(intIndex).Item( _
                "TuesdayHours")
            SaveTimeSheet = ExecuteStoredProcedure()
            'Update Wednesday's Hours
            MyBase.Command.Parameters.Item("inTimeSheetItemID").Value = _
                TimeSheet.Tables("TimeSheet").Rows(intIndex).Item( _
                "WednesdayTimeSheetItemID").ToString
            MyBase.Command.Parameters.Item("inHours").Value = _
                TimeSheet.Tables("TimeSheet").Rows(intIndex).Item( _
                "WednesdayHours")
            SaveTimeSheet = ExecuteStoredProcedure()
            'Update Thursday's Hours
            MyBase.Command.Parameters.Item("inTimeSheetItemID").Value = _
                TimeSheet.Tables("TimeSheet").Rows(intIndex).Item( _
                "ThursdayTimeSheetItemID").ToString
            MyBase.Command.Parameters.Item("inHours").Value = _
                TimeSheet.Tables("TimeSheet").Rows(intIndex).Item( _
                "ThursdayHours")
```

```
                    SaveTimeSheet = ExecuteStoredProcedure()
                    'Update Friday's Hours
                    MyBase.Command.Parameters.Item("inTimeSheetItemID").Value = _
                        TimeSheet.Tables("TimeSheet").Rows(intIndex).Item( _
                        "FridayTimeSheetItemID").ToString
                    MyBase.Command.Parameters.Item("inHours").Value = _
                        TimeSheet.Tables("TimeSheet").Rows(intIndex).Item( _
                        "FridayHours")
                    SaveTimeSheet = ExecuteStoredProcedure()
                Next
        Catch ExceptionErr As Exception
            Throw New System.Exception(ExceptionErr.Message, _
            ExceptionErr.InnerException)
        End Try
    End Function
```

7. Add the `SubmitTimeSheet` function in the same class next. Add the following code:

SQL Server

```
Public Function SubmitTimeSheet(ByVal TimeSheetID As Guid) As Boolean
    Try
        MyBase.SQL = "usp_SubmitTimeSheet"
        'Initialize the Command object
        MyBase.InitializeCommand()
        'Add the Parameters to the Parameters collection
        MyBase.AddParameter("@TimeSheetID", _
            SqlDbType.UniqueIdentifier, 16, TimeSheetID)
        'Execute the stored procedure
        SubmitTimeSheet = ExecuteStoredProcedure()
    Catch ExceptionErr As Exception
        Throw New System.Exception(ExceptionErr.Message, _
        ExceptionErr.InnerException)
    End Try
End Function
```

Oracle

```
Public Function SubmitTimeSheet(ByVal TimeSheetID As Guid) As Boolean
    Try
        MyBase.SQL = "usp_SubmitTimeSheet"
        'Initialize the Command object
        MyBase.InitializeCommand()
        'Add the Parameters to the Parameters collection
        MyBase.AddParameter("inTimeSheetID", _
            OracleClient.OracleType.Char, 36, TimeSheetID.ToString)
        'Execute the stored procedure
        SubmitTimeSheet = ExecuteStoredProcedure()
    Catch ExceptionErr As Exception
        Throw New System.Exception(ExceptionErr.Message, _
        ExceptionErr.InnerException)
    End Try
End Function
```

8. The final function to add in the WDATimeSheets class is the ApproveTimeSheet function. Add the following code to this class:

SQL Server

```
Public Function ApproveTimeSheet(ByVal TimeSheetID As Guid, _
    ByVal ManagerID As Guid) As Boolean
    Try
        MyBase.SQL = "usp_ApproveTimeSheet"
        'Initialize the Command object
        MyBase.InitializeCommand()
        'Add the Parameters to the Parameters collection
        MyBase.AddParameter("@TimeSheetID", _
            SqlDbType.UniqueIdentifier, 16, TimeSheetID)
        MyBase.AddParameter("@ManagerID", _
            SqlDbType.UniqueIdentifier, 16, ManagerID)
        'Execute the stored procedure
        ApproveTimeSheet = ExecuteStoredProcedure()
    Catch ExceptionErr As Exception
        Throw New System.Exception(ExceptionErr.Message, _
        ExceptionErr.InnerException)
    End Try
End Function
```

Oracle

```
Public Function ApproveTimeSheet(ByVal TimeSheetID As Guid, _
    ByVal ManagerID As Guid) As Boolean
    Try
        MyBase.SQL = "usp_ApproveTimeSheet"
        'Initialize the Command object
        MyBase.InitializeCommand()
        'Add the Parameters to the Parameters collection
        MyBase.AddParameter("inTimeSheetID", _
            OracleClient.OracleType.Char, 36, TimeSheetID.ToString)
        MyBase.AddParameter("inManagerID", _
            OracleClient.OracleType.Char, 36, ManagerID.ToString)
        'Execute the stored procedure
        ApproveTimeSheet = ExecuteStoredProcedure()
    Catch ExceptionErr As Exception
        Throw New System.Exception(ExceptionErr.Message, _
        ExceptionErr.InnerException)
    End Try
End Function
```

9. Now it's time to move to the WBLTimeSheets class in the business logic component to add the appropriate functions there. The first function to add is the SaveTimeSheet function. Add the following code to this class:

```
Public Function SaveTimeSheet(ByVal TimeSheet As DataSet) As Boolean
    Try
        'Call the data component to save the timesheet
        Return objWDATimeSheets.SaveTimeSheet(TimeSheet)
    Catch ExceptionErr As Exception
        Throw New System.Exception(ExceptionErr.Message, _
         ExceptionErr.InnerException)
    End Try
End Function
```

10. The `SubmitTimeSheet` function is next, so add the following code to the `WBLTimeSheets` class:

```
Public Function SubmitTimeSheet(ByVal TimeSheetID As Guid) As Boolean
    Try
        'Call the data component to submit the timesheet
        Return objWDATimeSheets.SubmitTimeSheet(TimeSheetID)
    Catch ExceptionErr As Exception
        Throw New System.Exception(ExceptionErr.Message, _
         ExceptionErr.InnerException)
    End Try
End Function
```

11. The `ApproveTimeSheet` function is the final function to be added to the business logic component. Add the following code:

```
Public Function ApproveTimeSheet(ByVal TimeSheetID As Guid, _
    ByVal ManagerID As Guid) As Boolean
    Try
        'Call the data component to approve the timesheet
        Return objWDATimeSheets.ApproveTimeSheet(TimeSheetID, ManagerID)
    Catch ExceptionErr As Exception
        Throw New System.Exception(ExceptionErr.Message, _
         ExceptionErr.InnerException)
    End Try
End Function
```

12. Now it's time to add some code to the TimeSheet form, so view the code in the Code Editor. When users are finished editing a timesheet, they click the Save button to save the changes. Click the Class Name combo box and select `btnSave`, and in the Method Name combo box, select the `Click` event. Add the following code to the `btnSave_Click` procedure:

```
Private Sub btnSave_Click(ByVal sender As Object, _
    ByVal e As System.EventArgs) Handles btnSave.Click

        'Initialize a new instance of the business logic component
        Using objTimeSheets As New WroxBusinessLogic.WBLTimeSheets( _
            strCompany, strApplication)
            Try
                'Save the timesheet changes
                If Not objTimeSheets.SaveTimeSheet(objTimeSheetDS) Then
                    Throw New Exception("Save TimeSheet Failed")
                End If
                'Display a statusbar message
                ToolStripStatus.Text = "Timesheet saved"
            Catch ExceptionErr As Exception
                MessageBox.Show(ExceptionErr.Message, strAppTitle)
            End Try
        End Using
End Sub
```

13. When users complete their timesheet for the week, they will submit their timesheet for approval. Click the Class Name combo box and select `btnSubmit`, and in the Method Name combo box select the `Click` event. Add the following code to the `btnSubmit_Click` procedure:

```
Private Sub btnSubmit_Click(ByVal sender As Object, _
    ByVal e As System.EventArgs) Handles btnSubmit.Click

    'Initialize a new instance of the business logic component
    Using objTimeSheets As New WroxBusinessLogic.WBLTimeSheets( _
        strCompany, strApplication)
        Try
            'Submit the timesheet
            If Not objTimeSheets.SubmitTimeSheet( _
                New Guid(objTimeSheetDS.Tables("TimeSheet").Rows(0).Item( _
                "TimeSheetID").ToString)) Then
                Throw New Exception("Submit TimeSheet Failed")
            End If
            'Reload the timesheet so it becomes read-only
            Call LoadTimeSheet(cboWeekEnding)
            'Display a statusbar message
            ToolStripStatus.Text = "Timesheet submitted"
        Catch ExceptionErr As Exception
            MessageBox.Show(ExceptionErr.Message, strAppTitle)
        End Try
    End Using
End Sub
```

14. When managers approve a timesheet for a user, they click the Approve button. You need to add some code to the Click event for that button. Click the Class Name combo box and select btnApprove, and in the Method Name combo box select the Click event. Add the following code to the btnApprove_Click procedure:

```
Private Sub btnApprove_Click(ByVal sender As Object, _
    ByVal e As System.EventArgs) Handles btnApprove.Click

    'Initialize a new instance of the business logic component
    Using objTimeSheets As New WroxBusinessLogic.WBLTimeSheets( _
        strCompany, strApplication)
        Try
            'Submit the timesheet
            If Not objTimeSheets.ApproveTimeSheet( _
            New Guid(objTimeSheetDS.Tables("TimeSheet").Rows(0).Item( _
                "TimeSheetID").ToString), New Guid(strManagerID)) Then
                Throw New Exception("Approve TimeSheet Failed")
            End If
            'Display a statusbar message
            ToolStripStatus.Text = "Timesheet approved"
        Catch ExceptionErr As Exception
            MessageBox.Show(ExceptionErr.Message, strAppTitle)
        End Try
    End Using
End Sub
```

That's all the code that's needed to complete the functionality in your TimeSheet form. To test your changes, start your project and log in as a user. When the TimeSheet form is displayed, complete the timesheet and then click the Save button. Your timesheet will be saved and you'll see a message in the status bar indicating that the timesheet was saved, as shown in Figure 13-3. You can continue to make changes to the timesheet and save it again if you want.

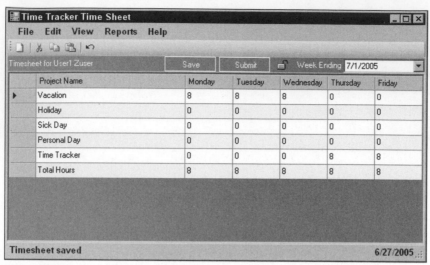

Figure 13-3

Now test the functionality of the Submit button. Click the Submit button and you see a message in the status bar indicating that the timesheet was submitted, as shown in Figure 13-4. You'll also notice that the icon next to the Submit button has been changed to a locked status and the timesheet is read-only and will not allow any changes.

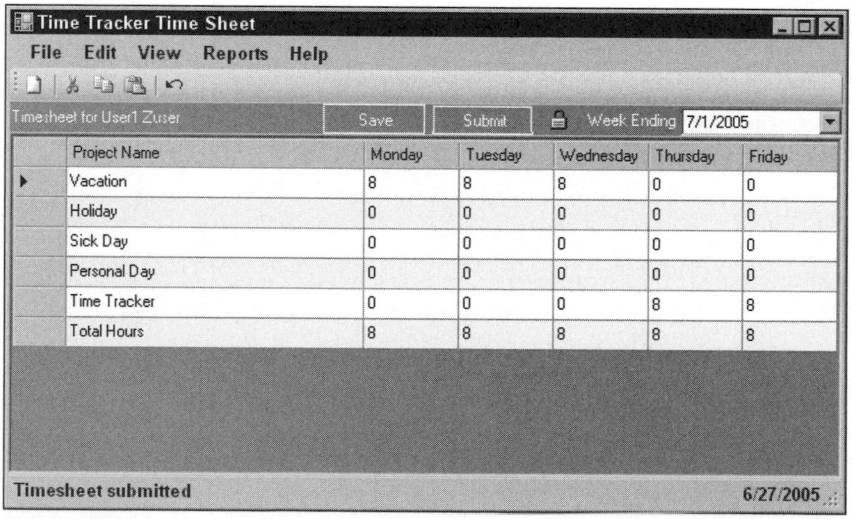

Figure 13-4

You have exercised all of the functionality from a user's standpoint so close the TimeSheet form. Start your project again and this time log in as a manager. When the TimeSheet form is displayed, select the user in the Employee combo box who you submitted the timesheet for and select the appropriate week ending date in the Week Ending combo box. When the timesheet appears, click the Approve button and you'll notice a message in the status bar indicating that the timesheet was approved, as shown in Figure 13-5.

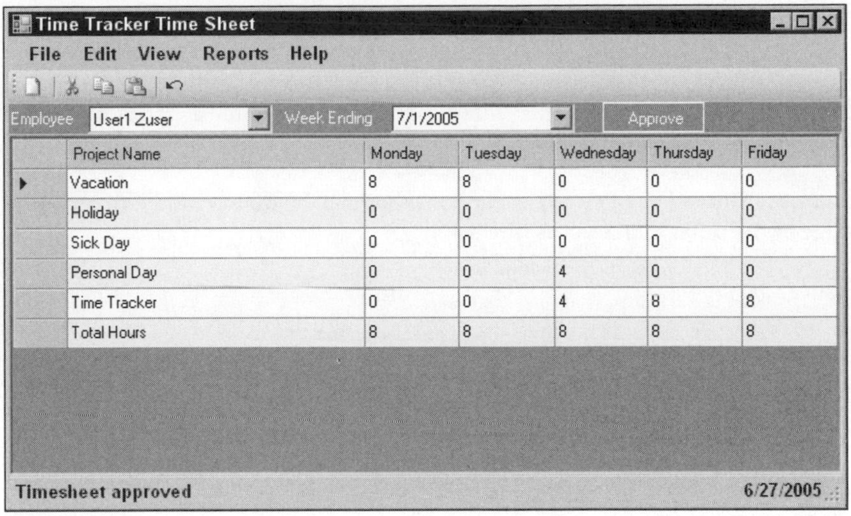

Figure 13-5

How It Works

The first stored procedure that you create in this exercise is the usp_UpdateTimeSheetItem stored procedure. This is a simple UPDATE stored procedure that will update a single row in the TimeSheetItems table.

In the SQL Server version that follows, you can see that there are only two input parameters to this stored procedure: the TimeSheetItemID of the timesheet item to be updated, and the hours that should be updated in the Hours column.

The UPDATE statement is also simple and updates the Hours column where the TimeSheetItemID in the TimeSheetItems table matches the @TimeSheetItemID input parameter. The appropriate error-handling code has been added to handle any errors that may occur.

SQL Server

```
CREATE PROCEDURE usp_UpdateTimeSheetItem
(
    @TimeSheetItemID    UNIQUEIDENTIFIER,
    @Hours              TINYINT
)
AS

BEGIN TRY
    UPDATE TimeSheetItems
        SET Hours = @Hours
        WHERE TimeSheetItemID = @TimeSheetItemID
END TRY
```

```
BEGIN CATCH
    BEGIN
    RAISERROR('Update timesheet item failed.',18,1)
    RETURN
    END
END CATCH
```

In the Oracle version, the same two input parameters have been supplied with data types appropriate for Oracle. The UPDATE statement in this stored procedure is the same as the SQL Server version and updates a single row of data in the TimeSheetItems table.

Error handling is included to catch any exceptions that may be thrown and will return an appropriate error message to the caller if an error is thrown.

Oracle

```
CREATE OR REPLACE PROCEDURE usp_UpdateTimeSheetItem
(
    inTimeSheetItemID    CHAR,
    inHours              NUMBER
)
AS
BEGIN
    UPDATE TimeSheetItems
        SET Hours = inHours
        WHERE TimeSheetItemID = inTimeSheetItemID;
    EXCEPTION
        WHEN OTHERS THEN
        RAISE_APPLICATION_ERROR( -20999,'Update timesheet item failed.');
        RETURN;
END;
```

Next, you create the usp_SubmitTimeSheet stored procedure. The TimeSheets table contains the Submitted column, which stores a BIT value in SQL Server and a NUMBER value in Oracle. When a timesheet is created, this column contains a value of 0, indicating that the timesheet has not been submitted. When users submit their timesheets, this column is updated to contain a value of 1, indicating that their timesheets have been submitted.

The TimeSheet form contains the necessary logic to make the timesheet read-only when the submitted column contains a value of 1.

The SQL Server version of this stored procedure accepts only one parameter, the TimeSheetID of the timesheet to be updated. The UPDATE statement sets the value in the Submitted column to a value of 1, indicating that the timesheet has been submitted.

The appropriate error handling is included in this stored procedure to handle any errors that may occur and will return the appropriate error message to the caller of this stored procedure.

SQL Server

```
CREATE PROCEDURE usp_SubmitTimeSheet
(
    @TimeSheetID    UNIQUEIDENTIFIER
)
```

```
AS

BEGIN TRY
   UPDATE TimeSheets
      SET Submitted = 1
      WHERE TimeSheetID = @TimeSheetID
END TRY
BEGIN CATCH
   BEGIN
   RAISERROR('Submit timesheet failed.',18,1)
   RETURN
   END
END CATCH
```

The Oracle version of this stored procedure is similar to the SQL Server version and accepts only the TimeSheetID of the timesheet being updated as its one and only input parameter. The UPDATE statement also mirrors its SQL Server counterpart, setting the value in the Submitted column to a value of 1.

Error-handling code is also included to handle any exceptions thrown and to return the appropriate error message back to the caller.

Oracle

```
CREATE OR REPLACE PROCEDURE usp_SubmitTimeSheet
(
    inTimeSheetID    CHAR
)
AS

BEGIN
   UPDATE TimeSheets
      SET Submitted = 1
      WHERE TimeSheetID = inTimeSheetID;
   EXCEPTION
      WHEN OTHERS THEN
      RAISE_APPLICATION_ERROR( -20999,'Submit timesheet failed.');
      RETURN;
END;
```

The final stored procedure you create in this exercise is usp_ApproveTimeSheet. Managers using the TimeSheet form execute this stored procedure when they click the Approve button on the TimeSheet form.

The SQL Server implementation of this stored procedure accepts two input parameters: the TimeSheetID of the timesheet to be approved and the ManagerID of the manager approving the timesheet.

The UPDATE statement sets the ApprovalDate to the current date and time and updates the ManagerID column with the ManagerID passed in the @ManagerID input parameter. The appropriate error handling is included to handle any errors that may occur and to pass the appropriate error message to the caller of this stored procedure.

SQL Server

```
CREATE PROCEDURE usp_ApproveTimeSheet
(
    @TimeSheetID    UNIQUEIDENTIFIER,
```

```
    @ManagerID      UNIQUEIDENTIFIER
)
AS

BEGIN TRY
   UPDATE TimeSheets
      SET ApprovalDate = GETDATE(),
      ManagerID = @ManagerID
      WHERE TimeSheetID = @TimeSheetID
END TRY
BEGIN CATCH
   BEGIN
   RAISERROR('Approve timesheet failed.',18,1)
   RETURN
   END
END CATCH
```

The Oracle version of this stored procedure also accepts the TimeSheetID and ManagerID as input parameters using the data types that are appropriate for the Oracle schema. The UPDATE statement mirrors the functionality of its SQL Server counterpart, updating the ApprovalDate and ManagerID columns.

The appropriate error handling is included and raises an application error if the UPDATE statement fails. It then returns the appropriate error message to the caller.

Oracle

```
CREATE OR REPLACE PROCEDURE usp_ApproveTimeSheet
(
   inTimeSheetID   CHAR,
   inManagerID     CHAR
)
AS

BEGIN
   UPDATE TimeSheets
      SET ApprovalDate = SYSDATE,
      ManagerID = inManagerID
      WHERE TimeSheetID = inTimeSheetID;
   EXCEPTION
      WHEN OTHERS THEN
      RAISE_APPLICATION_ERROR( -20999,'Approve timesheet failed.');
      RETURN;
END;
```

The SaveTimeSheet function is created next in the data access component. Only the SQL Server version is shown here. The only differences between the SQL Server and Oracle versions are the data types used in the Parameters collection.

The first thing to do in this function is to set the SQL property in the base class to the stored procedure to be executed. Then you initialize the Command object by calling the InitializeCommand method in the base class.

Because you will be making multiple calls to this stored procedure, you want to add the parameters to the `Parameters` collection, passing a value of `Nothing` to the `AddParameter` method. The actual values for these parameters are set in the `For` loop that follows:

```
Public Function SaveTimeSheet(ByVal TimeSheet As DataSet) As Boolean
    Try
        MyBase.SQL = "usp_UpdateTimeSheetItem"
        'Initialize the Command object
        MyBase.InitializeCommand()
        'Add the Parameters to the Parameters collection
        MyBase.AddParameter("@TimeSheetItemID", _
         SqlDbType.UniqueIdentifier, 16, Nothing)
        MyBase.AddParameter("@Hours", _
         SqlDbType.TinyInt, 1, Nothing)
```

Now you want to process each business day of the week for each project. This is done in a `For` loop that processes each row in the `TimeSheet DataSet`. Remember that each row in the `TimeSheet DataSet` contains the hours for each business day of the week for a single project. You use the `Count` property of the `Rows` property in the `DataSet` to determine the number of rows to process and subtract 2 from that. Normally you subtract 1 from the `Count` property because the index of the `Rows` property is a zero-based index. However, here you must subtract 2 to account for the last row in the `DataSet`, which you do not want to process. Remember that the last row in the `DataSet` contains the total row you added, which contains the total for each day of the week. This is merely done for the display of the timesheet, so users know how many hours they entered for each day.

```
'Process all rows in the table
For intIndex As Integer = 0 To _
    TimeSheet.Tables("TimeSheet").Rows.Count - 2
```

To update Monday's hours, you get the TimeSheetItemID for Monday from the `DataSet`, which is contained in the `MondayTimeSheetItemID` column, and set the value in the `@TimeSheetItemID` Parameter in the `Parameters` collection. Then you get the hours entered for Monday from the `MondayHours` column in the `DataSet` and set the value for the `@Hours` Parameter in the `Parameters` collection. Finally, you call the `ExecuteStoredProcedure` method in the base class to update the hours for Monday for this given project.

You repeat this process for Tuesday, Wednesday, Thursday, and Friday. This causes the hours for each day of the week to be updated for a single project. Then you start the loop over and update the hours for each day of the week for the next project:

```
'Update Monday's Hours
MyBase.Command.Parameters.Item("@TimeSheetItemID").Value = _
    TimeSheet.Tables("TimeSheet").Rows(intIndex).Item( _
    "MondayTimeSheetItemID")
MyBase.Command.Parameters.Item("@Hours").Value = _
    TimeSheet.Tables("TimeSheet").Rows(intIndex).Item( _
    "MondayHours")
SaveTimeSheet = ExecuteStoredProcedure()
'Update Tuesday's Hours
MyBase.Command.Parameters.Item("@TimeSheetItemID").Value = _
    TimeSheet.Tables("TimeSheet").Rows(intIndex).Item( _
    "TuesdayTimeSheetItemID")
```

```
        MyBase.Command.Parameters.Item("@Hours").Value = _
            TimeSheet.Tables("TimeSheet").Rows(intIndex).Item( _
            "TuesdayHours")
        SaveTimeSheet = ExecuteStoredProcedure()
        'Update Wednesday's Hours
        MyBase.Command.Parameters.Item("@TimeSheetItemID").Value = _
            TimeSheet.Tables("TimeSheet").Rows(intIndex).Item( _
            "WednesdayTimeSheetItemID")
        MyBase.Command.Parameters.Item("@Hours").Value = _
            TimeSheet.Tables("TimeSheet").Rows(intIndex).Item( _
            "WednesdayHours")
        SaveTimeSheet = ExecuteStoredProcedure()
        'Update Thursday's Hours
        MyBase.Command.Parameters.Item("@TimeSheetItemID").Value = _
            TimeSheet.Tables("TimeSheet").Rows(intIndex).Item( _
            "ThursdayTimeSheetItemID")
        MyBase.Command.Parameters.Item("@Hours").Value = _
            TimeSheet.Tables("TimeSheet").Rows(intIndex).Item( _
            "ThursdayHours")
        SaveTimeSheet = ExecuteStoredProcedure()
        'Update Friday's Hours
        MyBase.Command.Parameters.Item("@TimeSheetItemID").Value = _
            TimeSheet.Tables("TimeSheet").Rows(intIndex).Item( _
            "FridayTimeSheetItemID")
        MyBase.Command.Parameters.Item("@Hours").Value = _
            TimeSheet.Tables("TimeSheet").Rows(intIndex).Item( _
            "FridayHours")
        SaveTimeSheet = ExecuteStoredProcedure()
    Next
```

The Catch block contains the code to handle any errors that may be thrown from the execution of this stored procedure and will throw a new exception, passing the error received to the caller of this function:

```
    Catch ExceptionErr As Exception
        Throw New System.Exception(ExceptionErr.Message, _
        ExceptionErr.InnerException)
    End Try
End Function
```

The next function you add to your data access component is the SubmitTimeSheet function. This function executes the usp_SubmitTimeSheet stored procedure, which marks the timesheet as submitted. The only differences between the SQL Server and Oracle versions are the data types used in the Parameters collection, so only the SQL Server version is listed here.

This function accepts the TimeSheetID parameter as its one and only input parameter, as does the usp_SubmitTimeSheet stored procedure. The Submitted column in the TimeSheets table is set to a value of 1 in the stored procedure, which marks the timesheet as submitted.

```
Public Function SubmitTimeSheet(ByVal TimeSheetID As Guid) As Boolean
    Try
        MyBase.SQL = "usp_SubmitTimeSheet"
        'Initialize the Command object
        MyBase.InitializeCommand()
```

```
            'Add the Parameters to the Parameters collection
            MyBase.AddParameter("@TimeSheetID", _
                SqlDbType.UniqueIdentifier, 16, TimeSheetID)
            'Execute the stored procedure
            SubmitTimeSheet = ExecuteStoredProcedure()
        Catch ExceptionErr As Exception
            Throw New System.Exception(ExceptionErr.Message, _
            ExceptionErr.InnerException)
        End Try
    End Function
```

The last function you add to the data access component is the `ApproveTimeSheet` function, which is called when the manager clicks the Approve button in the TimeSheet form. This function accepts two parameters as input: the `TimeSheetID` of the timesheet to be approved and the `ManagerID` of the manager approving the timesheet.

The steps performed in this function are to set the `SQL` property in the base class to the stored procedure being executed and to initialize the `Command` object. Then you add the two parameters for this stored procedure to the `Parameters` collection and execute the stored procedure.

The appropriate code is included to handle any errors that may be thrown when executing this stored procedure.

```
    Public Function ApproveTimeSheet(ByVal TimeSheetID As Guid, _
        ByVal ManagerID As Guid) As Boolean
        Try
            MyBase.SQL = "usp_ApproveTimeSheet"
            'Initialize the Command object
            MyBase.InitializeCommand()
            'Add the Parameters to the Parameters collection
            MyBase.AddParameter("@TimeSheetID", _
                SqlDbType.UniqueIdentifier, 16, TimeSheetID)
            MyBase.AddParameter("@ManagerID", _
                SqlDbType.UniqueIdentifier, 16, ManagerID)
            'Execute the stored procedure
            ApproveTimeSheet = ExecuteStoredProcedure()
        Catch ExceptionErr As Exception
            Throw New System.Exception(ExceptionErr.Message, _
            ExceptionErr.InnerException)
        End Try
    End Function
```

Code is added to the business logic component next, starting with the `SaveTimeSheet` function, a simple function that accepts the `TimeSheet DataSet` as its input parameters and then calls the corresponding function in the data access component. The appropriate error handling is included to handle any errors that may occur.

```
    Public Function SaveTimeSheet(ByVal TimeSheet As DataSet) As Boolean
        Try
            'Call the data component to save the timesheet
            Return objWDATimeSheets.SaveTimeSheet(TimeSheet)
        Catch ExceptionErr As Exception
```

```
            Throw New System.Exception(ExceptionErr.Message, _
                ExceptionErr.InnerException)
        End Try
    End Function
```

The `SubmitTimeSheet` function is added next and accepts the `TimeSheetID` of the timesheet to be submitted as input. This function calls the corresponding function in the data access component and also includes the appropriate error-handling code:

```
    Public Function SubmitTimeSheet(ByVal TimeSheetID As Guid) As Boolean
        Try
            'Call the data component to submit the timesheet
            Return objWDATimeSheets.SubmitTimeSheet(TimeSheetID)
        Catch ExceptionErr As Exception
            Throw New System.Exception(ExceptionErr.Message, _
                ExceptionErr.InnerException)
        End Try
    End Function
```

The final function added to the business logic component is the `ApproveTimeSheet` function. This function accepts the `TimeSheetID` and `ManagerID` as input and calls the corresponding function in the data access component, also including the appropriate error handling:

```
    Public Function ApproveTimeSheet(ByVal TimeSheetID As Guid, _
        ByVal ManagerID As Guid) As Boolean
        Try
            'Call the data component to approve the timesheet
            Return objWDATimeSheets.ApproveTimeSheet(TimeSheetID, ManagerID)
        Catch ExceptionErr As Exception
            Throw New System.Exception(ExceptionErr.Message, _
                ExceptionErr.InnerException)
        End Try
    End Function
```

When a user clicks the Save button in the TimeSheet form, the `btnSave_Click` procedure is executed. Here you initialize a new instance of the business logic component and then the call the `SaveTimeSheet` function, passing it the timesheet in the `objTimeSheetDS` DataSet. The call to the `SaveTimeSheet` function is wrapped in an `If...Then` statement to handle any errors that may occur. If the timesheet is updated successfully, you display the appropriate message in the status bar.

The `Catch` block contains the necessary code to handle and display any errors that may occur in this procedure:

```
    Private Sub btnSave_Click(ByVal sender As Object, _
        ByVal e As System.EventArgs) Handles btnSave.Click

        'Initialize a new instance of the business logic component
        Using objTimeSheets As New WroxBusinessLogic.WBLTimeSheets( _
            strCompany, strApplication)
            Try
                'Save the timesheet changes
                If Not objTimeSheets.SaveTimeSheet(objTimeSheetDS) Then
```

```
                    Throw New Exception("Save TimeSheet Failed")
                End If
                'Display a statusbar message
                ToolStripStatus.Text = "Timesheet saved"
            Catch ExceptionErr As Exception
                MessageBox.Show(ExceptionErr.Message, strAppTitle)
            End Try
        End Using
    End Sub
```

When users submit their timesheet, they click the Submit button in the TimeSheet form and the btnSubmit_Click procedure executes. This procedure starts by initializing a new instance of the business logic component.

```
    Private Sub btnSubmit_Click(ByVal sender As Object, _
        ByVal e As System.EventArgs) Handles btnSubmit.Click

        'Initialize a new instance of the business logic component
        Using objTimeSheets As New WroxBusinessLogic.WBLTimeSheets( _
            strCompany, strApplication)
```

The SubmitTimeSheet function in the business logic component expects a Guid as input. However, the data type for the TimeSheetID in the DataSet is defined as a Guid data type in SQL Server and a String data type in Oracle. Therefore, to be consistent in your implementation of code, you convert the data in this column to a Guid using one of the overloaded versions of the constructor of the Guid structure and passing it the column in the DataSet. You must also use the ToString method on the column of the DataSet, because the constructor of the Guid structure assumes that the column is not a string value because it is coming from a DataSet:

```
        Try
            'Submit the timesheet
            If Not objTimeSheets.SubmitTimeSheet( _
                New Guid(objTimeSheetDS.Tables("TimeSheet").Rows(0).Item( _
                "TimeSheetID").ToString)) Then
                Throw New Exception("Submit TimeSheet Failed")
            End If
```

A call is made to the LoadTimeSheet function after the timesheet has been submitted. Calling this function causes the updated timesheet to be retrieved from the database, and the Submitted column in the DataSet will now contain a value of 1. This causes the timesheet to be displayed as read-only and no further updates are allowed to this timesheet.

```
            'Reload the timesheet so it becomes read-only
            Call LoadTimeSheet(cboWeekEnding)
            'Display a statusbar message
            ToolStripStatus.Text = "Timesheet submitted"
        Catch ExceptionErr As Exception
            MessageBox.Show(ExceptionErr.Message, strAppTitle)
        End Try
    End Using
End Sub
```

The final procedure you add to the TimeSheet form is the `btnApprove_Click` procedure, which is called when a manager clicks the Approve button on a timesheet. The first thing that happens in this procedure is that you initialize a new instance of the business logic component.

Then you encapsulate the rest of the code in a `Try...Catch` block. Inside the `Try` block, you make a call to the `ApproveTimeSheet` function, converting the value in the `TimeSheetID` column to a `Guid` using one of the overloaded constructors of the `Guid` structure. This is also done for the `ManagerID`. Converting the `TimeSheetID` column to a `Guid` is not necessary for SQL Server, as this column is already a `Guid` data type, but doing this for both SQL Server and Oracle helps to ensure a consistent interface.

After the call to the `ApproveTimeSheet` function is made, you display a message in the status bar indicating that the timesheet has been approved. The `Catch` block contains the code to handle any errors and the `Finally` block contains the code to clean up the resources used in this procedure.

```
Private Sub btnApprove_Click(ByVal sender As Object, _
    ByVal e As System.EventArgs) Handles btnApprove.Click

    'Initialize a new instance of the business logic component
    Using objTimeSheets As New WroxBusinessLogic.WBLTimeSheets( _
        strCompany, strApplication)
        Try
            'Submit the timesheet
            If Not objTimeSheets.ApproveTimeSheet( _
             New Guid(objTimeSheetDS.Tables("TimeSheet").Rows(0).Item( _
                "TimeSheetID").ToString), New Guid(strManagerID)) Then
                Throw New Exception("Approve TimeSheet Failed")
            End If
            'Display a statusbar message
            ToolStripStatus.Text = "Timesheet approved"
        Catch ExceptionErr As Exception
            MessageBox.Show(ExceptionErr.Message, strAppTitle)
        End Try
    End Using
End Sub
```

That wraps up the code for the TimeSheet form. A user can now view the timesheet, make and save changes to the timesheet, and also submit the timesheet for approval. Managers can view the timesheets for their employees and also approve their timesheets.

Summary

The UPDATE stored procedures that you implemented in this chapter are straightforward. You already had experience implementing conditional logic and error handling in stored procedures from Chapter 11, and this experience served you well in this chapter when writing the usp_UpdateRole stored procedure. The rest of the stored procedures were simple update stored procedures that contained only the UPDATE statement and error handling.

You completed the functionality in the Admin form, which was straightforward and included the necessary code to update a role and user. The corresponding code in the business logic component and data access component were also straightforward.

The stored procedures to save, submit, and approve a timesheet were also simple stored procedures. However, the code in the data access component to save a timesheet was a little more involved. You actually had to call the usp_UpdateTimeSheetItem stored procedure multiple times for each row of data in the DataSet. This enabled you to update the hours for each day of the week for each project.

To summarize, you should know how to:

❑   Use variables, conditional processing logic, and error handling in your stored procedures

❑   Write simple UPDATE stored procedures and UPDATE stored procedures that perform validations

❑   Iterate through the columns and rows of a DataSet to process data

❑   Effeciently execute the same stored procedure in a loop

In Chapter 14, you provide an alternative way for users to access and complete their timesheets by building a TimeSheet form using ASP.NET. This enables traveling users to access their timesheets without having to be connected to your network.

Exercises

Exercise 1

Write two stored procedures, with the appropriate error handling, to delete a role and to delete a user. Then modify your data access and business logic components to execute these stored procedures.

Exercise 2

In the Admin form, implement the appropriate code under the Case "Roles" and Case "Users" statements in the ActionDelete procedure to delete a role and to delete a user.

Accessing Data in ASP.NET

Using the technology offered by ASP.NET, you can develop Web applications for your local intranet, extranet, or even the Internet. A Web application differs from a typical Web site in that a Web application is driven mostly, if not entirely, by ASPX (Active Server Page Framework) pages instead of static HTML pages. This enables you to access and take advantage of Web forms and server resources such as access to your business logic components and data access components.

Now that you've completed the user functionality in the TimeSheet form in the Time Tracker project, it's time to take a look at how to implement the timesheet functionality on the Web. In this chapter, you learn how to access data in your database using ASP.NET and how to present that data to your users in Web forms. This will enable any user in your organization with a Web browser to access the timesheet form in your Web application.

In this chapter, you:

❑ Reference and leverage your business logic and data access components in ASP.NET

❑ Select data from your database and display that data in a Web form

❑ Perform client-side data validation in Web forms

❑ Handle data updates in a Web form and update that data in your database

It is recommended that you have read the chapters on Web programming in *Beginning VB 2005* to have a basic understanding of how Web forms and ASP.NET work as this chapter does not cover the basics of Web forms and ASP.NET.

Selecting and Displaying Data

Initially selecting and displaying data in ASP.NET does not present a major challenge. You access the methods in your business logic component to retrieve the data to be displayed and then either bind the data to a control on a Web form or process the rows of data in the DataSet and build a table to be displayed. The major hurdle comes when it's time to edit or update the data.

Remember that a Web form is built on the Web server and sent to the client as Hypertext Markup Language (HTML). Once the client's Web browser receives the Web page, the connection to the Web server is terminated. Any further requests for data or server resources require posting a form in a Web page back to the server for processing. This causes a lot of round trips between the client and the server.

In addition, a lot more data is traveling between the client and the server. Consider the Login form in the Time Tracker application, for example. When you ran the application, the Login form was built and displayed. After you entered your credentials, you clicked OK and the code in the form executed to validate your credentials. If your credentials were not validated, a MessageBox dialog box was displayed informing you that your credentials were not validated. However, the Login form was always displayed and the code in the form handled the events that were raised.

Now examine what must happen in ASP.NET. A user requests the Login form and the server builds the form and sends it to the user's browser. The user then enters credentials and clicks OK. The browser must then post the form data back to the server for processing. The server processes the data and if it determines that the credentials were not valid, it must build the Login form again and send it back to the client along with the appropriate message that the credentials were not valid.

In this last scenario, you can see that the Login form has been built twice and sent to the client twice. Additionally, there is a lot of data traveling back and forth between the client and the server, not to mention the additional resources used to process and send the HTML requests.

When building Web forms in ASP.NET, you must keep all this in mind and try to put as much validation code in the client as possible to minimize the number of round trips between the client and the server. Later in the chapter, you explore other alternatives to minimize the number of round trips when editing data.

In this first exercise, you start building the TimeSheets Web application. This application will provide a login screen where users can provide credentials to log in to the TimeSheets Web application. Once users have logged in, their timesheet is displayed and they are able to edit, save, and submit their timesheets.

In this exercise, you build the Login form and provide the code to validate a user. The rest of the functionality is covered in the exercises that follow.

Try It Out   Building the TimeSheets Web Application

To complete this exercise:

1. Start Visual Studio 2005 and on the Recent Projects tab of the Start page, click the Create Web Site link or select File ➪ New ➪ Web Site.

2. In the New Web Site dialog box, select the ASP.NET Web Site icon in the Templates pane, File System in the Location combo box, and Visual Basic in the Language combo box, and enter a project name of **TimeSheets** in the field next to the Browse button, as shown in Figure 14-1. After you click OK, Visual Studio 2005 creates the Web site for you and sets up your project.

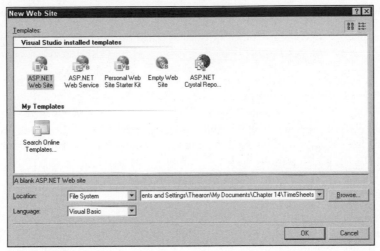

Figure 14-1

3. The default Web form created in your project is `Default.aspx` and this will be the start page for your Web site, but this is not the Web form that you want to be displayed when a user navigates to the TimeSheets Web site. You want the Web application to display the `Login.aspx` Web form, so you need to have the `Default.aspx` Web page redirect the client's browser to the `Login.aspx` page, which you'll be adding shortly. View the code for the `Default.aspx` page by right-clicking the `Default.aspx` page in the Solution Explorer and choosing the View Code context menu item or by clicking the View Code icon in Solution Explorer. Select (Page Events) in the Class Name combo box in the IDE and then select the Load event in the Method Name combo box. Add the following line of code in the `Page_Load` procedure:

```
Protected Sub Page_Load(ByVal sender As Object, _
    ByVal e As System.EventArgs) Handles Me.Load

    Response.Redirect("Login.aspx")
End Sub
```

4. Add a style sheet for the various formatting styles that will be applied to your text and controls. Right-click the TimeSheets project in Solution Explorer, and choose Add New Item from the context menu. In the Add New Item dialog box, select the Style Sheet icon in the Templates pane and accept the default name and then click Add. Modify the default Body style by adding the following code:

```
BODY
{
    BACKGROUND-COLOR: white;
    FONT-FAMILY: Verdana, Helvetica, sans-serif;
    FONT-SIZE: 9pt;
    FONT-WEIGHT: normal;
    LETTER-SPACING: normal;
    TEXT-TRANSFORM: none;
    WORD-SPACING: normal
}
```

5. To add a default style to be applied to all tables that you create, add the following code below the BODY style:

```
TABLE
{
    FONT-FAMILY: Verdana;
    FONT-SIZE: 9pt;
}
```

6. Now you want to create a style for the page header that will be displayed on each page in the TimeSheets Web application. Add the following code below the TABLE style. Notice the period preceding the style name, indicating a user-defined style:

```
.PageHeader
{
    BACKGROUND-COLOR: #4682B4;
    FONT-SIZE: 14pt;
    COLOR: White;
}
```

7. Now you want to create a style for the page footer that will be displayed on each page in the TimeSheets Web application. Add the following code:

```
.PageFooter
{
    FONT-SIZE: 7pt;
    COLOR: #4682B4;
}
```

8. Provide a standard look and feel to your Web site by incorporating the same header and footer in all Web pages displayed in your Web site. This can be accomplished by using a Master Page. Right-click the TimeSheets project in Solution Explorer, and choose Add New Item from the context menu. In the Add New Item dialog box, select the Master Page icon in the Templates pane and accept the default name and then click Add. Add the following code in the MasterPage file:

```
<head runat="server">
    <title>Time Tracker TimeSheets</title>
    <link rel="stylesheet" href="stylesheet.css" type="text/css">
</head>
<body>
    <table border="0" cellpadding="0" cellspacing="0" width="100%">
      <tr class="PageHeader">
        <td align="center">Time Tracker TimeSheets</td>
      </tr>
    </table>
    <form id="form1" runat="server">
    <div>
        <asp:contentplaceholder id="ContentPlaceHolder1" runat="server">
        </asp:contentplaceholder>
    </div>
    </form>
    <table border="0" cellpadding="0" cellspacing="0" width="100%">
      <tr class="PageFooter">
        <td align="center">Copyright &copy; 2005 Wrox Press. All rights
        reserved.</td>
```

```
      </tr>
    </table>
  </body>
```

9. Now you need to add the `Login.aspx` Web form. Right-click the TimeSheets project in Solution Explorer, choose Add New Item from the context menu. In the Add New Item dialog box, select the Web Form icon in the Templates pane, enter a name of **Login.aspx** in the Name field, and check the Select master page check box. Finally, click the Add button. You are prompted with the Select a Master Page dialog box with your master page listed and selected. Click OK in this dialog box.

10. Modify the contents of the Login Web form as follows:

```
<asp:Content ID="Content1" ContentPlaceHolderID="ContentPlaceHolder1"
Runat="Server">
    <table border="0" cellpadding="0" cellspacing="0" height="100%" width="100%"
      align="center">
      <tr valign="middle" align="center" height="300">
        <td>
          <table border="0" cellspacing="1" cellpadding="1"  width="300"
            align="center">
            <tr>
              <td nowrap>Login Name</td>
              <td></td>
              <td rowspan="2"></td>
            </tr>
            <tr>
              <td nowrap>Password</td>
              <td></td>
            </tr>
            <tr>
              <td colspan="3"></td>
            </tr>
            <tr>
              <td colspan="3"></td>
            </tr>
          </table>
        </td>
      </tr>
    </table>
</asp:Content>
```

11. Now switch to the design view for the Web form by clicking the Design tab at the bottom of the editor. The first control to be added is a TextBox control for users to enter their login names. Click the toolbox and then click the Standard tab if it is not already selected. Drag a TextBox control and drop it in the table cell next to the text Login Name. Set the following properties for this control in the Properties window:

❑ Set (ID) to **txtLoginName**.

❑ Set TabIndex to **1**.

❑ Set Width to **1.5in**.

12. Now drag another TextBox control from the toolbox and drop it in the cell next to the text Password. Set its properties as follows:

485

❑   Set (ID) to **txtPassword**.

❑   Set TabIndex to **2**.

❑   Set TextMode to **Password**.

❑   Set Width to **1.5in**.

13.   Drag a Button control from the toolbox and drop it in the last cell that spans both the Login Name and Password rows. Set its properties as follows:

❑   Set (ID) to **btnSubmit**.

❑   Set TabIndex to **3**.

❑   Set Text to **Submit**.

14.   Click on the Validation tab in the toolbox and drag a RequiredFieldValidator from the toolbox and drop it in the cell below the Password cell. Set its properties as follows:

❑   Set ControlToValidate to **txtLoginName**.

❑   Set ErrorMessage to **Login Name is a required field**.

15.   Drag a RequiredFieldValidator from the toolbox and drop it in the last cell in the table. Set its properties as follows:

❑   Set ControlToValidate to **txtPassword**.

❑   Set ErrorMessage to **Password is a required field**.

This would be a good place to stop and test the Login form. Start your project by clicking the Start button on the toolbar or clicking the Debug menu and selecting Start. You'll be prompted to add a Web.config file with debugging enabled so click OK in the Debugging Not Enabled dialog box.

When your Login form is displayed in your browser, you'll notice that the fields for the login credentials are centered in the browser window as shown in Figure 14-2. Resizing the browser window will cause the login fields to be re-centered.

Now click the Submit button and you see the error messages from the validation controls. Enter some text in the Login Name field and then click Submit. Now the only error message that you see is the one for the password. Enter some text in the Password field and click Submit. The form will be posted back to the server for processing. Of course, nothing will happen as you've yet to write any server-side code. Stop your project by closing the browser window.

1.   Switch to the HTML code for your Login form by clicking the Source tab at the bottom of the designer window. You'll need to add some JavaScript code to display a MessageBox dialog box when the user's credentials cannot be validated or the user's account has been suspended. Add the following code after the last closing </table> element:

```
    </table>
    <script language="javascript" for="window" event="onload">
    var sMessage = "<%=strErrorMessage%>";
    if (sMessage.length != 0)
    {
        alert(sMessage);
    }
    </script>
</asp:Content>
```

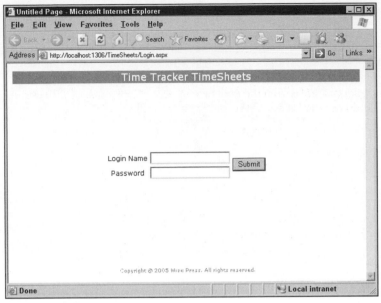

Figure 14-2

2. Before adding any VB code, you need to set a reference to your business logic component. Right-click the TimeSheets project in Solution Explorer and choose Add Reference. In the Add Reference dialog box, click Browse tab. Locate the `WroxBusinessLogic.dll` in your `WroxBusinessLogic\bin\Debug` folder and select it. Then click OK.

3. Because you'll be working with the `DataSet` class in your Login Web form, you need to set a reference to the `System.Data` namespace. View the code for the Login Web form and add the following `Imports` statement:

```
Imports System.Data

Partial Class Login
```

4. Now it's time to add some VB code to the Login form. You need to declare a public error message variable that was referenced in your JavaScript code. This enables a message to be set in your VB code and have that message accessible in your JavaScript code. Add the following variable declaration:

```
'Public variables
Public strErrorMessage As String = String.Empty
```

5. You need to add some code to the Submit button next so select btnSubmit in the Class Name combo box and the Click event in the Method Name combo box and then add the following code in the `btnSubmit_Click` procedure to validate a user's login credentials:

```
Protected Sub btnSubmit_Click(ByVal sender As Object, _
    ByVal e As System.EventArgs) Handles btnSubmit.Click

'Initialize a new instance of the business logic component
    Using objUsers As New WroxBusinessLogic.WBLUsers( _
```

```
              "Wrox", "Time Tracker")

            'Validate the user and get their role
            Using objDataSet As DataSet = objUsers.ValidateLogin( _
                txtLoginName.Text, txtPassword.Text)

                If objDataSet.Tables("User").Rows.Count > 0 Then
                    If objDataSet.Tables("User").Rows(0).Item("Status") Then
                        Response.Redirect("TimeSheet.aspx?UserID=" & _
                        objDataSet.Tables("User").Rows(0).Item( _
                        "UserID").ToString & "&UserName=" & _
                        objDataSet.Tables("User").Rows(0).Item( _
                        "UserName").ToString)
                    Else
                        strErrorMessage = "Your account has been suspended." & _
                         ControlChars.CrLf & "Please contact your administrator."
                    End If
                Else
                    strErrorMessage = "Your credentials were not validated."
                End If

            End Using

        End Using
    End Sub
```

6. To test the login process, add a TimeSheet Web form. Right-click the TimeSheets project in Solution Explorer, and choose Add New Item from the context menu. In the Add New Item dialog box, select the Web Form icon, enter a name of **TimeSheet.aspx** in the Name field, ensure the Select Master Page check box is checked, and then click the Add button. Your master page should already be selected in the Select a Master Page dialog box so click OK.

7. When your TimeSheet form is displayed, add the following text. This provides some simple text on the TimeSheet form for testing purposes.

```
<asp:Content ID="Content1" ContentPlaceHolderID="ContentPlaceHolder1"
Runat="Server">
TimeSheet Form
</asp:Content>
```

8. The final step is to set the Default Web form as the startup page. Right-click `Default.aspx` in the Solution Explorer and choose Set As Start Page.

You are now ready to test your code changes so start your project. When the Login Web form is displayed, enter some invalid data for the Login Name and Password. When you click the Submit button, your form is posted back to the server for processing and your credentials are checked. The "Your credentials were not validated" message is set and the Web form sent back to the browser. You then receive a MessageBox dialog box informing you that your credentials were not validated from the JavaScript code in the Login Web form.

Now enter a valid login name and password and click the Submit button. This time your credentials will be validated and you'll be redirected to the TimeSheet form. The words "TimeSheet Form" will be displayed on the Web form and you'll be able to see the query string values that were set in the Login form as part of the URL.

> Oracle readers: If you receive errors connecting to Oracle, please review Microsoft Knowledge Base Article – 255084. In most cases, following the instructions outlined in Step 10 in this article resolves the problem. You can find this Knowledge Base Article at http://support.microsoft.com/ default.aspx.

How It Works

You start this exercise by adding code to the Default.aspx Web form to redirect the browser to the Login.aspx Web form. The default documents in IIS are Default.htm, Default.asp, Index.htm, and Default.aspx. When users navigate to your Web application in a browser, all they need to do is enter the server name followed by the Web application name, such as http://someserver/timesheets. IIS will look in the default documents list for the Web site and look for a corresponding match in your Web application.

When IIS finds the Default.aspx page, it processes the Page_Load procedure in that page and then redirects the browser to the Login.aspx Web page because of the code that was added to the Default.aspx page to redirect to the Login.aspx Web page. The Login.aspx Web page is then processed and sent to the browser.

```
Protected Sub Page_Load(ByVal sender As Object, _
    ByVal e As System.EventArgs) Handles Me.Load

    Response.Redirect("Login.aspx")
End Sub
```

The next step was to add a style sheet and to add code to the empty the BODY style in the style sheet. This style specifies the background color of the Web pages, the font family and font size attributes to be used in the data displayed in all Web pages, and the letter spacing and word spacing styles to be applied.

```
BODY
{
    BACKGROUND-COLOR: white;
    FONT-FAMILY: Verdana, Helvetica, sans-serif;
    FONT-SIZE: 9pt;
    FONT-WEIGHT: normal;
    LETTER-SPACING: normal;
    TEXT-TRANSFORM: none;
    WORD-SPACING: normal
}
```

Note that when you are creating styles that should be applied to HTML elements, such as the <BODY> and <TABLE> elements, you specify the style name with the same name as the element to which it should be applied. This causes the style to be applied automatically to the corresponding HTML elements.

When defining a style, the style name is specified first and the style attributes are enclosed in a set of brackets, with each style terminated by a semicolon. In the style that follows, the style name is TABLE, and the style attributes are FONT-FAMILY and FONT-SIZE. The style attribute name is followed by a colon, followed by the value that should be set for that style attribute.

```
TABLE
{
    FONT-FAMILY: Verdana;
    FONT-SIZE: 9pt;
}
```

The next order of business was to create a style that would be used for the page header in each Web form. This helps create a consistent look across all Web forms in your application. When creating user-defined styles, the style name is always preceded by a period, followed by the style name, as shown in the code that follows.

The BACKGROUND-COLOR style attribute causes the background color to be set in the HTML element to which this style is applied. Colors in style attributes can be specified using the color name, such as Blue, or using the Red, Green, Blue (RGB) values, which is what is specified here. When using an RGB value, you must always precede the value with a pound (#) sign, as shown in the code that follows.

The COLOR style attribute shown in the following code will be applied to the text that is displayed in the HTML element to which this style is applied. Notice that here you have specified the color name of White.

```
.PageHeader
{
    BACKGROUND-COLOR: #4682B4;
    FONT-SIZE: 14pt;
    COLOR: White;
}
```

The last style that you added was for the page footer. Here you set the font size that will be applied to the text and the color of the text using a Red, Green, Blue (RGB) value.

```
.PageFooter
{
    FONT-SIZE: 7pt;
    COLOR: #4682B4;
}
```

To have the header and footer created consistently on each page, you use a master page. A master page allows you to create content in the page that will be applied to all pages across your Web site.

For the master page to gain access to the styles defined in your cascading style sheet, you must provide a link to the style sheet in your HTML code. This is always done inside of the <HEAD> element.

The <LINK> element is used by your Web page to establish a link to external documents and in this case, the style sheet. The rel attribute specifies the relationship between the external document and your Web page and has a value of stylesheet, indicating that the document being linked to is a cascading style sheet.

The `href` attribute specifies the URL of the document and can be fully qualified or you can just specify the path and page name of the document. The code that follows specifies the page name, as the style sheet exists in the same path as your Web pages.

Finally, the `type` attribute specifies the Multipurpose Internet Mail Extension (MIME) type of the document. A MIME type of `text/css` is used to specify that this is a text/cascading style sheet document and is used by the `type` attribute to retrieve the class identifier of the document type.

```
<head runat="server">
    <title>Time Tracker TimeSheets</title>
    <link rel="stylesheet" href="stylesheet.css" type="text/css">
```

Next, you build a table to display the page header using the `<TABLE>` element. This table contains one row of data, as is evident by the single `<TR>` element, and one column in that row, as indicated by the single `<TD>` element.

The attributes specified on the `<TABLE>` element define how the table will look. The `border` attribute specifies the width of the border around the table, while the `cellpadding` attribute specifies the amount of space between the border of a cell and the text in the cell. The `cellspacing` attribute, as you might have guessed, specifies the amount of space between the cells in your table. The `width` attribute specifies the width of the table, and has a value of `100%` in the code that follows. This causes the table to be resized to match the width of the Web page whenever the browser window is resized.

The `<TR>` element has but one attribute specified: `class`. The `class` attribute specifies the style name in your cascading style sheet that should be applied to this element — in this case, the `PageHeader` style. Remember that when you created this style in your style sheet you prefixed the style name with a period, but you do not specify the period here. This is not required here, but only in the style sheet to distinguish between user-defined style names and style names that are to be automatically applied to HTML elements.

The `<TD>` element has the `align` attribute specified to force the alignment of the cell contents. By default, all content in a cell is aligned to the left of the cell. However, the text specified here is for the page header and you want the text centered on the page, so you specify a value of `center` for the `align` attribute:

```
<table border="0" cellpadding="0" cellspacing="0" width="100%">
  <tr class="PageHeader">
    <td align="center">Time Tracker TimeSheets</td>
  </tr>
</table>
```

The next table that you add to your Web form is the table to display the footer. This table is added at the bottom of the master page and displays the copyright information. Again you specify that the text should be centered in the column and you specify the style that should be applied to the text in the table row.

```
<table border="0" cellpadding="0" cellspacing="0" width="100%">
  <tr class="PageFooter">
    <td align="center">Copyright &copy; 2005 Wrox Press. All rights
    reserved.</td>
  </tr>
</table>
```

You add the Login Web form next and specify that it should use a master page. This instructs Visual Studio 2005 to build the Web form in a manner that incorporates the master page so that the Login Web form gets the header and footer defined in the master page automatically.

You then add a table to the Login Web form that will be used to contain the controls that allow users to enter their login credentials and to submit them to the Web server for processing. To have the contents of the table centered vertically on the Web page, the table must fill the entire space of the Web page. You must specify the height of the table, which is done by including the `height` attribute, which has its value set to `100%`. The `width` attribute is also specified with a value of `100%` to fill the table horizontally. The `align` attribute, with a value of `center`, forces the contents of the table to be centered within the table.

This table has one row and one column. The `<TR>` element has the `valign` attribute, which specifies the vertical alignment of the contents of the row, and the `align` attribute, which specifies the horizontal alignment of the row. Inside of the column for this table, you specify another table that will hold the actual controls.

The first row inside of this inner table contains three columns. The first column contains the text Login Name and the second column contains the TextBox control for the login name. It's this third column that is of real interest. This third column contains the Button control, and this Button control is centered between the rows of the Login Name and Password, as previously shown in Figure 14-2. This is achieved by the inclusion of the `rowspan` attribute. You specify a value of 2 for this attribute, which causes this column in the table to span two rows and to be centered between the two rows.

The next row in the inner table contains only two columns because the previous row contains the third column that spans the two rows. The first column in this row will contain the text Password and the second column will contain the TextBox control for the password.

The last two rows in this inner table contain the validation controls. Notice that there is only one column in each of these rows and that they have the `colspan` attribute specified. The `colspan` attribute is used to make a column span multiple columns from the previous or following rows. Because the largest row in this inner table contains three columns, the value for the `colspan` attribute has been set to 3.

```
<table border="0" cellpadding="0" cellspacing="0" height="100%" width="100%"
    align="center">
  <tr valign="middle" align="center" height="300">
     <td>
        <table border="0" cellspacing="1" cellpadding="1"  width="300"
            align="center">
          <tr>
             <td nowrap>Login Name</td>
             <td></td>
             <td rowspan="2"></td>
          </tr>
          <tr>
             <td nowrap>Password</td>
             <td></td>
          </tr>
          <tr>
             <td colspan="3"></td>
```

```
            </tr>
            <tr>
                <td colspan="3"></td>
            </tr>
        </table>
    </td>
</tr>
</table>
```

At this point, you switch to the Form Designer for your Web form and drag the appropriate Web form controls from the toolbox and drop them in the appropriate cells in the inner table. The first control you add to your Web form is a TextBox control for the login name. You set the ID property for this control to txtLoginName, which corresponds to the Name property for a TextBox control in a Windows form. The TabIndex property is set next so that you can tab from one control to the next in the appropriate order. The Width property is set next to a value of 1.5in, which means that the TextBox control will be one and a half inches wide. This ensures that the TextBox control is sized appropriately and matches the size of the password TextBox control.

You add the txtPassword TextBox control next and set its properties appropriately. A Button control is added next and also has its properties set appropriately. The last two controls that you add are the RequiredFieldValidator controls.

The RequiredFieldValidator control automatically includes the appropriate code in your Web form to validate that a field contains data before allowing the form to be submitted. This control also checks for a blank space in case the user tries to enter a blank space in lieu of some actual text. The real beauty of this control is that all you have to specify is the control to be validated and the error message to be displayed; there is no code to write.

At this point, you test your Login Web form. When you start your project, the Default.aspx Web page is loaded and processed and the code in that form redirects the browser request to the Login.aspx form. This form is processed by IIS and sent to your browser. You can resize the browser window and see that the tables are resized accordingly.

You are also able to test the RequiredFieldValidator controls by trying to submit the Login Web form without entering any data. At this point, you have not written a single line of code but have a lot of functionality in your Login Web form. The RequiredFieldValidator controls don't allow the form to be submitted without any data in the Login Name and Password fields, which demonstrates the real power of these controls.

The next step in completing the Login Web form is to add some client-side JavaScript code to display a message if the user's credentials were not validated. You may be wondering why you use JavaScript instead of VBScript for the client-side validation code. It has become common practice to use JavaScript code for client-side scripts to ensure that your code runs in Netscape browsers as well as Internet Explorer browsers. In fact, if you view the source code for the Login.aspx Web page when it is displayed in the browser, you'll notice that JavaScript code has been added automatically to handle such things as validating the TextBox control's data as well as code to handle the submission of the Web form.

You may also be wondering why you wouldn't simply display the message in a label on the Web form with the appropriate message when a user is not validated. You want to really catch the user's attention when their credentials have not been validated—thus the use of a MessageBox dialog box.

You want this code to execute only after the Web form has been loaded in the browser, so you have included several attributes for the <SCRIPT> element. The language attribute specifies the language for the script and has been set to JavaScript. The for attribute specifies the object that this script is for and a value of window is specified to refer to the browser window. The event attribute specifies the event in the object to which this script should react, and a value of onload is specified. These attributes cause this script to be executed after the browser window loads the HTML document.

The first line of code in this script is a variable declaration. In JavaScript, you define a variable by specifying the var keyword followed by the variable name, which in this case is sMessage. Then you set the variable to the value contained in your strErrorMessage variable, which is defined in the next step. You can access your VB variables in your JavaScript by enclosing them in VBScript server-side script tags. A server-side script tag begins with the characters <% and ends with the characters %>. The equal sign causes the value of the server-side variable to be set in this string, which is enclosed in quotes. This line of code causes the sMessage variable to be populated with the value contained in the strErrorMessage variable when the form is being rendered by IIS before it is sent to the browser.

The next line of code checks the length of the sMessage variable to determine whether it should display a MessageBox dialog box. If the length of the sMessage variable is not equal to 0, a MessageBox dialog box is displayed by the alert method. The alert method accepts a variable or string value of the message to be displayed.

```
<script language="javascript" for="window" event="onload">
    var sMessage = "<%=strErrorMessage%>";
    if (sMessage.length != 0)
    {
        alert(sMessage);
    }
</script>
```

Before adding any VB code to your code-behind file for the Login.aspx page, you set a reference to your business logic component. This enables you to access the methods to validate a user. There is no need to set a reference to the data access component because the business logic component contains that reference.

The first thing that you have to do is to set a reference to the System.Data namespace by including the appropriate Imports statement.

```
Imports System.Data
```

Then you add a variable declaration for the strErrorMessage variable. This variable must be defined as public in scope so that it is accessible to the code in your Login.aspx page. You also want to set this variable to an empty string so that it is initialized. Otherwise, if the variable is not set to some string value, the JavaScript would cause an error because the variable would be set to Nothing.

```
'Public variables
Public strErrorMessage As String = String.Empty
```

The only logic that you add is in the btnSubmit_Click procedure. This procedure is executed every time the Submit button is clicked on the Login Web page.

The first thing that you do here is declare an object for the business logic component and call the constructor in your component, passing it the required parameters. This is the same code that you saw in your Time Tracker application:

```
Protected Sub btnSubmit_Click(ByVal sender As Object, _
    ByVal e As System.EventArgs) Handles btnSubmit.Click

    'Initialize a new instance of the business logic component
    Using objUsers As New WroxBusinessLogic.WBLUsers( _
        "Wrox", "Time Tracker")
```

Next, you declare a `DataSet` object and call the `ValidateLogin` method to validate the user's credentials. You get the `LoginName` parameter for the `ValidateLogin` method from the `txtLoginName` field in the Web form being posted. You get the password from the `txtPassword` field. Notice that these are the `ID` values that were set when you defined these controls on your Web form.

After the `ValidateLogin` method executes, you want to check the `Count` property of the `Rows` property in your `DataSet` to determine whether any rows were returned. The `DataSet` will contain a row of data if the user's credentials were validated.

If the user is validated, you use the Status column to determine whether the user is active or suspended. Remember that this column contains a Boolean value and can be used in the `If...Then` statement. You want to redirect active users to the `TimeSheet.aspx` Web page and this is done in the next line of code.

The `Redirect` method is called on the `Response` object to redirect the browser to another URL, which in this case is the `TimeSheet.aspx` Web page. You want to pass some credentials to this Web page, which is done in the form of a query string. A query string is specified as parameters appended to the end of a URL. To append a query string to a URL, you specify a question mark (?) and then the parameter name followed by an equal (=) sign followed by the parameter value. You separate multiple parameters by using the ampersand (&) character.

In the following line of code, you are appending two query string parameters to the URL: `UserID` and `UserName`. The values for these query strings are being set from the appropriate columns in your `DataSet`.

```
'Validate the user and get their role
Using objDataSet As DataSet = objUsers.ValidateLogin( _
    txtLoginName.Text, txtPassword.Text)

    If objDataSet.Tables("User").Rows.Count > 0 Then
        If objDataSet.Tables("User").Rows(0).Item("Status") Then
            Response.Redirect("TimeSheet.aspx?UserID=" & _
            objDataSet.Tables("User").Rows(0).Item( _
            "UserID").ToString & "&UserName=" & _
            objDataSet.Tables("User").Rows(0).Item( _
            "UserName").ToString)
```

If a user's account has been suspended, you set the `strErrorMessage` variable to the appropriate error message and it is displayed when the `Login.aspx` Web form is redisplayed. You may be wondering why the `Login.aspx` Web form will be redisplayed. This is because you have taken no action to redirect the browser to another Web page as shown in the previous code. Thus, when this code completes its execution, the `Login.aspx` Web form will be rebuilt and sent back to the browser.

```
        Else
            strErrorMessage = "Your account has been suspended." & _
                ControlChars.CrLf & "Please contact your administrator."
        End If
```

If the user's credentials are not validated, you set the `strErrorMessage` variable to a message indicating that the credentials were not validated.

```
        Else
            strErrorMessage = "Your credentials were not validated."
        End If

    End Using

    End Using
End Sub
```

At this point, you are able to test your logic and see how the JavaScript code is able to display a MessageBox dialog box when the credentials are not validated. In addition, you can see how your code redirects the browser to the `TimeSheet.aspx` Web page when the credentials are validated. You've also proven two important points. The first point is that you have taken advantage of code reuse by using the existing code in your business logic component. The second point is that your business logic component and data access component have been well designed and can be efficiently used by both a Windows application and a Web application.

Web Form DataGrid Control

Because of the stateless nature of Web forms, a GridView control on a Web form behaves very differently from a DataGridView control on a Windows form. They even have a different look; the Web form GridView control has an extra column that contains editing links, as shown in Figure 14-3.

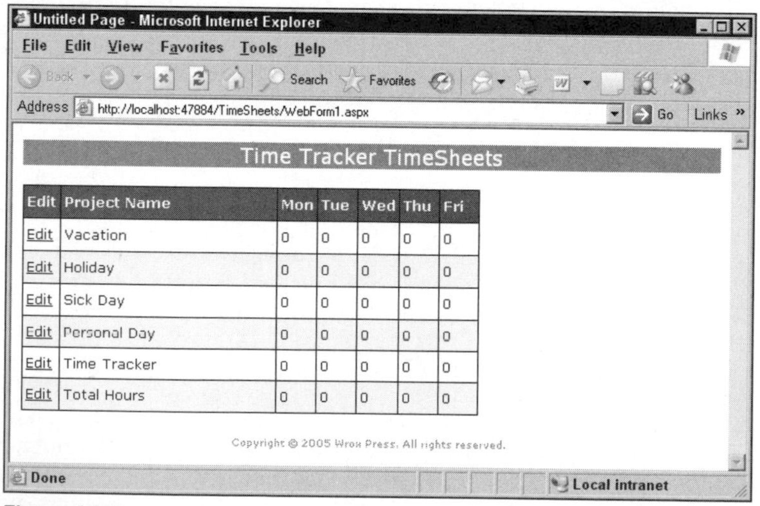

Figure 14-3

As you can see, the columns in the GridView control are not immediately editable. To edit a column in this GridView control, you must click the edit link for the row to be edited. This will cause your Web form to be posted back to the server and the edit row built for the GridView control. Then the Web form containing the updated GridView control will be posted back to the client; the results will look like the GridView shown in Figure 14-4.

Now you can make the necessary edits to the row that you have chosen. When you are finished with your edits, you must either click the Update link to update your changes or click the Cancel link to cancel your changes. Either way, the Web form is posted back to the server for processing and then rebuilt. The updated GridView control is then sent back to the client again and the process is repeated over and over until you have made all of the changes that you want.

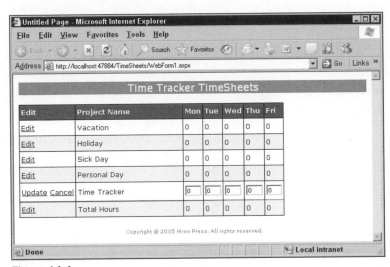

Figure 14-4

As you can see, there are a lot of round trips between the client browser and the Web server. And that's only half of the story. There's also a lot of up-front work to be done in the Web page, building the GridView control to bind the various columns to your `DataSet`. Once all the editing is done, you will be able to read the information that has changed and then perform the necessary updates to your database.

As you can see in the explanation and from looking at Figures 14-3 and 14-4, this is not an ideal situation for your users. You want your users to be able to make all of their edits to the timesheet without having the Web page posted back to the server for processing for each hour that they enter. Basically, you want to emulate the DataGridView control in a Windows form, enabling users to enter all of their times and then click the Save button to save their changes. This provides better performance for your users, your application, and your Web server.

In the next exercise, you implement the functionality in the TimeSheet Web form to build a table that looks similar to the GridView control in Figure 14-4, complete with text boxes in each editable column. This will enable users to enter all of their times without having the Web form posted back to the server for updates. After users have entered all of their times, they click the Save button to save their changes and click the Submit button to submit their timesheet. The overall look and feel of the TimeSheet form will mirror the TimeSheet form in the Time Tracker application as closely as possible.

Try It Out — Building the TimeSheet Web Form

To complete this exercise:

1. Open your TimeSheets Web project in Visual Studio 2005 if it is not still open.

2. The first order of business is to add some additional user-defined styles to the style sheet. Open the cascading style sheet in your project by double-clicking `StyleSheet.css` in Solution Explorer. Add the following styles:

```css
.PageFooter
{
    FONT-SIZE: 7pt;
    COLOR: #4682B4;
}
```

```css
.Spacer
{
    HEIGHT: 5px;
}

.General
{
    FONT-FAMILY: Verdana;
    FONT-SIZE: 10pt;
}

.FlatButton
{
    BORDER-RIGHT: black 1px solid;
    BORDER-TOP: black 1px solid;
    FONT-SIZE: 10pt;
    BORDER-LEFT: black 1px solid;
    BORDER-BOTTOM: black 1px solid;
    FONT-FAMILY: Verdana;
    BACKGROUND-COLOR: #F5F5F5;
    COLOR: #000066;
}

.CellOutline
{
    BORDER-LEFT: 1.5px solid #4682B4;
    BORDER-RIGHT: 1.5px solid #4682B4;
    BORDER-TOP: 1.5px solid #4682B4;
    BORDER-BOTTOM: 1.5px solid #4682B4;
    PADDING-LEFT: 10px;
    PADDING-RIGHT: 10px;
    PADDING-TOP: 10px;
    PADDING-BOTTOM: 10px;
}

.TimeSheetTable
```

```
{
   BACKGROUND-COLOR: White;
   BORDER-COLOR: Black;
   BORDER-WIDTH: 1px;
   BORDER-STYLE:  solid;
   BORDER-COLLAPSE: collapse;
   FONT-FAMILY: Verdana;
   FONT-SIZE: 10pt;
}


.TimeSheetTableHeader
{
   COLOR: White;
   BACKGROUND-COLOR: #006699;
   FONT-WEIGHT: bold;
}


.EvenRow
{
   COLOR: #000066;
   BACKGROUND-COLOR: #F5F5F5;
}


.OddRow
{
   COLOR: #000066;
}


.TransparentTextBox
{
   WIDTH: 30px;
   BORDER-TOP-STYLE: none;
   BORDER-RIGHT-STYLE: none;
   BORDER-LEFT-STYLE: none;
   BORDER-BOTTOM-STYLE: none;
   BACKGROUND-COLOR: transparent;
}
```

3. View the `TimeSheet.aspx` Web page by double-clicking it in Solution Explorer and then view the HTML for the Web page by clicking the Source tab at the bottom of the designer. You'll need to add some JavaScript code to check for numeric values in the text boxes that you'll be adding. Add the following JavaScript function replacing the text "TimeSheet Form":

```
<asp:Content ID="Content1" ContentPlaceHolderID="ContentPlaceHolder1"
Runat="Server">
<script language=javascript>
function IsNumeric()
{
   switch (event.keyCode)
   {
     case 8:
         //Backspace
         event.returnValue = true;
```

```
        break;
    case 9:
        //Tab
        event.returnValue = true;
        break;
    case 48:
        //0
        event.returnValue = true;
        break;
    case 96:
        //0
        event.returnValue = true;
        break;
    case 49:
        //1
        event.returnValue = true;
        break;
    case 97:
        //1
        event.returnValue = true;
        break;
    case 50:
        //2
        event.returnValue = true;
        break;
    case 98:
        //2
        event.returnValue = true;
        break;
    case 51:
        //3
        event.returnValue = true;
        break;
    case 99:
        //3
        event.returnValue = true;
        break;
    case 52:
        //4
        event.returnValue = true;
        break;
    case 100:
        //4
        event.returnValue = true;
        break;
    case 53:
        //5
        event.returnValue = true;
        break;
    case 101:
        //5
        event.returnValue = true;
        break;
```

```
        case 54:
           //6
           event.returnValue = true;
           break;
        case 102:
           //6
           event.returnValue = true;
           break;
        case 55:
           //7
           event.returnValue = true;
           break;
        case 103:
           //7
           event.returnValue = true;
           break;
        case 56:
           //8
           event.returnValue = true;
           break;
        case 104:
           //8
           event.returnValue = true;
           break;
        case 57:
           //9
           event.returnValue = true;
           break;
        case 105:
           //9
           event.returnValue = true;
           break;
        default:
           //All others
           event.returnValue = false;
           break;
     }
   }
</script>
```

4. You need one more JavaScript function to recalculate the total hours for a given day of the week. It is called when the user tabs out of a text box. Add the following code beneath the function just added in the previous step and before the closing the `</script>` element:

```
}
```

```
function Recalculate(dayofweek)
{
   //Get the number of rows
   var intCount = document.all.txtMondayHours.length;

   //Find the day of the week that you are working with
   switch (dayofweek)
   {
```

```
case "Monday":
    //Set the current total to 0 as it will be recalculated
    document.all.txtMondayTotal.value = 0;
    //Process each row of data adding it to the total
    for (i=0;i<intCount;i++)
    {
        document.all.txtMondayTotal.value =
            parseInt(document.all.txtMondayTotal.value) +
            parseInt(document.all.txtMondayHours[i].value);
    }
    break;
case "Tuesday":
    //Set the current total to 0 as it will be recalculated
    document.all.txtTuesdayTotal.value = 0;
    //Process each row of data adding it to the total
    for (i=0;i<intCount;i++)
    {
        document.all.txtTuesdayTotal.value =
            parseInt(document.all.txtTuesdayTotal.value) +
            parseInt(document.all.txtTuesdayHours[i].value);
    }
    break;
case "Wednesday":
    //Set the current total to 0 as it will be recalculated
    document.all.txtWednesdayTotal.value = 0;
    //Process each row of data adding it to the total
    for (i=0;i<intCount;i++)
    {
        document.all.txtWednesdayTotal.value =
            parseInt(document.all.txtWednesdayTotal.value) +
            parseInt(document.all.txtWednesdayHours[i].value);
    }
    break;
case "Thursday":
    //Set the current total to 0 as it will be recalculated
    document.all.txtThursdayTotal.value = 0;
    //Process each row of data adding it to the total
    for (i=0;i<intCount;i++)
    {
        document.all.txtThursdayTotal.value =
            parseInt(document.all.txtThursdayTotal.value) +
            parseInt(document.all.txtThursdayHours[i].value);
    }
    break;
case "Friday":
    //Set the current total to 0 as it will be recalculated
    document.all.txtFridayTotal.value = 0;
    //Process each row of data adding it to the total
    for (i=0;i<intCount;i++)
    {
        document.all.txtFridayTotal.value =
            parseInt(document.all.txtFridayTotal.value) +
            parseInt(document.all.txtFridayHours[i].value);
```

```
            }
            break;
        }
    }
}
</script>
```

5. You now want to create the table for the controls on your form. Add the following code above your JavaScript:

```
<asp:Content ID="Content1" ContentPlaceHolderID="ContentPlaceHolder1"
Runat="Server">
    <table border="0" cellpadding="0" cellspacing="0" width="100%">
        <tr>
            <td colspan="4"> </td>
        </tr>
        <tr>
            <td class="General" nowrap>TimeSheet for
                <b><%=Request.QueryString("UserName")%></b>
            </td>
            <td></td>
            <td></td>
            <td class="General">Week Ending Date</td>
        </tr>
        <tr>
            <td colspan="4" class="Spacer"></td>
        </tr>
        <tr>
            <td colspan="4" class="CellOutline">
                <%Call DisplayTimeSheet()%>
            </td>
        </tr>
    </table>
<script language=javascript>
```

6. Now switch to Design view for the Web form by clicking the Design tab at the bottom of the editor. You add the Save button first so click the toolbox, select the Standard tab, and drag a Button control from the toolbox and drop it in the second cell of the first row of the table that you just created. Set its properties as follows:

   ❑ Set (ID) to **btnSave**.

   ❑ Set CssClass to **FlatButton**.

   ❑ Set Text to **Save**.

7. Drag another Button control from the Toolbox and drop it in the third cell on the first row. Set its properties as follows:

   ❑ Set (ID) to **btnSubmit**.

   ❑ Set CssClass to **FlatButton**.

   ❑ Set Text to **Submit**.

8. Now drag a DropDownList control from the Toolbox and drop it in the last cell after the text "Week Ending Date." Set its properties as follows:

❑ Set (ID) to **cboWeekEndingDate**.

❑ Set AutoPostBack to **True**.

❑ Set CssClass to **General**.

9. Before adding any code to the TimeSheet Web form, create the week ending date functions that you created in your TimeSheet form in your Time Tracker application. However, you want these functions to be accessible to any Web form in this application. To that end, you want to add a class to this project, so right-click the TimeSheets project in Solution Explorer, and choose Add New Item from the context menu. In the Add New Item dialog box, select the Class icon in the Templates pane and enter a name of **Dates.vb** in the Name field. Then click the Add button. You'll be prompted with a dialog box that informs you that your class should be placed in the App_Code folder. Click Yes to have the folder automatically created in your project and the class added to that folder.

10. Add the following functions to this class:

```
Public Function GetCurrentWeekEndingDate() As String
    GetCurrentWeekEndingDate = DateSerial( _
        Year(Now), Month(Now), DateAndTime.Day(Now) - _
        DatePart("w", Now, Microsoft.VisualBasic.FirstDayOfWeek.Sunday) + 6)
End Function

Public Function GetPreviousWeekEndingDate() As String
    GetPreviousWeekEndingDate = DateSerial( _
        Year(Now), Month(Now), DateAndTime.Day(Now) - _
        DatePart("w", Now, Microsoft.VisualBasic.FirstDayOfWeek.Sunday) - 1)
End Function
```

11. You want to add VB code for the TimeSheet Web page, so right-click TimeSheet.aspx in Solution Explorer and choose View Code from the context menu. First you need to import the System.Data namespace so add the following Imports statement:

```
Imports System.Data

Partial Class TimeSheet
```

12. You need some variable declarations for the various tasks to be performed in the code. Add these declarations to your code:

```
'Private variables and objects
Private intIndex As Integer
Private intTotal As Integer

Private blnEvenRow As Boolean = True

Private strCompany As String = "Wrox"
Private strApplication As String = "Time Tracker"

Private dteWeekEndingDate As Date

Private objTimeSheets As WroxBusinessLogic.WBLTimeSheets
Private objDates As New Dates

Private objTimeSheetDS As DataSet
```

13. Add some code to the Page_Load procedure. Select (Page Events) in the Class Name combo box and the Load event in the Method Name combo box. Add the code that follows. You receive an error that the UpdateTimeSheetDS and GetTimeSheet procedures are not declared. You can ignore these errors, as you add those procedures in the following steps:

```
Protected Sub Page_Load(ByVal sender As Object, _
    ByVal e As System.EventArgs) Handles Me.Load

        If IsPostBack Then
            'Get the week ending date
            dteWeekEndingDate = CType(ViewState("WeekEndingDate"), Date)
            'Get the timesheet DataSet
            objTimeSheetDS = CType(ViewState("TimeSheetDS"), DataSet)

            'Update the timesheet DataSet
            Call UpdateTimeSheetDS()
        Else
            'Set the default week ending date
            dteWeekEndingDate = CType(objDates.GetCurrentWeekEndingDate, Date)

            'Load the week ending dates in the form
            cboWeekEndingDate.Items.Add(objDates.GetPreviousWeekEndingDate)
            cboWeekEndingDate.Items.Add(objDates.GetCurrentWeekEndingDate)
            cboWeekEndingDate.SelectedIndex = 1

            'Get the timesheet
            Call GetTimeSheet()

            'Save the data between requests
            ViewState("TimeSheetDS") = objTimeSheetDS
            ViewState("WeekEndingDate") = dteWeekEndingDate
        End If
End Sub
```

14. The GetTimeSheet procedure will call the business logic component to get the requested timesheet and will calculate the total row of data. Add the following code:

```
Private Sub GetTimeSheet()
    'Initialize a new instance of the business logic component
    Using objTimeSheets As New WroxBusinessLogic.WBLTimeSheets( _
        strCompany, strApplication)

        'Get the timesheet for the user
        objTimeSheetDS = objTimeSheets.GetTimeSheet( _
            New Guid(Request.QueryString("UserID")), dteWeekEndingDate)

        'Initialize a new DataRow object
        Dim objDataRow As DataRow = objTimeSheetDS.Tables("TimeSheet").NewRow

        'Set the values in the columns
        objDataRow.Item("ProjectName") = "Total Hours"

        'Calculate and set the total hours for Monday
        intTotal = 0
```

```
            For intIndex = 0 To objTimeSheetDS.Tables("TimeSheet").Rows.Count - 1
                intTotal += CType(objTimeSheetDS.Tables( _
                    "TimeSheet").Rows(intIndex).Item("MondayHours"), Integer)
            Next
            objDataRow.Item("MondayHours") = intTotal

            'Calculate and set the total hours for Tuesday
            intTotal = 0
            For intIndex = 0 To objTimeSheetDS.Tables("TimeSheet").Rows.Count - 1
                intTotal += CType(objTimeSheetDS.Tables( _
                    "TimeSheet").Rows(intIndex).Item("TuesdayHours"), Integer)
            Next
            objDataRow.Item("TuesdayHours") = intTotal

            'Calculate and set the total hours for Wednesday
            intTotal = 0
            For intIndex = 0 To objTimeSheetDS.Tables("TimeSheet").Rows.Count - 1
                intTotal += CType(objTimeSheetDS.Tables( _
                    "TimeSheet").Rows(intIndex).Item("WednesdayHours"), Integer)
            Next
            objDataRow.Item("WednesdayHours") = intTotal

            'Calculate and set the total hours for Thursday
            intTotal = 0
            For intIndex = 0 To objTimeSheetDS.Tables("TimeSheet").Rows.Count - 1
                intTotal += CType(objTimeSheetDS.Tables( _
                    "TimeSheet").Rows(intIndex).Item("ThursdayHours"), Integer)
            Next
            objDataRow.Item("ThursdayHours") = intTotal

            'Calculate and set the total hours for Friday
            intTotal = 0
            For intIndex = 0 To objTimeSheetDS.Tables("TimeSheet").Rows.Count - 1
                intTotal += CType(objTimeSheetDS.Tables( _
                    "TimeSheet").Rows(intIndex).Item("FridayHours"), Integer)
            Next
            objDataRow.Item("FridayHours") = intTotal

            'Add the row to the DataSet
            objTimeSheetDS.Tables("TimeSheet").Rows.Add(objDataRow)
        End Using
    End Sub
```

15. The `DisplayTimeSheet` procedure is called from the Web form and builds a table containing the timesheet and writes it to your Web form. You will receive an error that the `WriteTimeSheetRow` procedure is not declared. You can ignore this error because you add that procedure in the next step. Add the following code:

```
Public Sub DisplayTimeSheet()
    'Begin table
    Response.Write("<table cellpadding=""3"" cellspacing=""0"" " & _
        "bordercolor=""Black"" border=""1""" & _
        "class=""TimeSheetTable"" >")
```

```
    Response.Write("<tr class=""TimeSheetTableHeader"">")
    Response.Write("<td nowrap style=""width:200px;"">Project Name</td>")
    Response.Write("<td style=""width:30px;"">Mon</td>")
    Response.Write("<td style=""width:30px;"">Tue</td>")
    Response.Write("<td style=""width:30px;"">Wed</td>")
    Response.Write("<td style=""width:30px;"">Thu</td>")
    Response.Write("<td style=""width:30px;"">Fri</td>")
    Response.Write("</tr>")

    'Process all rows of data
    For intIndex = 0 To objTimeSheetDS.Tables("TimeSheet").Rows.Count - 2
        WriteTimeSheetRow(objTimeSheetDS.Tables("TimeSheet").Rows(intIndex))
    Next

    'Write the total row
    blnEvenRow = Not blnEvenRow
    If blnEvenRow Then
        Response.Write("<tr class=""EvenRow"">")
    Else
        Response.Write("<tr class=""OddRow"">")
    End If
    Response.Write("<td nowrap>Total Hours</td>")
    Response.Write("<td><INPUT type=""text"" name=""txtMondayTotal""" & _
        "class=""TransparentTextBox"" readonly " & _
        "onfocus=""javascript:txtMondayHours[0].select();" & _
        "txtMondayHours[0].focus();"" value=""" & _
        objTimeSheetDS.Tables("TimeSheet").Rows(intIndex).Item( _
        "MondayHours") & """></td>")
    Response.Write("<td><INPUT type=""text"" name=""txtTuesdayTotal""" & _
        "class=""TransparentTextBox"" readonly value=""" & _
        objTimeSheetDS.Tables("TimeSheet").Rows(intIndex).Item( _
        "TuesdayHours") & """></td>")
    Response.Write("<td><INPUT type=""text"" name=""txtWednesdayTotal""" & _
        "class=""TransparentTextBox"" readonly value=""" & _
        objTimeSheetDS.Tables("TimeSheet").Rows(intIndex).Item( _
        "WednesdayHours") & """></td>")
    Response.Write("<td><INPUT type=""text"" name=""txtThursdayTotal""" & _
        "class=""TransparentTextBox"" readonly value=""" & _
        objTimeSheetDS.Tables("TimeSheet").Rows(intIndex).Item( _
        "ThursdayHours") & """></td>")
    Response.Write("<td><INPUT type=""text"" name=""txtFridayTotal""" & _
        "class=""TransparentTextBox"" readonly value=""" & _
        objTimeSheetDS.Tables("TimeSheet").Rows(intIndex).Item( _
        "FridayHours") & """></td>")

    'End the table
    Response.Write("</tr>")
    Response.Write("</table>")
End Sub
```

16. The WriteTimeSheetRow procedure writes an actual row of data in the timesheet table using the values from the DataSet. Add the following code:

```
Private Sub WriteTimeSheetRow(ByVal objDataRow As DataRow)
    'Toggle the flag
    blnEvenRow = Not blnEvenRow
    If blnEvenRow Then
        Response.Write("<tr class=""EvenRow"">")
    Else
        Response.Write("<tr class=""OddRow"">")
    End If
    Response.Write("<td nowrap>" & objDataRow.Item("ProjectName") & _
        "</td>")
    If objTimeSheetDS.Tables("TimeSheet").Rows(0).Item("Submitted") Then
        'The data is read-only so just display it
        Response.Write("<td style=""width:30px;"">" & _
            objDataRow.Item("MondayHours") & "</td>")
        Response.Write("<td style=""width:30px;"">" & _
            objDataRow.Item("TuesdayHours") & "</td>")
        Response.Write("<td style=""width:30px;"">" & _
            objDataRow.Item("WednesdayHours") & "</td>")
        Response.Write("<td style=""width:30px;"">" & _
            objDataRow.Item("ThursdayHours") & "</td>")
        Response.Write("<td style=""width:30px;"">" & _
            objDataRow.Item("FridayHours") & "</td>")
    Else
        Response.Write("<td><input type=""textbox"" style=""width:30px;"" " & _
            "name=""txtMondayHours"" value=""" & _
            objDataRow.Item("MondayHours") & _
            """ onBlur=""javascript:Recalculate('Monday');"" " & _
            "onkeydown=""javascript:IsNumeric();""></td>")
        Response.Write("<td><input type=""textbox"" style=""width:30px;"" " & _
            "name=""txtTuesdayHours"" value=""" & _
            objDataRow.Item("TuesdayHours") & _
            """ onBlur=""javascript:Recalculate('Tuesday');"" " & _
            "onkeydown=""javascript:IsNumeric();""></td>")
        Response.Write("<td><input type=""textbox"" style=""width:30px;"" " & _
            "name=""txtWednesdayHours"" value=""" & _
            objDataRow.Item("WednesdayHours") & _
            """ onBlur=""javascript:Recalculate('Wednesday');"" " & _
            "onkeydown=""javascript:IsNumeric();""></td>")
        Response.Write("<td><input type=""textbox"" style=""width:30px;"" " & _
            "name=""txtThursdayHours"" value=""" & _
            objDataRow.Item("ThursdayHours") & _
            """ onBlur=""javascript:Recalculate('Thursday');"" " & _
            "onkeydown=""javascript:IsNumeric();""></td>")
        Response.Write("<td><input type=""textbox"" style=""width:30px;"" " & _
            "name=""txtFridayHours"" value=""" & _
            objDataRow.Item("FridayHours") & _
            """ onBlur=""javascript:Recalculate('Friday');"" " & _
            "onkeydown=""javascript:IsNumeric();""></td>")
    End If
    Response.Write("</tr>")
End Sub
```

17. The UpdateTimeSheetDS procedure processes the fields on the Web form and updates the timesheet DataSet. Add the following code to create this procedure:

```
Private Sub UpdateTimeSheetDS()
    If Request.Form("txtMondayHours") Is Nothing Then
        Exit Sub
    End If
    Dim strMondayHours() As String = _
        Split(Request.Form("txtMondayHours"), ",")
    Dim strTuesdayHours() As String = _
        Split(Request.Form("txtTuesdayHours"), ",")
    Dim strWednesdayHours() As String = _
        Split(Request.Form("txtWednesdayHours"), ",")
    Dim strThursdayHours() As String = _
        Split(Request.Form("txtThursdayHours"), ",")
    Dim strFridayHours() As String = _
        Split(Request.Form("txtFridayHours"), ",")

    'Process all rows of data minus the total row
    For intIndex = 0 To objTimeSheetDS.Tables("TimeSheet").Rows.Count - 2
        objTimeSheetDS.Tables("TimeSheet").Rows(intIndex).Item( _
            "MondayHours") = CType(strMondayHours(intIndex), Byte)
        objTimeSheetDS.Tables("TimeSheet").Rows(intIndex).Item( _
            "TuesdayHours") = CType(strTuesdayHours(intIndex), Byte)
        objTimeSheetDS.Tables("TimeSheet").Rows(intIndex).Item( _
            "WednesdayHours") = CType(strWednesdayHours(intIndex), Byte)
        objTimeSheetDS.Tables("TimeSheet").Rows(intIndex).Item( _
            "ThursdayHours") = CType(strThursdayHours(intIndex), Byte)
        objTimeSheetDS.Tables("TimeSheet").Rows(intIndex).Item( _
            "FridayHours") = CType(strFridayHours(intIndex), Byte)
    Next

    'Now process the total row - this is needed for when we build a new
    ' table to post back to the client
    objTimeSheetDS.Tables("TimeSheet").Rows(intIndex).Item( _
        "MondayHours") = CType(Request.Form("txtMondayTotal"), Byte)
    objTimeSheetDS.Tables("TimeSheet").Rows(intIndex).Item( _
        "TuesdayHours") = CType(Request.Form("txtTuesdayTotal"), Byte)
    objTimeSheetDS.Tables("TimeSheet").Rows(intIndex).Item( _
        "WednesdayHours") = CType(Request.Form("txtWednesdayTotal"), Byte)
    objTimeSheetDS.Tables("TimeSheet").Rows(intIndex).Item( _
        "ThursdayHours") = CType(Request.Form("txtThursdayTotal"), Byte)
    objTimeSheetDS.Tables("TimeSheet").Rows(intIndex).Item( _
        "FridayHours") = CType(Request.Form("txtFridayTotal"), Byte)
End Sub
```

18. When a user selects a new date in the combo box on the Web form, you want to get the timesheet for that date and display it. Select cboWeekEndingDate in the Class Name combo box at the top of the editor and in the Method Name combo box select the SelectedIndexChanged event. Add the following code to the cboWeekEndingDate_SelectedIndexChanged procedure:

```
Protected Sub cboWeekEndingDate_SelectedIndexChanged( _
    ByVal sender As Object, ByVal e As System.EventArgs) _
```

```
                    Handles cboWeekEndingDate.SelectedIndexChanged

            'If the date is different...
            If ViewState("WeekEndingDate").ToString <> _
                cboWeekEndingDate.SelectedValue Then

                'Set the new date from the Web form
                dteWeekEndingDate = CType(cboWeekEndingDate.SelectedValue, Date)

                'Get the timesheet
                Call GetTimeSheet()

                'Save the data between requests
                ViewState("TimeSheetDS") = objTimeSheetDS
                ViewState("WeekEndingDate") = dteWeekEndingDate
            End If
        End Sub
```

19. Add some code to save a timesheet when the user clicks the Save button on the Web form. Select
     btnSave in the Class Name combo box at the top of the editor and in the Method Name combo
     box select the Click event. Add the following code to the btnSave_Click procedure:

```
Protected Sub btnSave_Click(ByVal sender As Object, _
    ByVal e As System.EventArgs) Handles btnSave.Click

        'Initialize a new instance of the business logic component
        Using objTimeSheets As New WroxBusinessLogic.WBLTimeSheets( _
            strCompany, strApplication)
            Try
                'Save the timesheet changes
                If Not objTimeSheets.SaveTimeSheet(objTimeSheetDS) Then
                    Throw New Exception("Save TimeSheet Failed")
                End If
            Catch ExceptionErr As Exception
                Response.Write(ExceptionErr.Message)
            End Try
        End Using
    End Sub
```

20. When users click the Submit button on the Web form, you'll want to submit their timesheets. In
     the Class Name combo box, select btnSubmit, and in the Method Name combo box select the
     Click event. Add the following code to the btnSubmit_Click procedure:

```
Protected Sub btnSubmit_Click(ByVal sender As Object, _
    ByVal e As System.EventArgs) Handles btnSubmit.Click

        'Initialize a new instance of the business logic component
        Using objTimeSheets As New WroxBusinessLogic.WBLTimeSheets( _
            strCompany, strApplication)
            Try
                'Submit the timesheet
                If Not objTimeSheets.SubmitTimeSheet(New Guid( _
                    objTimeSheetDS.Tables("TimeSheet").Rows(0).Item( _
                    "TimeSheetID").ToString)) Then
                    Throw New Exception("Submit TimeSheet Failed")
```

```
                End If
                'Reload the timesheet so it becomes read-only
                Call GetTimeSheet()
            Catch ExceptionErr As Exception
                Response.Write(ExceptionErr.Message)
            End Try
        End Using
    End Sub
```

Now it's time to test your changes, so start your project. When the Login Web form is displayed, log in as a user. When your login credentials have been validated, the TimeSheet Web form is displayed, as shown in Figure 14-5.

As you can see, you can edit the hours for any given day for any project without having the Web form posted back to the server. This timesheet also has a very different look than the timesheet shown in the GridView in Figures 14-3 and 14-4.

Select a day and project, enter a numeric value, and press the Tab key. You'll notice that the total row is automatically updated to display the total for that day. Now enter a non-numeric value in the current text box. You'll notice that nothing appears to happen. What actually has happened is that the IsNumeric JavaScript function has been executed and has determined that the value you tried to enter was not a numeric value and therefore canceled the onkeydown event. This prevents a user from entering non-numeric data in these fields.

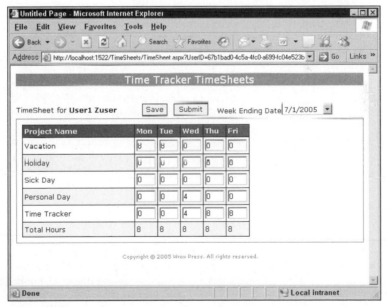

Figure 14-5

Now click the Save button and you'll notice that the TimeSheet Web form has been posted back to the server and the timesheet has been updated in the database. You can verify this by stopping your project and starting it again, and logging in. When the TimeSheet Web form is displayed, you see the changes that you saved. The behavior of the Save button provides the same functionality and uses the same code that was implemented for the Save button in the TimeSheet form in the Time Tracker application.

Now complete the timesheet with the hours that you want and then click the Save button to save the timesheet and then click Submit to have the timesheet submitted. The TimeSheet Web form is posted back to the server for processing, and once the timesheet has been updated in the database, the TimeSheet Web form is rebuilt and sent back to the client. However, you'll now notice that the timesheet has been formatted to be read-only, as the timesheet has been submitted for approval, as shown in Figure 14-6.

The Submit button exhibits the same behavior and uses the same code as the Submit button in the TimeSheet form in the Time Tracker application. This enables you to provide a similar interface in both the Time Tracker Windows application and the TimeSheets Web application. Only the user interface has changed; the business rules and data access rules have remained the same.

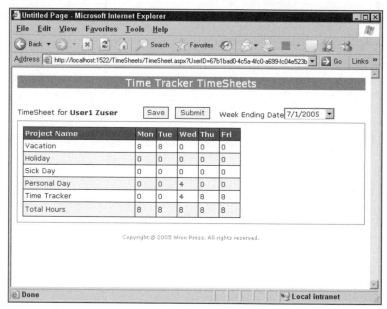

Figure 14-6

How It Works

You start this exercise by defining some more user-defined styles in your cascading style sheet. The Spacer style is used in your table to specify the height of an empty row of data between the controls and the timesheet table. The HEIGHT style attribute is used to define the height of the HTML element to which this style is applied, which in this case is a <TD> element.

The General style is used to specify the font name and size to be used for the HTML elements to which this style is applied. You used this style to specify the font for the text in the drop-down list control and the text in other various columns in your table.

```
.Spacer
{
    HEIGHT: 5px;
}

.General
{
    FONT-FAMILY: Verdana;
    FONT-SIZE: 10pt;
}
```

The FlatButton style is used to define the style of the Button controls on your Web form. Instead of having plain gray buttons, you use this style to give them the same look as the buttons on the TimeSheet form in the Time Tracker application. The BORDER-RIGHT, BORDER-TOP, BORDER-LEFT, and BORDER-BOTTOM style attributes are used to set the borders of the Button control. These style attributes accept three parameters: the color of the border, the size of the border, and the line style of the border. This style also defines the font to be used and the size of the font. The BACKGROUND-COLOR style attribute defines the background color of the Button control and the COLOR style attribute defines the color of the text on the Button control.

```
.FlatButton
{
    BORDER-RIGHT: black 1px solid;
    BORDER-TOP: black 1px solid;
    FONT-SIZE: 10pt;
    BORDER-LEFT: black 1px solid;
    BORDER-BOTTOM: black 1px solid;
    FONT-FAMILY: Verdana;
    BACKGROUND-COLOR: #F5F5F5;
    COLOR: #000066;
}
```

The CellOutline style is used in the table cell where the timesheet was built. This style defines the borders of the cell and specifies the padding to be used in the cell. The PADDING-LEFT, PADDING-RIGHT, PADDING-TOP, and PADDING-BOTTOM style attributes define the amount of space to leave between the borders of the cell and the content of the cell. Here you specify the padding space to be 10 pixels:

```
.CellOutline
{
    BORDER-LEFT: 1.5px solid #4682B4;
    BORDER-RIGHT: 1.5px solid #4682B4;
    BORDER-TOP: 1.5px solid #4682B4;
    BORDER-BOTTOM: 1.5px solid #4682B4;
    PADDING-LEFT: 10px;
    PADDING-RIGHT: 10px;
    PADDING-TOP: 10px;
    PADDING-BOTTOM: 10px;
}
```

The TimeSheetTable style is used in the table that contains the timesheet and defines the borders of the table. The BORDER-WIDTH style attribute defines the width of the borders in the table and has been set to use a border width of 1 pixel. The BORDER-STYLE attribute defines the styles of the borders of the table and is set to a value of `solid` to define a solid border line. The `BORDER-COLLAPSE` style attribute indicates whether the row and cell borders of a table are joined in a single border or detached. A value of `collapse`, as defined here, indicates that the borders of the cells and rows are collapsed to form a solid border around each cell and row.

The `TimeSheetTableHeader` style is used to define the header row of the timesheet. This is where the column labels are defined, and this style sets the background color of the cells, the color of the text, and the font weight.

```
.TimeSheetTable
{
    BACKGROUND-COLOR: White;
    BORDER-COLOR: Black;
    BORDER-WIDTH: 1px;
    BORDER-STYLE:  solid;
    BORDER-COLLAPSE: collapse;
    FONT-FAMILY: Verdana;
    FONT-SIZE: 10pt;
}

.TimeSheetTableHeader
{
    COLOR: White;
    BACKGROUND-COLOR: #006699;
    FONT-WEIGHT: bold;
}
```

The alternating style of the DataGrid control provides a means to have every other row a different color. To emulate this behavior, you define an `EvenRow` and `OddRow` style, which is used in the rows of your timesheet. The `EvenRow` style defines the background color to use in each cell and the color to be used for the text in the cells. The `OddRow` style simply defines the color to be used on the text in the cells.

Finally, the `TransparentTextBox` style is used to make the TextBox controls in the total row of the timesheet look like regular text. You need the TextBox controls in the total row to be able to calculate and display the total for each column in your JavaScript.

This style sets the width of the TextBox control and sets the border styles to none, meaning that no borders will be visible in the TextBox control. Also, the `BACKGROUND-COLOR` style attribute is set to a value of `transparent`, indicating that the background color of the text box will inherit the background color of the cell in which it is placed.

```
.EvenRow
{
    COLOR: #000066;
    BACKGROUND-COLOR: #F5F5F5;
}

.OddRow
{
    COLOR: #000066;
}
```

```
.TransparentTextBox
{
   WIDTH: 30px;
   BORDER-TOP-STYLE: none;
   BORDER-RIGHT-STYLE: none;
   BORDER-LEFT-STYLE: none;
   BORDER-BOTTOM-STYLE: none;
   BACKGROUND-COLOR: transparent;
}
```

You continue by adding two client-side JavaScript functions that are used to validate input and recalculate the total row in your timesheet.

The `IsNumeric` JavaScript function is lengthy but really quite simple. This function validates the key that has been pressed and determines whether it is a numeric key, a backspace key, or a Tab key. Any other key is invalid and this function will cause the invalid key to be canceled.

The text boxes on your form that contain the hours for the various projects call this function when the `onkeydown` event is fired for that text box. The `onkeydown` event is a cancelable event, meaning that your code can cancel the key being pressed. The `Event` object is an object of the `Window` object (the browser window) and represents the state of an event. HTML elements have different events and the text box element raises the `onkeydown` event when the user presses a key.

This function evaluates the event `keyCode` of the key being pressed in the `switch` statement. This is the equivalent to the `Case` statement in VB. If the `keyCode` of the key is equal to the backspace key, Tab key, or any of the numeric keys across the top of your keyword or any of the numeric keys in the keypad of your keyboard, the case statements will set the `returnValue` property of the `event` object to a value of `true`, meaning that the event may be processed. The `break` statement is required in each Case statement to exit the processing of the `switch` statement.

```
function IsNumeric()
{
   switch (event.keyCode)
   {
      case 8:
         //Backspace
         event.returnValue = true;
         break;
      case 9:
         //Tab
         event.returnValue = true;
         break;
      case 48:
         //0
         event.returnValue = true;
         break;
      case 96:
         //0
         event.returnValue = true;
         break;
      case 49:
         //1
```

```
        event.returnValue = true;
        break;
    case 97:
        //1
        event.returnValue = true;
        break;
    case 50:
        //2
        event.returnValue = true;
        break;
    case 98:
        //2
        event.returnValue = true;
        break;
    case 51:
        //3
        event.returnValue = true;
        break;
    case 99:
        //3
        event.returnValue = true;
        break;
    case 52:
        //4
        event.returnValue = true;
        break;
    case 100:
        //4
        event.returnValue = true;
        break;
    case 53:
        //5
        event.returnValue = true;
        break;
    case 101:
        //5
        event.returnValue = true;
        break;
    case 54:
        //6
        event.returnValue = true;
        break;
    case 102:
        //6
        event.returnValue = true;
        break;
    case 55:
        //7
        event.returnValue = true;
        break;
    case 103:
        //7
        event.returnValue = true;
        break;
```

```
    case 56:
        //8
        event.returnValue = true;
        break;
    case 104:
        //8
        event.returnValue = true;
        break;
    case 57:
        //9
        event.returnValue = true;
        break;
    case 105:
        //9
        event.returnValue = true;
        break;
```

The code in the `default` statement will execute when none of the previous `case` statements are matched, and here you set the `returnValue` property to a value of `false`. This causes the `onkeydown` event to be canceled, meaning that the key pressed by the user will not be processed.

```
    default:
        //All others
        event.returnValue = false;
        break;
    }
}
```

The `Recalculate` function recalculates the total for a given day of the week. This function has been designed to accept the day of the week as an input parameter so it knows which day of the week it should recalculate the totals for. This function will be called when the user tabs out of a text box in the timesheet.

The text boxes for a given day of the week for the various projects have the same name. For example, the text box for Monday has a name of `txtMondayHours` for each project listed. This effectively creates an array of TextBox controls named `txtMondayHours`. Therefore, the first thing that this function does is to declare a variable named `intCount` and get the number of elements in the array.

This is accomplished using the `length` property of the `TextBox` element `txtMondayHours`. The `length` property returns the actual number of elements in the array. You access this property by first specifying the `document` object, which represents the HTML document in the browser window. Then you access the `all` collection in the `document` object, and then access the text box by specifying the text box name.

You may have noticed that the text box for the Monday hours is always specified. Each column for each day of the week has the same number of TextBox controls, so this is a reliable method for determining how many elements are in the array of text boxes.

After getting the number of elements in the array, you use a `switch` statement to determine which day of the week you should recalculate the totals for. The value passed in the `dayofweek` input parameter is the actual day of the week.

After you determine which day of the week you should be processing, the first thing that you do is clear the total in the text box in the total row for that day of the week. Then you set up a `for` loop and process each element in the array. The `for` statement accepts three parameters: the `initialization` parameter, the `test` parameter, and the `increment` parameter.

The variable named `i` is declared and set to an initial value of 0 for the initialization parameter. This will represent the first item in the array, as the items in the array use a zero-based index. The test parameter is specified as `i<intCount`, meaning that this `for` statement should process as long as the value in the `i` parameter is less than the value in the `intCount` parameter. The increment parameter is specified as `i++`, meaning that for each iteration of the loop, the value of the `i` parameter is incremented by a value of 1.

Inside of the `for` loop, you set the `value` property of the total text box to the value that is already there plus the value of the text box in the array for the day of the week that you are processing. For example, if you are processing the totals for Monday, you set the `value` of the `txtMondayTotal` text box to equal the current value of the `txtMondayTotal` text box plus the value of the `txtMondayHours` text box in the array that you are processing.

The `parseInt` function returns an Integer value converted from a string, as all values in the `value` property of a text box are strings. Using this function just helps speed up the calculation of the totals, as the JavaScript engine does not have to go through the process of determining that this is a string value and then converting the string to an `Integer` data type.

```
function Recalculate(dayofweek)
{
    //Get the number of rows
    var intCount = document.all.txtMondayHours.length;

    //Find the day of the week that you are working with
    switch (dayofweek)
    {
        case "Monday":
            //Set the current total to 0 as it will be recalculated
            document.all.txtMondayTotal.value = 0;
            //Process each row of data adding it to the total
            for (i=0;i<intCount;i++)
            {
                document.all.txtMondayTotal.value =
                    parseInt(document.all.txtMondayTotal.value) +
                    parseInt(document.all.txtMondayHours[i].value);
            }
            break;
        case "Tuesday":
            //Set the current total to 0 as it will be recalculated
            document.all.txtTuesdayTotal.value = 0;
            //Process each row of data adding it to the total
            for (i=0;i<intCount;i++)
            {
                document.all.txtTuesdayTotal.value =
                    parseInt(document.all.txtTuesdayTotal.value) +
                    parseInt(document.all.txtTuesdayHours[i].value);
            }
```

```
            break;
        case "Wednesday":
            //Set the current total to 0 as it will be recalculated
            document.all.txtWednesdayTotal.value = 0;
            //Process each row of data adding it to the total
            for (i=0;i<intCount;i++)
            {
                document.all.txtWednesdayTotal.value =
                    parseInt(document.all.txtWednesdayTotal.value) +
                    parseInt(document.all.txtWednesdayHours[i].value);
            }
            break;
        case "Thursday":
            //Set the current total to 0 as it will be recalculated
            document.all.txtThursdayTotal.value = 0;
            //Process each row of data adding it to the total
            for (i=0;i<intCount;i++)
            {
                document.all.txtThursdayTotal.value =
                    parseInt(document.all.txtThursdayTotal.value) +
                    parseInt(document.all.txtThursdayHours[i].value);
            }
            break;
        case "Friday":
            //Set the current total to 0 as it will be recalculated
            document.all.txtFridayTotal.value = 0;
            //Process each row of data adding it to the total
            for (i=0;i<intCount;i++)
            {
                document.all.txtFridayTotal.value =
                    parseInt(document.all.txtFridayTotal.value) +
                    parseInt(document.all.txtFridayHours[i].value);
            }
            break;
    }
}
```

The next step is to create a table that will hold the controls and the actual timesheet. The first row in this table is just a filler row to create a space between the last row of data in the previous table and the first row of data in this table. If none of the columns in a row contain data, the row will not take up space in the resulting output that is displayed. To have this row create the space that you are looking for, you specify that a blank space should be created in the column using the text . This creates a place-holder for a space in the column, thus giving you the effect that you want.

The next row in this table contains the username and contains the Save and Submit buttons as well as the DropDownList control for the week ending dates. The third row in this table is an alternative way to create a spacer row instead of using the HTML characters, , used to create the first row in this table. Here you are using a user-defined style in your style sheet to specify the height of the row, which causes this row to take up space in the HTML output regardless of whether the row contains any data.

The final row in this table contains some server-side code to call the DisplayTimeSheet function. This function builds a timesheet table and writes it in the column of this row:

```
<table border="0" cellpadding="0" cellspacing="0" width="100%">
   <tr>
      <td colspan="4"> </td>
   </tr>
   <tr>
      <td class="General" nowrap>TimeSheet for
         <b><%=Request.QueryString("UserName")%></b>
      </td>
      <td></td>
      <td></td>
      <td class="General">Week Ending Date</td>
   </tr>
   <tr>
      <td colspan="4" class="Spacer"></td>
   </tr>
   <tr>
      <td colspan="4" class="CellOutline">
         <%Call DisplayTimeSheet()%>
      </td>
   </tr>
</table>
```

The next steps add the actual controls to the Web form and set their properties.

You add the Dates class next and add two functions to this class. The GetCurrentWeekEndingDate and GetPreviousWeekEndingDate functions are the same functions that you created in your TimeSheet form in the Time Tracker application. Placing these functions in this class makes them accessible to all Web forms in your application. You'll not only use these functions in your TimeSheet Web form, but also in another Web form that you create in Chapter 16.

```
Public Function GetCurrentWeekEndingDate() As String
    GetCurrentWeekEndingDate = DateSerial( _
        Year(Now), Month(Now), DateAndTime.Day(Now) - _
        DatePart("w", Now, Microsoft.VisualBasic.FirstDayOfWeek.Sunday) + 6)
End Function

Public Function GetPreviousWeekEndingDate() As String
    GetPreviousWeekEndingDate = DateSerial( _
        Year(Now), Month(Now), DateAndTime.Day(Now) - _
        DatePart("w", Now, Microsoft.VisualBasic.FirstDayOfWeek.Sunday) - 1)
End Function
```

The first thing you do when you start adding code to the code-behind file for your TimeSheet Web form is to import the System.Data namespace, for which the code is not shown here. Then you declare some variables. These variables are used throughout your code for the various tasks that you perform and all of these variables should look familiar from your TimeSheet form in the Time Tracker application.

```
'Private variables and objects
Private intIndex As Integer
Private intTotal As Integer

Private blnEvenRow As Boolean = True
```

```
            Private strCompany As String = "Wrox"
            Private strApplication As String = "Time Tracker"

            Private dteWeekEndingDate As Date

            Private objTimeSheets As WroxBusinessLogic.WBLTimeSheets
            Private objDates As New Dates

            Private objTimeSheetDS As DataSet
```

Remember that the Page_Load procedure is always executed first, before any HTML in your Web form is rendered. Here you have some tasks that need to be performed before a post back occurs and after a post back occurs.

Starting at the top, you want to check the IsPostBack property and if this Web form is being posted back to the server, you want to get the data that you stored in ViewState. ViewState is a field in a Web page inserted by ASP.NET in encrypted format and persists changes to the state of a Web form between post backs. You can add your data to the ViewState of a Web form on the server when building the Web page and then retrieve those values when the page is posted back to the server for processing.

The first value that you want to retrieve from ViewState is the initial week ending date that was stored there with a name of WeekEndingDate. You explicitly convert the value you retrieve from ViewState to a Date data type and set this value in your dteWeekEndingDate variable. Then you retrieve the DataSet containing the timesheet data from ViewState and explicitly convert this object to a DataSet data type and set it in your objTimeSheetDS object. Finally, you call the UpdateTimeSheetDS function to update the timesheet DataSet with any changes that the user may have made.

```
        Protected Sub Page_Load(ByVal sender As Object, _
            ByVal e As System.EventArgs) Handles Me.Load

        If IsPostBack Then
                'Get the week ending date
                dteWeekEndingDate = CType(ViewState("WeekEndingDate"), Date)
                'Get the timesheet DataSet
                objTimeSheetDS = CType(ViewState("TimeSheetDS"), DataSet)

                'Update the timesheet DataSet
                Call UpdateTimeSheetDS()
```

If the page is not being posted back then the code in the Else statement is executed and sets some initial values, loads the controls on the Web form, gets the timesheet data, and saves the data in ViewState.

First, you set the default week ending date in the dteWeekEndingDate variable using the week ending date for the current week, which is retrieved from the GetCurrentWeekEndingDate function in the Dates class. Then you add the previous and current week ending dates to the Items collection in the cboWeekEndingDate combo box on your Web form and set the SelectedIndex property to display the current week ending date.

Next, you call the GetTimeSheet procedure to get the timesheet for the specified week ending date that has been set in the dteWeekEndingDate variable. Finally, you save the timesheet DataSet and current week ending date in `ViewState` so that they will be available when the user posts the Web form back to the server for processing.

```
        Else
            'Set the default week ending date
            dteWeekEndingDate = CType(objDates.GetCurrentWeekEndingDate, Date)

            'Load the week ending dates in the form
            cboWeekEndingDate.Items.Add(objDates.GetPreviousWeekEndingDate)
            cboWeekEndingDate.Items.Add(objDates.GetCurrentWeekEndingDate)
            cboWeekEndingDate.SelectedIndex = 1

            'Get the timesheet
            Call GetTimeSheet()

            'Save the data between requests
            ViewState("TimeSheetDS") = objTimeSheetDS
            ViewState("WeekEndingDate") = dteWeekEndingDate
        End If
    End Sub
```

The `GetTimeSheet` procedure does not need much explanation as it pretty much mirrors the code in the `LoadTimeSheet` procedure in the TimeSheet form in the Time Tracker application. In the `LoadTimeSheet` procedure, you worked with a `DataView` object to build and calculate the total row. In this procedure you are working directly with the `DataSet` object to build and calculate the total row. Also, this procedure does not do any data binding to any controls, so you'll notice that it is much smaller than the `LoadTimeSheet` procedure in the TimeSheet form in the Time Tracker application.

```
        Private Sub GetTimeSheet()
            'Initialize a new instance of the business logic component
            Using objTimeSheets As New WroxBusinessLogic.WBLTimeSheets( _
                strCompany, strApplication)

                'Get the timesheet for the user
                objTimeSheetDS = objTimeSheets.GetTimeSheet( _
                    New Guid(Request.QueryString("UserID")), dteWeekEndingDate)

                'Initialize a new DataRow object
                Dim objDataRow As DataRow = objTimeSheetDS.Tables("TimeSheet").NewRow

                'Set the values in the columns
                objDataRow.Item("ProjectName") = "Total Hours"

                'Calculate and set the total hours for Monday
                intTotal = 0
                For intIndex = 0 To objTimeSheetDS.Tables("TimeSheet").Rows.Count - 1
                    intTotal += CType(objTimeSheetDS.Tables( _
                        "TimeSheet").Rows(intIndex).Item("MondayHours"), Integer)
                Next
                objDataRow.Item("MondayHours") = intTotal

                'Calculate and set the total hours for Tuesday
                intTotal = 0
```

```
        For intIndex = 0 To objTimeSheetDS.Tables("TimeSheet").Rows.Count - 1
            intTotal += CType(objTimeSheetDS.Tables( _
                "TimeSheet").Rows(intIndex).Item("TuesdayHours"), Integer)
        Next
        objDataRow.Item("TuesdayHours") = intTotal

        'Calculate and set the total hours for Wednesday
        intTotal = 0
        For intIndex = 0 To objTimeSheetDS.Tables("TimeSheet").Rows.Count - 1
            intTotal += CType(objTimeSheetDS.Tables( _
                "TimeSheet").Rows(intIndex).Item("WednesdayHours"), Integer)
        Next
        objDataRow.Item("WednesdayHours") = intTotal

        'Calculate and set the total hours for Thursday
        intTotal = 0
        For intIndex = 0 To objTimeSheetDS.Tables("TimeSheet").Rows.Count - 1
            intTotal += CType(objTimeSheetDS.Tables( _
                "TimeSheet").Rows(intIndex).Item("ThursdayHours"), Integer)
        Next
        objDataRow.Item("ThursdayHours") = intTotal

        'Calculate and set the total hours for Friday
        intTotal = 0
        For intIndex = 0 To objTimeSheetDS.Tables("TimeSheet").Rows.Count - 1
            intTotal += CType(objTimeSheetDS.Tables( _
                "TimeSheet").Rows(intIndex).Item("FridayHours"), Integer)
        Next
        objDataRow.Item("FridayHours") = intTotal

        'Add the row to the DataSet
        objTimeSheetDS.Tables("TimeSheet").Rows.Add(objDataRow)
    End Using
End Sub
```

The `DisplayTimeSheet` procedure is where the real work begins. Remember that this function is called from your Web form and builds a table in your Web form that represents a timesheet. This is accomplished using the `Write` method on the `Response` object, which writes HTML data to your Web form.

The first thing that you do in this procedure is start the table that represents the timesheet. Because the data to be written by the `Write` method is a string, the string must be enclosed in quotes. The various HTML attribute values must also be enclosed in quotes, so to accomplish this you must provide two consecutive quotes around the values of the HTML attributes in order to have a quote processed correctly for those attribute values.

The `<TABLE>` element is the first HTML element written to your Web form and has the various attributes specified to format the table appropriately. You specify the `TimeSheetTable` style for the `class` attribute so that the styles defined in this user-defined style are applied to this table.

The first row in this table has the `TimeSheetTableHeader` style applied so that this row in the table is formatted appropriately using the user-defined style that you created. You can see in the lines of code that follow that the columns in this row specify the column headers that appear on the timesheet report shown in Figures 14-5 and 14-6. The `width` style attribute is specified in these columns to control the width of each column.

```
Public Sub DisplayTimeSheet()
    'Begin table
    Response.Write("<table cellpadding=""3"" cellspacing=""0"" " & _
        "bordercolor=""Black"" border=""1""" & _
        "class=""TimeSheetTable"" >")
    Response.Write("<tr class=""TimeSheetTableHeader"">")
    Response.Write("<td nowrap style=""width:200px;"">Project Name</td>")
    Response.Write("<td style=""width:30px;"">Mon</td>")
    Response.Write("<td style=""width:30px;"">Tue</td>")
    Response.Write("<td style=""width:30px;"">Wed</td>")
    Response.Write("<td style=""width:30px;"">Thu</td>")
    Response.Write("<td style=""width:30px;"">Fri</td>")
    Response.Write("</tr>")
```

After the header row of the table has been built, you set up a `For...Next` loop to process the actual data in the timesheet `DataSet`. Remember that you want to process only the timesheet data and not the total row, so you specify the `Count` property minus 2 to account for the total row that you added to the `DataSet`. Inside of the loop, you call the `WriteTimeSheetRow` procedure, passing it the `DataRow` in the `DataSet` object.

```
'Process all rows of data
For intIndex = 0 To objTimeSheetDS.Tables("TimeSheet").Rows.Count - 2
    WriteTimeSheetRow(objTimeSheetDS.Tables("TimeSheet").Rows(intIndex))
Next
```

After all the rows of data for a timesheet have been processed, write the last row in the table. This row will contain the totals for each column in the timesheet table. Every even row in the table has a background color of WhiteSmoke applied. To keep track of whether a row is even or odd, you have a Boolean variable called `blnEvenRow`. Setting this variable not equal to itself forces the value from `True` to `False` and from `False` to `True`, effectively toggling the value in the variable.

Depending on whether the value in this variable is `True` or `False`, you write the appropriate `<TR>` element, applying the `EvenRow` or `OddRow` style to that row.

```
'Write the total row
blnEvenRow = Not blnEvenRow
If blnEvenRow Then
    Response.Write("<tr class=""EvenRow"">")
Else
    Response.Write("<tr class=""OddRow"">")
End If
```

The first column in the total row contains the text "Total Hours" and is written using the first line of code in the following code fragment. The next column contains the total hours for Monday, HTML elements, and some JavaScript.

First, you write an `<INPUT>` HTML element, setting its `type` attribute to `text`. You set the `name` attribute value to `txtMondayTotal` and set the `class` attribute using a value of `TransparentTextBox`.

Remember that this user-defined style removes the entire border of the TextBox control to make it appear as just plaintext. Specifying the readonly attribute makes the text in this TextBox control read-only.

Next, you specify the onfocus event for this TextBox control and specify which JavaScript function should be executed when the text box receives focus. Here you are shifting the focus from this text box back to the first text box in the Monday column by first calling the select method on the txtMondayHours text box. Remember that the txtMondayHours text box is a control array so you also specify which member in the array should be used. The select method causes the data in the text box to be selected. Then you call the focus method on the text box to give it focus.

The value attribute specifies the value that should be displayed in the text box and is set using the last row of data in the timesheet DataSet.

```
Response.Write("<td nowrap>Total Hours</td>")
Response.Write("<td><INPUT type=""text"" name=""txtMondayTotal""" & _
    "class=""TransparentTextBox"" readonly " & _
    "onfocus=""javascript:txtMondayHours[0].select();" & _
    "txtMondayHours[0].focus();"" value=""" & _
    objTimeSheetDS.Tables("TimeSheet").Rows(intIndex).Item( _
    "MondayHours") & """></td>")
```

The code for the rest of the columns in the total row mirrors that of the previous column minus the JavaScript functions. The reason behind this is that when a user tabs out of the last column in the Friday column, the next text box to get focus is the one in the total row in the Monday column. Although to a user this looks like static text, it is actually a TextBox control. Therefore, you specify the JavaScript functions to shift focus away from that text box back to the first text box in the Monday column.

```
Response.Write("<td><INPUT type=""text"" name=""txtTuesdayTotal""" & _
    "class=""TransparentTextBox"" readonly value=""" & _
    objTimeSheetDS.Tables("TimeSheet").Rows(intIndex).Item( _
    "TuesdayHours") & """></td>")
Response.Write("<td><INPUT type=""text"" name=""txtWednesdayTotal""" & _
    "class=""TransparentTextBox"" readonly value=""" & _
    objTimeSheetDS.Tables("TimeSheet").Rows(intIndex).Item( _
    "WednesdayHours") & """></td>")
Response.Write("<td><INPUT type=""text"" name=""txtThursdayTotal""" & _
    "class=""TransparentTextBox"" readonly value=""" & _
    objTimeSheetDS.Tables("TimeSheet").Rows(intIndex).Item( _
    "ThursdayHours") & """></td>")
Response.Write("<td><INPUT type=""text"" name=""txtFridayTotal""" & _
    "class=""TransparentTextBox"" readonly value=""" & _
    objTimeSheetDS.Tables("TimeSheet").Rows(intIndex).Item( _
    "FridayHours") & """></td>")
```

You end the table by writing the closing tag for the <TR> element and the closing tag for the <TABLE> element:

```
'End the table
Response.Write("</tr>")
Response.Write("</table>")
End Sub
```

The next procedure that you write is the `WriteTimeSheetRow` procedure. This procedure accepts the `DataRow` from the `DataSet` containing the timesheet data to be written to the Web form. The first thing you do in this procedure is toggle the `blnEvenRow` variable. Then you write the appropriate row using either the `EvenRow` or `OddRow` style.

The first column of data in this row is the project name and is written using the project name contained in the ProjectName column of the `DataRow` object. After the project name has been written, you need to determine if the timesheet should be displayed as read-only or editable. This is determined by querying the Submitted column in the `DataRow`. Remember that this column contains a Boolean value and can be used in an `If...Then` statement to determine which path to take.

If the timesheet data should be displayed as read-only, you merely write the data in the columns as static text.

```
Private Sub WriteTimeSheetRow(ByVal objDataRow As DataRow)
    'Toggle the flag
    blnEvenRow = Not blnEvenRow
    If blnEvenRow Then
        Response.Write("<tr class=""EvenRow"">")
    Else
        Response.Write("<tr class=""OddRow"">")
    End If
    Response.Write("<td nowrap>" & objDataRow.Item("ProjectName") & _
        "</td>")
    If objTimeSheetDS.Tables("TimeSheet").Rows(0).Item("Submitted") Then
        'The data is read-only so just display it
        Response.Write("<td style=""width:30px;"">" & _
            objDataRow.Item("MondayHours") & "</td>")
        Response.Write("<td style=""width:30px;"">" & _
            objDataRow.Item("TuesdayHours") & "</td>")
        Response.Write("<td style=""width:30px;"">" & _
            objDataRow.Item("WednesdayHours") & "</td>")
        Response.Write("<td style=""width:30px;"">" & _
            objDataRow.Item("ThursdayHours") & "</td>")
        Response.Write("<td style=""width:30px;"">" & _
            objDataRow.Item("FridayHours") & "</td>")
```

If the displayed timesheet data should be editable, then you need to display the data in TextBox controls, which is done in the following code. Here you write an `<INPUT>` element and set the `type` attribute to a value of `textbox`, indicating that this `<INPUT>` element should be displayed as a TextBox control.

Then you set the various attributes of the HTML element, starting with the `style` attribute. Here you specify the width of the text box by setting the `width` style attribute to a value of 30 pixels. Next, you specify the name of the text box and then the value. The value for the text box is retrieved from the appropriate column in the `DataRow` object.

You need to add some JavaScript functions to be executed for the various events of each text box. The first JavaScript function to be executed is the `Recalculate` function, which should be executed when the `onBlur` event is fired. This event is fired when the TextBox control loses focus, whether you tab out of the text box or click in another text box with the mouse. Therefore, you specify the `onBlur` event and the JavaScript function `Recalculate`, passing it the day of the week for which it should recalculate the totals.

Next, you specify the `onkeydown` event. This event fires when you press a key while in a text box. You specify the JavaScript function `IsNumeric`, which is executed to ensure that the value being entered is a numeric key.

The remaining columns for the timesheet row mirror the first, specifying the appropriate values for the `name` attribute and the appropriate day of the week for the `Recalculate` function.

```
        Else
            Response.Write("<td><input type=""textbox"" style=""width:30px;"" " & _
                "name=""txtMondayHours"" value=""" & _
                objDataRow.Item("MondayHours") & _
                """ onBlur=""javascript:Recalculate('Monday');"" " & _
                "onkeydown=""javascript:IsNumeric();""></td>")
            Response.Write("<td><input type=""textbox"" style=""width:30px;"" " & _
                "name=""txtTuesdayHours"" value=""" & _
                objDataRow.Item("TuesdayHours") & _
                """ onBlur=""javascript:Recalculate('Tuesday');"" " & _
                "onkeydown=""javascript:IsNumeric();""></td>")
            Response.Write("<td><input type=""textbox"" style=""width:30px;"" " & _
                "name=""txtWednesdayHours"" value=""" & _
                objDataRow.Item("WednesdayHours") & _
                """ onBlur=""javascript:Recalculate('Wednesday');"" " & _
                "onkeydown=""javascript:IsNumeric();""></td>")
            Response.Write("<td><input type=""textbox"" style=""width:30px;"" " & _
                "name=""txtThursdayHours"" value=""" & _
                objDataRow.Item("ThursdayHours") & _
                """ onBlur=""javascript:Recalculate('Thursday');"" " & _
                "onkeydown=""javascript:IsNumeric();""></td>")
            Response.Write("<td><input type=""textbox"" style=""width:30px;"" " & _
                "name=""txtFridayHours"" value=""" & _
                objDataRow.Item("FridayHours") & _
                """ onBlur=""javascript:Recalculate('Friday');"" " & _
                "onkeydown=""javascript:IsNumeric();""></td>")
        End If
        Response.Write("</tr>")
    End Sub
```

The `UpdateTimeSheetDS` procedure is added next and updates the timesheet `DataSet` with the values that were entered on the TimeSheet Web form. Remember that the text boxes for each day of the week were created as a control array, meaning that each text box in the Monday column has a name of `txtMondayHours`. This holds true for the rest of the columns as well, with the text boxes for Tuesday being `txtTusedayHours`, and those for Wednesday being `txtWednesday`, and so on.

When you request the values for the text boxes for a specific day of the week from the `Request.Form` collection, the values are returned as a comma-separated list of values. Therefore, you define your variables in this procedure as string arrays and then call the `Split` function, passing it the values for a specific day of the week and specifying that the data is separated by commas.

```
Private Sub UpdateTimeSheetDS()
    If Request.Form("txtMondayHours") Is Nothing Then
        Exit Sub
    End If
    Dim strMondayHours() As String = _
        Split(Request.Form("txtMondayHours"), ",")
    Dim strTuesdayHours() As String = _
        Split(Request.Form("txtTuesdayHours"), ",")
    Dim strWednesdayHours() As String = _
        Split(Request.Form("txtWednesdayHours"), ",")
    Dim strThursdayHours() As String = _
        Split(Request.Form("txtThursdayHours"), ",")
    Dim strFridayHours() As String = _
        Split(Request.Form("txtFridayHours"), ",")
```

Now you want to loop through the rows of the timesheet DataSet and update the hours in each column with the appropriate data from the string arrays defined previously. Your DataSet will contain the same number of rows, minus the total row, as there are bounds in the array. The data in the columns of your DataSet are defined as Byte data types, so you use the CType function to convert the hours in your string array to a Byte data type when adding it to your DataSet.

```
    'Process all rows of data minus the total row
    For intIndex = 0 To objTimeSheetDS.Tables("TimeSheet").Rows.Count - 2
        objTimeSheetDS.Tables("TimeSheet").Rows(intIndex).Item( _
            "MondayHours") = CType(strMondayHours(intIndex), Byte)
        objTimeSheetDS.Tables("TimeSheet").Rows(intIndex).Item( _
            "TuesdayHours") = CType(strTuesdayHours(intIndex), Byte)
        objTimeSheetDS.Tables("TimeSheet").Rows(intIndex).Item( _
            "WednesdayHours") = CType(strWednesdayHours(intIndex), Byte)
        objTimeSheetDS.Tables("TimeSheet").Rows(intIndex).Item( _
            "ThursdayHours") = CType(strThursdayHours(intIndex), Byte)
        objTimeSheetDS.Tables("TimeSheet").Rows(intIndex).Item( _
            "FridayHours") = CType(strFridayHours(intIndex), Byte)
    Next
```

The columns in the total row of the timesheet on the TimeSheet Web form have unique names, so you can use those columns to update the total row in your DataSet because they contain the updated totals for the modifications that the user made. This enables you to avoid recalculating the total row in your DataSet. Again, you convert the data from the Request.Form collection to a Byte data type when adding them to the DataSet.

```
    'Now process the total row - this is needed for when we build a new
    'table to post back to the client
    objTimeSheetDS.Tables("TimeSheet").Rows(intIndex).Item( _
        "MondayHours") = CType(Request.Form("txtMondayTotal"), Byte)
    objTimeSheetDS.Tables("TimeSheet").Rows(intIndex).Item( _
        "TuesdayHours") = CType(Request.Form("txtTuesdayTotal"), Byte)
    objTimeSheetDS.Tables("TimeSheet").Rows(intIndex).Item( _
        "WednesdayHours") = CType(Request.Form("txtWednesdayTotal"), Byte)
    objTimeSheetDS.Tables("TimeSheet").Rows(intIndex).Item( _
        "ThursdayHours") = CType(Request.Form("txtThursdayTotal"), Byte)
    objTimeSheetDS.Tables("TimeSheet").Rows(intIndex).Item( _
        "FridayHours") = CType(Request.Form("txtFridayTotal"), Byte)
End Sub
```

The next order of business is to add code for the combo box on your Web form. When a user selects a new week ending date in the combo box, it will automatically call this procedure to get the new week ending date and to get the corresponding timesheet data.

The first thing that you do in this procedure is compare the week ending date selected against the week ending date that you stored in ViewState. If they are different, you process the rest of the code in this procedure.

You set the date selected in the combo box in the dteWeekEndingDate variable and then call the GetTimeSheet procedure to get the new timesheet data. Then you save the new date and timesheet data in ViewState.

```
Protected Sub cboWeekEndingDate_SelectedIndexChanged( _
    ByVal sender As Object, ByVal e As System.EventArgs) _
    Handles cboWeekEndingDate.SelectedIndexChanged

    'If the date is different...
    If ViewState("WeekEndingDate").ToString <> _
        cboWeekEndingDate.SelectedValue Then

        'Set the new date from the Web form
        dteWeekEndingDate = CType(cboWeekEndingDate.SelectedValue, Date)

        'Get the timesheet
        Call GetTimeSheet()

        'Save the data between requests
        ViewState("TimeSheetDS") = objTimeSheetDS
        ViewState("WeekEndingDate") = dteWeekEndingDate
    End If
End Sub
```

Next, you add code for your Save and Submit buttons. Remember that the Save button saves the changes made to a timesheet in the database, whereas the Submit button marks the timesheet in the database as submitted, preventing the user from making any more changes to it.

The code that you write in the btnSave_Click procedure closely resembles the code that you wrote in the btnSave_Click procedure in the TimeSheet form in the Time Tracker application. You initialize a new instance of the business logic component and then call the SaveTimeSheet method, passing it the DataSet containing the timesheet. If an error is thrown, you write the error on the Web form using the Write method of the Response object.

```
Protected Sub btnSave_Click(ByVal sender As Object, _
    ByVal e As System.EventArgs) Handles btnSave.Click

    'Initialize a new instance of the business logic component
    Using objTimeSheets As New WroxBusinessLogic.WBLTimeSheets( _
        strCompany, strApplication)
        Try
            'Save the timesheet changes
            If Not objTimeSheets.SaveTimeSheet(objTimeSheetDS) Then
                Throw New Exception("Save TimeSheet Failed")
```

```
        End If
    Catch ExceptionErr As Exception
        Response.Write(ExceptionErr.Message)
    End Try
End Using
End Sub
```

The code for the Submit button is just as simple as the code for the Save button. You use your business
logic component to process the data and have it marked as submitted in the database. When you call the
SubmitTimeSheet method in your business logic component, you pass it the Guid of the TimeSheetID
column from the timesheet DataSet. After the call to the SubmitTimeSheet method, you want to
reload the timesheet DataSet as it will now be marked as submitted in the database, which means that
it is read-only for the user, so you call the GetTimeSheet procedure in this class.

```
Protected Sub btnSubmit_Click(ByVal sender As Object, _
    ByVal e As System.EventArgs) Handles btnSubmit.Click

    'Initialize a new instance of the business logic component
    Using objTimeSheets As New WroxBusinessLogic.WBLTimeSheets( _
        strCompany, strApplication)
        Try
            'Submit the timesheet
            If Not objTimeSheets.SubmitTimeSheet(New Guid( _
                objTimeSheetDS.Tables("TimeSheet").Rows(0).Item( _
                "TimeSheetID").ToString)) Then
                Throw New Exception("Submit TimeSheet Failed")
            End If
            'Reload the timesheet so it becomes read-only
            Call GetTimeSheet()
        Catch ExceptionErr As Exception
            Response.Write(ExceptionErr.Message)
        End Try
    End Using
End Sub
```

At this point, you can test your code and see how a timesheet is built and displayed on a Web form. You
saw that the TimeSheet Web form in Figures 14-5 and 14-6 looks similar to the TimeSheet form in your
Time Tracker application. This enables users to enter their time from a desktop Windows application or
through a Web browser, with no additional training required on the Web application. The Web form also
implemented the same functionality that the user was used to in the Time Tracker application; the users
must click the Save button to save their hours and they must click the Submit button to submit their
timesheet for approval.

Summary

In this chapter, you have taken a look at how to implement a TimeSheet Web form that provides the
same look and feel as the TimeSheet form in your Time Tracker application. This enables a user to transition from the Time Tracker Windows application to the TimeSheets Web application without any training whatsoever.

The major advantage of the exercises in this chapter is that you were able to reuse the code that you had previously written for the TimeSheet form in the Time Tracker application. This not only included reusing the code in your business logic component and data access component, but you were also able to reuse a lot of the logic and functions from the TimeSheet form in the Time Tracker application.

You were also able to reuse a lot of the code and logic needed to implement the Login Web form in the TimeSheets Web application. This provides a level of security to your Web application, enabling only authorized users to use the application.

From the discussions on how data is extracted and displayed in a Web form, you should realize the performance impact that a data-centric Web application can have on your Web server. This became apparent when I discussed how a GridView control was built and processed for a Web form. You should understand how Web form controls are built and processed so that you can make efficient use of them in your Web applications or look for alternative means as you did for the TimeSheet Web form.

To summarize, you should know:

❑   How to create styles that are automatically applied to HTML elements and how to create user-defined styles

❑   How to use a RequiredFieldValidator control on your Web form

❑   How to write client-side JavaScript code that can react to and cancel events

❑   That a GridView control requires being posted back to the server in order to edit a row of data and posted back again to either update or cancel the edit for a row

❑   That you can reuse and leverage business logic and data access components in your Web application

In Chapter 15, you write a Web Service that will be used to create report data. This Web Service will be accessible from either a Web application or a Windows application.

Creating a Web Service

Web Services have become the latest trend in creating applications that share data in a standard format, whether it is across the enterprise or across the Internet. Because Web Services use industry standard technologies such as XML to exchange data and HTTP to communicate with other applications, any program that supports these technologies can use and interact with Web Services. This makes the processing and sharing of data beyond the enterprise possible.

Web Services are an ideal way to share data and provide a common end point for processing that data. In this chapter you create a Web Service that produces report data, and in the next chapter you see how easy it is to access this data from other applications, specifically your Time Tracker Windows application and your TimeSheets Web application.

In this chapter, you:

❑ Create and implement new stored procedures to produce report data

❑ Enhance your business logic and data access components to support these stored procedures

❑ Design and build a Web Service to produce report data

❑ Leverage your business logic component by using it in your Web Service

I recommend that you read the chapter on Web Services in *Beginning VB 2005* for a basic understanding of how Web Services work and the basic terminology used in this chapter.

Design Goal

The design goal behind your Web Service is to generate report data for your Time Tracker application and to expose that data to both your Time Tracker application and your TimeSheets Web application. This will enable you to share this report data with different applications and provide a central point to generate report data.

When you set out to design a Web Service, you first need to determine the business requirements that you are trying to solve. In this case it is to provide a central location for generating report data for the Time Tracker application and to expose this reporting data to a variety of applications.

Another important design consideration that needs to be determined is how you plan to share the data that you generate from your Web Service. Because you will be generating report data in your Web Service, you know that the data will take on the shape of columns and rows and that the number of columns and rows will vary depending on the various reports and the amount of data being reported on.

Therefore, it only makes sense to return this reporting data in a DataSet that the requesting application can process as it needs. You should try to be consistent in your implementation of your interfaces, as you were when designing your business logic and data access components. Because the main goal of this Web Service will be to generate and return report data, all Web methods will return a DataSet as their return data type.

You want to generate five reports in your Web Service. These reports are briefly described in Table 15-1.

Table 15-1: Web Service Reports

Report	Description
TimeSheets Due	Provides a list of all users who have not submitted their timesheets for a given manager and week ending date
TimeSheets Submitted	Provides a list of all users who have submitted their timesheets for a given manager and week ending date
TimeSheets MTD	Provides a list of all timesheets submitted for a given manager for the current month to date
TimeSheets QTD	Provides a list of all timesheets submitted for a given manager for the current quarter to date
TimeSheets YTD	Provides a list of all timesheets submitted for a given manager for the current year to date

Once you know the reports that need to be generated, the next step before creating your Web Service is to create the stored procedures that will produce this data and to update your data access and business logic components to execute these stored procedures.

Date Functions

Now that you know what reports are to be generated, you can surmise that you will need to do some date calculations in the stored procedures that calculate the month to date, quarter to date, and year to date reports. When you created the usp_InsertTimeSheet stored procedure, you did a little date calculation by adding and subtracting days from a given date. You know that SQL Server and Oracle handle date calculations differently, and in this section you examine how to perform the various date calculations required to derive the necessary dates for your stored procedures.

Current week ending date

SQL Server and Oracle implement different functions to perform date calculations and you'll need to calculate several dates for your reports. One of the dates that you need for your reports is the current week ending date. Although this date is passed as an input parameter to some of your report stored procedures, you'll benefit from learning how to calculate the current week ending date in your stored procedures.

Take a look at the SELECT statement in the following code snippet, which demonstrates how to select the current week ending date for SQL Server. Right off the bat you'll notice that several built-in date functions are provided by SQL Server. The first of these is the DATEADD function, which is used to add different date parts to a date, such as days, weeks, months, and so on. The second date function that you see is the DATEDIFF function, which returns the difference between two dates. The final date function that you see in the SELECT statement is the GETDATE() function, which you've been using in your stored procedures to get the current date.

The DATEADD function accepts three parameters: the date part, a number, and a date. The date part can be specified as day, week, month, quarter, year, and so on. Abbreviations are typically used for each of these date parts, and in the following example an abbreviation of WK has been specified to represent week. The number parameter is the number used to increment the date part, and the date parameter represents the date to be incremented. In the following example, the number parameter is calculated using the DATEDIFF function and the date is specified as the day of the week that represents the last business day that you want. A value of 0 represents Monday, a value of 1 represents Tuesday, and so on.

The DATEDIFF function returns the difference between two dates using the date part that you specify. This function accepts three parameters: the date part, the starting date, and the end date. In the following example, the date part has been specified as week using the abbreviation WK, the starting date has been specified as 0, and the ending date has been specified as GETDATE(), to get the current date.

When the entire SELECT executes, it returns the Friday date for the current week.

```
SELECT DATEADD(WK, DATEDIFF(WK,0,GETDATE()), 4)
```

The Oracle version of calculating the current week ending date relies on the TO_CHAR function and some basic math. The TO_CHAR function converts a date to a string format and accepts two parameters: the date to be converted and the date format to which the date should be converted. In the following example, the TO_CHAR function will convert the current date as specified by the SYSDATE function to the day of the week as specified by the date format of D. The first day of the week in Oracle is Sunday and would have a value of 1, so if the current day were Monday then the TO_CHAR function would return a value of 2.

To calculate the week ending date for Friday of the current week, you need to specify a value of 6 minus the current day of the week as returned by the TO_CHAR function and then add that value to the current date, as shown in the following example:

```
SELECT (SYSDATE + (6 - TO_CHAR(SYSDATE, 'D'))) FROM DUAL;
```

First day of the month date

To return month-to-date reports, you first need to determine what the first day of the month is and then what the current week ending date is. You now know how to calculate the current week ending date so now you need to determine how to calculate the first day of the current month.

SQL Server uses the DATEADD and DATEDIFF functions in a manner similar to that in which it calculated the current week ending date. In the following code, you are using the DATEADD function, passing it a date part of MM for month, indicating that you want to add months to the date being passed. For the number parameter, you calculate a value using the DATEDIFF function, and for the date parameter you pass a value of 0, indicating that you do not want to add to the date, but rather that the DATEADD function should return the date using the number and date parameters.

The DATEDIFF function also gets a date part of MM passed to it, with a starting date of 0 and an ending date of the current date as indicated by the GETDATE() function. This combination of functions will return the first day of the current month.

```
SELECT DATEADD(MM, DATEDIFF(MM,0,GETDATE()), 0)
```

Oracle takes a different approach by using the ADD_MONTHS and LAST_DAY functions. The ADD_MONTHS function is an overloaded function that accepts two parameters in any order. One parameter is the date to be used in the calculation and the other parameter is a numeric value indicating the number to add to the month.

The LAST_DAY function returns the last day of the month for the date supplied. This is especially useful in determining the last day of the month of February, given that a leap year causes February to have 29 days.

In the following code, you use the LAST_DAY function to get the last day of the current month, and the current date is returned by the SYSDATE function and is supplied as the date to this function. The results of this function are passed as the date parameter to the ADD_MONTHS function and a value of –1 is passed as the number to add to the date. Using a negative value will cause the ADD_MONTHS function to subtract from the date, rather than add to it. The results of this calculation will be the last day of the previous month. Then you add a value of 1 to the results to get the first day in the current month.

```
SELECT ADD_MONTHS(LAST_DAY(SYSDATE), -1) + 1 FROM DUAL;
```

First day of the quarter

Calculating the first day of the current quarter is just as easy as calculating the first day of the month. SQL Server uses the same functions to achieve this result, while Oracle uses a slightly different, but simple, approach.

In the following SQL Server code, you can see that you are using the DATEADD and DATEDIFF functions, passing a date part of QQ, which represents quarter. Therefore, all date calculations using these functions will be based on quarters. Because the format of the following code is identical to the code for determining the first day of the month, I will not go into the details again. The only difference is that you are using a date part of QQ here versus a date part of MM for calculating months.

```
SELECT DATEADD(QQ, DATEDIFF(QQ,0,GETDATE()), 0)
```

The code for Oracle takes a different approach to calculating the first day of the quarter. The TRUNC function will round down dates to the beginning of the format mask provided. This function accepts two parameters: a date value and the format mask. A format mask is typically a one- or two-character abbreviation for the format that you want the TRUNC function to operate against.

In the following code, you pass the SYSDATE function, which returns the current date and a format mask of Q, indicating a quarter. The results returned from this function will be the first day of the current quarter.

```
SELECT TRUNC(SYSDATE, 'Q') FROM DUAL;
```

First day of the year

Now that you know how to calculate the first day of the quarter, calculating the first day of the year is just as simple. The functions that you use to calculate the first day of the year mirror the functions that you used to calculate the first day of the quarter. All you need to do is to replace the date part used in SQL Server and the format mask in Oracle.

Taking a look at the code for SQL Server first, you can see that this code resembles the code for calculating the first day of the quarter. Instead of supplying a date part of QQ for quarter, here you supply a date part of YY for year. The rest of the code is the same and this SELECT statement will return the first day of the year.

```
SELECT DATEADD(YY, DATEDIFF(YY,0,GETDATE()), 0)
```

In Oracle, the functions used are the same functions used in the previous example for Oracle to calculate the first day of the quarter. The only difference is the format mask used here, which is specified as YEAR, indicating that the TRUNC function should truncate the date to the first day of the current year.

```
SELECT TRUNC(SYSDATE, 'YEAR') FROM DUAL;
```

Now that you know how to calculate the various dates that will be used in your stored procedures for the various reports, it's time to create the stored procedures that will be used to produce the report data. In this next Try It Out, you create all of the required stored procedures necessary to produce the report data for the reports that will be generated from your Web Service.

Try It Out   Report Stored Procedures

To complete this exercise:

1. Open your Time Tracker application in Visual Studio 2005.

2. View the Server Explorer window and click the Auto Hide icon on the window to keep it visible and then view the Stored Procedures node for your database.

3. The first stored procedure that you want to create is the stored procedure to select a specific manager's name. The manager's name will be displayed in the heading of all reports. Readers using SQL Server should right-click the Stored Procedures and choose Add New Stored Procedure from the context menu. Readers using Oracle should use their favorite Oracle tool such as iSQL *Plus to create the stored procedures. Enter the code for the following stored procedure:

SQL Server

```
CREATE PROCEDURE usp_SelectManagerName
(
    @ManagerID      UNIQUEIDENTIFIER,
    @ManagerName    VARCHAR(61) OUTPUT
)
AS

SELECT @ManagerName = FirstName + ' ' + LastName
FROM Users
WHERE UserID = @ManagerID
```

Click the Save icon on the toolbar to create the stored procedure.

Oracle

```
CREATE OR REPLACE PROCEDURE usp_SelectManagerName
(
    inManagerID     IN  CHAR,
    outManagerName  OUT VARCHAR2
)
AS

BEGIN
    SELECT FirstName || ' ' || LastName INTO outManagerName
    FROM Users
    WHERE UserID = inManagerID;
END;
```

Click the Execute button to have the stored procedure created in your database.

4. The next stored procedure that you want to create is the stored procedure to select the timesheets that are due for a given week ending date and manager. Because this stored procedure will return data, Oracle readers need to create a package. SQL Server users should right-click the Stored Procedures node in the Server Explorer and choose Add New Stored Procedure and Oracle users should use their Oracle tool. Enter the following code:

SQL Server

```
CREATE PROCEDURE usp_SelectTimeSheetsDue
(
    @ManagerID        UNIQUEIDENTIFIER,
    @WeekEndingDate   DATETIME
)
AS

SELECT Email, FirstName + ' ' + LastName AS UserName, SUM(Hours) AS TotalHours
FROM TimeSheets
LEFT OUTER JOIN TimeSheetItems ON TimeSheets.TimeSheetID =
TimeSheetItems.TimeSheetID
LEFT OUTER JOIN Users ON TimeSheets.UserID = Users.UserID
WHERE Users.ManagerID = @ManagerID
AND WeekEndingDate = @WeekEndingDate
AND Submitted = 0
GROUP BY FirstName, LastName, Email
```

Click the Save icon on the toolbar to have the stored procedure created in your database.

Oracle

```
CREATE OR REPLACE PACKAGE TimeSheetsDuePackage
AS
    TYPE  CURSOR_TYPE IS REF CURSOR;
    PROCEDURE usp_SelectTimeSheetsDue (inManagerID IN CHAR, inWeekEndingDate IN
        DATE, results_cursor OUT CURSOR_TYPE);
END;
```

Click the Execute button to create the package in your database and then enter the following code to create the package body:

```
CREATE OR REPLACE PACKAGE BODY TimeSheetsDuePackage
AS
    PROCEDURE usp_SelectTimeSheetsDue (inManagerID IN CHAR, inWeekEndingDate IN
        DATE, results_cursor OUT CURSOR_TYPE)
    AS
    BEGIN
       OPEN results_cursor FOR
       SELECT Email, FirstName || ' ' || LastName AS UserName, SUM(Hours) AS
           TotalHours
       FROM TimeSheets
       LEFT OUTER JOIN TimeSheetItems ON TimeSheets.TimeSheetID =
           TimeSheetItems.TimeSheetID
       LEFT OUTER JOIN Users ON TimeSheets.UserID = Users.UserID
       WHERE Users.ManagerID = inManagerID
       AND WeekEndingDate = inWeekEndingDate
       AND Submitted = 0
       GROUP BY FirstName, LastName, Email;
    END;
END;
```

Click the Execute button to have the package body created in your database.

5. The next stored procedure that you want to create is the stored procedure to select the timesheets that have been submitted for a given week ending date and manager. This stored procedure also returns data, so Oracle readers need to create a package. SQL Server users should right-click the Stored Procedures node in the Server Explorer and choose Add New Stored Procedure and Oracle users should use their Oracle tool. Enter the following code:

SQL Server

```
CREATE PROCEDURE usp_SelectTimeSheetsSubmitted
(
    @ManagerID          UNIQUEIDENTIFIER,
    @WeekEndingDate     DATETIME
)
AS

SELECT FirstName + ' ' + LastName AS UserName, SUM(Hours) AS TotalHours
FROM TimeSheets
LEFT OUTER JOIN TimeSheetItems ON TimeSheets.TimeSheetID =
TimeSheetItems.TimeSheetID
LEFT OUTER JOIN Users ON TimeSheets.UserID = Users.UserID
WHERE Users.ManagerID = @ManagerID
```

```
AND WeekEndingDate = @WeekEndingDate
AND Submitted = 1
GROUP BY FirstName, LastName
```

Click the Save icon on the toolbar to create the stored procedure.

Oracle

```
CREATE OR REPLACE PACKAGE TimeSheetsSubmittedPackage
AS
    TYPE  CURSOR_TYPE IS REF CURSOR;
    PROCEDURE usp_SelectTimeSheetsSubmitted (inManagerID IN CHAR,
        inWeekEndingDate IN DATE, results_cursor OUT CURSOR_TYPE);
END;
```

Click the Execute button to create the package in your database and then enter the following code to create the package body:

```
CREATE OR REPLACE PACKAGE BODY TimeSheetsSubmittedPackage
AS
    PROCEDURE usp_SelectTimeSheetsSubmitted (inManagerID IN CHAR,
        inWeekEndingDate IN DATE, results_cursor OUT CURSOR_TYPE)
    AS
    BEGIN
        OPEN results_cursor FOR
        SELECT FirstName || ' ' || LastName AS UserName, SUM(Hours) AS TotalHours
        FROM TimeSheets
        LEFT OUTER JOIN TimeSheetItems ON TimeSheets.TimeSheetID =
            TimeSheetItems.TimeSheetID
        LEFT OUTER JOIN Users ON TimeSheets.UserID = Users.UserID
        WHERE Users.ManagerID = inManagerID
        AND WeekEndingDate = inWeekEndingDate
        AND Submitted = 1
        GROUP BY FirstName, LastName;
    END;
END;
```

Click the Execute button to have the package body created in your database.

6.   The next stored procedure that you want to create is the stored procedure to select the timesheets for the month-to-date report. As this stored procedure returns data, Oracle readers will need to create a package. SQL Server users should right-click the Stored Procedures node in the Server Explorer and choose Add New Stored Procedure and Oracle users should use their Oracle tool. Enter the following code:

SQL Server

```
CREATE PROCEDURE usp_SelectTimeSheetsMTD
(
    @ManagerID    UNIQUEIDENTIFIER
)
AS

-- Declare local variables
DECLARE @FirstDayOfMonth DATETIME,
```

```
        @WeekEndingDate DATETIME

-- Calculate the first day of the month date and current week ending date
SET @FirstDayOfMonth = DATEADD(MM, DATEDIFF(MM,0,GETDATE()), 0)
SET @WeekEndingDate = DATEADD(WK, DATEDIFF(WK,0,GETDATE()), 4)

-- Select month-to-date submitted timesheets
SELECT FirstName + ' ' + LastName AS UserName, SUM(Hours) AS TotalHours,
    WeekEndingDate, ApprovalDate
FROM TimeSheets
LEFT OUTER JOIN TimeSheetItems ON TimeSheets.TimeSheetID =
    TimeSheetItems.TimeSheetID
LEFT OUTER JOIN Users ON TimeSheets.UserID = Users.UserID
WHERE Users.ManagerID = @ManagerID
AND WeekEndingDate BETWEEN @FirstDayOfMonth AND @WeekEndingDate
AND Submitted = 1
GROUP BY WeekEndingDate, FirstName, LastName, ApprovalDate
```

Click the Save icon on the toolbar to create the stored procedure.

Oracle

```
CREATE OR REPLACE PACKAGE TimeSheetsMTDPackage
AS
    TYPE  CURSOR_TYPE IS REF CURSOR;
    PROCEDURE usp_SelectTimeSheetsMTD (inManagerID IN CHAR,
        results_cursor OUT CURSOR_TYPE);
END;
```

Click the Execute button to create the package in your database and then enter the following code to create the package body:

```
CREATE OR REPLACE PACKAGE BODY TimeSheetsMTDPackage
AS
    PROCEDURE usp_SelectTimeSheetsMTD (inManagerID IN CHAR,
        results_cursor OUT CURSOR_TYPE)
    AS
    -- Declare local variables
    varFirstDayOfMonth DATE;
    varWeekEndingDate DATE;
    BEGIN
        -- Calculate the first day of the month date and current week ending date
        SELECT ADD_MONTHS(LAST_DAY(SYSDATE), -1) + 1  INTO varFirstDayOfMonth
        FROM DUAL;
        SELECT (SYSDATE + (6 - TO_CHAR(SYSDATE, 'D'))) INTO varWeekEndingDate
        FROM DUAL;

        OPEN results_cursor FOR
        -- Select month-to-date submitted timesheets
        SELECT FirstName || ' ' || LastName AS UserName, SUM(Hours) AS TotalHours,
            WeekEndingDate, ApprovalDate
        FROM TimeSheets
        LEFT OUTER JOIN TimeSheetItems ON TimeSheets.TimeSheetID =
            TimeSheetItems.TimeSheetID
        LEFT OUTER JOIN Users ON TimeSheets.UserID = Users.UserID
        WHERE Users.ManagerID = inManagerID
        AND WeekEndingDate BETWEEN varFirstDayOfMonth AND varWeekEndingDate
        AND Submitted = 1
```

```
        GROUP BY WeekEndingDate, FirstName, LastName, ApprovalDate;
    END;
END;
```

Click the Execute button to have the package body created in your database.

7. The next stored procedure that you want to create is the stored procedure to select the timesheets for the quarter-to-date report. Again, Oracle readers need to create a package, as this stored procedure returns data. SQL Server users should right-click the Stored Procedures node in the Server Explorer and choose Add New Stored Procedure and Oracle users should use their Oracle tool. Enter the following code:

SQL Server

```
CREATE PROCEDURE usp_SelectTimeSheetsQTD
(
    @ManagerID    UNIQUEIDENTIFIER
)
AS

-- Declare local variables
DECLARE @FirstDayOfQuarter DATETIME,
        @WeekEndingDate DATETIME

-- Calculate the first day of the quarter date and current week ending date
SET @FirstDayOfQuarter = DATEADD(QQ, DATEDIFF(QQ,0,GETDATE()), 0)
SET @WeekEndingDate = DATEADD(WK, DATEDIFF(WK,0,GETDATE()), 4)

-- Select quarter-to-date submitted timesheets
SELECT FirstName + ' ' + LastName AS UserName, SUM(Hours) AS TotalHours,
    WeekEndingDate, ApprovalDate
FROM TimeSheets
LEFT OUTER JOIN TimeSheetItems ON TimeSheets.TimeSheetID =
TimeSheetItems.TimeSheetID
LEFT OUTER JOIN Users ON TimeSheets.UserID = Users.UserID
WHERE Users.ManagerID = @ManagerID
AND WeekEndingDate BETWEEN @FirstDayOfQuarter AND @WeekEndingDate
AND Submitted = 1
GROUP BY WeekEndingDate, FirstName, LastName, ApprovalDate
```

Click the Save icon on the toolbar to create the stored procedure.

Oracle

```
CREATE OR REPLACE PACKAGE TimeSheetsQTDPackage
AS
    TYPE  CURSOR_TYPE IS REF CURSOR;
    PROCEDURE usp_SelectTimeSheetsQTD (inManagerID IN CHAR,
        results_cursor OUT CURSOR_TYPE);
END;
```

Click the Execute button to create the package in your database and then enter the following code to create the package body:

```
CREATE OR REPLACE PACKAGE BODY TimeSheetsQTDPackage
AS
    PROCEDURE usp_SelectTimeSheetsQTD (inManagerID IN CHAR,
```

```
          results_cursor OUT CURSOR_TYPE)
    AS
    -- Declare local variables
    varFirstDayOfQuarter DATE;
    varWeekEndingDate DATE;
    BEGIN
        -- Calculate the first day of the quarter date and current week ending date
        SELECT TRUNC(SYSDATE, 'Q') INTO varFirstDayOfQuarter FROM DUAL;
        SELECT (SYSDATE + (6 - TO_CHAR(SYSDATE, 'D'))) INTO varWeekEndingDate
            FROM DUAL;

        OPEN results_cursor FOR
        -- Select quarter-to-date submitted timesheets
        SELECT FirstName || ' ' || LastName AS UserName, SUM(Hours) AS TotalHours,
            WeekEndingDate, ApprovalDate
        FROM TimeSheets
        LEFT OUTER JOIN TimeSheetItems ON TimeSheets.TimeSheetID =
            TimeSheetItems.TimeSheetID
        LEFT OUTER JOIN Users ON TimeSheets.UserID = Users.UserID
        WHERE Users.ManagerID = inManagerID
        AND WeekEndingDate BETWEEN varFirstDayOfQuarter AND varWeekEndingDate
        AND Submitted = 1
        GROUP BY WeekEndingDate, FirstName, LastName, ApprovalDate;
    END;
END;
```

Click the Execute button to have the package body created in your database.

8. The last stored procedure to create is one to select the timesheets for the year-to-date report. Again, Oracle readers need to create a package, as this stored procedure returns data. SQL Server users should right-click the Stored Procedures node in the Server Explorer and choose Add New Stored Procedure and Oracle users should use their Oracle tool. Enter the following code:

SQL Server

```
CREATE PROCEDURE usp_SelectTimeSheetsYTD
(
    @ManagerID    UNIQUEIDENTIFIER
)
AS

-- Declare local variables
DECLARE @FirstDayOfYear DATETIME,
        @WeekEndingDate DATETIME

-- Calculate the first day of the year date and current week ending date
SET @FirstDayOfYear = DATEADD(YY, DATEDIFF(YY,0,GETDATE()), 0)
SET @WeekEndingDate = DATEADD(WK, DATEDIFF(WK,0,GETDATE()), 4)

-- Select year-to-date submitted timesheets
SELECT FirstName + ' ' + LastName AS UserName, SUM(Hours) AS TotalHours,
    WeekEndingDate, ApprovalDate
FROM TimeSheets
```

```
LEFT OUTER JOIN TimeSheetItems ON TimeSheets.TimeSheetID =
TimeSheetItems.TimeSheetID
LEFT OUTER JOIN Users ON TimeSheets.UserID = Users.UserID
WHERE Users.ManagerID = @ManagerID
AND WeekEndingDate BETWEEN @FirstDayOfYear AND @WeekEndingDate
AND Submitted = 1
GROUP BY WeekEndingDate, FirstName, LastName, ApprovalDate
```

Click the Save icon on the toolbar to create the stored procedure.

Oracle

```
CREATE OR REPLACE PACKAGE TimeSheetsYTDPackage
AS
   TYPE  CURSOR_TYPE IS REF CURSOR;
   PROCEDURE usp_SelectTimeSheetsYTD (inManagerID IN CHAR,
      results_cursor OUT CURSOR_TYPE);
END;
```

Click the Execute button to create the package in your database and then enter the following code to create the package body:

```
CREATE OR REPLACE PACKAGE BODY TimeSheetsYTDPackage
AS
   PROCEDURE usp_SelectTimeSheetsYTD (inManagerID IN CHAR,
      results_cursor OUT CURSOR_TYPE)
   AS
   -- Declare local variables
   varFirstDayOfYear DATE;
   varWeekEndingDate DATE;
   BEGIN
      -- Calculate the first day of the year date and current week ending date
      SELECT TRUNC(SYSDATE, 'YEAR')  INTO varFirstDayOfYear FROM DUAL;
      SELECT (SYSDATE + (6 - TO_CHAR(SYSDATE, 'D'))) INTO varWeekEndingDate
      FROM DUAL;

      OPEN results_cursor FOR
      -- Select year-to-date submitted timesheets
      SELECT FirstName || ' ' || LastName AS UserName, SUM(Hours) AS TotalHours,
         WeekEndingDate, ApprovalDate
      FROM TimeSheets
      LEFT OUTER JOIN TimeSheetItems ON TimeSheets.TimeSheetID =
         TimeSheetItems.TimeSheetID
      LEFT OUTER JOIN Users ON TimeSheets.UserID = Users.UserID
      WHERE Users.ManagerID = inManagerID
      AND WeekEndingDate BETWEEN varFirstDayOfYear AND varWeekEndingDate
      AND Submitted = 1
      GROUP BY WeekEndingDate, FirstName, LastName, ApprovalDate;
   END;
END;
```

Click the Execute button to have the package body created in your database.

9. Now it's time to implement the necessary functions in your data access component to execute these stored procedures. View the code for the WDATimeSheets class in your data access component and add the following function to select and return the manager's name:

SQL Server

```
Public Function GetManagerName(ByVal ManagerID As Guid) As String
    Try
        MyBase.SQL = "usp_SelectManagerName"
        'Initialize the Command object
        MyBase.InitializeCommand()
        'Add the Parameters to the Parameters collection
        MyBase.AddParameter("@ManagerID", _
         SqlDbType.UniqueIdentifier, 16, ManagerID)
        MyBase.AddParameter("@ManagerName", _
         SqlDbType.VarChar, 61, Nothing)
        'Change the default direction for the @ManagerName parameter
        MyBase.Command.Parameters("@ManagerName").Direction = _
            ParameterDirection.Output
        'Execute the stored procedure
        MyBase.ExecuteStoredProcedure()
        'Retrieve the output
        GetManagerName = MyBase.Command.Parameters("@ManagerName").Value
    Catch ExceptionErr As Exception
        Throw New System.Exception(ExceptionErr.Message, _
        ExceptionErr.InnerException)
    End Try
End Function
```

Oracle

```
Public Function GetManagerName(ByVal ManagerID As Guid) As String
    Try
        MyBase.SQL = "usp_SelectManagerName"
        'Initialize the Command object
        MyBase.InitializeCommand()
        'Add the Parameters to the Parameters collection
        MyBase.AddParameter("inManagerID", _
         OracleClient.OracleType.Char, 36, ManagerID.ToString)
        MyBase.AddParameter("outManagerName", _
         OracleClient.OracleType.VarChar, 61, Nothing)
        'Change the default direction for the outManagerName parameter
        MyBase.Command.Parameters("outManagerName").Direction = _
            ParameterDirection.Output
        'Execute the stored procedure
        MyBase.ExecuteStoredProcedure()
        'Retrieve the output
        GetManagerName = MyBase.Command.Parameters("outManagerName").Value
    Catch ExceptionErr As Exception
        Throw New System.Exception(ExceptionErr.Message, _
        ExceptionErr.InnerException)
    End Try
End Function
```

10. Add the `TimeSheetsDue` function, which will return all timesheets for a given week ending date and manager. Enter the following code:

SQL Server

```
Public Function TimeSheetsDue(ByVal ManagerID As Guid, _
    ByVal WeekEndingDate As Date) As DataSet
    Try
```

```
            TimeSheetsDue = New DataSet
            MyBase.SQL = "usp_SelectTimeSheetsDue"
            'Initialize the Command object
            MyBase.InitializeCommand()
            'Add the Parameters to the Parameters collection
            MyBase.AddParameter("@ManagerID", _
             SqlDbType.UniqueIdentifier, 16, ManagerID)
            MyBase.AddParameter("@WeekEndingDate", _
             SqlDbType.DateTime, 8, WeekEndingDate)
            'Fill the DataSet
            MyBase.FillDataSet(TimeSheetsDue, "TimeSheets")
        Catch ExceptionErr As Exception
            Throw New System.Exception(ExceptionErr.Message, _
            ExceptionErr.InnerException)
        End Try
    End Function
```

Oracle

```
Public Function TimeSheetsDue(ByVal ManagerID As Guid, _
    ByVal WeekEndingDate As Date) As DataSet
        Try
            TimeSheetsDue = New DataSet
            MyBase.SQL = "TimeSheetsDuePackage.usp_SelectTimeSheetsDue"
            'Initialize the Command object
            MyBase.InitializeCommand()
            'Add the Parameters to the Parameters collection
            MyBase.AddParameter("inManagerID", _
             OracleClient.OracleType.Char, 36, ManagerID.ToString)
            MyBase.AddParameter("inWeekEndingDate", _
             OracleClient.OracleType.DateTime, 8, WeekEndingDate)
            MyBase.AddParameter("results_cursor", _
                OracleClient.OracleType.Cursor, ParameterDirection.Output)
            'Fill the DataSet
            MyBase.FillDataSet(TimeSheetsDue, "TimeSheets")
        Catch ExceptionErr As Exception
            Throw New System.Exception(ExceptionErr.Message, _
            ExceptionErr.InnerException)
        End Try
End Function
```

11. The next function that you want to create is the `TimeSheetsSubmitted` function. Enter the following code:

SQL Server

```
Public Function TimeSheetsSubmitted(ByVal ManagerID As Guid, _
    ByVal WeekEndingDate As Date) As DataSet
        Try
            TimeSheetsSubmitted = New DataSet
            MyBase.SQL = "usp_SelectTimeSheetsSubmitted"
            'Initialize the Command object
            MyBase.InitializeCommand()
            'Add the Parameters to the Parameters collection
            MyBase.AddParameter("@ManagerID", _
             SqlDbType.UniqueIdentifier, 16, ManagerID)
```

```
            MyBase.AddParameter("@WeekEndingDate", _
             SqlDbType.DateTime, 8, WeekEndingDate)
            'Fill the DataSet
            MyBase.FillDataSet(TimeSheetsSubmitted, "TimeSheets")
        Catch ExceptionErr As Exception
            Throw New System.Exception(ExceptionErr.Message, _
            ExceptionErr.InnerException)
        End Try
    End Function
```

Oracle

```
Public Function TimeSheetsSubmitted(ByVal ManagerID As Guid, _
        ByVal WeekEndingDate As Date) As DataSet
        Try
            TimeSheetsSubmitted = New DataSet
            MyBase.SQL = "TimeSheetsSubmittedPackage.usp_SelectTimeSheetsSubmitted"
            'Initialize the Command object
            MyBase.InitializeCommand()
            'Add the Parameters to the Parameters collection
            MyBase.AddParameter("inManagerID", _
             OracleClient.OracleType.Char, 36, ManagerID.ToString)
            MyBase.AddParameter("inWeekEndingDate", _
             OracleClient.OracleType.DateTime, 8, WeekEndingDate)
            MyBase.AddParameter("results_cursor", _
                OracleClient.OracleType.Cursor, ParameterDirection.Output)
            'Fill the DataSet
            MyBase.FillDataSet(TimeSheetsSubmitted, "TimeSheets")
        Catch ExceptionErr As Exception
            Throw New System.Exception(ExceptionErr.Message, _
            ExceptionErr.InnerException)
        End Try
    End Function
```

12. The TimeSheetsMTD function is next and returns the month-to-date report data. Enter the following code:

SQL Server

```
Public Function TimeSheetsMTD(ByVal ManagerID As Guid) As DataSet
        Try
            TimeSheetsMTD = New DataSet
            MyBase.SQL = "usp_SelectTimeSheetsMTD"
            'Initialize the Command object
            MyBase.InitializeCommand()
            'Add the Parameters to the Parameters collection
            MyBase.AddParameter("@ManagerID", _
             SqlDbType.UniqueIdentifier, 16, ManagerID)
            'Fill the DataSet
            MyBase.FillDataSet(TimeSheetsMTD, "TimeSheets")
        Catch ExceptionErr As Exception
            Throw New System.Exception(ExceptionErr.Message, _
            ExceptionErr.InnerException)
        End Try
    End Function
```

Oracle

```
Public Function TimeSheetsMTD(ByVal ManagerID As Guid) As DataSet
    Try
        TimeSheetsMTD = New DataSet
        MyBase.SQL = "TimeSheetsMTDPackage.usp_SelectTimeSheetsMTD"
        'Initialize the Command object
        MyBase.InitializeCommand()
        'Add the Parameters to the Parameters collection
        MyBase.AddParameter("inManagerID", _
         OracleClient.OracleType.Char, 36, ManagerID.ToString)
        MyBase.AddParameter("results_cursor", _
            OracleClient.OracleType.Cursor, ParameterDirection.Output)
        'Fill the DataSet
        MyBase.FillDataSet(TimeSheetsMTD, "TimeSheets")
    Catch ExceptionErr As Exception
        Throw New System.Exception(ExceptionErr.Message, _
        ExceptionErr.InnerException)
    End Try
End Function
```

13. The `TimeSheetsQTD` function returns the quarter-to-date report data. Enter the following code to create this function:

SQL Server

```
Public Function TimeSheetsQTD(ByVal ManagerID As Guid) As DataSet
    Try
        TimeSheetsQTD = New DataSet
        MyBase.SQL = "usp_SelectTimeSheetsQTD"
        'Initialize the Command object
        MyBase.InitializeCommand()
        'Add the Parameters to the Parameters collection
        MyBase.AddParameter("@ManagerID", _
         SqlDbType.UniqueIdentifier, 16, ManagerID)
        'Fill the DataSet
        MyBase.FillDataSet(TimeSheetsQTD, "TimeSheets")
    Catch ExceptionErr As Exception
        Throw New System.Exception(ExceptionErr.Message, _
        ExceptionErr.InnerException)
    End Try
End Function
```

Oracle

```
Public Function TimeSheetsQTD(ByVal ManagerID As Guid) As DataSet
    Try
        TimeSheetsQTD = New DataSet
        MyBase.SQL = "TimeSheetsQTDPackage.usp_SelectTimeSheetsQTD"
        'Initialize the Command object
        MyBase.InitializeCommand()
        'Add the Parameters to the Parameters collection
        MyBase.AddParameter("inManagerID", _
         OracleClient.OracleType.Char, 36, ManagerID.ToString)
        MyBase.AddParameter("results_cursor", _
            OracleClient.OracleType.Cursor, ParameterDirection.Output)
        'Fill the DataSet
        MyBase.FillDataSet(TimeSheetsQTD, "TimeSheets")
```

```
        Catch ExceptionErr As Exception
            Throw New System.Exception(ExceptionErr.Message, _
            ExceptionErr.InnerException)
        End Try
    End Function
```

14. The last function for your `WDATimeSheets` class is the `TimeSheetsYTD` function. Enter the following code:

SQL Server

```
Public Function TimeSheetsYTD(ByVal ManagerID As Guid) As DataSet
    Try
        TimeSheetsYTD = New DataSet
        MyBase.SQL = "usp_SelectTimeSheetsYTD"
        'Initialize the Command object
        MyBase.InitializeCommand()
        'Add the Parameters to the Parameters collection
        MyBase.AddParameter("@ManagerID", _
        SqlDbType.UniqueIdentifier, 16, ManagerID)
        'Fill the DataSet
        MyBase.FillDataSet(TimeSheetsYTD, "TimeSheets")
    Catch ExceptionErr As Exception
        Throw New System.Exception(ExceptionErr.Message, _
        ExceptionErr.InnerException)
    End Try
End Function
```

Oracle

```
Public Function TimeSheetsYTD(ByVal ManagerID As Guid) As DataSet
    Try
        TimeSheetsYTD = New DataSet
        MyBase.SQL = "TimeSheetsYTDPackage.usp_SelectTimeSheetsYTD"
        'Initialize the Command object
        MyBase.InitializeCommand()
        'Add the Parameters to the Parameters collection
        MyBase.AddParameter("inManagerID", _
        OracleClient.OracleType.Char, 36, ManagerID.ToString)
        MyBase.AddParameter("results_cursor", _
            OracleClient.OracleType.Cursor, ParameterDirection.Output)
        'Fill the DataSet
        MyBase.FillDataSet(TimeSheetsYTD, "TimeSheets")
    Catch ExceptionErr As Exception
        Throw New System.Exception(ExceptionErr.Message, _
        ExceptionErr.InnerException)
    End Try
End Function
```

15. You now need to create the corresponding functions in your business logic component. View the code for the `WBLTimeSheets` class in your business logic component. First, create the `GetManagerName` function to return the manager's name. Enter the following code:

```
Public Function GetManagerName(ByVal ManagerID As Guid) As String
    Try
        'Call the data component to get the manager's name
        GetManagerName = objWDATimeSheets.GetManagerName(ManagerID)
```

```
        Catch ExceptionErr As Exception
            Throw New System.Exception(ExceptionErr.Message, _
            ExceptionErr.InnerException)
        End Try
    End Function
```

16. The next function that you want to create is the `TimeSheetsDue` function. Enter the following code:

```
Public Function TimeSheetsDue(ByVal ManagerID As Guid, _
    ByVal WeekEndingDate As Date) As DataSet
    Try
        'Call the data component to get all timesheets that have
        'not been submitted for the given week ending date
        TimeSheetsDue = objWDATimeSheets.TimeSheetsDue( _
            ManagerID, WeekEndingDate)
    Catch ExceptionErr As Exception
        Throw New System.Exception(ExceptionErr.Message, _
        ExceptionErr.InnerException)
    End Try
End Function
```

17. The `TimeSheetsSubmitted` function returns all timesheets that have been submitted for a specific week ending date and manager. Enter the following code:

```
Public Function TimeSheetsSubmitted(ByVal ManagerID As Guid, _
    ByVal WeekEndingDate As Date) As DataSet
    Try
        'Call the data component to get all timesheets that have
        'been submitted for the given week ending date
        TimeSheetsSubmitted = objWDATimeSheets.TimeSheetsSubmitted( _
            ManagerID, WeekEndingDate)
    Catch ExceptionErr As Exception
        Throw New System.Exception(ExceptionErr.Message, _
        ExceptionErr.InnerException)
    End Try
End Function
```

18. The `TimeSheetsMTD` function returns the month-to-date reports for a specific manager. Enter the following code to create this function:

```
Public Function TimeSheetsMTD(ByVal ManagerID As Guid) As DataSet
    Try
        'Call the data component to get all timesheets that have
        'been submitted for the current month
        TimeSheetsMTD = objWDATimeSheets.TimeSheetsMTD(ManagerID)
    Catch ExceptionErr As Exception
        Throw New System.Exception(ExceptionErr.Message, _
        ExceptionErr.InnerException)
    End Try
End Function
```

19. Create the `TimeSheetsQTD` function, which will return all timesheets that have been submitted in the current quarter for a specific manager. Enter the following code:

```
Public Function TimeSheetsQTD(ByVal ManagerID As Guid) As DataSet
    Try
        'Call the data component to get all timesheets that have
        'been submitted for the current quarter
        TimeSheetsQTD = objWDATimeSheets.TimeSheetsQTD(ManagerID)
    Catch ExceptionErr As Exception
        Throw New System.Exception(ExceptionErr.Message, _
          ExceptionErr.InnerException)
    End Try
End Function
```

20. The final function to be created is `TimeSheetsYTD`, which returns all timesheets submitted for the current year for a given manager. Enter the following code:

```
Public Function TimeSheetsYTD(ByVal ManagerID As Guid) As DataSet
    Try
        'Call the data component to get all timesheets that have
        'been submitted for the current year
        TimeSheetsYTD = objWDATimeSheets.TimeSheetsYTD(ManagerID)
    Catch ExceptionErr As Exception
        Throw New System.Exception(ExceptionErr.Message, _
          ExceptionErr.InnerException)
    End Try
End Function
```

21. Recompile the entire solution. Because you are making changes to the business logic and data access components, the Time Tracker project also needs to be recompiled in order to pick up the new business logic component. Click the Build menu and choose the Build Solution menu item.

How It Works

The point of this exercise is to create all of the stored procedures needed to generate the reporting data that will be returned from the Web Service you'll be creating in the next exercise. Because you already have a framework in place for executing stored procedures (e.g., a data access and business logic component), it only makes sense to leverage that framework in your Web Service as you did in your Web application in Chapter 14.

The first stored procedure that you create is a little different from the stored procedures that you've created thus far in this book. This stored procedure returns data through an output parameter and not as a result set. Because this type of stored procedures is new to you, I want to explain the details for the stored procedure for both SQL Server and Oracle.

Starting with the SQL Server version, you see that you have one input parameter, which is named @ManagerID, and one output parameter named @ManagerName. The output parameter is clearly defined by the OUTPUT keyword following the parameter definition. The SELECT statement for this stored procedure selects the manager name from the Users table, where the UserID equals the @ManagerID parameter.

The manager's name is concatenated from the FirstName and LastName columns and the results of this concatenation are placed in the @ManagerName output parameter in the SELECT statement. In SQL Server, you specify the output parameter in the SELECT statement followed by an equal sign (=) and then the data that should be set in the output parameter. In this case, it is a concatenation of data from multiple columns.

```
CREATE PROCEDURE usp_SelectManagerName
(
    @ManagerID      UNIQUEIDENTIFIER,
    @ManagerName    VARCHAR(61) OUTPUT
)
AS

SELECT @ManagerName = FirstName + ' ' + LastName
FROM Users
WHERE UserID = @ManagerID
```

The Oracle version of this stored procedure operates on the same principle as the SQL Server version. You have your input parameter named inManagerID and because Oracle provides the IN keyword, it has been specified to clearly mark this parameter as an input parameter. The use of the IN keyword is not required here but has been used to clearly distinguish the input parameters from the output parameters. The output parameter is specified and named outManagerName and uses the OUT keyword to signify that this is an output parameter.

The SELECT statement here concatenates the data from the FirstName and LastName columns and places the results in the outManagerName output parameter. Notice that Oracle uses the INTO keyword to select the data from the columns into the output parameter.

```
CREATE OR REPLACE PROCEDURE usp_SelectManagerName
(
    inManagerID      IN   CHAR,
    outManagerName   OUT VARCHAR2
)
AS

BEGIN
    SELECT FirstName || ' ' || LastName INTO outManagerName
    FROM Users
    WHERE UserID = inManagerID;
END;
```

The next stored procedure that you create is the SelectTimeSheetsDue stored procedure. This stored procedure selects all timesheets that have not been submitted for a specific week ending date and manager. Because this stored procedure returns a result set, those readers using Oracle have to create a package and package body. I've already thoroughly covered creating a package and package body in Chapter 9, so I'll forgo the details again here and merely explain the SQL Server version of the stored procedure.

This stored procedure accepts the ManagerID and week ending date as input. The SELECT statement selects data from various columns, uses concatenation and column aliases, and sums the data from the Hours column. You've seen concatenation and column aliases before but the SUM function is new, so let me briefly explain it.

The SUM function returns the sum of all values in a column — in this case, the Hours column. Remember that the TimeSheetItems table contains a row of data for each project for each day of the week, and the

Hours column contains the number of hours entered for a given project for a given day of the week. What the SUM function does for you is to return the sum of all values in the Hours column so that you end up with only one row of data in your result set.

The primary table that you are selecting data from here is the TimeSheets table. Remember that the TimeSheets table contains only one row of data per user for any given week. The table also contains the Submitted column, which indicates which users have not submitted their timesheets. It also contains the WeekEndingDate column so that you can select the unsubmitted timesheets for the week ending date specified in the @WeekEndingDate input parameter.

Because you want to get the sum of all hours that the user has entered for his or her unsubmitted time-sheet, you perform a LEFT OUTER JOIN on the TimeSheetsItem table to join only the rows of data that match the TimeSheetID being selected from the TimeSheets table.

You want to get some user details such as e-mail addresses and first and last name, so you perform a LEFT OUTER JOIN on the Users table to get this information. This will join only the rows of data in the Users table for the users being selected in the TimeSheets table.

The WHERE clause specifies the condition for selecting the required data, and the first condition specifies that you want to select the data for a specific manager only. The second condition in the WHERE clause comes after the AND keyword. The AND keyword specifies that more than one condition applies to the WHERE clause, and this condition specifies that data should be selected only for a specific week ending date. The final condition in the WHERE clause specifies that you want to select only timesheets that have a value of 0 in the Submitted column, which indicates that the timesheet has not been submitted.

Because you have an aggregate function (SUM) in the SELECT statement, you cannot use the ORDER BY clause to order the results of your SELECT statement. Therefore, to return the results in a sorted fashion, you must use the GROUP BY clause. The GROUP BY clause specifies that the output data should be placed in a group, essentially sorting the data. Here you have specified FirstName, LastName, and Email, which will cause the data to be sorted by the user's first name, last name, and e-mail address, respectively:

```
CREATE PROCEDURE usp_SelectTimeSheetsDue
(
    @ManagerID          UNIQUEIDENTIFIER,
    @WeekEndingDate     DATETIME
)
AS

SELECT Email, FirstName + ' ' + LastName AS UserName, SUM(Hours) AS TotalHours
FROM TimeSheets
LEFT OUTER JOIN TimeSheetItems ON TimeSheets.TimeSheetID =
TimeSheetItems.TimeSheetID
LEFT OUTER JOIN Users ON TimeSheets.UserID = Users.UserID
WHERE Users.ManagerID = @ManagerID
AND WeekEndingDate = @WeekEndingDate
AND Submitted = 0
GROUP BY FirstName, LastName, Email
```

The next stored procedure that was created is usp_SelectTimeSheetsSubmitted. This stored procedure is the same as the usp_SelectTimeSheetsDue stored procedure except for one condition in the WHERE clause. Because you want to return all timesheets that have been submitted for a specific manager and week ending date, you specify that the Submitted column should contain a value of 1, which indicates that the timesheet has been submitted for approval:

```
CREATE PROCEDURE usp_SelectTimeSheetsSubmitted
(
    @ManagerID          UNIQUEIDENTIFIER,
    @WeekEndingDate     DATETIME
)
AS

SELECT FirstName + ' ' + LastName AS UserName, SUM(Hours) AS TotalHours
FROM TimeSheets
LEFT OUTER JOIN TimeSheetItems ON TimeSheets.TimeSheetID =
TimeSheetItems.TimeSheetID
LEFT OUTER JOIN Users ON TimeSheets.UserID = Users.UserID
WHERE Users.ManagerID = @ManagerID
AND WeekEndingDate = @WeekEndingDate
AND Submitted = 1
GROUP BY FirstName, LastName
```

The next stored procedure created is usp_SelectTimeSheetsMTD, which returns all submitted timesheets for the current month to date for a specific manager. Because the Oracle version is very similar to the SQL Server version, only the SQL Server version is listed here. The first day of the month date and the current week ending date will be calculated in the stored procedure, so they are not passed as input parameters. The only input parameter to this stored procedure is the ManagerID, which is used to select all timesheets that have been submitted by the manager's employees.

```
CREATE PROCEDURE usp_SelectTimeSheetsMTD
(
    @ManagerID    UNIQUEIDENTIFIER
)
AS
```

Because you will be calculating the first day of the month date and current week ending date, you need to declare a couple of variables, which is done in the next couple of lines of code. Then you calculate the appropriate dates and set them in your variables. I covered how to calculate these dates at the beginning of this chapter, so I'll forgo the details again. Remember, however, that these dates are calculated differently for SQL Server and Oracle, so readers using Oracle might want to review the stored procedure in Step 7 of this exercise to see how the date is calculated for Oracle.

```
-- Declare local variables
DECLARE @FirstDayOfMonth DATETIME,
        @WeekEndingDate DATETIME

-- Calculate the first day of the month date and current week ending date
SET @FirstDayOfMonth = DATEADD(MM, DATEDIFF(MM,0,GETDATE()), 0)
SET @WeekEndingDate = DATEADD(WK, DATEDIFF(WK,0,GETDATE()), 4)
```

The SELECT statement that follows concatenates the user's first and last names, sums the hours that the user submitted for a given week, and selects the week ending date and the date that the timesheet was approved by the manager.

The primary table that you are selecting data from is the TimeSheets table, and you join the TimeSheetsItems table using a LEFT OUTER JOIN to get the hours that were submitted. You also use a LEFT OUTER JOIN on the Users table to get the details for the users.

The WHERE clause specifies the ManagerID for whom the timesheets should be retrieved, the date range of the timesheets, and that only timesheets that have been submitted should be selected. The second condition in this WHERE clause is new. Here you have specified that the date in the WeekEndingDate column should fall between two dates. The BETWEEN operator is used to specify a range of dates; you specify the beginning date and ending date. Any date in the WeekEndingDate column that is equal to or greater than the date in the @FirstDayOfMonth variable and is less than or equal to the date in the @WeekEndingDate variable will be selected.

Again, the GROUP BY clause is used to order the results returned by this stored procedure and must be used because of the SUM function in the SELECT statement:

```
-- Select month-to-date submitted timesheets
SELECT FirstName + ' ' + LastName AS UserName, SUM(Hours) AS TotalHours,
    WeekEndingDate, ApprovalDate
FROM TimeSheets
LEFT OUTER JOIN TimeSheetItems ON TimeSheets.TimeSheetID =
    TimeSheetItems.TimeSheetID
LEFT OUTER JOIN Users ON TimeSheets.UserID = Users.UserID
WHERE Users.ManagerID = @ManagerID
AND WeekEndingDate BETWEEN @FirstDayOfMonth AND @WeekEndingDate
AND Submitted = 1
GROUP BY WeekEndingDate, FirstName, LastName, ApprovalDate
```

The usp_SelectTimeSheetsQTD and usp_SelectTimeSheetsYTD stored procedures mirror the usp_SelectTimeSheetsMTD stored procedure except that they specify the first day of the quarter and the first day of the year. Therefore, these stored procedures are not listed again. Please review the "Date Functions" section at the beginning of this chapter to review how the first day of the quarter and the first day of the year are calculated.

To preserve space, I'm going to cover only one function in the data access component, the GetManagerName function. The rest of the functions mirror the code that you've implemented in the data access component in previous chapters.

The GetManagerName function is a little different from the other functions that you've implemented because the usp_SelectManagerName stored procedure implements an output parameter. This function starts off like the other functions that you have created in your data access component in that you set the SQL property in the base class to the stored procedure to be executed. Then you initialize the Command object by calling the InitializeCommand method in the base class and add your parameters.

```
Public Function GetManagerName(ByVal ManagerID As Guid) As String
    Try
        MyBase.SQL = "usp_SelectManagerName"
        'Initialize the Command object
        MyBase.InitializeCommand()
        'Add the Parameters to the Parameters collection
        MyBase.AddParameter("@ManagerID", _
```

```
               SqlDbType.UniqueIdentifier, 16, ManagerID)
        MyBase.AddParameter("@ManagerName", _
               SqlDbType.VarChar, 61, Nothing)
```

The difference is apparent after you have added the second parameter. Because this is an output parameter, you must change the default direction of this parameter from being an input parameter to being an output parameter. This is done by accessing the @ManagerName parameter in the Parameters collection and setting the Direction property to Output. The Direction property is set using one of the values in the ParameterDirection enumeration, and in the code that follows the value being set is Output.

After you call the ExecuteStoredProcedure method, you need to retrieve the value returned in the output parameter. This is done by accessing the @ManagerName parameter in the Parameters collection and getting the value contained in the Value property. You set the value returned from this parameter to the function name, as this function returns a string value.

The rest of the code you've seen before and it is standard error-handling code.

```
            'Change the default direction for the @ManagerName parameter
            MyBase.Command.Parameters("@ManagerName").Direction = _
                ParameterDirection.Output
            'Execute the stored procedure
            MyBase.ExecuteStoredProcedure()
            'Retrieve the output
            GetManagerName = MyBase.Command.Parameters("@ManagerName").Value
        Catch ExceptionErr As Exception
            Throw New System.Exception(ExceptionErr.Message, _
            ExceptionErr.InnerException)
        End Try
    End Function
```

The functions that you added in your business logic component are all very straightforward. You've seen them before and they are very simple, so there's no need to cover them again.

Web Services

A Web Service consists of public functions that have been marked with the WebMethod attribute, as shown in the following code fragment. This causes these functions to be exposed in the Web Service for everyone to use and the Simple Object Access Protocol (SOAP) interfaces to be automatically generated for these Web methods.

```
        <WebMethod()> _
        Public Function HelloWorld() As String
            Return "Hello World"
        End Function
```

If you were to view the default service page for a Web Service you would see this Web method exposed as shown in Figure 15-1. From a user's perspective, you can see that the HelloWorld Web method is exposed but you really have no idea what this Web method does.

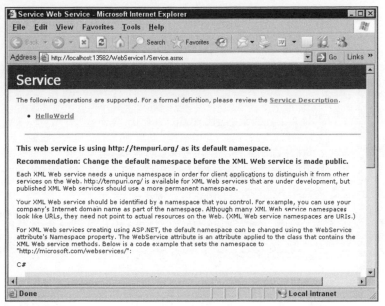

Figure 15-1

The `WebMethod` attribute contains the `Description` property, which can be set to provide a description for a Web method. This enables you to provide a description of what function the Web method serves, and this description will then be available for everyone to see. The code fragment that follows demonstrates how the `Description` property is set in the `WebMethod` attribute.

All properties for the `WebMethod` attribute are enclosed inside of the parentheses, and each property is separated by a comma. The property name is specified followed by a colon and equal sign, and the value for the property is set accordingly. Because the `Description` property contains a string value, the value has been enclosed in quotes, as shown here:

```
<WebMethod(Description:="This WebMethod returns a string " & _
    "containing the text 'Hello World'.")> _
Public Function HelloWorld() As String
    Return "Hello World"
End Function
```

Now when you access this Web Service, a description is shown for the Web method, making it apparent what function the Web method `HelloWorld` serves, as shown in Figure 15-2.

Just as a description helps document your Web methods, a description can be used to help document your Web Service in general. The `WebService` attribute also has a `Description` property that can be set to provide a general description of a Web Service. The following code fragment shows how to set a description in the `WebService` attribute.

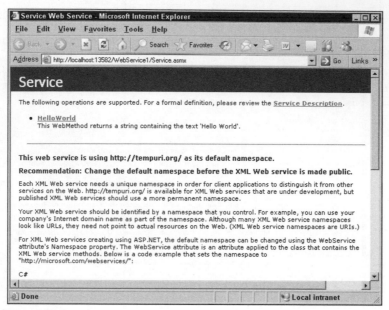

Figure 15-2

Again, you use the `Description` property followed by a colon and an equal sign and then the string value for the description. Notice that two properties are specified here and that the properties are separated by a comma, as described previously.

```
<System.Web.Services.WebService( _
    Namespace:="http://www.wrox.com/WebService1/Service", _
    Description:="This demo Web Service is used to " & _
    "demonstrate how descriptions can be provided to make " & _
    "your Web Service more user friendly and informative.")> _
```

Now when you access this Web Service, you can see a description for the Web Service in general and a description for the Web method, as shown in Figure 15-3. Also note that the namespace has been modified in the preceding code, which eliminates the namespace message that was shown in Figure 15-2.

Web methods are really just public functions that accept input parameters and return a value. What makes them available as a Web method is the use of the `WebMethod` attribute. Because these functions are just normal functions, they can accept any number of input parameters and return a single value. The data types available to a Web method are the same data types that are available to any other function that you've created in your Windows and Web applications. Basically, any .NET Framework data type can be used in a Web method.

In the next Try It Out, you create a Web Service that returns report data from the stored procedures that you created in the previous exercise. Because the majority of the work to be performed is done in your business logic and data access component, the amount of code that you need to implement in your Web Service is minimal.

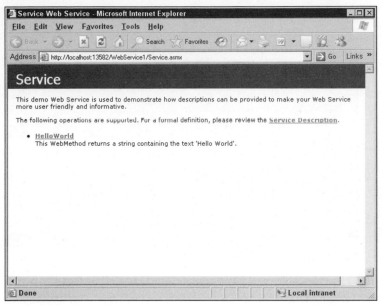

Figure 15-3

Try It Out   Creating a Web Service

To complete this exercise:

1. Start Visual Studio 2005 and from the Start page, click the create Web Site link or select File ⇨ New ⇨ Web Site.

2. In the New Web Site dialog box, shown in Figure 15-4, click the ASP.NET Web Service icon in the Templates pane and enter a name of **TimeSheetWS** in the Location name field. Also ensure that File System is selected in the Location type field. Then click OK to create this Web Service.

3. You want to rename the default service page from Service to Reports. Expand the App_Code folder in the Solution Explorer and right-click Service.vb and choose Rename. Enter a name of **Reports.vb**. Now double-click the file to view the code and change the class name from Service to **Reports**.

4. Right-click Service.asmx in the Solution Explorer and rename it to **Reports.asmx**. Now double-click the file to view the code and change the code-behind file to be Reports.vb and the class to be Reports.

5. At this point you just want to validate all of your changes so click Start on the toolbar. You are prompted with the Debugging Not Enabled dialog box and the Add a new Web.Config file with debugging enabled option selected. Click OK in this dialog box to have the Web.config file added to your project. When the browser opens, the Reports service page is displayed and you can click the HelloWord link to view the HelloWorld Web method. Close your browser to be returned to Visual Studio 2005.

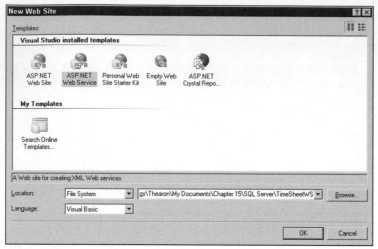

Figure 15-4

6. Now you need to set a reference to your business logic component. Right-click the project in the Solution Explorer and choose Add Reference from the context menu.

7. In the Add Reference dialog box, click the Browse tab and locate your `WroxBusinessLogic.dll` component, select it, and then click OK.

8. View the code for `Reports.vb` in the App_Code folder.

9. Add the following `Imports` statement as shown:

```
Imports System.Web
Imports System.Web.Services
Imports System.Web.Services.Protocols
Imports System.Data
```

10. Add a description for your Web Service. Modify the `WebService` attribute as shown:

```
<WebService(Namespace:="http://www.wrox.com/TimeSheetsWS/Reports", _
    Description:="This Web Service produces manager timesheet " & _
    "reports for the Time Tracker application.")> _
```

11. Add some variables that will be used by the various Web methods that you create. Add the following variable declarations:

```
'Private variables and objects
Private strCompany As String = "Wrox"
Private strApplication As String = "Time Tracker"

Private objTimeSheets As WroxBusinessLogic.WBLTimeSheets

Private objTimeSheetDS As DataSet
```

12. Each report that you create will have a header containing the report title, manager name, and week ending date. This report header will be created in the `GenerateHeaderDataSet` function. Add the following code to create this function:

```vb
Private Sub GenerateHeaderDataSet(ByVal ReportName As String, _
    ByVal ManagerID As Guid, ByVal ReportDate As Date)

    'Initialize a new instance of the business logic component
    Using objTimeSheets As New WroxBusinessLogic.WBLTimeSheets( _
        strCompany, strApplication)

        'Get all timesheets that have been submitted for the current year
        Dim strManagerName As String = objTimeSheets.GetManagerName(ManagerID)

        'Declare a new DataTable
        Dim objDataTable As New DataTable("ReportHeader")

        'Declare a DataColumn
        Dim objDataColumn As DataColumn

        'Create the Title column
        objDataColumn = New DataColumn
        objDataColumn.DataType = System.Type.GetType("System.String")
        objDataColumn.ColumnName = "Title"
        'Add the column to the DataTable
        objDataTable.Columns.Add(objDataColumn)

        'Create the ManagerName column
        objDataColumn = New DataColumn
        objDataColumn.DataType = System.Type.GetType("System.String")
        objDataColumn.ColumnName = "ManagerName"
        'Add the column to the DataTable
        objDataTable.Columns.Add(objDataColumn)

        'Create the Date column
        objDataColumn = New DataColumn
        objDataColumn.DataType = System.Type.GetType("System.DateTime")
        objDataColumn.ColumnName = "Date"
        'Add the column to the DataTable
        objDataTable.Columns.Add(objDataColumn)

        'Create a new DataRow
        Dim objDataRow As DataRow = objDataTable.NewRow

        'Set the values in the columns
        objDataRow.Item("Title") = ReportName
        objDataRow.Item("ManagerName") = strManagerName
        objDataRow.Item("Date") = ReportDate

        'Add the row to the DataSet
        objDataTable.Rows.Add(objDataRow)

        'Add the DataTable to the DataSet
        objTimeSheetDS.Tables.Add(objDataTable)
    End Using
End Sub
```

13. Delete the `HelloWorld` Web method as it will not be used.

14. Now you are ready to start creating the Web methods that will be accessible to everyone using your Web Service. First, create the `TimeSheetsDue` Web method, which generates the report data for timesheets that have not been submitted. Add the following code:

```
<WebMethod(Description:="Timesheets Due report for the " & _
    "employees of a specified manager and week ending date.")> _
Public Function TimeSheetsDue(ByVal ManagerID As Guid, _
    ByVal WeekEndingDate As Date) As DataSet

    'Initialize a new instance of the business logic component
    Using objTimeSheets As New WroxBusinessLogic.WBLTimeSheets( _
        strCompany, strApplication)

        'Get all timesheets that are due
        objTimeSheetDS = objTimeSheets.TimeSheetsDue(ManagerID, WeekEndingDate)
    End Using

    'Generate the report header
    Call GenerateHeaderDataSet("Timesheets Due", ManagerID, WeekEndingDate)

    'Return the TimeSheet DataSet
    Return objTimeSheetDS
End Function
```

15. Create the `TimeSheetsSubmitted` Web method. This Web method returns the report data for all timesheets that have been submitted for the specified manager and week ending date. Enter the following code:

```
<WebMethod(Description:="Timesheets Submitted report for the " & _
    "employees of a specified manager and week ending date.")> _
Public Function TimeSheetsSubmitted(ByVal ManagerID As Guid, _
    ByVal WeekEndingDate As Date) As DataSet

    'Initialize a new instance of the business logic component
    Using objTimeSheets As New WroxBusinessLogic.WBLTimeSheets( _
        strCompany, strApplication)

        'Get all timesheets that have been submitted
        objTimeSheetDS = objTimeSheets.TimeSheetsSubmitted( _
            ManagerID, WeekEndingDate)
    End Using

    'Generate the report header
    Call GenerateHeaderDataSet("Timesheets Submitted", _
        ManagerID, WeekEndingDate)

    'Return the TimeSheet DataSet
    Return objTimeSheetDS
End Function
```

16. The `TimeSheetsMTD` Web method is next and generates the month-to-date timesheet report. Add the following code to create this Web method:

```
<WebMethod(Description:="Timesheets Month-to-Date report for " & _
    "the employees of a specified manager.")> _
Public Function TimeSheetsMTD(ByVal ManagerID As Guid) As DataSet

    'Initialize a new instance of the business logic component
    Using objTimeSheets As New WroxBusinessLogic.WBLTimeSheets( _
        strCompany, strApplication)

        'Get all timesheets that have been submitted for the current month
        objTimeSheetDS = objTimeSheets.TimeSheetsMTD(ManagerID)
    End Using

    'Generate the report header
    Call GenerateHeaderDataSet("Timesheets Month-to-Date", ManagerID, Now)

    'Return the TimeSheet DataSet
    Return objTimeSheetDS
End Function
```

17. The `TimeSheetsQTD` Web method is next and generates the quarter-to-date timesheet report. Add the following code:

```
<WebMethod(Description:="Timesheets Quarter-to-Date report for " & _
    "the employees of a specified manager.")> _
Public Function TimeSheetsQTD(ByVal ManagerID As Guid) As DataSet

    'Initialize a new instance of the business logic component
    Using objTimeSheets As New WroxBusinessLogic.WBLTimeSheets( _
        strCompany, strApplication)

        'Get all timesheets that have been submitted for the current quarter
        objTimeSheetDS = objTimeSheets.TimeSheetsQTD(ManagerID)
    End Using

    'Generate the report header
    Call GenerateHeaderDataSet("Timesheets Quarter-to-Date", ManagerID, Now)

    'Return the TimeSheet DataSet
    Return objTimeSheetDS
End Function
```

18. The last Web method that needs to be added is the `TimeSheetsYTD` Web method. This Web method generates the year-to-date timesheet report. Add the following code to create this Web method:

```
<WebMethod(Description:="Timesheets Year-to-Date report for " & _
    "the employees of a specified manager.")> _
Public Function TimeSheetsYTD(ByVal ManagerID As Guid) As DataSet

    'Initialize a new instance of the business logic component
    Using objTimeSheets As New WroxBusinessLogic.WBLTimeSheets( _
        strCompany, strApplication)

        'Get all timesheets that have been submitted for the current year
```

```
              objTimeSheetDS = objTimeSheets.TimeSheetsYTD(ManagerID)
       End Using

       'Generate the report header
       Call GenerateHeaderDataSet("Timesheets Year-to-Date", ManagerID, Now)

       'Return the TimeSheet DataSet
       Return objTimeSheetDS
    End Function
```

At this point, you can run your Web Service by clicking the Start button on the toolbar. You will be able to view the Web Service description and see the available Web methods along with their descriptions, as shown in Figure 15-5. However, because these Web methods return a `DataSet` as their return types, you will be unable to test your Web methods until Chapter 16.

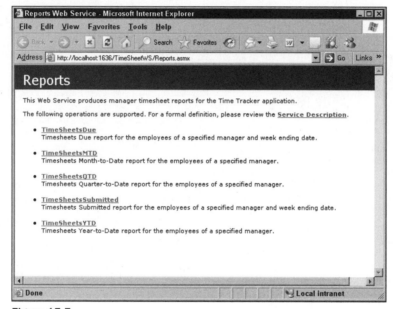

Figure 15-5

How It Works

The first thing that you do in this exercise after renaming the files to Reports is to set a reference to your business logic component, as it will be doing most of the work for this Web Service. The majority of the functionality that has been implemented in this Web Service uses the methods in your business logic component and this provides an excellent vehicle for code reuse.

You then import the `System.Data` namespace, not shown here, and then provide a description for your Web Service by setting the `Description` property of the `WebService` attribute. This provides an overall description of the purpose of this Web Service, as shown previously in Figure 15-5. You also change the default namespace to one that reflects this Web service.

```
<WebService(Namespace:="http://www.wrox.com/TimeSheetsWS/Reports", _
    Description:="This Web Service produces manager timesheet " & _
    "reports for the Time Tracker application.")> _
```

You add some private variable declarations next, which should look familiar to you. These are the same variables that you used in your Time Tracker application as well as your TimeSheets Web application. These variables will be used to access your business logic component and to return a timesheet DataSet.

```
'Private variables and objects
Private strCompany As String = "Wrox"
Private strApplication As String = "Time Tracker"

Private objTimeSheets As WroxBusinessLogic.WBLTimeSheets

Private objTimeSheetDS As DataSet
```

Every report will have a report header and this will be in the form of a separate table in the objTimeSheets DataSet. Therefore, the objTimeSheets DataSet will contain two tables for every report generated: one table named TimeSheets that will contain the actual timesheet report data, and one table named ReportHeader that will contain the header information for the report.

The GenerateHeaderDataSet procedure is responsible for generating the report header table in the objTimeSheets DataSet. This procedure accepts three input parameters: the name of the report, the ManagerID, and the report date.

The first thing that you do in this procedure is initialize a new instance of your business logic component. Then a call is made to get the manager's name because all you have is an ID in the form of a Guid. Remember that the GetManagerName method in the business logic component calls the corresponding method in the data access component, which in turn executes the usp_SelectManagerName stored procedure to return the manager's name.

```
Private Sub GenerateHeaderDataSet(ByVal ReportName As String, _
    ByVal ManagerID As Guid, ByVal ReportDate As Date)

    'Initialize a new instance of the business logic component
    Using objTimeSheets As New WroxBusinessLogic.WBLTimeSheets( _
        strCompany, strApplication)

        'Get all timesheets that have been submitted for the current year
        Dim strManagerName As String = objTimeSheets.GetManagerName(ManagerID)
```

Next, you declare a new DataTable object and set the table name in the constructor as shown in the next line of code. Because you are creating a new table in the objTimeSheetDS DataSet, you must create each column in the table and set its properties. Therefore, the next step is to declare a DataColumn object, which will be used to create each column in the table.

The first column that you create is the Title column, which will contain the title of the report being generated. First you set the objDataColumn variable to a new instance of the DataColumn class. Then you set the DataType property to the data type for the column. Because the report title is a string value, you use the string constant System.String when calling the GetType method on the System.Type class. Remember that the `System.Type` class is used to represent and return .NET Framework type declarations.

After you set the `DataType` property, you set the `ColumnName` property, which in this case is `Title`. Then you add the new column to the table by calling the `Add` method on the `Columns` collection.

```
'Declare a new DataTable
Dim objDataTable As New DataTable("ReportHeader")

'Declare a DataColumn
Dim objDataColumn As DataColumn

'Create the Title column
objDataColumn = New DataColumn
objDataColumn.DataType = System.Type.GetType("System.String")
objDataColumn.ColumnName = "Title"
'Add the column to the DataTable
objDataTable.Columns.Add(objDataColumn)
```

The next column added is the `ManagerName` column. It also contains a string value and has been defined with a String data type. The last column in the `ReportHeader` table is the `Date` column. This column will contain either the week ending date that was passed to a Web method or the current date. Because this column will contain a date, it has been defined with the `DateTime` data type.

```
'Create the ManagerName column
objDataColumn = New DataColumn
objDataColumn.DataType = System.Type.GetType("System.String")
objDataColumn.ColumnName = "ManagerName"
'Add the column to the DataTable
objDataTable.Columns.Add(objDataColumn)

'Create the Date column
objDataColumn = New DataColumn
objDataColumn.DataType = System.Type.GetType("System.DateTime")
objDataColumn.ColumnName = "Date"
'Add the column to the DataTable
objDataTable.Columns.Add(objDataColumn)
```

Now that all of the columns have been defined, you need to add a new row to the table so that you can add some data. A `DataRow` object has been defined in the next line of code.

Then you set the values in the various columns of this new row using the data that has been passed to this procedure and the data that was retrieved from your business logic component. After the values have been set, you add the new `DataRow` to the table by calling the `Add` method on the `Rows` collection of the table. Finally, you add the new table to the `objTimeSheetDS` DataSet.

```
'Create a new DataRow
Dim objDataRow As DataRow = objDataTable.NewRow

'Set the values in the columns
objDataRow.Item("Title") = ReportName
objDataRow.Item("ManagerName") = strManagerName
```

```
            objDataRow.Item("Date") = ReportDate

            'Add the row to the DataSet
            objDataTable.Rows.Add(objDataRow)

            'Add the DataTable to the DataSet
            objTimeSheetDS.Tables.Add(objDataTable)
        End Using
    End Sub
```

The next step is to start creating your Web methods. These are the public functions that are exposed as Web methods, making them available to anyone who uses your Web Service. The first Web method that you create is TimeSheetsDue. This Web method returns the report data for the Timesheets Due report for the specified manager and week ending date.

You specify the Description property for the WebMethod attribute, which provides a description for this Web method. The input parameters for this function are the ManagerID and WeekEndingDate for the report to be generated.

```
        <WebMethod(Description:="Timesheets Due report for the " & _
            "employees of a specified manager and week ending date.")> _
        Public Function TimeSheetsDue(ByVal ManagerID As Guid, _
            ByVal WeekEndingDate As Date) As DataSet
```

The first thing that you do in this function is initialize a new instance of your business logic component. Then you call the TimeSheetsDue method in your business logic component, passing it the appropriate parameters, and receive a DataSet returned with the report data.

```
        'Initialize a new instance of the business logic component
        Using objTimeSheets As New WroxBusinessLogic.WBLTimeSheets( _
            strCompany, strApplication)

            'Get all timesheets that are due
            objTimeSheetDS = objTimeSheets.TimeSheetsDue(ManagerID, WeekEndingDate)
        End Using
```

Next, you call the GenerateHeaderDataSet procedure to generate the report header for this report. You pass this function, the name of the report, the ManagerID, and the week ending date passed to this procedure. Finally, you return the complete DataSet, which contains two tables: TimeSheets and ReportHeader.

```
        'Generate the report header
        Call GenerateHeaderDataSet("Timesheets Due", ManagerID, WeekEndingDate)

        'Return the TimeSheet DataSet
        Return objTimeSheetDS
    End Function
```

The next Web method that you create is the TimeSheetsSubmitted Web method. This Web method produces the Timesheets Submitted report for the specified manager and week ending date. Again, you set the Description property for the WebMethod attribute to provide a description for this Web method. The input parameters to this Web method are the ManagerID and the WeekEndingDate.

This Web method and the other ones that you created all follow the same pattern: They initialize a new instance of the business logic component, call the appropriate method to generate a report DataSet, and then call the GenerateHeaderDataSet procedure to generate the report header.

```
<WebMethod(Description:="Timesheets Submitted report for the " & _
    "employees of a specified manager and week ending date.")> _
Public Function TimeSheetsSubmitted(ByVal ManagerID As Guid, _
    ByVal WeekEndingDate As Date) As DataSet

    'Initialize a new instance of the business logic component
    Using objTimeSheets As New WroxBusinessLogic.WBLTimeSheets( _
        strCompany, strApplication)

        'Get all timesheets that have been submitted
        objTimeSheetDS = objTimeSheets.TimeSheetsSubmitted( _
            ManagerID, WeekEndingDate)
    End Using

    'Generate the report header
    Call GenerateHeaderDataSet("Timesheets Submitted", _
        ManagerID, WeekEndingDate)

    'Return the TimeSheet DataSet
    Return objTimeSheetDS
End Function
```

The TimeSheetsMTD, TimeSheetsQTD, and TimeSheetsYTD Web methods all accept one input parameter, the ManagerID of the manager for whom the report should be generated. Because these Web methods all follow the same pattern as the previous two Web methods, the code will not be listed here again.

When you run your Web Service, the default service page, which is the Reports.asmx service page shown in Figure 15-5, is displayed. Here you are able to view the description for the Web Service, the available Web methods, and their descriptions. If you click a Web method, you are able to view the SOAP request and response documents for the Web method. This service page is the same service page that other users will see when locating this Web Service, and the descriptions that you provided will be extremely helpful, as you'll discover in Chapter 16 when you set a reference to this Web Service in your Time Tracker and TimeSheets projects.

Summary

This chapter has taken on a rather broad depth by examining additional SQL functions in SQL Server and Oracle, the use of stored procedure output parameters, and how to create a Web Service. You've already learned how to calculate the current week ending date in your Time Tracker application, and in this chapter you took that to the next level by calculating the current week ending date in some of your stored procedures.

You also discovered how to calculate the first day of the month, the first day of the quarter, and the first day of the year using the built-in functions in both SQL Server and Oracle. The knowledge that you have gained using these built-in date functions will serve you well as you move onto writing other database applications.

The Web Service that you created was pretty basic and didn't involve a lot of complex logic. This enabled you to leverage the existing code that you wrote in your business logic and data access components, providing excellent reuse of this code. The most complex logic that you wrote in your Web Service was the code to create the report header, which involved creating a new table in the DataSet, adding the columns to the table, and adding a row and populating it with data.

To summarize, you should know how to:

❑ Calculate dates in SQL Server and Oracle stored procedures

❑ Return data from a stored procedure through an output parameter

❑ Set a description for your Web Service and Web methods

❑ Use your business logic component in your Web Service

In Chapter 16, you discover how your Web Service also provides excellent code reuse when you access this Web Service from your Time Tracker and TimeSheets projects.

Accessing a Web Service

You know that Web Services use industry standard technologies, such as XML, to exchange data and HTTP to communicate with other applications. This makes Web Services available to any program that supports these technologies. But accessing a Web Service from a VB 2005 or ASP.NET program is probably more straightforward than you thought.

Accessing a Web Service from any .NET program is just as simple as accessing any other component that you have written. You set a reference to your Web Service, declare an object as a new instance of the Web Service, and then call the methods in the Web Service. Visual Studio 2005 takes care of implementing the required SOAP interfaces for you behind the scenes, which leaves you free to concentrate on using the functionality provided by the Web Service.

In this chapter, you see just how easy it is to access a Web Service from both a Windows application and a Web application. As you access your Web Service from both types of applications, you'll discover that a Web Service not only provides extensibility across your enterprise but also provides excellent code reuse by enabling the various types of applications to leverage the functionality available in the Web Service.

In this chapter, you:

- ❑ Reference a Web Service in your applications and call its Web methods
- ❑ Process a `DataSet` that contains multiple tables
- ❑ Generate HTML reports in a pop-up window

Referencing a Web Service in a Windows Application

To set a reference to a Web Service in your application, a *discovery process* must be performed. This is a process that Visual Studio 2005 goes through to locate or discover one or more related documents for a Web Service. When searching for Web Services on your local machine, Visual Studio

2005 looks for files that have the `.asmx` file extension, Web Services Description Language (WSDL) documents, and Discovery documents that contain a `.disco` file extension. When searching the Internet for Web Services, Visual Studio 2005 searches a Universal Discovery Description and Integration (UDDI) service, which provides a list of all registered Web Services along with their Discovery documents.

After you have located a Web Service to use, you can click that Web Service to see a full description of it and its available Web methods. If you choose to use that Web Service, you can either accept the default Web reference name or provide a new Web reference name for that Web Service.

At the point when you select a Web Service to use and accept or provide a new Web reference name, Visual Studio 2005 generates several documents in your project. The first of these is a *reference map*, which contains the SOAP interface for communicating with your Web Service. The other documents generated are a *Discovery document* and a *WSDL document*. All of these documents are used internally by Visual Studio 2005 to support communications with the Web Service and to provide the Web methods and their parameters through IntelliSense in the Visual Studio 2005 IDE.

You learn about all of these elements in detail as you work through the steps in the next Try It Out, which guides you through the process of referencing and using your TimeSheetsWS Web Service in your Time Tracker application.

Try It Out   Referencing a Web Service in a Windows Application

To complete this exercise:

1. Open your TimeSheetWS Web service application in Visual Studio 2005.

2. Click the Start button on the toolbar to start it.

3. Start another instance of Visual Studio 2005 and open your Time Tracker application.

4. Right-click the Time Tracker project in Solution Explorer and choose Add Web Reference from the context menu.

5. In the Add Web Reference dialog box shown in Figure 16-1, you can see that you have several options for browsing for Web Services. You would typically want to choose a Web Service on your local machine and so you would click the Web Services on the Local Machine link. This works fine if you have IIS installed on your machine and developed your Web service using IIS. However, you developed your Web service using the local file system so when Visual Studio 2005 starts your Web service it uses the Visual Web Developer Web Server and creates a port number for the Web service to run under.

6. Switch to the browser window where your Web service is running and copy the URL from the Address bar. Then switch back to your Time Tracker project and paste the URL in the URL field in the Add Web Reference dialog box and click the Go button.

7. Once your Web service has been located, enter a name of **TimeSheetsWS** in the Web reference name field as shown in Figure 16-2. Then click the Add Reference button to have Visual Studio 2005 add this Web reference to your project.

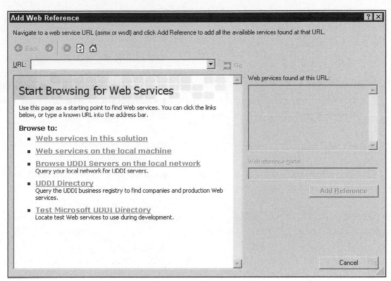

Figure 16-1

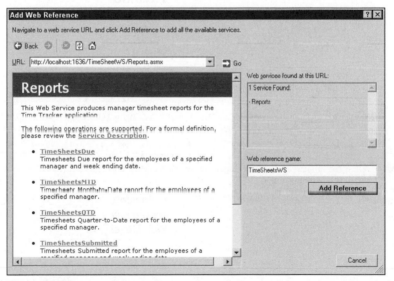

Figure 16-2

8. Now view the code for the TimeSheet form. You want to add an enumeration for various report types, so add the following code after the other variable declarations for your form:

```
Private objTimeSheetDV As Data.DataView
```

```
Private Enum ReportType
    TimeSheetsDue = 1
    TimeSheetsSubmitted = 2
```

```
            TimeSheetsMTD = 3
            TimeSheetsQTD = 4
            TimeSheetsYTD = 5
    End Enum
```

9. You'll be setting the `Text` property of the `ToolStripStatus` status bar when you display your reports, but you don't want the text visible when you display a timesheet. Modify the `LoadTimeSheet` procedure as follows:

```
Private Sub LoadTimeSheet(ByVal WeekEndingDate As ComboBox)
    'Clear previous bindings
    grdTimeSheet.DataSource = Nothing
    grdTimeSheet.DataMember = String.Empty
    grdTimeSheet.Columns.Clear()
```

```
    'Set the status bar message
    ToolStripStatus.Text = "Ready"
```

10. You can encapsulate all the reporting functionality in one generic procedure that uses the `ReportType` enumeration that you just declared. Add the code for the `DisplayReport` procedure as shown:

```
Private Sub DisplayReport(ByVal Report As ReportType)
    Try
        'Initialize a new instance of the Web service
        Using objReports As New TimeSheetsWS.Reports
            'Get the report
            Select Case Report
                Case ReportType.TimeSheetsDue
                    objTimeSheetDS = objReports.TimeSheetsDue( _
                        New Guid(strManagerID), _
                        cboEmployeeWeekEnding.SelectedItem)
                Case ReportType.TimeSheetsSubmitted
                    objTimeSheetDS = objReports.TimeSheetsSubmitted( _
                        New Guid(strManagerID), _
                        cboEmployeeWeekEnding.SelectedItem)
                Case ReportType.TimeSheetsMTD
                    objTimeSheetDS = objReports.TimeSheetsMTD( _
                        New Guid(strManagerID))
                Case ReportType.TimeSheetsQTD
                    objTimeSheetDS = objReports.TimeSheetsQTD( _
                        New Guid(strManagerID))
                Case ReportType.TimeSheetsYTD
                    objTimeSheetDS = objReports.TimeSheetsYTD( _
                        New Guid(strManagerID))
            End Select
        End Using

        'Clear previous bindings
        grdTimeSheet.DataSource = Nothing
        grdTimeSheet.DataMember = String.Empty
        grdTimeSheet.Columns.Clear()

        'Set the text in the status bar
```

```
            Select Case Report
                Case ReportType.TimeSheetsDue, ReportType.TimeSheetsSubmitted
                    ToolStripStatus.Text = "Report: " & _
                        objTimeSheetDS.Tables("ReportHeader").Rows(0).Item( _
                        "Title") & ", Manager: " & _
                        objTimeSheetDS.Tables("ReportHeader").Rows(0).Item( _
                        "ManagerName") & ", Week Ending Date: " & _
                        Format(objTimeSheetDS.Tables( _
                        "ReportHeader").Rows(0).Item("Date"), "Short Date")
                Case ReportType.TimeSheetsMTD, ReportType.TimeSheetsQTD, _
                    ReportType.TimeSheetsYTD
                    ToolStripStatus.Text = "Report: " & _
                        objTimeSheetDS.Tables("ReportHeader").Rows(0).Item( _
                        "Title") & ", Manager: " & _
                        objTimeSheetDS.Tables("ReportHeader").Rows(0).Item( _
                        "ManagerName") & ", Report Date: " & _
                        Format(objTimeSheetDS.Tables( _
                        "ReportHeader").Rows(0).Item("Date"), "Short Date")
            End Select

            'Bind the new DataSet to the DataGridView
            grdTimeSheet.AutoGenerateColumns = True
            grdTimeSheet.DataSource = objTimeSheetDS
            grdTimeSheet.DataMember = "TimeSheets"
        Catch ExceptionErr As Exception
            'Display the error
            MessageBox.Show(ExceptionErr.Message, strAppTitle)
        End Try
    End Sub
```

11. Now you need to start adding the event handlers for the various report menu items. In the Class Name combo box at the top of the Code Editor, select `TimesheetsDueToolStripMenuItem;` and in the Method Name combo box, select the `Click` event. Add the following code in the `TimesheetsDueToolStripMenuItem_Click` procedure:

```
Private Sub TimesheetsDueToolStripMenuItem_Click( _
    ByVal sender As Object, ByVal e As System.EventArgs) _
    Handles TimesheetsDueToolStripMenuItem.Click

    'Get and display the report
    Call DisplayReport(ReportType.TimeSheetsDue)
End Sub
```

12. You want to add the code for the TimesheetsSubmitted menu item next, so click the Class Name combo box and select `TimesheetsSubmittedToolStripMenuItem;` and in the Method Name combo box, select the `Click` event. Add the following code to the `TimesheetsSubmittedToolStripMenuItem_Click` procedure:

```
Private Sub TimesheetsSubmittedToolStripMenuItem_Click( _
    ByVal sender As Object, ByVal e As System.EventArgs) _
    Handles TimesheetsSubmittedToolStripMenuItem.Click

    'Get and display the report
    Call DisplayReport(ReportType.TimeSheetsSubmitted)
End Sub
```

13. The Timesheets MTD menu item is next so click in the Class Name combo box and select `TimesheetsMTDToolStripMenuItem`; and in the Method Name combo box, select the `Click` event. Add the following code to the `TimesheetsMTDToolStripMenuItem_Click` procedure:

```
Private Sub TimesheetsMTDToolStripMenuItem_Click( _
    ByVal sender As Object, ByVal e As System.EventArgs) _
    Handles TimesheetsMTDToolStripMenuItem.Click

    'Get and display the report
    Call DisplayReport(ReportType.TimeSheetsMTD)
End Sub
```

14. Now click in the Class Name combo box and select `TimesheetsQTDToolStripMenuItem`; and in the Method Name combo box, select the `Click` event to have the event handler for the Timesheets QTD menu item added. Add the following code to the `TimesheetsQTDToolStripMenuItem_Click` procedure:

```
Private Sub TimesheetsQTDToolStripMenuItem_Click( _
    ByVal sender As Object, ByVal e As System.EventArgs) _
    Handles TimesheetsQTDToolStripMenuItem.Click

    'Get and display the report
    Call DisplayReport(ReportType.TimeSheetsQTD)
End Sub
```

15. The final event handler to be added is for the Timesheets YTD menu item. Click in the Class Name combo box and select `TimesheetsYTDToolStripMenuItem`; then select the `Click` event in the Method Name combo box. Add the following code to the `TimesheetsYTDToolStripMenuItem_Click` procedure:

```
Private Sub TimesheetsYTDToolStripMenuItem_Click( _
    ByVal sender As Object, ByVal e As System.EventArgs) _
    Handles TimesheetsYTDToolStripMenuItem.Click

    'Get and display the report
    Call DisplayReport(ReportType.TimeSheetsYTD)
End Sub
```

You are now ready to run your project and test the reporting capabilities of the TimeSheet form. Start your project by clicking the Start icon on the toolbar or by clicking the Debug menu and selecting Start. When the Login form is displayed, log in as the first user that you defined. Fill in the time on a timesheet, save it, and then submit it. Then exit the application.

Start your project again and log in as the second user that you have defined. Enter some time on a timesheet and save it but do not submit it. Exit the application.

Finally, start your project again and this time log in as a manager. When the TimeSheet form is displayed, select the current week ending date in the Week Ending combo box, which causes the timesheet for the user displayed in the Employee combo box to be displayed. You need to select the week ending date for your reports, which causes the timesheet for the currently selected employee to be displayed.

Now click the Reports menu and select the Timesheets Due menu item. Your code calls the Web Service to produce the report data, which returns a `DataSet` containing two tables: TimeSheets and ReportHeader. The data in the ReportHeader table is used to populate the report header information that is displayed in the status bar as shown in Figure 16-3. The `DataGridView` is then bound to the TimeSheets table in the `DataSet` to produce the details of the report, as shown in the `DataGrid` itself in Figure 16-3.

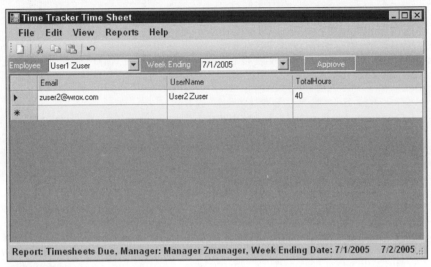

Figure 16-3

At this point, you can click the rest of the Report menu items to view the various reports from your Web Service. You'll notice the text in the status bar updated to reflect the current report being displayed.

How It Works

The first step in this exercise is to set a reference to your Web Service. When the Add Web Reference dialog box is displayed, as was shown in Figure 16-1, you can browse for Web Services on your local machine or browse the UDDI directory on your network, the Internet, or Microsoft's test UDDI directory.

You have to enter the URL of your Web Service as you developed your Web Service using the local file system so when Visual Studio 2005 starts your Web Service, it uses the Visual Web Developer Web Server and creates a port number for the Web Service to run under. Once you click the Go button and your Web Service is located, you enter a name for your Web reference name and then click the Add Reference button to have a reference to the Web Service added to your project. As a side note, when your Web Service is located it displays the Reports service page (as shown in Figure 16-2), the description that you entered for your Web Service, and the available Web methods and their descriptions. This is the same service page that you saw in Figure 15-5 in the previous chapter. You can now see how important it is to enter a description for your Web Service and each Web method.

The next step is to add an enumeration for the various report types that will be produced. This enumeration will be used in the `DisplayReport` procedure to determine which Web method to call in your Web Service:

```
      Private Enum ReportType
          TimeSheetsDue = 1
          TimeSheetsSubmitted = 2
          TimeSheetsMTD = 3
          TimeSheetsQTD = 4
          TimeSheetsYTD = 5
      End Enum
```

You modify the `LoadTimeSheet` procedure next to set the `Text` property of the status bar to Ready. When a timesheet report is displayed, the `DisplayReport` procedure sets this property to display the report header information. When you view a timesheet, you do not want to see the report header information so you set the text to Ready.

```
          'Set the status bar message
          ToolStripStatus.Text = "Ready"
```

The `DisplayReport` procedure is created next, and this procedure encapsulates all the functionality necessary to call your Web Service to have the report data generated and to display this report data in your `DataGridView`.

The first thing that you do in this procedure is declare an object as a new instance of the `Reports` class in your Web Service. Then, to determine which report is to be generated, you code a `Select Case` statement that uses the `Report` parameter that you pass to this procedure. Because the `Report` parameter is derived from the `ReportType` enumeration, the `Case` statements use the members of the enumeration, and Visual Studio 2005's IntelliSense helps you out when creating these `Case` statements by displaying a drop-down list of members in the `ReportType` enumeration.

For each `Case` statement, you call the appropriate Web method to generate the selected report, passing the Web method the required parameters and setting the results of that call in the `objTimeSheetDS` `DataSet`. Again, Visual Studio 2005's IntelliSense kicks in and displays the required parameters for each Web method as you write your code.

All of this built-in functionality makes calling the Web methods in a Web Service very easy and it behaves just like any other component that you reference in your projects. All this is possible because of the work done behind the scenes by Visual Studio 2005 when you set a reference to the Web Service. Visual Studio 2005 generates for your Web Service a reference map that defines all the SOAP interfaces required to communicate with your Web Service, as well as the WSDL and DISCO files for your Web Service.

```
      Private Sub DisplayReport(ByVal Report As ReportType)
          Try
              'Initialize a new instance of the Web service
              Using objReports As New TimeSheetsWS.Reports
                  'Get the report
                  Select Case Report
                      Case ReportType.TimeSheetsDue
                          objTimeSheetDS = objReports.TimeSheetsDue( _
                              New Guid(strManagerID), _
                              cboEmployeeWeekEnding.SelectedItem)
                      Case ReportType.TimeSheetsSubmitted
                          objTimeSheetDS = objReports.TimeSheetsSubmitted( _
```

```
                            New Guid(strManagerID), _
                            cboEmployeeWeekEnding.SelectedItem)
                    Case ReportType.TimeSheetsMTD
                        objTimeSheetDS = objReports.TimeSheetsMTD( _
                            New Guid(strManagerID))
                    Case ReportType.TimeSheetsQTD
                        objTimeSheetDS = objReports.TimeSheetsQTD( _
                            New Guid(strManagerID))
                    Case ReportType.TimeSheetsYTD
                        objTimeSheetDS = objReports.TimeSheetsYTD( _
                            New Guid(strManagerID))
                End Select
            End Using
```

The next step is to clear the previous bindings made to the `grdTimeSheet DataGridView`.

```
            'Clear previous bindings
            grdTimeSheet.DataSource = Nothing
            grdTimeSheet.DataMember = String.Empty
            grdTimeSheet.Columns.Clear()
```

Next, you start building the text that will be displayed in the status bar using the data in the ReportHeader table of your `DataSet`. You set the report title using the Title column in the ReportHeader table and set the manager's name using the ManagerName column. Finally, you set the week ending date or report date using the Date column in the ReportHeader table.

Next, you set the `AutoGenerateColumns` property of the `DataGridView` to `True` so that the columns from your report `DataSet` are automatically displayed in the `DataGridView`. Then you bind the `DataSet` to the `DataGridView` and set the `DataMember` property to the table in the `DataSet`, telling the `DataGridView` which table in the `DataSet` it should bind to.

```
            'Set the text in the status bar
            Select Case Report
                Case ReportType.TimeSheetsDue, ReportType.TimeSheetsSubmitted
                    ToolStripStatus.Text = "Report: " & _
                        objTimeSheetDS.Tables("ReportHeader").Rows(0).Item( _
                        "Title") & ", Manager: " & _
                        objTimeSheetDS.Tables("ReportHeader").Rows(0).Item( _
                        "ManagerName") & ", Week Ending Date: " & _
                        Format(objTimeSheetDS.Tables( _
                        "ReportHeader").Rows(0).Item("Date"), "Short Date")
                Case ReportType.TimeSheetsMTD, ReportType.TimeSheetsQTD, _
                    ReportType.TimeSheetsYTD
                    ToolStripStatus.Text = "Report: " & _
                        objTimeSheetDS.Tables("ReportHeader").Rows(0).Item( _
                        "Title") & ", Manager: " & _
                        objTimeSheetDS.Tables("ReportHeader").Rows(0).Item( _
                        "ManagerName") & ", Report Date: " & _
                        Format(objTimeSheetDS.Tables( _
                        "ReportHeader").Rows(0).Item("Date"), "Short Date")
            End Select

            'Bind the new DataSet to the DataGridView
```

```
            grdTimeSheet.AutoGenerateColumns = True
            grdTimeSheet.DataSource = objTimeSheetDS
            grdTimeSheet.DataMember = "TimeSheets"
        Catch ExceptionErr As Exception
            'Display the error
            MessageBox.Show(ExceptionErr.Message, strAppTitle)
        End Try
    End Sub
```

The event handler procedures that you create for each of the Report menu items are all basically the same so I cover only the first one here and you can refer to Steps 13 through 15 in the exercise to view the other procedures.

You add the `Click` event handler for each Report menu item so that this code is executed when you click a menu item. The only statement in each of these procedures is a call to the `DisplayReport` procedure, passing it the appropriate report type to be generated and displayed. This report type is set using the appropriate member from the `ReportType` enumeration.

Once again, Visual Studio 2005's IntelliSense displays a drop-down list of members from the `ReportType` enumeration, enabling you to select the appropriate report type.

```
    Private Sub TimesheetsDueToolStripMenuItem_Click( _
        ByVal sender As Object, ByVal e As System.EventArgs) _
        Handles TimesheetsDueToolStripMenuItem.Click

        'Get and display the report
        Call DisplayReport(ReportType.TimeSheetsDue)
    End Sub
```

This exercise, while rudimentary, has demonstrated how simple it is to reference and use a Web Service in a Windows application. Once a reference was set to a Web Service, you discovered just how easy it is to call the Web methods in a Web Service. You can see that using the Web methods in a Web Service is just like using the methods in any other component that you have referenced in your project.

Referencing a Web Service in a Web Application

Referencing and accessing a Web Service in an ASP.NET application is just as simple as referencing and accessing a Web Service in a Windows application. In fact, you go through the exact same steps as you did when referencing a Web Service in your Windows application.

Once you set a reference to a Web Service in ASP.NET, Visual Studio 2005 generates the exact same documents that are needed to communicate with the Web Service as it did in your Windows application. It generates a reference map, a WDSL document, and a DISCO file. These same files are generated regardless of whether your application is a Windows application or a Web application.

In this next Try It Out, you enhance your TimeSheets Web application to include a Reports Web page that will be used by managers to select which report they want generated. When a Button control is clicked on this page, you call your Web Service to generate the report data; and then you process that report data, creating an HTML report in a new browser window.

Try It Out   Referencing a Web Service in a Web Application

To complete this exercise:

1. Start Visual Studio 2005 and open your TimeSheets Web application.

2. You need to modify the Login Web page first to redirect any users who are managers to a different Web page when they log in. View the code for the Login form by clicking the `Login.aspx` form in Solution Explorer and then clicking the View Code icon or by right-clicking the `Login.aspx` page in Solution Explorer and choosing View Code. Modify the `Page_Load` procedure as shown:

```
If objDataSet.Tables("User").Rows(0).Item("Status") Then
        If objDataSet.Tables("User").Rows(0).Item( _
            "RoleName").ToString.ToLower Like "manager" Then
            Response.Redirect("Reports.aspx?UserID=" & _
            objDataSet.Tables("User").Rows(0).Item( _
            "UserID").ToString)
        Else
            Response.Redirect("TimeSheet.aspx?UserID=" & _
            objDataSet.Tables("User").Rows(0).Item( _
            "UserID").ToString & "&UserName=" & _
            objDataSet.Tables("User").Rows(0).Item( _
            "UserName").ToString)
        End If
    Else
```

3. Now you need to actually create the Reports Web page. Right-click the TimeSheets project in Solution Explorer, and choose Add New Item from the context menu. In the Add New Item dialog box, select the Web Form icon, enter a name of **Reports.aspx** in the Name field, and check the Select master page check box. Then click the Add button to have the page added to your project. Accept the default options in the Select a Master Page dialog box and click OK.

4. Now add a client-side JavaScript function to open a new window to display the actual timesheet report chosen. This function will cause a new browser window to be opened and cause the browser to navigate to the `TimeSheetReport.aspx` Web page that you'll be adding shortly:

```
<asp:Content ID="Content1" ContentPlaceHolderID="ContentPlaceHolder1"
Runat="Server">
  <script language=javascript>
      function TimeSheetReport(ReportType)
      {
          window.open("TimeSheetReport.aspx?Report=" + ReportType +
            "&ManagerID=" + "<%=Request.QueryString("UserID")%>" +
            "&WeekEndingDate=" +
    escape(document.all.ctl00$ContentPlaceHolder1$cboWeekEndingDate.options[
    document.all.ctl00$ContentPlaceHolder1$cboWeekEndingDate.options.selectedIndex]
    .value),
```

```
                "TimeSheetReport",
                "width=800,height=600,scrollbars=yes,resizable=yes,toolbar=yes");
        }
    </script>
    </asp:Content>
```

5. Add a `<TABLE>` element just below the JavaScript you just created. This table will hold the various HTML controls on your form. Add the following code:

```
    </script>
    <table border="0" cellpadding="1" cellspacing="2">
        <tr>
            <td>Week Ending Date</td>
            <td colspan="4"></td>
        </tr>
        <tr>
            <td></td>
            <td></td>
            <td></td>
            <td></td>
            <td></td>
        </tr>
    </table>
```

6. Click the Design tab at the bottom of the Form Designer window to return to the Design View for your Web form. Click the Toolbox and then click the Standard tab. Drag a Dropdown control from the toolbox and drop it in the column next to the text Week Ending Date. Set the following properties for this control in the Properties window:

    ❑   Set ID to **cboWeekEndingDate**.

    ❑   Set CssClass to **General**.

7. Now drag an Input (Button) control from the HTML tab of the toolbox and drop it in the first cell of the second row of the table below the text Week Ending Date. Set the following properties for this control:

    ❑   Set Class to **FlatButton**.

    ❑   Set Value to **Timesheets Due**.

8. Now drag another Input (Button) control from the HTML tab of the toolbox and drop it in the second cell of the second row and set the following properties for this control:

    ❑   Set Class to **FlatButton**.

    ❑   Set Value to **Timesheets Submitted**.

9. Drag another Input (Button) control from the HTML tab of the toolbox and drop it in the third cell of the second row and set the following properties for this control:

    ❑   Set Class to **FlatButton**.

    ❑   Set Value to **Timesheets MTD**.

10. Drag another Input (Button) control from the HTML tab of the toolbox and drop it in the fourth cell of the second row and set the following properties for this control:

- ❑ Set `Class` to **FlatButton**.
- ❑ Set `Value` to **Timesheets QTD**.

11. Drag another Button control from the HTML tab of the toolbox and drop it in the fifth cell of the second row and set the following properties for this control:

- ❑ Set `Class` to **FlatButton**.
- ❑ Set `Value` to **Timesheets YTD**.

12. You now need to add some code for the `onclick` event for each of the five Button controls that you've added so that they call the JavaScript `TimeSheetReport` function. Click the Source tab at the bottom of the IDE and modify the first Button control as follows:

```
<input class="FlatButton" id="Button1" type="button" value="Timesheets Due"
    onclick="JavaScript:TimeSheetReport('TimesheetsDue');"/>
```

13. Modify the second Button control as follows:

```
<input class="FlatButton" id="Button2" type="button" value="Timesheets Submitted"
    onclick="JavaScript:TimeSheetReport('TimesheetsSubmitted');"/>
```

14. Modify the third Button control as follows:

```
<input class="FlatButton" id="Button3" type="button" value="Timesheets MTD"
    onclick="JavaScript:TimeSheetReport('TimesheetsMTD');"/>
```

15. Modify the fourth Button control as follows:

```
<input class="FlatButton" id="Button4" type="button" value="Timesheets QTD"
    onclick="JavaScript:TimeSheetReport('TimesheetsQTD');"/>
```

16. Modify the fifth Button control as follows:

```
<input class="FlatButton" id="Button5" type="button" value="Timesheets YTD"
    onclick="JavaScript:TimeSheetReport('TimesheetsYTD');"/>
```

17. View the code for this form by clicking the `Reports.aspx` form in Solution Explorer and then clicking the View Code icon or by right-clicking the `Reports.aspx` page in Solution Explorer and choosing View Code from the context menu. Select (Page Events) in the Class Name combo box at the top of the Code Editor and select the `Load` event in the Method Name combo box. Add the following code to the `Page_Load` procedure:

```
Protected Sub Page_Load(ByVal sender As Object, ByVal e As System.EventArgs) _
    Handles Me.Load

        If Not IsPostBack Then
            'Load the week ending dates in the form
            Dim objDates As New Dates
            cboWeekEndingDate.Items.Add(objDates.GetPreviousWeekEndingDate)
            cboWeekEndingDate.Items.Add(objDates.GetCurrentWeekEndingDate)
            cboWeekEndingDate.SelectedIndex = 1
        End If
End Sub
```

18. Right-click the TimeSheets project in Solution Explorer, and choose Add New Item from the context menu. In the Add New Item dialog box, ensure the Web Form template is selected and enter a name of **TimeSheetReport.aspx** in the Name field, and then click the Add button. Accept the default values in the Select a Master Page dialog box and click OK.

Run your project by either clicking the Start button on the toolbar or by clicking the Debug menu and choosing Start. When the Login Web page is displayed, log in as a manager and you'll be redirected to the Reports Web page, as shown in Figure 16-4.

If you click any of the Button controls, the TimeSheetReport Web page is displayed in a new browser window. Notice that this browser window has been opened with a specific size and that it does not contain the menu bar, address bar, or status bar.

When you are done testing your project, stop the project by closing all browser windows.

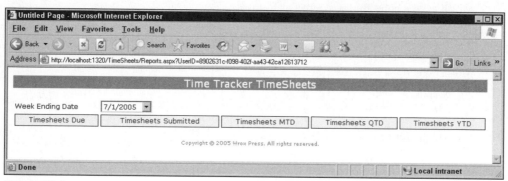

Figure 16-4

1. Now it's time to add a reference to your Web Service. Right-click the TimeSheets project in Solution Explorer and choose Add Web Reference.

2. Switch to the browser window where your Web service is running and copy the URL from the Address bar. Then switch back to your TimeSheets project and paste the URL in the URL field in the Add Web Reference dialog box and click the Go button.

3. Once your Web service has been located, enter a name of **TimeSheetsWS** in the Web reference name field as shown in Figure 16-2. Then click the Add Reference button to have Visual Studio 2005 add this Web reference to your project.

4. View the code for your style sheet and add the following code at the end:

```
.ReportTitle
{
COLOR: black;
FONT-SIZE: 12pt;
FONT-WEIGHT: bold;
}


.SubTitleBold
{
```

```
COLOR: black;
FONT-SIZE: 9pt;
FONT-WEIGHT: bold;
}


.SubTitleNormal
{
COLOR: black;
FONT-SIZE: 9pt;
}


.ReportHeader
{
    BACKGROUND-COLOR: #4682B4;
    FONT-SIZE: 8pt;
    COLOR: White;
    FONT-WEIGHT: bold;
}


.ReportText
{
COLOR: black;
FONT-SIZE: 8pt;
}
```

5. Now view the code for the TimeSheetReport Web page by clicking `TimeSheetReport.aspx` in Solution Explorer and then clicking the View Code icon or by right-clicking `TimeSheetReport .aspx` in Solution Explorer and choosing View Code from the context menu. Add the following `Imports` statement at the top of the class:

```
Imports System.Data

Partial Class TimeSheetReport
```

6. Now add some variable declarations that will be used by the various procedures you create. Add the following variable declarations:

```
'Private variables and objects
Private blnEvenRow As Boolean = True

Private strReport As String
Private strManagerID As String

Private dteWeekEndingDate As Date

Private objTimeSheetDS As New DataSet
```

7. When this Web form is called, it passes a couple of query string values that you'll need to save. The perfect place to do this is in the `Page_Load` procedure. Remember that this procedure is called first when the Web page is processed. Select `(Page Events)` in the Class Name combo box and the `Load` event in the Method Name combo box. Add the following code to this procedure:

```
Protected Sub Page_Load(ByVal sender As Object, ByVal e As System.EventArgs) _
    Handles Me.Load
```
```
    If Not IsPostBack Then
        'Save the QueryString values
        strReport = Request.QueryString("Report")
        dteWeekEndingDate = CType(Request.QueryString("WeekEndingDate"), Date)
        strManagerID = Request.QueryString("ManagerID")
    End If
End Sub
```

8. The first procedure that you want to create is the `Main` procedure. You'll be calling this procedure from server-side script code in your Web form to get the report data from your Web Service and to process the report data. Add the following code to create this procedure. You'll receive errors that the `WriteReportHeader`, `ProcessShortReport`, and `ProcessLongReport` procedures are not defined. You can ignore these errors as you create these procedures in the next few steps:

```
Public Sub Main()
    Using objReports As New TimeSheetsWS.Reports
        objReports.Credentials = _
            System.Net.CredentialCache.DefaultCredentials
        Select Case strReport
        Case "TimesheetsDue"
            objTimeSheetDS = objReports.TimeSheetsDue( _
                New Guid(strManagerID), dteWeekEndingDate)
            Call WriteReportHeader()
            Call ProcessShortReport()
        Case "TimesheetsSubmitted"
            objTimeSheetDS = objReports.TimeSheetsSubmitted( _
                New Guid(strManagerID), dteWeekEndingDate)
            Call WriteReportHeader()
            Call ProcessShortReport()
        Case "TimesheetsMTD"
            objTimeSheetDS = objReports.TimeSheetsMTD( _
                New Guid(strManagerID))
            Call WriteReportHeader()
            Call ProcessLongReport()
        Case "TimesheetsQTD"
            objTimeSheetDS = objReports.TimeSheetsQTD( _
                New Guid(strManagerID))
            Call WriteReportHeader()
            Call ProcessLongReport()
        Case "TimesheetsYTD"
            objTimeSheetDS = objReports.TimeSheetsYTD( _
                New Guid(strManagerID))
            Call WriteReportHeader()
            Call ProcessLongReport()
        End Select
    End Using
End Sub
```

9. Add the following code to create the `WriteReportHeader` procedure, which writes the header that is common to all reports:

```
Private Sub WriteReportHeader()
    Response.Write("<table cellspacing=""0"" cellpadding=""3""" & _
        "border=""0"">")

    Response.Write("<tr>")
    Response.Write("<td colspan=""3"" align=""center""" & _
        "class=""ReportTitle"">" & _
        objTimeSheetDS.Tables("ReportHeader").Rows(0).Item("Title") & _
        "</td>")
    Response.Write("</tr>")

    Response.Write("<tr>")
    Response.Write("<td nowrap><font class=""SubTitleBold"">" & _
        "Manager:</font><font class=""SubTitleNormal"">" & _
        objTimeSheetDS.Tables("ReportHeader").Rows(0).Item("ManagerName") & _
        "</font></td>")
    Response.Write("<td width=""100%""> </td>")
    Select Case strReport
        Case "TimesheetsDue", "TimesheetsSubmitted"
            Response.Write("<td align=""right"" nowrap>" & _
                "<font class=""SubTitleBold"">Week Ending Date:</font>" & _
                "<font class=""SubTitleNormal""> " & _
                Format(objTimeSheetDS.Tables("ReportHeader").Rows(0).Item( _
                "Date"), "Short Date") & "</font></td>")
        Case "TimesheetsMTD", "TimesheetsQTD", "TimesheetsYTD"
            Response.Write("<td align=""right"" nowrap>" & _
                "<font class=""SubTitleBold"">Report Date:</font>" & _
                "<font class=""SubTitleNormal""> " & _
                Format(objTimeSheetDS.Tables("ReportHeader").Rows(0).Item( _
                "Date"), "Short Date") & "</font></td>")
    End Select
    Response.Write("</tr>")

    Response.Write("<tr>")
    Response.Write("<td colspan=""3"" width=""100%""> </td>")
    Response.Write("</tr>")

    Response.Write("</table>")
End Sub
```

10. The `ProcessShortReport` procedure is used to process the report data from your Web Service for the Timesheets Due and Timesheets Submitted reports. Add the following code to create this procedure:

```
Private Sub ProcessShortReport()
    Response.Write("<table cellspacing=""0"" cellpadding=""3""" & _
        "border=""0"">")

    Response.Write("<tr class=""ReportHeader"">")
    Response.Write("<td nowrap width=""200px"">Employee</td>")
    Response.Write("<td nowrap>Total Hours</td>")
    Response.Write("<td width=""100%""> </td>")
    Response.Write("</tr>")

    For intIndex As Integer = 0 To _
```

```
        objTimeSheetDS.Tables("TimeSheets").Rows.Count - 1
    blnEvenRow = Not blnEvenRow
    If blnEvenRow Then
        Response.Write("<tr class=""EvenRow"">")
    Else
        Response.Write("<tr class=""OddRow"">")
    End If
    If strReport = "TimesheetsDue" Then
        Response.Write("<td class=""ReportText""><a href=""mailto:" & _
            objTimeSheetDS.Tables("TimeSheets").Rows(intIndex).Item( _
            "Email") & "?subject=Timesheet Due&body=Your timesheet " & _
            "for week ending date " & dteWeekEndingDate.ToString & _
            " is due. Please submit your timesheet for approval."">" & _
            objTimeSheetDS.Tables("TimeSheets").Rows(intIndex).Item( _
            "UserName") & "</a></td>")
    Else
        Response.Write("<td class=""ReportText"">" & _
            objTimeSheetDS.Tables("TimeSheets").Rows(intIndex).Item( _
            "UserName") & "</td>")
    End If
    Response.Write("<td class=""ReportText"" align=""right"">" & _
        objTimeSheetDS.Tables( _
        "TimeSheets").Rows(intIndex).Item("TotalHours") & "</td>")
    Response.Write("<td> </td>")
    Response.Write("</tr>")
Next

    Response.Write("</table>")
End Sub
```

11. The last procedure that you need to add is the `ProcessLongReport` procedure. This procedure will be called to process the report data for the Timesheets Month-to-Date, Timesheets Quarter-to-Date, and Timesheets Year-to-Date reports. Add the following code to create this procedure:

```
Private Sub ProcessLongReport()
    Response.Write("<table cellspacing=""0"" cellpadding=""3""" & _
        "border=""0"">")

    Response.Write("<tr class=""ReportHeader"">")
    Response.Write("<td nowrap width=""200px"">Employee</td>")
    Response.Write("<td nowrap>Total Hours</td>")
    Response.Write("<td width=""5px""> </td>")
    Response.Write("<td nowrap>Week Ending Date</td>")
    Response.Write("<td width=""5px""> </td>")
    Response.Write("<td nowrap>Approval Date</td>")
    Response.Write("<td width=""100%""> </td>")
    Response.Write("</tr>")

    For intIndex As Integer = 0 To _
        objTimeSheetDS.Tables("TimeSheets").Rows.Count - 1
        blnEvenRow = Not blnEvenRow
```

```
            If blnEvenRow Then
                Response.Write("<tr class=""EvenRow"">")
            Else
                Response.Write("<tr class=""OddRow"">")
            End If
            Response.Write("<td class=""ReportText"">" & objTimeSheetDS.Tables( _
                "TimeSheets").Rows(intIndex).Item("UserName") & "</td>")
            Response.Write("<td class=""ReportText"" align=""right"">" & _
                objTimeSheetDS.Tables("TimeSheets").Rows(intIndex).Item( _
                "TotalHours") & "</td>")
            Response.Write("<td> </td>")
            Response.Write("<td class=""ReportText"" align=""right"">" & _
                objTimeSheetDS.Tables( _
                "TimeSheets").Rows(intIndex).Item("WeekEndingDate") & "</td>")
            Response.Write("<td> </td>")
            Response.Write("<td class=""ReportText"" align=""right"">")
            If IsDBNull(objTimeSheetDS.Tables( _
                "TimeSheets").Rows(intIndex).Item("ApprovalDate")) Then
                Response.Write("</td>")
            Else
                Response.Write(Format(objTimeSheetDS.Tables( _
                    "TimeSheets").Rows(intIndex).Item( _
                    "ApprovalDate"), "Short Date") & "</td>")
            End If
            Response.Write("<td> </td>")
            Response.Write("</tr>")
        Next

        Response.Write("</table>")
    End Sub
```

12. Now view the Form Designer for the TimeSheetReport Web page. To display the report, you need to call the Main procedure, so add the following code:

```
<asp:Content ID="Content1" ContentPlaceHolderID="ContentPlaceHolder1"
Runat="Server">
    <%
    Call Main()
    %>
</asp:Content>
```

That's all the code that you need to implement to generate and process report data from your Web Service. Start your project by clicking the Start button on the toolbar or by clicking the Debug menu and selecting the Start menu item. When the Login form is displayed, log in as a manager so that you are redirected to the Reports Web page.

When the Reports Web page is displayed, click any report to see the report data in a new browser window. The Timesheets Due and Timesheets Submitted reports produce a report with only two columns: the employee name and total hours. The Timesheets Due report will display the employee name as a hyperlink, and clicking an employee opens a new e-mail message, as shown in Figure 16-5. You can see that the To line, the Subject line, and the body of the message are already filled in with the appropriate data.

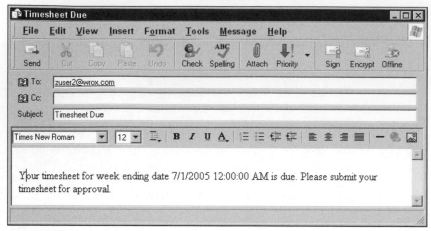

Figure 16-5

The Timesheets MTD, Timesheets QTD, and Timesheets YTD reports display four columns of data as shown in the Timesheets YTD report shown in Figure 16-6. These reports not only display the employee name and total hours, but also the week ending date for which a timesheet was submitted and the date that the timesheet was approved.

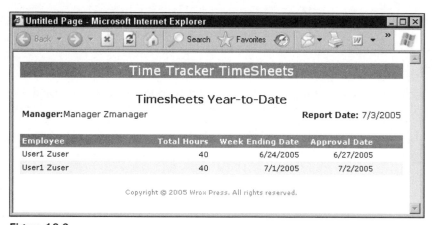

Figure 16-6

How It Works

You start this exercise by modifying the Login Web page to redirect users logging to the Reports Web page if they are managers. This is very similar to the code that you added to the `Main` module in your Time Tracker application to redirect users with the admin role to the Admin form.

Here you check the `RoleName` column in the `DataSet` to determine whether it contains text that is like the word `manager`. If it does, you redirect the user to the Reports Web page, passing it the `UserID` of the manager logging in. If the `RoleName` column doesn't contain text that is like the word `manager`, then you execute the previous code that you had in this Web page whereby you redirected the user to the TimeSheet Web page.

```
If objDataSet.Tables("User").Rows(0).Item( _
    "RoleName").ToString.ToLower Like "manager" Then
    Response.Redirect("Reports.aspx?UserID=" & _
    objDataSet.Tables("User").Rows(0).Item("UserID").ToString)
Else
```

You create the Reports Web page next, and add a JavaScript function that accepts the report type to be processed and opens a new browser window so the report can be processed and displayed. The `window` object represents an open window in a browser and the `open` method of the `window` object will cause a new browser window to be opened and to navigate to the URL passed as an input parameter to this method.

The `open` method accepts four optional parameters: `URL`, `window name`, `window features`, and `replace`. The `URL` parameter specifies the document to be displayed in the new window. In the code that follows, you are building the URL by specifying string constants, the input parameter to this function, and the `UserID` from the query string passed to the Reports Web page. You concatenate the values using a plus (+) sign.

Because the date value that you are passing as a query string value in the URL contains forward slashes, you must properly escape the date so that the forward slashes are not interpreted as part of the URL. This is done using the `escape` function, which encodes values so that they can be read on all computers. Basically, the `escape` function replaces special characters, such as a forward slash, using a `%xx` format. The percent (`%`) sign is a signifier that a two-digit hexadecimal value follows and that this constitutes a complete value.

The `window name` parameter of the `open` method has been specified as `TimeSheetReport`. This is a name that can be used by the `TARGET` attribute in a Web form. Whether or not this attribute is used, it is a good idea to specify the window name when opening new browser windows. This enables you to call this method again with a different report while the new window is open and the window will automatically display the new report; a new window will not be opened as long as a window with that name is already open.

When a new browser window is opened using the `open` method of the `window` object, all the features and the size of the browser are used when the window is opened. For example, if you have multiple toolbars displayed in your current browser window, they will be displayed when this new window is opened. You can control which features are displayed when the new window is opened by specifying the `window features` parameter. This is a comma-separated list of window features, as shown in the following code. Here you are specifying that the new window be opened with a specified width and height and that the scrollbars and toolbars be visible. Note that when the `window features` parameter is specified, any features not specified in this parameter are considered to be turned off, meaning that they will not be displayed. This was evident in the window displayed in Figure 16-5.

The `replace` parameter is not specified in the code, but if it were present it would be a Boolean value indicating whether the URL parameter that was specified should replace the existing entry in the history list or if a new entry should be created in the history list.

```
<script language=javascript>
    function TimeSheetReport(ReportType)
    {
        window.open("TimeSheetReport.aspx?Report=" + ReportType +
            "&ManagerID=" + "<%=Request.QueryString("UserID")%>" +
            "&WeekEndingDate=" +
escape(document.all.ct100$ContentPlaceHolder1$cboWeekEndingDate.options[
document.all.ct100$ContentPlaceHolder1$cboWeekEndingDate.options.selectedIndex]
.value),
            "TimeSheetReport",
            "width=800,height=600,scrollbars=yes,resizable=yes,toolbar=yes");
    }
</script>
```

The next table that you create contains all of your controls for this Web page, as shown in Figure 16-4. You basically create an empty table with text in only one column. The controls are added to the table when you switch to Design view.

```
<table border="0" cellpadding="1" cellspacing="2">
    <tr>
        <td>Week Ending Date</td>
        <td colspan="4"></td>
    </tr>
    <tr>
        <td></td>
        <td></td>
        <td></td>
        <td></td>
        <td></td>
    </tr>
</table>
```

In this exercise, you add mostly HTML controls, rather than Web Form controls, which were added to your Web forms in Chapter 14. Because there is no major implementation of code in the code-behind file, there is no need to implement server-side controls in the Reports Web page except for the combo box, which holds the week ending dates. Most of the processing done in this page is done via client-side script, so HTML controls suited your purpose very well. You drag the appropriate HTML controls from the toolbox, drop them into the appropriate cells in the table, and then set some basic properties for these controls to change their appearance.

When you switch back to the Source view for your Web form, you modify the code for these HTML controls to add code for the `onclick` event for each of the buttons. The following code causes the `TimeSheetReport` function to be executed when a user clicks this button on the Web form. Here you are passing the `TimeSheetReport` function an input parameter of `TimesheetsDue`. This value will be used in the `TimeSheetReport` function as part of the query string for the URL that is used to display a timesheet report.

You repeat this same process for each of the `<INPUT>` elements, passing the appropriate value to the `TimeSheetReport` function. Therefore, the code for each of these elements is not listed again here.

```
<input class="FlatButton" id="Button1" type="button" value="Timesheets Due"
    onclick="JavaScript:TimeSheetReport('TimesheetsDue');"/>
```

The only code you add in the code-behind file is the code to get the week ending dates and load them in the combo box on the Web form. Here you add the code to the Load event for the page and use the Dates class that you created in Chapter 14. You call the GetPreviousWeekEndingDate procedure to get and load the previous week ending date and the GetCurrentWeekEndingDate procedure to get and load the current week ending date. Then you set the current week ending date as the default date selected by setting the SelectedIndex property to 1.

```
Protected Sub Page_Load(ByVal sender As Object, ByVal e As System.EventArgs) _
    Handles Me.Load

    If Not IsPostBack Then
        'Load the week ending dates in the form
        Dim objDates As New Dates
        cboWeekEndingDate.Items.Add(objDates.GetPreviousWeekEndingDate)
        cboWeekEndingDate.Items.Add(objDates.GetCurrentWeekEndingDate)
        cboWeekEndingDate.SelectedIndex = 1
    End If
End Sub
```

Before testing your code, you add the TimeSheetReport Web page. Then you are able to run your Web application and log in as a manager, and you are redirected to the Reports Web page (refer to Figure 16-4). When you click each of the buttons, the TimeSheetReport Web page opens in a new window.

The next step in this exercise is to add a Web reference to your Web Service. The exact same steps were used in this exercise as the steps that were performed in the first exercise. You right-click the project in Solution Explorer, choose Add Web Reference from the context menu, and then paste the URL for your Web Service in the Add Web Reference dialog box. Then you enter a name for your Web Service that will be used to reference the Web service in your project.

You then add some new user defined styles, which are used when building your timesheet reports, to your style sheet. You have a style for the report title, styles for subtitles, a style for your report header, and a style for your report text.

```
.ReportTitle
{
 COLOR: black;
 FONT-SIZE: 12pt;
 FONT-WEIGHT: bold;
}

.SubTitleBold
{
 COLOR: black;
 FONT-SIZE: 9pt;
 FONT-WEIGHT: bold;
}

.SubTitleNormal
{
 COLOR: black;
 FONT-SIZE: 9pt;
```

```
}

.ReportHeader
{
    BACKGROUND-COLOR: #4682B4;
    FONT-SIZE: 8pt;
    COLOR: White;
    FONT-WEIGHT: bold;
}

.ReportText
{
 COLOR: black;
 FONT-SIZE: 8pt;
}
```

In your code-behind file for the TimeSheetReport Web page, you first import the `System.Data` namespace (code not shown here) and then declare some variables that will be accessible to all functions in this page. The `blnEvenRow` variable will be used to toggle the style used between even and odd rows in your TimeSheet report. The `strReport` variable will contain the report to be generated and the `strManagerID` variable will hold the GUID of the manager. The `dteWeekEndingDate` variable will be used to contain the date for the report and the `objTimeSheetDS` variable should be pretty obvious as you've used this one before; it will contain the timesheet report data.

```
'Private variables and objects
Private blnEvenRow As Boolean = True

Private strReport As String
Private strManagerID As String

Private dteWeekEndingDate As Date

Private objTimeSheetDS As New DataSet
```

When the TimeSheetReport Web page is processed, the first event that is executed is the `Load` event for the page. This is where you want to capture and save the query string values passed to this page. In the `Page_Load` procedure that follows, you save the type of report being processed in the `strReport` variable, the week ending date requested in the `dteWeekEndingDate` variable, and the manager ID in the `strManagerID` variable:

```
Protected Sub Page_Load(ByVal sender As Object, ByVal e As System.EventArgs) _
    Handles Me.Load

    If Not IsPostBack Then
        'Save the QueryString values
        strReport = Request.QueryString("Report")
        dteWeekEndingDate = CType(Request.QueryString("WeekEndingDate"), Date)
        strManagerID = Request.QueryString("ManagerID")
    End If
End Sub
```

The `Main` procedure is called from server-side code in the HTML code in your Web form. This procedure determines which report to process based on the value contained in the `strReport` variable. The first thing that you do in this procedure is initialize a new instance of the TimeSheetsWS Web Service and then set the Credentials property of the Web Service using the default credentials of your Web application.

Then, using a Select Case statement, you determine which report was requested and then call the appropriate Web method in your Web Service to have the report data generated and returned in a DataSet. There are two basic report types: a short report containing two columns and a long report containing four columns. The first two Case statements process the short report, while the last three Case statements process the long report.

```
Public Sub Main()
    Using objReports As New TimeSheetsWS.Reports
        objReports.Credentials = _
            System.Net.CredentialCache.DefaultCredentials
        Select Case strReport
            Case "TimesheetsDue"
                objTimeSheetDS = objReports.TimeSheetsDue( _
                    guidManagerID, dteWeekEndingDate)
                Call WriteReportHeader()
                Call ProcessShortReport()
            Case "TimesheetsSubmitted"
                objTimeSheetDS = objReports.TimeSheetsSubmitted( _
                    guidManagerID, dteWeekEndingDate)
                Call WriteReportHeader()
                Call ProcessShortReport()
            Case "TimesheetsMTD"
                objTimeSheetDS = objReports.TimeSheetsMTD( _
                    guidManagerID)
                Call WriteReportHeader()
                Call ProcessLongReport()
            Case "TimesheetsQTD"
                objTimeSheetDS = objReports.TimeSheetsQTD( _
                    guidManagerID)
                Call WriteReportHeader()
                Call ProcessLongReport()
            Case "TimesheetsYTD"
                objTimeSheetDS = objReports.TimeSheetsYTD( _
                    guidManagerID)
                Call WriteReportHeader()
                Call ProcessLongReport()
        End Select
    End Using
End Sub
```

The WriteReportHeader procedure is responsible for writing the report header in the Web page for all reports. The first line of code here calls the Write method of the Response object to begin writing a <TABLE> element in the HTML of your Web page. You set some basic attributes for the <TABLE> element, which controls how the table will look.

```
Private Sub WriteReportHeader()
    Response.Write("<table cellspacing=""0"" cellpadding=""3""" & _
        "border=""0"">")
```

The first row in the table contains the report title. There is only one table cell in this row and it spans three cells, as indicated by the colspan attribute. The text in this cell should be centered on the page, as specified by the align attribute. The data for the report title is retrieved from the Title column of the objTimeSheetDS DataSet.

```
Response.Write("<tr>")
Response.Write("<td colspan=""3"" align=""center""" & _
    "class=""ReportTitle"">" & _
    objTimeSheetDS.Tables("ReportHeader").Rows(0).Item("Title") & _
    "</td>")
Response.Write("</tr>")
```

The next row in the table contains three cells. The first cell contains the manager's name for which this report is produced, a filler cell, and the date for this report. You do not want the data in the first cell to wrap to the next line, so you specify the nowrap attribute. The text Manager: should be bold, so you have specified the <FONT> element and tell it to use the SubTitleBold class in your style sheet. The manager's name is retrieved from the ManagerName column in the objTimeSheetDS DataSet.

The next cell here is just a filler cell. The report that is displayed on this page contains the manager's name in the left side of the report and is aligned to the left. The date for this report is contained in the right side and is aligned to the right. To have the manager's name aligned to the left and the date aligned to the right, you need to specify a filler cell in between that takes up all the extra room in the row. To accomplish this, you specify the width attribute for this cell and set its value to 100%. You must also specify the text , which causes a blank space to be written in this cell, effectively creating white space in this cell.

```
Response.Write("<tr>")
Response.Write("<td nowrap><font class=""SubTitleBold"">" & _
    "Manager:</font><font class=""SubTitleNormal"">" & _
    objTimeSheetDS.Tables("ReportHeader").Rows(0).Item("ManagerName") & _
    "</font></td>")
Response.Write("<td width=""100%""> </td>")
```

The third cell in this row contains the report date, and a Select Case statement is used to determine what text to write in the cell. For the short reports, the text Week Ending Date: is written, followed by the date specified in the Date column of the objTimeSheetDS DataSet. For the long reports, the text Report Date: is written, followed by the date in the Date column of the DataSet.

Notice that there are only two Case statements here and that each Case statement contains multiple test expressions, with each one separated by a comma. Because the same action is to be performed for the short reports and the long reports, it only makes sense to combine the test expressions for the Case statement in one line. This prevents you from duplicating code for each test expression.

The align attribute specified for this cell aligns the data to the right. The nowrap attribute has also been specified and prevents the text in this cell from wrapping to the next line. Finally, the date displayed from the Date column of the DataSet is formatted using the Format function.

The Format function accepts two parameters: the expression to be formatted and the format style to use to format the expression. There are many defined styles, and the one being used here formats a date using the short date format, as shown in Figure 16-6.

```
        Select Case strReport
            Case "TimesheetsDue", "TimesheetsSubmitted"
                Response.Write("<td align=""right"" nowrap>" & _
                    "<font class=""SubTitleBold"">Week Ending Date:</font>" & _
                    "<font class=""SubTitleNormal""> " & _
                    Format(objTimeSheetDS.Tables("ReportHeader").Rows(0).Item( _
                    "Date"), "Short Date") & "</font></td>")
            Case "TimesheetsMTD", "TimesheetsQTD", "TimesheetsYTD"
                Response.Write("<td align=""right"" nowrap>" & _
                    "<font class=""SubTitleBold"">Report Date:</font>" & _
                    "<font class=""SubTitleNormal""> " & _
                    Format(objTimeSheetDS.Tables("ReportHeader").Rows(0).Item( _
                    "Date"), "Short Date") & "</font></td>")
        End Select
        Response.Write("</tr>")
```

The final row in the header table is just a filler row to take up space between the header of the report and the actual report data.

```
        Response.Write("<tr>")
        Response.Write("<td colspan=""3"" width=""100%""> </td>")
        Response.Write("</tr>")

        Response.Write("</table>")
    End Sub
```

The `ProcessShortReport` procedure processes the report data for the Timesheets Due and Timesheets Submitted reports. The first thing that you do in this procedure is start a new table for the actual report data.

The first row in the table is the header row, which contains a steel-blue background with the header text in white, as specified in the `ReportStyle` style in your style sheet. The first column in this table has the `width` attribute specified so that this column will always be the same width. The second column does not need a width specified as it contains the total hours. However, the `nowrap` attribute has been specified to prevent the data in this column from wrapping.

Finally, the third column in this table is used as a filler column to keep the data in the first two columns aligned to the left of the report. This ensures that the data is displayed in a consistent manner when the browser window is resized.

```
    Private Sub ProcessShortReport()
        Response.Write("<table cellspacing=""0"" cellpadding=""3""" & _
            "border=""0"">")

        Response.Write("<tr class=""ReportHeader"">")
        Response.Write("<td nowrap width=""200px"">Employee</td>")
        Response.Write("<td nowrap>Total Hours</td>")
        Response.Write("<td width=""100%""> </td>")
        Response.Write("</tr>")
```

After the header row of the report data has been written, it's time to process the data in the `DataSet` and write the report data. Using a `For...Next` loop, you process all rows of data in the `DataSet`. The first thing that you do inside this loop is toggle the blnEvenRow variable so that each row of data is written using an alternating style.

Next, you query the blnEvenRow variable to determine whether it is True or False. When the variable is set to True, you write the <TR> element and specify the EvenRow style to set the background color of the row to White Smoke. When the variable is False, you simply write the <TR> element and specify the OddRow style, which causes the background color of the row to be white.

```
For intIndex As Integer = 0 To _
        objTimeSheetDS.Tables("TimeSheets").Rows.Count - 1
    blnEvenRow = Not blnEvenRow
    If blnEvenRow Then
        Response.Write("<tr class=""EvenRow"">")
    Else
        Response.Write("<tr class=""OddRow"">")
    End If
```

Now you determine whether the report being processed is the Timesheets Due report, in which case you want to write the employee's name in the report using a hyperlink. This enables you to click the employee's name in the report and have a mail message pop up with the details of the message filled in, as shown in Figure 16-5.

The <A> element provides a hyperlink in your Web page and the href attribute can be used to specify a link to another Web page or a link to a mail message. Because you want a new mail message to be generated, you have specified a value of mailto in the href attribute and have provided the details of the mail message.

Notice that the value specified in the href attribute looks similar to a normal URL in that it contains a query string, with each query string name and value pair separated by an ampersand (&) character. The first parameter for the mailto protocol is the recipient's e-mail address, which is set using the Email column from the DataSet. Then you specify a question mark (?) indicating the query string part of the address, and specify the text of subject as the first query string name. The value for subject is set to the static text of Timesheet Due. The body of the message is specified next and consists of static text and the date from the Date column of your DataSet. Finally, the text for the <A> element is written using the UserName column from the DataSet.

```
If strReport = "TimesheetsDue" Then
    Response.Write("<td class=""ReportText""><a href=""mailto:" & _
        objTimeSheetDS.Tables("TimeSheets").Rows(intIndex).Item( _
        "Email") & "?subject=Timesheet Due&body=Your timesheet " & _
        "for week ending date " & dteWeekEndingDate.ToString & _
        " is due. Please submit your timesheet for approval."">" & _
        objTimeSheetDS.Tables("TimeSheets").Rows(intIndex).Item( _
        "UserName") & "</a></td>")
```

If the report being generated is the Timesheet Submitted report, the code for the Else statement is processed, and here you simply write the user's name in the cell as plaintext using the UserName column in the DataSet.

After the username has been written in the first cell, you want to write out the total number of hours on the user's timesheet, which is done in the next line of code. Notice that you specify the align attribute for this cell so that all hours are aligned to the right of the cell. You typically want to right-align numbers in a column, which is what is being done here. The hours are retrieved from the TotalHours column in your DataSet and written to the cell.

The final cell in this row simply contains the text   which causes a blank space to be written in this cell. The final line of code in this procedure closes the table by writing the closing element for the table.

```
            Else
                Response.Write("<td class=""ReportText"">" & _
                    objTimeSheetDS.Tables("TimeSheets").Rows(intIndex).Item( _
                    "UserName") & "</td>")
            End If
            Response.Write("<td class=""ReportText"" align=""right"">" & _
                objTimeSheetDS.Tables( _
                "TimeSheets").Rows(intIndex).Item("TotalHours") & "</td>")
            Response.Write("<td> </td>")
            Response.Write("</tr>")
        Next

        Response.Write("</table>")
    End Sub
```

The ProcessLongReport report procedure is called to produce the Timesheets Month-to-Date, Timesheets Quarter-to-Date, and Timesheets Year-to-Date reports. Remember that these reports have four columns each that list the employee name, the total hours submitted, the timesheet week ending date, and the date the timesheet was approved by a manager.

Like the ProcessShortReport procedure, you start this procedure by creating a table for the report header row that will contain the column headers for the report. Then you create the header row and write the data to each cell in this row. A filler cell is specified between each cell in the header row to provide some extra space between each column in the report. This is just a normal cell that has the width attribute specified and the text   in the cell. When the report is produced, this cell will take up white space in the report and help to keep the data in the report columns from looking crowded.

```
    Private Sub ProcessLongReport()
        Response.Write("<table cellspacing=""0"" cellpadding=""3""" & _
            "border=""0"">")

        Response.Write("<tr class=""ReportHeader"">")
        Response.Write("<td nowrap width=""200px"">Employee</td>")
        Response.Write("<td nowrap>Total Hours</td>")
        Response.Write("<td width=""5px""> </td>")
        Response.Write("<td nowrap>Week Ending Date</td>")
        Response.Write("<td width=""5px""> </td>")
        Response.Write("<td nowrap>Approval Date</td>")
        Response.Write("<td width=""100%""> </td>")
        Response.Write("</tr>")
```

Now you set up a For...Next loop to process each row of data in the objTimeSheetDS DataSet. The first thing that you do in this loop is toggle the blnEvenRow variable so that the even rows written in the table are written using the background color of White Smoke.

```
For intIndex As Integer = 0 To _
    objTimeSheetDS.Tables("TimeSheets").Rows.Count - 1
    blnEvenRow = Not blnEvenRow
    If blnEvenRow Then
        Response.Write("<tr class=""EvenRow"">")
    Else
        Response.Write("<tr class=""OddRow"">")
    End If
```

Next, you start writing the data in each cell. You write the username in the first cell using the data from the `UserName` column in the `DataSet`. The text in the cell is left-aligned by default when no `align` attribute has been specified. Then you write the total hours submitted on the user's timesheet in the next cell, and this data is right-aligned in the cell because the `align` attribute has been specified with a value of `right`.

The filler cell is specified next, and the text ` ` is specified in this cell to create a blank space in the cell. The week ending date for the timesheet is written next using data from the `WeekEndingDate` column of the `DataSet`. Dates look better when they are right-aligned in a column so you also specify the `align` attribute for this cell.

Another filler cell is written and again you have specified the text ` ` to take up space in that cell. Finally, you write the last column of data, which is the date that the timesheet was approved. Again, the data in this column is right-aligned, as is evident by the `align` attribute with a value of `right`.

Because a timesheet may not have been approved when this report is generated, you first check to see whether the value returned in the `ApprovalDate` column of the `DataSet` contains a `Null` value by using the `IsDBNull` function. Remember that this function checks the value of an object to determine whether it contains a `DBNull` value and returns a value of `True` if it does. If the value in the `ApprovalDate` column is `Null`, you simply write the ending element for the cell. If it is not `Null`, you write the date in this cell using the date in the `ApprovalDate` column of the `DataSet` and then write the ending element for the cell.

The last few lines of code here simply write the last filler cell in this table, the ending table row element, and the ending table element:

```
Response.Write("<td class=""ReportText"">" & objTimeSheetDS.Tables( _
    "TimeSheets").Rows(intIndex).Item("UserName") & "</td>")
Response.Write("<td class=""ReportText"" align=""right"">" & _
    objTimeSheetDS.Tables("TimeSheets").Rows(intIndex).Item( _
    "TotalHours") & "</td>")
Response.Write("<td> </td>")
Response.Write("<td class=""ReportText"" align=""right"">" & _
    objTimeSheetDS.Tables( _
    "TimeSheets").Rows(intIndex).Item("WeekEndingDate") & "</td>")
Response.Write("<td> </td>")
Response.Write("<td class=""ReportText"" align-""right"">")
If IsDBNull(objTimeSheetDS.Tables( _
    "TimeSheets").Rows(intIndex).Item("ApprovalDate")) Then
    Response.Write("</td>")
Else
    Response.Write(Format(objTimeSheetDS.Tables( _
        "TimeSheets").Rows(intIndex).Item( _
```

```
                          "ApprovalDate"), "Short Date") & "</td>")
                End If
                Response.Write("<td> </td>")
                Response.Write("</tr>")
        Next

        Response.Write("</table>")
    End Sub
```

The final step is to add some server-side VBScript in your Web page. This code just calls the Main procedure in your code-behind file to process the report. You may be wondering why this code is here and not in the Page_Load procedure in your code-behind file. You have to take into account the order in which the events are fired for a Web page and when the Web page is actually rendered. The Page_Load event is fired when the Web page is requested and is also fired before any HTML in the Web page is actually rendered.

Therefore, you want the HTML to start being rendered before calling your procedures to produce and write the report data, as you are using the Write method of the Response object to write HTML to your Web page. Calling the Main procedure here ensures that the HTML in your Web form has been rendered up until this point, which means that the headers for the Web page have already been processed, which also means that your style sheet has already been linked in, giving you access to the styles in the style sheet.

```
<body>
    <%
    Call Main()
    %>
</body>
```

When you tested your reports, you saw that the Timesheets Due report displayed the username as a hyperlink. This enables you to provide the code in the HTML to display a new mail message with all the details already filled in, which in turn enables a manager to run this report, click the hyperlink, and then e-mail the message to the user, requesting that he or she submit the timesheet for approval.

All of the reports were displayed in a browser window with only the toolbar displayed. This provides the manager running the report with a quick way to print it. Yes, you could omit the toolbar and simply right-click the Web page and choose Print from the context menu. However, many users will be confused if they do not see a menu item or toolbar button to print the report. Therefore, including the toolbar in the browser window just provides a good user experience and reduces the support calls on how to print a report.

Summary

This chapter has shown you how easy it is to reference and access a Web Service in both your Windows applications and your Web applications. You have seen how once a reference is set to a Web Service, calling the Web methods in the Web Service is just as easy as calling the methods in your business logic component. Visual Studio 2005 takes care of all of the details of communicating with the Web Service behind the scenes, in particular the SOAP interfaces.

You also had a chance to work more with DataSets by working with one that contained multiple tables. In the last chapter you saw how easy it is to create a DataSet that contained multiple tables, and in this chapter you saw how easy it is to process data from each table in the DataSet and to also bind a specific table in a DataSet to a DataGrid control in a Windows form.

Finally, you learned a little more about HTML and JavaScript, and had the opportunity to create a report Web page that was displayed in a new browser window. This provides an alternative way of creating Web-based reports without using the Crystal Reports components included with Visual Studio 2005. You saw how easy it is to use the Write method of the Response object in your code-behind file to write the report data to the Web page, eliminating the need for Crystal Reports components.

To summarize, you should know:

❑ How to set a reference to a Web Service in both a Windows application and a Web application

❑ How to call the Web methods in a Web Service

❑ How to bind a DataSet with multiple tables to a DataGrid control

❑ How to open a new browser window using JavaScript

This wraps up your learning experience with this book. However, this is by no means the end of your learning experience with VB 2005, ADO.NET, or database programming in general. While you have learned a lot and have covered a lot of ground, there are still volumes of information to learn. As you progress in your career and sharpen your database programming skills with VB 2005, you'll want to network with your peers to share experiences and information. This can be an invaluable source of information for you.

I hope you have enjoyed this book and have found it to be very useful and informative. I have enjoyed writing it and sharing my knowledge with you and I hope that you find it to be an invaluable reference not only for database programming with VB 2005 but also for VB 2005 in general. The Wrox team of editors and I wish you much success in your ventures.

Data Type Cross-Reference

This appendix provides a general data type cross-reference between Microsoft Access, Microsoft SQL Server, and Oracle. Table A-1 lists the most common data types in each database and their capacities. These are the data types that you are most likely to use in your everyday programming tasks; the table does not contain every data type supported by each of the databases. In Table A-1, characters refer to character data, and bytes refer to binary data.

Table A-1: Data Type Cross-Reference

Access	SQL Server	Oracle
	BIGINT -9,223,372,036,854,775,808 to -9,223,372,036,854,775,807	
	BINARY Fixed-length up to 8,000 bytes	
YES/NO Yes/No, True/False or On/Off	BIT 0 or 1	
	CHAR Fixed-length up to 8,000 bytes	CHAR Fixed-length up to 2,000 bytes
DATE/TIME January 1, 100 through December 31, 9999	DATETIME January 1, 1753 through December 31, 9999	DATE January 1, 4712 BC to December 31, 4712 AD
NUMBER: DECIMAL $-10^{28}-1$ through $10^{28}-1$	DECIMAL $-10^{38}+1$ through $10^{38}-1$	NUMBER $-10^{38}+1$ through $10^{38}-1$

Table continued on following page

Table A-1: Data Type Cross-Reference *(continued)*

Access	SQL Server	Oracle
NUMBER: DOUBLE -1.79769313486231E308 to -4.94065645841247E-324 for negative values and from 1.79769313486231E308 to 4.94065645841247E-324 for positive values	FLOAT -1.79E + 308 through -2.23E - 308, 0 and 2.23E + 308 through 1.79E + 308	NUMBER -10^38 +1 through 10^38 -1
OLE OBJECT Variable-length up to 1,073,741,823 bytes	Image Variable-length up to 2,147,483,647 bytes	LONGRAW Variable-length up to 2,147,483,648 bytes
		BLOB Variable-length up to 4,294,967,296 bytes
NUMBER: LONG INTEGER -2,147,483,648 to 2,147,483,647 AUTONUMBER: LONG INTEGER 1 to 2,147,483,647	INTEGER -2,147,483,648 to 2,147,483,647	NUMBER -10^38 +1 through 10^38 -1
	NCHAR Fixed-length up to 4,000 Unicode characters	NCHAR Fixed-length up to 2,000 Unicode characters
	NTEXT Variable-length up to 1,073,741,823 Unicode characters	
		NCLOB Variable-length up to 4,294,967,296 Unicode characters
	NVARCHAR Variable-length up to 4,000 Unicode characters	NVARCHAR2 Variable-length up to 4,000 Unicode characters
NUMBER: SINGLE -3.402823E38 to -1.401298E-45 for negative values and from 1.401298E-45 to 3.402823E38 for positive values	REAL -3.40E + 38 through -1.18E - 38, 0 and 1.18E - 38 through 3.40E + 38	NUMBER -10^38 +1 through 10^38 -1

Access	SQL Server	Oracle
	SMALLDATETIME January 1, 1900 through June 6, 2079	
NUMBER: INTEGER -32,768 to 32,767	SMALLINT -32,768 to 32,767	NUMBER -10^38 +1 through 10^38 -1
	SMALLMONEY -214,748.3648 through +214,748.3647	
MEMO Variable-length up to 65,535 characters	TEXT Variable-length up to 2,147,483,647 characters	LONG Variable-length up to 2,147,483,648 characters
		CLOB Variable-length up to 4,294,967,296 characters
NUMBER: BYTE 0 to 255	TINYINT 0 to 255	NUMBER -10^38 +1 through 10^38 -1
NUMBER: REPLICATION ID Globally unique identifier (Guid) AUTONUMBER: REPLICATION ID Globally unique identifier (Guid)	UNIQUEIDENTIFIER Globally unique identifier (Guid)	RAW: defined as RAW(16) Globally unique identifier without dashes
	VARBINARY Variable-length up to 8,000 bytes	RAW Variable-length up to 2,000 bytes
TEXT Variable-length up to 255 characters	VARCHAR Variable-length up to 8,000 characters	VARCHAR2 Variable-length up to 4,000 characters

Time Tracker Project UI

This appendix guides you through the steps required to build the user interface for the Time Tracker project. It's a long process with multiple steps, so you have the option of following the steps outlined here or downloading the complete UI along with the rest of the code for this book from the Wrox Web site at www.wrox.com/dynamic/books/download.aspx.

The steps outlined here are broken into sections. Each section guides you through the steps of adding controls to a form or adding code to a class or module. Certain icons and images are used in building the UI, so it is suggested that you download the code for this appendix to have access to those icons and images.

This appendix does not provide a detailed explanation of the steps performed here to build the interface or of the code added. When the code built here is used in your exercises, it is thoroughly explained as part of the exercise's How It Works section.

Building an Outlook Style Interface

The Time Tracker application has a functional Outlook 2003 style interface that is familiar to most users. The feature set for this application will be kept to a minimum, as you want to focus your attention on interacting with the database and not on all the bells and whistles of an application.

The major components of the interface are a menu, a toolbar, a status bar, an Outlook 2003–style navigation bar, and navigation panels for each of the screens.

Admin form

The Admin form provides the administrative features of your application. This form is used to view, insert, update, and delete data in your database tables.

To create this form:

1. Start Visual Studio 2005 and start a new project by clicking the New Project button on the Projects tab of the Start page or by selecting File ⇨ New ⇨ Project.

2. In the New Project dialog box, select a Windows Application template and enter a project name of `Time Tracker`. Click OK to create this project.

3. Right-click `Form1` in Solution Explorer and choose Delete from the context menu.

4. Right-click the Time Tracker project in the Solution Explorer window, choose Add from the context menu, and then choose the Add ➪ Windows Form submenu item. In the Add New Item – Time Tracker dialog box, give the new form a name of **Admin.vb** and then click the Add button.

5. Right-click the Time Tracker project in Solution Explorer and choose Properties from the context menu. In the Time Tracker Properties window, choose Admin in the combo box for Startup Object and then close this window.

6. Set the following properties for form Admin:

- ❑ Set `Size` to **760, 510**.

- ❑ Set `StartPosition` to CenterScreen.

- ❑ Set `Text` to **Time Tracker Administration**.

7. Drag a MenuStrip control from the Toolbox and drop it on your form. At the bottom of the IDE, right click on the MenuStrip1 control and select the `Insert Standard Items` context menu item to have the standard menus and menu items inserted.

8. You do not need the Tools menu so right-click the Tools menu and choose Delete.

9. In the Type Here box next to the Help menu enter the text **&View**.

10. In the Type Here box next to the View menu enter the text **&Action**.

11. Now click the View menu and drag it to the left so it is positioned after the Edit menu.

12. You need images that can represent Projects, Groups, Group Projects, Roles, and Users. Either create these images or find some icons or bitmaps that will represent these categories. Visual Studio 2005 contains a collection of bitmaps and icons that can be used in your menus and toolbars. In a default installation, these bitmaps and icons are located at `C:\Program Files\ Microsoft Visual Studio 8\Common7\ VS2005ImageLibrary`. You'll find that using icons, with their transparent backgrounds, in your menus and toolbars provides a better look. If you have a graphics tool, you can edit bitmaps and save them as icons for use in your application. If not, you can just use the bitmaps.

13. In the Type Here box under the View menu enter **&Projects**. In the Properties window, click the `Image` property and click the ellipse button to invoke the Select Resource dialog box. Click the Import button in the Select Resource dialog box and browse for and select a suitable icon or bitmap file for Projects. This should be a 16×16 pixel icon or bitmap. Click the Open button in the Open dialog box to have the image imported into the Select Resource dialog box. Then click OK to close the Select Resource dialog box.

14. In the Type Here box under the Projects menu item, enter the text **&Groups**. In the Properties window click the `Image` property and then click the ellipse button to invoke the Select Resource dialog box. Select an appropriate image to represent Groups and then click OK to assign the image to this menu item.

15. Repeat the previous step adding the menu items **Group Project&s**, **&Roles**, and **&Users**.

16. Click the Action menu and drag it to the left of the Help menu.

17. In the Type Here box under the Action menu, enter the text **&Add**. In the Properties window click the `Image` property and then click the ellipse button to invoke the Select Resource dialog box. Select an appropriate image to represent Add and then click OK to assign this image to the menu item.

18. Repeat the previous step adding menu items for **&Update** and **&Delete**.

19. You need only three menu items on the File menu: New, Menu Separator, and Exit. Right-click all the other menu items on the File menu and choose Delete from the context menu to delete them.

20. On the Edit menu you do not need the Redo menu item so you can delete it by right-clicking it and choosing Delete from the context menu. You can also assign an image for the Undo menu item if desired.

21. The only menu item you need on the Help menu is the About menu item. Delete the other menu items.

22. Now drag a ToolStrip control from the Toolbox and drop it on your form. Right click the ToolStrip1 control at the bottom of the IDE and select `Insert Standard Items` from the context menu to have the standard buttons inserted on the toolbar.

23. You'll need to get rid of the toolbar buttons that you do not need so right-click the following buttons and choose Delete from the context menu.

- ❏ Open
- ❏ Save
- ❏ Print
- ❏ Help

24. Now click the Add ToolStripButton icon on the toolbar to add a new button. The button is added to the left of this icon. Click the button and set the `Name` property to **UndoToolStripButton**. Now click the ellipse button on the `Image` property to invoke the Select Resource dialog box and then click the ellipse button. Locate an image for Undo, and then select Open in the Open dialog box and then OK in the Select Resource dialog box. Set the `ToolTipText` property to **Undo**.

25. Add another Separator bar on the toolbar by clicking the down arrow on the Add ToolStripButton icon on the toolbar and selecting Separator.

26. Add another button to the toolbar and set its `Name` property to **AddToolStripButton**, its `Image` property to the add image you used on the menu and its `ToolTipText` property to **Add**.

27. Add another button to the toolbar and set its `Name` property to **UpdateToolStripButton**, its `Image` property to the update image you used on the menu and its `ToolTipText` property to **Update**.

28. Add a final button to the toolbar and set its `Name` property to **DeleteToolStripButton**, its `Image` property to the delete image you used on the menu, and its `ToolTipText` property to **Delete**.

29. Drag a StatusStrip control from the Toolbox and drop it on your form. Now click the Add ToolStripStatusLabel icon on the StatusStrip to add a label to it. Click the label just added and set the following properties in the Properties window:

- ❏ Set `Name` to **ToolStripStatus**.
- ❏ Set `Spring` to True.
- ❏ Set `Text` to **Ready**.
- ❏ Set `TextAlign` to MiddleLeft.

30. Add another ToolStripStatusLabel to the StatusStrip and set the following properties:

❑ Set `Name` to **ToolStripDate**.

❑ Set `Text` to **date**.

31. At this point it would be a good idea to save your form. Click the Save All button on the toolbar.

32. You need some images for the Outlook style navigation pane. You can provide your own or use the ones that are available for download for this book from the Wrox Web site at `www.wrox.com/dynamic/books/download.aspx`. Drag an ImageList control from the Toolbox and drop it onto your form. Set the following properties of the ImageList control:

❑ Set `Name` to **imlNavigation**.

❑ Set `ColorDepth` to Depth32Bit.

❑ Ensure that `ImageSize` is set to **1, 32**.

33. Click the `Images` property and then click the ellipse button to invoke the Image Collection Editor dialog box. Add the following images from the images folder that you downloaded for this appendix or your own images:

❑ `Selection Bar Selected.bmp`

❑ `Selection Bar Unselected.bmp`

❑ `Selection Bar Highlighted.bmp`

34. Drag a Panel control from the Toolbox and drop it onto your form. Set the following properties for this control:

❑ Set `Name` to **pnlBackground**.

❑ Set `BackColor` to White.

❑ Set `Dock` to Fill.

❑ Set `Padding.All` to **3**.

35. Drag a SplitContainer control onto the pnlBackground panel and set the following properties:

❑ Set `BorderStyle` to FixedSingle.

❑ Set `SplitterDistance` to **167**.

36. Drag a Panel control onto Panel1 of the SplitContainer1 control and set the following properties:

❑ Set `Name` to **pnlNavigationBackground**.

❑ Set `Dock` to Fill.

37. Drag a Panel control onto the pnlNavigationBackground panel and set the following properties:

❑ Set `Name` to **pnlCurrentScreen**.

❑ Set `BackColor` to ControlDark.

❑ Set `Dock` to Top.

❑ Set `Size` to **165, 22**.

38. Now drag a Label control onto the pnlCurrentScreen panel and set the following properties:

- ❑ Set Name to **lblCurrentScreen**.
- ❑ Set Dock to Fill.
- ❑ Set Font to Arial, 12pt, Bold.
- ❑ Set ForeColor to White.
- ❑ Set Text to **Projects**.
- ❑ Set TextAlign to MiddleLeft.

39. Drag another Panel control from the Toolbox and drop it onto the pnlNavigationBackground panel. Set the following properties for this control:

- ❑ Set Name to **pnlNavigationTitle**.
- ❑ Set BackgroundImage to images\Titlebar.bmp.
- ❑ Set Dock to Top.
- ❑ Set Size to **165, 19**.

40. Drag a Label control from the Toolbox and drop it onto the pnlNavigationTitle panel. Set the following properties for this control:

- ❑ Set Name to **lblAllScreens**.
- ❑ Set BackColor to Transparent.
- ❑ Set Font to Tahoma, 8pt.
- ❑ Set Location to **4, 2**.
- ❑ Set Text to **All Projects**.
- ❑ Set TextAlign to MiddleLeft.

41. Drag a Panel control from the Toolbox and drop it onto the pnlNavigationBackground panel. Set the following properties for this control:

- ❑ Set Name to **pnlNavigationCurrentScreen**.
- ❑ Set Dock to Top.
- ❑ Set Size to **165, 26**.

42. Drag a PictureBox control from the Toolbox and drop it onto the pnlNavigationCurrentScreen panel. Set the following properties for this control:

- ❑ Set Name to **imgScreen**.
- ❑ Set BackColor to Transparent.
- ❑ Set Image to your Projects icon.
- ❑ Set Location to **16, 5**.
- ❑ Set Size to **16, 16**.

43. Drag a Label control from the Toolbox and drop it onto the pnlNavigationCurrentScreen panel. Set the following properties for this control:

- ❑ Set Name to **lblScreen**.
- ❑ Set Font to Tahoma, 8pt.
- ❑ Set Location to **40, 6**.
- ❑ Set Text to **Projects**.
- ❑ Set TextAlign to MiddleLeft.

44. Drag a Panel control from the Toolbox and drop it onto the pnlNavigationBackground panel. Set the following properties for this control:

- ❑ Set Name to **pnlNavigationCurrentView**.
- ❑ Set BackgroundImage to images\Titlebar.bmp.
- ❑ Set Dock to Top.
- ❑ Set Size to **165, 19**.

45. Drag a Label control from the Toolbox and drop it onto the pnlNavigationCurrentView panel. Set the following properties for this control:

- ❑ Set Name to **lblCurrentView**.
- ❑ Set BackColor to Transparent.
- ❑ Set Font to Tahoma, 8pt.
- ❑ Set Location to **4, 3**.
- ❑ Set Text to **Current View**.
- ❑ Set TextAlign to MiddleLeft.

46. Drag a Panel control from the Toolbox and drop it onto the pnlNavigationBackground panel. Set the following properties for this control:

- ❑ Set Name to **pnlNavigationCurrentViewOptions**.
- ❑ Set Dock to Top.
- ❑ Set Size to **165, 105**.

47. Drag a RadioButton control from the Toolbox and drop it onto the pnlNavigationCurrent-ViewOptions panel. Set the following properties for this control:

- ❑ Set Name to **optOption1**.
- ❑ Set FlatStyle to Flat.
- ❑ Set Location to **16, 8**.
- ❑ Set Text to **Name**.

48. Drag another RadioButton control from the Toolbox and drop it onto the pnlNavigationCurrent-ViewOptions panel. Set the following properties for this control:

- ❑ Set Name to **optOption2**.
- ❑ Set FlatStyle to Flat.

- ❑ Set `Location` to **16, 31**.
- ❑ Set `Text` to **Description**.

49. Drag another RadioButton control from the Toolbox and drop it onto the pnlNavigationCurrent-ViewOptions panel. Set the following properties for this control:

- ❑ Set `Name` to **optOption3**.
- ❑ Set `Checked` to True.
- ❑ Set `FlatStyle` to Flat.
- ❑ Set `Location` to **16, 56**.
- ❑ Set `Text` to **Sequence Number**.

50. Drag another RadioButton control from the Toolbox and drop it onto the pnlNavigationCurrent-ViewOptions panel. Set the following properties for this control:

- ❑ Set `Name` to **optOption4**.
- ❑ Set `FlatStyle` to Flat.
- ❑ Set `Location` to **16, 80**.
- ❑ Set `Text` to **Date**.

51. Drag a Panel control onto the pnlNavigationBackground panel. Set the following properties for this control:

- ❑ Set `Name` to **pnlSeparator**.
- ❑ Set `BackColor` to Control.
- ❑ Set `Dock` to Top.
- ❑ Set `Size` to **165, 2**.

52. Drag another Panel control onto the pnlNavigationBackground panel. Set the following properties for this control:

- ❑ Set `Name` to **pnlNavUsers**.
- ❑ Set `BackgroundImage` to `images\Selection Bar Unselected.bmp`.
- ❑ Set `Dock` to Bottom.
- ❑ Set `Size` to **165, 32**.

53. Drag a PictureBox control from the Toolbox and drop it onto the pnlNavUsers panel. Set the following properties for this control:

- ❑ Set `Name` to **imgUsers**.
- ❑ Set `BackColor` to Transparent.
- ❑ Set `Image` to your Users icon.
- ❑ Set `Location` to **16, 8**.
- ❑ Set `Size` to **16, 16**.

54. Drag a Label control from the Toolbox and drop it onto the pnlNavUsers panel. Set the following properties for this control:

- ❏ Set Name to **lblUsers**.
- ❏ Set BackColor to Transparent.
- ❏ Set Font to Tahoma, 8pt.
- ❏ Set Location to **36, 9**.
- ❏ Set Text to **Users**.
- ❏ Set TextAlign to MiddleLeft.

55. Drag another Panel control onto the pnlNavigationBackground panel .Set the following properties for this control:

- ❏ Set Name to **pnlNavRoles**.
- ❏ Set BackgroundImage to images\Selection Bar Unselected.bmp.
- ❏ Set Dock to Bottom.
- ❏ Set Size to **165, 32**.

56. Drag a PictureBox control from the Toolbox and drop it onto the pnlNavRoles panel. Set the following properties for this control:

- ❏ Set Name to **imgRoles**.
- ❏ Set BackColor to Transparent.
- ❏ Set Image to your Roles icon.
- ❏ Set Location to **16, 8**.
- ❏ Set Size to **16, 16**.

57. Drag a Label control from the Toolbox and drop it onto the pnlNavRoles panel. Set the following properties for this control:

- ❏ Set Name to **lblRoles**.
- ❏ Set BackColor to Transparent.
- ❏ Set Font to Tahoma, 8pt.
- ❏ Set Location to **36, 9**.
- ❏ Set Text to **Roles**.
- ❏ Set TextAlign to MiddleLeft.

58. Drag another Panel control onto the pnlNavigationBackground panel. Set the following properties for this control:

- ❏ Set Name to **pnlNavGroupProjects**.
- ❏ Set BackgroundImage to images\Selection Bar Unselected.bmp.
- ❏ Set Dock to Bottom.
- ❏ Set Size to **165, 32**.

59. Drag a PictureBox control from the Toolbox and drop it onto the pnlNavGroupProjects panel. Set the following properties for this control:

- ❑ Set Name to **imgGroupProjects**.
- ❑ Set BackColor to Transparent.
- ❑ Set Image to your Group Projects icon.
- ❑ Set Location to **16, 8**.
- ❑ Set Size to **16, 16**.

60. Drag a Label control from the Toolbox and drop it onto the pnlNavGroupProjects panel. Set the following properties for this control:

- ❑ Set Name to **lblGroupProjects**.
- ❑ Set BackColor to Transparent.
- ❑ Set Font to Tahoma, 8pt.
- ❑ Set Location to **36, 9**.
- ❑ Set Text to **Group Projects**.
- ❑ Set TextAlign to MiddleLeft.

61. Drag another Panel control onto the pnlNavigationBackground panel. Set the following properties for this control:

- ❑ Set Name to **pnlNavGroups**.
- ❑ Set BackgroundImage to images\Selection Bar Unselected.bmp.
- ❑ Set Dock to Bottom.
- ❑ Set Size to **165, 32**.

62. Drag a PictureBox control from the Toolbox and drop it onto the pnlNavGroups panel. Set the following properties for this control:

- ❑ Set Name to **imgGroups**.
- ❑ Set BackColor to Transparent.
- ❑ Set Image to your Groups icon.
- ❑ Set Location to **16, 8**.
- ❑ Set Size to **16, 16**.

63. Drag a Label control from the Toolbox and drop it onto the pnlNavGroups panel. Set the following properties for this control:

- ❑ Set Name to **lblGroups**.
- ❑ Set BackColor to Transparent.
- ❑ Set Font to Tahoma, 8pt.
- ❑ Set Location to **36, 9**.
- ❑ Set Text to **Groups**.
- ❑ Set TextAlign to MiddleLeft.

64. Drag another Panel control onto the pnlNavigationBackground panel. Set the following properties for this control:

- ❑ Set Name to **pnlNavProjects**.
- ❑ Set BackgroundImage to images\Selection Bar Selected.bmp.
- ❑ Set Dock to Bottom.
- ❑ Set Size to **165, 32**.

65. Drag a PictureBox control from the Toolbox and drop it onto the pnlNavProjects panel. Set the following properties for this control:

- ❑ Set Name to **imgProjects**.
- ❑ Set BackColor to Transparent.
- ❑ Set Image to your Projects icon.
- ❑ Set Location to **16, 8**.
- ❑ Set Size to **16, 16**.

66. Drag a Label control from the Toolbox and drop it onto the pnlNavProjects panel. Set the following properties for this control:

- ❑ Set Name to **lblProjects**.
- ❑ Set BackColor to Transparent.
- ❑ Set Font to Tahoma, 8pt.
- ❑ Set Location to **36, 9**.
- ❑ Set Text to **Projects**.
- ❑ Set TextAlign to MiddleLeft.

67. Drag one final Panel control onto the pnlNavigationBackground panel. Set the following properties for this control:

- ❑ Set Name to **pnlGrabbar**.
- ❑ Set BackgroundImage to images\Grabbar Background.bmp.
- ❑ Set Dock to Bottom.
- ❑ Set Size to **165, 7**.

68. Drag a PictureBox control from the Toolbox and drop it onto the pnlGrabbar panel. Set the following properties for this control:

- ❑ Set Name to **imgGrabbarHandle**.
- ❑ Set Image to images\Grabbar Handle.bmp.
- ❑ Set Location to **64, 0**.
- ❑ Set Size to **37, 7**.

69. Save your project again at this point by clicking the Save All button on the toolbar.

70. Drag a Panel control onto Panel2 of the SplitContainer1 control and set the following properties:

- ❑ Set Name to **pnlScreens**.
- ❑ Set Dock to Fill.

71. Drag a Panel control onto the pnlScreens panel. Set the following properties for this control:

- ❑ Set Name to **pnlProjects**.
- ❑ Set Size to 576, 403.
- ❑ Set Dock to Fill.

72. Drag a Panel control from the Toolbox and drop it onto pnlProjects. Set the following properties for this control:

- ❑ Set Name to **pnlProjectsTitle**.
- ❑ Set BackColor to ControlDark.
- ❑ Set Dock to Top.
- ❑ Set Size to **573, 22**.

73. Drag a Label control from the Toolbox and drop it onto pnlProjectsTitle. Set the following properties for this control:

- ❑ Set Dock to Fill.
- ❑ Set Font to Arial, 12pt, Bold.
- ❑ Set ForeColor to White.
- ❑ Set Text to **Projects**.
- ❑ Set TextAlign to MiddleLeft.

74. Drag a ListView control from the Toolbox and drop it onto pnlProjects. Set the following properties for this control:

- ❑ Set Name to **lvwProjects**.
- ❑ Set Anchor to Top, Bottom, Left, Right
- ❑ Click the ellipse button for the Columns property to invoke the ColumnHeader Collection Editor dialog box. Click the Add button to add a column and set the Text property to **Name** and the Width property to **150**.
- ❑ Click the Add button again to add another column and set the Text property to **Description** and the Width property to **200**.
- ❑ Click the Add button again and set the Text property to **Seq #**, TextAlign to Right, and Width to **50**.
- ❑ Click the Add button again and set the Text property to **Last Update Date** and Width to **125**. Then click OK to close the ColumnHeader Collection Editor dialog box.
- ❑ Set FullRowSelect to True.
- ❑ Set Location to **2, 28**.
- ❑ Set Size to **570, 200**.
- ❑ Set View to Details.

75. Drag a GroupBox control from the Toolbox and drop it onto pnlProjects. Set the following properties for this control:

- ❑ Set Anchor to Bottom, Left, Right.
- ❑ Set Location to **2, 234**.
- ❑ Set Size to **570, 168**.
- ❑ Set Text to **Project Details**.

76. Drag a Label control from the Toolbox and drop it onto GroupBox1. Set the following properties for this control:

- ❑ Set Location to **61, 18**.
- ❑ Set Text to **ID**.
- ❑ Set TextAlign to MiddleRight.

77. Drag a TextBox control from the Toolbox and drop it onto GroupBox1. Set the following properties for this control:

- ❑ Set Name to **txtProjectID**.
- ❑ Set Location to **82, 15**.
- ❑ Set ReadOnly to True.
- ❑ Set Size to **246, 20**.

78. Drag a Label control from the Toolbox and drop it onto GroupBox1. Set the following properties for this control:

- ❑ Set Location to **42, 47**.
- ❑ Set Text to **Name**.
- ❑ Set TextAlign to MiddleRight.

79. Drag a TextBox control from the Toolbox and drop it onto GroupBox1. Set the following properties for this control:

- ❑ Set Name to **txtProjectName**.
- ❑ Set Location to **82, 44**.
- ❑ Set Size to **176, 20**.

80. Drag a Label control from the Toolbox and drop it onto GroupBox1. Set the following properties for this control:

- ❑ Set Location to **15, 76**.
- ❑ Set Text to **Description**.
- ❑ Set TextAlign to MiddleRight.

81. Drag a TextBox control from the Toolbox and drop it onto GroupBox1. Set the following properties for this control:

- ❑ Set Name to **txtProjectDescription**.
- ❑ Set Anchor to Top, Left, Right.

❑ Set Location to **82, 73**.

❑ Set Size to **480, 20**.

82. Drag a Label control from the Toolbox and drop it onto GroupBox1. Set the following properties for this control:

❑ Set Location to **42, 105**.

❑ Set Text to **Seq #.**

❑ Set TextAlign to MiddleRight.

83. Drag a TextBox control from the Toolbox and drop it onto GroupBox1. Set the following properties for this control:

❑ Set Name to **txtSequenceNumber**.

❑ Set Location to **82, 102**.

❑ Set Size to **32, 20**.

84. Drag a Label control from the Toolbox and drop it onto GroupBox1. Set the following properties for this control:

❑ Set Location to **8, 134**.

❑ Set Text to **Update Date**.

❑ Set TextAlign to MiddleRight.

85. Drag a TextBox control from the Toolbox and drop it onto GroupBox1. Set the following properties for this control:

❑ Set Name to **txtProjectUpdateDate**.

❑ Set Location to **82, 131**.

❑ Set ReadOnly to True.

❑ Set Size to **134, 20**.

At this point, go ahead and run your project by clicking the Start button on the toolbar to get a sense of what your application will look like. You'll be able to resize the Outlook style navigation bar on the left, resize the form, and have the ListView control and GroupBox control resize with the form. Your form at this point should look similar to the one shown in Figure B-1. Stop your project and return to the Form Designer to add some more controls.

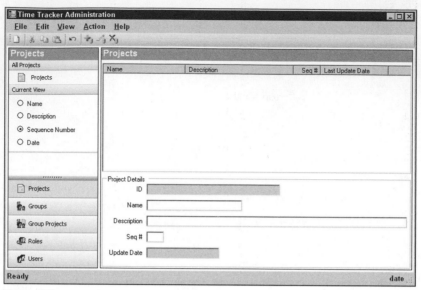

Figure B-1

86. Click pnlProjects and set the `Dock` property to None. Then set the `Location` property to **5000, 5000**. This will cause the Panel control to be undocked and moved out of the way for development on the next Panel control.

87. Drag a Panel control from the Toolbox and drop it onto the pnlScreens control. Set the following properties for this control:

❑ Set `Name` to **pnlGroups**.

❑ Set `Size` to **576, 427**.

❑ Set `Dock` to Fill.

88. Drag a Panel control from the Toolbox and drop it onto pnlGroups. Set the following properties for this control:

❑ Set `Name` to **pnlGroupsTitle**.

❑ Set `BackColor` to ControlDark.

❑ Set `Dock` to Top.

❑ Set `Size` to **573, 22**.

89. Drag a Label control from the Toolbox and drop it onto pnlGroupsTitle. Set the following properties for this control:

❑ Set `Dock` to Fill.

❑ Set `Font` to Arial, 12pt, Bold.

❑ Set `ForeColor` to White.

❑ Set `Text` to **Groups**.

❑ Set `TextAlign` to MiddleLeft.

90. Drag a ListView control from the Toolbox and drop it onto pnlGroups. Set the following properties for this control:

- ❑ Set Name to **lvwGroups**.
- ❑ Set Anchor to Top, Bottom, Left, Right.
- ❑ Click the ellipse button for the Columns property to invoke the ColumnHeader Collection Editor dialog box. Click the Add button to add a column and set the Text property to **Name** and the Width property to **150**.
- ❑ Click the Add button again to add another column, and set the Text property to **Description** and the Width property to **200**.
- ❑ Click the Add button again and set the Text property to **Last Update Date** and Width to **125**. Then click OK to close the ColumnHeader Collection Editor dialog box.
- ❑ Set FullRowSelect to True.
- ❑ Set Location to **2, 28**.
- ❑ Set Size to **570, 243**.
- ❑ Set View to Details.

91. Drag a GroupBox control from the Toolbox and drop it onto pnlGroups. Set the following properties for this control:

- ❑ Set Anchor to Bottom, Left, Right.
- ❑ Set Location to **2, 276**.
- ❑ Set Size to **570, 126**.
- ❑ Set Text to **Group Details**.

92. Drag a Label control from the Toolbox and drop it onto GroupBox2. Set the following properties for this control:

- ❑ Set Location to **61, 21**.
- ❑ Set Text to **ID**.
- ❑ Set TextAlign to MiddleRight.

93. Drag a TextBox control from the Toolbox and drop it onto GroupBox2. Set the following properties for this control:

- ❑ Set Name to **txtGroupID**.
- ❑ Set Location to **82, 18**.
- ❑ Set ReadOnly to True.
- ❑ Set Size to **246, 20**.

94. Drag a Label control from the Toolbox and drop it onto GroupBox2. Set the following properties for this control:

- ❑ Set Location to **42, 47**.
- ❑ Set Text to **Name**.
- ❑ Set TextAlign to MiddleRight.

95. Drag a TextBox control from the Toolbox and drop it onto GroupBox2. Set the following properties for this control:

- ❑ Set Name to **txtGroupName**.
- ❑ Set Location to **82, 44**.
- ❑ Set Size to **176, 20**.

96. Drag a Label control from the Toolbox and drop it onto GroupBox2. Set the following properties for this control:

- ❑ Set Location to **15, 73**.
- ❑ Set Text to **Description**.
- ❑ Set TextAlign to MiddleRight.

97. Drag a TextBox control from the Toolbox and drop it onto GroupBox2. Set the following properties for this control:

- ❑ Set Name to **txtGroupDescription**.
- ❑ Set Anchor to Top, Left, Right.
- ❑ Set Location to **82, 70**.
- ❑ Set Size to **480, 20**.

98. Drag a Label control from the Toolbox and drop it onto GroupBox2. Set the following properties for this control:

- ❑ Set Location to **8, 99**.
- ❑ Set Text to **Update Date**.
- ❑ Set TextAlign to MiddleRight.

99. Drag a TextBox control from the Toolbox and drop it onto GroupBox2. Set the following properties for this control:

- ❑ Set Name to **txtGroupUpdateDate**.
- ❑ Set Location to **82, 96**.
- ❑ Set ReadOnly to True.
- ❑ Set Size to **134, 20**.

100. Save your project again by clicking the Save All button on the toolbar.

Run your project to see how this screen will look. Your form at this point should look similar to the one shown in Figure B-2. You add code later to synchronize the navigation bar with the current screen. Stop your project and return to the Form Designer to add some more controls.

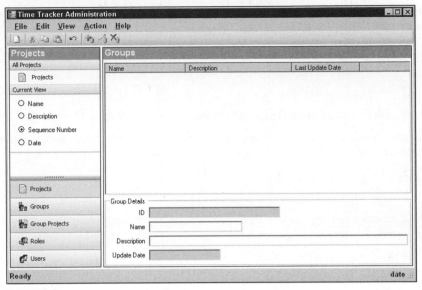

Figure B-2

101. Click pnlGroups and set the Dock property to None. Then set the Location property to **5000, 5000**. This causes the Panel control to be undocked and moved out of the way for development on the next Panel control

102. Drag a Panel control from the Toolbox and drop it onto the pnlScreens control. Set the following properties for this control:

- ❏ Set Name to **pnlGroupProjects**.
- ❏ Set Size to **576, 427**.
- ❏ Set Dock to Fill.

103. Drag a Panel control from the Toolbox and drop it onto pnlGroupProjects. Set the following properties for this control:

- ❏ Set Name to **pnlGroupProjectsTitle**.
- ❏ Set BackColor to ControlDark.
- ❏ Set Dock to Top.
- ❏ Set Size to **573, 22**.

104. Drag a Label control from the Toolbox and drop it onto pnlGroupProjectsTitle. Set the following properties for this control:

- ❏ Set Dock to Fill.
- ❏ Set Font to Arial, 12pt, Bold.
- ❏ Set ForeColor to White.
- ❏ Set Text to **Group Projects**.
- ❏ Set TextAlign to MiddleLeft.

105. Drag a GroupBox control from the Toolbox and drop it onto pnlGroupProjects. Set the following properties for this control:

- ❑ Set `Anchor` to Top, Bottom, Left, Right.
- ❑ Set `Location` to **2, 25**.
- ❑ Set `Size` to **570, 377**.
- ❑ Set `Text` to **Group Projects Details**.

106. Drag a Label control from the Toolbox and drop it onto GroupBox3. Set the following properties for this control:

- ❑ Set `Location` to **8, 16**.
- ❑ Set `Text` to **Groups**.

107. Drag a ComboBox control from the Toolbox and drop it onto GroupBox3. Set the following properties for this control:

- ❑ Set `Name` to **cboGroups**.
- ❑ Set `DropDownStyle` to DropDownList.
- ❑ Set `Location` to **8, 32**.
- ❑ Set `Size` to **240, 21**.

108. Drag a Label control from the Toolbox and drop it onto GroupBox3. Set the following properties for this control:

- ❑ Set `Location` to **8, 60**.
- ❑ Set `Text` to **Available Projects**.

109. Drag a ListBox control from the Toolbox and drop it onto GroupBox3. Set the following properties for this control:

- ❑ Set `Name` to **lstProjects**.
- ❑ Set `Anchor` to Top, Bottom, Left.
- ❑ Set `IntegralHeight` to False.
- ❑ Set `Location` to **8, 76**.
- ❑ Set `Size` to **240, 295**.

110. Drag a Label control from the Toolbox and drop it onto GroupBox3. Set the following properties for this control:

- ❑ Set `Location` to **255, 60**.
- ❑ Set `Text` to **Group Projects**.

111. Drag a ListBox control from the Toolbox and drop it onto GroupBox3. Set the following properties for this control:

- ❑ Set `Name` to **lstGroupProjects**.
- ❑ Set `AllowDrop` to True.
- ❑ Set `Anchor` to Top, Bottom, Left.

❏ Set IntegralHeight to False.

❏ Set Location to **255, 76**.

❏ Set Size to **240, 295**.

112. Save your project by clicking the Save All button on the toolbar.

Run your project to see how this screen will look. Your form at this point should look similar to the one shown in Figure B-3. Stop your project and return to the Form Designer to add some more controls.

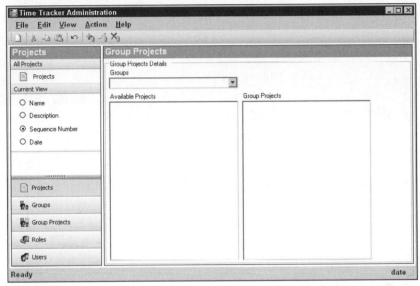

Figure B-3

113. Click pnlGroupProjects and set the Dock property to None and the Location property to **5000, 5000**.

114. Drag a Panel control from the Toolbox and drop it onto the pnlScreens control. Set the following properties for this control:

❏ Set Name to **pnlRoles**.

❏ Set Size to **576, 427**.

❏ Set Dock to Fill.

115. Drag a Panel control from the Toolbox and drop it onto pnlRoles. Set the following properties for this control:

❏ Set Name to **pnlRolesTitle**.

❏ Set BackColor to ControlDark.

❏ Set Dock to Top.

❏ Set Size to **573, 22**.

116. Drag a Label control from the Toolbox and drop it onto pnlRolesTitle. Set the following properties for this control:

- ❏ Set `Dock` to Fill.
- ❏ Set `Font` to Arial, 12pt, Bold.
- ❏ Set `ForeColor` to White.
- ❏ Set `Text` to **Roles**.
- ❏ Set `TextAlign` to MiddleLeft.

117. Drag a ListView control from the Toolbox and drop it onto pnlProjects. Set the following properties for this control:

- ❏ Set `Name` to **lvwRoles**.
- ❏ Set `Anchor` to Top, Bottom, Left, Right.
- ❏ Click the ellipse button for the `Columns` property to invoke the ColumnHeader Collection Editor dialog box. Click the Add button to add a column and set the `Text` property to **Name** and the `Width` property to **150**.
- ❏ Click the Add button again to add another column, and set the `Text` property to **Description** and the `Width` property to **200**.
- ❏ Click the Add button again and set the `Text` property to **Ranking**, `TextAlign` to Right, and `Width` to **60**.
- ❏ Click the Add button again and set the `Text` property to **Last Update Date** and `Width` to **125**. Then click OK to close the ColumnHeader Collection Editor dialog box.
- ❏ Set `FullRowSelect` to True.
- ❏ Set `Location` to **2, 28**.
- ❏ Set `Size` to **570, 217**.
- ❏ Set `View` to Details.

118. Drag a GroupBox control from the Toolbox and drop it onto pnlRoles. Set the following properties for this control:

- ❏ Set `Anchor` to Bottom, Left, Right.
- ❏ Set `Location` to **2, 250**.
- ❏ Set `Size` to **570, 152**.
- ❏ Set `Text` to **Role Details**.

119. Drag a Label control from the Toolbox and drop it onto GroupBox4. Set the following properties for this control:

- ❏ Set `Location` to **61, 21**.
- ❏ Set `Text` to **ID**.
- ❏ Set `TextAlign` to MiddleRight.

120. Drag a TextBox control from the Toolbox and drop it onto GroupBox4. Set the following properties for this control:

- ❏ Set Name to **txtRoleID**.
- ❏ Set Location to **82, 18**.
- ❏ Set ReadOnly to True.
- ❏ Set Size to **246, 20**.

121. Drag a Label control from the Toolbox and drop it onto GroupBox4. Set the following properties for this control:

- ❏ Set Location to **42, 47**.
- ❏ Set Text to **Name**.
- ❏ Set TextAlign to MiddleRight.

122. Drag a TextBox control from the Toolbox and drop it onto GroupBox4. Set the following properties for this control:

- ❏ Set Name to **txtRoleName**.
- ❏ Set Location to **82, 44**.
- ❏ Set Size to **176, 20**.

123. Drag a Label control from the Toolbox and drop it onto GroupBox4. Set the following properties for this control:

- ❏ Set Location to **15, 73**.
- ❏ Set Text to **Description**.
- ❏ Set TextAlign to MiddleRight.

124. Drag a TextBox control from the Toolbox and drop it onto GroupBox4. Set the following properties for this control:

- ❏ Set Name to **txtRoleDescription**.
- ❏ Set Anchor to Top, Left, Right.
- ❏ Set Location to **82, 70**.
- ❏ Set Size to **480, 20**.

125. Drag a Label control from the Toolbox and drop it onto GroupBox4. Set the following properties for this control:

- ❏ Set Location to **30, 99**.
- ❏ Set Text to **Ranking**.
- ❏ Set TextAlign to MiddleRight.

126. Drag a TextBox control from the Toolbox and drop it onto GroupBox4. Set the following properties for this control:

- ❏ Set Name to **txtRanking**.
- ❏ Set Location to **82, 96**.
- ❏ Set Size to **32, 20**.

127. Drag a Label control from the Toolbox and drop it onto GroupBox4. Set the following properties for this control:

- ❏ Set Location to **8, 125**.
- ❏ Set Text to **Update Date**.
- ❏ Set TextAlign to MiddleRight.

128. Drag a TextBox control from the Toolbox and drop it onto GroupBox4. Set the following properties for this control:

- ❏ Set Name to **txtRoleUpdateDate**.
- ❏ Set Location to **82, 122**.
- ❏ Set ReadOnly to True.
- ❏ Set Size to **134, 20**.

129. Save your project by clicking the Save All button on the toolbar.

Run your project to see how this screen will look. Your form at this point should look similar to the one shown in Figure B-4. Stop your project and return to the Form Designer to add some more controls.

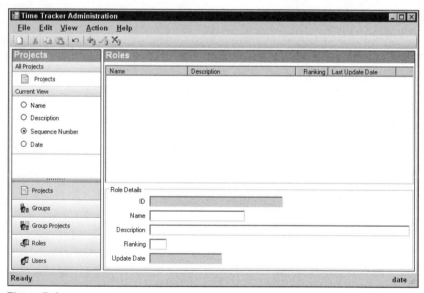

Figure B-4

130. Click pnlRoles and set the Dock property to None and the Location property to **5000, 5000**.

131. Drag a Panel control from the Toolbox and drop it onto the pnlScreens control. Set the following properties for this control:

- ❏ Set Name to **pnlUsers**.
- ❏ Set Size to **576, 427**.
- ❏ Set Dock to Fill.

132. Drag a Panel control from the Toolbox and drop it onto pnlUsers. Set the following properties for this control:

❏ Set `Name` to **pnlUsersTitle**.

❏ Set `BackColor` to ControlDark.

❏ Set `Dock` to Top.

❏ Set `Size` to **573, 22**.

133. Drag a Label control from the Toolbox and drop it onto pnlUsersTitle. Set the following properties for this control:

❏ Set `Dock` to Fill.

❏ Set `Font` to Arial, 12pt, Bold.

❏ Set `ForeColor` to White.

❏ Set `Text` to **Users**.

❏ Set `TextAlign` to MiddleLeft.

134. Drag a ListView control from the Toolbox and drop it onto pnlUsers. Set the following properties for this control:

❏ Set `Name` to **lvwUsers**.

❏ Set `Anchor` to Top, Bottom, Left, Right.

❏ Click the ellipse button for the `Columns` property to invoke the ColumnHeader Collection Editor dialog box. Click the Add button to add a column, set the `Text` property to **Login**, and set the `Width` property to **75**.

❏ Click the Add button again to add another column, set the `Text` property to **Name**, and set the `Width` property to **150**.

❏ Click the Add button again and set the `Text` property to **Email** and the `Width` property to **125**.

❏ Click the Add button again and set the `Text` property to **Phone** and the `Width` property to **100**.

❏ Click the Add button again and set the `Text` property to **Status** and `Width` to **100**. Then click OK to close the ColumnHeader Collection Editor dialog box.

❏ Set `FullRowSelect` to True.

❏ Set `Location` to **2, 28**.

❏ Set `Size` to **570, 190**.

❏ Set `View` to Details.

135. Drag a GroupBox control from the Toolbox and drop it onto pnlUsers. Set the following properties for this control:

❏ Set `Anchor` to Bottom, Left, Right.

❏ Set `Location` to **2, 223**.

❏ Set `Size` to **570, 179**.

❏ Set `Text` to **User Details**.

136. Drag a Label control from the Toolbox and drop it onto GroupBox5. Set the following properties for this control:

- ❑ Set Location to **61, 21**.
- ❑ Set Text to **ID**.
- ❑ Set TextAlign to MiddleRight.

137. Drag a TextBox control from the Toolbox and drop it onto GroupBox5. Set the following properties for this control:

- ❑ Set Name to **txtUserID**.
- ❑ Set Location to **82, 18**.
- ❑ Set ReadOnly to True.
- ❑ Set Size to **246, 20**.

138. Drag a RadioButton control from the Toolbox and drop it onto GroupBox5. Set the following properties for this control:

- ❑ Set Name to **optStatusActive**.
- ❑ Set Checked to True.
- ❑ Set Location to **392, 20**.
- ❑ Set Text to **Active**.

139. Drag a RadioButton control from the Toolbox and drop it onto GroupBox5. Set the following properties for this control:

- ❑ Set Name to **optStatusSuspended**.
- ❑ Set Location to **448, 20**.
- ❑ Set Text to **Suspended**.

140. Drag a Label control from the Toolbox and drop it onto GroupBox5. Set the following properties for this control:

- ❑ Set Location to **44, 47**.
- ❑ Set Text to **Login**.
- ❑ Set TextAlign to MiddleRight.

141. Drag a TextBox control from the Toolbox and drop it onto GroupBox5. Set the following properties for this control:

- ❑ Set Name to **txtLogin**.
- ❑ Set Location to **82, 44**.
- ❑ Set Size to **100, 20**.

142. Drag a Label control from the Toolbox and drop it onto GroupBox5. Set the following properties for this control:

- ❑ Set Location to **262, 47**.
- ❑ Set Text to **Password**.
- ❑ Set TextAlign to MiddleRight.

143. Drag a TextBox control from the Toolbox and drop it onto GroupBox5. Set the following properties for this control:

- ❑ Set Name to **txtPassword**.
- ❑ Set Location to **322, 44**.
- ❑ Set PasswordChar to *.
- ❑ Set Size to **100, 20**.

144. Drag a Label control from the Toolbox and drop it onto GroupBox5. Set the following properties for this control:

- ❑ Set Location to **17, 73**.
- ❑ Set Text to **First Name**.
- ❑ Set TextAlign to MiddleRight.

145. Drag a TextBox control from the Toolbox and drop it onto GroupBox5. Set the following properties for this control:

- ❑ Set Name to **txtFirstName**.
- ❑ Set Location to **82, 70**.
- ❑ Set Size to **100, 20**.

146. Drag a Label control from the Toolbox and drop it onto GroupBox5. Set the following properties for this control:

- ❑ Set Location to **257, 73**.
- ❑ Set Text to **Last Name**.
- ❑ Set TextAlign to MiddleRight.

147. Drag a TextBox control from the Toolbox and drop it onto GroupBox5. Set the following properties for this control:

- ❑ Set Name to **txtLastName**.
- ❑ Set Location to **322, 70**.
- ❑ Set Size to **100, 20**.

148. Drag a Label control from the Toolbox and drop it onto GroupBox5. Set the following properties for this control:

- ❑ Set Location to **43, 99**.
- ❑ Set Text to **Email**.
- ❑ Set TextAlign to MiddleRight.

149. Drag a TextBox control from the Toolbox and drop it onto GroupBox5. Set the following properties for this control:

- ❑ Set Name to **txtEmail**.
- ❑ Set Location to **82, 96**.
- ❑ Set Size to **165, 20**.

150. Drag a Label control from the Toolbox and drop it onto GroupBox5. Set the following properties for this control:

- ❏ Set Location to **279, 99**.
- ❏ Set Text to **Phone**.
- ❏ Set TextAlign to MiddleRight.

151. Drag a TextBox control from the Toolbox and drop it onto GroupBox5. Set the following properties for this control:

- ❏ Set Name to **txtPhone**.
- ❏ Set Location to **322, 96**.
- ❏ Set Size to **100, 20**.

152. Drag a Label control from the Toolbox and drop it onto GroupBox5. Set the following properties for this control:

- ❏ Set Location to **40, 125**.
- ❏ Set Text to **Group**.
- ❏ Set TextAlign to MiddleRight.

153. Drag a ComboBox control from the Toolbox and drop it onto GroupBox5. Set the following properties for this control:

- ❏ Set Name to **cboUserGroup**.
- ❏ Set DropDownStyle to DropDownList.
- ❏ Set Location to **82, 122**.
- ❏ Set Size to **165, 21**.

154. Drag a Label control from the Toolbox and drop it onto GroupBox5. Set the following properties for this control:

- ❏ Set Location to **267, 125**.
- ❏ Set Text to **Manager**.
- ❏ Set TextAlign to MiddleRight.

155. Drag a ComboBox control from the Toolbox and drop it onto GroupBox5. Set the following properties for this control:

- ❏ Set Name to **cboUserManager**.
- ❏ Set DropDownStyle to DropDownList.
- ❏ Set Location to **322, 122**.
- ❏ Set Size to **165, 21**.

156. Drag a Label control from the Toolbox and drop it onto GroupBox5. Set the following properties for this control:

- ❏ Set Location to **48, 151**.
- ❏ Set Text to **Role**.
- ❏ Set TextAlign to MiddleRight.

157. Drag a ComboBox control from the Toolbox and drop it onto GroupBox5. Set the following properties for this control:

- ❑ Set `Name` to **cboUserRole**.
- ❑ Set `DropDownStyle` to DropDownList.
- ❑ Set `Location` to **83, 148**.
- ❑ Set `Size` to **165, 21**.

158. Drag a Label control from the Toolbox and drop it onto GroupBox5. Set the following properties for this control:

- ❑ Set `Location` to **248, 151**.
- ❑ Set `Text` to **Update Date**.
- ❑ Set `TextAlign` to MiddleRight.

159. Drag a TextBox control from the Toolbox and drop it onto GroupBox5. Set the following properties for this control:

- ❑ Set `Name` to **txtUserUpdateDate**.
- ❑ Set `Location` to **322, 148**.
- ❑ Set `ReadOnly` to True.
- ❑ Set `Size` to **134, 20**.

160. Save your project by clicking the Save All button on the toolbar.

Run your project to see how this screen will look. Your form at this point should look similar to the one shown in Figure B-5. Stop your project and return to the Form Designer to rearrange some controls.

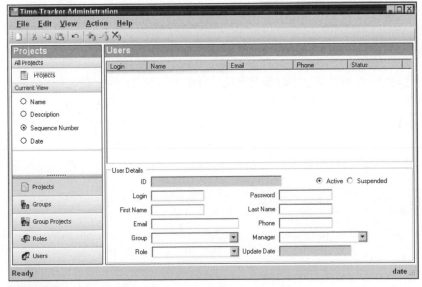

Figure B-5

161. Click pnlUsers and set the Dock property to None and the Location property to **5000, 5000**.

162. Select pnlProjects in the Properties window and set its Dock property to Fill.

TimeSheet form

The TimeSheet form will be used by users to enter time spent on various projects and by managers to approve timesheets.

To create this form:

1. Right-click the Time Tracker project in Solution Explorer, choose Add from the context menu, and then choose Windows Form. In the Add New Item – Time Tracker dialog box, enter a form name of **TimeSheet.vb** and then click the Add button.

2. Set the following properties for the form:

- ❑ Set Size to **624, 372**.
- ❑ Set StartPosition to CenterScreen.
- ❑ Set Text to **Time Tracker Time Sheet**.

3. Drag a MenuStrip control from the Toolbox and drop it on your form. At the bottom of the IDE, right click MenuStrip1 and select Insert Standard Items from the context menu to have the standard menus and menu items inserted.

4. You do not need the Tools menu so right-click the Tools menu and choose Delete from the context menu.

5. In the Type Here box next to the Help menu, enter the text **&View**.

6. In the Type Here box next to the View menu, enter the text **&Reports**.

7. Now click the View menu and drag it to the left so it is positioned after the Edit menu.

8. In the Type Here box under the View menu, enter the text **&My Time Sheet**.

9. In the next Type Here box down, enter the text **&Employee Time Sheets**.

10. Now click the Reports menu and drag it immediately to the left of the Help menu.

11. In the box below the &Reports menu, enter the text **Timesheets &Due**.

12. In the next Type Here box, enter the text **Timesheets &Submitted**.

13. In the next Type Here box, enter a dash (-) character.

14. In the next Type Here box, enter the text **Timesheets &MTD**.

15. In the next Type Here box, enter the text **Timesheets &QTD**.

16. In the next box, enter the text **Timesheets &YTD**.

17. On the Edit menu you do not need the Redo menu item so you can delete it by right-clicking it and choosing Delete from the context menu. You can also assign an image for the Undo menu item if desired.

18. The only menu item you need on the Help menu is the About menu item. Delete the other menu items.

19. Now drag a ToolStrip control from the Toolbox and drop it on your form. Right click on ToolStrip1 at the bottom of the IDE and select `Insert Standard Items` from the context menu to have the standard buttons inserted on the toolbar.

20. You'll need to get rid of the toolbar buttons that you do not need so right-click the following buttons and choose Delete from the context menu.

- ❑ Open
- ❑ Save
- ❑ Print
- ❑ Help

21. Now click the Add ToolStripButton icon on the toolbar to add a new button. The button is added to the left of this icon. Click the button and set the `Name` property to **UndoToolStripButton**. Now click the ellipse button on the `Image` property to invoke the Select Resource dialog box and then click the ellipse button in this dialog box. Locate an image for Undo, select Open in the Open dialog box, and then click OK in the Select Resource dialog box. Set the `ToolTipText` property to **Undo.**

22. Drag a StatusStrip control from the Toolbox and drop it on your form. Now click the Add ToolStripStatusLabel icon on the StatusStrip to add a label to it. Click the label just added and set the following properties in the Properties window:

- ❑ Set `Name` to **ToolStripStatus**.
- ❑ Set `Spring` to True.
- ❑ Set `Text` to **Ready**.
- ❑ Set `TextAlign` to MiddleLeft.

23. Add another ToolStripStatusLabel to the StatusStrip and set the following properties:

- ❑ Set `Name` to **ToolStripDate**.
- ❑ Set `Text` to **date**.

24. Drag an ImageList control and drop it on your form; it will dock at the bottom of the designer. Set the following properties:

- ❑ Set `ColorDepth` to Depth32Bit.
- ❑ Set `ImageSize` to **16, 16**.

25. Click on the ellipse button on the `Images` property to invoke the Images Collection Editor. Add two images, an unlocked icon and a locked icon. Then click OK to close the Images Collection Editor.

26. You are now ready to start adding some controls. Drag a Panel control from the Toolbox and drop it onto your form. Set its properties as follows:

- ❑ Set `Name` to **pnlEmployee**.
- ❑ Set `BackColor` to ControlDark.
- ❑ Set `Size` to **616, 22**.
- ❑ Set `Dock` to Top.

27. Drag a Label control from the Toolbox and drop it onto pnlEmployee. Set its properties as follows:

- ❏ Set Name to **lblEmployee**.
- ❏ Set ForeColor to White.
- ❏ Set Location to **0, 4**.
- ❏ Set Text to **Timesheet for**.
- ❏ Set TextAlign to MiddleLeft.

28. Drag a Button control from the Toolbox and drop it onto pnlEmployee. Set its properties as follows:

- ❏ Set Name to **btnSave**.
- ❏ Set Anchor to Top, Right.
- ❏ Set FlatStyle to Flat.
- ❏ Set ForeColor to White.
- ❏ Set Location to **232, 0**.
- ❏ Set Size to **75, 22**.
- ❏ Set Text to **Save**.

29. Drag another Button control from the Toolbox and drop it onto pnlEmployee. Set its properties as follows:

- ❏ Set Name to **btnSubmit**.
- ❏ Set Anchor to Top, Right.
- ❏ Set FlatStyle to Flat.
- ❏ Set ForeColor to White.
- ❏ Set Location to **312, 0**.
- ❏ Set Size to **75, 22**.
- ❏ Set Text to **Submit**.

30. Drag a PictureBox control from the Toolbox and drop it onto pnlEmployee. Set its properties as follows:

- ❏ Set Name to **imgStatus**.
- ❏ Set Anchor to Top, Right.
- ❏ Set Image to a 16 × 16–pixel image of an unlocked lock.
- ❏ Set Location to **398, 2**.
- ❏ Set Size to **16, 16**.

31. Drag a Label control from the Toolbox and drop it onto pnlEmployee. Set its properties as follows:

- ❏ Set Anchor to Top, Right.
- ❏ Set ForeColor to White.
- ❏ Set Location to **424, 4**.

    ❑   Set Text to **Week Ending**.

    ❑   Set TextAlign to MiddleRight.

32. Drag a ComboBox control from the Toolbox and drop it onto pnlEmployee. Set its properties as follows:

    ❑   Set Name to **cboWeekEnding**.

    ❑   Set Anchor to Top, Right.

    ❑   Set DropDownStyle to DropDownList.

    ❑   Set Location to **496, 1**.

    ❑   Set Size to **121, 21**.

33. Drag a DataGridView control from the Toolbox and drop it onto your form. Set its properties as follows:

    ❑   Set Name to **grdTimeSheet**.

    ❑   Set Anchor to Top, Bottom, Left, Right.

    ❑   Set BorderStyle to Fixed3D.

    ❑   Set Location to **0, 72**.

    ❑   Set Size to **616, 250**.

34. Right-click the Time Tracker project in the Solution Explorer window and choose Properties from the context menu. In the Startup Object combo box, select TimeSheet, and click the X in the upper-right corner to close the Properties page.

35. Save your project by clicking the Save All button on the toolbar.

Run your project to get a feel for how this form will look. It should look similar to the one shown in Figure B-6. When you are done, stop your project and return to the Form Designer so you can add controls.

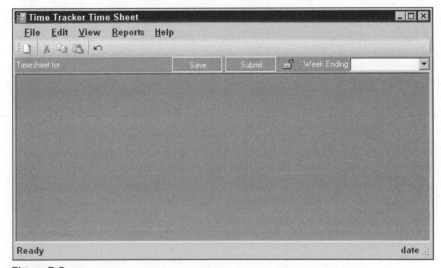

Figure B-6

36. Click pnlEmployee and set the `Dock` property to None and `Location` to **5000, 5000**.

37. Drag a Panel control from the Toolbox and drop it onto your form. Set its properties as follows:

- ❑ Set `Name` to **pnlManager**.
- ❑ Set `BackColor` to ControlDark.
- ❑ Set `Size` to **616, 22**.
- ❑ Set `Dock` to Top.

38. Drag a Label control from the Toolbox and drop it onto pnlManager. Set its properties as follows:

- ❑ Set `ForeColor` to White.
- ❑ Set `Location` to **0, 4**.
- ❑ Set `Text` to **Employee**.
- ❑ Set `TextAlign` to MiddleLeftt.

39. Drag a ComboBox control from the Toolbox and drop it onto pnlManager. Set its properties as follows:

- ❑ Set `Name` to **cboEmployee**.
- ❑ Set `DropDownStyle` to DropDownList.
- ❑ Set `Location` to **58, 1**.
- ❑ Set `Size` to **136, 21**.

40. Drag a Label control from the Toolbox and drop it onto pnlManager. Set its properties as follows:

- ❑ Set `ForeColor` to White.
- ❑ Set `Location` to **200, 4**.
- ❑ Set `Text` to **Week Ending**.
- ❑ Set `TextAlign` to MiddleRight.

41. Drag a ComboBox control from the Toolbox and drop it onto pnlManager. Set its properties as follows:

- ❑ Set `Name` to **cboEmployeeWeekEnding**.
- ❑ Set `DropDownStyle` to DropDownList.
- ❑ Set `Location` to **282, 1**.
- ❑ Set `Size` to **136, 21**.

42. Drag a Button control from the Toolbox and drop it onto pnlManager. Set its properties as follows:

- ❑ Set `Name` to **btnApprove**.
- ❑ Set `FlatStyle` to Flat.
- ❑ Set `ForeColor` to White.
- ❑ Set `Location` to **440, 0**.

❑   Set Size to **75, 22**.

❑   Set Text to **Approve**.

43.   Save your project by clicking the Save All button on the toolbar.

Run your project to get a feel for how this form will look. It should currently look similar to the one shown in Figure B-7. When you are done, stop your project and return to the Form Designer so you can rearrange some controls.

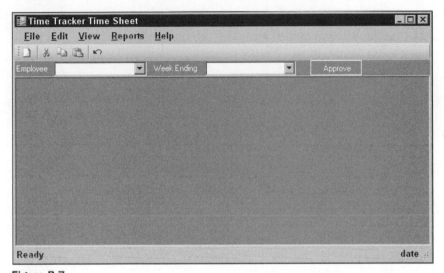

Figure B-7

44.   Click pnlManager and set its Dock property to None and its Location property to **5000, 5000**.

45.   In the Properties window, select pnlEmployee and set its Dock property to Top.

Login form

The Login form will be used by all users to log into the Time Tracker application.

To create this form:

1.   Right-click the Time Tracker project in Solution Explorer, choose Add from the context menu, and then choose Windows Form. In the Add New Item – Time Tracker dialog box, enter a form name of **Login.vb** and then click the Add button.

2.   Set the following properties for the form:

❑   Set FormBorderStyle to FixedDialog.

❑   Set MaximizeBox to False.

❑   Set MinimizeBox to False.

- ❑ Set Size to **272, 144**.
- ❑ Set StartPosition to CenterScreen.
- ❑ Set Text to **Time Tracker Login**.

3. Drag a Label control from the Toolbox and drop it onto your form. Set its properties as follows:

- ❑ Set Location to **24, 27**.
- ❑ Set Text to **User Name**.

4. Drag a TextBox control from the Toolbox and drop it onto your form. Set its properties as follows:

- ❑ Set Name to **txtLoginName**.
- ❑ Set Location to **96, 24**.
- ❑ Set Size to **155, 20**.

5. Drag a Label control from the Toolbox and drop it onto your form. Set its properties as follows:

- ❑ Set Location to **24, 51**.
- ❑ Set Text to **Password**.

6. Drag a TextBox control from the Toolbox and drop it onto your form. Set its properties as follows:

- ❑ Set Name to **txtPassword**.
- ❑ Set Location to **96, 48**.
- ❑ Set PasswordChar to *****.
- ❑ Set Size to **155, 20**.

7. Drag a Button control from the Toolbox and drop it onto your form. Set its properties as follows:

- ❑ Set Name to **btnOK**.
- ❑ Set DialogResult to OK.
- ❑ Set Location to **96, 80**.
- ❑ Set Size to **75, 23**.
- ❑ Set Text to **OK**.

8. Drag a Button control from the Toolbox and drop it onto your form. Set its properties as follows:

- ❑ Set Name to **btnCancel**.
- ❑ Set DialogResult to Cancel.
- ❑ Set Location to **176, 80**.
- ❑ Set Size to **75, 23**.
- ❑ Set Text to **Cancel**.

9. Save your project by clicking the Save All button on the toolbar.

Your completed Login form in the designer should look similar to the one shown in Figure B-8.

Figure B-8

About form

You now want to add an About form that provides general information about your application. This form will be accessible when the user clicks the Help menu and chooses the About menu item.

To create this form:

1. Right-click the Time Tracker project in Solution Explorer, choose Add from the context menu, and then choose Windows Form. In the Add New Item – Time Tracker dialog box, enter a form name of **About.vb** and then click the Add button.

2. Set the following properties for the About form:

   ❑ Set `FormBorderStyle` to FixedDialog.

   ❑ Set `MaximizeBox` to False.

   ❑ Set `MinimizeBox` to False.

   ❑ Set `Size` to **360, 216**.

   ❑ Set `StartPosition` to CenterParent.

   ❑ Set `Text` to **About**.

3. Drag a PictureBox control from the Toolbox onto the form. Set its properties as follows:

   ❑ Set `Name` to **imgApplicationIcon**.

   ❑ Set `BorderStyle` to Fixed3D.

   ❑ Set `Location` to **12, 12**.

   ❑ Set `Size` to **32, 32**.

   ❑ Set `SizeMode` to StretchImage.

4. Drag a Label control from the Toolbox onto the form. Set its properties as follows:

   ❑ Set `Name` to **lblTitle**.

   ❑ Click the button for the `Font` property to invoke the Font dialog box. In the Font dialog box, set the Font style to Bold and the Size to 12. Then click OK to close this dialog box.

   ❑ Set `Location` to **68, 12**.

   ❑ Set `Text` to **Application Title**.

5. Drag a Label control from the Toolbox onto the form. Set its properties as follows:

- ❑ Set Name to **lblVersion**.
- ❑ Set Location to **68, 48**.
- ❑ Set Text to **Application Version**.

6. Drag a Label control from the Toolbox onto the form. Set its properties as follows:

- ❑ Set Name to **lblCopyright**.
- ❑ Set Location to **68, 72**.
- ❑ Set Text to **Application Copyright**.

7. Drag a Label control from the Toolbox onto the form. Set its properties as follows:

- ❑ Set Name to **lblDescription**.
- ❑ Set AutoSize to False.
- ❑ Set Location to **68, 96**.
- ❑ Set Size to **274, 58**.
- ❑ Set Text to **Application Description**.

8. Drag a Button control from the Toolbox onto the form. Set its properties as follows:

- ❑ Set Name to **btnOK**.
- ❑ Set DialogResult to OK.
- ❑ Set Location to **272, 160**.
- ❑ Set Size to **75, 23**.
- ❑ Set Text to **OK**.

9. Save your project by clicking the Save All button on the toolbar.

Your completed About form in the Designer should look similar to the one shown in Figure B-9.

Figure B-9

MainEntry class

As you're developing your application, you'll want to display and work with various forms in your project. In the end, you'll want to display the Login form and then perform some logic to determine which form should be displayed after that. To that end, you want to add a class to your project with a procedure that will be called at startup. This procedure will determine which form should be displayed.

To add this class:

1. Right-click the Time Tracker project in the Solution Explorer window, select Add from the context menu, and then select the Class submenu item to invoke the Add New Item – Time Tracker dialog box. In the Name field, enter a name of **MainEntry.vb**, and click the Add button to close this dialog box and have the class added to your project.

2. You need a Main procedure to be executed when your project starts, so add this procedure in the module and add the following code to this procedure:

```
Public Shared Sub Main()
    Dim objAdmin As New Admin
    objAdmin.ShowDialog()
    objAdmin.Dispose()
    objAdmin = Nothing
End Sub
```

3. Right-click the Time Tracker project in the Solution Explorer window and choose Properties from the context menu to invoke the Time Tracker Property Pages. Uncheck the Enable application framework checkbox and then select MainEntry in the Startup Object combo box. Leave the Property Pages open as you'll be adding some more information in the next section.

AssemblyInfo file

You want to set some values for the assembly as these values will be read and displayed in your About form.

To set these values:

1. In the Property pages, click the Assembly Information button to invoke the Assembly Information dialog box.

2. Set the values for the assembly attributes as follows:

   ❑ Set Title to **Time Tracker**.

   ❑ Set Description to **This application allows users to enter time spent on various projects. The time spent on the various projects is tracked and displayable in report form.**

   ❑ Set Company to **Wrox**.

   ❑ Set Product to **Time Tracker**.

   ❑ Set Copyright to **Copyright (c) 2005 Wrox. All rights reserved.**.

3. Click OK to close the Assembly Information dialog box and then click the Save All button on the toolbar to save your changes. Leave the Property Pages open as you'll be adding some more information in the next section.

App.config file

In Chapters 2 through 5, you see how to use string constants in your code to provide a connection string to be used when making a database connection. You also see how to prompt the user for database information and then build a dynamic connection string using that information when you work through the exercises in Chapter 5. Now it's time to see how you can provide this information in an application configuration file that enables you to change this information after your program has been compiled.

To add your custom settings:

1. Click the Settings tab on the side of the Property pages.

2. In the Name column, enter a name of **Provider** and in the Value column enter a value of **Microsoft.Jet.OLEDB.4.0**.

3. In the next row, enter a name of **DataSource** in the Name column and a value of **C:\Chapter 6\ ProjectTimeTracker.mdb** in the Value column.

4. In the next row, enter a name of **InitialCatalog** and the text string **Nothing** in the value column.

5. In the next row, enter a name of **UserID** and the text string **Nothing** in the value column.

6. In the next row, enter a name of **Password** and the text string **Nothing** in the value column.

7. Click the Save All button on the toolbar to save your changes and then close the Property pages by clicking the X in the upper-right corner.

WDABase class

As you work through the chapters up through Chapter 9, you access various databases. In Chapter 10, you build a business logic component and a data access component. To aid in the transition to these components in Chapter 10, it makes sense to encapsulate the core database functionality in a class.

To create the WDABase class:

1. Right-click the Time Tracker project in the Solution Explorer window, select Add from the context menu, and then select Class to invoke the Add New Item – Time Tracker dialog box. In the Name field, enter a name of **WDABase.vb** and then click the Add button to add this class to your project.

2. Right-click the Time Tracker project in the Solution Explorer window, select Add Reference from the context menu. Scroll down the list on the .NET tab of the Add Reference dialog box until you find the System.Data namespace. Select it and then click the OK button to have this reference added to your project.

3. You need to be able to access the OleDb namespace to access your database. To that end, add the following Imports statements at the top of this class:

```
Imports System.Data
Imports System.Data.OleDb
```

4. Implement a disposable interface in this class that can be called from the client using this class. In the `Dispose` method, you perform the necessary code to clean up the resources used in this class. Add the `Implements IDisposable` statement and press Enter. When you do, the procedure `Dispose` will be automatically added to your class. You don't want to enter any code in that procedure just yet.

```
Public Class WDABase
    Implements IDisposable
```

5. Add some variable declarations that are available to all procedures in the class and available to classes that instantiate this class. Add the following variables above the `Dispose` procedure:

```
'Class level variables that are available to classes that instantiate me
Public SQL As String

Public Connection As OleDbConnection
Public Command As OleDbCommand
Public DataAdapter As OleDbDataAdapter
Public DataReader As OleDbDataReader
```

6. When this class is instantiated, your code will read the connection string values from your application configuration file and initialize the connection object. To do this, add a constructor for this class. Add this procedure above the `Dispose` procedure and add the following code to it:

```
Public Sub New()
    'Build the SQL connection string and initialize the Connection object
    Connection - New OleDbConnection( _
    "Provider=" & My.Settings.Provider & ";" & _
    "Data Source=" & My.Settings.DataSource & ";")
End Sub
```

7. Now add some code to the `Dispose` procedure to dispose of the objects used in this class. Add the following code to the `Dispose` procedure:

```
Private Overloads Sub Dispose(ByVal disposing As Boolean)
    If Not Me.disposed Then
        If disposing Then
            ' TODO: put code to dispose managed resources
            If Not DataReader Is Nothing Then
                DataReader.Close()
                DataReader = Nothing
            End If
            If Not DataAdapter Is Nothing Then
                DataAdapter.Dispose()
                DataAdapter = Nothing
            End If
            If Not Command Is Nothing Then
                Command.Dispose()
                Command = Nothing
            End If
            If Not Connection Is Nothing Then
                Connection.Close()
                Connection.Dispose()
                Connection = Nothing
```

```
                    End If
            End If


                ' TODO: put code to free unmanaged resources here
        End If
        Me.disposed = True
    End Sub
```

8. Start adding some public procedures that can be called in this class to perform some rudimentary database operations. You add error-handling code to all of these procedures so that it throws an error if something goes wrong. It will be up to the client calling this class to add its own error-handling code to test for and handle any errors thrown. Add a public procedure called `OpenConnection` below the `Dispose` procedure and add the following code to it:

```
Public Sub OpenConnection()
    Try
        Connection.Open()
    Catch OleDbExceptionErr As OleDbException
        Throw New System.Exception(OleDbExceptionErr.Message, _
            OleDbExceptionErr.InnerException)
    Catch InvalidOperationExceptionErr As InvalidOperationException
        Throw New System.Exception(InvalidOperationExceptionErr.Message, _
            InvalidOperationExceptionErr.InnerException)
    End Try
End Sub
```

9. Add a public procedure called `CloseConnection` to close the database connection. Add this procedure and then add the following code to it:

```
Public Sub CloseConnection()
    Connection.Close()
End Sub
```

10. The next public procedure that you want to add is one that will initialize a `Command` object. To properly set the `CommandType` property, you need to determine whether the SQL variable contains a SQL string, a query, or a stored procedure. You can accomplish this by comparing the beginning of the text in the SQL variable with the values of SELECT, INSERT, UPDATE, and DELETE, followed by a space. If the SQL variable does not contain these values, then it is safe to assume that the SQL variable contains the name of a query or stored procedure, and the `CommandType` property should be set to a value of `StoredProcedure`. Add the `InitializeCommand` procedure and add the following code to it:

```
Public Sub InitializeCommand()
    If Command Is Nothing Then
        Try
            Command = New OleDbCommand(SQL, Connection)
            'See if this is a stored procedure
            If Not SQL.ToUpper.StartsWith("SELECT ") _
                And Not SQL.ToUpper.StartsWith("INSERT ") _
                And Not SQL.ToUpper.StartsWith("UPDATE ") _
                And Not SQL.ToUpper.StartsWith("DELETE ") Then
                Command.CommandType = CommandType.StoredProcedure
            End If
        Catch OleDbExceptionErr As OleDbException
```

```
        Throw New System.Exception(OleDbExceptionErr.Message, _
                OleDbExceptionErr.InnerException)
        End Try
    End If
End Sub
```

11. You need to be able to support using a `Command` object and adding parameters to the `Parameters` collection. To that end, you need to add a public procedure named `AddParameter`. Add this procedure to your code and then add the following code to it:

```
Public Sub AddParameter(ByVal Name As String, ByVal Type As OleDbType, _
    ByVal Size As Integer, ByVal Value As Object)
    Try
        Command.Parameters.Add(Name, Type, Size).Value = Value
    Catch OleDbExceptionErr As OleDbException
        Throw New System.Exception(OleDbExceptionErr.Message, _
            OleDbExceptionErr.InnerException)
    End Try
End Sub
```

12. Add a public procedure named `InitializeDataAdapter` to your class. This procedure initializes a new instance of the `OleDbDataAdapter` class and sets the `SelectCommand` property to the `Command` object. Add the following code to this procedure:

```
Public Sub InitializeDataAdapter()
    Try
        DataAdapter = New OleDbDataAdapter
        DataAdapter.SelectCommand = Command
    Catch OleDbExceptionErr As OleDbException
        Throw New System.Exception(OleDbExceptionErr.Message, _
        OleDbExceptionErr.InnerException)
    End Try
End Sub
```

13. You want to provide a procedure that can fill a `DataSet` object and take care of all of the details associated with performing this task. This procedure accepts the `DataSet` object by reference and populates the `DataSet` with data. Add the procedure and the following code:

```
Public Sub FillDataSet(ByRef oDataSet As DataSet, ByVal TableName As String)
    Try
        InitializeCommand()
        InitializeDataAdapter()
        DataAdapter.Fill(oDataSet, TableName)
    Catch OleDbExceptionErr As OleDbException
        Throw New System.Exception(OleDbExceptionErr.Message, _
            OleDbExceptionErr.InnerException)
    Finally
        Command.Dispose()
        Command = Nothing
        DataAdapter.Dispose()
        DataAdapter = Nothing
    End Try
End Sub
```

14. You want to provide a procedure that can fill a `DataTable` object and take care of all of the details associated with performing this task. This procedure accepts the `DataTable` object by reference and populates the `DataTable` with data. Add the procedure and the following code:

```
Public Sub FillDataTable(ByRef oDataTable As DataTable)
    Try
        InitializeCommand()
        InitializeDataAdapter()
        DataAdapter.Fill(oDataTable)
    Catch OleDbExceptionErr As OleDbException
        Throw New System.Exception(OleDbExceptionErr.Message, _
            OleDbExceptionErr.InnerException)
    Finally
        Command.Dispose()
        Command = Nothing
        DataAdapter.Dispose()
        DataAdapter = Nothing
    End Try
End Sub
```

15. The final code that you add to this class is a function that can execute a stored procedure that does not return any data. This would be a stored procedure that inserts, updates, or deletes data. This function should return a value of the number of records affected by the stored procedure that is executed. Add the following code to your class:

```
Public Function ExecuteStoredProcedure() As Integer
    Try
        OpenConnection()
        ExecuteStoredProcedure = Command.ExecuteNonQuery()
    Catch ExceptionErr As Exception
        Throw New System.Exception(ExceptionErr.Message, _
            ExceptionErr.InnerException)
    Finally
        CloseConnection()
    End Try
End Function
```

Admin form code

In this section, you add some common code to make the Admin form functional. This is not database-related code, as that code will be added in the appropriate chapters.

To add this code:

1. Right-click the Admin form in Solution Explorer and choose View Code from the context menu.

2. Add some variable declarations that are available to the entire form class. Add the following variables:

```
Public Class Admin
    'Private variables and objects
    Private intIndex As Integer

    Private strActiveScreen As String = "Projects"
```

```
        Private strAppTitle As String

        Private objData As WDABase

        Private imgCurrentNavImage As Image

        Private Const ImageSelected As Integer = 0
        Private Const ImageUnselected As Integer = 1
        Private Const ImageHighlighted As Integer = 2
```

3. Create a procedure that can be called to dock the panel controls on your form. Add the following procedure:

```
        Private Sub DockPanel(ByRef objPanel As Panel)
            'Set the Dock property to Fill
            '(this will cause the location to change to 0,0)
            objPanel.Dock = DockStyle.Fill
            'Set the navigation panel information
            optOption1.Visible = True
            optOption2.Visible = True
            optOption3.Visible = True
            optOption4.Visible = True
            Select Case objPanel.Name
                Case "pnlProjects"
                    strActiveScreen = "Projects"
                    lblCurrentScreen.Text = "Projects"
                    lblAllScreens.Text = "All " & "Projects"
                    imgScreen.Image = imgProjects.Image
                    lblScreen.Text = "Projects"
                    optOption1.Text = "Name"
                    optOption2.Text = "Description"
                    optOption3.Text = "Sequence Number"
                    optOption3.Checked = True
                    optOption4.Text = "Date"
                Case "pnlGroups"
                    strActiveScreen = "Groups"
                    lblCurrentScreen.Text = "Groups"
                    lblAllScreens.Text = "All " & "Groups"
                    imgScreen.Image = imgGroups.Image
                    lblScreen.Text = "Groups"
                    optOption1.Text = "Name"
                    optOption1.Checked = True
                    optOption2.Text = "Description"
                    optOption3.Text = "Date"
                    optOption4.Visible = False
                Case "pnlGroupProjects"
                    strActiveScreen = "Group Projects"
                    lblCurrentScreen.Text = "Group Projects"
                    lblAllScreens.Text = "All " & "Group Projects"
                    imgScreen.Image = imgGroupProjects.Image
                    lblScreen.Text = "Group Projects"
                    optOption1.Visible = False
                    optOption2.Visible = False
                    optOption3.Visible = False
                    optOption4.Visible = False
```

```
            Case "pnlRoles"
                strActiveScreen = "Roles"
                lblCurrentScreen.Text = "Roles"
                lblAllScreens.Text = "All " & "Roles"
                imgScreen.Image = imgRoles.Image
                lblScreen.Text = "Roles"
                optOption1.Text = "Name"
                optOption2.Text = "Description"
                optOption3.Text = "Ranking"
                optOption3.Checked = True
                optOption4.Text = "Date"
            Case "pnlUsers"
                strActiveScreen = "Users"
                lblCurrentScreen.Text = "Users"
                lblAllScreens.Text = "All " & "Users"
                imgScreen.Image = imgUsers.Image
                lblScreen.Text = "Users"
                optOption1.Text = "Login"
                optOption2.Text = "Name"
                optOption2.Checked = True
                optOption3.Text = "Email"
                optOption4.Text = "Status"
        End Select
    End Sub
```

4. Now create a procedure that can be called to undock the panel controls on your form. Add the following code:

```
Private Sub UnDockPanel(ByRef objPanel As Panel, _
    ByRef objNavControl As Control)

    'Undock the Panel
    objPanel.Dock = DockStyle.None
    'Move it out of the way
    objPanel.Location = New Point(5000, 5000)
    'Set the image to be unselected
    objNavControl.BackgroundImage = imlNavigation.Images(ImageUnselected)
End Sub
```

5. The next thing that you add is a `Navigate` procedure that can be called to navigate to the various screens that you created in the panel controls. Add the following procedure and its code:

```
Private Sub Navigate(ByVal Shortcut As String)
    'Process each control in the pnlNavigationBackground Control collection
    For Each objControl As Control In pnlNavigationBackground.Controls
        'If the type of control is a Panel then process it
        If TypeOf objControl Is Panel Then
            Select Case objControl.Name
                Case "pnlNavProjects"
                    'If this is the shortcut chosen...
                    If Shortcut = "pnlNavProjects" Then
                        Call DockPanel(pnlProjects)
                    Else
                        Call UnDockPanel(pnlProjects, objControl)
```

```
                            End If
                   Case "pnlNavGroups"
                        'If this is the shortcut chosen...
                        If Shortcut = "pnlNavGroups" Then
                            Call DockPanel(pnlGroups)
                        Else
                            Call UnDockPanel(pnlGroups, objControl)
                        End If
                   Case "pnlNavGroupProjects"
                        'If this is the shortcut chosen...
                        If Shortcut = "pnlNavGroupProjects" Then
                            Call DockPanel(pnlGroupProjects)
                        Else
                            Call UnDockPanel(pnlGroupProjects, objControl)
                        End If
                   Case "pnlNavRoles"
                        'If this is the shortcut chosen...
                        If Shortcut = "pnlNavRoles" Then
                            Call DockPanel(pnlRoles)
                        Else
                            Call UnDockPanel(pnlRoles, objControl)
                        End If
                   Case "pnlNavUsers"
                        'If this is the shortcut chosen...
                        If Shortcut = "pnlNavUsers" Then
                            Call DockPanel(pnlUsers)
                        Else
                            Call UnDockPanel(pnlUsers, objControl)
                        End If
                End Select
           End If
       Next
End Sub
```

6. When you move your mouse over and out of the shortcut Panel, Label, and PictureBox controls in the navigation panel, you want the image in the `BackgroundImage` property of the shortcut Panel control to change. When you select a shortcut Panel control, you want the `BackgroundImage` property to contain the image of a selected shortcut. Finally, you want the Panel controls to invoke the `Navigate` procedure. You can do this with generic procedures for each of the mouse events for the Panel, Label, and PictureBox controls on the navigation panel. Add the following procedures and their code:

```
Private Sub NavigationPanel_MouseEnter(ByVal sender As Object, _
    ByVal e As System.EventArgs)

    imgCurrentNavImage = sender.backgroundimage
    sender.backgroundimage = imlNavigation.Images(ImageHighlighted)
    sender.Cursor = Cursors.Hand
End Sub

Private Sub NavigationPanel_MouseLeave(ByVal sender As Object, _
    ByVal e As System.EventArgs)

    sender.backgroundimage = imgCurrentNavImage
```

```
        sender.Cursor = Cursors.Default
    End Sub

    Private Sub NavigationPanel_MouseUp(ByVal sender As Object, _
        ByVal e As System.Windows.Forms.MouseEventArgs)

        imgCurrentNavImage = imlNavigation.Images(ImageSelected)
        Call Navigate(sender.name)
    End Sub

    Private Sub NavigationChildControl_MouseEnter( _
        ByVal sender As Object, ByVal e As System.EventArgs)

        NavigationPanel_MouseEnter(sender.Parent, e)
    End Sub

    Private Sub NavigationChildControl_MouseLeave( _
        ByVal sender As Object, ByVal e As System.EventArgs)

        NavigationPanel_MouseLeave(sender.Parent, e)
    End Sub

    Private Sub NavigationChildControl_MouseUp( _
        ByVal sender As Object, ByVal e As System.Windows.Forms.MouseEventArgs)

        NavigationPanel_MouseUp(sender.parent, e)
    End Sub
```

7. When you resize the navigation panel, you want the grabbar image to be re-centered in the grabbar panel. In the Class Name combo box, select pnlGrabbar; and in the Method Name combo box, select the Resize event. Add the following code to the pnlGrabbar_Resize procedure:

```
    Private Sub pnlGrabbar_Resize(ByVal sender As Object, _
        ByVal e As System.EventArgs) Handles pnlGrabbar.Resize

        'Recenter PictureBox control
        imgGrabbarHandle.Location = New Point( _
            (pnlGrabbar.Size.Width - imgGrabbarHandle.Size.Width) \ 2, _
            (pnlGrabbar.Size.Height - imgGrabbarHandle.Size.Height) \ 2)
    End Sub
```

8. Now that you have some generic procedures defined for the mouse events of the shortcut Panel, Label, and PictureBox controls, you need to associate the mouse events for these controls with the event handling procedures that you just created. Select (Admin Events) in the Class Name combo box and the Load event in the Method Name combo box. Add the following code in the Admin_Load procedure:

```
    Private Sub Admin_Load(ByVal sender As Object, _
        ByVal e As System.EventArgs) Handles MyBase.Load

        'Add handlers for shortcut Panel controls MouseEnter event
        AddHandler pnlNavProjects.MouseEnter, AddressOf NavigationPanel_MouseEnter
        AddHandler pnlNavGroups.MouseEnter, AddressOf NavigationPanel_MouseEnter
        AddHandler pnlNavGroupProjects.MouseEnter, _
            AddressOf NavigationPanel_MouseEnter
```

```
    AddHandler pnlNavRoles.MouseEnter, AddressOf NavigationPanel_MouseEnter
    AddHandler pnlNavUsers.MouseEnter, AddressOf NavigationPanel_MouseEnter

    'Add handlers for shortcut Panel controls MouseLeave event
    AddHandler pnlNavProjects.MouseLeave, AddressOf NavigationPanel_MouseLeave
    AddHandler pnlNavGroups.MouseLeave, AddressOf NavigationPanel_MouseLeave
    AddHandler pnlNavGroupProjects.MouseLeave, _
        AddressOf NavigationPanel_MouseLeave
    AddHandler pnlNavRoles.MouseLeave, AddressOf NavigationPanel_MouseLeave
    AddHandler pnlNavUsers.MouseLeave, AddressOf NavigationPanel_MouseLeave

    'Add handlers for shortcut Panel controls MouseUp event
    AddHandler pnlNavProjects.MouseUp, AddressOf NavigationPanel_MouseUp
    AddHandler pnlNavGroups.MouseUp, AddressOf NavigationPanel_MouseUp
    AddHandler pnlNavGroupProjects.MouseUp, AddressOf NavigationPanel_MouseUp
    AddHandler pnlNavRoles.MouseUp, AddressOf NavigationPanel_MouseUp
    AddHandler pnlNavUsers.MouseUp, AddressOf NavigationPanel_MouseUp

    'Add handlers for shortcut Label controls MouseEnter event
    AddHandler lblProjects.MouseEnter, _
        AddressOf NavigationChildControl_MouseEnter
    AddHandler lblGroups.MouseEnter, _
        AddressOf NavigationChildControl_MouseEnter
    AddHandler lblGroupProjects.MouseEnter, _
        AddressOf NavigationChildControl_MouseEnter
    AddHandler lblRoles.MouseEnter, AddressOf NavigationChildControl_MouseEnter
    AddHandler lblUsers.MouseEnter, AddressOf NavigationChildControl_MouseEnter

    'Add handlers for shortcut Label controls MouseLeave event
    AddHandler lblProjects.MouseLeave, _
        AddressOf NavigationChildControl_MouseLeave
    AddHandler lblGroups.MouseLeave, _
        AddressOf NavigationChildControl_MouseLeave
    AddHandler lblGroupProjects.MouseLeave, _
        AddressOf NavigationChildControl_MouseLeave
    AddHandler lblRoles.MouseLeave, AddressOf NavigationChildControl_MouseLeave
    AddHandler lblUsers.MouseLeave, AddressOf NavigationChildControl_MouseLeave

    'Add handlers for shortcut Label controls MouseUp event
    AddHandler lblProjects.MouseUp, AddressOf NavigationChildControl_MouseUp
    AddHandler lblGroups.MouseUp, AddressOf NavigationChildControl_MouseUp
    AddHandler lblGroupProjects.MouseUp, _
        AddressOf NavigationChildControl_MouseUp
    AddHandler lblRoles.MouseUp, AddressOf NavigationChildControl_MouseUp
    AddHandler lblUsers.MouseUp, AddressOf NavigationChildControl_MouseUp

    'Add handlers for shortcut PictureBox controls MouseEnter event
    AddHandler imgProjects.MouseEnter, _
        AddressOf NavigationChildControl_MouseEnter
    AddHandler imgGroups.MouseEnter, _
        AddressOf NavigationChildControl_MouseEnter
    AddHandler imgGroupProjects.MouseEnter, _
        AddressOf NavigationChildControl_MouseEnter
    AddHandler imgRoles.MouseEnter, AddressOf NavigationChildControl_MouseEnter
```

```
            AddHandler imgUsers.MouseEnter, AddressOf NavigationChildControl_MouseEnter

            'Add handlers for shortcut PictureBox controls MouseLeave event
            AddHandler imgProjects.MouseLeave, _
                AddressOf NavigationChildControl_MouseLeave
            AddHandler imgGroups.MouseLeave, _
                AddressOf NavigationChildControl_MouseLeave
            AddHandler imgGroupProjects.MouseLeave, _
                AddressOf NavigationChildControl_MouseLeave
            AddHandler imgRoles.MouseLeave, AddressOf NavigationChildControl_MouseLeave
            AddHandler imgUsers.MouseLeave, AddressOf NavigationChildControl_MouseLeave

            'Add handlers for shortcut PictureBox controls MouseUp event
            AddHandler imgProjects.MouseUp, AddressOf NavigationChildControl_MouseUp
            AddHandler imgGroups.MouseUp, AddressOf NavigationChildControl_MouseUp
            AddHandler imgGroupProjects.MouseUp, _
                AddressOf NavigationChildControl_MouseUp
            AddHandler imgRoles.MouseUp, AddressOf NavigationChildControl_MouseUp
            AddHandler imgUsers.MouseUp, AddressOf NavigationChildControl_MouseUp

            'Set the current date in the date panel in the status bar
            ToolStripDate.Text = Date.Today

            'Get the applicataion title
            strAppTitle = My.Application.Info.Title
        End Sub
```

At this point, you can run your project to test the code that you've added. You'll be able to click all of the shortcut controls in the navigation panel and navigate to each of the screens that you defined on the various Panel controls. When your mouse enters a shortcut control, the background image of the shortcut panel will become highlighted; and when you click a shortcut panel, the background image will be changed to the selected image. When you have finished testing, stop your project and return to the Code Editor.

9. Add some procedures that can be called by the menu items and toolbar buttons next. The first procedure that you want to add is a procedure for the New menu item and toolbar button. This procedure will clear the fields on the current screen. Add this procedure and code as follows:

```
Private Sub FileNew()
    'Clear the contents on the active screen
    Select Case strActiveScreen
        Case "Projects"
            txtProjectID.Text = String.Empty
            txtProjectName.Text = String.Empty
            txtProjectDescription.Text = String.Empty
            txtSequenceNumber.Text = String.Empty
            txtProjectUpdateDate.Text = String.Empty
        Case "Groups"
            txtGroupID.Text = String.Empty
            txtGroupName.Text = String.Empty
            txtGroupDescription.Text = String.Empty
            txtGroupUpdateDate.Text = String.Empty
        Case "Group Projects"
            cboGroups.SelectedIndex = -1
```

```
                        lstGroupProjects.Items.Clear()
            Case "Roles"
                txtRoleID.Text = String.Empty
                txtRoleName.Text = String.Empty
                txtRoleDescription.Text = String.Empty
                txtRanking.Text = String.Empty
                txtRoleUpdateDate.Text = String.Empty
            Case "Users"
                txtUserID.Text = String.Empty
                optStatusActive.Checked = True
                txtLogin.Text = String.Empty
                txtPassword.Text = String.Empty
                txtFirstName.Text = String.Empty
                txtLastName.Text = String.Empty
                txtEmail.Text = String.Empty
                txtPhone.Text = String.Empty
                cboUserGroup.SelectedIndex = -1
                cboUserManager.SelectedIndex = -1
                cboUserRole.SelectedIndex = -1
                txtUserUpdateDate.Text = String.Empty
        End Select
    End Sub
```

10. You also want to add some procedures that can be called by the Edit menu and Edit toolbar buttons. These procedures operate on the TextBox control that has focus and perform the edit function requested. Starting with the Undo function, add the following procedure and code:

```
Private Sub EditUndo()
    'Process each control in the pnlScreens Panel
    For Each objPanel As Control In pnlScreens.Controls
        'If this is a Panel...
        If TypeOf objPanel Is Panel Then
            'Now process each control in all child
            'Panels(e.g.pnlProjects, pnlGroups, pnlGroupProjects)
            For Each objPanelControl As Control In objPanel.Controls
                'If this is a GroupBox...
                If TypeOf objPanelControl Is GroupBox Then
                    'Process each control in the GroupBox
                    For Each objControl As Control In objPanelControl.Controls
                        'If this is a TextBox...
                        If TypeOf objControl Is TextBox Then
                            'If it has focus...
                            If objControl.Focused Then
                                'Set a reference to it so the properties and
                                'methods are available
                                Dim objTextBox As TextBox = objControl
                                'See if last operation can be undone
                                If objTextBox.CanUndo = True Then
                                    'Undo the last operation
                                    objTextBox.Undo()
                                End If
                                'The work is all done so exit the procedure
                                Exit Sub
                            End If
                        End If
                    End If
```

```
                        Next
                    End If
                Next
            End If
        Next
    End Sub
```

11. Add the EditCut procedures and code next:

```
Private Sub EditCut()
    'Process each control in the pnlScreens Panel
    For Each objPanel As Control In pnlScreens.Controls
        'If this is a Panel...
        If TypeOf objPanel Is Panel Then
            'Now process each control in all child
            'Panels(e.g.pnlProjects, pnlGroups, pnlGroupProjects)
            For Each objPanelControl As Control In objPanel.Controls
                'If this is a GroupBox...
                If TypeOf objPanelControl Is GroupBox Then
                    'Process each control in the GroupBox
                    For Each objControl As Control In objPanelControl.Controls
                        'If this is a TextBox...
                        If TypeOf objControl Is TextBox Then
                            'If it has focus...
                            If objControl.Focused Then
                                'Set a reference to it so the properties and
                                'methods are available
                                Dim objTextBox As TextBox = objControl
                                'See if any text has been selected
                                If objTextBox.SelectionLength > 0 Then
                                    'Cut the text and place it on the clipboard
                                    objTextBox.Cut()
                                End If
                                'The work is all done so exit the procedure
                                Exit Sub
                            End If
                        End If
                    Next
                End If
            Next
        End If
    Next
End Sub
```

12. Add the EditCopy procedures and code next:

```
Private Sub EditCopy()
    'Process each control in the pnlScreens Panel
    For Each objPanel As Control In pnlScreens.Controls
        'If this is a Panel...
        If TypeOf objPanel Is Panel Then
            'Now process each control in all child
            'Panels(e.g.pnlProjects, pnlGroups, pnlGroupProjects)
            For Each objPanelControl As Control In objPanel.Controls
                'If this is a GroupBox...
                If TypeOf objPanelControl Is GroupBox Then
```

```
                         'Process each control in the GroupBox
                 For Each objControl As Control In objPanelControl.Controls
                     'If this is a TextBox...
                     If TypeOf objControl Is TextBox Then
                         'If it has focus...
                         If objControl.Focused Then
                             'Set a reference to it so the properties and
                             'methods are available
                             Dim objTextBox As TextBox = objControl
                             'See if any text has been selected
                             If objTextBox.SelectionLength > 0 Then
                                 'Copy the text and place it on the
                                 'Clipboard
                                 objTextBox.Copy()
                             End If
                             'The work is all done so exit the procedure
                             Exit Sub
                         End If
                     End If
                 Next
             End If
         Next
     End If
   Next
End Sub
```

13. Add the `EditPaste` procedures and code next:

```
Private Sub EditPaste()
    'Process each control in the pnlScreens Panel
    For Each objPanel As Control In pnlScreens.Controls
        'If this is a Panel...
        If TypeOf objPanel Is Panel Then
            'Now process each control in all child
            'Panels(e.g.pnlProjects, pnlGroups, pnlGroupProjects)
            For Each objPanelControl As Control In objPanel.Controls
                'If this is a GroupBox...
                If TypeOf objPanelControl Is GroupBox Then
                    'Process each control in the GroupBox
                    For Each objControl As Control In objPanelControl.Controls
                        'If this is a TextBox...
                        If TypeOf objControl Is TextBox Then
                            'If it has focus...
                            If objControl.Focused Then
                                'Set a reference to it so the properties and
                                'methods are available
                                Dim objTextBox As TextBox = objControl
                                'See if there is any text on the Clipboard
                                If Clipboard.GetDataObject().GetDataPresent( _
                                    DataFormats.Text) = _
                                    True Then
                                    'Paste the text from Clipboard
                                    objTextBox.Paste()
                                End If
                                'The work is all done so exit the procedure
                                Exit Sub
```

```
                           End If
                      End If
                 Next
             End If
          Next
       End If
    Next
End Sub
```

14. And finally, add the `EditSelectAll` procedures and code:

```
Private Sub EditSelectAll()
    'Process each control in the pnlScreens Panel
    For Each objPanel As Control In pnlScreens.Controls
        'If this is a Panel...
        If TypeOf objPanel Is Panel Then
            'Now process each control in all child
            'Panels(e.g.pnlProjects, pnlGroups, pnlGroupProjects)
            For Each objPanelControl As Control In objPanel.Controls
                'If this is a GroupBox...
                If TypeOf objPanelControl Is GroupBox Then
                    'Process each control in the GroupBox
                    For Each objControl As Control In objPanelControl.Controls
                        'If this is a TextBox...
                        If TypeOf objControl Is TextBox Then
                            'If it has focus...
                            If objControl.Focused Then
                                'Set a reference to it so the properties and
                                'methods are available
                                Dim objTextBox As TextBox = objControl
                                'Select all available text
                                objTextBox.SelectAll()
                                'The work is all done so exit the procedure
                                Exit Sub
                            End If
                        End If
                    Next
                End If
            Next
        End If
    Next
End Sub
```

15. Next, add three generic procedures that can be called by the Add, Update, and Delete menu items and toolbar buttons. Add the following procedures and code:

```
Private Sub ActionAdd()
    'Add database row based on the active screen
    Select Case strActiveScreen
        Case "Projects"
        Case "Groups"
        Case "Group Projects"
        Case "Roles"
        Case "Users"
    End Select
```

```
        End Sub

        Private Sub ActionUpdate()
            'Update database row based on the active screen
            Select Case strActiveScreen
                Case "Projects"
                Case "Groups"
                Case "Group Projects"
                Case "Roles"
                Case "Users"
            End Select
        End Sub

        Private Sub ActionDelete()
            'Delete database row based on the active screen
            Select Case strActiveScreen
                Case "Projects"
                Case "Groups"
                Case "Group Projects"
                Case "Roles"
                Case "Users"
            End Select
        End Sub
```

16. Now it's time to start adding the procedures for the menu items. Click the Class Name combo box and choose newToolStripMenuItem; and in the Method Name combo box, choose the `Click` event. Add the following code to the `newToolStripMenuItem_Click` procedure:

```
Private Sub newToolStripMenuItem_Click(ByVal sender As Object, _
    ByVal e As System.EventArgs) Handles newToolStripMenuItem.Click

        FileNew()
End Sub
```

17. Click the Class Name combo box and choose exitToolStripMenuItem; and in the Method Name combo box, choose the `Click` event. Add the following code to the exitToolStripMenuItem `Click` procedure:

```
Private Sub exitToolStripMenuItem_Click(ByVal sender As Object, _
    ByVal e As System.EventArgs) Handles exitToolStripMenuItem.Click

        Me.Close()
End Sub
```

18. Click the Class Name combo box and choose undoToolStripMenuItem; and in the Method Name combo box, choose the `Click` event. Add the following code to the undoToolStripMenuItem_Click procedure:

```
Private Sub undoToolStripMenuItem_Click(ByVal sender As Object, _
    ByVal e As System.EventArgs) Handles undoToolStripMenuItem.Click

        EditUndo()
End Sub
```

19. Click the Class Name combo box and choose cutToolStripMenuItem; and in the Method Name combo box, choose the Click event. Add the following code to the cutToolStripMenuItem_Click procedure:

```
Private Sub cutToolStripMenuItem_Click(ByVal sender As Object, _
    ByVal e As System.EventArgs) Handles cutToolStripMenuItem.Click

        EditCut()
End Sub
```

20. Click the Class Name combo box and choose copyToolStripMenuItem; and in the Method Name combo box, choose the Click event. Add the following code to the copyToolStripMenuItem_Click procedure:

```
Private Sub copyToolStripMenuItem_Click(ByVal sender As Object, _
    ByVal e As System.EventArgs) Handles copyToolStripMenuItem.Click

        EditCopy()
End Sub
```

21. Click the Class Name combo box and choose pasteToolStripMenuItem; and in the Method Name combo box, choose the Click event. Add the following code to the pasteToolStripMenuItem_Click procedure:

```
Private Sub pasteToolStripMenuItem_Click(ByVal sender As Object, _
    ByVal e As System.EventArgs) Handles pasteToolStripMenuItem.Click

        EditPaste()
End Sub
```

22. Click the Class Name combo box and choose selectAllToolStripMenuItem; and in the Method Name combo box, choose the Click event. Add the following code to the selectAllToolStripMenuItem_Click procedure:

```
Private Sub selectAllToolStripMenuItem_Click(ByVal sender As Object, _
    ByVal e As System.EventArgs) Handles selectAllToolStripMenuItem.Click

        EditSelectAll()
End Sub
```

23. Click the Class Name combo box and choose ProjectsToolStripMenuItem; and in the Method Name combo box, choose the Click event. Add the following code to the ProjectsToolStripMenuItem_Click procedure:

```
Private Sub ProjectsToolStripMenuItem_Click(ByVal sender As Object, _
    ByVal e As System.EventArgs) Handles ProjectsToolStripMenuItem.Click

        Navigate("pnlNavProjects")
        pnlNavProjects.BackgroundImage = imlNavigation.Images(ImageSelected)
End Sub
```

24. Click the Class Name combo box and choose GroupsToolStripMenuItem; and in the Method Name combo box, choose the Click event. Add the following code to the GroupsToolStripMenuItem_Click procedure:

```
Private Sub GroupsToolStripMenuItem_Click(ByVal sender As Object, _
    ByVal e As System.EventArgs) Handles GroupsToolStripMenuItem.Click

    Navigate("pnlNavGroups")
    pnlNavGroups.BackgroundImage = imlNavigation.Images(ImageSelected)
End Sub
```

25. Click the Class Name combo box and choose GroupProjectsToolStripMenuItem; and in
the Method Name combo box, choose the Click event. Add the following code to the
GroupProjectsToolStripMenuItem_Click procedure:

```
Private Sub GroupProjectsToolStripMenuItem_Click(ByVal sender As Object, _
    ByVal e As System.EventArgs) Handles GroupProjectsToolStripMenuItem.Click

    Navigate("pnlNavGroupProjects")
    pnlNavGroupProjects.BackgroundImage = imlNavigation.Images(ImageSelected)
End Sub
```

26. Click the Class Name combo box and choose RolesToolStripMenuItem; and in
the Method Name combo box, choose the Click event. Add the following code to the
RolesToolStripMenuItem_Click procedure:

```
Private Sub RolesToolStripMenuItem_Click(ByVal sender As Object, _
    ByVal e As System.EventArgs) Handles RolesToolStripMenuItem.Click

    Navigate("pnlNavRoles")
    pnlNavRoles.BackgroundImage = imlNavigation.Images(ImageSelected)
End Sub
```

27. Click the Class Name combo box and choose UsersToolStripMenuItem; and in
the Method Name combo box, choose the Click event. Add the following code to the
UsersToolStripMenuItem_Click procedure:

```
Private Sub UsersToolStripMenuItem_Click(ByVal sender As Object, _
    ByVal e As System.EventArgs) Handles UsersToolStripMenuItem.Click

    Navigate("pnlNavUsers")
    pnlNavUsers.BackgroundImage = imlNavigation.Images(ImageSelected)
End Sub
```

28. Click the Class Name combo box and choose AddToolStripMenuItem; and in
the Method Name combo box, choose the Click event. Add the following code to the
AddToolStripMenuItem_Click procedure:

```
Private Sub AddToolStripMenuItem_Click(ByVal sender As Object, _
    ByVal e As System.EventArgs) Handles AddToolStripMenuItem.Click

    ActionAdd()
End Sub
```

29. Click the Class Name combo box and choose UpdateToolStripMenuItem; and in
the Method Name combo box, choose the Click event. Add the following code to the
UpdateToolStripMenuItem_Click procedure:

```
Private Sub UpdateToolStripMenuItem_Click(ByVal sender As Object, _
    ByVal e As System.EventArgs) Handles UpdateToolStripMenuItem.Click
```

```
        ActionUpdate()
```
```
    End Sub
```

30. Click the Class Name combo box and choose DeleteToolStripMenuItem; and in the Method Name combo box, choose the Click event. Add the following code to the DeleteToolStripMenuItem_Click procedure:

```
Private Sub DeleteToolStripMenuItem_Click(ByVal sender As Object, _
    ByVal e As System.EventArgs) Handles DeleteToolStripMenuItem.Click
```

```
        ActionDelete()
```
```
    End Sub
```

31. Click the Class Name combo box and choose AboutToolStripMenuItem; and in the Method Name combo box, choose the Click event. Add the following code to the AboutToolStripMenuItem_Click procedure:

```
Private Sub AboutToolStripMenuItem_Click(ByVal sender As Object, _
    ByVal e As System.EventArgs) Handles AboutToolStripMenuItem.Click
```

```
        Dim objAbout As New About
        objAbout.ShowDialog(Me)
        objAbout.Dispose()
        objAbout = Nothing
```
```
    End Sub
```

32. Now its time to add the Click event handler for all your toolbar buttons. Click the Class Name combo box and choose newToolStripButton; and in the Method Name combo box, choose the Click event. Add the following code to the newToolStripButton_Click procedure:

```
Private Sub newToolStripButton_Click(ByVal sender As Object, _
    ByVal e As System.EventArgs) Handles newToolStripButton.Click
```

```
        FileNew()
```
```
    End Sub
```

33. Click the Class Name combo box and choose cutToolStripButton; and in the Method Name combo box, choose the Click event. Add the following code to the cutToolStripButton_Click procedure:

```
Private Sub cutToolStripButton_Click(ByVal sender As Object, _
    ByVal e As System.EventArgs) Handles cutToolStripButton.Click
```

```
        EditCut()
```
```
    End Sub
```

34. Click the Class Name combo box and choose copyToolStripButton; and in the Method Name combo box, choose the Click event. Add the following code to the copyToolStripButton_Click procedure:

```
    Private Sub copyToolStripButton_Click(ByVal sender As Object, _
        ByVal e As System.EventArgs) Handles copyToolStripButton.Click

        EditCopy()
    End Sub
```

35. Click the Class Name combo box and choose pasteToolStripButton; and in the Method Name combo box, choose the Click event. Add the following code to the pasteToolStripButton_Click procedure:

```
    Private Sub pasteToolStripButton_Click(ByVal sender As Object, _
        ByVal e As System.EventArgs) Handles pasteToolStripButton.Click

        EditPaste()
    End Sub
```

36. Click the Class Name combo box and choose UndoToolStripButton; and in the Method Name combo box, choose the Click event. Add the following code to the UndoToolStripButton_Click procedure:

```
    Private Sub UndoToolStripButton_Click(ByVal sender As Object, _
        ByVal e As System.EventArgs) Handles UndoToolStripButton.Click

        EditUndo()
    End Sub
```

37. Click the Class Name combo box and choose AddToolStripButton; and in the Method Name combo box, choose the Click event. Add the following code to the AddToolStripButton_Click procedure:

```
    Private Sub AddToolStripButton_Click(ByVal sender As Object, _
        ByVal e As System.EventArgs) Handles AddToolStripButton.Click

        ActionAdd()
    End Sub
```

38. Click the Class Name combo box and choose UpdateToolStripButton; and in the Method Name combo box, choose the Click event. Add the following code to the UpdateToolStripButton_Click procedure:

```
    Private Sub UpdateToolStripButton_Click(ByVal sender As Object, _
        ByVal e As System.EventArgs) Handles UpdateToolStripButton.Click

        ActionUpdate()
    End Sub
```

39. Click the Class Name combo box and choose DeleteToolStripButton; and in the Method Name combo box, choose the Click event. Add the following code to the DeleteToolStripButton_Click procedure:

```
    Private Sub DeleteToolStripButton_Click(ByVal sender As Object, _
        ByVal e As System.EventArgs) Handles DeleteToolStripButton.Click

        ActionDelete()
    End Sub
```

This is all of the code that you need to add to the Admin form. At this point, you can save and run your project and test the menu items and toolbar buttons. You'll be able to exit the application, cut, copy, paste, undo, and select all functions in the text boxes, and display the Help form.

TimeSheet form code

In this section, you add some common code to make the TimeSheet form functional. This is not database-related code, as that code will be added in the appropriate chapters.

To add this code:

1. Right-click the TimeSheet form in the Solution Explorer window and choose View Code from the context menu.

2. Add some variable declarations to the form first. These variables will be accessible to all procedures in this form. Add the following variables at the top of your class:

```
Public Class TimeSheet
    'Private variables
    Private intIndex As Integer

    Private blnEmployeeDisplay As Boolean = True

    Private strAppTitle As String
```

3. Get the application title from the executable name and set the current date in the status bar. The form's Load procedure is the ideal place to perform these operations. Click (Timesheet Events) in the Class Name combo box; and in the Method Name combo box, choose the Load event. Add the following code to the TimeSheet_Load procedure:

```
Private Sub TimeSheet_Load(ByVal sender As Object, _
    ByVal e As System.EventArgs) Handles Me.Load

    'Set the current date in the date panel in the status bar
    ToolStripDate.Text = Date.Today

    'Get the process title from the executable name
    strAppTitle = My.Application.Info.Title
End Sub
```

4. Now add some code to exit the application. Click exitToolStripMenuItem in the Class Name combo box and the Click event in the Method Name combo box. Add the following code to the exitToolStripMenuItem_Click procedure:

```
Private Sub exitToolStripMenuItem_Click(ByVal sender As Object, _
    ByVal e As System.EventArgs) Handles exitToolStripMenuItem.Click

    Me.Close()
End Sub
```

5. Now add some code to navigate from the Managers view to the Employees view. Click MyTimeSheetToolStripMenuItem in the Class Name combo box and the Click event in the Method Name combo box. Add the following code to the MyTimeSheetToolStripMenuItem_Click procedure:

```
Private Sub MyTimeSheetToolStripMenuItem_Click(ByVal sender As Object, _
    ByVal e As System.EventArgs) Handles MyTimeSheetToolStripMenuItem.Click
```

```
    'Undock the Panel
    pnlManager.Dock = DockStyle.None
    'Move it out of the way
    pnlManager.Location = New Point(5000, 5000)
    'Set the Dock property to Fill
    '(this will cause the location to change to 0,0)
    pnlEmployee.Dock = DockStyle.Top
    'Set the view flag
    blnEmployeeDisplay = True
```
```
End Sub
```

6. Add some code to navigate from the Employees view to the Managers view. Click EmployeeTimeSheetsToolStripMenuItem in the Class Name combo box and the `Click` event in the Method Name combo box. Add the following code to the `EmployeeTimeSheetsToolStripMenuItem_Click` procedure:

```
Private Sub EmployeeTimeSheetsToolStripMenuItem_Click(ByVal sender As Object, _
    ByVal e As System.EventArgs) Handles _
    EmployeeTimeSheetsToolStripMenuItem.Click
```

```
    'Undock the Panel
    pnlEmployee.Dock = DockStyle.None
    'Move it out of the way
    pnlEmployee.Location = New Point(5000, 5000)
    'Set the Dock property to Fill
    '(this will cause the location to change to 0,0)
    pnlManager.Dock = DockStyle.Top
    'Set the view flag
    blnEmployeeDisplay - False
```
```
End Sub
```

7. Finally, add some code to display the About form. Click aboutToolStripMenuItem in the Class Name combo box and the `Click` event in the Method Name combo box. Add the following code to the aboutToolStripMenuItem_Click procedure.

```
Private Sub aboutToolStripMenuItem_Click(ByVal sender As Object, _
    ByVal e As System.EventArgs) Handles aboutToolStripMenuItem.Click
```

```
    Dim objAbout As New About
    objAbout.ShowDialog(Me)
    objAbout.Dispose()
    objAbout = Nothing
```
```
End Sub
```

About form code

In this section, you add some common code to make the About form functional. The About form can be called from both the Admin form and the TimeSheet form.

To add this code:

1. Right-click the About form in the Solution Explorer window and choose View Code from the context menu.

2. Set the Text property of the various labels on the About form when the form loads. Click the Class Name combo box and choose (About Events); and in the Method Name combo box, choose the Load event. Add the following code to the About_Load procedure:

```
Private Sub About_Load(ByVal sender As Object, _
    ByVal e As System.EventArgs) Handles Me.Load

        'Set this form's Text property by using the
        'Text property of the parent form
        Me.Text = "About " & Owner.Text

        'Set the application icon using the parent form's icon
        imgApplicationIcon.Image = Owner.Icon.ToBitmap()

        'Get a reference to the AssemblyInfo for this application
        Dim objAssemblyInfo As Type = sender.GetType()

        'Set the Text property for the title, version, copyright
        'and description labels
        lblTitle.Text = My.Application.Info.Title
        lblVersion.Text = My.Application.Info.Version.ToString
        lblCopyright.Text = My.Application.Info.Copyright
        lblDescription.Text = My.Application.Info.Description
End Sub
```

That's all the code that you need for this project at this time. You can test the code for the About form by running your project and choosing the About menu item from the Help menu. When your About form is displayed, you see the information that was read from your Assembly, and it should look similar to the form shown in Figure B-10.

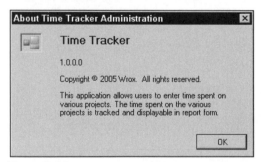

Figure B-10

C

Exercise Solutions

Chapter 2

Exercise 1 solution

The first thing that you do after creating a new Windows application is set a reference to the System.Data.dll namespace. This is done by right-clicking the project in the Solution Explorer and choosing Add Reference from the context menu. Then in the .NET tab of the Add Reference dialog box, you should scroll down the list until you find System.Data.dll, select it, and then click OK.

After adding the list box to your form, you switch to the Code Editor for Form1 and then add the following Imports statements:

```
Imports System.Data
Imports System.Data.OleDb

Public Class Form1
```

In the Load event for the form, you should have code similar to the code shown here to populate the list box:

```
Private Sub Form1_Load(ByVal sender As System.Object, _
    ByVal e As System.EventArgs) Handles MyBase.Load

    'Declare variables and objects
    Dim strConnectionString As String = _
        "Provider=Microsoft.Jet.OLEDB.4.0;" & _
        "Data Source=C:\Program Files\Microsoft Office\Office11\" & _
        "Samples\Northwind.mdb;"
    Dim objConnection As New OleDbConnection(strConnectionString)
    Dim strSQL As String = _
        "SELECT FirstName, LastName FROM Employees"
    Dim objCommand As New OleDbCommand(strSQL, objConnection)
    Dim objDataAdapter As New OleDbDataAdapter(objCommand)
    Dim objDataTable As New Data.DataTable("Employees")
```

```
            Dim objDataRow As DataRow

            Try
                'Open the database connection
                objConnection.Open()

                'Fill the DataTable object
                objDataAdapter.Fill(objDataTable)

                'Load the list box on the form
                For Each objDataRow In objDataTable.Rows
                    ListBox1.Items.Add(objDataRow.Item("FirstName") & " " & _
                        objDataRow.Item("LastName"))
                Next
            Catch OleDbExceptionErr As OleDbException
                'Write the exception
                Debug.WriteLine(OleDbExceptionErr.Message)
            Catch InvalidOperationExceptionErr As InvalidOperationException
                'Write the exception
                Debug.WriteLine(InvalidOperationExceptionErr.Message)
            End Try

            'Close the database connection
            objConnection.Close()

            'Clean up
            objDataRow = Nothing
            objDataTable.Dispose()
            objDataTable = Nothing
            objDataAdapter.Dispose()
            objDataAdapter = Nothing
            objCommand.Dispose()
            objCommand = Nothing
            objConnection.Dispose()
            objConnection = Nothing
        End Sub
```

Exercise 2 solution

The code created for this exercise should look very similar to the last Try It Out in this chapter, except that instead of using a DataTable and DataAdapter object, you use just a DataReader object and populate the list box on your form using the DataReader object.

The code in the Load event of your form should look similar to the code shown here and your form results should look identical to those shown in Figure 2-3.

```
        Private Sub Form1_Load(ByVal sender As System.Object, _
            ByVal e As System.EventArgs) Handles MyBase.Load

            'Declare variables and objects
            Dim strConnectionString As String = _
                "Provider=Microsoft.Jet.OLEDB.4.0;" & _
                "Data Source=C:\Program Files\Microsoft Office\Office11\" & _
```

```
            "Samples\Northwind.mdb;"
        Dim objConnection As New OleDbConnection(strConnectionString)
        Dim strSQL As String = _
            "SELECT FirstName, LastName FROM Employees"
        Dim objCommand As New OleDbCommand(strSQL, objConnection)
        Dim objReader As OleDbDataReader

        Try
            'Open the database connection
            objConnection.Open()

            'Initialize the DataReader object
            objReader = objCommand.ExecuteReader()

            'Load the list box on the form
            While objReader.Read
                ListBox1.Items.Add(objReader.Item("FirstName") & " " & _
                    objReader.Item("LastName"))
            End While
        Catch OleDbExceptionErr As OleDbException
            'Write the exception
            Debug.WriteLine(OleDbExceptionErr.Message)
        Catch InvalidOperationExceptionErr As InvalidOperationException
            'Write the exception
            Debug.WriteLine(InvalidOperationExceptionErr.Message)
        End Try

        'Close the DataReader object
        objReader.Close()

        'Close the database connection
        objConnection.Close()

        'Clean up
        objReader.Dispose()
        objReader = Nothing
        objCommand.Dispose()
        objCommand = Nothing
        objConnection.Dispose()
        objConnection = Nothing
    End Sub
```

Chapter 3

Exercise 1 solution

After configuring your data source for the DataGridView control, your DataGridView control will be bound to the `ProductsBindingSource` component, which is automatically generated. Your DataGridView control will also contain columns for ProductName, UnitPrice, UnitsInStock, and UnitsOnOrder. When you run your project, the DataGridView control is populated with the data from these fields in your database.

Exercise 2 solution

After adding your labels and text boxes to your form, you should click the Text property of the DataBindings property to configure your data source as you did in the "Binding Data to TextBox Controls" Try It Out exercise in this chapter. After your data source is configured, you set the Text property of the DataBindings property of each of the text boxes using the appropriate fields in the SuppliersBindingSource component, which was automatically added to your project. Finally, you add a BindingNavigator control to your form and set the BindingSource property to the SuppliersBindingSource component.

Chapter 4

Exercise 1 solution

The SELECT statement for your query should look like the example shown here:

```
SELECT ProjectName, SequenceNumber
FROM Projects
ORDER BY ProjectName DESC;
```

Exercise 2 solution

The UPDATE statement for your query should look like the example shown here:

```
UPDATE Projects
SET ProjectDescription = @ProjectDescription
WHERE ProjectID = @ProjectID;
```

Chapter 5

Exercise 1 solution

The first thing that you should do is set a reference to the System.Data namespace and add the following Imports statements:

```
Imports System.Data
Imports System.Data.OleDb
```

The variables that need to be declared can be declared at the form level or at the procedure level. You should declare the following variables:

```
'Form level variables
Private strConnectionString As String = _
    "Provider=Microsoft.Jet.OLEDB.4.0;" & _
    "Data Source=C:\Chapter 5\ProjectTimeTracker.mdb;"

Private objConnection As OleDbConnection
Private objCommand As OleDbCommand
Private objDataAdapter As OleDbDataAdapter
Private objDataTable As DataTable
```

The code to load the combo box could be placed in the Form Load event or in a button Click event and should look similar to this:

```
'Initialize the Connection object
objConnection = New OleDbConnection(strConnectionString)

'Initialize the Command object
objCommand = New OleDbCommand("SELECT ProjectID, ProjectName " & _
    "FROM Projects", objConnection)

'Initialize the DataAdapter object and set the SelectCommand property
objDataAdapter = New OleDbDataAdapter
objDataAdapter.SelectCommand = objCommand

'Initialize the DataTable object
objDataTable = New DataTable

'Populate the DataTable
objDataAdapter.Fill(objDataTable)

'Bind the DataTable to the ComboBox
ComboBox1.DataSource = objDataTable
ComboBox1.DisplayMember = "ProjectName"
ComboBox1.ValueMember = "ProjectID"

'Clean up
objDataAdapter.Dispose()
objDataAdapter = Nothing
objCommand.Dispose()
objCommand = Nothing
objConnection.Dispose()
objConnection = Nothing
```

Exercise 2 solution

If you coded the variables in Exercise 1 at the form level, you need only two additional variables as shown here:

```
Private objDataReader As OleDbDataReader
Private blnIsLoading As Boolean = True
```

You need to modify the code that binds the DataTable to the combo box as follows to turn off the blnIsLoading flag:

```
'Bind the DataTable to the ComboBox
ComboBox1.DataSource = objDataTable
ComboBox1.DisplayMember = "ProjectName"
ComboBox1.ValueMember = "ProjectID"

'Turn off the loading flag
blnIsLoading = False
```

The code you added to the `ComboBox1_SelectedValueChanged` event handler should look similar to the code shown here:

```
Private Sub ComboBox1_SelectedValueChanged(ByVal sender As Object, _
    ByVal e As System.EventArgs) Handles ComboBox1.SelectedValueChanged

    'Exit if the combo box is being loaded
    If blnIsLoading Then
        Exit Sub
    End If

    'Initialize the Connection object and open it
    objConnection = New OleDbConnection(strConnectionString)
    objConnection.Open()

    'Initialize the Command object
    objCommand = New OleDbCommand

    'Set the objCommand object properties
    objCommand.CommandText = "usp_SelectProject"
    objCommand.CommandType = CommandType.StoredProcedure
    objCommand.Connection = objConnection

    'Add the required parameter for the query
    objCommand.Parameters.Add("@ProjectID", OleDbType.Guid, 16).Value = _
        New Guid(ComboBox1.SelectedValue.ToString)

    'Execute the Query
    objDataReader = objCommand.ExecuteReader()

    'If we have data then display the project description
    If objDataReader.HasRows Then
        objDataReader.Read()
        TextBox1.Text = objDataReader.Item("ProjectDescription")
    End If

    'Close the DataReader and Connection
    objDataReader.Close()
    objConnection.Close()

    'Clean up
    objDataReader = Nothing
    objCommand.Dispose()
    objCommand = Nothing
    objConnection.Dispose()
    objConnection = Nothing
End Sub
```

Chapter 6

Exercise 1 solution

The first thing that you do after adding your controls is create your application configuration settings and then set a reference to the System.Data namespace. Then you should add the following Imports statements:

```
Imports System.Data
Imports System.Data.OleDb
```

In the Click event for the button, the first thing you do is declare and initialize a Connection object using the configuration settings that you specified.

```
'Declare and initialize a Connection object
Dim objConnection As New OleDbConnection( _
"Provider=" & My.Settings.Provider & ";" & _
"Data Source=" & My.Settings.DataSource & ";")
```

Next, you use the same code from the btnDataReader_Click procedure from the Access SQL project adding the necessary code to open and close the database connection.

```
'Declare and initialize a new instance of the OleDbCommand class
Dim objCommand As New OleDbCommand(TextBox1.Text, objConnection)

'Declare an OleDbDataReader object
Dim objDataReader As OleDbDataReader

'Declare a String variable
Dim strData As String

Try
    'Open the database connection
    objConnection.Open()

    'Execute the SQL text
    objDataReader = objCommand.ExecuteReader()

    'Check to see if we have data
    If objDataReader.HasRows Then

        'Process all rows
        While objDataReader.Read()

            'Clear the variable
            strData = String.Empty

            'Get the data in each column
            For intIndex As Integer = 0 To objDataReader.FieldCount - 1
                strData &= objDataReader.Item(intIndex).ToString & ", "
            Next

            'Remove the last comma from the string
```

```
                           strData = strData.Remove(strData.Length - 2, 2)

                           'Write the data to the TextBox
                           TextBox1.Text &= ControlChars.CrLf & strData

                       End While

                   End If

                   'Close the reader
                   objDataReader.Close()

                   'Close the database
                   objConnection.Close()

               Catch OleDbExceptionErr As OleDbException
                   MessageBox.Show(OleDbExceptionErr.Message, "Access SQL")
               End Try

               'Cleanup
               objCommand.Dispose()
               objCommand = Nothing
               objDataReader = Nothing
               objConnection.Dispose()
               objConnection = Nothing
           End Sub
```

When you run your project, enter a SQL statement, and click the button, you should receive results of that query listed in the text box on the form.

Chapter 7

Exercise 1 solution

Your queries should look similar to the following.

Query to select all scores:

```
SELECT ScoreID, Opposition, OurScore, TheirScore, DatePlayed
FROM Scores
ORDER BY DatePlayed;
```

Query to select a specific score:

```
SELECT ScoreID, Opposition, OurScore, TheirScore, DatePlayed
FROM Scores
WHERE ScoreID = @ScoreID;
```

Query to insert a score:

```
INSERT INTO Scores (ScoreID, Opposition, OurScore, TheirScore, DatePlayed)
VALUES (@ScoreID,@Opposition, @OurScore, @TheirScore, @DatePlayed);
```

Query to update a score:

```
UPDATE Scores
SET Opposition = @Opposition,
OurScore = @OurScore,
TheirScore = @TheirScore,
DatePlayed = @DatePlayed
WHERE ScoreID = @ScoreID;
```

Query to delete a score:

```
DELETE
FROM Scores
WHERE ScoreID = @ScoreID;
```

Exercise 2 solution

The first thing that you should do after designing your form is add a reference to the System.Data namespace. Then you should add the following Imports statement at the top of your Form class:

```
Imports System.Data.OleDb

Public Class Form1
```

The private variables needed in your form include:

```
'Private variables and objects
Private intRowsAffected As Integer

Private strConnection As String

Private objConnection As OleDbConnection
Private objCommand As OleDbCommand
Private objDataReader As OleDbDataReader
```

Next, you should add three private procedures: one to open the database connection, one to close the database connection, and one to load the scores list.

```
Private Sub OpenConnection()
    Try
        objConnection.Open()
    Catch OleDbExceptionErr As OleDbException
        Throw New System.Exception(OleDbExceptionErr.Message, _
            OleDbExceptionErr.InnerException)
    Catch InvalidOperationExceptionErr As InvalidOperationException
        Throw New System.Exception(InvalidOperationExceptionErr.Message, _
            InvalidOperationExceptionErr.InnerException)
    End Try
End Sub

Private Sub CloseConnection()
    objConnection.Close()
```

```
    End Sub

Private Sub LoadScores()
    'Declare variables
    Dim objListViewItem As ListViewItem

    Try
        'Initialize the Command object and set its properties
        objCommand = New OleDbCommand("usp_SelectScores", objConnection)
        objCommand.CommandType = Data.CommandType.StoredProcedure

        'Open the database connection
        OpenConnection()

        'Get the data
        objDataReader = objCommand.ExecuteReader

        'See if any data exists before continuing
        If objDataReader.HasRows Then

            'Clear previous list
            lvwScores.Items.Clear()

            'Process all rows
            While objDataReader.Read()

                'Create a new ListViewItem
                objListViewItem = New ListViewItem

                'Add the data to the ListViewItem
                objListViewItem.Text = _
                    objDataReader.Item("Opposition")
                objListViewItem.Tag = objDataReader.Item("ScoreID")

                'Add the sub items to the listview item
                objListViewItem.SubItems.Add( _
                    objDataReader.Item("OurScore"))
                objListViewItem.SubItems.Add( _
                    objDataReader.Item("TheirScore"))
                objListViewItem.SubItems.Add( _
                    Format(objDataReader.Item("DatePlayed"), "g"))

                'Add the ListViewItem to the ListView control
                lvwScores.Items.Add(objListViewItem)

            End While

        End If

        'Close the DataReader object
        objDataReader.Close()

        'Close the database connection
        CloseConnection()

    Catch OleDbExceptionErr As OleDbException
```

```
                    MessageBox.Show(OleDbExceptionErr.Message)
        End Try
    End Sub
```

The form's `Load` and `Closing` events are ideal places to put your code to initialize your `Connection` object and to perform the final cleanup of your resources. These procedures should contain code similar to the code shown here:

```
    Private Sub Form1_Load(ByVal sender As System.Object, _
        ByVal e As System.EventArgs) Handles MyBase.Load

        'Build the SQL connection string and initialize the Connection object
        objConnection = New OleDbConnection( _
        "Provider=Microsoft.Jet.OLEDB.4.0;" & _
        "Data Source=..\..\ProjectTimeTracker.mdb;")

        'Load the scores
        LoadScores()
    End Sub

    Private Sub Form1_FormClosing(ByVal sender As Object, _
        ByVal e As System.Windows.Forms.FormClosingEventArgs) _
        Handles Me.FormClosing

        'Clean up
        If Not objDataReader Is Nothing Then
            objDataReader.Close()
            objDataReader = Nothing
        End If
        If Not Command() Is Nothing Then
            objCommand.Dispose()
            objCommand = Nothing
        End If
        If Not objConnection Is Nothing Then
            objConnection.Close()
            objConnection.Dispose()
            objConnection = Nothing
        End If
    End Sub
```

When you click an item in the `ListView` control, you should populate the fields on your form with the selected item. The code to perform this is shown here:

```
    Private Sub lvwScores_Click(ByVal sender As Object, _
        ByVal e As System.EventArgs) Handles lvwScores.Click

        Try
            'Initialize the Command object and set its properties
            objCommand = New OleDbCommand("usp_SelectScore", objConnection)
            objCommand.CommandType = Data.CommandType.StoredProcedure

            'Add the Parameter to the Parameters collection
            objCommand.Parameters.Add("@ScoreID", OleDbType.Guid, 16).Value = _
```

```
                    lvwScores.SelectedItems.Item(0).Tag

            'Open the database connection
            OpenConnection()

            'Get the data
            objDataReader = objCommand.ExecuteReader

            'See if any data exists before continuing
            If objDataReader.HasRows Then

                'Read the first and only row of data
                objDataReader.Read()

                'Populate the Project Details section
                txtScoreID.Text = _
                    objDataReader.Item("ScoreID").ToString.ToUpper
                txtOpposition.Text = _
                    objDataReader.Item("Opposition")
                txtOurScore.Text = _
                    objDataReader.Item("OurScore")
                txtTheirScore.Text = _
                    objDataReader.Item("TheirScore")
                txtDatePlayed.Text = _
                    Format(objDataReader.Item("DatePlayed"), "g")

            End If

            'Close the DataReader object
            objDataReader.Close()

            'Close the database connection
            CloseConnection()

        Catch OleDbExceptionErr As OleDbException
            MessageBox.Show(OleDbExceptionErr.Message)
        End Try
    End Sub
```

The code for your Add, Update, and Delete buttons is shown here:

```
Private Sub btnAdd_Click(ByVal sender As Object, _
    ByVal e As System.EventArgs) Handles btnAdd.Click

    Try
        'Initialize the Command object and set its properties
        objCommand = New OleDbCommand("usp_InsertScore", objConnection)
        objCommand.CommandType = Data.CommandType.StoredProcedure

        'Add the Parameters to the Parameters collection
        objCommand.Parameters.Add("@ScoreID", _
            OleDbType.Guid, 16).Value = Guid.NewGuid()
        objCommand.Parameters.Add("@Opposition", _
            OleDbType.VarChar, 50).Value = txtOpposition.Text
        objCommand.Parameters.Add("@OurScore", _
```

```
            OleDbType.UnsignedTinyInt, 1).Value = _
            CType(txtOurScore.Text, Byte)
        objCommand.Parameters.Add("@TheirScore", _
            OleDbType.UnsignedTinyInt, 1).Value = _
            CType(txtTheirScore.Text, Byte)
        objCommand.Parameters.Add("@DatePlayed", _
            OleDbType.DBDate, 8).Value = _
            CType(txtDatePlayed.Text, DateTime)

        'Open the database connection
        OpenConnection()

        'Execute the query
        intRowsAffected = objCommand.ExecuteNonQuery()

        'Close the database connection
        CloseConnection()

        'Check the rows affected
        If intRowsAffected = 0 Then
            Throw New Exception("Insert Score Failed")
        End If

        'Clear the input fields
        txtScoreID.Text = String.Empty
        txtOpposition.Text = String.Empty
        txtOurScore.Text = String.Empty
        txtTheirScore.Text = String.Empty
        txtDatePlayed.Text = String.Empty

        'Reload the Scores list
        LoadScores()

    Catch OleDbExceptionErr As OleDbException
        MessageBox.Show(OleDbExceptionErr.Message)
    End Try
End Sub

Private Sub btnUpdate_Click(ByVal sender As Object, _
    ByVal e As System.EventArgs) Handles btnUpdate.Click

    Try
        'Initialize the Command object and set its properties
        objCommand = New OleDbCommand("usp_UpdateScore", objConnection)
        objCommand.CommandType = Data.CommandType.StoredProcedure

        'Add the Parameters to the Parameters collection
        objCommand.Parameters.Add("@Opposition", _
            OleDbType.VarChar, 50).Value = txtOpposition.Text
        objCommand.Parameters.Add("@OurScore", _
            OleDbType.UnsignedTinyInt, 1).Value = _
            CType(txtOurScore.Text, Byte)
        objCommand.Parameters.Add("@TheirScore", _
            OleDbType.UnsignedTinyInt, 1).Value = _
            CType(txtTheirScore.Text, Byte)
```

```
            objCommand.Parameters.Add("@DatePlayed", _
                OleDbType.DBDate, 8).Value = _
                CType(txtDatePlayed.Text, DateTime)
            objCommand.Parameters.Add("@ScoreID", _
                OleDbType.Guid, 16).Value = _
                New Guid(txtScoreID.Text)

            'Open the database connection
            OpenConnection()

            'Execute the query
            intRowsAffected = objCommand.ExecuteNonQuery()

            'Close the database connection
            CloseConnection()

            'Check the rows affected
            If intRowsAffected = 0 Then
                Throw New Exception("Update Score Failed")
            End If

            'Clear the input fields
            txtScoreID.Text = String.Empty
            txtOpposition.Text = String.Empty
            txtOurScore.Text = String.Empty
            txtTheirScore.Text = String.Empty
            txtDatePlayed.Text = String.Empty

            'Reload the Scores list
            LoadScores()

        Catch OleDbExceptionErr As OleDbException
            MessageBox.Show(OleDbExceptionErr.Message)
        End Try
    End Sub

    Private Sub btnDelete_Click(ByVal sender As Object, _
        ByVal e As System.EventArgs) Handles btnDelete.Click

        Try
            'Initialize the Command object and set its properties
            objCommand = New OleDbCommand("usp_DeleteScore", objConnection)
            objCommand.CommandType = Data.CommandType.StoredProcedure

            'Add the Parameter to the Parameters collection
            objCommand.Parameters.Add("@ScoreID", _
                OleDbType.Guid, 16).Value = _
                New Guid(txtScoreID.Text)

            'Open the database connection
            OpenConnection()

            'Execute the query
            intRowsAffected = objCommand.ExecuteNonQuery()

            'Close the database connection
```

```
                    CloseConnection()

                'Check the rows affected
                If intRowsAffected = 0 Then
                    Throw New Exception("Delete Score Failed")
                End If

                'Clear the input fields
                txtScoreID.Text = String.Empty
                txtOpposition.Text = String.Empty
                txtOurScore.Text = String.Empty
                txtTheirScore.Text = String.Empty
                txtDatePlayed.Text = String.Empty

                'Reload the Scores list
                LoadScores()

            Catch OleDbExceptionErr As OleDbException
                MessageBox.Show(OleDbExceptionErr.Message)
            End Try
        End Sub
```

Chapter 8

Exercise 1 solution

After you design your form, you should add the WDABase class to your project and set a reference to the System.Data namespace. You should add the following Imports statement at the top of your Form class:

```
Imports System.Data
```

Next, in your Form Load event, you add code similar to the code that follows. There are two Using statements shown, with the first being commented out. The first Using statement is the one that you use for connecting to SQL Server and you replace the parameters with values that are specific to your environment. The second Using statement is used for connecting to Oracle and again you replace the parameters with values that are specific to your environment.

```
        Private Sub Form1_Load(ByVal sender As System.Object, _
            ByVal e As System.EventArgs) Handles MyBase.Load

        'SQL Server connection
        'Using objData As New WDABase("SQL Server", "OracleSql", _
        '    "ProjectTimeTracker", "thearon", "thearon")

        'Oracle connection
        Using objData As New WDABase("Oracle", "wrox", _
            "", "thearon", "thearon")

            Try
                'Open the database connection
                objData.OpenConnection()

                'Build an SELECT SQL statement
                objData.SQL = "SELECT ProjectID, ProjectName FROM Projects " & _
```

```
                    "ORDER BY ProjectName"

            'Declare a DataTable object and populate it
            Dim objDataTable As New DataTable
            objData.FillDataTable(objDataTable)

            'Bind the DataTable to the list box
            ListBox1.DataSource = objDataTable
            ListBox1.DisplayMember = "ProjectName"
            ListBox1.ValueMember = "ProjectID"

            'Close the database connection
            objData.CloseConnection()

        Catch ExceptionErr As Exception
            'Display the error
            MessageBox.Show(ExceptionErr.Message)
        End Try

    End Using
End Sub
```

Exercise 2 solution

You add code to the Click event of the list box and it should look similar to the code shown here. The first Using statement is the one that you use for connecting to SQL Server and you replace the parameters with values that are specific to your environment. The second Using statement is used for connecting to Oracle and again you replace the parameters with values that are specific to your environment:

```
Private Sub ListBox1_Click(ByVal sender As Object, _
    ByVal e As System.EventArgs) Handles ListBox1.Click

        'SQL Server connection
        'Using objData As New WDABase("SQL Server", "OracleSql", _
        '    "ProjectTimeTracker", "thearon", "thearon")
        'Oracle connection
        Using objData As New WDABase("Oracle", "wrox", _
            "", "thearon", "thearon")

            Try
                'Build a SELECT SQL statement
                objData.SQL = "SELECT SequenceNumber, LastUpdateDate " & _
                    "FROM Projects " & _
                    "WHERE ProjectID = ?"

                'Initialize the Command object
                objData.InitializeCommand()

                'Add a Parameter to the Parameters collection
                objData.AddParameter("ProjectID", _
                    Data.OleDb.OleDbType.Char, 36, ListBox1.SelectedValue)

                'Open the connection
```

```
                                objData.OpenConnection()

                            'Get the data in a DataReader object
                            objData.DataReader = objData.Command.ExecuteReader

                            'See if any data exists before continuing
                            If objData.DataReader.HasRows Then

                                'Read the first row
                                objData.DataReader.Read()

                                'Populate the fields on the form
                                txtSequenceNumber.Text = objData.DataReader.Item( _
                                    "SequenceNumber")
                                txtUpdateDate.Text = objData.DataReader.Item("LastUpdateDate")

                                'Close the DataReader
                                objData.DataReader.Close()

                                'Close the database connection
                                objData.CloseConnection()

                            End If

                        Catch ExceptionErr As Exception
                            'Display the error
                            MessageBox.Show(ExceptionErr.Message)
                        End Try
                End Using
            End Sub
```

Chapter 9

Exercise 1 solution

The view that you create should look similar to the following code:

SQL Server

```
CREATE VIEW vw_SelectProjects
AS
SELECT    ProjectID, ProjectName, ProjectDescription
FROM      Projects
```

Oracle

```
CREATE OR REPLACE VIEW vw_SelectProjects
AS
SELECT ProjectID, ProjectName, ProjectDescription
FROM Projects;
```

After designing your form, you should set a reference to the System.Data namespace. Readers using Oracle should also set a reference to the System.Data.OracleClient namespace. Next, you right-click the project in the Solution Explorer and choose Add ⇨ Existing Item from the context menu. You then add the app.config file and the WDABase class from your Time Tracker application.

The app.config file needs to be modified directly so you should view the code by double-clicking the app.config file in the Solution Explorer. Next, you rename all instances of Time_Tracker to Exercise_1.

For your application to recognize the new settings that were imported, you need to view the Property pages for your application by right-clicking the project in the Solution Explorer and choosing Properties from the context menu. Then you click the Settings tab in the Property Pages and Visual Studio 2005 displays a dialog box informing you that new settings were imported from the app.config file. At this point, you save your project to save the changes.

Next, you import the System.Data namespace in Form1:

```
Imports System.Data
```

You add your code to populate the list box to the form's Load event. Optionally, you can add a button to your form and put the code in the button's Click event. Your code to execute the view and load the list box should look similar to the code shown here:

```
Private Sub Form1_Load(ByVal sender As System.Object, _
    ByVal e As System.EventArgs) Handles MyBase.Load

    'Initialize a new instance of the data access base class
    Using objData As New WDABase
        Try
            'Declare local variables
            Dim objDataTable As New Data.DataTable("Projects")

            'Get all Projects in a DataSet
            objData.SQL = "SELECT ProjectID, ProjectName " & _
                "FROM vw_SelectProjects " & _
                "ORDER BY ProjectName"
            objData.InitializeCommand()
            Call objData.FillDataTable(objDataTable)

            'Bind ListBox control
            ListBox1.DataSource = objDataTable
            ListBox1.DisplayMember = "ProjectName"
            ListBox1.ValueMember = "ProjectID"

        Catch ExceptionErr As Exception
            MessageBox.Show(ExceptionErr.Message, "Exercise 1")
        End Try
    End Using
End Sub
```

Exercise 2 solution

The exercise requires you to add a text box to your form and code to the list box's Click event. Your code should look similar to the code shown here:

SQL Server and Oracle

```
Private Sub ListBox1_Click(ByVal sender As Object, _
    ByVal e As System.EventArgs) Handles ListBox1.Click

    'Initialize a new instance of the data access base class
    Using objData As New WDABase
        Try
```

SQL Server

```
        'Build the SQL string
        objData.SQL = "SELECT ProjectDescription " & _
            "FROM vw_SelectProjects " & _
            "WHERE ProjectID = @ProjectID"

        'Initialize the Command object
        objData.InitializeCommand()

        'Add a Parameter to the Parameters collection
        objData.AddParameter("@ProjectID", _
            Data.SqlDbType.UniqueIdentifier, 16, ListBox1.SelectedValue)
```

Oracle

```
        'Build the SQL string
        objData.SQL = "SELECT ProjectDescription " & _
            "FROM vw_SelectProjects " & _
            "WHERE ProjectID = :inProjectID"

        'Initialize the Command object
        objData.InitializeCommand()

        'Add a Parameter to the Parameters collection
        objData.AddParameter("inProjectID", _
            Data.OracleClient.OracleType.Char, 36, ListBox1.SelectedValue)
```

SQL Server and Oracle

```
        'Open the connection
        objData.OpenConnection()

        'Get the data in a DataReader object
        objData.DataReader = objData.Command.ExecuteReader

        'See if any data exists before continuing
        If objData.DataReader.HasRows Then

            'Read the first row
```

```
                        objData.DataReader.Read()

                        'Populate the fields on the form
                        txtProjectDescription.Text = _
                            objData.DataReader.Item("ProjectDescription")

                    End If

                    'Close the DataReader
                    objData.DataReader.Close()

                    'Close the database connection
                    objData.CloseConnection()

            Catch ExceptionErr As Exception
                MessageBox.Show(ExceptionErr.Message, "Exercise 1")
            End Try
        End Using
    End Sub
```

Chapter 10

Exercise 1 solution

The first thing that you do is set a reference to the WroxBusinessLogic.dll. This is done by clicking the Browse tab in the Add Reference dialog box and browsing to the compiled DLL for the WroxBusinessLogic project.

Next, you delete the WDABase class from your project as it is no longer needed.

The following variable declarations are needed at the top of your form class:

```
'Private variables and objects
Private strCompany As String = "Wrox"
Private strApplication As String = "Time Tracker"

Private objProjects As WroxBusinessLogic.WBLProjects

Private objDataSet As Data.DataSet
Private objProjectsDS As Data.DataSet
```

Next, you modify the procedure to load the list box to use the GetProjects method in the business logic component. Your code for this procedure should now look similar to the code shown here:

```
'Initialize a new instance of the business logic component
Using objProjects As New WroxBusinessLogic.WBLProjects( _
    strCompany, strApplication)

    Try
        'Get all projects in a DataSet object
        objProjectsDS = objProjects.GetProjects()

        'Bind ListBox control
```

```
                    ListBox1.DataSource = objProjectsDS.Tables("Projects")
                    ListBox1.DisplayMember = "ProjectName"
                    ListBox1.ValueMember = "ProjectID"

            Catch ExceptionErr As Exception
                MessageBox.Show(ExceptionErr.Message, "Exercise 1")
            End Try
        End Using
```

Your code to retrieve a specific project should now look similar to the code shown here, which calls the `GetProject` method in your business logic component:

```
        'Initialize a new instance of the business logic component
        Using objProjects As New WroxBusinessLogic.WBLProjects( _
            strCompany, strApplication)

            Try
                'Get the specific project selected in the ListView control
                objDataSet = objProjects.GetProject( _
                    New Guid(ListBox1.SelectedValue.ToString))

                txtProjectDescription.Text = _
                    objDataSet.Tables("Project").Rows(0).Item( _
                    "ProjectDescription")

            Catch ExceptionErr As Exception
                MessageBox.Show(ExceptionErr.Message, "Exercise 1")
            End Try
        End Using
```

As you can see from this exercise, the amount of code in your application was dramatically reduced and you were able to reuse your business logic and data access components that you built in this chapter.

Chapter 11

Exercise 1 solution

Your code modifications to the `ListBox1_Click` procedure should look similar to the code shown here:

```
        If objDataSet.Tables("Project").Rows(0).Item( _
            "ProjectDescription") = String.Empty Then

            txtProjectDescription.Text = "No Data Available"
        Else
            txtProjectDescription.Text = _
                objDataSet.Tables("Project").Rows(0).Item( _
                "ProjectDescription")
        End If
```

Exercise 2 solution

The modifications to your stored procedure should be as follows:

SQL Server

```
ALTER PROCEDURE usp_InsertRole
(
    @RoleID             UNIQUEIDENTIFIER,
    @RoleName           VARCHAR(50),
    @RoleDescription    TEXT,
    @Ranking            TINYINT
)
AS
IF EXISTS (SELECT Ranking FROM Roles WHERE Ranking = @Ranking)
    BEGIN
    RAISERROR('Ranking already exists and cannot be duplicated',18,1)
    END
ELSE
    BEGIN
    BEGIN TRY
        INSERT INTO Roles
            (RoleID, RoleName, RoleDescription, Ranking, LastUpdateDate)
            VALUES(@RoleID, @RoleName, @RoleDescription, @Ranking, GETDATE())
    END TRY
    BEGIN CATCH
        RAISERROR('Insert into Roles failed.',18,1)
    END CATCH
    END
```

Oracle

```
CREATE OR REPLACE PROCEDURE usp_InsertRole
(
inRoleID            CHAR,
inRoleName          VARCHAR2,
inRoleDescription   CLOB,
inRanking           NUMBER
)
AS

RankAvailable number(3,0);

BEGIN
    BEGIN
        SELECT Ranking INTO RankAvailable
        FROM Roles
        WHERE Ranking - inRanking;
        RAISE_APPLICATION_ERROR (-20999,
            'Ranking already exists and cannot be duplicated');
    EXCEPTION
        WHEN NO_DATA_FOUND THEN
        BEGIN
            INSERT INTO Roles
                (RoleID, RoleName, RoleDescription, Ranking, LastUpdateDate)
```

```
                VALUES(inRoleID, inRoleName, inRoleDescription, inRanking, SYSDATE);
        EXCEPTION
            WHEN OTHERS THEN
            RAISE_APPLICATION_ERROR( -20999,'Insert into Roles failed.');
    END;
  END;
END;
```

Chapter 12

Exercise 1 solution

Your stored procedure should look similar to the one shown here. Readers using Oracle will have created a package and package body for their stored procedure:

SQL Server

```
CREATE PROCEDURE usp_Chapter12Ex1
AS

SELECT FirstName + ' ' + LastName AS UserName, RoleName
FROM Users
JOIN Roles ON Users.RoleID = Roles.RoleID
ORDER BY UserName
```

Oracle

```
CREATE OR REPLACE PACKAGE Chapter12Ex1Package
AS
    TYPE CURSOR_TYPE IS REF CURSOR;
    PROCEDURE usp_Chapter12Ex1 (results_cursor OUT CURSOR_TYPE);
END;
```

```
CREATE OR REPLACE PACKAGE BODY Chapter12Ex1Package
AS
    PROCEDURE usp_Chapter12Ex1 (results_cursor OUT CURSOR_TYPE)
    AS
    BEGIN
        OPEN results_cursor FOR
        SELECT FirstName || ' ' || LastName AS UserName, RoleName
        FROM Users
        JOIN Roles ON Users.RoleID = Roles.RoleID
        ORDER BY UserName;
    END;
END;
```

Exercise 2 solution

After adding the DataGridView control to your form, you should switch to the Code Editor and set a reference to the `System.Data` namespace. Readers using Oracle will also have to set a reference to the `System.Data.OracleClient` namespace. The next step is to import the appropriate namespace in your class as follows:

SQL Server

```
Imports System.Data.SqlClient
```

Oracle

```
Imports System.Data.OracleClient
```

The next step is to add code to the `Load` event of the form to execute your stored procedure and to bind the `DataSet` to the DataGridView control. Your code should look similar to the following code. You'll need to update the connection string with the appropriate information to connect to your SQL Server database or Oracle database:

SQL Server

```
Private Sub Form1_Load(ByVal sender As System.Object, _
    ByVal e As System.EventArgs) Handles MyBase.Load

    Try
        'Declare variables and objects
        Dim strConnection As String = _
            "Data Source=OracleSql;" & _
            "Database=ProjectTimeTracker;" & _
            "User ID=thearon;" & _
            "Password=thearon;"

        Dim objDataSet As New Data.DataSet
        Dim objConnection As New SqlConnection(strConnection)

        Dim objCommand As New SqlCommand("usp_Chapter12Ex1", objConnection)
        objCommand.CommandType = Data.CommandType.StoredProcedure

        Dim objDataAdapter As New SqlDataAdapter
        objDataAdapter.SelectCommand = objCommand

        'Fill the DataSet
        objDataAdapter.Fill(objDataSet, "Users")

        'Bind the DataSet to the DataGridView
        DataGridView1.AutoGenerateColumns = False
        DataGridView1.DataSource = objDataSet
        DataGridView1.DataMember = "Users"

        'Set the DataGridView properties
        DataGridView1.AlternatingRowsDefaultCellStyle.BackColor = _
            Color.WhiteSmoke

        'Create and add DataGridView text box columns
        Dim objColumn As New DataGridViewTextBoxColumn
        With objColumn
            .HeaderText = "User Name"
            .DataPropertyName = "UserName"
            .Width = 200
        End With
        DataGridView1.Columns.Add(objColumn)

        objColumn = New DataGridViewTextBoxColumn
```

```
                With objColumn
                    .HeaderText = "Role Name"
                    .DataPropertyName = "RoleName"
                    .Width = 100
                End With
                DataGridView1.Columns.Add(objColumn)

                'Clean up
                objDataAdapter.Dispose()
                objDataAdapter = Nothing
                objCommand.Dispose()
                objCommand = Nothing
                objConnection.Dispose()
                objConnection = Nothing
                objDataSet.Dispose()
                objDataSet = Nothing
            Catch SqlExceptionErr As SqlException
                MessageBox.Show(SqlExceptionErr.Message)
            End Try
        End Sub
```

Oracle

```
        Private Sub Form1_Load(ByVal sender As System.Object, _
            ByVal e As System.EventArgs) Handles MyBase.Load

            Try
                'Declare variables and objects
                Dim strConnection As String = _
                    "Data Source=Wrox;" & _
                    "User ID=thearon;" & _
                    "Password=thearon;"

                Dim objDataSet As New Data.DataSet
                Dim objConnection As New OracleConnection(strConnection)

                Dim objCommand As New OracleCommand( _
                    "Chapter12Ex1Package.usp_Chapter12Ex1", objConnection)
                objCommand.CommandType = Data.CommandType.StoredProcedure
                objCommand.Parameters.Add("results_cursor", OracleType.Cursor)
                objCommand.Parameters.Item(0).Direction = _
                    Data.ParameterDirection.Output

                Dim objDataAdapter As New OracleDataAdapter
                objDataAdapter.SelectCommand = objCommand

                'Fill the DataSet
                objDataAdapter.Fill(objDataSet, "Users")

                'Bind the DataSet to the DataGridView
                DataGridView1.AutoGenerateColumns = False
                DataGridView1.DataSource = objDataSet
                DataGridView1.DataMember = "Users"

                'Set the DataGridView properties
```

```
                DataGridView1.AlternatingRowsDefaultCellStyle.BackColor = _
                    Color.WhiteSmoke

                'Create and add DataGridView text box columns
                Dim objColumn As New DataGridViewTextBoxColumn
                With objColumn
                    .HeaderText = "User Name"
                    .DataPropertyName = "UserName"
                    .Width = 200
                End With
                DataGridView1.Columns.Add(objColumn)

                objColumn = New DataGridViewTextBoxColumn
                With objColumn
                    .HeaderText = "Role Name"
                    .DataPropertyName = "RoleName"
                    .Width = 100
                End With
                DataGridView1.Columns.Add(objColumn)

                'Clean up
                objDataAdapter.Dispose()
                objDataAdapter = Nothing
                objCommand.Dispose()
                objCommand = Nothing
                objConnection.Dispose()
                objConnection = Nothing
                objDataSet.Dispose()
                objDataSet = Nothing
            Catch OracleExceptionErr As OracleException
                MessageBox.Show(OracleExceptionErr.Message)
            End Try
        End Sub
```

Chapter 13

Exercise 1 solution

Your stored procedure to delete a role should look similar to this stored procedure:

SQL Server

```
CREATE PROCEDURE usp_DeleteRole
(
    @RoleID    UNIQUEIDENTIFIER
)
AS

BEGIN TRY
    DELETE FROM ROles
    WHERE RoleID = @RoleID
END TRY
BEGIN CATCH
    BEGIN
```

```
         RAISERROR('Delete role failed.',18,1)
         RETURN
         END
   END CATCH
```

Oracle

```
CREATE OR REPLACE PROCEDURE usp_DeleteRole
(
    inRoleID   CHAR
)
AS

BEGIN
    DELETE FROM Roles
    WHERE RoleID = inRoleID;
    EXCEPTION
        WHEN OTHERS THEN
        RAISE_APPLICATION_ERROR( -20999,'Delete role failed.');
        RETURN;
END;
```

Your stored procedure to delete a user should look similar to this stored procedure:

SQL Server

```
CREATE PROCEDURE usp_DeleteUser
(
    @UserID   UNIQUEIDENTIFIER
)
AS

BEGIN TRY
    DELETE FROM Users
    WHERE UserID = @UserID
END TRY
BEGIN CATCH
    BEGIN
    RAISERROR('Delete user failed.',18,1)
    RETURN
    END
END CATCH
```

Oracle

```
CREATE OR REPLACE PROCEDURE usp_DeleteUser
(
    inUserID   CHAR
)
AS

BEGIN
    DELETE FROM Users
    WHERE UserID = inUserID;
    EXCEPTION
```

```
            WHEN OTHERS THEN
            RAISE_APPLICATION_ERROR( -20999,'Delete user failed.');
            RETURN;
    END;
```

The `DeleteRole` function in your `WDARoles` class in your data access component should look similar to the following code:

SQL Server

```
    Public Function DeleteRole(ByVal RoleID As Guid) As Boolean
        Try
            MyBase.SQL = "usp_DeleteRole"
            'Initialize the Command object
            MyBase.InitializeCommand()
            'Add the Parameters to the Parameters collection
            MyBase.AddParameter("@RoleID", _
                SqlDbType.UniqueIdentifier, 16, RoleID)
            'Execute the stored procedure
            DeleteRole = ExecuteStoredProcedure()
        Catch ExceptionErr As Exception
            Throw New System.Exception(ExceptionErr.Message, _
            ExceptionErr.InnerException)
        End Try
    End Function
```

Oracle

```
    Public Function DeleteRole(ByVal RoleID As Guid) As Boolean
        Try
            MyBase.SQL = "usp_DeleteRole"
            'Initialize the Command object
            MyBase.InitializeCommand()
            'Add the Parameters to the Parameters collection
            MyBase.AddParameter("inRoleID", _
                OracleClient.OracleType.Char, 36, RoleID.ToString)
            'Execute the stored procedure
            DeleteRole = ExecuteStoredProcedure()
        Catch ExceptionErr As Exception
            Throw New System.Exception(ExceptionErr.Message, _
            ExceptionErr.InnerException)
        End Try
    End Function
```

The `DeleteUser` function in your `WDAUsers` class in your data access component should look similar to the following code:

SQL Server

```
    Public Function DeleteUser(ByVal UserID As Guid) As Boolean
        Try
            MyBase.SQL = "usp_DeleteUser"
            'Initialize the Command object
            MyBase.InitializeCommand()
            'Add the Parameters to the Parameters collection
```

```
            MyBase.AddParameter("@UserID", _
                SqlDbType.UniqueIdentifier, 16, UserID)
            'Execute the stored procedure
            DeleteUser = ExecuteStoredProcedure()
        Catch ExceptionErr As Exception
            Throw New System.Exception(ExceptionErr.Message, _
            ExceptionErr.InnerException)
        End Try
    End Function
```

Oracle

```
    Public Function DeleteUser(ByVal UserID As Guid) As Boolean
        Try
            MyBase.SQL = "usp_DeleteUser"
            'Initialize the Command object
            MyBase.InitializeCommand()
            'Add the Parameters to the Parameters collection
            MyBase.AddParameter("inUserID", _
                OracleClient.OracleType.Char, 36, UserID.ToString)
            'Execute the stored procedure
            DeleteUser = ExecuteStoredProcedure()
        Catch ExceptionErr As Exception
            Throw New System.Exception(ExceptionErr.Message, _
            ExceptionErr.InnerException)
        End Try
    End Function
```

The `DeleteRole` function in the `WBLRoles` class in your business logic component should look similar to this code:

```
    Public Function DeleteRole(ByVal RoleID As Guid) As Boolean
        Try
            'Call the data component to delete the role
            Return objWDARoles.DeleteRole(RoleID)
        Catch ExceptionErr As Exception
            Throw New System.Exception(ExceptionErr.Message, _
                ExceptionErr.InnerException)
        End Try
    End Function
```

Finally, the `DeleteUser` function in the `WBLUsers` class in your business logic component should look similar to this code:

```
    Public Function DeleteUser(ByVal UserID As Guid) As Boolean
        Try
            'Call the data component to delete the user
            Return objWDAUsers.DeleteUser(UserID)
        Catch ExceptionErr As Exception
            Throw New System.Exception(ExceptionErr.Message, _
                ExceptionErr.InnerException)
        End Try
    End Function
```

Exercise 2 solution

Your code under the `Case "Roles"` statement should look similar to this:

```
Case "Roles"
        'Initialize a new instance of the business logic component
        Using objRoles As New WroxBusinessLogic.WBLRoles( _
            strCompany, strApplication)
            'Delete the role
            If Not objRoles.DeleteRole( _
                New Guid(txtRoleID.Text)) Then
                Throw New Exception("Delete Role Failed")
            End If
        End Using

        'Clear the input fields
        txtRoleID.Text = String.Empty
        txtRoleName.Text = String.Empty
        txtRoleDescription.Text = String.Empty
        txtRanking.Text = String.Empty
        txtRoleUpdateDate.Text = String.Empty

        'Reload the Roles list
        Call LoadRoles()
```

Your code under the `Case "Users"` statement should look similar to this:

```
Case "Users"
        'Initialize a new instance of the business logic component
        Using objUsers As New WroxBusinessLogic.WBLUsers( _
            strCompany, strApplication)
            'Delete the user
            If Not objUsers.DeleteUser( _
                New Guid(txtUserID.Text)) Then
                Throw New Exception("Delete User Failed")
            End If
        End Using

        'Clear the input fields
        txtUserID.Text = String.Empty
        txtLogin.Text = String.Empty
        txtPassword.Text = String.Empty
        txtFirstName.Text = String.Empty
        txtLastName.Text = String.Empty
        txtEmail.Text = String.Empty
        txtPhone.Text = String.Empty
        optStatusActive.Checked = True
        txtUserUpdateDate.Text = String.Empty

        'Reload the Managers combo box
        Call LoadManagers()

        'Reload the Users list
        Call LoadUsers()
        cboUserGroup.SelectedIndex = -1
        cboUserRole.SelectedIndex = -1
        cboUserManager.SelectedIndex = -1
```

Index

Index

SYMBOLS

A

D

H

deleting groups, 215–216
deleting projects, 219
drag-and-drop functions, 218–219, 229,
   230–231
Group ID, 224
index changed event, 217–218
initializing `Command` object, 227–228
keys, pressed and released, 232
loading groups, 216–217, 226–227
mouse button, linking, 229
parameters, 213–214, 222–223
projects, list of available, 225
rows, adding, 231
testing changes, 220–221
updating, 223–224
updating groups, 214
variables, adding, 221–222
VBScript, 601
viewing
node, 185
roles, data validation, 328–329
views
Oracle
   columns or rows, restricting users to, 206–207
   creating, 207–213
   described, 8, 10
   input parameters, restriction against, 205–206
   retrieving data, 206
SQL Server
   columns or rows, restricting users to, 206–207
   creating, 207–213
   described, 4, 7
   input parameters, restriction against, 205–206
   retrieving data, 206
VB 2005
   adding groups, 229–230
   binding data, 228
   deleting groups, 215–216
   deleting projects, 219
   drag-and-drop functions, 218–219, 229,
      230–231
   Group ID, 224
   index changed event, 217–218
   initializing `Command` object, 227–228
   keys, pressed and released, 232
   loading groups, 216–217, 226–227

mouse button, linking, 229
parameters, 213–214
parameters, adding, 222–223
projects, list of available, 225
rows, adding, 231
testing changes, 220–221
updating, 223–224
updating groups, 214
variables, adding, 221–222
Visual Basic. See VB 2005
Visual Studio 2005 data wizards
data access components
   `BindingNavigator`, 49
   `BindingSource`, 49
   `DataGridView`, 48
   `DataSet`, 48
   described, 47–48
   `TableAdapter`, 49
data binding
   to `DataGridView` control, 50–53
   described, 49
   to `TextBox` controls, 53–56

W

Web applications
described, 481
selecting and displaying, 481–482
Web forms, GridView control, 496–497
Web Services, referencing, 580–581
Web browser–type interface
Admin form
   button controls, 630
   creating, 607–608
   e-mail, 631
   grabber handle, 616
   groups section, 618–622, 632–633
   images, 608–609
   navigation pane, 610–616
   phone number, 632
   projects done by groups section, 623–625, 628
   projects section, 617–618
   roles, 625–627
   status strip, 609–610
   toolbar buttons, 609

X